Programming Flex™ 3

Chafic Kazoun and Joey Lott

O'REILLY®
Beijing • Cambridge • Farnham • Köln • Sebastopol • Tokyo

Adobe Developer Library, a copublishing partnership between O'Reilly Media Inc. and Adobe Systems, Inc., is the authoritative resource for developers using Adobe technologies. These comprehensive resources offer learning solutions to help developers create cutting-edge interactive web applications that can reach virtually anyone on any platform.

With top-quality books and innovative online resources covering the latest tools for rich-Internet application development, the *Adobe Developer Library* delivers expert training, straight from the source. Topics include ActionScript, Adobe Flex®, Adobe Flash®, and Adobe Acrobat® software.

Get the latest news about books, online resources, and more at *adobedeveloper-library.com*.

Programming Flex™ 3
by Chafic Kazoun and Joey Lott

Printed in the United States of America.

Published by O'Reilly Media, Inc., 1005 Gravenstein Highway North, Sebastopol, CA 95472.

O'Reilly books may be purchased for educational, business, or sales promotional use. Online editions are also available for most titles (*http://safari.oreilly.com*). For more information, contact our corporate/institutional sales department: (800) 998-9938 or *corporate@oreilly.com*.

Editor: Audrey Doyle
Production Editor: Michele Filshie
Proofreader: Kim Wimpsett
Indexer: Ellen Troutman Zaig
Cover Designer: Karen Montgomery
Interior Designer: David Futato
Illustrators: Robert Romano and Jessamyn Read

Printing History:
September 2008: First Edition.

ISBN: 978-0-596-51621-5

[LSI] [2010-11-30]

1290986208

Table of Contents

Foreword

I remember 2004. That was the year the Olympics were held in Greece. Oil rose above $50 per barrel. *The Return of the King* swept the Oscars. The Red Sox won the World Series. The Serendib Scops Owl was discovered in Sri Lanka... What a year! Okay, that last one I ripped off from Wikipedia. But 2004 *was* a big year for those owls... and it was also a big year for Internet applications. It was the year Flex was born.

A lot has changed in just a few short years. Flex 1 was very exclusive and its applications were tied to a server. It required expensive licenses and few resources were available to help you out. Flex 1.5 cut the cord between the application and the server. Suddenly, anyone could write and deploy a killer Flex app, but most folks still had not heard of Flex. When Flex 2 came out, it was really making some headway into the mindshare of rich Internet application (RIA) developers, even as the industry struggled to define what a RIA developer was. Flex got more and more press, and the SDK was finally released for free. By the time the 2.0.1 update shipped, Flex had an impressive following of designers, developers, so-called *devigners*, and that rarest of beasts, the Serendib developer.

And now comes Flex 3, the most complete and usable version of Flex yet. You get a profiler, OLAP, CS3 integration, refactoring, framework RSLs, deep linking, an AJAX bridge, code generation for servers, automation, just about everything you could dream of. And if something isn't in the box, you can bet someone in the community is working on it: frameworks, 3D libraries, maps, mashups, configurators, dashboards, monitors, widgets, you name it.

But with all those new features and functionality, what's the biggest change in Flex 3?

Well, it's not a new feature, or a refactored API. It's not the splashy new box cover, and it's not the low, low price. It's not even that snazzy new "Getting Started Experience." No, it's none of these things. To see the biggest change in Flex 3, to really see it, you need to stand up, walk down the hall, step into the bathroom (after knocking politely, of course), and look in the mirror. The biggest change in Flex 3 is *you*. That's right. With Flex 3, you, I, or anyone else can contribute to the open source Flex SDK. You can stick your hand into the belly of the beast, tweak its spleen, sew it up, and reawaken a whole new beast. With just a text editor and an Internet connection, you can become a contributor on this leading RIA technology.

So, where does this book fit in? Looking at the existing Flex 3 product documentation, I see more than 2,300 pages of content and nearly 1,200 example applications. I even wrote a couple of those, although if you corner me with a compiler error, I'll deny it. And that doesn't even include the Language Reference, with thousands more "virtual" pages of developer doc. So, why do we need a book about Flex 3 if so much content is already available?

Well, when they wrote *Programming Flex 2*, the first edition of this book, Chafic and Joey learned how to use Flex 2 from the outside in. This was before the source code was even available to look at. They managed to figure out how to do such things as work with remote data, navigate the complexities of the Flex layout schemes, and create incredible custom components. They were real developers solving real problems and writing real code. I remember looking at many of the topics in that edition and saying to myself, "I wish I had written that." These guys took incredibly complex topics and distilled them into the information you needed.

For this edition, Chafic and Joey looked at the product from the inside out. They peeled back the skin and saw the sinewy skeleton of a dynamic framework that will define the next generation of web apps. If you're designing a video player, there's a chapter for you. If you've got a yen for currency formatters, this book has you covered. If you just want to get a handle on the application life cycle, you came to the right place.

So, this book will tell you what Flex 3 is. And after you read it, you might discover something that Flex 3 isn't. But now there's something you can do about it. At some late hour, when everyone else is asleep, if the inspiration strikes you, you might screw up your courage and heap on the moxie, and put your mark on the Flex world by joining the forces at *http://opensource.adobe.com/flex*. This book is just the beginning.

—Matt Horn
Adobe

Preface

It literally took us several years to write *Programming Flex 2*, the predecessor to this book. We worked hard on that book, and when it was finally written and edited and proofread and off to the printer we sighed and looked forward to a break from writing about Flex. However, Flex 3 followed close on the heels of Flex 2, and as the saying goes, there's no rest for the weary. We again picked up our keyboards and started updating the book for Flex 3. The result is what you have in your hands. And it is more than a simple update.

We thought *Programming Flex 2* was one of the best books available for Flex 2. However, we knew we could do better. There were topics we just didn't have time to include in that book. With *Programming Flex 3* we wanted to not only update the book for Flex 3, but also expand our coverage to include things that weren't in the first book. We think we achieved that goal.

The most notable additions to *Programming Flex 3* are in Chapter 20, Chapter 21, and Chapter 22. In Chapter 20, we go into great detail on everything you need to know to add Flex applications to web pages, which we think is an important (if not crucial) topic. Chapter 21 covers building Adobe AIR desktop applications using Flex. And Chapter 22 contains the synthesis of everything else we discuss throughout the book. This is the one addition we think is perhaps the most important, since it helps explain how to take everything you've learned about Flex in preceding chapters and use that knowledge to build a real-world application.

However, we didn't merely add new chapters to the book. We also revised and updated all the chapters in the book. Some chapters didn't require much updating because there were minimal changes for the relevant features between Flex 2 and Flex 3. On the other hand, other chapters required extensive updates and additions. If you read Programming Flex 2 then you'll find lots of new or revised content in this book.

Flex 3 is huge in scope, even bigger than Flex 2. Although the learning curve is not steep (it's actually very easy to get started building Flex 3 applications), it is a long learning curve simply because of the massive amount of features packed into the framework. The official Flex documentation is quite good at telling you how to do something once you know what you're looking for. Therefore, we made it our goal to present to you a book that fills in the gaps and helps you to get comfortable enough with Flex that you can start using it right away. It is our intention in this book to provide you with practical advice from our own experiences learning Flex, and from our longer-term experiences building rich Internet applications using Flash Platform technologies.

We really feel that Flex 3 is a fantastic product and a great way to build applications. Although this is a technical book, we have poured our enthusiasm into our writing, and we'd like to think you will share our enthusiasm as you read this book. We feel that Flex 3 is a far better way to build rich Internet applications than any alternative currently on the market, and we think that as you read this book and learn how to work with Flex, you'll agree. With Flex, you have few (if any) problems involving cross-browser compatibility, network data communication is a snap, and the framework is built with solid object-oriented principles and standards in mind. In short, we feel it's the fastest way to build the coolest, most stable applications.

Who This Book Is For

This book is intended for anyone looking to learn more about Flex 3. We recognize that the audience for this book represents a very diverse group of people with many different backgrounds. Some readers may already be experts at working with Flex 2 (though they may be new to Flex 3), whereas others may never have heard of Flex before picking up this book. Some readers may have years of experience working with Flash Platform technologies, and others may be completely new to creating content that runs in Flash Player. Some readers may have computer science degrees or may have worked in the software industry for years. Yet others may be self-taught. We have done our best to write a book that will cater to this diverse group.

However, be aware that to get the most from this book, it is best that you have a solid understanding of object-oriented principles and that you are comfortable with understanding concepts such as runtime environments, byte code, and compilers. Furthermore, you will get the most from this book if you already know ActionScript, Java, C, C#, or another language that uses similar syntax. Although we did include a chapter dedicated to covering the basics of ActionScript (the programming language that Flex applications utilize), we don't discuss any of the core APIs in detail. If you are interested in learning more about the ActionScript language, we encourage you to find a good ActionScript 3.0 book such as Essential ActionScript 3 and ActionScript 3 Cookbook.

How This Book Is Organized

We spent a lot of time organizing and reorganizing the content of this book. Although there is likely no one way to present the content that will seem perfect to all readers, we've done our best to present it in an order that we feel makes sense:

Chapter 1, Introducing Flex
: What is Flex? What are rich Internet applications (RIAs)? This chapter answers these questions, providing a context for the rest of the book.

Chapter 2, Building Applications with the Flex Framework
: In this chapter, we discuss the various elements and steps involved in building a Flex application. Topics include using the compilers, building scripts, and more.

Chapter 3, MXML
: MXML is the declarative language used by Flex. In this chapter, you'll learn the basics of MXML.

Chapter 4, ActionScript
: ActionScript is the object-oriented programming language used by Flex. In this chapter, you'll learn the basics of ActionScript 3.0.

Chapter 5, Framework Fundamentals
: Flex vastly simplifies many aspects of building applications. Although you don't often have to look under the hood, understanding the fundamentals of how the framework works is useful. In this chapter, you'll learn about Flex application life cycles, bootstrapping, and more.

Chapter 6, Managing Layout
: Flex provides many layout containers that allow you to quickly and easily create all sorts of layouts within your applications. This chapter explains how to work with those containers.

Chapter 7, Working with UI Components
: In this chapter, you'll learn about the user interface components (buttons, lists, menus, etc.) that are part of the Flex framework.

Chapter 8, Customizing Application Appearance
: Customizing the appearance of Flex applications is important because it allows you to create applications that adhere to a corporate style guide or to a creative vision. This chapter explains how to change the appearance of Flex applications.

Chapter 9, Application Components
: To make Flex application development manageable it's important to know how to break up the application into discrete parts. This chapter discusses strategies for this.

Chapter 10, Framework Utilities and Advanced Component Concepts
: Once you've learned the basics of working with components, you'll likely want to know how to expand on that knowledge. In this chapter, you'll learn about such topics as tool tips, customizing lists, pop-up windows, and more.

Chapter 11, Working with Media
: Flex allows you to include all sorts of assets and media in your applications, from images to animations to video and audio. In this chapter, you'll learn how to work with these elements.

Chapter 12, Managing State
: Flex applications and components within those applications can change from one view to another. Flex refers to these changes as *states*. Sometimes managing state is as simple as adding a new component to a form, and other times it involves changing the entire contents of the screen. How to manage state is the subject of this chapter.

Chapter 13, Using Effects and Transitions
: For animated changes between states or in response to user events or system events, Flex includes features called *transitions* and *effects*. You will learn about transitions and effects in this chapter.

Chapter 14, Working with Data
: In this chapter, you'll learn how to model data in Flex applications as well as how to link components so that they automatically update when data values change.

Chapter 15, Validating and Formatting Data
: In this chapter, you'll learn how to validate user input and how to format data such as numbers, phone numbers, and so on.

Chapter 16, Client Data Communication
: Client data communication is any transfer of data into or out of Flash Player where the data remains on the client computer. Examples of this are communication between two or more Flex applications running on the same computer, and storing persistent data on the computer. These topics are discussed in this chapter.

Chapter 17, Remote Data Communication
: In this chapter, you'll learn how to communicate from a Flex application running on a client computer to a remote data service. In the process, you'll learn how to use XML, SOAP, AMF, and more.

Chapter 18, Application Debugging
: Debugging applications is just as important as writing them. It's unusual to build an application that has no errors, and therefore it's crucial that you be able to track down those errors efficiently. In this chapter, you'll learn how to work with the debugging features of Flex.

Chapter 19, Building Custom Components
: Custom components are an important part of Flex applications because they allow you to create elements that can be used, customized, and distributed. This chapter discusses the steps necessary to create custom components using the Flex framework.

Chapter 20, Embedding Flex Applications in a Web Browser
: Many (if not most) Flex applications are deployed on the Web. That requires embedding Flex applications in web browsers. In this chapter, we talk about strategies for achieving this, as well as how to integrate Flex applications with browsers for back and forward button functionality and deep linking features.

Chapter 21, Building AIR Applications
: In this chapter, you'll learn how to use Flex to build desktop applications that run on the Adobe AIR runtime environment. This allows you to use your Flex skills to build applications that also have access to desktop-only features such as the local filesystem and system-level drag-and-drop.

Chapter 22, Building a Flex Application
: This chapter looks at the challenge of building a complete and working Flex application. In this chapter, you'll get a chance to examine different architectural challenges and possible solutions.

What You Need to Use This Book

To use this book, you should have the Flex SDK and a text editor. Our intention with this book is that those with the (free) SDK can follow along. However, we recommend that anyone who is serious about developing Flex applications use Flex Builder. If you're just starting with Flex, you might want to use the free trial version of Flex Builder initially for an optimal experience building Flex applications.

Conventions Used in This Book

The following typographical conventions are used in this book:

Italic
: Indicates new terms, URLs, email addresses, filenames, file extensions, pathnames, directories, and Unix utilities

`Constant width`
: Indicates commands, options, switches, variables, attributes, keys, functions, types, classes, namespaces, methods, modules, properties, parameters, values, objects, events, event handlers, XML tags, HTML tags, macros, the contents of files, and the output from commands

`Constant width bold`
: Shows commands and other text that should be typed literally by the user

`Constant width italic`
: Shows text that should be replaced with user-supplied values

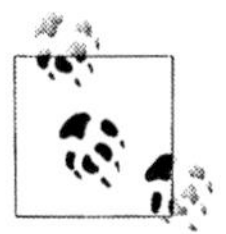

This icon signifies a tip, suggestion, or general note.

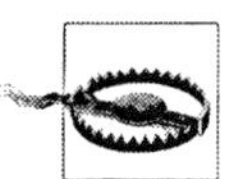

This icon signifies a caution or warning.

Using Code Examples

This book is here to help you get your job done. In general, you may use the code in this book in your programs and documentation. You do not need to contact us for permission unless you're reproducing a significant portion of the code. For example, writing a program that uses several chunks of code from this book does not require permission. Selling or distributing a CD-ROM of examples from O'Reilly books *does* require permission. Answering a question by citing this book and quoting example code does not require permission. Incorporating a significant amount of example code from this book into your product's documentation *does* require permission.

We appreciate, but do not require, attribution. An attribution usually includes the title, author, publisher, and ISBN. For example: "*Programming Flex 3* by Chafic Kazoun and Joey Lott. Copyright 2008 O'Reilly Media, Inc., 978-0-596-51621-5."

If you feel your use of code examples falls outside fair use or the permission given here, feel free to contact us at *permissions@oreilly.com*.

Safari® Books Online

When you see a Safari® Books Online icon on the cover of your favorite technology book, that means the book is available online through the O'Reilly Network Safari Bookshelf.

Safari offers a solution that's better than e-books. It's a virtual library that lets you easily search thousands of top tech books, cut and paste code samples, download chapters, and find quick answers when you need the most accurate, current information. Try it for free at *http://safari.oreilly.com*.

Comments and Questions

Please address comments and questions concerning this book to the publisher:

O'Reilly Media, Inc.
1005 Gravenstein Highway North
Sebastopol, CA 95472
(800) 998-9938 (in the United States or Canada)
(707) 829-0515 (international or local)
(707) 829-0104 (fax)

We have a web page for this book, where we list errata, examples, and any additional information. You can access this page at:

http://www.oreilly.com/catalog/9780596516215

To comment or ask technical questions about this book, send email to:

bookquestions@oreilly.com

For more information about our books, conferences, Resource Centers, and the O'Reilly Network, see our website at:

http://www.oreilly.com

Acknowledgments

This book, perhaps more than most, represents the efforts and contributions of many people. We'd like to acknowledge the following individuals.

Many thanks are due to the many folks at O'Reilly who made this book possible. Special thanks to Steve Weiss and Audrey Doyle, not only for their hard work and patience on this book, but also for their longevity for having also seen us through the previous book. We'd also like to thank Dennis Fitzgerald for keeping us on task and as close to our deadlines as possible. We don't envy Dennis's job, since he had to push and prod us every week, but we are thankful for it. Each of these individuals has continuously gone above and beyond the call of duty, and we very much appreciate their efforts.

We'd also like to thank the many people at Adobe for working to create such a fantastic product as Flex 3, as well as for answering our questions and helping us to see what things we might have missed. We'd especially like to thank a few select people who helped with this book, or who provided content we included from the previous book: Matt Chotin, Alex Harui, Andrew Spaulding, and Manish Jethani, who not only answered our questions, but also took the time to review our chapters and provide valuable comments. We're also very grateful to Matt Horn from Adobe for graciously accepting our invitation to write the Foreword to this book.

The technical quality of this book is not due just to the work of the authors. The technical editors for this book dedicated hours and hours of time to tell us when we were wrong so that we could correct it before you read it. Therefore, we'd like to thank this book's technical editors, Romin Irani and Derek Wischusen.

From Chafic

I would first like to thank Joey. Working with him has been more than a pleasure. His experience in both the technical realm and the publishing industry, along with his patience throughout the process, were an asset to completing this book to the highest standards possible. I would also like to thank my friends, my family, and my team at Atellis for their support.

From Joey

I'd like to thank Chafic for asking me to participate in writing this book. It is an honor to work with Chafic. He is a perfectionist in the best possible way, and he sets high standards that I think show in this book. I would also like to thank my colleagues at The Morphic Group for their helpful comments on the book. And I would like to thank my friends and family for their generosity of spirit.

CHAPTER 1
Introducing Flex

Flex is a collection of technologies that enables you to rapidly build applications deployed to Flash Player, a runtime environment for delivering sophisticated user interfaces and interactivity. Flex leverages existing, matured technologies and standards such as XML, web services, HTTP, Flash Player, and ActionScript. Even though Flex allows you to create complete rich Internet and desktop applications, it does so in a relatively simple and intuitive manner. Although Flex does allow you to get under the hood for more granular control over all the elements, it significantly lowers the learning curve in that it allows you to compose applications rapidly by assembling off-the-shelf components, including UI controls, layout containers, data models, and data communication components.

In this chapter, we'll introduce Flex and Flex technologies in more detail so that you can better understand what Flex is and how you can best get started working with it. You'll learn what elements a Flex application uses and how they work together. We'll also compare and contrast Flex with other technologies for creating both standard and rich Internet applications (RIAs). Additionally, we'll review the changes and additions to Flex 3 from earlier versions.

Understanding Flex Application Technologies

If you're new to Flex, you may not yet have a clear understanding of what a Flex application is, how it works, and what benefits it has over alternative technologies and platforms. You build Flex applications utilizing the Flex framework, and you run or view them using Flash Player. In the following sections, you'll learn more about Flash Player, the Flex framework, and additional technologies that may be part of a Flex application.

Adobe has a new open source initiative, and Flex is included. As of this writing, the Flex framework and compiler are open source. You can learn more about this at *http://opensource.adobe.com/flex*.

Flash Player

Flex is part of the Adobe Flash Platform, which is a set of technologies with Flash Player at the core. Flex applications are intended to be deployed to Flash Player, meaning Flash Player runs all Flex applications. With nearly every computer connected to the Internet having some version of Flash Player installed, and an increasing number of mobile devices being Flash-enabled, Flash Player is one of the most ubiquitous pieces of software anywhere. Adobe estimates that each new version of Flash Player has adoption rates reaching 80% in less than 12 months (Flash Player 8 reached 86% within nine months). The reasons for such quick adoption rates are debatable, but there are a few factors that are almost certainly causative:

- Flash Player content is potentially more compelling and engaging than static HTML content.
- Flash Player is capable of providing integrated solutions that utilize data services, interactive UI design, media elements such as audio and video, and even real-time communications.
- Well-made Flash Player content can provide a refreshing user experience that utilizes metaphors from desktop computing, such as drag-and-drop and double-click. Flash Player frees the UI design from scrolling pages of text and images.
- Flash Player is a relatively small (one-time) download. Even with the multitude of new features added with every release, the Flash Player download is less than 1 MB. And with built-in features such as Express Install, upgrading Flash Player versions is very simple.
- Stability and security are important considerations. Flash Player is a stable program that has been around for more than a decade. Adobe is very careful with Flash Player security as well. Flash Player has very little access to the client's local system. It cannot save arbitrary files to the local system, and it cannot access Internet resources unless they meet very strict requirements.
- Flash Player is cross-platform (and cross-browser) compatible. Flash Player runs on Windows, OS X, and Linux, and on all major browsers, including Firefox, Internet Explorer, Safari, and Opera.

Flex 3 content relies on features of Flash Player 9, meaning that users must be running Flash Player 9 or later to correctly view Flex 3 content. You can read more about deploying Flex applications and detecting player versions in Chapter 20.

Using the Flex framework you can build and compile to the *.swf* format. The compiled *.swf* file is an intermediate bytecode format that Flash Player can read. Flash Player 9 has two virtual machines for running Flash and Flex content. These virtual machines are called AVM1 and AVM2. AVM1 is used to run legacy content and Flash content designed for older versions of Flash Player. AVM2 is written from the ground up, and it functions in a fundamentally different way than AVM1. With AVM2, *.swf* content is no longer interpreted. Rather, it is compiled (the equivalent of just-in-time compilation) and run such that it can take advantage of lower-level computing power. This is very similar to how Java and .NET applications work. Flex applications always run in AVM2, meaning that Flex applications make use of the most advanced features of Flash Player.

AVM2 brings the best of both worlds. Since *.swf* content is compiled to bytecode that the ActionScript virtual machine can understand, the *.swf* format is platform-independent. That also means Flash Player ultimately dictates the functionality allowed by a Flex application. As mentioned previously, that means Flash Player can guarantee certain security safeguards so that you can deploy applications that users can trust. Yet at the same time, AVM2 compiles the content so that it runs significantly faster and more efficiently than previous versions of Flash Player.

The Flex Framework

The Flex framework is synonymous with the Flex class library and is a collection of ActionScript classes used by Flex applications. (ActionScript is the programming language used by Flash Player. We discuss it in more detail later in this chapter.) The Flex framework is written entirely in ActionScript classes and defines controls, containers, and managers designed to simplify building RIAs.

The Flex class library is the subject of much of this book. It consists of the following categories:

Form controls
: Form controls are standard controls such as buttons, text inputs, text areas, lists, radio buttons, checkboxes, and combo boxes. In addition to the standard form controls familiar to most HTML developers, the Flex class library also includes controls such as a rich text editor, a color selector, a date selector, and more.

Menu controls
: Flex provides a set of menu controls such as pop-up menus and menu bars.

Media components
: One of the hallmarks of Flex applications is rich media support. The Flex class library provides a set of components for working with media such as images, audio, and video.

Layout containers
: Flex applications enable highly configurable screen layout. You can use the layout containers to place contents within a screen and determine how they will change over time or when the user changes the dimensions of Flash Player. With a diverse set of container components you can create sophisticated layouts using grids, forms, boxes, canvases, and more. You can place elements with absolute or relative coordinates so that they can adjust correctly to different dimensions within Flash Player.

Data components and data binding
: Flex applications are generally distributed applications that make remote procedure calls to data services residing on servers. The data components consist of connectors that simplify the procedure calls, data models to hold the data that is returned, and data binding functionality to automatically associate form control data with data models.

Formatters and validators
: Data that is returned from remote procedure calls often needs to be formatted before getting displayed to the user. The Flex class library includes a robust set of formatting features (format a date in a variety of string representations, format a number with specific precision, format a number as a phone number string, etc.) to accomplish that task. Likewise, when sending data to a data service from user input, you'll frequently need to validate the data beforehand to ensure that it is in the correct form. The Flex class library includes a set of validators for just that purpose.

Cursor management
: Unlike traditional web applications, Flex applications are stateful, and they don't have to do a complete screen refresh each time data is sent or requested from a data service. However, since remote procedure calls often incur network and system latency, it's important to notify the user when the client is waiting on a response from the data service. Cursor management enables Flex applications to change the cursor appearance to notify the user of such changes.

State management
: A Flex application will frequently require many state changes. For example, standard operations such as registering for a new account or making a purchase usually require several screens. The Flex class library provides classes for managing those changes in state. State management works not only at the macro level for screen changes, but also at the micro level for state changes within individual components. For example, a product display component could have several states: a base state displaying just an image and a name, and a details state that adds a description, price, and shipping availability. Furthermore, Flex provides the ability to easily apply transitions so that state changes are animated.

Effects
: Flex applications aren't limited by the constraints of traditional web applications. Since Flex applications run within Flash Player, they can utilize the animation features of Flash. As such, the Flex class library enables an assortment of effects, such as fades, zooms, blurs, and glows.

Deep linking and browser back and forward button integration
: The browser integration features of Flex allow for deep linking (unique URLs for different application states allowing for linking directly to a state) as well as allowing the browser's back and forward buttons to correctly navigate through states of the Flex application.

Drag-and-drop management
: The Flex class library simplifies adding drag-and-drop functionality to components with built-in drag-and-drop functionality on select components and a manager class that allows you to quickly add drag-and-drop behaviors to components.

Tool tips
: Use this feature of the Flex class library to add tool tips to elements as the user moves the mouse over them.

Style management
: The Flex class library enables a great deal of control over how nearly every aspect of a Flex application is styled. You can apply style changes such as color and font settings to most controls and containers directly to the objects or via Cascading Style Sheets (CSS).

Localization
: Using Flex you can localize applications by way of the resource management part of the Flex framework. This allows you to use resource bundles containing localized text, images, and other resources.

Flex Builder 3

Flex Builder 3 is the official Adobe IDE for building and debugging Flex applications. Built on the popular Eclipse IDE, Flex Builder has built-in tools for writing, debugging, and building applications using Flex technologies such as MXML and ActionScript.

The Flex framework ships as part of Flex Builder. Flex Builder and the Flex framework, however, are not synonymous. You don't have to use Flex Builder to use the Flex framework. Instead, you can opt to install the free Flex SDK, which includes the compiler and the Flex framework. You can then integrate the Flex framework with a different IDE, or you can use any text editor to edit the MXML and ActionScript files, and you can run the compiler from the command line.

Flex Builder is a commercial product. See *http://www.adobe.com/go/flexbuilder* for more information.

Integrating with Data Services

Data services are an important aspect of most Flex applications. They are the way in which the Flex application can load and send data originating from a data tier such as a database [we discuss the concept of tiers in "The Differences Between Traditional and Flex Web Applications" later in this chapter]. Flash Player supports any text data, XML, a binary messaging format called AMF, and persistent socket connections, allowing for real-time data pushed from the server to the client.

Each data format that Flex supports may or may not require special server resources. For example, a Flex application can request XML data from a static resource or from a dynamic resource such as a PHP page. AMF is a binary messaging format that Flash Player understands natively, but for a server to interact with Flash Player via AMF it requires an AMF translator on the server, such as the remote object services that are part of LiveCycle Data Services.

Flex simplifies working with data services by way of classes and components that are part of the framework. We discuss working with data services in more detail in Chapter 17.

Integrating with Media Servers

Since Flex applications are deployed using Flash Player, they can leverage the media support for Flash video and audio. Although Flash Player can play back Flash video and MP3 audio as progressive downloads, you can benefit from true streaming media by way of a technology such as Flash Media Server (*http://www.adobe.com/go/fms*) or Red5 (*http://www.osflash.org/red5*).

Additional Flex Libraries and Components

Additional Flex libraries and components are available for you to use when building Flex applications. The most obvious of these are the additional components available with the Professional edition of Flex Builder 3. The advanced data grid and the charting component set are available only with the Professional edition of Flex Builder 3, and they're not included with the free Flex SDK or with the Standard edition of Flex Builder 3.

However, the advanced data grid and charting components are far from the only examples of add-on libraries and components for Flex. There are many such examples, available both commercially and free. A good list of available libraries and components is available at *http://www.flex.org/components*.

Add-on libraries enable more rapid application development because they provide prebuilt functionality. For example, with the addition of the charting component set you can quickly and simply add robust charting and graphing features to Flex applications.

Using Flex Elements

The Flex framework includes a core set of languages and libraries that are the basis of any Flex application. Using MXML, ActionScript, and the Flex class library you can construct and compile *.swf* content that you can then deploy to Flash Player.

MXML

MXML is an XML-based markup language primarily for describing screen layout. In that respect, it is much like HTML. Using MXML tags you can add components such as form controls and media playback components to layout containers such as grids.

In addition to screen layout, you can use MXML to describe effects, transitions, data models, and data binding. MXML is robust enough that it is possible to build many applications entirely with MXML. Flex Builder enables you to construct MXML with a WYSIWYG approach, enabling you to build basic Flex applications without writing any code.

Although the WYSIWYG approach is helpful for basic prototypes and simple applications, writing MXML code is still necessary for more complex tasks. Additionally, sophisticated Flex applications generally require both MXML and ActionScript.

MXML is a declarative way to create Flex content, but the simplicity should not fool you into thinking that MXML is not powerful. MXML provides a fast and powerful way to create layout and UI content. However, MXML documents get compiled in several steps, the first of which converts the MXML to an ActionScript class. This means MXML documents provide you with all the power of object-oriented design, but with the convenience of a markup language. Furthermore, MXML documents are treated as ActionScript classes at runtime.

ActionScript

ActionScript is the programming language understood by Flash Player and is the fundamental engine of all Flex applications. MXML simplifies screen layout and many basic tasks, but all of what MXML does is made possible by ActionScript, and ActionScript can do many things that MXML cannot do. For example, ActionScript is necessary to respond to events such as mouse clicks.

Although it is possible to build an application entirely with MXML or entirely with ActionScript, it is more common and more sensible to build applications with the appropriate balance of both MXML and ActionScript. Each offers benefits, and they work well together. MXML is best suited for screen layout and basic data features. ActionScript is best suited for user interaction, complex data functionality, and any custom functionality not included in the Flex class library.

ActionScript is supported natively by Flash Player and does not require any additional libraries to run. All the native ActionScript classes (classes that are built into Flash Player) are packaged in the `flash` package or in the top-level package. In contrast, the Flex framework is written in ActionScript, but those classes are included in an *.swf* file at compile time. All the Flex framework classes are in the `mx` package.

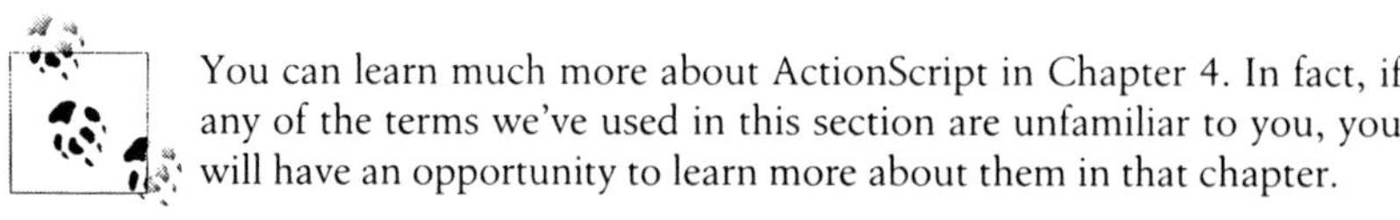

You can learn much more about ActionScript in Chapter 4. In fact, if any of the terms we've used in this section are unfamiliar to you, you will have an opportunity to learn more about them in that chapter.

Working with Data Services (Loading Data at Runtime)

Flex applications are generally distributed applications. That means several computers work in conjunction to create one system. For example, all Flex applications have a client tier (discussed shortly) that runs on the user's computer in the form of an *.swf* running in Flash Player. In most cases, the client tier communicates with a server or servers to send and retrieve data. The servers provide what are called *data services*, which are essentially programs that have public interfaces (APIs) whereby a client can make a request to a method of that program. When a client makes such a request, it's called a *remote procedure call*, or RPC.

There are many types of data services. In its simplest form a data service could consist of a static text file or XML document served from a web server. A slightly more sophisticated data service might be a dynamic XML document generated via a server-side script or program, such as a PHP or ASPX page. Many data services require greater sophistication. One of the most common types of such a sophisticated data service is the web service. Web services use XML (generally in the form of SOAP) as a messaging format, and they enable RPCs using HTTP for requests and responses. Although a SOAP web service is an example of a standards-based data service, many types of data services don't necessarily conform to a particular standard set by the W3C. Many programs on the Web, for example, expose primitive data services that use arbitrary messaging formats and protocols. One such program is used by MapQuest, a popular mapping web site. For instance, you would use the following URL to view a MapQuest page with a map of Los Angeles:

http://www.mapquest.com/maps/map.adp?country=US&city=Los+Angeles&state=CA

Notice that the query string uses arbitrary parameters to determine what to map. Therefore, if you wanted to display a map of New York, you would change the city and state parameter values in the URL as follows:

http://www.mapquest.com/maps/map.adp?country=US&city=New+York&state=NY

Flash Player is capable of making RPCs to many types of data services. For example, Flash Player can make requests to any web resource using HTTP, which means it can make requests to many primitive data services such as a static or a dynamic XML document, or the MapQuest example mentioned previously. That also means it can make requests to web services. Moreover, the Flex class library simplifies requests to most data services.

In addition to the types of data services previously mentioned, Flex applications can also make calls to methods of classes on the server, using a technology called

Remoting. Remoting uses a binary messaging format called *AMF*, which is supported natively by Flash Player. AMF has all the benefits of SOAP, but since it is binary, the bandwidth overhead is greatly reduced. And since AMF is natively supported by Flash Player, no special coding is necessary to use Remoting data services from the client tier. However, for a Remoting data service to be available to the client tier, it must be made accessible via a piece of software that resides on the server and can read and write AMF packets as well as delegate the requests to the correct services. You can find a list of Remoting server products in Chapter 17.

The Differences Between Traditional and Flex Web Applications

Many applications deployed on the Web use HTML as the user interface. Flex applications are similar in many respects, but they have distinct differences. If you're used to building applications that use an HTML UI, it's important to take a few moments to shift how you approach building applications when you start working with Flex. What works for HTML-based applications may or may not work for Flex applications.

Both traditional and Flex applications are generally *n*-tiered. The exact number and types of tiers an application has depend on many factors. Most traditional applications have, at a minimum, a data tier, a business tier, and a presentation tier. Flex applications have a data tier and a business tier; however, as noted earlier, they also introduce a client tier, which is what strongly differentiates them from traditional web applications. The client tier of Flex applications enables clients to offload computation from the server, freeing up network latency and making for responsive and highly interactive user interfaces.

Data tiers generally consist of databases or similar resources. Business tiers consist of the core application business logic. As an example, a business tier may accept requests from a client or presentation tier, query the data tier, and return the requested data.

In traditional applications, the presentation tier consists of HTML, CSS, JavaScript, JSP, ASP, PHP, or similar documents. Typically a request is made from the user's web browser for a specific presentation tier resource, and the web server runs any necessary interpreters to convert the resource to HTML and JavaScript, which is then returned to the web browser running on the client computer. Technically the HTML rendered in the browser is a client tier in a traditional web application. However, since the client tier of a traditional web application is stateless and fairly unresponsive, it is generally not considered a full-fledged tier. (The exception to that generalization is the case of Ajax applications, which use client-side JavaScript and XML to build responsive and sophisticated client tiers.)

Flex applications generally reside embedded within the presentation tier. In addition, Flex applications can integrate with the presentation tier to create tightly coupled client-side systems. Flex applications use Flash Player to run sophisticated client-tier portions of the application. The Flex application client is *stateful*, which means it can make changes to the view without having to make a request to the server. Furthermore, the Flex application client is responsive. For example, Flash Player can respond to user interaction such as mouse movement, mouse clicks, and keyboard presses, and it can respond to events such as notifications from the business tier when data is returned or pushed to the client. Flash Player also can respond to timer events. Since Flash Player is a smart client, it is capable of saving on network overhead and bandwidth usage by managing client-side logic without having to consult the business tier. For example, Flex applications can walk the user through a step-based or wizard-like interface, collect and validate data, and allow the user to update and edit previous steps, all without having to make requests to the business tier until the user wants to submit the data. All of this makes Flex clients potentially far more compelling, responsive, and engaging than traditional web applications.

Because the Flex application client tier is so much more sophisticated than the presentation tier of a traditional web application, the Flex client tier requires significantly more time and resources to build successfully. A common mistake is to assume that Flex client tiers require the same time and resources as a traditional web application presentation tier. Successful Flex client tiers often require the same time and resources during design, implementation, and testing phases as the business tier.

Understanding How Flex Applications Work

Flex applications deployed on the Web work differently than HTML-based applications. It's important to understand how Flex applications work in order to build them most effectively. When you understand how Flex applications work, you can know what elements are necessary for an application and how to build the application for the best user experience. Figure 1-1 summarizes the basic concepts discussed in this section.

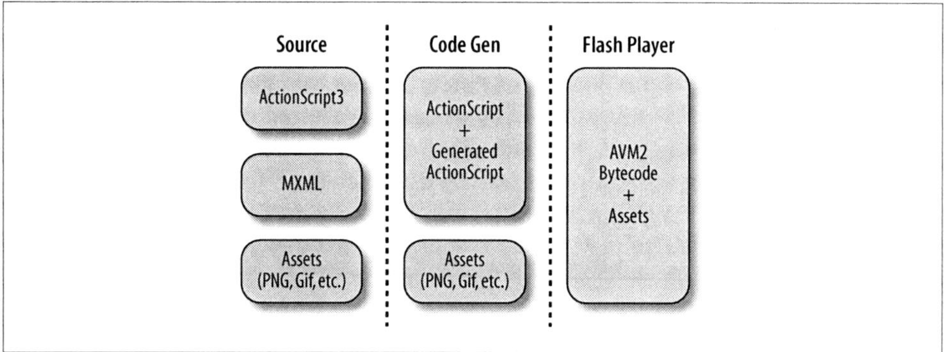

Figure 1-1. Understanding Flex application source-compile-deploy workflow

Every Flex application deployed on the Web utilizes Flash Player as the deployment platform. That means a fundamental understanding of Flash Player is essential to understanding Flex. Additionally, all Flex applications use the Flex framework at a minimum to compile the application. As such, it's important to understand the relationship between the source code files, the compiler, and Flash Player.

All Flex applications require at least one MXML file or ActionScript class file, and most Flex applications utilize both MXML and ActionScript files. The MXML and ActionScript class files comprise the source code files for the application. Flash Player does not know how to interpret MXML or uncompiled ActionScript class files. Instead, it is necessary to compile the source code files to the *.swf* format, which Flash Player can interpret. A typical Flex application compiles to just one *.swf* file. You then deploy that one *.swf* to the server, and when requested, it plays back in Flash Player. That means that unlike HTML-based applications, the source code files remain on the development machine, and you do not deploy them to the production server.

Asset files such as MP3s, CSS documents, and PNGs can be embedded within an *.swf* or they can be loaded at runtime. When an asset is embedded within an *.swf*, it's not necessary to deploy the file to the production server, since it is compiled within the *.swf* file. However, since embedding assets within the *.swf* often makes for a less streamlined downloading experience and a less dynamic application, it is far more common to load such assets at runtime. That means the asset files are not compiled into the *.swf*, and much like an HTML page the assets are loaded into Flash Player when requested by the *.swf* at runtime. In that case, the asset files must be deployed to a valid URL when the *.swf* is deployed.

Data services are requested at runtime. That means the services must be available at a valid URL when requested at runtime. For example, if a Flex application utilizes a web service, that web service must be accessible from the client when requested. Media servers and Flex Enterprise Services must also be accessible when utilized by Flex applications.

Understanding Flex and Flash Authoring

Many developers first learning about Flex 3 may still be unclear as to the relationship between Flex and Flash authoring, the traditional tool for creating content for Flash Player. First, you do not have to understand Flash authoring in order to work with Flex. In fact, you can get started with Flex without any prior knowledge of or experience in Flash authoring.

Flash authoring is a product that was developed in 1996 as a vector animation tool primarily aimed at creating animation content for the Web. In the many versions since that time, both Flash authoring and Flash Player (the deployment platform for Flash authoring content) have enabled greater and greater capabilities, and developers began to create RIAs with the tools. However, although Flash authoring is a fantastic tool for creating animations, it is not the ideal tool for creating applications. The metaphors that Flash authoring uses at its core (such as timelines) are simply not applicable to application development.

Flex 3 is a product aimed primarily at creating applications. The framework includes a rich set of layout and user interface components, and the technology uses metaphors such as states and transitions that are appropriate to application development.

Both Flex and Flash authoring allow you to create *.swf* content that runs in Flash Player. In theory, you can achieve the same things using both products. However, Flash is a tool that allows you to create timeline-based animations and to use drawing tools best suited for expressiveness, whereas Flex allows you to much more rapidly assemble screens of content with transitions and data communication behaviors. As with any craft, it is advisable to use the best tool for the job. Until now, Flash authoring was one of the only tools for creating *.swf* content. But with Flex 3, we now have a tool with a more specific focus.

Although many people may initially try to frame the Flex and Flash authoring debate as a winner-takes-all scenario, it's rather naïve to think of them as competing technologies. Rather, they are two complementary technologies that allow all Flash platform developers to utilize specialized tools when creating rich Internet content. In fact, Flex and Flash authoring can work very well together. As you'll see in this book, Flex can import content created in Flash authoring, allowing you to create RIAs that utilize timeline-based content.

What's New in Flex 3

If you are familiar with earlier versions of Flex (Flex 1, Flex 1.5, and Flex 2), you may be interested in the relationship between Flex 3 and those earlier versions and what is new in Flex 3. In this section, we'll look at this subject in more detail.

If you're familiar with Flex 1 or Flex 1.5, but you haven't used Flex 2, you will find that Flex 3 is dramatically different from the version or versions of Flex you have used. Although Flex 3 continues to utilize MXML and ActionScript (both supported in Flex 1 and 1.5), it is vastly different from Flex 1 and Flex 1.5 in other respects. Flex 3 allows you to compile and deploy independent *.swf* files without any sort of expensive server-side services as was required by Flex 1 and 1.5. Flex 3 requires Flash Player 9, which allows for (and requires) the use of ActionScript 3. This latest ActionScript version introduces significant changes to the Flash Player API that enable a much improved way to add and remove display objects (including components) to the view.

If you've used Flex 2, but you're new to Flex 3, you may be interested in knowing what is new in Flex 3 that wasn't available in Flex 2. Some of the most significant changes/additions to Flex 3 are as follows:

Runtime localization/internationalization
: Although Flex 2 had built-in localization features, they were compile-time only, and they didn't allow for runtime switching of locales. In Flex 3, the locale can be changed at runtime, and the resource bundles can even be downloaded on demand.

Flex framework caching
: Flex 3 allows you to use the new Flash Player caching feature to cache the Flex framework, reducing the file size for Flex *.swf* files.

Support for Adobe AIR
: Adobe AIR is a runtime environment that allows Flex developers to build applications for the desktop. Flex 3 has native support for building AIR applications.

You can learn about these new features and more throughout the book.

Summary

In this chapter, we introduced the basics of what Flex is and what technologies and products are used to create Flex applications. You learned that Flex 3 consists of a framework (a class library) and a compiler that allow you to rapidly create Flex applications. These applications are *.swf* files that you can then run in Flash Player 9.

CHAPTER 2

Building Applications with the Flex Framework

The majority of this book is dedicated to programming Flex applications, with detailed discussions of working with MXML and ActionScript. However, to meaningfully use most of what we discuss in the chapters that follow, you'll need to know how to create a Flex project, how to compile the project, and how to deploy that project so that you can view it.

In this chapter, we'll discuss important topics like the tools needed to create Flex applications and how to create new projects for Flex applications. We'll look at elements comprising a Flex project and discuss compiling and deploying Flex applications.

Using Flex Tool Sets

To work with Flex and build Flex applications, you'll need tools. At a minimum, you must have a compiler capable of converting all your source files and assets into the formats necessary to deploy the application. That means you need to be able to compile MXML and ActionScript files into an *.swf* file.

There are two primary tools you can use that include the necessary compilers:

- The Flex Software Development Kit (SDK)
- Flex Builder 3

The Flex SDK is a free product that includes the entire Fl`ex framework as well as the `mxmlc` and `compc` compilers (see "Building Applications later in this chapter for more details on the compilers). Download the SDK at *http://www.adobe.com/products/flex/flexdownloads/*.

Flex Builder 3 is a professional IDE designed for Flex development, and it too includes the `mxmlc` and `compc` compilers. You can download a trial version of Flex Builder 3 or purchase a license at *http://www.adobe.com/go/flex*.

Flex Builder includes the entire copy of the SDK. Beginning with Flex Builder 3, it contains support for targeting different versions of the SDK. You can find the different versions of the SDK in *<Flex Builder Install Folder>\sdks*.

You can work with Flex Builder 3 in two ways: as a standalone application and as a plug-in for Eclipse. The standalone version of Flex Builder 3 is built on Eclipse, so it and the plug-in version are essentially equivalent. The primary differences are:

- Flex Builder 3 standalone does not require that you already have Eclipse installed, making it an optimal solution for those who have no other use for Eclipse. On the other hand, if you already use Eclipse, or if you intend to use Eclipse for other purposes, the standalone version would essentially require you to have two installations of Eclipse—one running Flex Builder and one standard installation. If you use or plan to use Eclipse for other reasons, you should definitely install the plug-in version of Flex Builder 3.
- The standalone version disables Java Development Tools (JDT), a plug-in used by some standard Eclipse features such as Ant. If you want to use JDT, you should install the plug-in version of Flex Builder 3.

Since Flex Builder is built on Eclipse, you can use any third-party Eclipse plug-ins with the standalone version of Flex Builder.

Many factors might drive your decision as to whether to use the Flex SDK or Flex Builder 3. The following is a list of just a few to consider:

Price
: The Flex SDK is a free product. It includes the entire Flex framework. Flex Builder 3, on the other hand, is a commercial product. There is no difference in price between the standalone and plug-in versions of Flex Builder 3.

Commitment to an existing IDE
: If you already have a considerable investment in an IDE in terms of time and resources, and if that IDE works very well for you, you may want to integrate the Flex SDK with your existing IDE. On the other hand, if you're already using Eclipse, consider that you can install the Flex Builder 3 plug-in for an existing installation of Eclipse.

Debugging capabilities
: The Flex SDK includes a command-line debugger. However, Flex Builder 3 includes an integrated debugger that allows you to set breakpoints and step through code, all from within your IDE.

Efficiency
: Unless and until other IDEs have increased support for Flex (ActionScript and MXML), Flex Builder is the fastest way to build Flex applications. With its built-in code hinting, code completion, error detection, and debugging capabilities, Flex Builder is far superior to the SDK for serious Flex application developers.

The majority of the content of this book is not dependent on any one tool. Much of our focus is on working with the Flex framework and ActionScript 3.0 and will require only the Flex SDK. When there are specific topics that do have dependencies on a particular tool, we make that clear. For example, in this chapter we discuss the differences between configuring a Flex Builder project versus a Flex SDK project.

Creating Projects

A Flex application consists of potentially many files. Although it's possible that a Flex project could consist of as little as one source file, most use tens if not hundreds of files. A typical Flex project might utilize the following:

MXML files
: These files contain the majority of the application view—the layout and UI components. You can read an introduction to MXML in Chapter 3. You can also learn about application and MXML components (both written in MXML) in Chapter 9.

ActionScript classes
: These files contain the source code for all the custom components, data models, client-side business logic, and server proxies. You will find an introduction to ActionScript in Chapter 4.

XML files
: Although XML is frequently loaded from a server as a dynamic response to an HTTP request from Flash Player, many applications also utilize static XML files as configuration parameters.

Image files
: Flex applications can embed image files or load them at runtime. We cover working with images in Chapter 11.

Audio and video files
: Flex applications can load audio and video content for playback within the application. Audio and video are almost always loaded at runtime. We discuss audio and video in Chapter 11.

Runtime shared libraries
: Runtime shared libraries are *.swf* files that contain code libraries that are shared between two or more Flex applications deployed on the same domain. To utilize a runtime shared library, you need two files: an *.swf* and an *.swc*. The *.swf* file contains the libraries, and the *.swc* file is used by the compiler to determine which

libraries to exclude from the application *.swf*. We discuss runtime shared libraries in more detail in Chapter 20.

HTML wrapper file
: Flex applications are deployed on the Web or as an AIR application. The HTML wrapper file is used when deploying to the Web. The published application is an *.swf* file. The most common way to play back an *.swf* on the Web is to embed it in an HTML page and execute it with Flash Player. The HTML wrapper file is the file that embeds the *.swf*.

Setting Up a New Project

How you configure a new Flex project depends in large part on what tool set you are using. If you're using the Flex SDK, that tool set generally requires the most work to configure a new project. We'll first discuss creating a project using the SDK. If you only ever intend to use Flex Builder to create and work with projects, you can go ahead and skip to "Creating a Flex Builder 3 project."

Creating an SDK project

Presumably, if you're using the Flex SDK, you're integrating it with an IDE such as Eclipse (*http://www.eclipse.org*), PrimalScript (*http://www.sapien.com*), or FlashDevelop (*http://www.flashdevelop.org*). If you are indeed using an IDE, you most likely want to start a new project (or workspace or whatever particular terminology your IDE uses). If you are not using an IDE (you like to edit code using a plain-text editor), you will want to create a new directory for the project.

You'll place all the project files in the project directory, likely organizing them into subdirectories. Which subdirectory structure you use is ultimately up to you. You'll need to know where and how you're organizing all the source code and assets so that you can configure the appropriate compiler options when building the application. (We discuss compiler options in "Building Applications," later in this chapter.) Files typically are organized into the following directories:

src
: A directory containing all the source MXML and ActionScript class files. The files are then generally organized into packages. You can organize both MXML and ActionScript files into packages in a Flex project. We discuss packages in more detail in Chapter 3 and Chapter 4.

bin
: A directory to which you save the compiled version of the application.

html
: A directory in which you keep the HTML wrapper file(s).

src/assets_embed
: A directory in which you save all the asset files embedded by the application at compile time. Assets that will be loaded at runtime should be placed in another directory where your application can access them at runtime.

build
: A directory in which you can place build scripts if using Apache Ant.

Creating a Flex Builder 3 project

With Flex Builder 3, you can easily create a new project. From the Flex Builder menu select File→New→Flex Project to open the Flex Project dialog and follow these steps:

1. Step 1 asks for a project name, location, application type, and server technology. The application type specifies if it's a web application that generates an *.swf* file to run in a browser or a Flex application for Adobe AIR runtime. For server technology, all examples in this book will work via the None option (Figure 2-1).

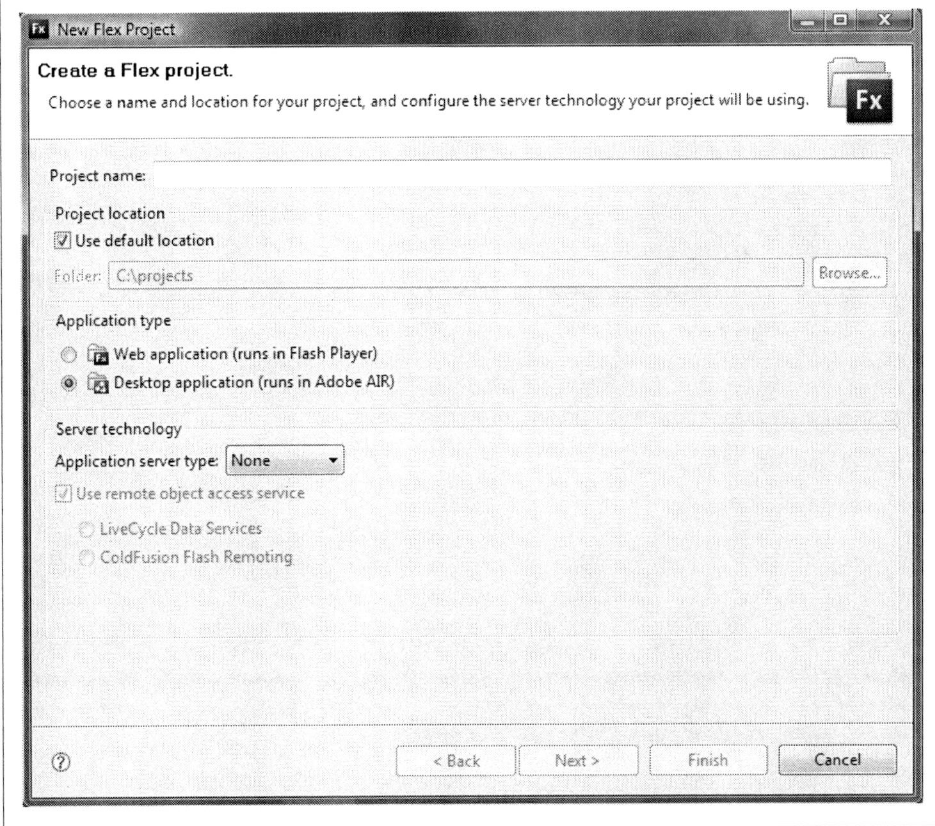

Figure 2-1. Specifying how the application will access data

2. At the completion of step 1, you can click Finish. If you click Next, you'll see a second step asking you to customize the source path and library path. These settings specify classes and libraries that you want to use but that reside outside the project directory or in a nonstandard location within the project directory. Unless stated otherwise, no examples in this book require you to customize the source path or library path. See Figure 2-2.

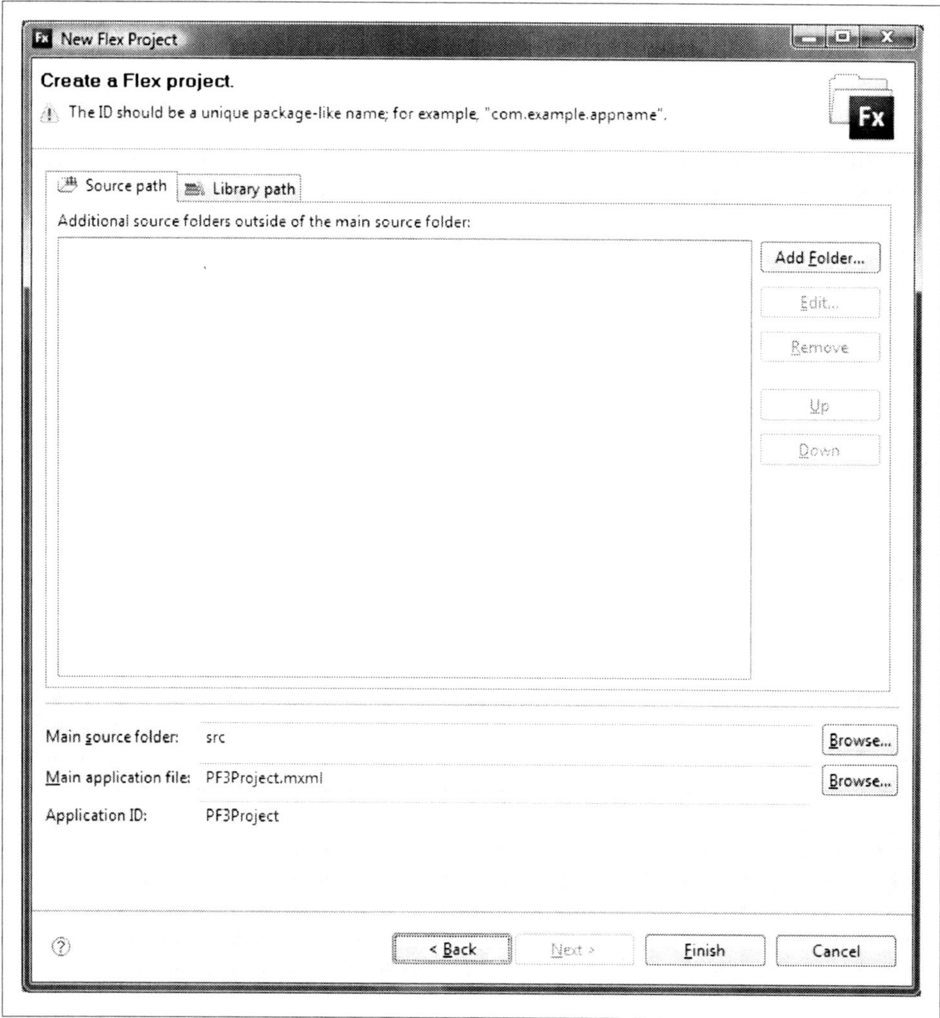

Figure 2-2. Setting the build paths for the new Flex project

When you create a Flex Builder project, you'll see that the new directory has a *bin-debug* directory to which Flex Builder saves the compiled application by default, as well as an *html-template* directory that stores the templates used by Flex Builder to generate the HTML wrapper file. You'll also see that the new project automatically created an MXML document with the same name as the project within the *.src* directory by default.

Building Applications

Once you've created a project and written some code, you'll want to build the project, which means compiling it and deploying it. How you accomplish these tasks depends, in part, on what tools you're using. The following sections discuss how to compile using the `mxmlc` compiler. If you're using Flex Builder, you may want to skip directly to "Compiling Using Flex Builder" later in this chapter, although it is always good to know about `mxmlc`, especially if you intend to use Ant or any build tool.

Compiling Using mxmlc

The `mxmlc` compiler is used to compile Flex applications (versus `compc`, which is used to compile components and libraries). When you use Flex Builder to compile, it automatically calls `mxmlc` (Flex Builder includes the SDK).

There are several ways you can use `mxmlc`, including from the command line, from a *.bat* or shell script, from an IDE, and from Apache Ant. Initially, we'll look at using `mxmlc` from the command line since it's the most basic way to use the compiler (though we'll also look at using the compiler via Apache Ant later in this chapter). The compiler flags we'll look at from the command line also apply to any other use of the compiler.

Configuring for Windows

When you want to work with `mxmlc` from the command line, it's generally a good idea to make sure you add it to your system path. If you're running Windows and you're uncertain how to edit your system path, follow these steps:

1. Right-click My Computer from the desktop or from the Start menu, and select Properties.
2. Click the Advanced tab, and then click the Environment Variables button.
3. In the System Variables list in the bottom part of the dialog, scroll until you see a variable called Path. Then edit the variable either by double-clicking on it or by selecting it and then clicking the Edit button.
4. At the end of the existing value, add the path to the Flex SDK's *bin* directory. If you're using Flex Builder, the default location is *C:\Program Files\Adobe\Flex Builder 3\sdks\<sdk version>*. If you're using the SDK and you installed the SDK in *C:\FlexSDK*, the location is *C:\FlexSDK\bin*. Windows uses a semicolon (`;`) as a delimiter. If necessary, add a semicolon between the existing value and the new addition.
5. Click OK on each open dialog.

Configuring for OS X and Linux

For OS X and Linux, you'll want to set the PATH environment variable in your shell. If you are using *.bash* or any shell that supports *.profile* files, you will want to add a *.profile* file in your user directory (or edit the file if it already exists). You can edit the file with any text editor that you want. If you are familiar with *vi*, for example, you can simply open a Terminal and type **vi ~/.profile**. The *.profile* should contain a line such as the following:

```
export PATH=$PATH:/Users/username/FlexSDK/bin
```

The preceding line of code assumes that you have installed the SDK in your user directory (you'll need to change *username* to your actual username). If you've installed the SDK elsewhere, you should modify the path correspondingly. Also note that the preceding code assumes that you don't want to add additional directories to your path. If you have an existing *.profile* file that already contains an export PATH line, you should simply append the Flex *bin* path to that line using a colon (:) as a delimiter. For example:

```
export PATH=$PATH:/existing/directories:/Users/username/FlexSDK/bin
```

Once you've edited the *.profile* you'll need to run the following command from any existing Terminal window or command prompt:

```
source ~/.profile
```

Beginning with the command line

To use the compiler from the command line you simply specify the compiler name followed by the options. The only required option is called file-specs, and it allows you to specify the entry point to the application you want to compile, that is, the main MXML document (or ActionScript class):

```
mxmlc -file-specs SampleApplication.mxml
```

Notice that file-specs is preceded by a hyphen. All options are preceded by a hyphen.

You can get help for the compiler by running mxmlc with the help option:

```
mxmlc -help
```

The file-specs option is the default option for mxmlc. That means a value that is not preceded by an option flag will be interpreted as the value for file-specs. The following example is equivalent to the preceding example:

```
mxmlc SampleApplication.mxml
```

The examples that follow attempt to compile *SampleApplication.mxml* to *SampleApplication.swf*.

Specifying an output location

By default, mxmlc compiles the application to an *.swf* with the same name as the input file (i.e., *SampleApplication.mxml* compiles to *SampleApplication.swf*) in the same directory as the input file. However, you can specify an output path and *.swf* name using the output option. The following compiles *SampleApplication.mxml* to *bin/main.swf*:

```
mxmlc SampleApplication.mxml -output bin/main.swf
```

Specifying source paths

The source path is the path in which the compiler looks for required MXML and ActionScript files. By default, the compiler looks in the same directory as the compile target (the file specified by file-specs). This means it will also look in subdirectories for documents and classes that are in packages. However, any files located outside the same directory structure won't be found using the default source path compiler settings.

You can use the source-path option to specify one or more directories in which the compiler should look for the MXML and ActionScript files. You can specify a list of directories by using spaces between directories. The following example looks for files in the current directory as well as in *C:\FlexApplicationCommonLibraries*:

```
mxmlc -source-path . C:\FlexApplicationCommonLibraries -file-specs
SampleApplication.mxml
```

Customizing the application background color

The default background color is the blue you see for most Flex applications. Use the default-background-color option to customize the background value. You can specify the value using 0x-prefixed hexadecimal representation in the form of RRGGBB. Use this in cases where you customize the appearance of an application and want the initial color seen by the user to match the overall look of your application. The following sets the default background color of *SampleApplication* to white:

```
mxmlc -default-background-color=0xFFFFFF SampleApplication.mxml
```

Note that the background color in this case is the background color of Flash Player. A Flex application being deployed to the Web has several places where its background is set. There is the background color in the HTML document, the *.swf* file, and the Flex root container. Setting the -default-background-colorph compiler setting will set only the background color of the *.swf* file. The most common way to set the background color for all three values is to set the root Application tag's backgroundProperty style. Setting the value of this style will instruct the Flex compiler to set the values of the root container (Application), the *.swf* file, and the HTML document background if you are using the provided templates.

Changing script execution settings

Flash Player automatically places restrictions on script execution in an attempt to prevent applications from crashing client systems. This means that if too many levels of recursion occur, or if a script takes too long to execute, Flash Player will halt the script.

The `default-script-limits` option allows you to customize each of these settings. The option requires two values: one for the maximum level of recursion and one for the maximum script execution time. The default maximum level of recursion is 1000, and the default maximum script execution time is 60 seconds (you cannot specify a value larger than 60 for this parameter):

```
mxmlc -default-script-limits 200 15 -file-specs SampleApplication.mxml
```

Although it's important to know about the existence of `default-script-limits`, it's also important to know that it should rarely be used. If you have to increase the `default-script-limits` setting for an application to avoid an error, frequently it's because there is a problem in the code or in the application logic.

Setting metadata

The *.swf* format allows you to encode metadata in the application file. The allowable metadata includes the following: `title`, `description`, `creator`, `publisher`, `language`, and `date`. You can set these values using options with the same names as the metadata elements:

```
mxmlc -title "Sample Application" -description "A Flex Sample Application" -file-
specs SampleApplication.mxml
```

Using incremental builds

By default, when you compile from the command line, `mxmlc` compiles a clean build every time. That means that it recompiles every source file, even if it hasn't changed since you last compiled. That is because by default, `mxmlc` doesn't have a way of knowing what has changed and what hasn't.

There are times when a clean build is exactly the behavior you want from `mxmlc`. However, in most cases you'll find that it's faster to use *incremental builds*. An incremental build is one in which the compiler recompiles only those elements that have changed since you last compiled. For all other elements it uses the previously compiled versions. Assuming that not much has changed since the previous compile, an incremental build can be much faster than a clean build.

If you want to use incremental builds, you need a way to determine what things have changed between builds. When you set the `-incremental` option to `true`, `mxmlc` writes to a file in the same directory as the target file you are compiling, and it shares the same name. The name of the cache file is *TargetFile_<#>.cache*, in which the # is a number generated by the compiler. For example, the following might write to a file called *SampleApplication_302345.cache* (where the number is determined by the compiler):

```
mxmlc -incremental=true -file-specs SampleApplication.mxml
```

Storing compiler settings in configuration files

Although it is undoubtedly great fun to specify compiler options on the command line, you can also store settings in configuration files. You can then specify the configuration file as a single option from the command line. The `load-config` option lets you specify the file you want to load to use as the configuration file:

```
mxmlc -load-config=configuration.xml SampleApplication.mxml
```

By default, `mxmlc` uses a configuration file called *flex-config.xml* located in the *frame works* directory of the SDK or Flex Builder installation. If you specify a value for the `load-config` option, that can override *flex-config.xml*. Many, though not all, of the settings in *flex-config.xml* are required. That means it's important that you do one of the following:

- Copy and modify the content of *flex-config.xml* for use in your custom configuration file. When you do so, you will likely have to modify several values in the file so that they point to absolute paths rather than relative paths. Specifically, you have to modify:
  - The `<external-library-path>` setting from the relative *libs/playerglobal.swc* to a valid path pointing to the actual *.swc* file
  - The `<library-path>` settings from `libs` and `locale/{locale}` to the valid paths pointing to those resources (you can keep the `{locale}` variable)
- Load your custom file in addition to the default. When you use the = operator to assign a value to the `load-config` option, you load the file in place of the default. When you use the += operator, you load the file in addition to the default. Any values specified in the custom configuration file override the same settings in the default file:

  ```
  mxmlc -load-config+=configuration.xml SampleApplication.mxml
  ```

Configuration files must have exactly one root node, and that root node must be a `<flex-config>` tag. The `<flex-config>` tag should define a namespace, as in the following example:

```
<flex-config xmlns="http://www.adobe.com/2006/flex-config">
</flex-config>
```

Within the root node you can nest nodes corresponding to compiler options. You can configure any and every compiler option from a configuration file. However, the option nodes must appear in the correct hierarchy. For example, some option nodes must appear within a `<compiler>` tag, and others must appear within a `<metadata>` tag. You can determine the correct hierarchy from the compiler help.

The following is a list of the options returned by `mxmlc -help list advanced`:

```
-benchmark
-compiler.accessible
-compiler.actionscript-file-encoding <string>
-compiler.allow-source-path-overlap
-compiler.as3
-compiler.context-root <context-path>
-compiler.debug
-compiler.defaults-css-files [filename] [...]
-compiler.defaults-css-url <string>
-compiler.define <name> <value>
-compiler.es
-compiler.external-library-path [path-element] [...]
-compiler.fonts.advanced-anti-aliasing
-compiler.fonts.flash-type
-compiler.fonts.languages.language-range <lang> <range>
-compiler.fonts.local-fonts-snapshot <string>
-compiler.fonts.managers [manager-class] [...]
-compiler.fonts.max-cached-fonts <string>
-compiler.fonts.max-glyphs-per-face <string>
-compiler.headless-server
-compiler.include-libraries [library] [...]
-compiler.incremental
-compiler.keep-all-type-selectors
-compiler.keep-as3-metadata [name] [...]
-compiler.keep-generated-actionscript
-compiler.library-path [path-element] [...]
-compiler.locale [locale-element] [...]
-compiler.mxml.compatibility-version <version>
-compiler.namespaces.namespace <uri> <manifest>
-compiler.optimize
-compiler.services <filename>
-compiler.show-actionscript-warnings
-compiler.show-binding-warnings
-compiler.show-shadowed-device-font-warnings
-compiler.show-unused-type-selector-warnings
-compiler.source-path [path-element] [...]
-compiler.strict
-compiler.theme [filename] [...]
-compiler.use-resource-bundle-metadata
-compiler.verbose-stacktraces
-compiler.warn-array-tostring-changes
-compiler.warn-assignment-within-conditional
-compiler.warn-bad-array-cast
-compiler.warn-bad-bool-assignment
-compiler.warn-bad-date-cast
-compiler.warn-bad-es3-type-method
-compiler.warn-bad-es3-type-prop
-compiler.warn-bad-nan-comparison
-compiler.warn-bad-null-assignment
-compiler.warn-bad-null-comparison
-compiler.warn-bad-undefined-comparison
-compiler.warn-boolean-constructor-with-no-args
-compiler.warn-changes-in-resolve
-compiler.warn-class-is-sealed
```

```
-compiler.warn-const-not-initialized
-compiler.warn-constructor-returns-value
-compiler.warn-deprecated-event-handler-error
-compiler.warn-deprecated-function-error
-compiler.warn-deprecated-property-error
-compiler.warn-duplicate-argument-names
-compiler.warn-duplicate-variable-def
-compiler.warn-for-var-in-changes
-compiler.warn-import-hides-class
-compiler.warn-instance-of-changes
-compiler.warn-internal-error
-compiler.warn-level-not-supported
-compiler.warn-missing-namespace-decl
-compiler.warn-negative-uint-literal
-compiler.warn-no-constructor
-compiler.warn-no-explicit-super-call-in-constructor
-compiler.warn-no-type-decl
-compiler.warn-number-from-string-changes
-compiler.warn-scoping-change-in-this
-compiler.warn-slow-text-field-addition
-compiler.warn-unlikely-function-value
-compiler.warn-xml-class-has-changed
-debug-password <string>
-default-background-color <int>
-default-frame-rate <int>
-default-script-limits <max-recursion-depth> <max-execution-time>
-default-size <width> <height>
-dump-config <filename>
-externs [symbol] [...]
-frames.frame [label] [classname] [...]
-help [keyword] [...]
-include-resource-bundles [bundle] [...]
-includes [symbol] [...]
-licenses.license <product> <serial-number>
-link-report <filename>
-load-config <filename>
-load-externs <filename>
-metadata.contributor <name>
-metadata.creator <name>
-metadata.date <text>
-metadata.description <text>
-metadata.language <code>
-metadata.localized-description <text> <lang>
-metadata.localized-title <title> <lang>
-metadata.publisher <name>
-metadata.title <text>
-output <filename>
-raw-metadata <text>
-resource-bundle-list <filename>
-runtime-shared-libraries [url] [...]
-runtime-shared-library-path [path-element] [rsl-url] [policy-file-url]
[rsl-url] [policy-file-url]
-static-link-runtime-shared-libraries
-target-player <version>
-use-network
```

```
-verify-digests
-version
-warnings
```

You'll notice that some of the options you already know, such as incremental and title, are prefixed (e.g., compiler.incremental and metadata.title). These prefixed commands are the full commands. The compiler defines aliases that you can use from the command line. That way, the compiler knows when you type **incremental**, you really mean compiler.incremental. However, when you use a configuration file, you must use the full option names. Prefixes translate to parent nodes. For example, the following sets the incremental option to true and the title option to Example:

```
<flex-config xmlns="http://www.adobe.com/2006/flex-config">
  <compiler>
    <incremental>true</incremental>
  </compiler>
  <metadata>
    <title>Example</title>
  </metadata>
</flex-config>
```

In the options list you'll notice that some options are followed by a value enclosed in <>. For example, the title option is followed by <text>. These values indicate that the option value should be a string. For example, as you can see in the preceding sample code, the <title> tag has a nested string value of Example. If an option is followed by two or more <value> values, the option node should contain child tags with the specified names. For example, the localized-title option is followed by <text> <lang>. Therefore, the following is an example of a configuration file that correctly describes the localized-title option:

```
<flex-config xmlns="http://www.adobe.com/2006/flex-config">
  <metadata>
    <localized-title>
      <text>Example</text>
      <lang>en_US</lang>
    </localized-title>
  </metadata>
</flex-config>
```

If an option is followed by [value] [...], it means the option node must contain one or more tags with the name specified. For example, file-specs is followed by [path-element] [...]. This means that the following is a valid configuration file specifying a file-specs value:

```
<flex-config xmlns="http://www.adobe.com/2006/flex-config">
  <file-specs>
    <path-element>Example.mxml</path-element>
  </file-specs>
</flex-config>
```

The following example is also a valid configuration file. This time, it defines several target files to compile.

```
<flex-config xmlns="http://www.adobe.com/2006/flex-config">
  <file-specs>
    <path-element>Example.mxml</path-element>
    <path-element>Example2.mxml</path-element>
    <path-element>Example3.mxml</path-element>
    <path-element>Example4.mxml</path-element>
  </file-specs>
</flex-config>
```

When an option is not followed by anything, it indicates that the value should be Boolean. For example, `incremental` is not followed by anything in the list.

If you would like to get more details on each compiler option, you can review the help documentation provided with Flex as well as issue a help command for a single command. For example, if you want to find what the `-use-network` command is for, you would issue:

```
mxmlc -help use-network
```

Using Ant

Using the compiler from the command line is not the best way to build applications, for the following reasons:

- It's inconvenient because you have to open a command line and type the command each time.
- Because you have to type the command each time, there's a greater chance of introducing errors.
- Not only is opening a command line and typing a command inconvenient, but it's also slow.
- Compiling from the command line doesn't allow you much in the way of features, such as copying and deploying files, testing for dependencies, and so on.

A standard tool used by application developers for scripting application builds is a program called Apache Ant. Ant is an open source tool that runs on Java to automate the build process. This includes testing for dependencies (e.g., the existence of directories), compiling, moving, and copying files, and launching applications. Although you can use *.bat* files or shell scripts to achieve many of Ant's basic tasks, Ant is extremely feature-rich (it offers support for compressing and uncompressing archives, email support, and FTP support, to name just a few) and can better handle potential errors than *.bat* or shell scripts.

If you're not familiar with Ant, the first thing you should do is to download and install Ant from *http://ant.apache.org*. Once you've installed Ant, you should add a new environment variable, called `ANT_HOME`, as well as the Ant *bin* directory to the system path. The `ANT_HOME` environment variable should point to the root directory of the Ant installation on the computer. For example, if Ant is installed at *C:\Ant* on a Windows system, the `ANT_HOME` environment variable should point to *C:\Ant*. Additionally, you should add the Ant *bin* directory to the system path. For example, if Ant is installed at *C:\Ant*, add *C:\Ant\bin* to the system path.

Ant works by executing a set of tasks, and by default it does not include a task for compiling Flex applications. We could use a task to manually invoke the `mxmlc` compiler, as we would via the command line, but instead Adobe has provided us a set of Flex tasks to simplify Ant use. The tasks allow you to invoke `mxmlc` and `compc` and generate an HTML wrapper. The tasks are included within the SDK distribution in *<sdk dir>\ant*. Installing the provided tasks is easy. You simply copy the *<sdk dir>\ant\lib\flexTasks.jar* file to your *lib* folder within your Ant installation. Once the file is installed, Ant will recognize the new tasks. Ant uses XML files named *build.xml*. The *build.xml* file for a project contains all the instructions that tell Ant how to compile and deploy all the necessary files (e.g., the application). The *build.xml* file consists of a `<project>` root node that contains nested target nodes. The project node allows you to define three attributes:

`name`
: The name of the project

`default`
: The name of the target to run when no other target is specified

`basedir`
: The directory to use for all relative directory calculations

For our sample *build.xml*, the `<project>` node looks like this to start:

```
<?xml version="1.0" encoding="utf-8"?>
<project name="FlexTest" default="compile" basedir="./">
</project>
```

This says that the base directory is the directory in which the file is stored, and the default target is called `compile`. Once the `<project>` root node is set up, you need to instruct Ant to load the Flex tasks and set some basic properties that every Ant build file must contain:

```
<?xml version="1.0" encoding="utf-8"?>
<project name="FlexTest" default="compile" basedir="./">
    <taskdef resource="flexTasks.tasks"
classpath="${basedir}/flexTasks/lib/flexTasks.jar"/>
    <property name="FLEX_HOME" value="C:/flex/sdk"/>
    <property name="APP_ROOT" value="myApp"/>
</project>
```

The basic setup of a build file is now complete. `FLEX_HOME` and `APP_ROOT` are Ant properties that will be useful when configuring tasks later on. As when you declare a variable in code, it is common practice to define properties in Ant in a single location toward the top and to reference them throughout, as we will see in a bit. You can declare any property you wish, but it is common to create at least these two. `FLEX_HOME` should point to the Flex `sdk` root, and `APP_ROOT` should reference your application directory.

Now that we have a basic build file ready, the final step is to set up a <target> within the <project> node. Multiple <target> nodes can exist within a build file, and each target node represents a named collection of tasks. Ant tasks could involve compiling an application, moving files, creating directories, launching applications, creating ZIP archives, using FTP commands, and so on. You can read all about the types of tasks available within Ant at *http://ant.apache.org/manual/tasksoverview.html*. The following defines the compile target for our sample *build.xml* file, which makes use of the newly installed task, mxmlc:

```
<?xml version="1.0" encoding="utf-8"?>
<project name="FlexTest" default="compile" basedir="./">
    <taskdef resource="flexTasks.tasks"
classpath="${basedir}/flexTasks/lib/flexTasks.jar"/>
    <property name="FLEX_HOME" value="C:/flex/sdk"/>
    <property name="APP_ROOT" value="myApp"/>
    <target name="compile">
        <mxmlc file="${APP_ROOT}/FlexTest.mxm">
        <load-config filename="${FLEX_HOME}/frameworks/flex-config.xml"/>
        <source-path path-element="${FLEX_HOME}/frameworks"/>
    </target>
</project>
```

This compile target runs by default because it is set as the default for the project. When you run the Ant build, the compile target runs the mxmlc task. Nested within the <mxmlc> tag you specify the framework and Flex configuration using the <load-config> and <source-path> nodes. In this build file, we didn't specify that you can place one or more <arg> tags that allow you to add arguments to the command. In this case, we're simply adding the file-specs option when calling the compiler.

Once you have a valid *build.xml* file you can run it from the command line by running the ant command from the same directory as the file:

```
ant
```

This runs the default target in the *build.xml* file located in the same directory. To run a nondefault target, you can specify the target name after the command. To run several targets, specify each target in a list, separated by spaces:

```
ant target1 target2
```

Ant integrates well with most IDEs and is often the preferred choice for build environments. Full coverage of Ant is beyond the scope of this book. For further information on Ant you can review *http://ant.apache.org/*, and for Flex-specific coverage you can review the documentation provided with the Flex SDK.

Compiling Using Flex Builder

If you work with Flex Builder, you can use the built-in options for building. Flex Builder automatically compiles your application for development purposes as you work, but the application produced by this automatic compilation is not suitable for deployment as it contains debug code that you will want to avoid for deployment unless you intend to debug in a production environment. To compile a production-ready application, use the Export Releaser Build option in the Project→Export release build menu item. By default, the compiled application will be placed in the *bin-release* folder of your Flex project.

Flex Builder runs the application in your default web browser unless you configure it to do otherwise. You can configure what web browser Flex Builder uses by selecting Window→Preferences→General→Web Browser.

Flex Builder builds all projects incrementally by default in debug mode within the *bin-debug* folder. That means it compiles only the elements that have changed since the last build. If you need to recompile all the source code, you need to clean the project, meaning that you instruct the compiler to recompile every necessary class, not just those that have changed since the last compile. You can do that by selecting Project→Clean. This opens the Clean dialog. The Clean dialog has two options: "Clean all projects" and "Clean projects selected below." If you select "Clean projects selected below," it cleans only the projects that you have selected in the list that appears in the dialog. Flex Builder then builds the project or projects the next time it is prompted, either by automatic triggers (saving a file) or when explicitly directed to run a build.

If you want to manually control a build, you must disable the automatic build feature by deselecting Project→Build Automatically. You can then select the Build All, Build Project, or Build Working Set option from the Project menu to manually run a build. The automatic build option is convenient for smaller projects that compile quickly. However, it's frequently helpful to disable automatic build for larger projects that require more time to compile. In such cases, the automatic build feature can cause delays every time you save a file rather than allowing you to build on demand.

Publishing Source Code

Since Flex applications are compiled, the source code for the application is not available by default. This is in contrast with traditional HTML applications in which the user has the option to view the source code from the browser. Although not appropriate for all applications, you do have the option to publish the source code for Flex applications using a Flex Builder feature. When you publish the source code, the user can select a View Source context menu item from Flash Player. The menu option will launch a new browser window that allows the user to view the published source code.

From Flex Builder you can select Project→Export Release Build. The Export Release Build dialog will open, where you can enable the view source. You may also select which source elements you want to publish by clicking on the Choose Source Files button. By default, all project source code and assets are selected. You can also specify the subdirectory to which to publish the source code files. All the selected ActionScript and MXML files are saved as HTML files.

If the main application entry point is an MXML file, Flex Builder automatically adds the necessary code to enable the View Source context menu item. To manually enable the View Source context menu for an MXML document, you should add the `viewSourceURL` attribute to the `<mx:Application>` tag such that it points to the *index.html* page in the published source code directory.

If you're publishing the source code for an application that uses an ActionScript class as the main entry point, you'll have to enable the context menu item using ActionScript code. This step requires the `com.adobe.viewsource.ViewSource` class. You should then call the static `addMenuItem()` method, passing it a reference to the main class instance and the URL for the source code, like so:

```
ViewSource.addMenuItem(this, "sourcecode/index.html");
```

Deploying Applications

Once you've compiled a Flex application, you next need to deploy the application. Many Flex applications are deployed on the Web, and that will be our focus in this section. If you want to learn more about deploying desktop applications (AIR applications), see Chapter 21.

Every Flex application consists of at least one main *.swf* file. Therefore, at a minimum you will always need to copy at least this one file to the deployment location (typically a web server). However, in addition to the main *.swf*, a Flex application may consist of the following deployable elements:

- An HTML wrapper file
- Data services (web services, Flash Remoting services, etc.)
- Text and XML assets loaded at runtime
- Images loaded at runtime
- Audio and video assets loaded at runtime
- Additional *.swf* files loaded at runtime
- Runtime shared libraries
- Modules

When you deploy an application, you need to make sure that you copy all the necessary files to the deployment locations.

We cover embedding applications in a web browser, along with deeper integration with a web browser, in more detail in Chapter 20.

If you are using Ant, you can easily write a *build.xml* file that copies the necessary files to the deployment directories. Ant natively supports filesystem tasks such as copy and move. It also supports FTP tasks for deploying applications to remote servers.

Summary

This chapter introduced the tool sets and techniques you need to create, configure, compile, and deploy Flex applications to the Web. You learned how to use the command-line compilers and well as how to use build tools such as Apache Ant.

CHAPTER 3
MXML

MXML is a declarative markup language used to create the user interface and to view portions of Flex applications. As the name implies, MXML is an XML-based language. If you're familiar with XML or even HTML, many of the basic MXML concepts we discuss in this chapter will already be familiar to you in a general sense. In this chapter, we'll look at all the basics of working with MXML, including the syntax and structure of the language, the elements of which MXML is composed, creating interactivity in MXML, and how you can use MXML to build applications.

Understanding MXML Syntax and Structure

If you've ever worked with XML or HTML, the structure of MXML will be familiar to you. Even if XML and HTML are unfamiliar to you, you will likely find MXML fairly intuitive. MXML uses tags to create components such as user interface controls (buttons, menus, etc.), and to specify how those components interact with one another and with the rest of the application, including data sources. In the following sections we'll look at how to write MXML code.

Creating MXML Documents

All MXML must appear within MXML documents, which are plain-text documents. You can use any text editor, XML editor, or IDE that can work with text or XML to write MXML, including those listed in the preceding chapter. To create a new MXML document, you can create a new text file with the *.mxml* file extension. If you are using Flex Builder, you can use the program's menus to add either a new MXML application, MXML module, or MXML component. All are MXML documents, differing only in the root element added to the document (as you'll see in this chapter).

XML encoding

Every document can and should have an XML declaration. Many IDEs and XML editors automatically add an XML declaration. Flex Builder adds an XML declaration by default using UTF-8 as the encoding. You must place the declaration as the first line of code in the MXML document, and unless you have a compelling reason to use a different encoding, you should use UTF-8 for the best compatibility:

```
<?xml version="1.0" encoding="utf-8"?>
```

Note that an XML declaration is not strictly required by the Flex compilers. However, for well-formed MXML, you should always include the XML declaration as it is recommended by the XML 1.0 specification.

Applications, modules, and components

All MXML documents can have just one root node. There are three types of MXML documents, and they are defined by the type of root node they have. The first type of MXML document is an application document. Application documents use `Application` nodes as the root node. All Flex applications must have one application document, and application documents are the only type of document you can compile into a Flex application. The following is an example of a basic application document that Flex Builder creates by default:

```
<?xml version="1.0" encoding="utf-8"?>
<mx:Application xmlns:mx="http://www.adobe.com/2006/mxml" layout="absolute">

</mx:Application>
```

Note that the `layout` attribute is not strictly required, but it is shown here because this is the default tag Flex Builder creates.

There are a few items to notice about this example:

- The `Application` node has matching opening and closing tags. The closing tag is prefixed by a forward slash (/). All MXML nodes must be closed as in any well-formed XML.
- The tag name uses an `mx` namespace. You can identify a namespace in a tag because the tag name is prefixed with the namespace identifier followed by a colon. We'll talk more about namespaces in the next section.
- The `Application` tag in this example has two attributes, called `xmlns` and `layout`. You use attributes to set values for a node. In this case, the `xmlns` attribute defines the `mx` namespace prefix (more about this in the next section), and the `layout` attribute defines the way in which the contents of the document will be positioned. The `layout` attribute is optional (we discuss this attribute in more detail in Chapter 6). For now, you can define application documents with an absolute layout or with no explicit layout attribute value. We'll talk more about attributes in "Setting component properties" later in this chapter.

Component documents are used to define *MXML components*, which are encapsulated elements of your application that you can abstract and isolate into their own documents to make your applications more manageable. We'll talk more about custom components in Chapter 9, and Chapter 19. The structure of component documents is similar to that of application documents in all respects except that the root node is not an `Application` tag. Rather, a component document uses an existing component as the root node (which is the superclass for the new MXML document/class). Again, we'll discuss this in much more detail later in this chapter and later in the book. However, for illustrative purposes, here we'll look at a simple example of a component document that is based on a standard Flex framework component called `Canvas`:

```
<?xml version="1.0" encoding="utf-8"?>
<mx:Canvas xmlns:mx="http://www.adobe.com/2006/mxml">

</mx:Canvas>
```

While the preceding is a complete component document, you can't compile an application from it. All Flex applications require an application document in order to compile, and you can use instances of component documents within the application document. You'll learn more about how to create custom components and use them in a Flex application in Chapter 9.

As you can see in this example, the structure of the document is much the same as that of the application document, but with a difference: the root node is a `Canvas` tag rather than an `Application` tag.

A module document is also remarkably similar to application and component documents, the primary difference being the root tag. A module document is used to define an MXML module, which you'll learn more about in Chapter 9. The root tag for a module document is `Module` as in the following example:

```
<?xml version="1.0" encoding="utf-8"?>
<mx:Module xmlns:mx="http://www.adobe.com/2006/mxml">

</mx:Module>
```

All other MXML code appears within the root node of a document. For example, if you want to add a button to an application, the document might look like this:

```
<?xml version="1.0" encoding="utf-8"?>
<mx:Application xmlns:mx="http://www.adobe.com/2006/mxml" layout="absolute">
  <mx:Button label="Example Button"></mx:Button>
</mx:Application>
```

Although we haven't yet discussed the button component, you can see quite clearly that the tag that adds the component is nested within the opening and closing tags of the root node. You'll also see that the syntax for the tag that adds the button is similar to that of the `Application` tag. It uses `<` and `>` characters to demarcate the tag, and it uses the same syntax for attributes. The Button tag in this example also has an opening and closing tag. If you omitted the closing tag, the compiler would not be able to compile the application. However, in the case of the button component, you would not typically nest any tags within it. Therefore, it is sometimes convenient to be able to open and close a node with just one tag. There is a shortcut to achieve this goal. You can simply add a forward slash immediately prior to the > character of the opening tag. That means you can rewrite the preceding example in the following way:

```
<?xml version="1.0" encoding="utf-8"?>
<mx:Application xmlns:mx="http://www.adobe.com/2006/mxml" layout="absolute">
    <mx:Button label="Example Button" />
</mx:Application>
```

That covers the fundamentals of MXML structure. We'll be elaborating on how to work with specific components and specialized tags throughout the remainder of the book.

Understanding namespaces

As shown in the preceding section, MXML uses something called a *namespace*. Simply put, a namespace is a unique grouping for elements—in this case Flex libraries. The entire Flex framework is written in ActionScript classes and a few MXML component documents that are stored in external libraries within *.swc* files. These external libraries contain tens if not hundreds of classes (and MXML components). Using these elements from ActionScript is not difficult. However, to use the elements from MXML you have to be able to map the library classes and MXML components to tags. You do this through manifest files and namespaces.

As shown in Chapter 2, a manifest file maps an ActionScript class to an identifier: the MXML tag name. A manifest file in and of itself would be enough to enable access to ActionScript classes and MXML components by way of MXML tags. However, the difficulty is that you need a way to ensure uniqueness of scope for the mappings. For example, the Flex framework defines a mapping called Button that points to a class called mx.controls.Button—a component that creates a simple user interface button. Yet what if you wanted to create your own class that maps to a Button identifier? This poses a problem because you cannot meaningfully have two Button identifiers within the same scope. If you did, how would the application know which button you are referencing? This highlights the utility of namespaces.

A namespace allows you to create a unique uniform resource identifier (URI) that corresponds to a particular manifest document. This namespace URI is set when the *.swc* file is compiled, as described in Chapter 2. You may recognize this particular URI from the MXML examples shown in the previous section. Within the MXML document you must tell Flex which namespaces you want the document to use. You can do that using the xmlns attribute. If you use the xmlns attribute by itself, it defines the default namespace for the document. Therefore, the example that follows on the next page is a valid MXML application document that adds a button component.

```
<?xml version="1.0" encoding="utf-8"?>
<Application xmlns="http://www.adobe.com/2006/mxml" layout="absolute">
  <Button label="Example Button" />
</Application>
```

This example says to use the Flex framework namespace as the default namespace for the document. This means that every tag used in the document is assumed to correspond to one of the mappings in the Flex framework manifest file. Therefore, the `Application` tag maps to the class that corresponds to the `Application` identifier in the manifest file. This is perfectly valid. However, this is not the way in which MXML documents typically utilize the Flex framework namespace; an MXML document may contain tags that shouldn't map to the Flex framework namespace by default. Therefore, it is better not to define that namespace as the default, but rather to use a namespace prefix. By convention we use the `mx` prefix for the Flex framework namespace. You can use a namespace prefix by following `xmlns` with a colon and the prefix before assigning the value, as in the following example:

```
<?xml version="1.0" encoding="utf-8"?>
<mx:Application xmlns:mx="http://www.adobe.com/2006/mxml" layout="absolute">
  <mx:Button label="Example Button" />
</mx:Application>
```

This example, which is exactly the same as an earlier example, adds the `mx` prefix for the Flex framework namespace. That means you must then prefix all tags that are part of that namespace with the `mx` prefix (e.g., `<mx:Button>`).

By using namespace prefixes, you can create additional namespaces and utilize them within Flex applications. Each namespace can use a different prefix within the MXML document, ensuring that even if two namespaces use the same mapping identifiers, they will not be in conflict. The following example illustrates this:

```
<?xml version="1.0" encoding="utf-8"?>
<mx:Application xmlns:mx="http://www.adobe.com/2006/mxml"
                xmlns:example="http://www.example.com" layout="absolute">
  <mx:Button label="Example Button" />
  <example:Button />
</mx:Application>
```

This example presupposes that a valid external library is already compiled with the namespace URI of *http://www.example.com* and that the library's manifest file contains a mapping identifier of `Button`. In this example, the application creates one button from the Flex framework and one button from the example library. We'll see more examples of creating custom namespaces for custom libraries in Chapter 20. Although no rule states that you must use the `mx` prefix for the Flex framework namespace, it is the standard convention, and we use that convention in this book.

Components

Flex applications are largely composed of *components*, or modular elements. Technically, a component is an ActionScript class or an MXML component document that you can instantiate in an application. In some cases the class or component document has been mapped to an identifier via a manifest file, and in some cases you can merely reference the class or component document by way of the fully qualified name. There are many different types of components, but in terms of the Flex framework components, there are two basic categories: visual and non-visual. The visual components consist of the following:

- Containers
- User interface controls

The non-visual components consist of the following:

- Data components
- Utility components

Containers

Containers are types of components that can contain other components. Every application must use containers. At a minimum, the `Application` element itself is a container because you can place other components within it. You use containers for layout. There are containers for vertical layout, horizontal layout, grids, tiles, and all sorts of layout configurations. When you use layout containers, you place other components within them using nested tags. The following uses a `VBox` (a container that automatically arranges the child elements so that they are stacked vertically) to stack two buttons:

```
<?xml version="1.0" encoding="utf-8"?>
<mx:Application xmlns:mx="http://www.adobe.com/2006/mxml" layout="absolute">
  <mx:VBox>
    <mx:Button label="Example Button 1" />
    <mx:Button label="Example Button 2" />
  </mx:VBox>
</mx:Application>
```

You can nest containers within containers, as the following example shows, by placing an `HBox` (a container that automatically arranges the child elements so that they are placed side by side horizontally) inside a `VBox`:

```
<?xml version="1.0" encoding="utf-8"?>
<mx:Application xmlns:mx="http://www.adobe.com/2006/mxml" layout="absolute">
  <mx:VBox>
    <mx:Button label="Example Button 1" />
    <mx:Button label="Example Button 2" />
    <mx:HBox>
      <mx:Button label="Example Button 3" />
      <mx:Button label="Example Button 4" />
    </mx:HBox>
  </mx:VBox>
</mx:Application>
```

You can read more about layout containers in Chapter 6.

UI controls

User interface controls are visible interface elements such as buttons, text inputs, lists, and data grids. There are many types of UI controls, and we discuss them in more detail in Chapter 7. You've already had a chance to see several examples with a button control.

Setting component properties

When you work with components, you often need to configure them by setting properties. For example, a `button` component lets you apply a label by setting a property. Every component type has its own unique set of properties that you can set. For example, a `button` and a `VBox` clearly have different properties because they do different things. However, despite the difference in the specific properties available for components, you can set the properties using the same techniques. You can set properties of components in several ways:

- Using tag attributes
- Using nested tags
- Using ActionScript

The simplest and most common way to set properties for a component is to use the tag attributes. We already showed several examples of this technique in earlier code examples. For instance, the `Application` tag allows you to set a `layout` property using a tag attribute, as in the following example:

```
<?xml version="1.0" encoding="utf-8"?>
<mx:Application xmlns:mx="http://www.adobe.com/2006/mxml" layout="absolute">

</mx:Application>
```

You'll notice that tag attributes always appear in the opening tag following the tag name. A tag can have many attributes, each separated by spaces. The attributes themselves consist of the attribute name, an equals sign, and the value enclosed in quotation marks.

Almost all components (all visible components) have an `id` property. In most instances of containers and UI controls, you should set the `id` property, because that is how to reference the instance using data binding or ActionScript. The `id` property is the name of the component instance, and it must be unique within the document. The value must also follow a few naming rules. Specifically, the `id` property for a component should consist only of letters, numbers, and underscores, and it should start with either an underscore or a letter, but not a number. The following assigns an `id` value to a button:

```
<mx:Button id="exampleButton" label="Example Button" />
```

You can set most properties (though not the `id` property) using nested tags as an alternative to tag attributes. The nested tags use the same name as the property/attribute, but they must be prefixed with the correct namespace prefix.

The following example assigns a button label using a nested tag:

```
<mx:Button id="exampleButton">
  <mx:label>Example Button</mx:label>
</mx:Button>
```

In most cases, it's preferable to set properties using attributes rather than nested tags because attributes are a more compact and more readable format. However, there are legitimate use cases that justify using nested tags. For example, some properties require complex values that cannot be represented by a string value placed within quotation marks. One such example is the `dataProvider` property for a combo box (a drop-down menu component). The `dataProvider` property of a combo box must be some sort of collection of values. The following example creates a combo box and uses a nested `dataProvider` tag to populate it with values:

```
<mx:ComboBox id="exampleComboBox">
  <mx:dataProvider>
    <mx:ArrayCollection>
      <mx:Array>
        <mx:String>A</mx:String>
        <mx:String>B</mx:String>
        <mx:String>C</mx:String>
        <mx:String>D</mx:String>
      </mx:Array>
    </mx:ArrayCollection>
  </mx:dataProvider>
</mx:ComboBox>
```

Note that you can also set the `dataProvider` property using ActionScript, which would not require nested tags. However, when you want to use MXML to set the `dataProvider` property, you must use nested tags, as in this example.

You can also set properties using ActionScript. When you set an `id` property for a component, you can reference it using that name as an ActionScript object. Most (though not all) component properties have the same names as attributes and as ActionScript properties. We'll look at working with ActionScript in the next chapter.

Non-visual components

As mentioned earlier, there are two types of non-visual components: data components and utility components. *Data components* are used to create data structures, such as arrays and collections, and for making remote procedure calls with protocols like SOAP for web services or AMF for Flash Remoting. You can read more about data components in Chapter 17.

Utility components are components used to achieve functionality. Examples of utility components are those used for creating repeating components and for creating data binding between components. Since utility components are responsible for varied, generally unrelated tasks, we haven't grouped them all in one chapter. Rather, you'll find discussions of utility components in the context of the topics when you'd most likely use the components. For example, the data binding component is discussed in Chapter 14, and the repeater component is discussed in Chapter 6.

Making MXML Interactive

MXML is useful for creating user interfaces—layout and controls. However, static content is not the hallmark of rich Internet applications. Users expect to be able to interact with Flex applications. There are two basic ways to create interactivity in MXML: handling events and data binding.

Handling Events

Every component does certain things. For example, at a minimum, all visual components can initialize themselves and resize. Most components can do things specific to that component type. For example, a button can respond to a user click. All of these things translate into something called an *event*. An event is a way that a component can notify other parts of the application when some action occurs. When a component sends out this notification, we say that it *dispatches an event*.

The Flex event model is based on the W3C specification. (See *http://www.w3.org/TR/DOM-Level-3-Events*.)

In Flex all events are dispatched in the form of Event objects. Some events are a more specific type, meaning the event objects are actually instances of a subclass of the Event class. For example, when an Image component loads a file, it dispatches events of type ProgressEvent, which is a subclass of Event. Because all events are of type Event (or a subclass of Event), they all contain the same type of information, including the type of event (i.e., was it a click event or a progress event or an initialize event?) as well as what object dispatched the event. You'll learn more about events and event dispatching details in Chapter 4.

Every type of component has set events that it dispatches. For example, a button component will always dispatch a click event when the user clicks on it (assuming the button is enabled). However, just because a component dispatches an event doesn't mean that anything is receiving a notification. If you want your application to respond to an event, you must tell it to handle the event.

There are several ways you can handle events. One way is to use ActionScript to register listeners. We'll talk about that solution in Chapter 4, when we talk about ActionScript in more detail. In this chapter, we're more interested in the MXML solutions. Within

MXML, you can add inline event handler attributes within a component tag. The event handler attribute name always matches the event name. For example, to handle a click event for a button you use the `click` attribute within the component tag. The value that you assign to an event attribute gets interpreted as ActionScript. The following example handles a button click event and launches an alert window:

```
<?xml version="1.0" encoding="utf-8"?>
<mx:Application xmlns:mx="http://www.adobe.com/2006/mxml" layout="absolute">
  <mx:Script>
  <![CDATA[
    import mx.controls.Alert;
  ]]>
  </mx:Script>
  <mx:Button id="alertButton" label="Show Alert"
             click="Alert.show('Example')" />
</mx:Application>
```

Even though we haven't yet talked about ActionScript or the `Alert` component, you can see that in this example that the click event attribute is defined to call `Alert.show('Example')`. If you test this example, you'll find that when you click the button, an alert dialog opens with the message that says `Example`.

In this section, our goal was simply to explain the concept of MXML event handling and to show the basic syntax. We'll discuss specific events throughout the book when talking about the components that dispatch the events.

Using Data Binding

Data binding is a feature you can use to link a component to another component or an ActionScript object. Data binding automates changing the value of one object when the value of another object changes. Data binding is an important concept for building Flex applications, and we've dedicated much of Chapter 14 to a detailed discussion of the topic. However, you'll need to understand data binding basics for some of the examples in the intervening chapters.

There are several syntaxes you can employ to enable data binding, but the simplest is a syntax that uses curly braces ({}) to evaluate a statement inline within an MXML tag. In Chapter 14, we'll discuss the additional ways to enable data binding, but before that point, we'll use only the curly brace syntax. The following example uses a text control and a text input control stacked vertically. Each of these controls is a standard Flex framework UI control. The `text` property of each of these controls allows you to read and write the value displayed in the control. In this first example, the text control displays the value `Example`:

```
<?xml version="1.0" encoding="utf-8"?>
<mx:Application xmlns:mx="http://www.adobe.com/2006/mxml" layout="absolute">
  <mx:VBox>
    <mx:Text id="output" text="Example" width="200" height="200"  />
    <mx:TextInput id="input" />
```

```
  </mx:VBox>
</mx:Application>
```

Now we'll use data binding to link the two controls so that as the user changes the value in the text input, the value displayed in the text control also changes:

```
<?xml version="1.0" encoding="utf-8"?>
<mx:Application xmlns:mx="http://www.adobe.com/2006/mxml" layout="absolute">
  <mx:VBox>
    <mx:Text id="output" text="{input.text}" width="200" height="200" />
    <mx:TextInput id="input" />
  </mx:VBox>
</mx:Application>
```

You can see that this example uses curly braces to surround an expression. The expression in this case points to the text input control (with an `id` of `input`)—specifically, the `text` property of that control. This data binding statement tells the Flex application that the text value for the text control should always use the value of the `text` property of the text input control, even when that value changes.

The preceding example was extremely simple and fairly impractical. However, it does illustrate the basic concept and syntax for data binding. We'll be using data binding to link components in a similar (though more useful) fashion in the following chapters.

Summary

This chapter discussed the fundamentals of the MXML language, including its purpose and syntax. We showed how to create MXML documents, add containers and UI components, and make the elements of an MXML document interactive.

CHAPTER 4
ActionScript

ActionScript is the programming language that you can use along with MXML to create sophisticated Flex applications. Although MXML is an important part of a Flex application, it is mostly used for creating the user interface, and it can go only so far in creating a complete application. For data models and sophisticated client-side business logic, you'll need to use ActionScript as well.

Flex applications require ActionScript 3.0, which represents a significant maturation from earlier versions of the language. ActionScript 3.0 is compliant with the ECMA-262 specification and leverages parts of the pending ECMAScript Edition 4 specification. ActionScript 3.0 supports a wide range of features, including formalized classes, interfaces, packages, runtime exception handling, runtime data types, reflection, regular expressions, E4X (XML), and more.

ActionScript is a standards-based, object-oriented language. Because ActionScript is an object-oriented language, it can be viewed as a collection of APIs generally in the form of classes. There are three tiers of ActionScript APIs:

Flash Player APIs
: These APIs are part of the Flash Player itself, and they run natively in that runtime environment. Flash Player APIs consist of core classes such as `String`, `Number`, `Date`, and `Array` as well as Flash Player-specific classes such as `DisplayObject`, `URLLoader`, `NetConnection`, `Video`, and `Sound`.

Flex framework APIs
: These are the APIs that make up the Flex framework itself. The Flex framework is written in ActionScript, so it leverages the lower-level Flash Player APIs. The Flex framework is effectively a layer on top of the Flash Player APIs. The Flex framework APIs consist of all the Flex containers (`Application`, `VBox`, etc.), controls (`Button`, `TextInput`, etc.), and other assorted data, manager, and utility classes that are discussed throughout much of this book.

Custom APIs
: These APIs are for the classes you build for use in custom applications. Custom classes can use Flash Player APIs as well as the Flex framework APIs.

The APIs that are intrinsic to Flash Player are far too large a category to attempt to discuss in this chapter, and in fact there are books spanning many hundreds of pages that still can't cover all of the Flash Player APIs. Our assumption in this book is that either you're already basically familiar with the Flash Player APIs or you're also reading a companion reference specific to Flash Player APIs. Most ActionScript 3.0 books focus primarily on the Flash Player APIs. You will most likely find that the Flex documentation API reference is quite helpful in this regard.

Much of this book is dedicated to the Flex framework APIs, via either ActionScript or MXML. For that reason, this chapter doesn't focus on the Flex framework APIs. ActionScript 3.0 is an object-oriented language, which means that in one form or another, the ActionScript code you write is part of a class. This book assumes you're already familiar with basic object-oriented programming concepts. It's not our intention to attempt to teach object-oriented theory in this chapter. Yet you will need to have a fundamental understanding of object-oriented concepts to make the most of this chapter.

ActionScript is an important and essential part of Flex applications. In fact, ActionScript is the foundation upon which the entire Flex framework is written. This chapter teaches you the important fundamental concepts about ActionScript, including the relationship between MXML and ActionScript, ActionScript syntax, events, error handling, XML, and reflection.

Using ActionScript

When you want to use ActionScript within Flex, you have four basic options for where to place the code:

- Inline within MXML tags
- Nested within MXML tags
- In MXML scripts
- Within ActionScript classes

The preceding lists the techniques for working with ActionScript code, from the simplest to the most complex form. We'll look at each of these techniques in the following sections.

Inline ActionScript

Inline ActionScript appears within MXML tags. Believe it or not, you've already seen several examples of this in Chapter 3. Inline event handling and data binding using curly brace syntax necessarily uses basic ActionScript. The following example uses ActionScript to display an alert dialog box when the user clicks on a button:

```
<mx:Button id="alertButton" label="Show Alert"
        click=" Alert.show('Example')" />
```

In this example, the text assigned to the `click` event handler attribute is ActionScript code, which calls a `show()` method of an ActionScript class called `Alert`.

The preceding example shows how to open an `Alert` component from a button. The code is a snippet and is not provided in the context of a complete MXML document. The `Alert` component is in the `mx.controls` package, and to use the component you must add an `import` statement to the document. If you're using Flex Builder, it automatically adds the `import` statement for you. Otherwise, you'll need to add a `Script` tag with the `import` statement.

The next example uses data binding syntax (curly braces) to indicate that the ActionScript expression contained within it should be evaluated at runtime:

```
<mx:VBox>
  <mx:TextInput id="input" />
  <mx:Text id="output" text="{input.text}" />
</mx:VBox>
```

This example uses the ActionScript expression `input.text`. The `input` object referenced is the text input control with an ID of `input`. At runtime, this expression is evaluated and then assigned to the `text` property of a `Text` component.

Inline data binding represents the most limited use of ActionScript, because it can evaluate only one expression. For instance, the preceding example evaluates the expression `input.text`. You could use a more complex expression, such as the following:

```
<mx:VBox>
  <mx:TextInput id="input" />
  <mx:Text id="output" text="{'User input: ' + input.text}" />
</mx:VBox>
```

This example concatenates the string `User input:` with the user input from the text input control. You can also create even more complex expressions using inline data binding.

Inline event handlers allow you to write more complex ActionScript that can consist of several statements. ActionScript statements generally end with semicolons. The following example illustrates a button with slightly more complex event handler code, consisting of two expressions:

```
<mx:Button id="alertButton" label="Show Alert" click="Alert.
show('Example');alertButton.x += 40;" />
```

The preceding example and subsequent examples will show the button moving only if placed in a container using canvas layout rules. If you test this code inside an `Application` container, make sure the container's layout style is absolute.

This example first displays an alert dialog box. It then moves the button to the right by 40 pixels. Although you can string together many statements (as in this example), it is very uncommon. It's not difficult to understand why this would be. Rather simply: the code is difficult to read and manage when you try to use several inline statements in that fashion. If an event handler needs to run several statements, it is far more common to simply call a function. We'll look at functions in more detail in the next section, and then later in the chapter, in the "Methods section.

Nested ActionScript

You also can nest ActionScript code within MXML tags. Just as you can nest values for most properties, you can nest the values (ActionScript) for event handlers. You must place the code within a `CDATA` block. Here's an example:

```
<mx:Button id="alertButton" label="Show Alert">
  <mx:click>
    <![CDATA[
      Alert.show("Example");
    ]]>
  </mx:click>
</mx:Button>
```

Nesting code in `CDATA` blocks within tags in this fashion looks much better than trying to cram a bunch of code inline within a tag. This might give you the idea that you should place large blocks of code nested within a tag in this fashion:

```
<mx:Button id="alertButton" label="Show Alert">
  <mx:click>
    <![CDATA[
      Alert.show("Example");
      alertButton.x += 40;
      alertButton.y += 20;
    ]]>
  </mx:click>
</mx:Button>
```

Although this certainly is more readable than a block of inline code, it is not the recommended way to use blocks of code with components. Instead, it is far better to centralize your code blocks within functions in MXML scripts or in classes. You can then limit ActionScript on components to one line of code.

MXML Scripts

The second way to add ActionScript code to an application is to place the code within an MXML script. An MXML script appears in an MXML document within a `Script` element:

```
<mx:Script>
</mx:Script>
```

Because ActionScript code may use special characters otherwise interpreted by the MXML compiler, you must place ActionScript code within `Script` tags and also within a `CDATA` block, as in the following example:

```
<mx:Script>
<![CDATA[

  import mx.controls.Alert;

  private function alertButtonClickHandler():void {
    Alert.show("Example");
    alertButton.x += 40;
    alertButton.y += 20;
  }

]]>
</mx:Script>
```

By placing code in functions within `Script` tags, you can limit the amount of code you need to place on component tags. For example, using the preceding script block, you could simplify the code on a button component as follows:

```
<mx:Button id="alertButton" label="Show Alert" click="alertButtonClickHandler();" />
```

You can optionally place ActionScript code blocks in separate files, and you can embed them in a script block using the `source` attribute of a `Script` tag:

```
<mx:Script source="code.as" />
```

Unlike class files (which are discussed in the next section), ActionScript files such as *code.as* from the preceding example do not require special syntax. Instead, you can think of an external ActionScript file included via the `source` attribute of a `Script` tag as nothing more than a way to move the code from the MXML file to an external file. At compile time, the code from the external ActionScript file gets inserted inside the `Script` tag. If you're using Flex Builder, you can create new ActionScript files by selecting File→New→ActionScript File.

Within MXML scripts, you can import classes and declare properties and methods. We discuss each of these in more detail in "Understanding ActionScript Syntax" later in this chapter.

Classes

Classes are the most sophisticated and powerful use of ActionScript. Although it's not wrong to use inline code and MXML scripts, it's generally advisable to have a bias for placing ActionScript code within ActionScript classes.

ActionScript class code exists within separate files apart from the MXML application and component documents. ActionScript class files are text files that use the file extension *.as*. We'll talk more about creating classes later in this chapter, in "Declaring Classes."

MXML and ActionScript Correlations

MXML is a powerful way to simplify the creation of user interfaces. In most cases, it is far better to use MXML for layout than to attempt the same thing with ActionScript. ActionScript is far better suited for business logic and data models. However, MXML and ActionScript are not really so different. In fact, MXML actually gets converted to ActionScript during compilation, and the MXML structure can be understood in terms of an ActionScript class. This can be useful because it allows you to better understand how MXML works and how it relates to ActionScript.

Because MXML is compiled into ActionScript, there is no runtime performance difference between components written in MXML and components written in ActionScript. The difference is primarily seen at authoring time. When you're writing a component, you will find there are differences between using MXML and using ActionScript. MXML is usually faster to write than ActionScript, but it also has its limitations. When you need to create something that is dynamic or can be highly parameterized, ActionScript is usually the better approach simply because it gives you greater low-level control. Furthermore, although an MXML component gets converted to an ActionScript class during compilation, it is not possible to customize the constructor for an MXML component. Therefore, if you need to customize the constructor, you must use ActionScript.

When you use an MXML tag to create a component instance, it is the equivalent of calling the component class's constructor as part of a `new` statement. For example, the following MXML tag creates a new button:

```
<mx:Button id="button" />
```

That is equivalent to the following piece of ActionScript code:

```
public var button:Button = new Button();
```

If you assign property values using MXML tag attributes, that's equivalent to setting the object properties via ActionScript. For example, the following creates a button and sets the label:

```
<mx:Button id="button" label="Click" />
```

The following code is the ActionScript equivalent (assuming that button is already defined as we've already seen):

```
button.label = "Click";
```

This demonstrates that MXML component tags correspond to ActionScript classes. Furthermore, MXML documents themselves are essentially ActionScript classes, simply authored in a different syntax. This is an extremely important point to understand. An application document is a class that extends the mx.core.Application, and component documents are classes that extend the corresponding component class (e.g., mx.containers.VBox).

MXML simplifies writing these classes because the MXML tags automatically translate into many lines of ActionScript code that handle important Flex framework tasks such as initialization, layout rules, and so forth.

When you create components with IDs in an MXML document, those are really *properties* of the class formed by the document. For example, the following creates a new class that extends mx.core.Application and creates one property called Button of type mx.controls.Button:

```
<?xml version="1.0" encoding="utf-8"?>
<mx:Application xmlns:mx="http://www.adobe.com/2006/mxml" layout="absolute">
  <mx:Button id="button" />
</mx:Application>
```

The preceding example is essentially the same as the following ActionScript class:

```
package {
  import mx.core.Application;
  import mx.controls.Button;
  public class Example extends Application {
    public var button:Button;
    public function Example() {
      super();
      button = new Button();
      addChild(button);
    }
  }
}
```

The preceding example is an oversimplification. The actual equivalent ActionScript class would be more complex due to the initialization requirements of Flex framework components. However, it illustrates the basic relationship between MXML and ActionScript.

When code is placed in an MXML script, it is equivalent to placing code within a class body. Variable declarations within MXML scripts are treated as properties of the class, and functions are methods of the class. This means that the rules that apply to writing pure ActionScript classes also apply to MXML scripts. For this reason, we'll focus almost exclusively on writing pure ActionScript class code throughout the remainder of this chapter. However, note that you can apply what you learn to MXML scripts as well.

Understanding ActionScript Syntax

Whether you're writing ActionScript code inline, in an MXML script, or in a class, you'll need to understand its basic syntax. The following sections look at the basic elements of ActionScript, such as class syntax, variables, statements, expressions, functions, and objects.

Understanding Packages

The majority of classes are organized into structures called *packages*. To understand most of ActionScript, you must understand what packages are and how you can work with them.

A package groups together classes so that you can ensure uniqueness of scope. For example, you can have only one `Button` class within a scope. If you tried to declare two `Button` classes in the same scope, there would be a conflict; the compiler wouldn't know which one to use.

A package allows you to create several classes with the same name by placing them in different scopes. For example, the `Button` class that's part of the Flex framework (i.e., the button UI component) exists within a package called `mx.controls`. When a class is placed within a package, it has what's called a *fully qualified class name*. Therefore, the fully qualified class name for `Button` is `mx.controls.Button`. That ensures that if you want to create another `Button` class in a different package, you can do so without conflicting with `mx.controls.Button`. For example, `mx.controls.Button` and `com.example.ui.Button` (a fictitious class) could exist within the same application without causing a problem.

When classes are in packages, it can be quite cumbersome to have to refer to the class by its fully qualified name. For example, if you want to declare a `Button` variable, you have to use the following code if you wish to use the fully qualified class name:

```
var button:mx.controls.Button;
```

And if you wanted to use the constructor, you'd have to use the following code:

```
button = new mx.controls.Button();
```

Obviously, it's much more convenient to use the shorthand form of a class name (i.e., `Button`). ActionScript allows you to reference a class by the shorthand notation if you first add an `import` statement. An `import` statement tells the compiler that you can refer to the class by its shorthand notation from that point forward. The following is an `import` statement for the `Button` class:

```
import mx.controls.Button;
```

You can simply refer to `Button` as such from that point forward.

If you import two `Button` classes (from different packages) in the same class, you must still refer to them using their fully qualified class names within that class.

Many developers understand how to reference packages using `import` statements, but they are uncertain as to how to go about creating package names for classes they might write. Although there is no right or wrong way to name packages, there is a strong convention. The convention is to use the reverse domain as the first part of the package name. For example, if you were to write classes for a company with a domain name of examplecompany.com (*http://examplecompany.com*), all classes would be in the `com.example` package or subpackages. The exception to this is when the classes transcend ownership by one company or organization. In such cases, the package name generally starts with a unique value that represents the project. For example, Flex classes exist within an `mx` package.

Typically, most classes are further organized into subpackages. For example, rather than placing a class directly into the `com.example` package, it generally makes more sense to further organize the class into a subpackage, such as `com.example.ui`, `com.example.services`, or `com.example.utils`. These subpackages simply help you to logically organize classes.

Declaring Classes

Next, let's look at the basic syntax and structure of a class. At a minimum, all ActionScript 3.0 classes consist of the following elements:

- Class package declaration
- Class declaration

Additionally, classes almost always also have `import` statements.

Creating class files

Each class must be defined in its own file. (There are a few unique exceptions, but in most practical cases, a class must be defined in its own file.) The name of the file must be the same as the name of the class it contains, and the file must use the *.as* file extension. For instance, if you want to define an `Example` class, you must create a file named *Example.as*.

Package declarations

The syntax for all ActionScript 3.0 classes begins with a package declaration. As discussed earlier in this chapter, packages are used to organize classes. A package name in ActionScript corresponds to the directory structure within which the ActionScript file is stored. Each directory and subdirectory is delimited by a dot (.) in a package name. For example, if a class is stored in the *example* subdirectory of a *com* directory, the package name would be `com.example`. A class's package declaration uses the `package` keyword followed by the package name. Opening and closing curly braces, which contain any `import` statements and class declarations, follow the `package` declaration. The following `package` declaration says that the enclosed class exists within the `com.example` package. This also means that the file must exist within a *com/example* directory relative to one of the source path directories.

```
package com.example {
  // Import statements go here.
  // Class declaration goes here.
}
```

It's considered a best practice to place all class files within packages, with the possible exception of main class files, when creating ActionScript 3.0-only (non-Flex) applications.

Import statements

As noted earlier, `import` statements should appear within the `package` declaration, but not within the class declaration. (Technically, `import` statements can be placed anywhere, but by convention, they should be placed within the `package` declaration, but not in the class declaration.) You must `import` any and all classes you intend to use. ActionScript 3.0 classes don't automatically import classes. The following example imports the `URLLoader` and `URLRequest` classes from the Flash Player API:

```
package com.example {
  import flash.net.URLLoader;
  import flash.net.URLRequest;
  // Class declaration goes here.
}
```

Class declaration

All public ActionScript 3.0 classes placed within `package` declarations must be declared using the `public` keyword, followed by the `class` keyword and the name of the class. (You'll learn about the differences between public, private, protected, and internal classes in the next section.) Opening and closing curly braces then follow, within which you place the class definition. Class names always start with initial capital letters by convention. The next example declares an `Example` class in the `com.example` package.

```
package com.example {
  import flash.net.URLLoader;
  import flash.net.URLRequest;
  public class Example {
    // Class code goes here.
  }
}
```

Variables and Properties

A *variable* is a named element you can use to store data or a reference to data. You can assign values to and read values from a variable.

When you want to work with a variable, the first thing you'll need to do is declare it. Declaring a variable allocates memory for it and tells the application that the variable exists. You can declare a variable using the `var` keyword as follows:

```
var variableName;
```

The `var` keyword is followed by the name of the variable. Variable names in ActionScript are arbitrary, but they must follow a few simple rules:

- The variable name can consist only of letters, numbers, dollar signs, and underscores.
- The variable name must not start with a number.

By convention, all ActionScript variables use initial lowercase letters rather than initial uppercase letters. The following declares a variable called `userName`:

```
var userName;
```

Although you can declare a variable without a data type, it's always recommended that you declare a variable *with* a data type. You can add a data type to the variable declaration using post-colon syntax as follows:

```
var variableName:DataType;
```

If you declare a variable without a data type, Flash Player allows any data to be assigned to the variable regardless of the type. The result is that there is no runtime type-checking for the variable, and there is no compile-time or runtime optimization because the type is not known ahead of time.

The data type determines the kind of data you can store in the variable. There are many data types, ranging from simple strings and numbers to reference types (such as arrays), and all the types defined by the Flex framework (e.g., `TextInput`, `Button`, etc.). There are far too many data types to list comprehensively here (especially because you can define custom data types). However, some of the most common core data types are `String`, `Number`, `Int`, `Uint`, `Boolean`, `Date`, and `Array`, as defined in Table 4-1.

Table 4-1. Common data types and their descriptions

Data type	Description
`String`	One or more characters, including all Unicode characters
`Number`	Any numeric value, including floating-point numbers
`Int`	Positive and negative integers and 0
`Uint`	Positive integers and 0
`Boolean`	True or false
`Date`	The date and time
`Array`	An index-ordered collection of data

When a variable is declared with a data type, you'll receive errors if you attempt to assign an invalid value to the variable. Flex applications provide both compile-time and runtime type checking.

The following example declares the `userName` variable with the data type `String`:

```
var userName:String;
```

Once you've declared a variable, the next thing to do is to assign values using an *assignment operator* (an equals sign), as in the following example:

```
userName = "Flex User";
```

You can also combine a declaration and assignment into one line:

```
var userName:String = "Flex User";
```

When you want to retrieve a value from a variable, simply reference the variable in a statement or expression that expects that type of value. The next example assigns the value from the `userName` variable to the `text` property of a `text` input component:

```
textInput.text = userName;
```

Variables are placed within class methods (you can find more on method syntax in "Methods later in this chapter). Variables declared outside methods are called *properties*, and they are scoped to the entire class. In most respects, variables and properties are the same. However, there is one key difference that shows up syntactically, which is simply a matter of scope. Here we describe the contrast between variable and property scope:

- Variables declared within methods are scoped exclusively to those methods. That means you can't reference a variable outside the method in which it is declared.
- Properties, on the other hand, have much greater scope. At a minimum, a property is accessible within the entire class. However, you can also opt to allow the property to be accessible outside the class with various settings called *modifiers*.

Classes define properties using quite a few possible modifiers. A property can be one of the following: public; private; protected; or internal.

`public`
: The `public` modifier means the property is accessible outside the class (e.g., from an instance of the class).

`private`
: The `private` modifier makes the property accessible only within the class.

`protected`
: The `protected` modifier makes the property accessible only within the class and its subclasses.

`internal`
: The `internal` modifier makes the property accessible only within the package.

Practically, you should always declare properties as `private` or `protected`. It is not a good idea to declare `public` properties because a class should always manage its state (the values of its properties). `internal` properties are a bad idea for the same reason.

You can declare properties in much the same way as you would declare variables using the `var` keyword. In addition, property names must follow the same rules as variable names. A common convention (and one used in this book) names `private` and `protected` properties with an initial underscore (_) to help distinguish them from local variables declared within methods. The following example declares a `private` property called `_loader` of type `URLLoader`:

```
package com.example {
  import flash.net.URLLoader;
  import flash.net.URLRequest;
  public class Example {
    private var _loader:URLLoader;
  }
}
```

In addition to the `public`, `private`, `protected`, and `internal` modifiers, you can also combine these modifiers with the `static` modifier. The `static` modifier says that the property is directly accessible from the class rather than from instances. Static modifiers are used for many purposes, including design patterns such as the Singleton pattern. The following example adds a static `private` property called `_instance` of type `Example`:

```
package com.example {
  import flash.net.URLLoader;
  import flash.net.URLRequest;
  public class Example {
    private var _loader:URLLoader;
    static private var _instance:Example;
  }
}
```

A concept related to properties is that of the *constant*. A constant is a container for data, much like a variable/property, except that once it has a value, you cannot change the value (hence the name, *constant*). You've likely seen constants in the Flash Player and Flex framework APIs. A few examples of constants are `Event.COMPLETE`,

MouseEvent.CLICK, TimerEvent.TIMER, and Math.PI. Although not a requirement, most constants are declared as static, and most are also declared as public (unlike properties, constants aren't part of a class's state and can therefore be declared as public). To declare a constant, use the const keyword rather than var. By convention, constant names are all uppercase, as shown here:

```
package com.example {
  import flash.net.URLLoader;
  import flash.net.URLRequest;
  public class Example {
    private var _loader:URLLoader;
    static private var _instance:Example;
    static public const TEST:String = "test constant";
  }
}
```

Methods

A *method* is a way to group together statements, give that group a name, and defer the execution of those statements until the method is called by its name. All method definitions must be placed within a class body, and they use the function keyword followed by the name of the method. Following the method name is a pair of parentheses enclosing any parameters that the method might accept. That is followed by a colon and the return type of the method. If the function does not return a value, the return type is declared as *void*. Following the return type declaration is the function definition enclosed in opening and closing curly braces. The following is a declaration for a function called test():

```
function test():void {
}
```

The test() method is declared so that it does not expect any parameters, and it does not expect to return a value. Currently, the test() method doesn't do anything either. Next, add a few statements inside the function so that it does something:

```
function test():void {
  var message:String = "function message";
  trace(message);
}
```

The trace() function writes text to an output such as a console or logfile. Chapter 18 discusses trace() and application debugging in more detail.

Now the test() method declares a variable called message, assigns a value to it (function message), and then uses trace() to output the value to the console (if debugging).

To call a method, use the method name followed by the `function` call operator (the parentheses). For example, if you want to call the `test()` method, you would use the following statement:

```
test();
```

The preceding example assumes that `test()` is declared in the same MXML component or ActionScript class from which you are trying to call it. Otherwise, if you want to call a method that is defined in a different ActionScript class or MXML component, the method must be declared as `public` (see later in this section for more information on declaring methods as `public`) and you must use dot notation to call the method from an instance of the class or component in which the method is defined.

If you want to declare a method so that you can pass it parameters, you must declare the parameters within the parentheses as a comma-delimited list. The parameter declarations consist of the parameter name and post-colon data typing. The following example rewrites `test()` so that it expects two parameters (`a` and `b`):

```
function test(a:String, b:String):void {
  trace("Your message is " + a + " and " + b);
}
```

When you want to call a method with parameters, simply pass the values within the function call operator, as in the following example:

```
test("one", "two");
```

ActionScript does not allow *overloading*. That means you cannot have two methods with the same name but different signatures (different parameter lists). However, ActionScript does allow for optional and *rest parameters*. Optional parameters allow you to define default values for parameters; this means the method does not require that a value be explicitly passed to the method when it is called.

To define a parameter as optional you need only to add an assignment operator and a default value when declaring the method. The following example makes `b` optional by giving it a default value of `two`:

```
function test(a:String, b:String = "two"):void {
  trace("Your message is " + a + " and " + b);
}
```

The default value for a parameter must be defined as a literal value at authoring time.

Now that test() is defined with an optional parameter, you can call it with one or two parameters. If you specify just one parameter, the default value is used for the second parameter. If you specify two parameters, the value you specify for the second overrides the default value.

```
test("one");  // Displays: Your message is one and two
test("three", "four");  // Displays: Your message is three and four
```

Rest parameters let you pass zero or more additional parameters of unknown types to a function. You declare a rest parameter using a parameter name preceded immediately by three dots. Within the method, you can access the rest parameter values as an array. The following code rewrites test() so that it always requires at least one parameter, but it also allows for zero or more additional parameters. By convention, the rest parameter is called rest (though you may use arbitrary names for the parameter).

```
function test(a:String, ...rest):void {
  var message:String = "Your message is " + a;
  var i:uint;
  for(i = 0; i < rest.length; i++) {
    message += " " + rest[i];
  }
  trace(message);
}
```

If you want to return a value from a method, you need to do two things: specify the correct return type, and add a return statement. When you specify a return type, you'll get both compile-time and runtime checking. A function set to return a String value must return a string, not a number, date, array, or any other type. A return statement immediately exits the function and returns the specified value to the expression or statement from which the function was called. The following rewrite of test() returns a string:

```
function test(a:String, ...rest):String {
  var message:String = "Your message is " + a;
  var i:uint;
  for(i = 0; i < rest.length; i++) {
    message += " " + rest[i];
  }
  return message;
}
```

Methods use the same public, private, protected, internal, and static modifiers as properties. If you omit the modifiers (as in the preceding examples), Flex assumes the methods are internal. The following declares two methods, one public and one both public and static:

```
package com.example {
  import flash.net.URLLoader;
  import flash.net.URLRequest;
  public class Example {
    private var _loader:URLLoader;
    static private var _instance:Example;
    static public const TEST:String = "test constant";
```

```
        public function traceMessage(message:String):void {
            trace("Your message is " + message);
        }
        static public function getInstance():Example {
            if(_instance == null) {
                _instance = new Example();
            }
            return _instance;
        }
    }
}
```

Unlike properties, it's common and acceptable to declare public methods. However, it's considered best practice that methods are carefully designed, especially if they're public. A public method can be called at any time, and it's important that they allow access in only very controlled ways.

Classes can and should have a special type of method called a *constructor*. A constructor is called when an instance of the class is created. An example is when you explicitly call a constructor as part of a new statement. The constructor method has these rules:

- The method name must be the same as that of the class.
- The method must be declared as public.
- The method must not declare a return type or return a value.

The following constructor assigns a new value to the _loader property:

```
package com.example {
  import flash.net.URLLoader;
  import flash.net.URLRequest;
  public class Example {
    private var _loader:URLLoader;
    static private var _instance:Example;
    static public const TEST:String = "test constant";
    public function Example() {
       _loader = new URLLoader();
    }
    public function traceMessage(message:String):void {
      trace("Your message is " + message);
    }
    static public function getInstance():Example {
      if(_instance == null) {
        _instance = new Example();
      }
      return _instance;
    }
  }
}
```

There are two additional special method types, called *implicit getter* and *setter* methods. These are declared as methods, but they are accessible as though they were public properties. The method declarations are identical to normal method declarations, except for the following:

- Getter methods use the `get` keyword.
- Setter methods use the `set` keyword.
- Getter methods must not expect any parameters and must return a value.
- Setter methods must expect exactly one parameter and must be declared with a `void` return type.

The following example declares a getter and a setter method, each called `sampleProperty`. In this example, a new `private` property is declared using the getter and setter methods as *accessors*. This is not a requirement for getter and setter methods, but it is a common use case.

```
package com.example {
  import flash.net.URLLoader;
  import flash.net.URLRequest;
  public class Example {
    private var _loader:URLLoader;
    static private var _instance:Example;
    private var _sampleProperty:String;
    public function get sampleProperty():String {
      return _sampleProperty;
    }
    public function set sampleProperty(value:String):void {
      _sampleProperty = value;
    }
    static public const TEST:String = "test constant";
    public function Example() {
      _loader = new URLLoader();
    }
    public function traceMessage(message:String):void {
      trace("Your message is " + message);
    }
    static public function getInstance():Example {
      if(_instance == null) {
        _instance = new Example();
      }
      return _instance;
    }
  }
}
```

You can call the getter method by using the method name as a property in a context that attempts to read the value. You can call the setter method by using the method name as a property in a context that attempts to write a value. The following example creates an instance of the `Example` class, then writes and reads a value to and from the instance using the getter and setter methods:

```
var example:Example = new Example();
example.sampleProperty = "A";   // Call the setter, passing it A as a parameter
trace(example.sampleProperty);  // Call the getter
```

Expressions

An *expression* is any ActionScript that can be evaluated. At its simplest, an expression might consist of just one literal value or one variable. More complex expressions combine several values and/or variables using *operators*. There are many types of operators in ActionScript, ranging from mathematical operators to Boolean operators to bitwise operators. Most operators operate on two operands. For example, the following uses variables as operands in conjunction with a multiplication operator:

```
unitValue * quantity
```

Generally, expressions aren't used in isolation. The preceding code multiplies the values from two variables, but it doesn't do anything with that product. That value would typically be used in an assignment statement or as part of a larger expression. Boolean expressions are often used in `if` and `for` statements, which we'll see next.

Statements

Statements are the building blocks of an application. They define the actions and program flow. Statements tell the application to do something. They can consist of variable declarations, assignments, function calls, loops, and conditionals. You've already seen examples of variable declaration statements, as in the following:

```
var total:Number;
```

An assignment statement uses the equals sign (=) to apply the value on the right side to the variable on the left. For example, the following code assigns the product of `unitValue` and `quantity` to a variable called `total`:

```
total = unitValue * quantity;
```

A statement can also be a call to a function. The following example calls a `trace()` function, which is a built-in Flash Player function that writes to the console when running a debug version of an application in the debug player:

```
trace("This is a simple statement.");
```

So far, you'll notice that each statement ends with a semicolon. All statements of these types should end with semicolons in ActionScript. These types of statements comprise the majority of ActionScript statements. However, there are some statements that do not end in semicolons. Those statements are looping and conditional statements, including `while`, `for`, and `if` statements.

Looping statements, like `while` and `for`, let you loop the execution of a group of statements as long as a condition is met. Here's an example of a `while` statement in ActionScript. This statement increments `total` as long as `total` is less than `maxTotal`:

```
while(total < maxTotal) {
  total += 5;
}
```

You can use `for` statements as a compact way to write common loops. The `for` statement syntax is similar to that of the `while` statement, except that in place of the one conditional expression, a `for` statement uses three expressions: initialization, condition, and update. The following `for` statement calls `trace()` five times:

```
for(var i:int = 0; i < 5; i++) {
  trace(i);
}
```

Conditional statements use Boolean expressions to make the execution of some statement or statements conditional. The following example adds five to `total` if `total` is less than `maxTotal`:

```
if(total < maxTotal) {
  total += 5;
}
```

You can use `if` statements on their own, as in the preceding example. You can also use `if` statements in conjunction with `else` clauses. You can use these clauses only as part of an `if` statement. If the `if` statement conditional expression evaluates to `false`, `else` clauses that follow are run until one of the conditions evaluates to `true`. It is possible to nest conditionals, and by convention the nested `if` statement starts on the same line as the `else` clause within which it is nested, creating what are often thought of as `else if` clauses (though they are technically `else` clauses with nested `if` statements). The following example adds five to `total` if `total` is less than `maxTotal`; otherwise, the code subtracts five:

```
if(total < maxTotal) {
  total += 5;
}
else {
  total -= 5;
}
```

The following example interjects an `else if` clause that tests whether the `total` is 20 more than `maxTotal`. If it is 20 more, it subtracts 10; otherwise, it goes to the `else` clause.

```
if(total < maxTotal) {
  total += 5;
}
else if(total > maxTotal + 20) {
  total -= 10;
}
else {
  total -= 5;
}
```

Arrays

Arrays are sets of data organized by integer indexes or keys. In ActionScript, arrays are instances of the `Array` class. New arrays are defined using an `Array` constructor as part of a `new` statement (which we'll talk about in the next section), or using *literal notation*. The literal notation uses square brackets to create an array. The following creates a new empty array and assigns it to a variable:

```
var books:Array = [];
```

You can also populate an array by adding a comma-delimited list of values between the square brackets:

```
var books:Array = ["Programming Flex 3", "ActionScript 3.0 Cookbook"];
```

You can access specific elements of the array using *array access notation*. The following example retrieves the first element from the array (ActionScript arrays are 0-indexed) and displays it in the console (again, if you are debugging the application):

```
trace(book[0]);
```

You can also assign values to elements using array access notation, as follows:

```
book[2] = "Web Services Essentials";
```

Arrays are objects in ActionScript, and they have methods and properties like most objects. It's beyond the scope of this book to delve into the `Array` API in depth. However, of the `Array` API, the `length` property and `push()` method are the most commonly used. The `length` property returns the number of elements in the array, and it is commonly used with a `for` statement to loop through all the elements of an array. The `push()` method allows you to append elements to an array.

ActionScript arrays are not strongly typed nor are they of fixed length. That means you can store any sort of data in an array, even mixed types. You could store numbers, strings, dates, custom types, and even other arrays in an array. Furthermore, because arrays are not of a fixed length, you can add items without concern for the allocated size of the array.

ActionScript has two ways of simulating *hashmaps*. The first of these is the `Object` type, which is the most basic of all object types. Unlike the majority of ActionScript classes, the `Object` class is dynamic, which means you can add arbitrary properties to `Object` instances. Although it is generally better to write data model classes than to store data in `Object` instances using arbitrary properties, there are cases when it is useful to use an `Object` instance as a hashmap/associative array.

The following example creates an `Object` instance and assigns several keys and values:

```
var authorsByBook:Object = new Object();
authorsByBook["Programming Flex 3"] = "Chafic Kazoun,Joey Lott";
authorsByBook["ActionScript 3.0 Cookbook"] = "Joey Lott,Keith Peters,Darron Schall";
```

ActionScript also has the `flash.utils.Dictionary` class, which can be used in a similar fashion to `Object`. However, the keys for `Dictionary` are evaluated using strict equality for nonprimitive types, and objects used as keys must point to the same identity. In contrast, when using an `Object` as an associative array, the keys are tested using standard equality for nonprimitives, and objects used as keys can point to different identities as long as the `toString()` methods return the same value. Consider the following example.

In this code, we create four keys to use: two are objects with `toString()` methods that return the same value, one is a primitive string, and one is a primitive integer. We then create two associative arrays—one an `Object` and one a `Dictionary`—and we populate them each with one element using the primitive string `1` as the key. Then we trace the values for each of the four keys for each of the associative arrays.

```
var key1:Object = new Object();
key1.toString = function():String {
    return "1";
};
var key2:Object = new Object();
key2.toString = function():String {
    return "1";
};
var key3:String = "1";
var key4:int = 1;

var object:Object = new Object();
object["1"] = "a";

var dictionary:Dictionary = new Dictionary();
dictionary["1"] = "a";

trace(object[key1]); // a
trace(object[key2]); // a
trace(object[key3]); // a
trace(object[key4]); // a

trace(dictionary[key1]); // undefined
trace(dictionary[key2]); // undefined
trace(dictionary[key3]); // a
trace(dictionary[key4]); // a
```

Because the `Object` always uses standard equality and evaluates the `toString()` method of objects used as keys, all four of the keys will work for access to the one element stored in the `Object`. The case is different for the `Dictionary` object. Because objects used as keys in this case must point to the same identity, neither of the object keys can be used to access the value. Because strict equality doesn't apply to primitive types used as keys, either a string of `1` or an integer of `1` will work as a key to access the value.

Objects

Objects are composites of state and functionality that you can use as elements within ActionScript code. There are potentially an infinite range of object types, including those from the built-in Flash Player types to Flex framework types to custom types.

An object is an instance of a class, which is a blueprint of sorts. Although there are other mechanisms for creating objects, the most common is to use a `new` statement with a constructor. The constructor for a class is a special function that shares the same name as the class. For example, the constructor for the `Array` class is called `Array`. Like any other functions, a constructor may or may not expect parameters. The only way to know whether a particular constructor expects parameters is to consult the API documentation. However, unlike most functions, a constructor must be used as part of a new statement, and it always creates a new instance of the class. The following example creates a new array using a new statement:

```
var books:Array = new Array();
```

Objects may have properties and methods depending on the type. Properties are essentially variables associated with an object, and methods are essentially functions associated with an object. You can reference properties and methods of an object in ActionScript using *dot syntax*. Dot syntax uses a dot between the name of the object and the property of the method. The following example uses dot syntax to call the push() method of the array object (the push() method appends the value as an array element):

```
books.push("Programming Flex 3");
```

The next example uses dot syntax to reference the length property of the array object:

```
trace(books.length);
```

Inheritance

You can create new classes (called *subclasses*) that inherit from existing classes (called *superclasses*). You achieve this using the extends keyword when declaring the class. The extends keyword should follow the class name and be followed by the class from which you want to inherit. The following defines class B, so it inherits from a fictional class, A:

```
package com.example {
  import com.example.A;
  public class B extends A {
  }
}
```

ActionScript 3.0 allows a class to inherit from just one superclass. The subclass inherits the entire implementation of the superclass, but it can access only properties and methods declared as public or protected. Properties that are declared as private and methods are never accessible outside a class—not even to subclasses. Classes in the same package can access properties declared as internal. Consider the class A and class B example, if A is defined as follows:

```
package com.example {
  public class A {
    private var _one:String;
    protected var _two:String;
    public function A() {
      initialize();
    }
    private function initialize():void {
      _one = "one";
      _two = "two";
    }
```

```
        public function run():void {
          trace("A");
        }
      }
    }
```

In this example, B (which is defined as a subclass of A) can access _two and run(), but it cannot access _one or initialize().

If a subclass wants to create its own implementation for a method that it inherits from a superclass, it can do so by overriding it. Normally, a subclass blindly inherits all of the superclass implementation. However, when you override a method, you tell the subclass that it should disregard the inherited implementation and use the overridden implementation instead. To override a method, you must use the override keyword in the method declaration. The following overrides the run() method:

```
package com.example {
  import com.example.A;
  public class B extends A {
    override public function run():void {
      trace("B");
    }
  }
}
```

When a subclass overrides a superclass method, the subclass method's signature must be identical to the superclass method's signature, that is, the parameters, return type, and access modifier must be the same.

Interfaces

ActionScript 3.0 also allows you to define *interfaces*. Interfaces allow you to separate the interface from the implementation, which enables greater application flexibility.

Much of what you learned about declaring classes applies to declaring interfaces as well. In fact, it's easier to list the differences:

- Interfaces use the interface keyword rather than the class keyword.
- Interfaces cannot declare properties.
- Interface methods declare the method signature but not the implementation.
- Interfaces declare only the public interface for implementing classes, and therefore method signature declarations do not allow for modifiers.

By convention, interface names start with an uppercase I. The following is an example of an interface:

```
package com.example {
  public interface IExample {
    function a():String;
    function b(one:String, two:uint):void;
```

```
        function get example():String;
        function set example(value:String):void;
    }
}
```

In the preceding example, interface says that any implementing class must declare methods a() and b() using the specified signatures.

You can declare a class so that it implements an interface using the implements keyword, following the class name or following the superclass name if the class extends a superclass. The following example implements IExample:

```
package com.example {
  import com.example.IExample;
  public class Example implements IExample {
    private var _example:String;
    public function get example():String {
      return _example;
    }
    public function set example(value:String):void {
      _example = value;
    }
    public function Example() {
    }
    public function a():String {
      return "a";
    }
    public function b(one:String, two:uint):void {
      trace(one + " " + two);
    }
  }
}
```

When a class implements an interface, the compiler verifies that it implements all the required methods. If it doesn't, the compiler throws an error. A class can implement methods beyond those specified by an interface, but it must always implement at least those methods. A class can also implement more than one interface with a comma-delimited list of interfaces following the implements keyword.

Handling Events

ActionScript 3.0 and the Flex framework use *events* to notify and receive notification when things occur. Events occur in response to the user (e.g., the user clicks on something), time (timer events), and asynchronous messaging (such as remote procedure calls). Regardless of the cause of an event, nearly all ActionScript events use the same event model.

In Chapter 3, you saw how to use event handler attributes. In ActionScript, you can handle events by registering *listeners*. A listener is a function or method that should receive notifications when an event is dispatched. For example, you can register a method to receive a notification when the user clicks a button.

You need at least two elements to register a listener: an object that dispatches events, and a function that listens for events. Objects capable of dispatching events either extend the `flash.events.EventDispatcher` class or implement the `flash.events.IEventDispatcher` interface. When an object can dispatch events, it has a public `addEventListener()` method that requires at least two parameters: the name of the event for which you want to listen and the function/method that should listen for the event.

```
object.addEventListener("eventName", listenerFunction);
```

In most cases, the event names are stored in *constants* of the corresponding event type class. For example, the click event name is stored in the `MouseEvent.CLICK` constant.

The listener function must expect one parameter of type `mx.events.Event` or the relevant subclass of `Event`. For example, if the object dispatches an event of type `MouseEvent`, the listener should accept a `MouseEvent` parameter. The event parameter contains information about the event that occurred, including a reference to the object dispatching the event (the `target` property of the event object) and the object that most recently bubbled (relayed) the event (the `currentTarget` property). (In many cases, the `target` and `currentTarget` properties reference the same object.) The following example adds an event listener using ActionScript, and when the user clicks the button, the listener displays the event object in an alert dialog box:

```
<?xml version="1.0" encoding="utf-8"?>
<mx:Application xmlns:mx="http://www.adobe.com/2006/mxml" layout="absolute"
initialize="initializeHandler(event)">
  <mx:Script>
    <![CDATA[

      import mx.controls.Alert;

      private function initializeHandler(event:Event):void {
        button.addEventListener(MouseEvent.CLICK, clickHandler);
      }

      private function clickHandler(event:MouseEvent):void {
        Alert.show("Event: " + event.type + " with target: " + event.target);
      }

    ]]>
  </mx:Script>

  <mx:Button id="button" />

</mx:Application>
```

In the preceding example, you may notice that `clickHandler()` is defined such that it expects a `MouseEvent` parameter. When you register an event handler method using the `addEventListener()` method, the event handler method will always be passed an `Event` parameter (or a subclass of `Event`, as in this example).

You can also unregister an event listener using the `removeEventListener()` method. This method requires the same parameters as `addEventListener()`. The method unregisters the specified listener function as a listener for the specified event.

It is extremely important that you remove event listeners when they are no longer necessary. This includes all cases where you want to remove from memory the object listening for the events. Flash Player will not garbage-collect an object if there are any references to it still in memory. That means that even if an object is no longer used anywhere in the application, except for a reference held by an event dispatcher, it will not be garbage-collected.

The following example removes the event listener added in the previous example:

```
button.removeEventListener(MouseEvent.CLICK, onClick);
```

Error Handling

ActionScript 3.0 supports *runtime error handling*. That means that if and when an error occurs, the application can respond to the error in an elegant fashion rather than simply failing to work without any notification to the user. ActionScript 3.0 uses two types of runtime errors: *synchronous* and *asynchronous*.

Handling Synchronous Errors

Synchronous errors occur immediately when trying to execute a statement. Use `try/catch/finally` to handle synchronous errors. When you have code that may throw runtime errors, surround it with a `try` statement:

```
try {
  // Code that might throw errors
}
```

You must then include one or more `catch` blocks following a `try`. If the code in the `try` block throws an error, the application attempts to match the error to the `catch` blocks in the order in which they appear. Every `catch` block must specify the specific type of error that it handles. The application runs the first `catch` block that it encounters to see whether it matches the type of error thrown. All error types are either `flash.errors.Error` types or subclasses of `Error`. Therefore, you should try to catch more specific error types first and more generic types (e.g., `Error`) later; for example:

```
try {
  // Code that might throw errors
}
catch (error:IOError) {
  // Code in case the specific error occurs
}
catch (error:Error) {
```

```
    // Code in case a non-specific error occurs
}
```

In addition, you can add a `finally` clause that runs regardless of whether the `try` statement is successful. A `finally` clause is used to run any code necessary based on any part of the `try` or `catch` blocks having run. For example, if you open something in a `try` block, you might close it in a `finally` clause.

```
try {
  // Code that might throw errors
}
catch (error:IOError) {
  // Code in case the specific error occurs
}
catch (error:Error) {
  // Code in case a non-specific error occurs
}
finally {
  // Code to run in any case
}
```

Most Flash Player and Flex framework classes use *asynchronous errors* rather than synchronous errors, so the following example may seem impractical, but it does illustrate the syntax for using `try/catch`. The `browse()` method for a `FileReference` object opens a browse dialog box that lets the user select a file from his local filesystem. However, Flash Player can display only one browse dialog box at a time. If you call `browse()` while a browse dialog box is already open, it throws a `flash.errors.IOError` type of error. If you don't handle the error, the user receives a notification in a default error dialog box.

```
<?xml version="1.0" encoding="utf-8"?>
<mx:Application xmlns:mx="http://www.adobe.com/2006/mxml" layout="absolute"
initialize="initializeHandler(event)">
  <mx:Script>
    <![CDATA[

      import flash.net.FileReference;

      private function initializeHandler(event:Event):void {
        var file:FileReference = new FileReference();
        file.browse();
        file.browse();
      }

    ]]>
  </mx:Script>

</mx:Application>
```

The following example rewrites the preceding code using error handling:

```
<?xml version="1.0" encoding="utf-8"?>
<mx:Application xmlns:mx="http://www.adobe.com/2006/mxml" layout="absolute"
initialize="initializeHandler(event)">
```

```
  <mx:Script>
    <![CDATA[

      import flash.net.FileReference;

      private function initializeHandler(event:Event):void {
        var file:FileReference = new FileReference();
        try {
          file.browse();
          file.browse();
        }
        catch(error:Error) {
          errors.text += error + "\n";
        }
      }

    ]]>
  </mx:Script>

  <mx:TextArea id="errors" />

</mx:Application>
```

Handling Asynchronous Errors

Many objects in ActionScript can potentially throw *asynchronous errors*. Asynchronous errors are those that occur in response to network operations. For example, if a requested file is not found, the network operation fails asynchronously, and an asynchronous error is thrown. All asynchronous errors are in the form of events, and they use the same event model as standard events. For example, if a URLLoader object attempts to load data outside the Flash Player security sandbox, it dispatches a securityError event.

The following example illustrates how to handle error events:

```
<?xml version="1.0" encoding="utf-8"?>
<mx:Application xmlns:mx="http://www.adobe.com/2006/mxml" layout="absolute"
initialize="initializeHandler(event)">
  <mx:Script>
    <![CDATA[

      private function initializeHandler(event:Event):void {
        var loader:URLLoader = new URLLoader();

         // In order to test this you'll need to specify a URL of a file that
         // exists outside of the security sandbox.
        loader.load(new URLRequest("data.xml"));
        loader.addEventListener(SecurityErrorEvent.SECURITY_ERROR,
securityErrorHandler);
      }

      private function securityErrorHandler(event:SecurityErrorEvent):void {
        errors.text += event + "\n";
```

```
        }

      ]]>
    </mx:Script>

    <mx:TextArea id="errors" />

</mx:Application>
```

Using XML

XML is a standard protocol for transferring, storing, and reading data for several purposes, including application initialization parameters, data sets, and remote procedure calls. Flex applications work with XML by using Flash Player's native support.

Flash Player 9 supports two mechanisms for working with XML: a legacy `XMLDocument` class and the new `XML` class that implements the ECMAScript for XML (E4X) standard. All XML examples in this book use E4X unless otherwise noted.

Creating XML Objects

There are two ways to create `XML` objects in ActionScript: using XML literals or with the `XML` constructor. XML literals are useful when you want to define the XML data directly in the code and you know the exact XML data you want to use. The following example defines an XML literal and assigns it to a variable:

```
var xml:XML = <books>
              <book>
                <title>Programming Flex 3</title>
                <authors>
                  <author first="Chafic" last="Kazoun" />
                  <author first="Joey" last="Lott" />
                </authors>
              </book>
              <book>
                <title>ActionScript 3.0 Cookbook</title>
                <authors>
                  <author first="Joey" last="Lott" />
                  <author first="Keith" last="Peters" />
                  <author first="Darron" last="Schall" />
                </authors>
              </book>
            </books>;
```

We'll assume that this is the `XML` object referenced by the remainder of the XML examples in this chapter.

If you aren't able to define the XML data directly in ActionScript, you can load the data as a string and pass it to the `XML` constructor. In the following example, `loadedXMLData` is a variable containing XML data loaded from an external source at runtime:

```
var xml:XML = new XML(loadedXMLData);
```

When you use the `XML` constructor, any string data you pass to the constructor is parsed into the `XML` object as XML nodes. By default, Flash Player attempts to interpret all string data as XML. That means it interprets whitespace (carriage returns, tabs, etc.) as XML nodes. That can cause unexpected results. Therefore, if the XML string data you pass to an `XML` constructor contains extra whitespace (for formatting purposes) that you don't want interpreted as XML nodes, you should first set the static `ignoreWhitespace` property to `true` for the `XML` class, as shown here:

```
XML.ignoreWhitespace = true;
var xml:XML = new XML(loadedXMLData);
```

Reading XML Data

Once you have an `XML` object, you can read from the object. There are two basic ways in which you can read the data: by traversing the Document Object Model (DOM) or by accessing the data using E4X syntax. The two techniques are not exclusive of one another: you can use them in conjunction with one another.

In each case that outputs an XML node, the following examples use the `toXMLString()` method to format the XML node as a string.

When viewing the XML data in light of the DOM, treat it simply as a hierarchical structure of data consisting of parent and child nodes. When looking at the DOM, focus primarily on the structure rather than the content. You can retrieve all the content from an `XML` object by treating it in this manner, but you access the data by structure by stepping into the XML one node at a time. The `XML` class defines a host of methods for retrieving DOM structure information, including the following:

`children()`
: The `children()` method returns an `XMLList` object with all the child nodes of an `XML` object. The `XMLList` class implements a very similar interface to that of XML, and all of the methods discussed in this section apply to both `XML` and `XMLList`. An `XMLList` object is essentially an array of `XML` or `XMLList` objects. You can even retrieve elements from an `XMLList` object using array access notation. For example, the following code retrieves the book nodes as an `XMLList`. It then displays the first element from that list.

```
var bookNodes:XMLList = xml.children();
trace(bookNodes[0].toXMLString());
```

`length()`
: The `length()` method returns the number of elements. For `XML` objects, this always returns `1`. For `XMLList` objects, it may return more than `1`. The following example illustrates the `children()` and `length()` methods used in conjunction. This example displays the titles of each of the books:

```
var bookNodes:XMLList = xml.children();
for(var i:uint = 0; i < bookNodes.length(); i++) {
  trace(bookNodes[i].children()[0].toXMLString());
}
```

`parent()`
: You can retrieve the parent of an `XML` or `XMLList` object using the `parent()` method. For example, the following displays the first book node by accessing the title node first, and then it retrieves the parent of that node:

```
trace(xml.children()[0].children()[0].parent().toXMLString());
```

`attributes()`
: The `attributes()` method returns an `XMLList` object with all the data from the attributes contained within an `XML` object. You can call the `name()` method for each attribute in the `XMLList` to retrieve the name of the attribute as a string. You can then use that value as a parameter, which you can pass to the `attribute()` method of the `XML` object to retrieve the value of the attribute. The following example illustrates how this works:

```
var author0:XML = xml.children()[0].children()[1].children()[0];
var attributes:XMLList = author0.attributes();
var attributeName:String;
for(var i:uint = 0; i < attributes.length(); i++) {
  attributeName = attributes[i].name();
  trace(attributeName + " " + author0.attribute(attributeName));
}
```

As you can see, traversing the XML DOM is effective but laborious. Often, it's far more effective to use E4X syntax, particularly when you already know the structure. E4X syntax allows you to access child nodes by name as properties of parent nodes. For example, the following accesses the first book node:

```
trace(xml.book[0]);
```

You can chain together this simple E4X syntax as in the following example, which retrieves the first author node of the first book node:

```
trace(xml.book[0].authors.author[0].toXMLString());
```

E4X also allows you to easily access attributes using the `@` symbol. The following uses this syntax to retrieve the value of the first attribute of the author node:

```
trace(xml.book[0].authors.author[0].@first);
```

You can also use E4X filters. Filters are enclosed in parentheses within which you specify conditions. The following example retrieves all the author nodes in which the last attribute is Kazoun:

```
var authors:XMLList = xml.book.authors.author.(@last == "Kazoun");
for(var i:uint = 0; i < authors.length(); i++) {
  trace(authors[i].parent().parent().toXMLString());
}
```

Writing to and Editing XML Objects

You can also write to and edit XML objects using ActionScript. There are three things you can do in this category:

- Modify existing data.
- Add new data.
- Remove existing data.

You can modify existing data using the same E4X syntax you use to read the data on the left side of an assignment statement. For example, the following changes the title of the first book:

```
xml.book[0].title = "Programming Flex 3: Edition 1";
```

The following example changes the name of the second author of the first book:

```
xml.book[0].authors.author[1].@first = "Joseph";
```

If you want to add new data, you can use the appendChild(), prependChild(), insertChildBefore(), and insertChildAfter() methods. Each method inserts a new XML node into an XML or XMLList structure. The appendChild() and prependChild() methods each accept one parameter and insert the node at the end and at the beginning of the structure, respectively. The following adds a new publisher node to each book:

```
xml.book[0].appendChild(<publisher>O'Reilly</publisher>);
xml.book[1].appendChild(<publisher>O'Reilly</publisher>);
```

You can use the insertChildBefore() and insertChildAfter() methods to add a new node before or after an existing node. The methods each require two parameters: the new node to add, and a reference to the existing node. The following adds a new publication date node (publicationDate) between the authors and publisher nodes:

```
xml.book[0].insertChildAfter(xml.book[0].authors, <publicationDate>2006</
publicationDate>);
xml.book[1].insertChildAfter(xml.book[1].authors, <publicationDate>2006</
publicationDate>);
```

You can remove elements using the delete operator. The following example first adds a new middle attribute to an author node and then removes it:

```
xml.book[0].authors.author[1] = <author first="Joey" middle="Persnippity" last="Lott"
/>;
trace(xml.book[0].authors);
```

```
delete xml.book[0].authors.author[1].@middle;
trace(xml.book[0].authors);
```

Reflection

ActionScript 3.0 supports class reflection using the following functions in the `flash.utils` package:

- `getQualifiedClassName`
- `getQualifiedSuperclassName`
- `getDefinitionByName`
- `describeType`

Getting the Class Name

You can retrieve the name of the class for which an object is an instance using the `getQualifiedClassName()` function. The function requires that you pass it a reference to an object; it then returns the fully qualified class name.

```
var loader:URLLoader = new URLLoader();
var className:String = getQualifiedClassName(loader);
trace(className); // Displays flash.net::URLLoader
```

If you want to retrieve the fully qualified superclass name for an object, you can use the `getQualifiedSuperclassName()` function:

```
var loader:URLLoader = new URLLoader();
var className:String = getQualifiedSuperclassName(loader);
trace(className); // Displays flash.events::EventDispatcher
```

Getting the Class by Name

If you have a class name, you can retrieve a reference to the class using the `getDefinitionByName()` function. The function requires a string parameter specifying a fully qualified class name, and it returns an `Object` type. The function returns an `Object` type rather than a `Class` type because it could also theoretically return a reference to a function if you pass it a fully qualified function name (e.g., `flash.util.getTimer`).

If you're certain that you're retrieving a class reference, you can cast the return value to `Class`, as in the following example:

```
var classReference:Class = Class(getDefinitionByName("flash.net.URLLoader"));
```

Once you've retrieved a reference to a class, you can create a `new` instance, as follows:

```
var instance:Object = new classReference();
```

Obviously, you can use the return value from getQualifiedClassName() or getQualifiedSuperclassName() in conjunction with getDefinitionByName(), as in the following example:

```
var loader:URLLoader = new URLLoader();
var className:String = getQualifiedClassName(loader);
var classReference:Class = Class(getDefinitionByName(className));
var instance:Object = new classReference();
```

Class Introspection

You can use describeType() to return a description of all the events, public properties, and public methods of an object. Simply pass the method a reference to the object you want to introspect. The method returns an XML object that details the class name, superclass, various class settings, implemented interfaces, constructor signature, public method signatures, and public properties descriptions.

The following example retrieves the description for a URLLoader object:

```
var loader:URLLoader = new URLLoader();
var description:XML = describeType(loader);
trace(description);
```

The preceding example outputs the following:

```
<type name="flash.net::URLLoader" base="flash.events::EventDispatcher"
isDynamic="false" isFinal="false" isStatic="false">
  <metadata name="Event">
    <arg key="name" value="httpStatus"/>
    <arg key="type" value="flash.events.HTTPStatusEvent"/>
  </metadata>
  <metadata name="Event">
    <arg key="name" value="securityError"/>
    <arg key="type" value="flash.events.SecurityErrorEvent"/>
  </metadata>
  <metadata name="Event">
    <arg key="name" value="ioError"/>
    <arg key="type" value="flash.events.IOErrorEvent"/>
  </metadata>
  <metadata name="Event">
    <arg key="name" value="progress"/>
    <arg key="type" value="flash.events.ProgressEvent"/>
  </metadata>
  <metadata name="Event">
    <arg key="name" value="complete"/>
    <arg key="type" value="flash.events.Event"/>
  </metadata>
  <metadata name="Event">
    <arg key="name" value="open"/>
    <arg key="type" value="flash.events.Event"/>
  </metadata>
  <extendsClass type="flash.events::EventDispatcher"/>
  <extendsClass type="Object"/>
  <implementsInterface type="flash.events::IEventDispatcher"/>
```

```
  <constructor>
    <parameter index="1" type="flash.net::URLRequest" optional="true"/>
  </constructor>
  <variable name="bytesTotal" type="uint"/>
  <variable name="data" type="*"/>
  <method name="load" declaredBy="flash.net::URLLoader" returnType="void">
    <parameter index="1" type="flash.net::URLRequest" optional="false"/>
  </method>
  <method name="close" declaredBy="flash.net::URLLoader" returnType="void"/>
  <variable name="dataFormat" type="String"/>
  <variable name="bytesLoaded" type="uint"/>
  <method name="dispatchEvent" declaredBy="flash.events::EventDispatcher"
returnType="Boolean">
    <parameter index="1" type="flash.events::Event" optional="false"/>
  </method>
  <method name="toString" declaredBy="flash.events::EventDispatcher"
returnType="String"/>
  <method name="willTrigger" declaredBy="flash.events::EventDispatcher"
returnType="Boolean">
    <parameter index="1" type="String" optional="false"/>
  </method>
  <method name="addEventListener" declaredBy="flash.events::EventDispatcher"
returnType="void">
    <parameter index="1" type="String" optional="false"/>
    <parameter index="2" type="Function" optional="false"/>
    <parameter index="3" type="Boolean" optional="true"/>
    <parameter index="4" type="int" optional="true"/>
    <parameter index="5" type="Boolean" optional="true"/>
  </method>
  <method name="hasEventListener" declaredBy="flash.events::EventDispatcher"
returnType="Boolean">
    <parameter index="1" type="String" optional="false"/>
  </method>
  <method name="removeEventListener" declaredBy="flash.events::EventDispatcher"
returnType="void">
    <parameter index="1" type="String" optional="false"/>
    <parameter index="2" type="Function" optional="false"/>
    <parameter index="3" type="Boolean" optional="true"/>
  </method>
</type>
```

Summary

In this chapter, we discussed the fundamentals of ActionScript 3.0. ActionScript is the ECMAScript-standard-based programming language used by Flex applications. Although the topic of ActionScript is far too complex to discuss comprehensively in one chapter, we have covered many of the basics you'll need to get started writing ActionScript code, including where to place the code, basic syntax, common data types, how to write classes, the event model, error handling, working with XML, and reflection.

CHAPTER 5

Framework Fundamentals

When you build a Flex application, you create an *.swf* file. Users can then run the application using Flash Player, just as they would any other *.swf* file that was created by any other means (e.g., by using the Flash authoring tool). Flex *.swf* files have two distinct characteristics:

- When building Flex applications, the developer has access to and uses a vast library of ActionScript classes known as the *Flex framework*. The parts of the framework the developer uses are compiled into the resultant *.swf* file.
- At runtime, the Flex framework code that is compiled into the *.swf* dictates a particular way in which the application will load, initialize, and run.

The Flex framework has been designed in such a way that it "just works" without you, the developer, needing to know too much about it. Yet, having a better understanding of the inner workings of the Flex framework will aid you in many ways. For example, the Flex framework provides built-in preloading functionality, and it uses a default progress indicator (unless you tell it otherwise). That means you get these capabilities for free, and they will work without any extra effort on your part. However, you can also customize the progress indicator, as well as customize what happens while the application is downloading and/or initializing, to suit your needs. Without a better understanding of the Flex framework, customizing Flex in this way may be difficult. This is also true of other scenarios, including customizing component creation policies, localizing applications, and using shared libraries.

In this chapter, we'll take an in-depth look at the Flex framework. We'll talk about some practical topics, such as how to localize an application using resource bundles. We'll also talk about some things that you probably won't feel are immediately and directly applicable to the work you do. For example, we'll talk about something known as an application domain, which determines how content loaded at runtime is partitioned. However, don't spend too much time worrying about whether you fully understand the more complex topics just yet. It's likely that sometime after reading this chapter, you'll be working on a Flex application that requires a customized solution that takes you into realms of code and framework knowledge you hadn't had to venture into previously. At that time, you may want to return to sections of this chapter to review how the Flex framework handles initialization, component life cycles, or any of the other topics we'll talk about in the following sections.

Understanding How Flex Applications Are Structured

How is a Flex application structured? At first glance, the answer to that question may seem obvious: every Flex application has an `Application` container object with lots of other components nested inside it. That is true, but it's only part of the story. Behind the scenes, the Flex framework does more than just create instances of the components and the `Application` container you know about because you wrote the corresponding MXML code. The `Application` is clearly an important part, but it's just one of the following three major pieces of a complete Flex application:

- `SystemManager`
- `Preloader`
- `Application`

This breakdown of `SystemManager`, `Preloader`, and `Application` as the three most significant pieces of a Flex application is not something you'll find anywhere in the Flex documentation. This is a purely subjective determination by the authors of this book. However, it is very helpful to focus on these three significant parts both to learn about their individual roles and to better understand how they relate to each other.

SystemManager Instance

The `mx.managers.SystemManager` class is arguably the most important class in a Flex application. Without `SystemManager`, no Flex application could run. However, despite its importance, you will see very few references to `SystemManager` in most works on Flex, including this book. Why is that? In part it's because `SystemManager` does its job well enough that you don't even have to know about it 99% of the time. Another reason you don't hear too much about `SystemManager` is that you cannot do much to configure or change it. Yet, you shouldn't overlook `SystemManager`; otherwise, you will not fully understand what a Flex application is.

It's natural enough to assume that the root container or display object in a Flex application is the `Application` object created by the MXML application document. After all, you never write any code to create a parent for the `Application` object. However, behind the scenes the Flex framework does create a parent for the `Application` object, and that parent is an instance of the `SystemManager` class. You can verify this by outputting the description of the parent of an application using the test code in Example 5-1.

Example 5-1. Displaying the description of the parent of an application

```
<?xml version="1.0" encoding="utf-8"?>
<mx:Application xmlns:mx="http://www.adobe.com/2006/mxml" layout="absolute"
creationComplete="creationCompleteHandler();">
    <mx:Script>
        <![CDATA[
            import flash.utils.describeType;

            private function creationCompleteHandler():void {
                textArea.text = flash.utils.describeType(parent);
            }

        ]]>
    </mx:Script>
    <mx:TextArea id="textArea" width="100%" height="100%" />
</mx:Application>
```

If you run this test, you'll see a description of the application's parent property type. In the description, you can see that the parent is of type `SystemManager`. The description contains a great deal of text. You can see the type of the application's parent by looking at the `base` attribute of the top-level `type` tag.

`SystemManager` has a property called `topLevelSystemManager`. This is a reference to the `SystemManager` instance that is at the root of everything running in Flash Player at that time. For a Flex application loaded as the main application within Flash Player, this property will always be self-referencing. However, a Flex application loaded into another Flex application also has its own `SystemManager`, and that `SystemManager` object's `topLevelSystemManager` will reference the `SystemManager` object of the parent Flex application rather than itself. For more information on loading Flex applications into other Flex applications, see the discussion of `ApplicationDomain` in "Understanding Application Domains" later in this chapter.

The `SystemManager` instance of an application is responsible for managing application startup, and it is also the container for not only the application, but also all the tool tips and pop ups in the application.

Although you don't frequently need to reference `SystemManager` for an application, you can do so if necessary. All subclasses of `UIComponents` (including `Application`) have a `systemManager` property that references `SystemManager` for the application. The primary way in which developers are likely to use `SystemManager` is to listen for events that are dispatched by any display object in the application. When those events bubble up, the last object to have an opportunity to handle the event is `SystemManager`.

Preloader Instance

When the Flex application first starts it creates the `SystemManager` instance. The `SystemManager` instance needs to do a few internal things first, but one of its primary responsibilities is to create a `Preloader` instance. The `Preloader` object is responsible for monitoring the download progress of the main application, gathering the list of runtime shared libraries and starting to download them, as well as creating a progress indicator to display to the user.

Application Instance

When you create a Flex application, you must have a main application MXML document, usually with a root tag of `Application`. All components that you include in the application are added directly or indirectly to the `Application` instance (although when you programmatically add a pop up using `PopUpManager`, the component is technically added to the `SystemManager` instance, not the `Application`). For instance, in Example 5-1 the root tag is `Application`, and it contains a text area component nested within it. It is evident that the `Application` component plays a major role in all Flex applications. Much of this book is focused on code that you can write that has an effect on the `Application` component or its contents.

Loading and Initializing Flex Applications

When you load a Flex application and run it, it may appear that not much is going on. As a user, you typically see a progress indicator until the application has loaded and initialized. However, behind the scenes an intricate process kicks off and runs its course until the application is ready to display to the user. As a Flex developer, you don't often have to concern yourself with exactly what is happening behind the scenes, but this knowledge can help you to better understand how to build an application and how to diagnose problems.

As we mentioned earlier in this chapter, Flex applications are *.swf* files that run in Flash Player. Historically, Flash Player was created to play back vector animations. Therefore, although the capabilities of Flash Player have grown tremendously since its earliest stages, its historical roots remain, and Flash Player still uses a timeline metaphor when running *.swf* content. Flash Player supports the concept of frames—much like frames of a movie. These frames occur sequentially over time, and unless otherwise instructed, Flash Player will automatically play back the frames of an *.swf* file as they are available because the *.swf* format is a progressive download format. That means Flash Player doesn't need to wait for an entire *.swf* file to download before it can begin to read the *.swf* content and play it back or run it. As we'll see in just a moment, the Flex framework uses this fact to its advantage. Each frame can contain elements of the application, be they code or embedded assets. As soon as the contents of a frame are downloaded, they're available for use.

If you ran the test from Example 5-1, you may have noticed that the `SystemManager` class is a subclass of the `flash.display.MovieClip` class because the `type` attribute of the `extendsClass` tag is `flash.display.MovieClip`. The `MovieClip` class is used frequently when creating Flash content using the Flash authoring tool because `MovieClip` supports multiple frames, something that is useful when using the timelines of Flash authoring. On the other hand, Flex really doesn't rely on timelines much. All Flex components have just one frame. Therefore, the `MovieClip` class isn't used much in Flex development. The `SystemManager` class is one notable exception. The reason that `SystemManager` extends `MovieClip` is that `SystemManager` instances have exactly two frames: the first frame is very lightweight, containing only enough content to manage and monitor download progress. The second frame contains everything else, including the majority of the Flex framework, the `Application` instance, all custom classes, and embedded assets. Because of `SystemManager`'s two-frame nature, it can quickly display a progress indicator to the user (because the first frame downloads quickly) while the second frame continues to download and initialize.

The `SystemManager` instance is the only major part of a Flex application that exists for the entire application life cycle. The `Preloader` instance exists for the first frame and only for a brief time on the second frame while the application is initializing. The `Application` instance exists on the second frame only. Figure 5-1 shows the relationship of these three parts to the two-frame timeline.

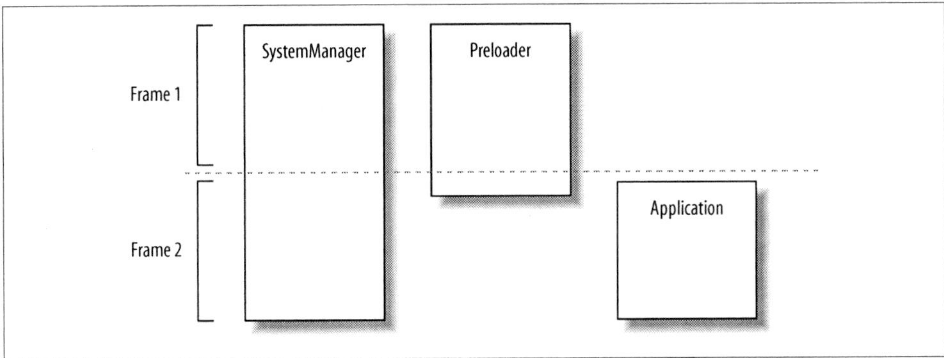

Figure 5-1. The SystemManager, Preloader, and Application objects as they exist over time

The details of how an application downloads and initializes are as follows. This sequence is condensed and simplified. We've omitted many cumbersome details for the sake of clarity and readability.

1. The first frame of the *.swf* downloads, and a `SystemManager` instance is automatically created.
2. The `SystemManager` loads resource bundles.

Simply put, *resource bundles* are collections of text or embedded resources that are accessible via keys. Resource bundles can be used at compile time or at runtime. You can read more about resource bundles later, in the "Localization" section of this chapter.

3. The SystemManager stops the timeline on frame 1, preventing anything from frame 2 from running until later.
4. The SystemManager creates a Preloader instance.
5. The SystemManager registers the ResourceManager class (you can learn more about this in the "Localization" section of this chapter) to make it available in frame 1, and passes the ResourceManager any resource modules specified using a query string or FlashVars.

FlashVars are variables passed into the Flex application via an HTML page. You can read more about FlashVars in Chapter 20.

6. The SystemManager starts the Preloader sequence.
7. The Preloader instance creates a preloader display.
8. The Preloader starts to download runtime shared libraries.
9. The Preloader monitors the progress of the main *.swf* download as well as the runtime shared libraries, dispatching events to notify the display when there is progress.
10. When everything has downloaded (the runtime shared libraries and the main *.swf*), the Preloader instance dispatches an initProgress event, which notifies the SystemManager that everything is ready to start initializing the Application object.
11. Once the SystemManager receives an initProgress event, it goes to the next frame, causing the Application object to instantiate.
12. The Application object begins to start up, and it runs through its startup life cycle, including layout management.
13. When the Application has initialized, it dispatches a creationComplete event, notifying the Preloader object.
14. The Preloader dispatches a complete event notifying the SystemManager that it is complete.
15. The SystemManager adds the Application instance to the display list and removes the Preloader and preloader display.
16. Both the SystemManager and the Application objects dispatch an applicationComplete event.

At that point, everything is downloaded and initialized, the application is visible, and the user can start to interact with it.

One important point to remember is that the overwhelming majority of the code for a Flex application is placed on frame 2. That means that most of the Flex framework, including all the UI components and data components, is available only on frame 2. It also means that by default, all your custom classes and components are available only starting on frame 2.

Understanding the Component Life Cycles

All Flex components, including `Application`, have a common, standard life cycle. These life cycles are most easily described and understood from the view of the events they dispatch. We are primarily concerned with the following three major events in a component life cycle:

`preinitialize`
: The component's been instantiated but hasn't yet created any child components.

`initialize`
: The component has created child components but has not yet laid out those components.

`creationComplete`
: The component has been completely instantiated and has laid out all child components.

The events always occur in this order: `preinitialize`, `initialize`, and `creationComplete`.

See Chapter 19 for more details on component life cycles and events.

Components are always created from descriptors. The use of descriptors allows the Flex framework a lot of flexibility in terms of how and when it instantiates components. Each component that can contain child components will have a list of descriptors for the child components. As you'll see in Chapter 10, you can control the creation policy for some components. In those cases, if you were to defer instantiation of child components, such a component would dispatch a `preinitialize` event right away, but it would not dispatch the `initialize` event until the code explicitly created the child components from the descriptors.

The `initialize` event occurs when the child components have been created. However, at this point the layout of the child components has not yet occurred. The `initialize` event means you can successfully reference the child components, targeting them with ActionScript commands.

The creationComplete event occurs at the point when we would conventionally think of a component as being truly complete: the child components are created, and everything is laid out.

These life cycle events occur within all components, and we'll return to these events throughout the book. We mention this life cycle in this chapter because it can help you to better understand what happens when an application first starts. That is, once an Application instance is created, it dispatches a preinitialize event. However, it hasn't yet created any child components. It then recursively creates child components. Here's an example to help you better understand the process. If an Application contains a VBox that contains a Label component, the Application instantiates its child, the VBox. The VBox then dispatches a preinitialize event. The VBox creates its child, the Label component. The VBox can then dispatch an initialize event. The Application can then do the same. Only after everything is laid out will the Application dispatch a creationComplete event.

Loading One Flex Application into Another Flex Application

Loading one Flex application into another Flex application is actually remarkably simple. All you need to do is create an SWFLoader instance and set the source property, as shown here:

```
<mx:SWFLoader source="application.swf" />
```

However, it gets slightly more challenging when you want to interact with the content you are loading. For example, if you want to call a public method defined in the loaded application, you must know two important things:

- What is the path to the loaded application relative to the SWFLoader used to load the application?
- When has the loaded application actually initialized?

The answers to these questions are as follows. When an SWFLoader loads a Flex application, the SWFLoader object's content property provides a reference to the root of the loaded Flex application. As we've already discussed, that root is a SystemManager object. The SystemManager class defines an application property that references the Application object. However, it's important to understand that the application property of a SystemManager object for a Flex application that has just loaded will be null because the loaded content will still be on its first frame, and the Application instance isn't constructed until the second frame. This might seem to pose a problem, but there is a relatively elegant solution.

When an SWFLoader loads and initializes the content, it dispatches an init event. You should first handle the init event. This tells you when you can reference the SystemManager for the loaded content. You must then add an event listener for the applicationComplete event for the SystemManager. When the applicationComplete event occurs, you can reference the Application object for the loaded content.

Let's look at an example that illustrates the proper way to load one Flex application into another and use events to wait until the application has actually initialized before trying to communicate with the loaded content. In this example, we'll first look at the code for the Flex application that will load into another application. This is the code for a runnable MXML application file called *B.mxml*. This application creates a canvas with a background color of white. It also adds a public method that allows loading applications to set the background color.

```
<?xml version="1.0" encoding="utf-8"?>
<mx:Application xmlns:mx="http://www.adobe.com/2006/mxml" layout="absolute">
    <mx:Script>
        <![CDATA[

            public function setBackground(color:Number):void {
                canvas.setStyle("backgroundColor", color);
            }

        ]]>
    </mx:Script>
    <mx:Canvas id="canvas" backgroundColor="#FFFFFF" width="100" height="100" />
</mx:Application>
```

Here's the runnable MXML application file for the Flex application that loads *B.swf*. Note that we first listen for the init event. Once the init event occurs, we add a listener to the SystemManager object for applicationComplete. Then, once applicationComplete occurs, we can call the public method of the loaded content.

```
<?xml version="1.0" encoding="utf-8"?>
<mx:Application xmlns:mx="http://www.adobe.com/2006/mxml" layout="absolute">
    <mx:Script>
        <![CDATA[
            import mx.managers.SystemManager;
            import mx.events.FlexEvent;

            private function initHandler(event:Event):void {
                event.target.content.addEventListener(FlexEvent.APPLICATION_COMPLETE,
applicationCompleteHandler);
            }

            private function applicationCompleteHandler(event:Event):void {
                event.target.application.setBackground(0xFFFF00);
            }

        ]]>
    </mx:Script>
    <mx:SWFLoader source="B.swf" init="initHandler(event)" />
</mx:Application>
```

With this simple example, you can see how to load one application into another application.

Flex 3 has a built-in feature for building modular applications that use several *.swf* files stitched together at runtime. In many cases, using modules is a much simpler way to achieve the same goals as loading one *.swf* into another. See Chapter 9 for more information on modules.

Differentiating Between Flash Player and the Flex Framework

One of the most important concepts to understand about Flex is the relationship between the Flex framework and Flash Player. Flash Player is a runtime environment for Flash and Flex applications. It can run *.swf* files, which contain bytecode that can communicate with Flash Player, instructing it to perform operations such as loading images, drawing graphics, making HTTP requests, and so on. Flash and Flex applications can do only what Flash Player allows them to do. Flash Player provides an API for all the operations it can perform.

Flex applications run in the same Flash Player as Flash applications. That means the *.swf* files for Flex applications cannot contain anything that a standard Flash application can't contain, and therefore, both applications have the same behaviors. This is because the applications contain only the instructions, and Flash Player is what runs the instructions. Therefore, what differentiates Flash and Flex applications is not the content, but how you create that content.

Flex consists of a compiler that is capable of compiling MXML and ActionScript. The entire Flex framework is written in ActionScript and MXML. It provides a layer of abstraction. The Flex framework consists of many thousands of lines of code, all of which ultimately run instructions that Flash Player can understand. This means that when you utilize the Flex framework, the compiler will include the necessary libraries in the *.swf* files. As a result, you can much more rapidly develop applications. For example, although you could write your own custom grid layout container or combo box UI control, doing so takes a lot longer than simply using the components that are part of the Flex framework.

The trade-off of using the framework is that the file size of the *.swf* increases over an *.swf* created without the use of the framework. This is in contrast to ActionScript 3.0-only projects that use none of the Flex framework. If you don't use the framework, increases in *.swf* file size are in pace with the amount of code you write (or libraries you use) and the assets you compile into the file. Native Flash Player ActionScript classes already exist within Flash Player itself; they don't have to be compiled into the *.swf*. Yet, when you work with the Flex framework, a single line of code that adds a framework component can add a nontrivial amount to the file size because it requires the compiler to include a class or a library of classes that aren't part of Flash Player.

You must determine on a case-by-case basis whether the trade-off in added file size is worth the benefits of using the Flex framework. This is a very subjective issue. However, noting that Flex applications are rich Internet applications (RIAs) targeted at broadband audiences, the few hundred kilobytes added by the framework in the typical application are often viewed as inconsequential.

You can also leverage the Flash Player caching feature to cache the Flex framework in order to reduce *.swf* file size. This feature is discussed in more detail shortly, in "Caching the Framework.[]

You can easily differentiate between Flash Player and Flex framework classes using these guidelines:

- If the class is in a package starting with the word *flash* (e.g., `flash.net.URLLoader`), it is part of Flash Player.
- If the class is in a package starting with the letters *mx* (e.g., `mx.controls.Button`), it is part of the Flex framework.
- MXML tags almost always (with few exceptions) correspond to Flex framework classes.

Caching the Framework

Flash Player 9, Update 3 (which is Flash Player 9.0.115) has a feature called *Flash Player cache*. Flash Player cache isn't entirely dissimilar from typical browser caching in that it is capable of storing persistent local copies of files and using the local copies instead of remote copies upon subsequent requests. However, Flash Player cache is significantly different from browser cache in two key ways:

- Flash Player cache works only with signed runtime shared libraries (must be signed by Adobe).
- Flash Player cache works across domains. That means you can download a signed runtime shared library from www.a.com (*http://www.a.com*) and when an *.swf* from www.b.com (*http://www.b.com*) needs that same signed runtime shared library, it will have access to it.

Flash Player cache is a way in which you can dramatically reduce the size of a Flex *.swf* file. Keep in mind that this does not necessarily mean you're reducing the number of bytes a user must download to access the application correctly. If the user doesn't already have the necessary signed runtime shared library files (*.swz* files) in cache, he will still have to download those. In fact, because the runtime shared libraries are the entire Flex framework instead of only the parts required by the specific application, the total download can potentially be greater than if the framework was statically linked and compiled in the application *.swf* file. However, if the user does have the required *.swz* files in cache, all he will have to download is the *.swf* file. Because the *.swf* file won't have to include all the classes in the *.swz* files it uses, the *.swf* file can be quite a bit smaller than it would be if all the classes were statically linked to it (i.e., compiled into it).

Typically, when you compile a Flex application, all the Flex framework libraries are statically linked. That means that all the libraries you use in the application are compiled into the resultant *.swf* file. That's why a typical Flex *.swf* file, even with nothing more than a blank application canvas, is at least several hundred kilobytes. All Flex applications always use the *framework.swc* library, which consists of the core Flex framework classes. However, many other libraries (*.swc* files) make up the Flex framework and can be linked to a Flex application. These include libraries for remote procedure calls and utilities, to name a few. Of the core libraries, though, only two are large enough to warrant *.swz* files. You'll find that in the Flex SDK in the *rsls* directory there are two core *.swz* files: one that corresponds to *framework.swc* and one that corresponds to *rpc.swc*. If you have the professional version of Flex, you will also have an *.swz* file corresponding to *datavisualization.swc*. You can dynamically link your Flex application to these *.swz* files instead of statically linking to the *.swc* files. This will cause the application to use the Flash Player cache for these libraries.

See Chapter 20 for more information about how to statically and dynamically link to libraries.

Also, note that if a Flex application is dynamically linked to *.swz* files that are different from those stored in a user's cache, Flash Player will download the required *.swz* files. An example of this would be if an application required a more recent version of the Flex framework than was stored in the *.swz* file in a user's cache. The detection and downloading are handled automatically by Flash Player.

Understanding Application Domains

Application domains are critically important in terms of how Flex applications function, but in most cases, you don't even know they are there. An application domain is the partition within which an application runs in Flash Player. In many cases, just one application is running in Flash Player, and in such cases, there is just one application domain. However, when you load additional *.swf* files into an existing application, you can create additional application domains for some or all of those additional applications.

When you load a *.swf* file, three possible things can occur:

- The loaded *.swf* runs in a new application domain that is completely partitioned from all other application domains.
- The loaded *.swf* runs in a new application domain that is a child of an existing application domain.
- The loaded *.swf* runs in an existing application domain.

Each scenario is subtly different. However, subtle differences can have a big effect, and it's important to understand these differences so that you can understand what choices to make in each case.

All Flex and Flash applications are composed of collections of classes. An application domain holds the collections of classes for an application or applications. When just one application is running in Flash Player, the concept of an application domain is practically a formality because you are guaranteed that an *.swf* will never contain more than one definition for a class. However, when you load an additional *.swf* file, there is a possibility that it will contain a definition for a class by the same name as one that is already loaded from another *.swf* file. An application domain ensures that within the domain there is only one definition for each class. Therefore, it has a set of rules for determining how to choose between conflicting definitions if such a scenario presents itself.

If an application is loaded into an application domain with a parent, it essentially inherits all the class definitions from the parent application domain. The result is that the child application domain cannot have class definitions for classes that are otherwise defined in the parent application domain. For example, if you load one Flex application *.swf* into another Flex application *.swf* with the default settings, there would be two application domains but one would be a child of the other, and all duplicate Flex framework classes from the child would be disregarded in favor of the same classes from the parent application domain. This is often appropriate, and it has several possible benefits:

- It uses less memory. If the duplicate classes were not disregarded, memory usage would increase.
- Singleton manager classes are accessible to both the parent and the child applications (meaning that just one instance of the class is shared by parent and child applications).
- Theoretically, it is possible to compile the child *.swf* files by excluding any duplicate classes the child *.swf* would inherit at runtime from the parent application domain. This would reduce the file size overhead in child *.swf* files.

Just as there are cases in which this default child domain behavior is useful, sometimes it works at cross purposes with a project's needs or requirements. For example, consider a scenario in which two applications are built using two classes with the same name but very different implementations. If one is loaded into the other, the child will not work as intended because that class will be discarded in the child, and the parent version will be used in both applications. In such a case, it is clear that there is a need to be able to completely partition the applications into separate application domains. Separate application domains ensure that the sorts of conflicts just described don't occur. However, it is important to use these sorts of exclusive application domains only when necessary because they will increase memory usage.

The third scenario is one in which an *.swf* is loaded into the same application domain as the loading/requesting application. This is the behavior utilized by runtime shared libraries. It is also useful when you want to load libraries of fonts and other assets at runtime for use in the requesting application.

You create each scenario (exclusive application domains, parent/child application domains, and same application domains) by specifying a `flash.system.LoaderContext` with the appropriate setting when calling the `load()` method of a `flash.display.Loader` or a `flash.net.URLLoader` object. The `LoaderContext` class defines an `applicationDomain` property. Setting the value of this property determines the application domain for the loaded content. The `applicationDomain` property is of type `flash.system.ApplicationDomain`. The `ApplicationDomain` class has a static property called `currentDomain` that is a reference to the application domain of the requesting code.

It's possible to use a `LoaderContext` and an `ApplicationDomain` object (in conjunction with the `currentDomain` property) to achieve the necessary behavior for each of the aforementioned scenarios. For instance, you can achieve the default behavior (the content is loaded into a child domain) by passing no second parameter to the `load()` method. You can achieve the same behavior when passing a `LoaderContext` object with the `applicationDomain` set to a new `ApplicationDomain` object that uses `ApplicationDomain.currentDomain` as the parent application domain. You do this by passing `ApplicationDomain.currentDomain` to the constructor of the constructor, as shown here:

```
var context:LoaderContext = new LoaderContext();
context.applicationDomain = new ApplicationDomain(ApplicationDomain.currentDomain);
var request:URLRequest = new URLRequest("RuntimeLoadingExample.swf");
var loader:Loader = new Loader();
loader.load(request, context);
```

You can achieve an exclusive, separate application domain for loaded content by constructing an `ApplicationDomain` object with no parameter passed to the constructor:

```
var context:LoaderContext = new LoaderContext();
context.applicationDomain = new ApplicationDomain();
var request:URLRequest = new URLRequest("RuntimeLoadingExample.swf");
var loader:Loader = new Loader();
loader.load(request, context);
```

If you want to load the content into the same application domain, you can simply use `ApplicationDomain.currentDomain`:

```
var context:LoaderContext = new LoaderContext();
context.applicationDomain = ApplicationDomain.currentDomain;
var request:URLRequest = new URLRequest("RuntimeLoadingExample.swf");
var loader:Loader = new Loader();
loader.load(request, context);
```

You can read more about `ApplicationDomain` in the Flex documentation and at *http://livedocs.adobe.com/flex/3/langref/flash/system/ApplicationDomain.html.*

Localization

Localization refers to enabling an application to display different resources at different locations. The most obvious and common example of localization is displaying text in different languages based on location or user selection. Localization is different from building entirely unique applications for each locale. Instead, the same code base is used for all locales, but different resource bundles are used for different locales. There are two basic variations on how this is implemented: compile time and runtime.

Compile-time localization means that you create a unique *.swf* for each locale. For example, if you want to support both French and Spanish, with compile-time localization you must create two *.swf* files: one for French and one for Spanish. Although with compile-time localization you create unique *.swf* files for each locale, each file uses the same code base. That means you don't have to build and maintain separate application code bases. What is different between the *.swf* files is the resource bundle(s) that gets compiled into the *.swf*. We'll talk more about resource bundles in just a minute.

Runtime localization allows you to create and deploy just one *.swf* containing your main application architecture. Runtime localization still uses resource bundles just like compile-time localization. However, rather than compiling the resource bundles for just one locale into the application runtime localization, necessitating different *.swf* files for each locale, runtime localization means one of two things: compiling in all resource bundles for all locales (allowing for changes between locales at runtime), or loading resource *modules* at runtime. We'll talk more about resource modules later in this chapter when we talk about the details of loading resources at runtime.

Resource Bundles

All Flex applications use resource bundles, whether you are aware of them or not. The Flex framework has a bunch of resource bundles for things such as containers, controls, effects, skins, and styles. These resource bundles are compiled into an application by default. You can also create your own custom resource bundles to use for things such as localization. You create a resource bundle by creating a new UTF-8 encoded text file and populating it with keys and values. Each key and value is delimited by an equals sign, and each key-value pair should be on its own line in the file. The following is an example of such a file:

```
instruction=Select a value
color=Color
send=Send
```

The keys in this example are `instruction`, `color`, and `send`. You probably noticed that all the values are strings. However, you can also embed objects and classes in a resource bundle using the `Embed()` and `ClassReference()` directives.

The following example not only uses string values, but also embeds an image:

```
instruction=Select a value
color=Color
send=Send
flag=Embed('../../usa.jpg')
```

All resource bundle files should be saved using UTF-8 encoding. This is important because it allows any character in the Unicode standard to be accurately stored. That means you can store and use characters outside the 128 characters used in the US-ASCII standard, allowing for use of characters in other languages and character sets.

You must save resource bundle files using the *.properties* extension. For example, you can save a resource bundle file as *languageResources.properties*. You will almost always want to save resource bundle files maintaining parity in naming, but placing them in subdirectories each named by locale. For example, if you want to support both French and Spanish, you might create two resource bundle files, both called *languageResources.properties*, but place them in different subdirectories called *fr_FR* and *es_ES*, respectively. Generally, you should place all the localization resource bundle files in subdirectories of one parent directory. For example, in the preceding scenario, the paths to the files might be *locale/fr_FR/languageResources.properties* and *locale/es_ES/languageResources.properties*. You could continue this pattern for as many locales as you need to support. For example, you could support English in the United States by adding a new file called *locale/en_US/languageResources.properties*. Usually, each file will contain the same set of keys, but with different, locale/language-specific values. For the examples that follow in the next few sections, we'll use the resource bundle files shown in Example 5-2, Example 5-3, and Example 5-4. For each resource bundle we'll assume that the files are saved in subdirectories of a *locale* directory that is a sibling of the *src* directory for the Flex project.

The code in Example 5-2 is saved in *locale/en_US/languageResources.properties*. This also assumes that there's an *assets* directory in the project root, and that the *.jpg* files referenced in the following code examples are stored in that *assets* directory.

Example 5-2. U.S. English resource bundle

```
instruction=Select a value
color=Color
send=Send
flag=Embed('../../assets/usa.jpg')
```

The code in Example 5-3 is saved in *locales/en_CA/languageResources.properties*.

Example 5-3. Canadian English resource bundle

```
instruction=Select a value
color=Colour
send=Send
flag=Embed('../../assets/canada.jpg')
```

The code in Example 5-4 is saved in *locales/es_ES/languageResources.properties*.

Example 5-4. Spanish (Spain) resource bundle

```
instruction=Seleccione un valor
color=Color
send=Envíe
flag=Embed('../../assets/spain.jpg')
```

As we mentioned earlier, Flex includes a bunch of resource bundles that it uses when compiling most Flex applications. For example, there are bundles for controls, containers, styles, and effects. Some of these bundles are locale-specific, and the Flex SDK has only the bundles for the locale for which the SDK was intended. As an example, in the United States some of the Flex resource bundles are stored in the *frameworks/locale/en_US* directory of the SDK because they are specific to U.S. English. If you want to use resource bundles other than the locales already supported by the version of the SDK you have, you will need to create copies of the existing resource bundles, saving them to directories within *frameworks/locale* with the locale names you intend to use. For example, if you want to support Spanish (from Spain), you'll need to make sure you have a *frameworks/locale/es_ES* directory in your SDK containing all the necessary resource bundles (compiled and packaged as *.swc* files). The simplest way to accomplish this is to use the `copylocale` utility provided in the *bin* directory of the SDK. The `copylocale` utility will copy an existing locale's resource bundles to a new locale. The syntax is as follows:

```
copylocale existingLocale newLocale
```

For example, if you already have the `en_US` locale and you want to support French, you could run `copylocale` as follows:

```
copylocale en_US fr_FR
```

The preceding code assumes you are running the command from a command prompt and that you have added the *bin* directory of your SDK installation to your system's path.

For the examples that we'll see in the following sections, we'll assume that we've already run `copylocale` as necessary to ensure that we have the following locales in the SDK: `en_US`, `en_CA`, and `es_ES`.

Using ResourceManager

One of the many manager classes that are included in the Flex framework is the ResourceManager class. As the name implies, this class is responsible for managing resources from resource bundles. In the next few sections, we'll see ways in which you can tell a ResourceManager what resource bundle(s) to use. However, first we'll look at how to access a ResourceManager as well as how to access the data from resource bundles via a ResourceManager.

The ResourceManager class uses the Singleton design pattern; therefore, there is just one instance per application. You can access that instance in one of two ways:

- Use the ResourceManager.getInstance() method.
- Use the resourceManager property of a UIComponent instance, including an Application instance.

A ResourceManager object contains all the data for all the resource bundles that have been loaded into an application. You can retrieve that data in two ways:

- Use the Resource() directive.
- Use the get methods of the ResourceManager instance.

The Resource() directive allows you to access data once, at application startup. That means you should use the Resource() directive only for compile-time localization. The directive requires that you pass it two attributes: bundle and key. The bundle is the name of the resource bundle file (minus the *.properties* extension) in which the key is defined. The key is the name of the key from the file for which you want the value. For example, the following uses the Resource() directive to retrieve the color value from the languageResources resource bundle:

```
<mx:Label text="@Resource(bundle='languageResources', key='color')" />
```

When using the Resource() directive for an attribute value in an MXML tag, you must precede the directive with an @ character.

If you would like to retrieve a value from ResourceManager using ActionScript or in a data binding expression, you will need to use one of the following get methods of ResourceManager: getString(), getNumber(), getInt(), getUint(), getBoolean(), getObject(), getStringArray(), or getClass(). All of these methods require two parameters: the resource bundle name and the key name. For example, the following code retrieves the value for the color key from the languageResources resource bundle:

```
var color:uint = ResourceManager.getInstance().getInt("languageResources", "color");
```

As you've already seen, most data is stored in a *.properties* file as strings. The exceptions to that are embedded assets (using the Embed() directive) and classes (using the Class

Reference() directive). Since there is no formal way to distinguish values as string, number, integer, Boolean, and so on, when storing the values in a *.properties* file, the responsibility of differentiating is left to the ResourceManager and you, the developer. You can use the get methods to specify how you'd like the ResourceManager to coerce the value for a key. For example, getBoolean() will attempt to coerce the value to a Boolean value whereas getInt() will attempt to coerce the value to an integer. You should use the getClass() method to retrieve all values stored using the Embed() or ClassReference() directive.

Compile-Time Localization

When you want to implement compile-time localization, you need to do two things:

- Add the Resource() directive or appropriate ResourceManager get method call at the point in the code where you need to retrieve the value from the resource bundle.
- Tell the compiler what resource bundles to include in the *.swf*.

The following code illustrates how an MXML document might look when using compile-time localization:

```
<?xml version="1.0" encoding="utf-8"?>
<mx:Application xmlns:mx="http://www.adobe.com/2006/mxml" layout="vertical">
    <mx:Form>
        <mx:FormHeading label="@Resource(key='instruction', bundle=
'languageResources')" />
        <mx:FormItem label="@Resource(bundle='languageResources', key='color')">
            <mx:ColorPicker id="color" />
        </mx:FormItem>
        <mx:FormItem>
            <mx:Button label="@Resource(bundle='languageResources', key='send')" />
        </mx:FormItem>
    </mx:Form>
    <mx:Image source="@Resource(bundle='languageResources', key='flag')" />
</mx:Application>
```

When compiling the application, you must tell it what resource bundles to use by adding a locale attribute to the compiler options. You also need to tell the compiler where it can find custom resource bundle *.properties* files by adding the directory for the resource bundle files to the source path. The following code tells the compiler to compile an application using the en_CA resource bundle, and it tells the compiler where it can find custom resource bundle files:

```
mxmlc -locale en_CA -source-path=../locale/{locale} Example.mxml
```

The {locale} in the preceding code is a variable that tells the compiler to use the value of the locale attribute.

If you are using Flex Builder, you should do the following:

1. Open the properties for the Flex project (Project→Properties).
2. Select the Flex Compiler option from the list of tabs appearing on the left side of the window.
3. In the "Additional compiler arguments" field, specify something such as the following:

```
-local en_CA -source-path=../locale/{locale}
```

Runtime Localization

Runtime localization occurs in one of two ways:

- Two or more resource bundles get compiled into the *.swf*.
- No resource bundles are compiled into the *.swf* because they are loaded at runtime from external resource modules.

We'll look at each option in the following sections.

Compiling multiple resource bundles into an .swf

You can compile two or more resource bundles into an *.swf* by adding a space-delimited list of locales to the `locale` compiler attribute. For example, if you'd like to compile the `en_US`, `en_CA`, and `es_ES` resource bundles into an *.swf*, the compiler attributes might look like the following:

```
-locale en_US en_CA es_ES -source-path=../locales/{locale}
```

That tells the compiler to include all the resource bundles for the locales in the main application *.swf* file. Then, at runtime, you can use ActionScript to change which locale is currently being used. The `localeChain` property of the `ResourceManager` instance controls which of the available resource bundles the Flex application should use. The `localeChain` property is an array of strings. Therefore, if you want to use the `en_US` resource bundles, you should set the `localeChain` property as follows:

```
resourceManager.localeChain = ["en_US"];
```

If you specify more than one locale in the `localeChain` array, any key-value pairs not found in the first locale will be retrieved from the next locale.

When you allow for runtime selection of locales, you cannot use the `Resource()` directive to retrieve resource bundle values. You must use only the `get` methods of the `ResourceManager` instance. Because of this, the Flex application must also specify one more piece of information via a metadata tag. That piece of data is the name of the resource bundle(s) to use. The `ResourceBundle` metadata tag will tell the compiler to include a particular custom resource bundle.

The following is an example of such a metadata tag in an MXML document:

```
<mx:Metadata>
    [ResourceBundle("languageResources")]
</mx:Metadata>
```

The following code illustrates how you can build an application that allows the user to select a locale at runtime. In Example 5-5, the user selects a locale and the language of the application changes.

Example 5-5. Selecting a locale at runtime

```
<?xml version="1.0" encoding="utf-8"?>
<mx:Application xmlns:mx="http://www.adobe.com/2006/mxml" layout="vertical">
    <mx:Metadata>
        [ResourceBundle("languageResources")]
    </mx:Metadata>
    <mx:Script>
        <![CDATA[

            private function selectLanguage():void {
                resourceManager.localeChain = [language.value];
            }

        ]]>
    </mx:Script>
    <mx:ComboBox id="language" change="selectLanguage();">
        <mx:dataProvider>
            <mx:ArrayCollection>
                <mx:Object label="English (US)" data="en_US" />
                <mx:Object label="English (Canada)" data="en_CA" />
                <mx:Object label="Espanol (Espana)" data="es_ES" />
            </mx:ArrayCollection>
        </mx:dataProvider>
    </mx:ComboBox>
    <mx:Form>
        <mx:FormHeading
label="{resourceManager.getString('languageResources', 'instruction')}" />
        <mx:FormItem
label="{resourceManager.getString('languageResources', 'color')}">
            <mx:ColorPicker id="color" />
        </mx:FormItem>
        <mx:FormItem>
            <mx:Button
label="{resourceManager.getString('languageResources', 'send')}" />
        </mx:FormItem>
    </mx:Form>
    <mx:Image
source="{resourceManager.getClass('languageResources', 'flag')}" />
</mx:Application>
```

Loading resource modules at runtime

Resource modules are resource bundles compiled into *.swf* files that are external to the main application *.swf* file. Resource modules allow you to build applications that can load resources at runtime. This allows users to change the locale at runtime, just as we saw in the preceding section. Resource modules are ideal when the number and size of the resource bundles are significant enough that compiling them all into the main *.swf* file would unnecessarily increase the main *.swf* file size beyond acceptable limits. Resource modules allow you to keep the main *.swf* file relatively small. Resource modules are loaded only when requested, as we'll see shortly.

Resource modules include not only custom resource bundles, but all the framework resource bundles for a locale as well. That means that to create a resource module you must know which resource bundles the application is using. To determine that, run `mxmlc` with the `locale` attribute set to an empty string using the `resource-bundle-list` attribute. The `resource-bundle-list` attribute specifies a file to which the compiler will write a list of resource bundles. The following is an example:

```
mxmlc -locale= -resource-bundle-list=listOfResourceBundles.txt Example.mxml
```

The preceding line of code will write to the specified file (e.g., *listOfResourceBundles.txt*) a space-delimited list of resource bundles, such as the following:

```
bundles = collections containers controls core effects languageResources skins styles
```

Next, you can use that list of resource bundles to compile the resource module using `mxmlc`. The syntax is as follows:

```
mxmlc -locale=locale -source-path=locale/{locale} -include-resource-
bundles=commaDelimitedListOfResourceBundles -output resourceModuleName.swf
```

The following is an example:

```
mxmlc -locale=en_US -source-path=locale/{locale}
-include-resource-bundles=languageResources,collections,containers,
controls,core,effects,skins,styles -output en_US_ResourceModule.swf
```

You must create the resource modules for each locale. Then, in the application, you can use the `loadResourceModule()` method of `ResourceManager` to load a resource module. The `loadResourceModule()` method returns an instance of an event dispatcher object that you can use to register a listener for a complete event to receive notification when the resource module has loaded. At that point, you can set the `localeChain` property.

When you compile an application using resource modules, you have available two basic strategies:

- You can compile with `locale` set to an empty string to compile no resource bundles into the application.

- You can compile with locale set to a default locale. The resource bundles for that locale will get compiled into the application, and all other locales can be loaded at runtime using resource modules.

If you're using the first strategy, consider that no resource bundles will be available by default on application initialization. That can cause errors if your application depends on resource bundles on startup. If you'd like to load a default module automatically on startup, you can specify that via the FlashVars variables localeChain and resourceModuleURLs. The following FlashVars value will tell the Flex application to load a resource module named *en_US_ResourceModule.swf* and set the localeChain to en_US:

```
localeChain=en_US&resourceModuleURLs=en_US_ResourceModule.swf
```

If you're not familiar with FlashVars, you can read more about it in Chapter 20.

The following example is an application that loads resource modules at runtime when the user selects a locale from a combo box. The example assumes that the default locale and resource module are specified via FlashVars.

```
<?xml version="1.0" encoding="utf-8"?>
<mx:Application xmlns:mx="http://www.adobe.com/2006/mxml" layout="vertical">
    <mx:Metadata>
        [ResourceBundle("languageResources")]
    </mx:Metadata>
    <mx:Script>
        <![CDATA[

            import mx.events.ResourceEvent;

            private var _selectedResourceName:String;

            private function changeResourceHandler(resourceName:String):void {
                _selectedResourceName = resourceName;
                var eventDispatcher:IEventDispatcher = resourceManager.
loadResourceModule(resourceName + "_ResourceModule.swf");
                eventDispatcher.addEventListener(ResourceEvent.COMPLETE,
languageModuleLoadedHandler);
            }

            private function languageModuleLoadedHandler(event:Event):void {
                resourceManager.localeChain = [_selectedResourceName];
            }

            private function selectLanguage():void {
                changeResourceHandler(language.value as String);
            }

        ]]>
    </mx:Script>
```

```
    <mx:ComboBox id="language" change="selectLanguage();">
        <mx:dataProvider>
            <mx:ArrayCollection>
                <mx:Object label="English (US)" data="en_US" />
                <mx:Object label="English (Canada)" data="en_CA" />
                <mx:Object label="Espanol (Espana)" data="es_ES" />
            </mx:ArrayCollection>
        </mx:dataProvider>
    </mx:ComboBox>
    <mx:Form>
        <mx:FormHeading
label="{resourceManager.getString('languageResources', 'instruction')}" />
        <mx:FormItem label="{resourceManager.getString('resources', 'color')}">
            <mx:ColorPicker id="color" />
        </mx:FormItem>
        <mx:FormItem>
            <mx:Button
label="{resourceManager.getString('languageResources', 'send')}" />
        </mx:FormItem>
    </mx:Form>
    <mx:Image
source="{resourceManager.getClass('languageResources', 'flag')}"
width="60" height="40" />
</mx:Application>
```

Summary

In this chapter, you learned about the low-level workings of the Flex framework. Although it's not always necessary to work directly with these aspects of a Flex application, understanding these topics can help you when building applications that might require lower-level changes. We also discussed the Flex application life cycle, differentiating between the Flex framework and Flash Player API, bootstrapping a Flex application, application domains, and preloader events.

CHAPTER 6
Managing Layout

One of the key features of Flex is its ability to simplify application layout. Traditional application development requires writing layout code, or working with layout components in a nonintuitive manner. With MXML and Flex's layout containers, you can lay out most applications without having to write a single line of custom layout code.

In this chapter, we will provide an overview of Flex layout containers and discuss the layout rules they use. We will also cover how to work with containers and children, how to nest containers, and how to build fluid interfaces.

Flex Layout Overview

Container components are the basis of how Flex provides layout logic. At the most basic level, the `Application` class is a container, and subitems within the `Application` class (tag) are called *children*. In MXML, placing nodes within a container declaration signifies that the objects are instantiated and are added to the container as children, and the container automatically handles their positioning and sizing.

For example, in the following code two children are added to the `Application` container —a `TextInput` instance and a `Button` instance:

```
<?xml version="1.0" encoding="utf-8"?>
<mx:Application xmlns:mx="http://www.adobe.com/2006/mxml">
    <mx:TextInput/>
    <mx:Button label="Submit"/>
</mx:Application>
```

If you are using Flex Builder, the default MXML template sets the `layout` property of the root `Application` instance to `absolute`; when not specified, the default value `vertical` is used. The `layout` property of the `Application` container controls how children are positioned and sized, and if the value is set, the examples may not work as expected.

In the preceding code, you added two children to the `Application` container by simply placing the children as subnodes of the container using MXML. This adds the children to the container's display list, which, under the hood, is the same display list Flash Player uses. Containers allow for several different types of layout management. In this example, we're allowing the container to apply its own default layout rules to stack the children vertically. Other layout containers have different layout rules, and some containers even allow you to specify fixed coordinates for children. We'll see lots of examples of these throughout the chapter. Containers also are noninteractive objects, in that they don't receive keyboard/mouse input themselves; instead, they house children that receive all input.

The `tabEnabled` property built into Flash Player is part of the `InteractiveObject` class from which containers inherit. The property controls whether an object can receive user focus, which is not the purpose of containers. So, by default, the `tabEnabled` property of containers is usually set to `false`. The `tabChildren` property, inherited from `DisplayObjectContainer`, is what instructs Flash Player to allow children of a container to receive user focus. With these properties set, children of containers will receive focus while the container itself will not.

In the previous code sample, we added children to a container using MXML. You can also do this using ActionScript, as shown in Example 6-1. Understanding the code in Example 6-1 will give you insight into how MXML works.

Example 6-1. Adding children to a container using ActionScript

```
<?xml version="1.0" encoding="utf-8"?>
<mx:Application xmlns:mx="http://www.adobe.com/2006/mxml" initialize="addItems()">
    <mx:Script>
        <![CDATA[
            import mx.controls.Button;
            import mx.controls.TextInput;
            private function addItems():void
            {
                var ti:TextInput = new TextInput();
                this.addChild(ti);
                var btn:Button = new Button();
                btn.label = "Submit";
                this.addChild(btn);
            }
        ]]>
    </mx:Script>
</mx:Application>
```

As you can see in Example 6-1, the ActionScript code is more verbose than the MXML code. This is a prime example of why MXML is ideal for rapidly developing application user interfaces. In general, you should write application layout in MXML whenever possible, and choose ActionScript only when you want to do more at runtime, such as add an arbitrary number of children, or in cases where MXML doesn't provide enough control to achieve the desired layout. Keep in mind that you can mix both ActionScript and MXML in an application's layout, so it's important for you to learn how to code in both ways. If you find that a portion of your layout requires dynamic control over child instantiation, you may opt to handle that with ActionScript and the display list API and handle the rest of the layout using MXML.

Working with Children

In addition to adding children, you also have the ability to remove, reorder, and retrieve the children of a container's display list. In Flex, container children are synonymous with children that inherit from the `UIComponent` class.

In Flex, container children must implement the `IUIComponent` interface. Because the `UIComponent` class implements this interface, we typically will refer to `UIComponent`-based components as *valid container children*. If you plan to implement a custom child, you'll need to ensure you implement `IUIComponent` and inherit from `flash.display.DisplayObject` for containers to handle the child properly.

Setting up the initial state of a container via MXML is simple enough, but managing change afterward requires a better understanding of the ActionScript display list API. The methods `addChild()`, `addChildAt()`, `getChildAt()`, `getChildByName()`, `getChildIndex()`, `getChildren()`, `removeAllChildren()`, `contains()`, and `setChildIndex()`, as well as the `numChildren` property, are the `Container` class members related to working with children. Most of them are self-explanatory. Example 6-2 takes the last child and moves it to the first position in a container's children when the button is pressed.

Example 6-2. Reordering children using the display list API

```
<?xml version="1.0" encoding="utf-8"?>
<mx:Application xmlns:mx="http://www.adobe.com/2006/mxml">
    <mx:Script>
        <![CDATA[
        private function moveToTheBeginning():void
        {

            // Retrieve the index of the last child. Child indexes are zero-based
            var lastChildIndex:int = tileOfLabels.numChildren - 1;

            // Get a reference to the last child
            var child:DisplayObject = tileOfLabels.getChildAt(lastChildIndex);

            // Change the index of the child
            tileOfLabels.setChildIndex(child,0);
        }
        ]]>
    </mx:Script>
    <mx:Tile id="tileOfLabels">
        <mx:Label text="1"/>
        <mx:Label text="2"/>
```

```
        <mx:Label text="3"/>
        <mx:Label text="4"/>
        <mx:Label text="5"/>
        <mx:Label text="6"/>
    </mx:Tile>
    <mx:Button label="Move to the beginning" click="moveToTheBeginning()"/>
</mx:Application>
```

This basic example covers a few important concepts. First, the initial layout contains six buttons within a `Tile` container, each labeled according to its order within the `Tile`. A button at the bottom is used to call a function to move the last child to the beginning of the `Tile` container. In `moveToTheBeginning()`, the index of the last child is retrieved, which is zero-based. Next, a reference to the last child in the display list is obtained using `getChildAt()`. After the last child index is retrieved, `setChildIndex()` is called and passes a reference to the button instance and a new index.

A good thing to keep in mind is that although MXML is ideal for laying out an application, you have full control of that layout at runtime using ActionScript. For instance, in ActionScript you can achieve tasks such as hiding containers depending on user interaction, as well as reordering containers and changing their sizes.

If you are familiar with how Flash Player handles display objects, handling children within containers should already look familiar as Flex implements the same API for handling child objects that Flash Player does. Note, however, that although the API between Flash Player and Flex is the same, there is a subtle difference in how Flash Player and Flex handle children. Flex containers, unlike Flash Player, do not return at runtime a reference to all children that are actually part of a container. Children in Flex are divided into two types: chrome and content. Children used to draw the outline, header, or other unique rendered items related to the container are added automatically by the component, are hidden from the display list API in Flex, and are referred to as *chrome children*. Children added to a container by the developer, such as `Button` or `Label`, are *content children*. Flex differentiates the two to simplify the process of dealing with children, because typically a developer is more interested in the content children.

Although Flex hides the chrome-related children, you can still access the complete display list and manipulate its children using the `rawChildren` container property. Flex provides this property to grant access to the entire display list, which you may need if you plan to manipulate chrome-related children or add display objects that do not implement `IUIComponent`. Working with `rawChildren` is an advanced topic that will require more understanding of Flash Player's display list, which we do not cover in this book. Also, if you need to add a child that does not inherit from `UIComponent`, you may want to consider implementing the `IUIComponent` interface for the display object rather than working with `rawChildren` directly.

Container Types

Every container provided by the Flex framework has a set of rules by which it lays out its children. Flex uses these rules to measure the available space for children and to decide where children are positioned. A `VBox` container, for example, arranges its children vertically, placing only one item per row. Similarly, an `HBox` container arranges its children horizontally. Every container in Flex was designed with a purpose (see Figure 6-1). Knowing when to use a particular container is important as you build your Flex applications.

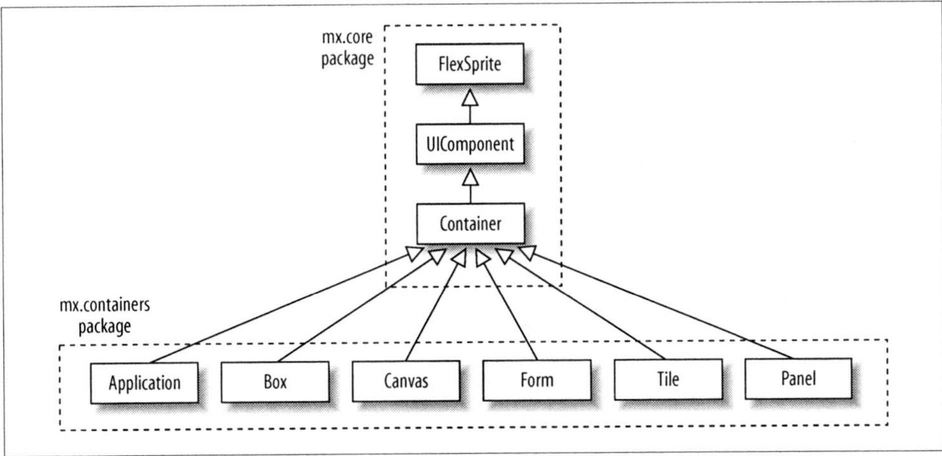

Figure 6-1. Class diagram of container components

Table 6-1 lists the different container types in Flex and describes how each is used.

Table 6-1. The different Flex container types

Container type	Description
Application	This special container is the root of a Flex application. By default, it behaves like a VBox container. The layout property controls how children are laid out. The possible values are ContainerLayout.ABSOLUTE, ContainerLayout.VERTICAL, and ContainerLayout.HORIZONTAL. Setting the layout property to ABSOLUTE causes this container to behave as a Canvas container and allows you to specify absolute positions for each child. Setting the value to HORIZONTAL or VERTICAL causes the layout to behave like an HBox or VBox, respectively.
Box	Typically, you will not use this container directly, but it is an important container to understand because many containers base their layout rules on it. This container lays out its children, one after the other, in a single column (or row), depending on the direction of the property value. By default, the contents are laid out vertically. Possible values for the direction property are BoxDirection.VERTICAL and BoxDirection.HORIZONTAL. Box is the base implementation for the Application, VBox, HBox, ControlBar, HDividedBox, VDividedBox, NavBar, Panel, and TitleWindow containers.
Canvas	This container is for absolute positioning and constraint-based layout. Children are laid out using the x and y properties, and the top, bottom, right, left, verticalCenter, and horizontalCenter properties are used for achieving a constraint-based layout.
ControlBar	This container is used to provide a reserved region at the bottom of a Panel or TitleWindow container for placing children. This container lays out its content in the same way that an HBox does.
DividedBox	This container lays out children in the same way that Box does, except it places an interactive divider bar between each child. This container is ideal for separating regions of an application and allowing a user to resize regions by dragging a divider. As with Box, children can be laid out horizontally or vertically.
Form	This special container is designed specifically for laying out forms. It allows you to easily position form labels, headings, and input controls.
Grid	This container allows you to position children within columns and rows. This container's behavior is very similar to that of HTML tables.
HBox	This container is derived from Box with the direction property set to BoxDirection.HORIZONTAL. Otherwise, it behaves as Box does.
HDividedBox	This container is derived from DividedBox with the direction property set to BoxDirection.HORIZONTAL by default.
Panel	This is a layout container that contains a chrome border with a title bar area. The content area by default behaves like a VBox. The layout property controls how children are laid out and the default value is ContainerLayout.VERTICAL. Additional possible values are ContainerLayout.ABSOLUTE and ContainerLayout.HORIZONTAL. Setting the layout property to ABSOLUTE causes this container to behave as a Canvas container. Setting the value to HORIZONTAL or VERTICAL causes the layout to behave like an HBox or VBox, respectively.
Tile	This container tiles children, and by default it tries to keep the number of rows and columns equal to each other. If the width or height property of the container is specified, the container will try to satisfy the available area. If no width or height is specified, it tries its best to keep the number of rows and columns equal to each other. The Tile container contains a direction property, which by default is set to VERTICAL. Possible values are TileDirection.VERTICAL and TileDirection.HORIZONTAL.
TitleWindow	Ideal for pop-up windows, TitleWindow inherits from Panel, with the addition of a button in the title bar to allow users to close the window.

Container type	Description
VBox	This container is derived from Box with the direction property set to BoxDirection.VERTICAL. Otherwise, it behaves as Box does.
VDividedBox	This container is derived from DividedBox, with the direction property set to BoxDirection.VERTICAL by default.

Layout Rules

Many containers internally make use of two main layout rules: box and canvas. These rules define how containers internally implement child positioning and sizing. Understanding the different layout rules will help you to understand how layout containers work and to develop application layouts more effectively.

Layout rules are executed when children containers are initially instantiated, anytime children are added or removed, and whenever a container is resized. The only time that is not the case is when the `autoLayout` property is set to `false`. In this case, the layout rules execute only on initialization and when children are added or removed.

Setting the `autoLayout` property to `false` still causes the container to measure and position children on initial rendering and when children are added or removed. However, this won't cause the container to lay out its children again when the container is resized. This is beneficial in cases when you do not want to implement a liquid interface that automatically resizes or when the exact layout needs to remain the same when the container is resized.

It is also important to note that measuring and positioning in a container can sometimes be a processor-intensive process, so you may opt to set `autoLayout` to `false` to handle such cases as well.

When layout rules are executing, they go through two steps. First, the container measures the space needed for each child. This allows the container to decide how much space it needs to best fit all of its children, and it allows the container to decide where everything should be positioned if it is responsible for positioning the children. During this process, if a child's `includeInLayout` property is set to `false`, the child will be ignored and won't be factored into the positioning of children. In the second step, the container repositions and sizes the children as needed.

Setting a child's `visible` property alone to `false` does not exclude the child from the layout routines of a container, resulting in a layout where hidden children will occupy a space within the container even though it is not visible. In cases where this is not the desired behavior, setting the `includeInLayout` and `visible` properties of a child to `false` will instruct the container to ignore that child when deciding how to lay out children and will visually hide the child.

Box-based layout

Now that you understand a bit about how layout rules work, let's discuss each type of layout rule in more detail. The containers `HBox`, `VBox`, `HDividedBox`, `VDividedBox`, `ApplicationControlBar`, and `ControlBar` all base their layout rules on those of the `Box` container. For this reason, you will often find people refer to these as *box-based layout containers*.

The box layout rule dictates that each child occupies its own row or column, depending on the direction under which the rule is operating. The two directions supported are vertical and horizontal. All box-based layout containers implement the `direction` property, and the default value of the `direction` property depends on the container. You can set the value of the `direction` property to horizontal or vertical using the constant values `BoxDirection.HORIZONTAL` and `BoxDirection.VERTICAL`.

In `Box`, the default direction is set to `vertical`, as shown in Figure 6-2. Each child occupies its own row, and the children are stacked one on top of the other.

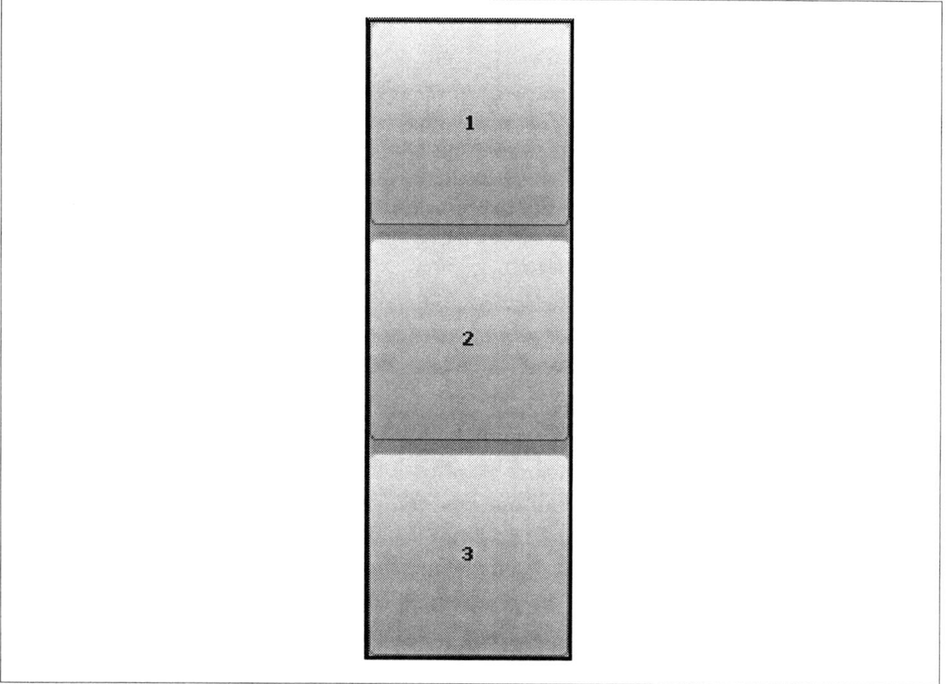

Figure 6-2. A Box container with three child objects

If the width of the container is not specified, the container determines it by identifying the child with the largest width and adjusting its own width so that it can display the child with little or no clipping. If an explicit width is set, the container will adhere to the specified width, and if the width of the child objects exceeds the set width, by default the child objects will be clipped and a scroll bar will be displayed. In the same manner, the height of the container expands to allow all children to fit accordingly, unless an explicit height for the box-based container is set, at which point the container uses a scroll bar to allow the user access to all the children. Changing the number of children or their width or height at runtime causes the container to be marked for invalidation, which will cause the layout rule to be reevaluated and the children to be automatically repositioned and sized as required.

In an attempt to minimize unnecessary redraws, which can cause severe performance degradation, Flex components mark parts of a component that need to be redrawn as *invalid*. We discuss invalidation in Chapter 19 in the context of component development, but the same process applies to all components in Flex, including containers.

When the box layout rule is operating with the `direction` property set to `horizontal`, the rules apply in the same way as when the `direction` property is set to `vertical`, except that the box attempts to grow and lay out children horizontally rather than vertically.

In this layout rule, the size of the container depends on a few factors:

- If the container's width and height are set, those values are used.
- If the size that is set is smaller than the area needed for the children to be displayed, a scroll bar is automatically displayed unless `verticalScrollPolicy` and `horizontalScrollPolicy` are set to `ScrollPolicy.OFF`.
- If no size is explicitly set, the container attempts to grow as needed within the available space. If enough space is not available, a scroll bar is used to allow the user access to the content.

Canvas-based absolute layout

The `Canvas` container implements the canvas-based layout rule. The canvas layout rule provides a lot of flexibility in attaining sophisticated layout while attempting to ensure that application layout routines perform well. That's because you must provide all the positioning logic, which means that Flex doesn't have to do all the work of measuring the `Canvas` container's children and calculating optimal positions.

Canvas-based layout allows you to position children using explicit `x` and `y` coordinates. This allows you to accurately control the position of each child. Example 6-3 shows two children positioned using exact `x` and `y` positions, relative to the position of the `Canvas` itself.

Example 6-3. Absolute positioning using a Canvas container

```
<?xml version="1.0" encoding="utf-8"?>
<mx:Application xmlns:mx="http://www.adobe.com/2006/mxml">
    <mx:Canvas>
```

```
        <mx:Label x="0" y="50" text="Enter your name:"/>
        <mx:TextInput x="110" y="50"/>
    </mx:Canvas>
</mx:Application>
```

As you can see, the Canvas container is most suitable for reproducing a pixel-perfect layout. Unlike other containers, where layout rules set the positions of children, the Canvas container doesn't prevent you from overlapping children. If the positions of the children need to change, you can handle it on your own by setting the x and y values at runtime.

Canvas-based constraint layout

Canvas also supports the ability to lay out children using what is called *constraint-based layout*. Constraint-based layout lets you lay out children at predefined positions relative to their parent or a constraint. This gives you the flexibility of positioning children in a predefined position while at the same time repositioning them as needed to satisfy the constraints set. This tends to be a more practical method of accurately positioning children than simply supplying a specific location, because it allows you to position children precisely within a plane and be able to reposition the children dynamically according to the constraints set. To position children using the constraint-based layout method you set one or several of their style properties—**top**, **bottom**, **left**, **right**, **horizontalCenter**, and **verticalCenter**—with a value based on the parent's or constraint's position in relation to the child. For now, we will focus on positioning in relationship to a parent, and later in this chapter we will see how we can use constraints for a more powerful layout. For example, when you set the **right** style to **10**, you're positioning the child 10 pixels away from the right edge of the parent container. When the container is resized, the child automatically repositions itself 10 pixels from the right edge.

Example 6-4 shows two buttons positioned using container-based layout. One is positioned 10 pixels from the bottom right, and the other is positioned 10 pixels from the right. Both buttons will automatically be repositioned whenever the browser is resized.

Example 6-4. Positioning children using constraint-based layout

```
<?xml version="1.0" encoding="utf-8"?>
<mx:Application xmlns:mx="http://www.adobe.com/2006/mxml">
    <mx:Canvas width="100%" height="100%">
        <mx:Button right="10" label="Rightmost button"/>
        <mx:Button right="10" bottom="10" label="Right bottommost button"/>
    </mx:Canvas>
</mx:Application>
```

Figure 6-3 shows the results.

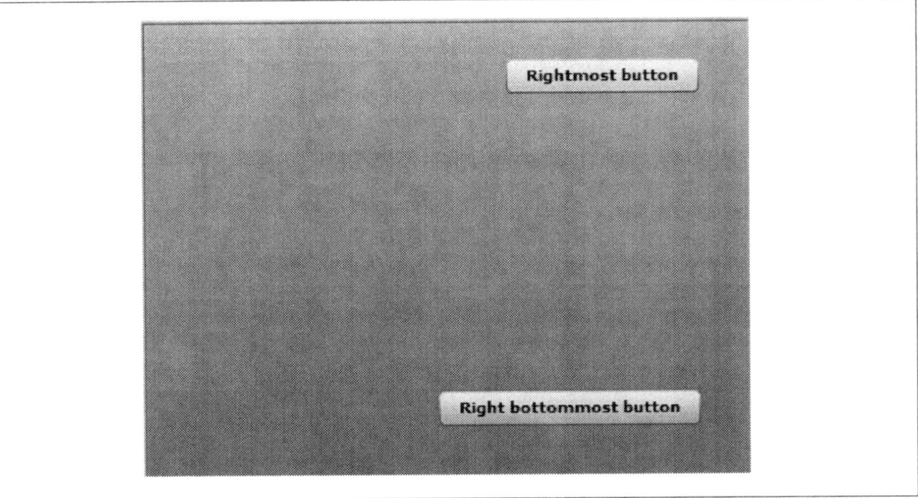

Figure 6-3. Results from Example 6-4, in which children are positioned using constraint-based layout

In Example 6-4, two buttons are positioned within a `Canvas`. The first button is positioned 10 pixels away from the right edge, with the default `y` value of `0` (if a child doesn't have its position set in a `Canvas` container, the default `x` and `y` values are `0, 0`). The second button is positioned to the bottom right of the `Canvas` container. This is accomplished by setting the first button's **`right`** style property to `10`. The second button's **`right`** and `bottom` style properties also are set to `10`, thus resulting in the button being offset 10 pixels from the bottom-right edge of the parent container. Also note that the `width` and `height` properties of the `Canvas` container are set to `100%`. This is to ensure that the canvas automatically resizes to occupy as much space as possible. Like all style properties, you can set constraint-based layout styles directly inline within MXML tags, via ActionScript using the `setStyle()` method, or via any other method that style properties support.

One final capability that constraint-based layout containers support is that of subdividing the container into regions and laying out the children according to those regions. The best way to think about this is to imagine a single plane that is divided into columns and rows, and within each table cell is a new parent for the children. You can achieve this by creating many instances of the `Canvas` container side by side or, optimally, by using a single `Canvas` container and dividing it into regions using `ConstraintColumn` and `ConstraintRow`.

As of this writing, Flex Builder does not support `ConstraintColumn`, `ConstraintRow`, and their associated syntax in design view. Adobe plans to support this in a future release, but if you plan to use Flex Builder and you need design view, you may decide against using this feature.

To understand this better, let's look at Example 6-5, which uses the additional constraints.

Example 6-5. Positioning children using constraint-based layout

```
<?xml version="1.0" encoding="utf-8"?>
<mx:Application xmlns:mx="http://www.adobe.com/2006/mxml">
    <mx:Canvas width="100%" height="100%">
         <mx:constraintColumns>
              <mx:ConstraintColumn id="column1" width="30%"/>
              <mx:ConstraintColumn id="column2" width="70%"/>
         </mx:constraintColumns>
        <mx:Button right="column1:10" label="Right of 1st Column"/>
        <!-- This will ignore the column constraints and will just use the main
parent Canvas -->
        <mx:Button horizontalCenter="0" label="Always centered"/>
        <!-- This makes use of the column constraint for the left but also uses the
main parent Canvas for the bottom -->
        <mx:Button left="column2:10" bottom="10" label="Left of 2nd Column"/>
    </mx:Canvas>
</mx:Application>
```

Figure 6-4 shows the results.

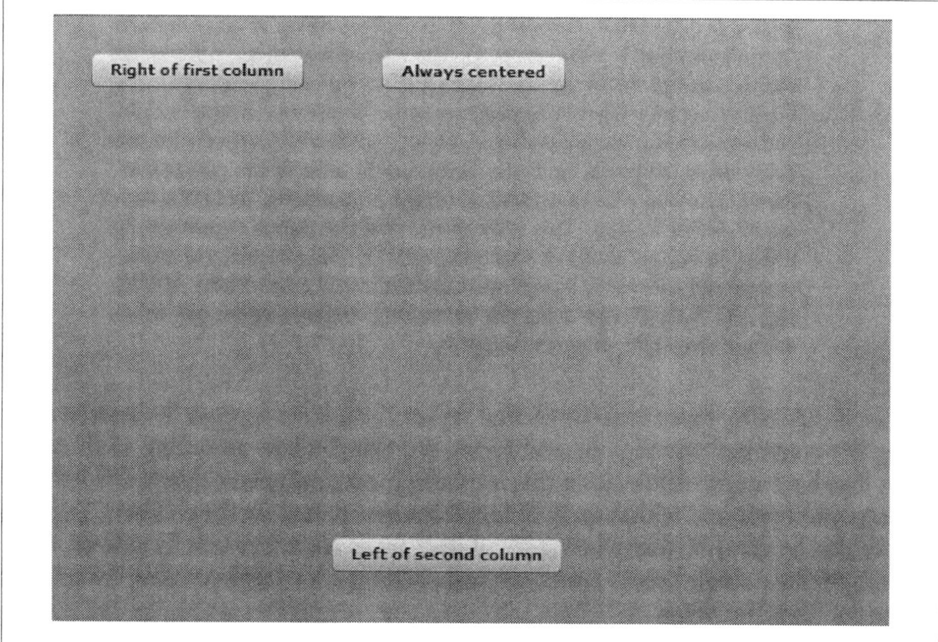

Figure 6-4. Results of Example 6-3

In Example 6-5, we defined two column constraints and positioned the children accordingly. The two columns in this example span the entire canvas, with the first column having a width of 30% and the second a width of 70%. In this example, we declared two `ColumnConstraint` instances and set their `id` property values to `column1` and `column2`. We then referenced the constraints using these `id` values when setting the positioning properties (`left`, `right`, `top`, `bottom`, `horizontalCenter`, and `verticalCenter`) of the children. In every case, we need to use the syntax `constraintID:value`. For example, in the preceding code, we set the `right` property of the first button to `column1:10`, meaning that the button should always appear 10 pixels from the right edge of the column constraint with an `id` of `column1`.

The second button in Example 6-5 is centered horizontally, but unlike the first and third buttons, it does not make use of the new constraint regions. This might not seem obvious at first, but using a column or row constraint doesn't prohibit you from still using the main canvas for positioning children. Thus, the second button will be positioned in relation to the entire canvas region and not within any of the columns in the example.

Finally, the third button in Example 6-5 is positioned 10 pixels from the bottom and left of the second column region. The second column has a width of 70%, and as no row constraint has been defined, the column spans the entire region vertically.

Here are some additional things to remember concerning constraint-based layouts:

- Setting the `top` style property causes the child's `y` value to be set to that many pixels away from the parent container's top edge.
- Setting the `bottom` style property causes the `y` property of the child to be set to the `height` of the container, minus the child's `height`.
- You can set both the `bottom` and `top` values of a child, thus resulting in the child `height` being resized automatically, while always satisfying the `top` and `bottom` constraints.
- Setting the `left` style property sets the `x` value of the child at runtime to that many pixels away from the parent's edge.
- Setting the `right` style property at runtime sets the `x` value to the total `width` of the container minus the `right` value and the `width` of the child.
- Setting both the `right` and `left` style properties causes the child to be resized to satisfy the constraint rules.
- Setting the values `top`, `bottom`, `left`, and `right` causes the child to be resized and positioned to meet the conditions.
- As with explicitly positioning items in a `Canvas` container, children you position using constraint-based layout rules can overlap each other.
- You can set a child's `width` and `height` to a percentage; the canvas positions and sizes them appropriately.

You can mix constraint-based layout with absolute positioning within the same `Canvas` container.

Hybrid layout containers

The containers `Application`, `Panel`, and `TitleWindow` are based on both box and canvas layout rules; that's why we call them *hybrid layout containers*. The rules by which these children are laid out depend on the value of the container's `layout` property. The `layout` property accepts three valid values: `ContainerLayout.ABSOLUTE`, `ContainerLayout.HORIZONTAL`, and `ContainerLayout.VERTICAL`.

When you set the `layout` property value to `absolute` the container behaves as a `Canvas`-based container. Setting the value to `horizontal` or `vertical` causes the container to act as a `Box`-based container with the appropriate direction (either a horizontal or a vertical layout, respectively).

Additional layout rules

Flex provides three other layout rules you can use in your application: `Tile`, `Grid`, and `Form`. These don't serve a general purpose like the others do, and they're not shared across containers. Instead, they are embedded within specific containers, as discussed in the following sections.

The tile layout rule. The tile layout rule is found in the `Tile` container. Its purpose is to lay out children in a grid form, while optimally keeping the number of rows and columns equal. If it cannot keep them equal, it creates an extra row or column, depending on the `direction` property of the `Tile` container instance.

The `direction` property for the `Tile` container can accept two values: `TileDirection.HORIZONTAL` and `TileDirection.VERTICAL`. The default is for children to be laid out horizontally first (see Figure 6-5). This means that each child is instantiated one next to the other, horizontally, starting from left to right. When the intended number of children per row is reached depending on the optimal number of rows versus columns, it places the next child on the row below. Vertical orientation, of course, works the same way, except it begins laying children out next to each other from the top left and moving down until it reaches the current number of rows before continuing on to the next column.

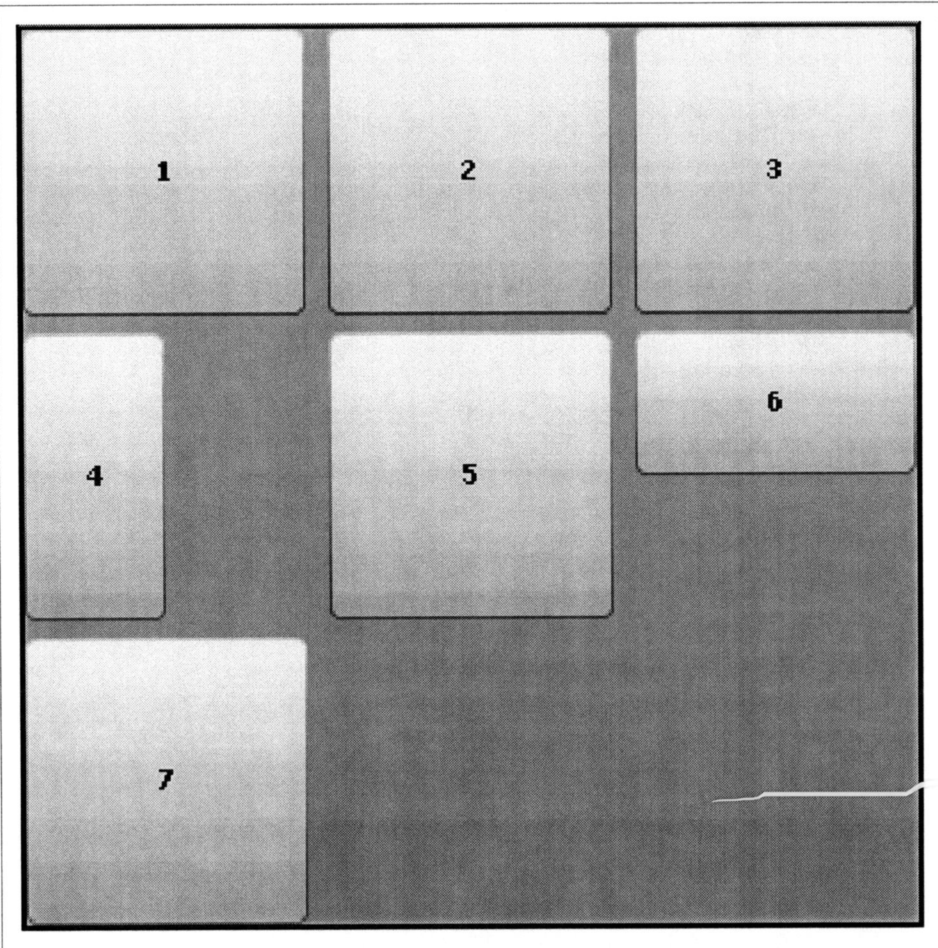

Figure 6-5. Results from having a Tile container with seven children, using the default horizontal direction

The `width` and `height` properties, when set, play a key role in terms of how a `Tile` container lays out children. A `Tile` with a set width and height will be forced to satisfy those limits, thus causing the rule of rows to columns to be adjusted. Under such cases, the `direction` property will still behave the same.

The grid layout rule. The grid layout rule is used by the `Grid` container component. This layout rule/container replicates how an HTML table works in Flex, as shown in Example 6-6.

Example 6-6. Grid container example

```
<?xml version="1.0" encoding="utf-8"?>
<mx:Application xmlns:mx="http://www.adobe.com/2006/mxml">
```

```
    <mx:Grid>
        <mx:GridRow>
            <mx:GridItem width="100">
                <mx:Label text="Select a Color:"/>
            </mx:GridItem>
            <mx:GridItem>
                <mx:ColorPicker/>
            </mx:GridItem>
        </mx:GridRow>
        <mx:GridRow>
                <mx:GridItem colSpan="2" horizontalAlign="right">
                    <mx:Button label="Submit"/>
                </mx:GridItem>
        </mx:GridRow>
    </mx:Grid>
</mx:Application>
```

Example 6-6 contains two rows. The first row contains a `Label` and a `ColorPicker`. The second contains a Submit button, which is aligned to the right of the table. To understand this example, it is helpful to take a look at how `Grid`-related classes relate to traditional HTML tables:

- An HTML `<table>` is synonymous with a `Grid`.
- An HTML `<tr>` (table row) is synonymous with a `GridRow`.
- An HTML `<td>` (table data) is synonymous with a `GridItem`.
- The `colspan` and `rowspan` properties in HTML are properties of the `GridItem` as `colSpan` and `rowSpan`.
- The HTML `align` attribute is a style called `horizontalAlign`.
- The HTML `valign` property is a style called `verticalAlign`.

If you are familiar with HTML, you may initially feel more comfortable using the `Grid` container over others.

Although the `Grid` container is a good representation of a familiar layout model, you should use the `Grid` container only as a last resort when laying out an application. Other containers such as `Canvas` and box-based containers are easier to maintain, provide better performance, and offer most of what `Grid` provides.

The form layout rule. The best way to introduce the form layout rule is to show an example of it in use (see Figure 6-6).

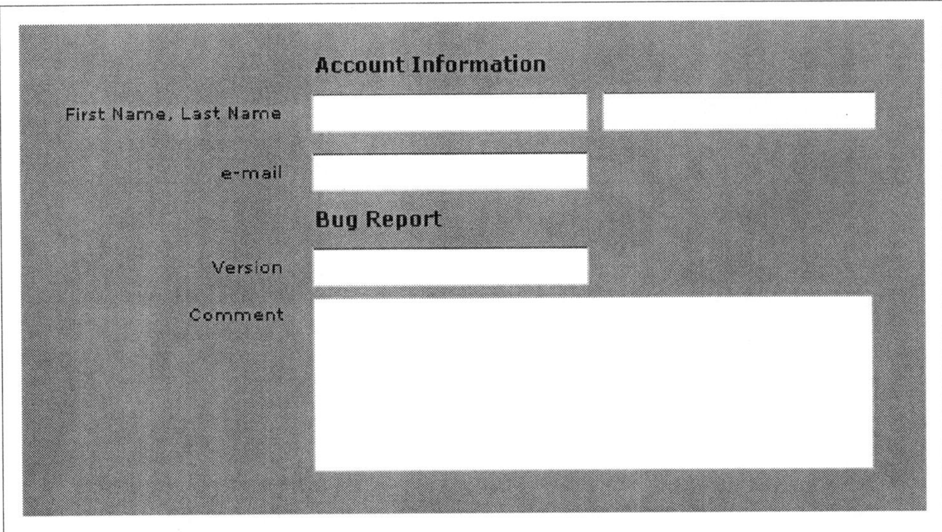

Figure 6-6. A typical form using the form layout rule

The form layout rule is found in the `Form` container. This container is used for laying out forms such as those you'd see on a web page, which typically include headings and input controls in a Flex application. The `Form` container, like the `Grid` container, has associated components and exists for convenience. You could reproduce the same layout using other containers, but for traditional forms you may find this container ideal.

The `Form` container's related components are `FormHeading` and `FormItem`:

`FormHeading`
: You use this to place a heading over a group of multiple `FormItems` within a `Form` by setting the `label` property. You can use multiple `FormHeading` controls within a form; you should place them before the group of form items the `FormHeading` represents. The label text is positioned and aligned to the body of the form items. You can control spacing between `FormHeading` children using the `paddingTop`, `paddingLeft`, and `paddingRight` style properties.

`FormItem`
: You use this when a `Form` container needs to contain items such as input boxes and combo boxes. You can place multiple instances of `FormItem` within a single form. `FormItem` implements the box-based layout rule, which allows you to place multiple children within a `FormItem` and exposes a `direction` property in the same way that other box-based containers do. Finally, `FormItem` exposes a `label` property that allows you to place text to the left of a row in a form.

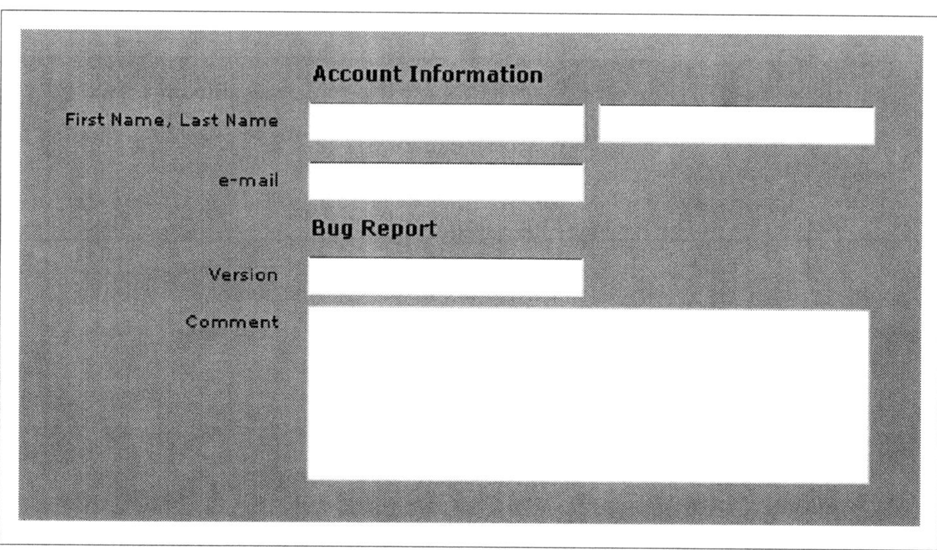

Figure 6-7. Application output from Example 6-7

Example 6-7 shows the code you would use to reproduce Figure 6-7 using the `Form` container.

Example 6-7. Example of using the Form container

```
<?xml version="1.0" encoding="utf-8"?>
<mx:Application xmlns:mx="http://www.adobe.com/2006/mxml">
    <mx:Form>
        <mx:FormHeading label="Account Information"/>
        <mx:FormItem label="First Name, Last Name" direction="horizontal">
            <mx:TextInput id="firstName"/>
            <mx:TextInput id="lastName"/>
        </mx:FormItem>
        <mx:FormItem label="e-mail">
            <mx:TextInput id="email"/>
        </mx:FormItem>
        <mx:FormHeading label="Bug Report"/>
        <mx:FormItem label="Version">
            <mx:TextInput id="version"/>
        </mx:FormItem>
        <mx:FormItem label="Comment">
            <mx:TextArea id="comment" width="326" height="100"/>
        </mx:FormItem>
    </mx:Form>
</mx:Application>
```

Notice how the form neatly positions and sizes all the children. This is the convenience of using a `Form` container.

Padding, Borders, and Gaps

Thus far, we have worked with containers using many of their default behaviors. In this section, we will discuss the important issue of style properties for padding, borders, and gaps.

Padding, borders, and gaps are style properties that control how children are positioned. Padding controls the space between a child and the container's border, and it is typically seen in box-, tile-, and grid-based layout containers. Borders are found in most containers, and they control the border surrounding the containers' bounding box. Finally, gaps control the space between each child when working with box-, tile-, and grid-based layout containers. To better understand how these style properties work, look at Figure 6-8, which shows some of the style properties and their purposes.

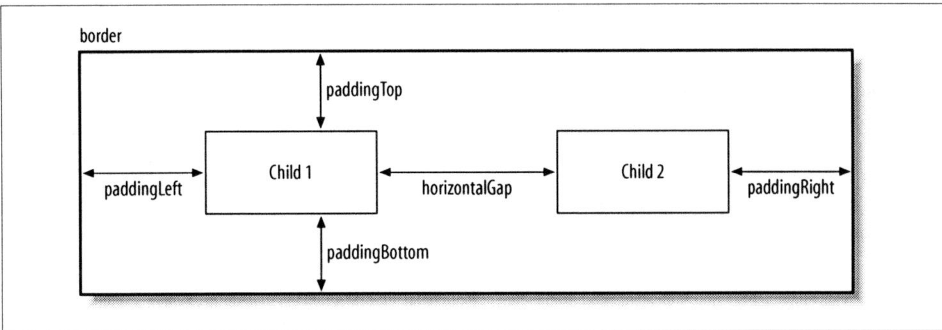

Figure 6-8. Diagram of children within an HBox and corresponding padding, borders, and gaps

It's important when laying out applications to keep these style properties in mind, as these properties are taken into account when a container performs its measurement routines to determine how much space is available. Some containers, such as `Application`, for example, default to having 24-pixel padding on all four sides. If you wanted to lay out an application that would truly occupy 100% of the browser window, you would set the `paddingTop`, `paddingBottom`, `paddingLeft`, and `paddingRight` properties to `0`. Let's take a look at such an example:

```
<?xml version="1.0" encoding="utf-8"?>
<mx:Application xmlns:mx="http://www.adobe.com/2006/mxml" paddingBottom="0"
paddingLeft="0" paddingRight="0" paddingTop="0">
    <mx:Button label="Max sized button" width="100%" height="100%"/>
</mx:Application>
```

The preceding code will result in an application with one large button that truly occupies 100% of the available space in the browser, as shown in Figure 6-9 on the next page.

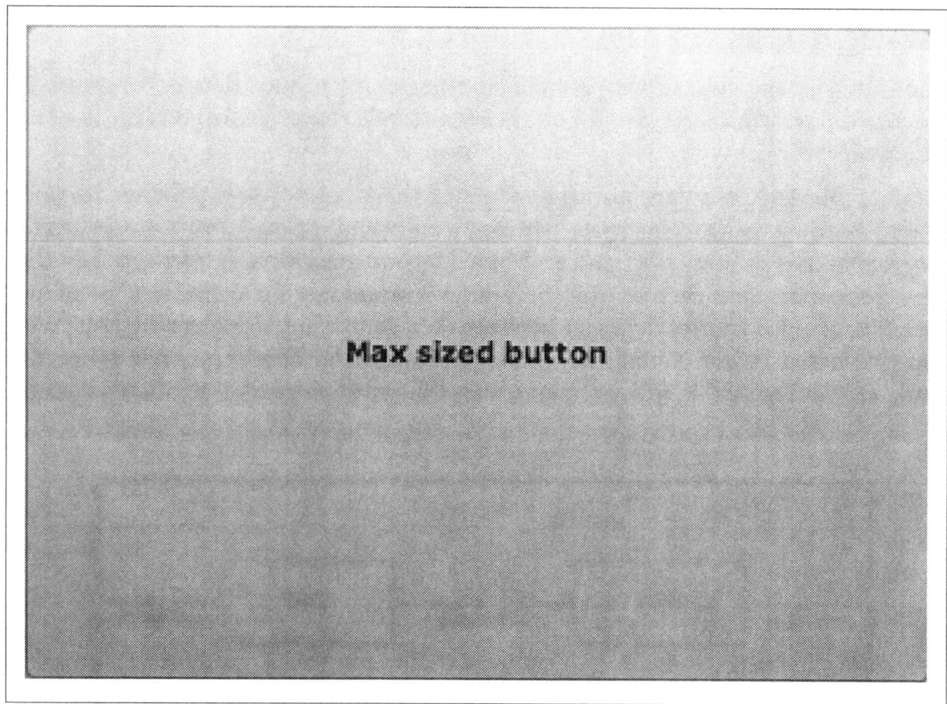

Figure 6-9. Application with zero padding

Nesting Containers

Most applications will require more than just one container to achieve the layout you desire. In such cases, you'll want to use multiple containers, and perhaps mix `Box`- and `Canvas`-based containers in the same application. Flex allows you to easily nest containers within other containers, and although you may not have realized it earlier, you have been nesting containers all along, because `Application` is itself a container. When you nest containers, children of containers will act like any other children. Example 6-8 shows how to nest containers; Figure 6-10 shows the results.

Example 6-8. Example of nesting containers

```
<?xml version="1.0" encoding="utf-8"?>
<mx:Application xmlns:mx="http://www.adobe.com/2006/mxml" layout="absolute">
    <mx:HBox width="100%" height="100%">
        <mx:Canvas width="50%" height="100%">
            <mx:Button label="Button 1" bottom="10" right="10"/>
            <mx:Button label="Button 2" bottom="40" right="10"/>
        </mx:Canvas>
        <mx:Panel width="50%" height="100%" layout="absolute">
        </mx:Panel>
    </mx:HBox>
</mx:Application>
```

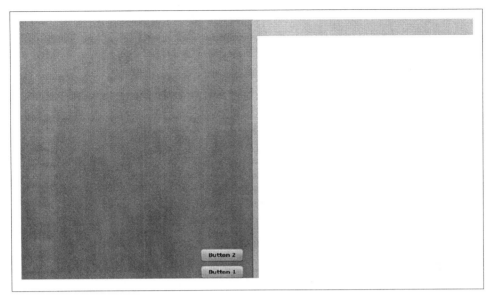

Figure 6-10. Results of Example 6-8

Example 6-8 combines multiple container types to achieve a layout that you could not easily attain with just one container. In this example, two areas in the application have been separated. To do this, we used an `HBox` container and placed two containers, one `Panel` and one `Canvas`, within, each occupying 50% of the total area. In this example, `HBox` is managing the positioning and layout of the two subcontainers. Also, each child container has its own area where the children rely on its layout rules and not on those of `HBox`.

Although this is a simple example, nested containers provide a powerful and easy way to lay out complex Flex applications. It is good to keep in mind, however, that excessive container nesting can lead to poor performance, and generating the layout you desire using constraint- or canvas-based layout may lead to a better overall application experience for the user.

Nested containers are ideal in another scenario as well. At times, you may want to use a container because of its chrome appearance. For example, a `Panel` container does not implement the form layout rule, but it does provide a chrome appearance that you might be interested in using. For such a case, you can nest a `Form` container (or any other container) within a `Panel` to obtain the chrome appearance of the `Panel` and the layout rules of the nested container.

Handling Scrolling and Clipping

Containers can't always fit their children within the available viewing area. This can occur because, for example, screen resolutions are different among end-users, the children need more space than what's available, or the canvas was resized. As a result, sooner or later you will have to deal with containers that have a scroll bar. Thankfully, Flex makes the process of dealing with this problem simple.

If a container doesn't have enough available space, a scroll bar (shown in Figure 6-11) appears by default, which allows the user to reach the content he desires.

Figure 6-11. The scroll bar that appears when clipping occurs by default in containers

You can override this default behavior and have a container always display a scroll bar, or none at all even if one is needed. Each container has the properties `horizontalScrollPolicy` and `verticalScrollPolicy`. These properties accept the values `ScrollPolicy.ON`, `ScrollPolicy.OFF`, and `ScrollPolicy.AUTO`, the latter which is the default value for containers.

Another functionality that containers perform on children when they exceed the available area is *clipping*. Clipping is the process whereby a container will clip (hide) the parts that exceed its viewable area. In the preceding example, the content was clipped, but a scroll bar was provided to allow the user to scroll. Flex containers allow you to disable clipping, if needed, using the `clipContent` property. By default, the `clipContent` property is set to `true`; if it is set to `false`, the content will not be clipped. Disabling clipping will also cause the children to extend beyond the container's boundaries. This can have adverse effects on your application layout, as the container boundaries are not adhered to when clipping is disabled.

The Spacer Component

The `Spacer` component is a component that can assist in handling layout within Flex. It is commonly used when you need to reposition a child when you're using a container that does not give you precise control, such as the `Canvas` container. The `Spacer` component is treated like any other container child component. You can add it to a container and give it width and height. Once you add it to a component, it does not render to the user's screen. Instead, it will just occupy the space a regular component would occupy.

Figure 6-12 shows a simple application in which three buttons are displayed. The buttons are placed within an HBox component, and the first and second buttons, unlike the second and third, require extra space in between. To achieve this, a Spacer component is used in between the first and second buttons.

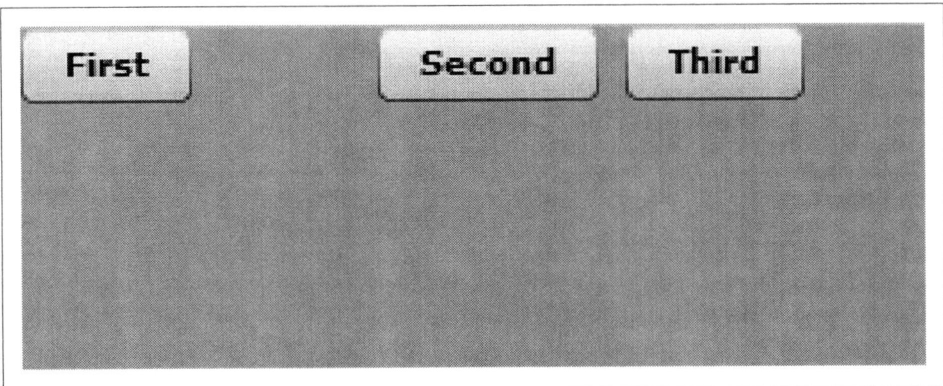

Figure 6-12. Three buttons within an HBox, with a Spacer component separating the first and second buttons

Here is the code used to create Figure 6-12:

```
<?xml version="1.0" encoding="utf-8"?>
<mx:Application xmlns:mx="http://www.adobe.com/2006/mxml" layout="absolute">
    <mx:HBox>
        <mx:Button label="First"/>
        <mx:Spacer width="40"/>
        <mx:Button label="Second"/>
        <mx:Button label="Third"/>
    </mx:HBox>
</mx:Application>
```

Spacers make it easy to adjust child positioning rules. Although you may be tempted to use Spacers everywhere, it is recommended that you first review why you need Spacers instead of assuming that Spacers may be the ideal solution, because often you may find that your layout can be handled in a more ideal manner.

Making Fluid Interfaces

Another benefit of using Flex is the ability to build *fluid interfaces* (i.e., interfaces that expand or contract when their available real estate changes). For applications deployed to the Web, this usually occurs when the browser window is resized. Without Flex, you would need to handle the Flash Player resize event manually and adjust the sizes of all the containers and their children to handle the change in available space.

In Flex, all layout containers and controls support the ability to set some values as percentages, the most basic of which are the width and height properties that set the available real estate for the container. Setting the width and height properties to a percentage value causes the container to occupy a percentage of the container of which it is currently a child.

Example 6-9 shows the code for a Panel container that occupies 70% of the width and 40% of the height of the Application container.

Example 6-9. A panel that occupies 70% of the width and 40% of the height of the available area

```
<?xml version="1.0" encoding="utf-8"?>
<mx:Application xmlns:mx="http://www.adobe.com/2006/mxml">
    <mx:Panel width="70%" height="40%">
    </mx:Panel>
</mx:Application>
```

The Application container's width and height values are set by default to occupy all the space available to it. As such, in Example 6-9, the Panel automatically adjusts to changes in the browser's size during runtime, as Application automatically grows to satisfy its size.

You can use percentage values in MXML for the width and height properties of any UI control in Flex, but percentage values are not valid in ActionScript. Instead, you have to use the percentWidth and percentHeight properties of a component. This is actually how the Flex compiler translates the percentage values from MXML to ActionScript at compile time.

Putting It All Together

Now that we have covered the many concepts related to managing layout within Flex, let's dig a bit deeper and learn how to put it all together.

The layout shown in Figure 6-13 contains a fixed left region for two List components that are stacked with a draggable divider, and a Canvas region that expands and repositions the Save button as needed to keep it at the bottom right.

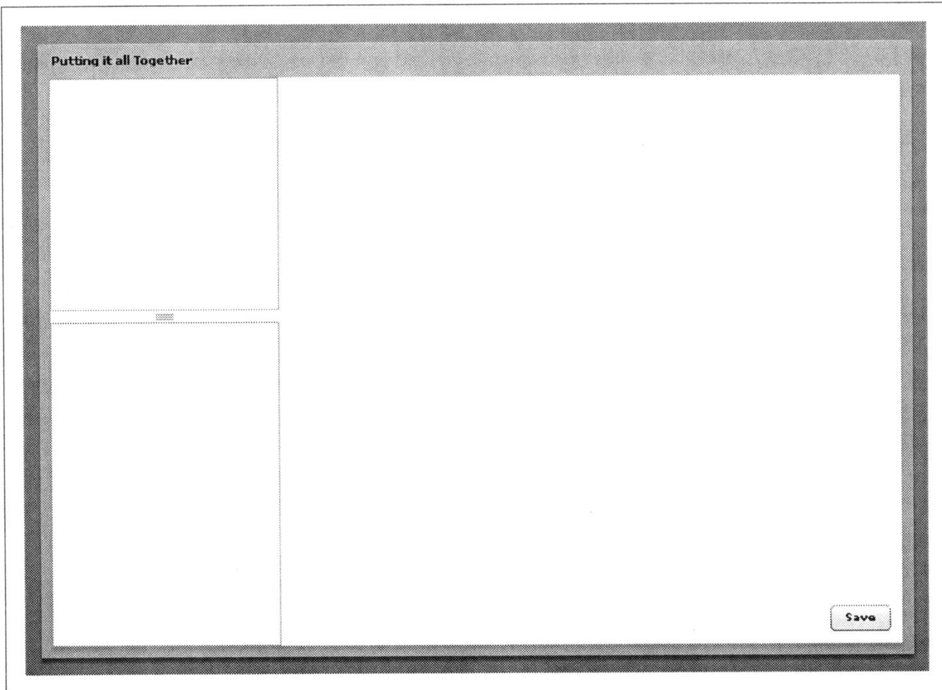

Figure 6-13. Layout example that contains different nested container types and controls

In Figure 6-13, the application is contained within a `Panel`, and the `width` and `height` properties are set to `resize` to maximize the application area. When resizing occurs, the left `VDividedBox` continues to have the same width, but it expands to fill the maximum vertical space. The `Canvas` on the right expands to fill the entire region, which allows the children to be laid out with the `Canvas` using constraint-based layout techniques (discussed earlier). Example 6-10 shows the code used to produce Figure 6-13.

Example 6-10. Code used to produce the layout in Figure 6-13

```
<?xml version="1.0" encoding="utf-8"?>
<mx:Application xmlns:mx="http://www.adobe.com/2006/mxml">
    <mx:Panel layout="horizontal" width="100%" height="100%" title="Putting it
all Together">
        <mx:VDividedBox width="200" height="100%">
            <mx:List width="100%" height="200"/>
            <mx:List width="100%"/>
        </mx:VDividedBox>
        <mx:Canvas width="100%" height="100%">
            <mx:Button bottom="10" right="10" label="Save"/>
        </mx:Canvas>
    </mx:Panel>
</mx:Application>
```

Now let's walk through the code. First, we declared the application, as shown in Example 6-11. Our intent is not to use the `Application` layout rules because the entire application is contained within a `Panel` that will serve as the root container.

Example 6-11. Adding the application

```
<?xml version="1.0" encoding="utf-8"?>
<mx:Application xmlns:mx="http://www.adobe.com/2006/mxml">

</mx:Application>
```

Next, we added the `Panel` container and set the `width` and `height` to `100%` to ensure that the interface expands as needed. This also ensures that the interface's children get the maximum possible real estate available to the application. As shown in Example 6-12, the layout value of `Panel` is set to `horizontal`, as you want the children to be positioned horizontally, one next to the other, using the box layout rule.

Example 6-12. Adding the Panel container

```
<?xml version="1.0" encoding="utf-8"?>
<mx:Application xmlns:mx="http://www.adobe.com/2006/mxml">
    <mx:Panel layout="horizontal" width="100%" height="100%" title="Putting it
all Together"/>
</mx:Application>
```

Next, we added the two `List` controls within a `VDividedBox`, as shown in Example 6-13.

Example 6-13. Adding the VDividedBox

```
<?xml version="1.0" encoding="utf-8"?>
<mx:Application xmlns:mx="http://www.adobe.com/2006/mxml">
    <mx:Panel layout="horizontal" width="100%" height="100%" title="Putting it
all Together">
        <mx:VDividedBox width="200" height="100%">
            <mx:List width="100%" height="200"/>
            <mx:List width="100%"/>
        </mx:VDividedBox>
    </mx:Panel>
</mx:Application>
```

The `VDividedBox`'s direction is set to `vertical` by default, so there is no need to set a `direction` value. The `VDividedBox`'s `width` property is set to a fixed pixel value of `200`. This ensures that the `VDividedBox` always has a 200-pixel width—no more and no less. The `height` is set to `100%` to ensure that the panel expands as the canvas is resized. The `VDividedBox` expands too, and its children get to take advantage of the extra space.

Next, we placed two `List` controls. Each `List` control has a `width` of `100%`. You could achieve the same result by setting the `List` controls to occupy `200` pixels rather than `100%`. However, we've found that setting the value to `100%` makes it easier in the future to resize the parent container (in this case, the `VDividedBox`) without having to change the behavior of the children. The `height` of the first `List` control is set to an explicit 200 pixels to ensure that on initial load, the top List control is given at least 200 pixels of real estate, both in height and in width, for displaying content to the user. (Omit this if you don't have a preference on its size.) After the initial load, if the user decides there's no need for the space, he can resize the VDividedBox children interactively.

Finally, we added the Canvas container with a Button, as shown in Example 6-14.

Example 6-14. Adding the Canvas to complete the example

```
<?xml version="1.0" encoding="utf-8"?>
<mx:Application xmlns:mx="http://www.adobe.com/2006/mxml">
    <mx:Panel layout="horizontal" width="100%" height="100%" title="Putting it
all Together">
        <mx:VDividedBox width="200" height="100%">
            <mx:List width="100%" height="200"/>
            <mx:List width="100%"/>
        </mx:VDividedBox>
        <mx:Canvas width="100%" height="100%">
            <mx:Button bottom="10" right="10" label="Save"/>
        </mx:Canvas>
    </mx:Panel>
</mx:Application>
```

The Canvas container's width and height properties are set to 100% to ensure that the Canvas container grows as needed. The container's x and y properties aren't set, so x and y both take the default value of 0. The Canvas container is a child of the Panel, which uses the horizontal BoxLayout rule. This ensures that the canvas is positioned to the right of the VDividedBox.

Within the Canvas container, the Button is positioned using constraint-based layout rules to anchor it to the bottom right. To achieve that, the bottom and right style properties are set to 10. That ensures that the Button is always 10 pixels away from the bottom-right corner of the Canvas container, even when the user resizes the Canvas container.

The techniques covered in this section will help you achieve many different layouts. It's important to keep in mind that you can mix many containers together to attain a desired layout. Deciding when to use more containers is a skill that varies widely, although as a general rule, completing a layout with fewer containers is better. With the power of the canvas-based layout rule along with constraint functionality, you often can achieve your application layout with fewer containers.

Summary

In this chapter, we covered the many mechanisms for performing application layout rapidly and efficiently in Flex. Flex has powerful layout containers that you can combine to achieve different results. As you've seen, Flex offers many layout containers that can greatly assist you in rapidly laying out applications.

CHAPTER 7

Working with UI Components

The Flex framework consists, in large part, of components. Within the framework there are many types of components, from data components to layout components to user interface (UI) components. You can read about each type of component in the appropriate chapters throughout this book. In this chapter, we focus on UI components. UI components are visual components that display something to the user and/or prompt the user to interact with the application.

Although there's no formal classification for the majority of the UI components in the Flex framework, it is useful to categorize them just for the purposes of discussion. We've organized our discussion of the Flex framework UI components based on the categories listed in Table 7-1.

Table 7-1. UI component categories

Category	Components
Buttons	Button, LinkButton, RadioButton, CheckBox
Value selectors	HSlider, VSlider, NumericStepper, ColorPicker, DateField, DateChooser
Text components	Label, Text, TextInput, TextArea, RichTextEditor
List-based controls	List, ComboBox, DataGrid, HorizontalList, TileList, Tree
Advanced data controls	AdvancedDataGrid
Pop-up controls	PopUpButton, PopUpMenuButton
Windows	Panel, TitleWindow
Navigators	ViewStack, Accordion, ButtonBar, LinkBar, MenuBar, TabBar, TabNavigator, ToggleButtonBar
Control bars	ControlBar, ApplicationControlBar
Media and progress indicators	Image, SWFLoader, VideoDisplay, ProgressBar

Layout containers are not included in Table 7-1 because we discuss them in depth in Chapter 6.

In this chapter, we will discuss each category of component listed in Table 7-1, with the exception of windows and media and progress containers, which we discuss in Chapter 6 and Chapter 11, respectively. Although you'll find a lot of good information about how to use UI components in this chapter, you will not find a complete reference for every component and its API. To do that would require a much larger volume than this. Furthermore, the official Flex documentation does a good job of providing this information already. You can read the online version of the Flex documentation at *http://livedocs.adobe.com/flex/3/html/index.html*. The information in this chapter complements the official documentation in that this chapter explains which components exist, how they are related, and when to use each one.

Understanding UI Components

All UI components (and all layout components) are related because they inherit from a common superclass called `mx.core.UIComponent`. This `UIComponent` class is part of the Flex framework. The class is abstract, meaning you would never create a `UIComponent` instance directly. However, it's important to understand `UIComponent` because it will tell you a lot about all the components that inherit from it.

The `UIComponent` class itself inherits from `mx.core.FlexSprite`, which directly inherits from `flash.display.Sprite`, which is part of the Flash Player API. This means that all Flex UI components behave very much like standard Flash display objects because they inherit from the display object inheritance chain. Figure 7-1 illustrates the inheritance relationship of UI components, showing only a partial list of the UI components (`Button`, `ComboBox`, `DateField`, etc.) in the interest of brevity.

Creating Component Instances

You can create UI component instances either with MXML or with ActionScript. If you use MXML, you should use the tag that has the same name as the component. For example, the following code creates a button instance:

```
<mx:Button />
```

When you want to use ActionScript you should use the constructor of the component class in a new statement. The following code creates a button instance using ActionScript:

```
var button:Button = new Button();
```

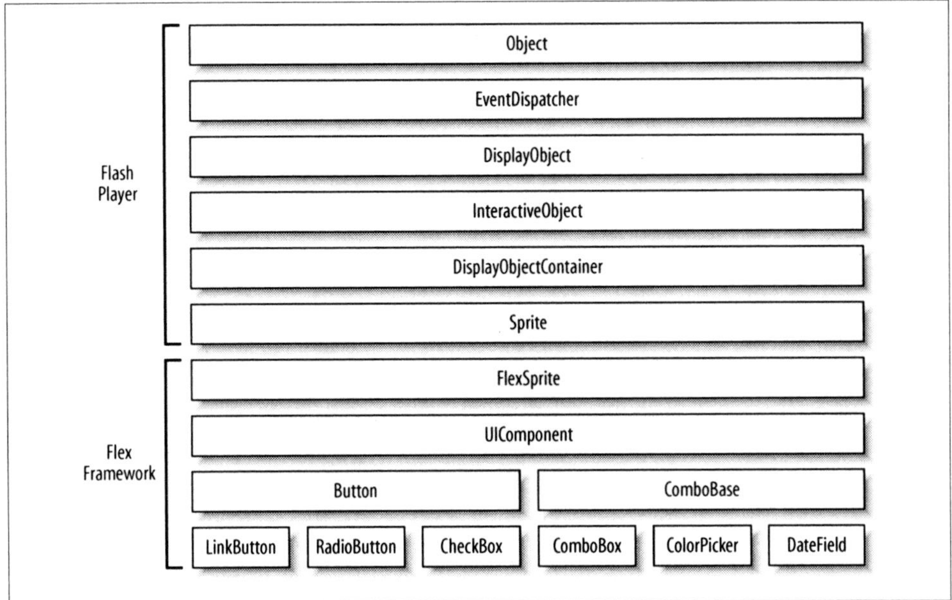

Figure 7-1. A partial list of the UI components and the inheritance relationship of UI components and Flash Player classes

When you create a component using ActionScript, the component is not automatically added to the display list as it is when you use MXML. If you want to add the component to the display list so that it is visible, you must use the `addChild()` method of a container:

```
addChild(button);
```

You can read more about adding components to containers in Chapter 6.

Common UI Component Properties

When you work with UI components, you can always count on certain properties being implemented. Those properties are as follows:

`x`
: The x coordinate of the component relative to its parent container's content area. You can set the property to move the component, and you can read the property to get the current x coordinate of the component.

`y`
: The y coordinate of the component relative to its parent container. Like the `x` property, you can both read and write the `y` property.

`width`
: The width of the component in pixels. You can read the property to retrieve the current width, and you can set the property to change the width of the component.

`height`
: The height of the component in pixels. Like the `width` property, you can both read and write the `height` property.

`scaleX`
: The scale of the component in the horizontal direction relative to its original width. The `scaleX` and `width` properties are linked. When you change the `scaleX`, the `width` changes as well, yet the opposite is not true. You can both read and write the `scaleX` property. Both `scaleX` and `scaleY` values are on a scale whereby 0 is 0% and 1 is 100%. For example, setting `scaleX` to .5 will halve the horizontal scale of a component.

`scaleY`
: The scale of the component in the vertical direction relative to its original height. The `scaleY` and `height` properties are linked just as the `scaleX` and `width` properties are linked. The values for `scaleY` are on the same range as are those for `scaleX`. And you can both read and write the `scaleY` property.

`rotation`
: The number of degrees of rotation of the component relative to its original orientation. Rotation is always clockwise and is always relative to the origin point of the component's internal coordinate system. In almost all cases, a component's origin exists at the upper-left corner. You can both read and write the `rotation` property.

`alpha`
: The opacity of the component. The default value is `1`, which means the component is fully opaque. The effective range for `alpha` is from 0 (transparent) to 1 (opaque). You can read and write the `alpha` property.

`visible`
: The visibility of the component. The default value is `true`, meaning the component is visible. A value of `false` means the component is not visible. You can both read and write the `visible` property.

`enabled`
: Whether a component is interactive. For example, if a button is enabled, it can accept mouse clicks. The default value is `true`. A value of `false` disables the component. You can both read and write the `enabled` property.

`parent`
: A reference to the parent container for the component. The `parent` property is read-only. If you want to change the parent of a component, you must use the `removeChild()` method of the parent container to remove the component, or use `addChild()` to add the component to a new container.

The preceding list is not intended to be comprehensive by any means. However, it does represent some of the most commonly used properties of all UI components.

You can work with most of these properties both in MXML and in ActionScript (except when a property is read-only, in which case you must use ActionScript to read the value). The following example sets several properties of a button instance using MXML:

```
<mx:Button id="button" label="Example Button"
    width="200" height="50" enabled="false" />
```

Here's the equivalent ActionScript code:

```
var button:Button = new Button();
button.label = "Example Button";
button.width = 200;
button.height = 50;
button.enabled = false;
addChild(button);
```

Handling Events

Events are the way in which objects (such as Flex UI components) can communicate with the rest of the application. There are two basic types of events: *user events* and *system events*. User events are events that occur directly because of user interaction with the application. For example, when the user clicks a button, a click event occurs, and when the user expands a drop-down menu (a combo box component), an open event occurs. On the other hand, a system event occurs because something happens within the application in response to initialization, asynchronous operations, or other such non-user-driven behavior. For example, when a component is created several events occur during the stages of creation indicating that various aspects of the component are accessible.

When an event occurs, we say the event is *dispatched* (or *broadcasted*). The object that dispatches an event is called the *target*. All Flex UI components are potential event targets, meaning all UI components dispatch events. The event that gets dispatched is in the form of an object of type `flash.events.Event` (or a subtype). The `Event` instance provides information about the event, including the type of event (click, open, etc.) and the target that dispatched the event.

When a component dispatches an event, nothing occurs in response unless something (called a *listener*) is configured to receive notifications. There are two ways that you can handle events in a Flex application: one uses MXML attributes and the other uses ActionScript.

As you saw in Figure 7-1, all UI components inherit from the Flash Player `EventDispatcher` class, meaning that all UI components are capable of dispatching events to listeners.

Handling events with MXML

When you create a component using MXML, you can add an event handler using an attribute that has the same name as the event you want to handle. For example, buttons dispatch click events when the user clicks on them. Therefore, you can add a `click` attribute to the `Button` tag to handle the click event. You also can assign ActionScript to the attribute. For example, the following code lowers the alpha of the button by .1 each time the user clicks on the button:

```
<mx:Button id="button" label="Alpha Button" click="button.alpha -= .1" />
```

Although you can assign ActionScript expressions to event handler attributes, as in the preceding example, it is more common (and useful) to assign a function call to the event handler attribute. This allows you to define more complex functionality in response to the event. When you call a function/method from an event handler attribute, you should pass a parameter called `event` to the function. In MXML, the `event` parameter will automatically pass along the event object that the component dispatches:

```
<mx:Button id="button" label="Alpha Button" click="clickHandler(event)" />
```

You then need to define the method that is intended to handle the event. The method should accept a parameter of type `Event` (or the appropriate subtype). The following example accomplishes the same thing as the inline expression did previously. However, in addition it resets the alpha to 1 if and when the alpha is less than 0:

```
private function clickHandler(event:MouseEvent):void {
  var target:Button = event.target as Button;
  target.alpha -= .1;
  if(target.alpha < 0) {
    target.alpha = 1;
  }
}
```

Some event types, such as `MouseEvent`, contain additional information beyond what a basic `Event` object would contain. For example, a `MouseEvent` contains information about whether a mouse button is currently pressed.

As you can see in the preceding code, we can retrieve a reference to the object that dispatched the event using the `target` property of the `event` object. This allows one event listener to be used with more than one event dispatcher.

Handling events with ActionScript

You can use ActionScript to add event listeners to a component as an alternative to using MXML event attributes. This is useful for a couple of reasons. First, it is useful to add event listeners using ActionScript when you are creating the component instance using ActionScript as opposed to MXML. Second, when you add event listeners using

ActionScript, you can also remove the event listeners later. This is useful if you want to temporarily or permanently stop listening for a specific event for a component.

To register a listener for an event using ActionScript you should use the `addEventListener()` method. This method requires that you pass it at least two parameters: the name of the event for which you want to listen and the function to use as the listener. Typically, you should use constants for event names rather than quoted strings to avoid typos that would introduce bugs that the compiler would not catch. The event name constants are members of the associated event class. For example, the `Event` class defines `OPEN`, `CLOSE`, `SCROLL`, `SELECT`, and many other constants. The `MouseEvent` class defines `CLICK`, `MOUSE_OVER`, and other mouse-related event constants. The `FlexEvent` class defines constants for many of the Flex-specific events such as `ADD`, `REMOVE`, `CREATION_COMPLETE`, and `INITIALIZE`. The following code creates a button and then adds a listener for the click event:

```
var button:Button = new Button();
button.label = "Click This Button";
button.addEventListener(MouseEvent.CLICK, clickHandler);
addChild(button);
```

The event listener function is automatically passed an `Event` object as a parameter:

```
private function clickHandler(event:MouseEvent):void {
  var target:Button = event.target as Button;
  target.alpha -= .1;
  if(target.alpha < 0) {
    target.alpha = 1;
  }
}
```

Event objects

The `flash.events.Event` class is the base class for all events in Flex applications. However, many event objects are instances of event subtypes. For example, events related to mouse behavior (`click`, `mouseOver`, etc.) are of type `MouseEvent`.

Event objects always have a `type` property indicating the type of event the object represents. For example, a click event will dispatch an object with a `type` property of `click`. Event objects also have `target` properties that reference the actual object that dispatched the event. In some cases, the target may not be the object for which you have registered a listener. This can occur when the object for which you have registered a listener contains a child component that also dispatches the same event (and the event bubbles). If you want to ensure that you are getting a reference to the object for which the listener is registered to listen for the event, use the `currentTarget` property. The following example illustrates this point:

```
<?xml version="1.0" encoding="utf-8"?>
<mx:Application xmlns:mx="http://www.adobe.com/2006/mxml" layout="vertical">
    <mx:Script>
        <![CDATA[
```

```
            private function clickHandler(event:MouseEvent):void {
                textArea.text = event.target + "\n" + event.currentTarget;
            }

        ]]>
    </mx:Script>
    <mx:Canvas id="canvas" click="clickHandler(event);">
        <mx:Button id="button" label="Click This Button" />
    </mx:Canvas>
    <mx:TextArea id="textArea" />
</mx:Application>
```

If you run this example and click the button, you'll see that the text area tells you that the target of the event is the button while the current target is the canvas. That is because the button is what actually dispatched the event, but the canvas is the object with which you registered the listener.

Standard Flex component events

Each UI component type may have events that are specific to that type. For example, combo boxes dispatch open events when the menu is expanded. However, all UI components have a set of events in common. Table 7-2 lists these common events.

Table 7-2. Common UI component events

Event	Constant	Description
`add`	`FlexEvent.ADD`	The component has been added to a container.
`remove`	`FlexEvent.REMOVE`	The component has been removed from a container.
`show`	`FlexEvent.SHOW`	The component has been made visible (the `visible` property is now `true`).
`hide`	`FlexEvent.HIDE`	The component has been made nonvisible (the `visi ble` property is now `false`).
`resize`	`FlexEvent.RESIZE`	The component dimensions have changed.
`preinitialize`	`FlexEvent.PREINITIALIZE`	The component has started to initialize, but children haven't yet been created.
`initialize`	`FlexEvent.INITIALIZE`	The component has been constructed, but it has not yet been measured and laid out.
`creationComplete`	`FlexEvent.CREATION_COMPLETE`	The component is completely created, measured, and laid out.

The list of common events in Table 7-2 isn't comprehensive. The `UIComponent` class (from which all UI components inherit) defines many more events. For a comprehensive list, look at the Flex documentation listing for `mx.core.UIComponent`. We'll also discuss many of the events in this book in the sections where they're most appropriate (e.g., we'll discuss drag-and-drop events in the "Drag-and-Drop section of Chapter 10).

Buttons

There are four basic button types of controls: Button, LinkButton, RadioButton, and CheckBox. Although each type behaves similarly, they have different intended uses. Figure 7-2 shows instances of each type.

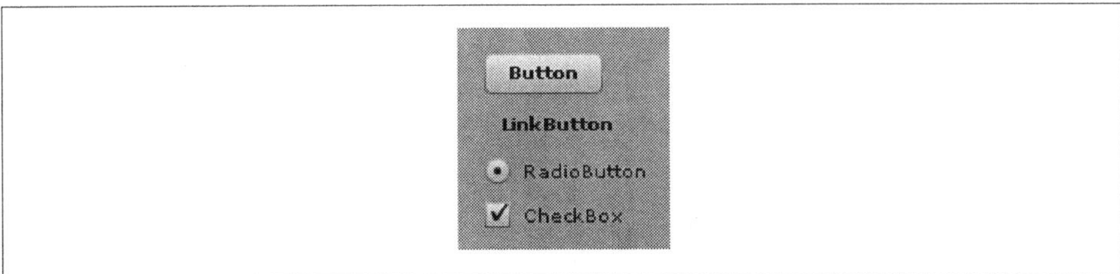

Figure 7-2. Button components

Of the four types, Button and LinkButton are the most similar in use. In fact, the primary difference between Button and LinkButton is purely cosmetic: buttons have borders and backgrounds and link buttons do not. However, you'll typically use both types for similar purposes—generally to initiate some behavior when the user clicks on the button or link button. Buttons are typically more common than link buttons.

By default, buttons and link buttons respond to every click in the same way. However, you can set the toggle property of a button or link button to true, in which case the button will have two states—selected and deselected—and it will toggle between those states each time the user clicks it.

Radio buttons are quite different in use from standard buttons. Radio buttons are typically used in groups. Radio buttons can be selected or deselected, and only one button can be selected per group. For this reason, radio buttons are often used when you want to allow the user to select just one from a group of options. You should typically first create a RadioButtonGroup instance when using radio buttons. Then, assign the ID of the group to the groupName property of each radio button in the group, as shown here:

```
<mx:RadioButtonGroup id="exampleGroup" />
<mx:RadioButton groupName="exampleGroup" label="A" value="a" />
<mx:RadioButton groupName="exampleGroup" label="B" value="b" />
```

Checkboxes are also buttons. They are most similar to standard buttons that have been set to toggle. When a user clicks a checkbox, it toggles the selected state of the component (toggling the value of the selected property). The following creates a checkbox with a label of A and toggled to selected:

```
<mx:CheckBox id="exampleCheckbox" label="A" selected="true" />
```

Value Selectors

Value selectors are components that allow the user to select a value. This is a fairly diverse category of components because the types of values they allow the user to select and the ways in which they allow the user to select the values are quite different. Figure 7-3 shows the basic value selector components (except for `VSlider`, because it is the vertical version of `HSlider`, which is shown).

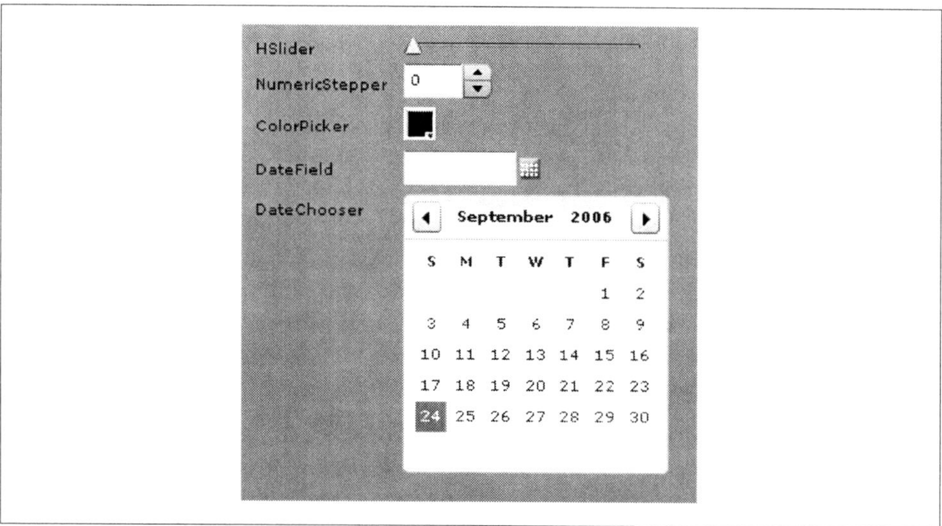

Figure 7-3. Value selector components

The slider components (`HSlider` and `VSlider`) differ only in that one is horizontal and one is vertical. Otherwise, they behave identically. The slider components allow the user to select a numeric value along a range from a minimum to a maximum value. The default range is 0 to 10, but you can adjust the range using the `minimum` and `maximum` properties. The slider components allow the user to drag a thumb along that range. Optionally, you can add more than one thumb and allow the user to select a range of values. Use the `thumbCount` property to specify the number of thumbs. The following example adds a new thumb when the user clicks on the button:

```
<?xml version="1.0" encoding="utf-8"?>
<mx:Application xmlns:mx="http://www.adobe.com/2006/mxml" layout="vertical">

    <mx:Script>
        <![CDATA[

            private function addThumb():void {
                hslider.thumbCount++;
            }

        ]]>
```

```
    </mx:Script>
    <mx:HSlider id="hslider" />
    <mx:Button label="Add Thumb" click="addThumb();" />
</mx:Application>
```

You may notice that when you add a new thumb, all the thumbs are reset back to 0 even if you had moved them previously. To maintain the values you must read the values prior to incrementing the thumbs and then reassign them just after incrementing the thumbs. When there's just one thumb, you can read the value using the `value` property. When there are many thumbs, you must use the `values` property, which is an array of values. The following rewrite of `addThumb()` reads the values, increments `thumbCount`, and then reassigns the preexisting values to the slider:

```
private function addThumb():void {
                var values:Array = hslider.values;
                hslider.thumbCount++;
               values.unshift(0);
               hslider.values = values;
            }
```

The numeric stepper control allows the user to select a numeric value as well. However, the interface for a numeric stepper is quite different from that of a slider interface. Whereas a slider interface is very graphical, the numeric stepper interface actually displays the current numeric value in digits, allowing the user to scroll through the list of possible values in the range.

The color picker component is very useful for allowing the user to select a color value from an expandable/collapsible grid of color swatches. The following simple example uses a color picker and a text area. The color style of the text area is data-bound to the color picker value, effectively changing the text color when the user changes the color picker value.

```
<mx:ColorPicker id="colorPicker" />
    <mx:TextArea color="{colorPicker.value as int}" />
```

The date field and date chooser components are useful for allowing the user to select date values. The date field component is a good way to allow the user to select a single date in a compact form. Although the date field component expands to display a calendar while the user is selecting a date, it again collapses to a compact form once the user has selected a value. The date chooser component, on the other hand, is an expanded format component that always displays the calendar from which the user can select a date. The date chooser component also allows the user to select multiple dates and ranges of dates.

Text Components

There are five basic text components that we can further categorize into display and input components. Figure 7-4 on the next page shows these components.

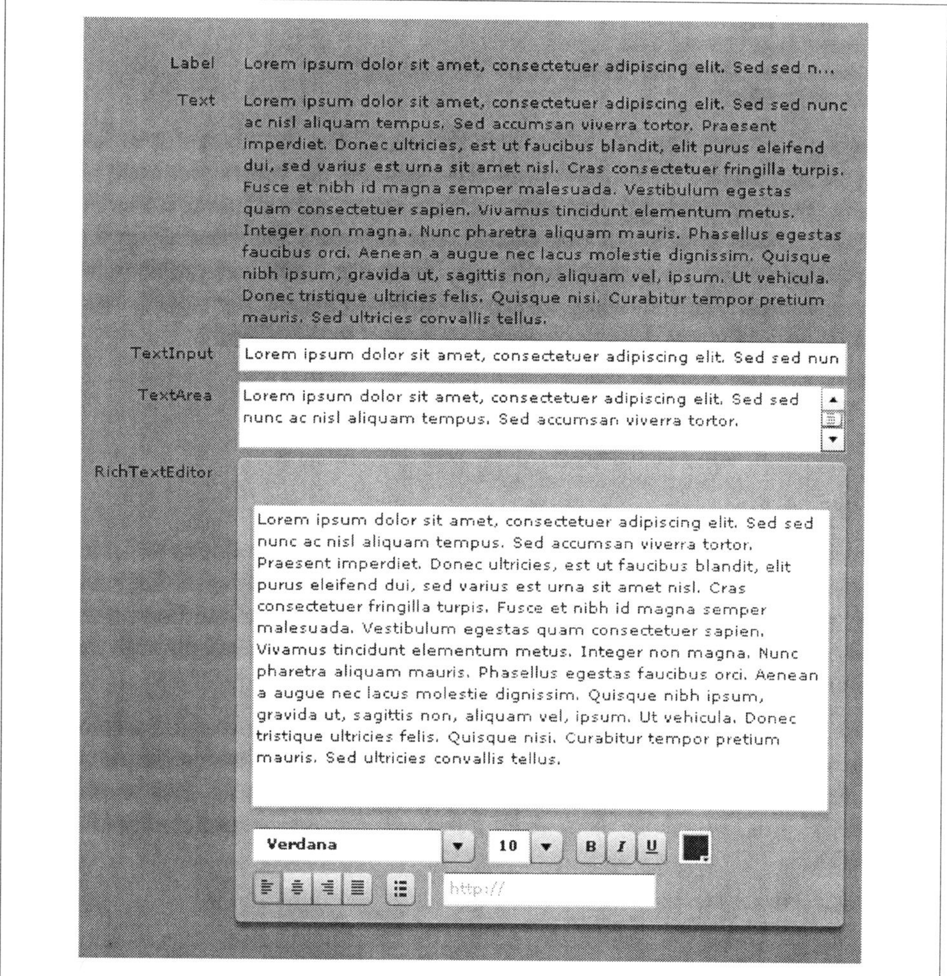

Figure 7-4. Text components

The label and text components are display-only components. The user cannot edit the contents of either of these types. The label component is useful for displaying one line of text whereas the text component is useful for displaying multiple lines of text.

The text input, text area, and rich text editor components are user input text controls. The text input component allows the user to input one line of text. The text area component allows the user to input multiple lines of text, and it automatically adds scroll bars when necessary. The rich text editor component not only allows the user to input multiple lines of text, but also allows the user to apply formatting styles such as bold, italic, underline, text align, and so forth.

List-Based Controls

List-based controls are among the most sophisticated of the standard controls. These are the components that allow the user to select an item or items from a list of options. In the simplest form, a list might be a vertical, scrollable list of text labels from which the user can select. However, list-based controls can be increasingly complex from there, supporting columns, horizontal and grid-based layouts, hierarchical and collapsible structures, and even icons, images, and more. Figure 7-5 shows the list-based controls.

The most fundamental of all the list-based controls is the list. Lists are vertically scrolling, single-column controls. These lists are among the most common types of lists.

Horizontal lists are mostly identical to standard lists except that they scroll horizontally rather than vertically. Horizontal lists are typically useful for scrolling icons and/or images (thumbnails), though you could also use a horizontal list for simple text.

Combo boxes are lists that collapse to a single line when not activated. Users often refer to these types of controls as *drop-down menus*; they allow the user to select from a vertically scrolling list of options when in an expanded state. Once a value has been selected, the control returns to the collapsed state.

Tile lists are scrollable lists in which the contents are arranged in a grid. Tile lists are useful when you want to display contents in a grid, but you need the grid to scroll.

Data grids are vertically scrolling, multicolumn lists. Data grids are good for displaying data that consists of records of multiple values that a user might need to see at the same time. For example, a data grid would be a good choice for displaying the details of a user's phone use history where each row displays the time, the duration, and the destination phone number, each in a different column.

Tree controls are hierarchical types of lists. They are very similar to standard lists in that they are vertically scrolling. However, whereas standard lists have linear data models, trees have hierarchical data models where individual elements can expand and collapse to reveal and hide nested elements.

UI components have a `data` property as well as a `dataProvider` property. Although it is easy enough to initially confuse the two, they are different properties with different purposes. The `dataProvider` property allows you to set the data model for a component. The `data` property is used by the Flex framework only when using a component as an item renderer for a list-based component, as discussed in Chapter 10, though you could conceivably use the `data` property in other contexts to assign data to a custom component.

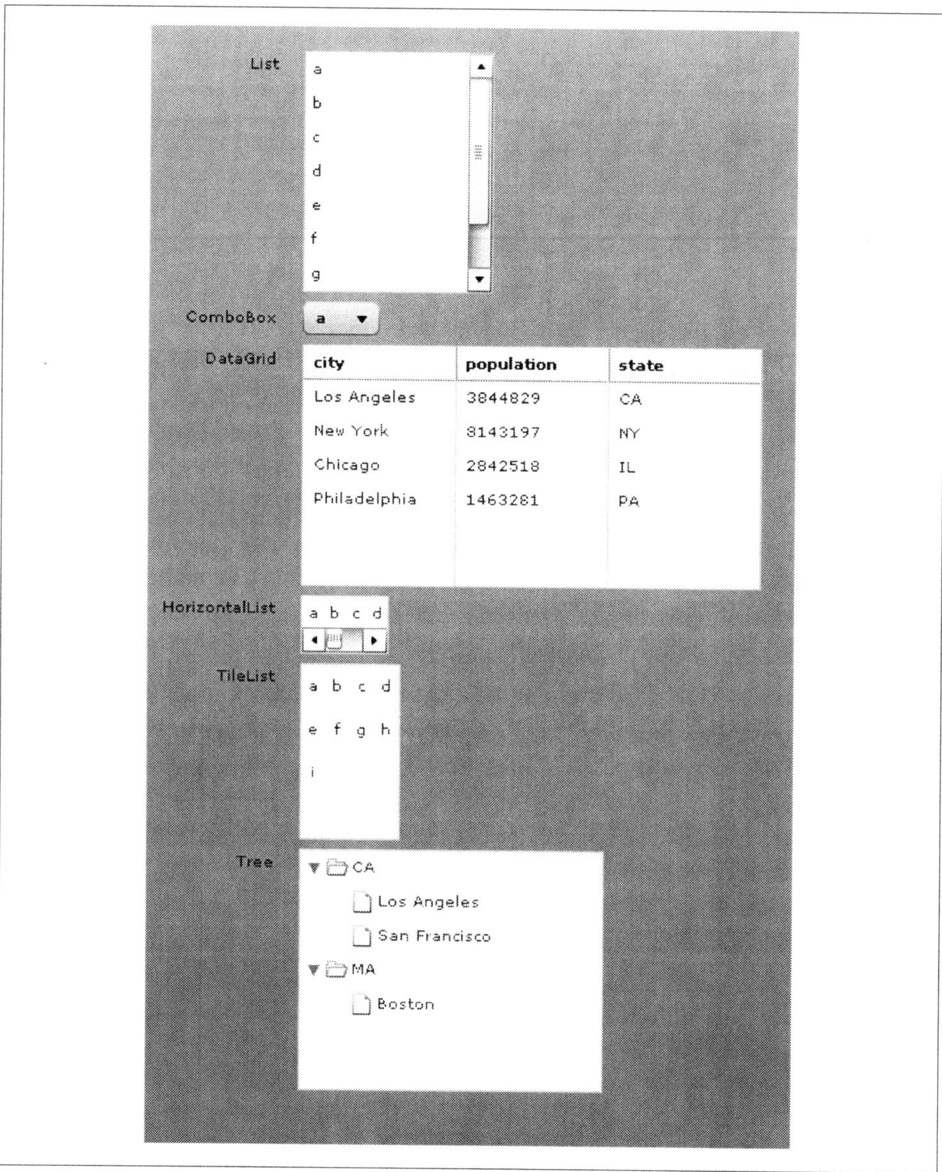

Figure 7-5. List-based controls

Data Models

Flex controls use Model-View-Controller (though not in a strict fashion), a software pattern that differentiates between the display of data and the data itself. This is very evident in the list-based controls. All list-based controls utilize data models. In the language used by these components, the data models are called *data providers*. Data providers are independent objects that you can associate with a control. The control then uses that object's data to render its view.

Data providers always implement the `mx.collections.ICollectionView` interface. Although you can assign an array or an `XML` object to the `dataProvider` property of most list-based components, Flex converts the object behind the scenes to a type that implements `ICollectionView`. That means that arrays get converted to a type called `mx.collections.ArrayCollection` and `XML` and `XMLList` objects get converted to `mx.collections.XMLListCollection`. It's generally best to always explicitly wrap the object as a collection first before assigning it as the data provider. That way you are assured of having a reference to the actual data provider collection rather than the object wrapped by the collection.

Creating a Collection Object

There are two basic ways to create collections: using ActionScript and using MXML. The ActionScript solution involves creating a new collection type, typically with the constructor. The following ActionScript example creates a new `ArrayCollection` object that wraps an array:

```
var collection:ICollectionView = new ArrayCollection(["a", "b", "c", "d"]);
```

The variables in these examples are typed as `ICollectionView` rather than the concrete types (e.g., `ArrayCollection`) so that polymorphism can be utilized in later examples. In the case of the preceding example, you could technically type the variable as `ArrayCollection`.

Likewise, this ActionScript example creates an `XMLListCollection` that wraps an `XMLList` object:

```
var xml:XML = <items><item>a</item><item>b</item>
              <item>c</item><item>d</item></items>;
var collection:ICollectionView = new XMLListCollection(xml.children());
```

You can create the same collections using MXML. The following example creates an `ArrayCollection` object using MXML:

```
<mx:ArrayCollection id="collection">
    <mx:Array>
        <mx:String>a</mx:String>
        <mx:String>b</mx:String>
        <mx:String>c</mx:String>
        <mx:String>d</mx:String>
    </mx:Array>
</mx:ArrayCollection>
```

This creates an `XMLListCollection` using MXML:

```
<mx:XMLListCollection id="collection">
    <mx:XMLList id="example">
```

```
        <item>a</item>
        <item>b</item>
        <item>c</item>
        <item>d</item>
    </mx:XMLList>
</mx:XMLListCollection>
```

Setting the Data Provider

You can use any sort of collection (as long as it implements `ICollectionView`) with any sort of list-based control, allowing for versatility of data structures. All you have to do is set the `dataProvider` property of the list-based control to be equal to the collection. For example, the following uses an `ArrayCollection` to populate a list:

```
var collection:ICollectionView = new ArrayCollection(["a", "b", "c", "d"]);
list.dataProvider = collection;
```

On the other hand, if the data happens to be in XML format, you can easily use an `XMLListCollection` instead:

```
var xml:XML = <items><item>a</item><item>b</item>
              <item>c</item><item>d</item></items>;
var collection:ICollectionView = new XMLListCollection(xml.children);
list.dataProvider = collection;
```

If you're using MXML to set the data provider, you can simply nest the collection within the list-based control tag. Because the `dataProvider` property is the default property for list-based controls, you don't need to explicitly state that the value should be assigned to the `dataProvider` property. The following example assigns an `ArrayCollection` to the `dataProvider` for a list:

```
<mx:List id="list" width="100">
    <mx:ArrayCollection>
        <mx:Array>
            <mx:String>a</mx:String>
            <mx:String>b</mx:String>
            <mx:String>c</mx:String>
            <mx:String>d</mx:String>
        </mx:Array>
    </mx:ArrayCollection>
</mx:List>
```

Using Data Grids

The preceding examples illustrated how to work with simple list-based controls such as lists, combo boxes, tile lists, and horizontal lists. Data grids inherit from standard lists, and therefore they function in much the same way. However, because data grids are more complex than standard lists, they have behavior that is specific to them. In the following sections, we'll look at working with data grids.

Using data providers

Data grid data providers are quite similar to standard data providers except that each element of a data grid data provider should consist of an object whose properties correspond to the columns of the data grid. The following example creates a data grid with columns named city, state, and population:

```
<mx:DataGrid>
    <mx:ArrayCollection>
        <mx:Array>
            <mx:Object city="Los Angeles" state="CA" population="3844829" />
            <mx:Object city="New York" state="NY" population="8143197" />
            <mx:Object city="Chicago" state="IL" population="2842518" />
            <mx:Object city="Philadelphia" state="PA" population="1463281" />
        </mx:Array>
    </mx:ArrayCollection>
</mx:DataGrid>
```

You can, of course, achieve the same result using ActionScript. Here's an example that displays the same content using ActionScript:

```
<?xml version="1.0"?>
<mx:Application xmlns:mx="http://www.adobe.com/2006/mxml"
creationComplete="creationCompleteHandler(event)">
    <mx:Script>
        <![CDATA[
            import mx.collections.ArrayCollection;

            private function creationCompleteHandler(event:Event):void {
                var array:Array = new Array({city: "Los Angeles",
                                             state: "CA",
                                             population: 3844829},
                                            {city: "New York",
                                             state: "NY",
                                             population: 8143197},
                                            {city: "Chicago",
                                             state: "IL",
                                             population: 2842518},
                                            {city: "Philadelphia",
                                             state: "PA",
                                             population: 1463281});
                var collection:ArrayCollection = new ArrayCollection(array);
                grid.dataProvider = collection;
            }

        ]]>
    </mx:Script>
    <mx:DataGrid id="grid" width="500" />

</mx:Application>
```

Working with data grid columns

By default, data grids automatically display columns corresponding to all the properties of the elements of the data provider. The code in the preceding section creates a data grid with three columns with the headings "city," "state," and "population". Although this may be the intended behavior, in many cases it is not very versatile. For this reason, it is possible to explicitly control the columns of a data grid.

You can specify which columns will display within a data grid by setting the `columns` property of the data grid to an array of `DataGridColumn` objects. Using these column objects, you can filter which columns get displayed, the widths of the columns, the editability of the columns, the heading text for the columns, and more. Here's an example that displays the city and population values with custom labels, but does not display the state data:

```
<mx:DataGrid id="grid" width="500">
    <mx:columns>
        <mx:DataGridColumn headerText="City" dataField="city" />
        <mx:DataGridColumn headerText="Population (within city limits)"
                           dataField="population" />
    </mx:columns>
    <mx:dataProvider>
        <mx:ArrayCollection>
            <mx:Array>
                <mx:Object city="Los Angeles" state="CA" population="3844829" />
                <mx:Object city="New York" state="NY" population="8143197" />
                <mx:Object city="Chicago" state="IL" population="2842518" />
                <mx:Object city="Philadelphia" state="PA" population="1463281" />
            </mx:Array>
        </mx:ArrayCollection>
    </mx:dataProvider>
</mx:DataGrid>
```

The Advanced Data Control

The advanced data grid control (`AdvancedDataGrid`) is available with the Professional version of Flex Builder 3 and is not part of the standard SDK. However, since the advanced data grid does represent significant new features above and beyond the standard data grid, it's worth taking a look at some of its features and how you can work with it.

In addition to providing the standard features of the normal data grid, the advanced data grid control can also do the following:

- Allow the user to sort on more than one column
- Select cells as well as rows
- Display hierarchical data (such as an advanced tree control)

Creating an advanced data grid

In the simplest implementation, you can use an advanced data grid just as you would a normal data grid. For instance, Example 7-1 creates an advanced data grid and populates it using an `ArrayCollection` object of countries.

Example 7-1. Using an advanced data grid in the simplest way

```
<?xml version="1.0" encoding="utf-8"?>
<mx:Application xmlns:mx="http://www.adobe.com/2006/mxml" layout="absolute"
creationComplete="creationCompleteHandler();">
    <mx:Script>
        <![CDATA[
            import mx.collections.ArrayCollection;

            [Bindable]
            private var _populations:ArrayCollection;

            private function creationCompleteHandler():void {
                _populations = new ArrayCollection();
                _populations.addItem({country:  "Canada",
                                      continent: "North America",
                                      population: 31612897});
                _populations.addItem({country:  "Venezuela",
                                      continent: "South America",
                                      population: 23054210});
                _populations.addItem({country:  "United States",
                                      continent: "North America",
                                      population: 281421906});
                _populations.addItem({country:  "Brazil",
                                      continent: "South America",
                                      population: 169799170});
            }

        ]]>
    </mx:Script>
    <mx:AdvancedDataGrid id="advancedDataGrid" width="100%" height="100%"
dataProvider="{_populations}" />
</mx:Application>
```

The result of the code in this example is that the advanced data grid is almost identical to a standard data grid. The one notable exception is that the advanced data grid allows the user to sort by multiple columns. The default behavior is that each column heading has two clickable regions. The larger clickable region sorts by that column and only that column. The smaller region adds the column to the chain of sortable columns. For instance, in the preceding example the advanced data grid displays three columns: `name`, `continent`, and `population`. As you can see in Figure 7-6, the smaller portion of the "continent" and "name" column headings designates in which order those columns will be sorted. In Figure 7-6, the data is sorted first by the `continent` column and then by the `name` column.

If you prefer that the column headings not show the sorting order and instead show only the header text, you can set `sortExpertMode` to `true` for the advanced data grid. In expert mode, the grid is still sortable by multiple columns, but the sorting requires that the user knows how to use the grid correctly to achieve the sorting: holding down the Ctrl key while clicking a header will add it to the sort chain.

continent 1 ▲	name 2 ▲	population
North America	Canada	31612897
North America	United States	281421906
South America	Brazil	169799170
South America	Venezuela	23054210

Figure 7-6. Sorting by multiple columns in default mode

Continent	Country	Population
▼ North America		
North America	United States	281421906
North America	Canada	31612897
▼ South America		
South America	Venezuela	23054210
South America	Brazil	169799170

Figure 7-7. Grouping data displays in a tree interface

Selecting rows and columns

With a standard data grid it is possible to select one row or multiple rows. With an advanced data grid you have other options, including:

- Selecting one cell
- Selecting multiple cells

You can use the `selectionMode` property to determine which mode the grid should use. The possible values are `none`, `singleRow`, `multipleRows`, `singleCell`, and `multipleCells`.

Working with grouping data

Normally when you work with data in a grid, it's fairly flat and two-dimensional. However, the advanced data grid allows you to group data to create an added dimension to the grid. For example, say we want to group the data set we used earlier by continent, allowing the user to look at only the North America rows or only the South America rows if she wants. The advanced data grid achieves this by using a tree-like interface, as you can see in Figure 7-7.

Grouped data is two-dimensional data that you wrap in an `mx.collections.GroupingCollection` instance. The `GroupingCollection` type allows you to specify fields on which the data should be grouped. For example, the data that is displayed in the grid in Figure 7-7 is grouped by continent. The code for this appears in Example 7-2.

Example 7-2. Working with grouping data

```
<?xml version="1.0" encoding="utf-8"?>
<mx:Application xmlns:mx="http://www.adobe.com/2006/mxml" layout="absolute"
creationComplete="creationCompleteHandler();">
    <mx:Script>
        <![CDATA[
            import mx.collections.Grouping;
            import mx.collections.GroupingField;
            import mx.collections.GroupingCollection;
            import mx.collections.ArrayCollection;

            [Bindable]
            private var _populations:GroupingCollection;

            private function creationCompleteHandler():void {
                var arrayCollection:ArrayCollection = new ArrayCollection();
                arrayCollection.addItem({country:  "Canada",
                                        continent: "North America",
                                        population: 31612897});
                arrayCollection.addItem({country:  "Venezuela",
                                        continent: "South America",
                                        population: 23054210});
                arrayCollection.addItem({country:  "United States",
                                        continent: "North America",
                                        population: 281421906});
                arrayCollection.addItem({country:  "Brazil",
                                        continent: "South America",
                                        population: 169799170});
                _populations = new GroupingCollection();
                _populations.source = arrayCollection;
                var grouping:Grouping = new Grouping();
                grouping.fields = [new GroupingField("continent")];
                _populations.grouping = grouping;
                _populations.refresh();
            }

        ]]>
    </mx:Script>
    <mx:AdvancedDataGrid id="advancedDataGrid" width="100%" height="100%"
dataProvider="{_populations}">
        <mx:columns>
            <mx:AdvancedDataGridColumn headerText="Continent" dataField="continent" />
            <mx:AdvancedDataGridColumn headerText="Country" dataField="country" />
            <mx:AdvancedDataGridColumn headerText="Population" dataField=
"population" />
        </mx:columns>
    </mx:AdvancedDataGrid>
</mx:Application>
```

You'll notice that the `GroupingCollection` instance in Example 7-2 wraps an `ArrayCollection` instance, though it could also wrap XML-based data. You can specify the data that the `GroupingCollection` instance should wrap by way of the `source` property. Simply assign the two-dimensional data to the `source` property as in Example 7-2.

Once you've set the source of the `GroupingCollection` you next need to tell it how to group the data. You can do that by assigning a `Grouping` object to the `grouping` property. A `Grouping` object has fields, which are instances of `GroupingField`. The fields that you specify are those that are used to group the data. In the example, we group the data by continent. All items in the data set with the same continent value are automatically grouped because we set the `grouping` field to `continent`. Once we set the `grouping` property we need to call the `refresh()` method of the `GroupingCollection` instance to tell the system that the data has updated. That will notify listeners to update themselves.

You may also have noticed that in the example we specified columns for the advanced data grid. We can specify columns using the `columns` property, just as we would for a standard data grid. However, as you can see in the example, the column instances are instances of `AdvancedDataGridColumn` rather than simply `DataGridColumn`. Otherwise, we would set the same properties as we would for a column of a standard data grid: `headerText` and `dataField`. Setting the columns is required when using grouping data.

Grouping columns

Sometimes data sets have columns of related data, and in these cases you may want to be able to group those columns when displaying them in a grid. The advanced data grid allows you to do that by using `AdvancedDataGridColumnGroup` objects. Figure 7-8 shows what grouped columns look like. In this image, you can see that the census and estimated population columns are grouped together.

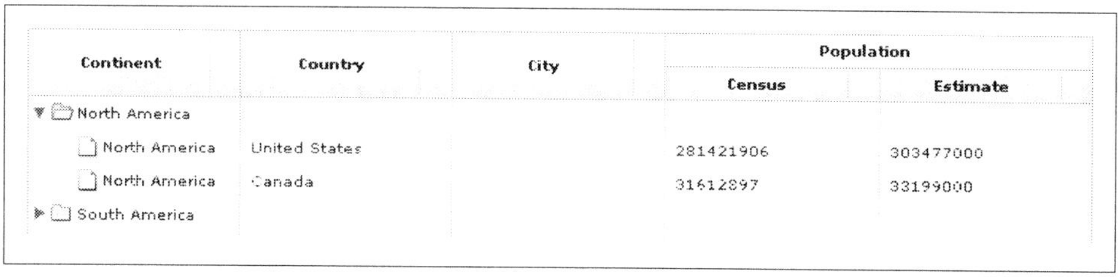

Continent	Country	City	Population	
			Census	Estimate
North America				
North America	United States		281421906	303477000
North America	Canada		31612897	33199000
South America				

Figure 7-8. Grouping columns together using AdvancedDataGridColumnGroup

To group columns, follow these guidelines:

- Instead of assigning the columns to the `columns` property of the grid, assign them to the `groupedColumns` property.
- Wrap all grouped columns in an `AdvancedDataGridColumnGroup` object.

Example 7-3 shows the code used to create the grid shown in Figure 7-8.

Example 7-3. Creating column groups

```
<?xml version="1.0" encoding="utf-8"?>
<mx:Application xmlns:mx="http://www.adobe.com/2006/mxml" layout="absolute"
creationComplete="creationCompleteHandler();">
    <mx:Script>
```

```
        <![CDATA[
            import mx.collections.Grouping;
            import mx.collections.GroupingField;
            import mx.collections.GroupingCollection;
            import mx.collections.ArrayCollection;

            [Bindable]
            private var _populations:GroupingCollection;

            private function creationCompleteHandler():void {
                var arrayCollection:ArrayCollection = new ArrayCollection();
              arrayCollection.addItem({country: "Canada",
                                       continent: "North America",
                                       censusPopulation: 31612897,
                                       estimatedPopulation: 33199000});
              arrayCollection.addItem({country: "Venezuela",
                                       continent: "South America",
                                       censusPopulation: 23054210,
                                       estimatedPopulation: 23423158});
              arrayCollection.addItem({country: "United States",
                                       continent: "North America",
                                       censusPopulation: 281421906,
                                       estimatedPopulation: 303477000});
              arrayCollection.addItem({country: "Brazil",
                                       continent: "South America",
                                       censusPopulation: 169799170,
                                       estimatedPopulation: 170035512});
              _populations = new GroupingCollection();
              _populations.source = arrayCollection;
              var grouping:Grouping = new Grouping();
              grouping.fields = [new GroupingField("continent")];
              _populations.grouping = grouping;
              _populations.refresh();

            }

        ]]>
    </mx:Script>
    <mx:AdvancedDataGrid id="advancedDataGrid" sortExpertMode="false"
        width="100%" height="100%" dataProvider="{_populations}">
        <mx:groupedColumns>
            <mx:AdvancedDataGridColumn headerText="Continent"
                dataField="continent" />
            <mx:AdvancedDataGridColumn headerText="Country"
                dataField="country" />
            <mx:AdvancedDataGridColumnGroup headerText="Population">
                <mx:AdvancedDataGridColumn headerText="Census"
                    dataField="censusPopulation" />
                <mx:AdvancedDataGridColumn headerText="Estimate"
                    dataField="estimatedPopulation" />
            </mx:AdvancedDataGridColumnGroup>
        </mx:groupedColumns>
    </mx:AdvancedDataGrid>
</mx:Application>
```

Working with hierarchical data

The results of working with grouping data and hierarchical data are very similar, but the starting points are different. As you saw in the previous section, grouping data is the result of taking two-dimensional data such as an array and creating a sense of a third dimension by specifying a field or fields on which to group the data. The result is that the data appears in a tree—data grid hybrid. Hierarchical data is already multidimensional in nature. It does not need to be grouped. An example of hierarchical data is XML data. This data already (potentially) contains three or more dimensions. All that is necessary in such a case is to display the data in a hierarchical fashion. The result is that the data gets displayed in a tree—grid hybrid just as grouped data gets displayed.

When you want to display hierarchical data in an advanced data grid, you must wrap the data in an `mx.collections.HierarchicalData` instance. The `HierarchicalData` object needs to know what fields of the data set should be expandable. By default, all `HierarchicalData` objects assume the expandable field is called `children`. Example 7-4 shows hierarchical data that uses a property called `children` to indicate the expandable field. In this case, the `continent` objects use the `children` property to store an array of `country` objects.

Example 7-4. Using hierarchical data

```
<?xml version="1.0" encoding="utf-8"?>
<mx:Application xmlns:mx="http://www.adobe.com/2006/mxml" layout="absolute"
creationComplete="creationCompleteHandler();">
    <mx:Script>
        <![CDATA[
            import mx.collections.HierarchicalData;
            import mx.collections.ArrayCollection;

            [Bindable]
            private var _populations:HierarchicalData;

            private function creationCompleteHandler():void {
                var unitedStates:Object = {country: "United States",
                                           censusPopulation: 281421906,
                                           estimatedPopulation: 303477000};
              var canada:Object = {country: "Canada",
                                   censusPopulation: 31612897,
                                   estimatedPopulation: 33199000};
              var venezuela:Object = {country: "Venezuela",
                                      censusPopulation: 23054210,
                                      estimatedPopulation: 23423158};
              var brazil:Object = {country: "Brazil",
                                   censusPopulation: 169799170,
                                   estimatedPopulation: 170035512};
              var northAmerica:Object = {continent: "North America",
                                         children: [unitedStates, canada]};
              var southAmerica:Object = {continent: "South America",
                                         children: [venezuela, brazil]};
              _populations =
new HierarchicalData(new ArrayCollection([northAmerica, southAmerica]));
```

```
            }

        ]]>
    </mx:Script>
    <mx:AdvancedDataGrid id="advancedDataGrid" sortExpertMode="false"
        width="100%" height="100%" dataProvider="{_populations}">
         <mx:groupedColumns>
              <mx:AdvancedDataGridColumn headerText="Continent"
                  dataField="continent" />
              <mx:AdvancedDataGridColumn headerText="Country" dataField="country" />
              <mx:AdvancedDataGridColumn headerText="City" dataField="city" />
              <mx:AdvancedDataGridColumnGroup headerText="Population">
                  <mx:AdvancedDataGridColumn headerText="Census"
                      dataField="censusPopulation" />
                  <mx:AdvancedDataGridColumn headerText="Estimate"
                      dataField="estimatedPopulation" />
              </mx:AdvancedDataGridColumnGroup>
         </mx:groupedColumns>
    </mx:AdvancedDataGrid>
</mx:Application>
```

However, it's not always possible or practical to depend on a field called `children`. Instead, it is far more advantageous to be able to specify the name of the expandable field. For instance, consider what would happen if the preceding example didn't just use generic objects, but also used custom data types, called `Continent` and `Country`, each specifying subregions by way of a property called `regions`. Since the property isn't called `children`, we need to tell Flex how to locate the correct field to expand. We can do that by setting the value of the `childrenField` property of the `HierarchicalData` object to the name of the property:

```
_populations.childrenField = "regions";
```

Using Tree Controls

Like data grids, tree controls inherit from standard lists but have specialized behavior. In the case of trees, the specialized behavior is that trees are capable of rendering hierarchical data providers.

Although most lists display a linear list of elements (whether vertically, horizontally, or in grid format), tree controls allow you to render elements that themselves have nested child elements. These sorts of data providers are called *hierarchical data providers*. The following simple XML snippet demonstrates a hierarchical relationship in which the cities are child elements of states:

```
<state label="CA">
   <city label="Los Angeles" />
   <city label="San Francisco" />
</state>
<state label="MA">
   <city label="Boston" />
</state>
```

A tree control can represent this sort of data. Tree controls have two types of elements: branch elements and leaf nodes. When a data provider element has child elements, it's automatically treated as a branch element, meaning it is expandable within the tree. Here's an example that uses a tree to display state and city data:

```
<mx:Tree labelField="@label" width="200">
    <mx:XMLListCollection>
        <mx:XMLList>
                <state label="CA">
                    <city label="Los Angeles" />
                    <city label="San Francisco" />
                </state>
                <state label="MA">
                    <city label="Boston" />
                </state>
        </mx:XMLList>
    </mx:XMLListCollection>
</mx:Tree>
```

You'll notice that in this example, the tree requires a `labelField` property value indicating what to use as the label for the elements. The `@label` value uses E4X syntax (see Chapter 4) to indicate that the tree should use the label attributes of each XML node for the label of the corresponding tree element.

Although it's easiest to visualize hierarchical relationships with XML, you are not restricted to using XML-based data providers for trees. You can use any sort of collection. For example, you can use an `ArrayCollection` object as a data provider. However, when you want to establish hierarchical relationships using collection types that aren't intrinsically hierarchical, you must follow certain rules. Specifically, to add children to an element, you must add them as an array for a property called `children`. The following example illustrates this using the city/state example from before:

```
<mx:Tree labelField="label" width="200">
    <mx:ArrayCollection>
        <mx:Array>
                <mx:Object label="CA">
                    <mx:children>
                        <mx:Object label="Los Angeles" />
                        <mx:Object label="San Francisco" />
                    </mx:children>
                </mx:Object>
                <mx:Object label="MA">
                    <mx:children>
                        <mx:Object label="Boston" />
                    </mx:children>
                </mx:Object>
        </mx:Array>
    </mx:ArrayCollection>
</mx:Tree>
```

Of course, you can achieve the same result using ActionScript in every case. First, here's an example that populates a tree using XML data:

```
<?xml version="1.0"?>
<mx:Application xmlns:mx="http://www.adobe.com/2006/mxml"
creationComplete="creationCompleteHandler(event)">
    <mx:Script>
        <![CDATA[
            import mx.collections.XMLListCollection;
            import mx.controls.List;

            private function creationCompleteHandler(event:Event):void {
                var xml:XML =         <items>
                                        <item label="CA">
                                            <item label="Los Angeles" />
                                            <item label="San Francisco" />
                                        </item>
                                        <item label="MA">
                                            <item label="Boston" />
                                        </item>
                                      </items>;
                var collection:XMLListCollection = new
XMLListCollection(xml.children());
                tree.dataProvider = collection;
            }

        ]]>
    </mx:Script>
    <mx:Tree id="tree" labelField="@label" width="200" />
</mx:Application>
```

And here's an example that achieves the same goal using an array:

```
<?xml version="1.0"?>
<mx:Application xmlns:mx="http://www.adobe.com/2006/mxml"
creationComplete="creationCompleteHandler(event)">
    <mx:Script>
        <![CDATA[
            import mx.collections.ArrayCollection;
            import mx.controls.List;

            private function creationCompleteHandler(event:Event):void {
                var array:Array = new Array({label: "CA", children: new Array(
                                        {label: "Los Angeles"},
                                        {label: "San Francisco"})},
                                    {label: "MA", children: new Array(
                                        {label: "Boston"})});
                var collection:ArrayCollection = new ArrayCollection(array);
                tree.dataProvider = collection;
            }

        ]]>
    </mx:Script>
    <mx:Tree id="tree" labelField="label" width="200" />
</mx:Application>
```

Working with Selected Values and Items

List-based controls allow for programmatic and user selection of elements. An application may frequently need to be able to detect which item the user has selected. For this purpose, list-based controls have the following properties:

`allowMultipleSelection`
: By default, lists allow for one selected item at a time. By setting `allowMultipleSelection` to `true`, you allow a user to select more than one item at a time.

`value`
: This is the value of the selected item. The value of the `value` property depends on the structure of the data provider. Because it has very strict requirements, to get predictable results it is frequently better not to rely on the `value` property.

`selectedItem`
: This is the element from the data provider corresponding to the selected item in the list. This is a very predictable property because it will always be a reference rather than an interpretation. That means that if the data provider is a collection of strings, the `selectedItem` will be a string. If the data provider is a collection of XML elements, however, the `selectedItem` will be an XML element.

`selectedItems`
: This is an array of elements. This is the multiselect equivalent to `selectedItem`.

`selectedIndex`
: This is the integer index of the selected item. For all controls using linear data providers, this is a predictable and useful property. If the `selectedIndex` property of a standard list is `0`, the first element is selected. This property is complicated only when using hierarchical data providers, because the relationship of the index of a visible element and the data provider depends on the expanded/collapsed state of the rest of the control's elements.

`selectedIndices`
: This is an array of the indexes of the selected items. This is the multiselect equivalent of `selectedIndex`.

Now let's look at a few examples using these properties. First, here's an example that sets the selected index of a list based on an index from a numeric stepper:

```
<mx:VBox>
    <mx:List id="list" width="100" selectedIndex="{stepper.value}">
        <mx:ArrayCollection>
            <mx:Array>
                <mx:String>a</mx:String>
                <mx:String>b</mx:String>
                <mx:String>c</mx:String>
                <mx:String>d</mx:String>
            </mx:Array>
        </mx:ArrayCollection>
```

```
    </mx:List>
    <mx:NumericStepper id="stepper" minimum="0" maximum="3" />
</mx:VBox>
```

Here's an example that displays the selected values from a data grid when the user selects them:

```
<mx:VBox>
    <mx:DataGrid id="grid" width="500" change="output.text =
grid.selectedItem.city">
        <mx:columns>
            <mx:DataGridColumn headerText="City" dataField="city" />
            <mx:DataGridColumn headerText="Population (within city limits)"
dataField="population" />
        </mx:columns>
        <mx:ArrayCollection>
            <mx:Array>
                <mx:Object city="Los Angeles" state="CA" population="3844829" />
                <mx:Object city="New York" state="NY" population="8143197" />
                <mx:Object city="Chicago" state="IL" population="2842518" />
                <mx:Object city="Philadelphia" state="PA" population="1463281" />
            </mx:Array>
        </mx:ArrayCollection>
    </mx:DataGrid>
    <mx:TextInput id="output" width="200" />
</mx:VBox>
```

Pop-Up Controls

Apart from the ability to programmatically create menus and menu bar navigator (discussed in the next section), there are two Flex framework controls that you can use to create pop-up controls: PopUpButton and PopUpMenuButton. Both of these controls allow a user to display a pop up. PopUpMenuButton allows the user to pop up a menu, whereas PopUpButton is more generic, allowing a user to pop up any control.

Using PopUpButton

The PopUpButton control allows you to associate the button with a pop up. The pop up can be any other UI component. Typically, you would use a pop-up button to display a small window or something similar. As you can see in Figure 7-9, the pop up appears adjacent to the button, appearing and disappearing from the button.

For the example shown in Figure 7-9, we created a simple MXML component that looks like the following:

```
<?xml version="1.0" encoding="utf-8"?>
<mx:TitleWindow xmlns:mx="http://www.adobe.com/2006/mxml" width="400" height="300">
    <mx:VBox>
        <mx:Label text="Select a color:" />
        <mx:RadioButton groupName="colors" label="grey" />
        <mx:RadioButton groupName="colors" label="brown" />
        <mx:Button label="Select As Color" />
```

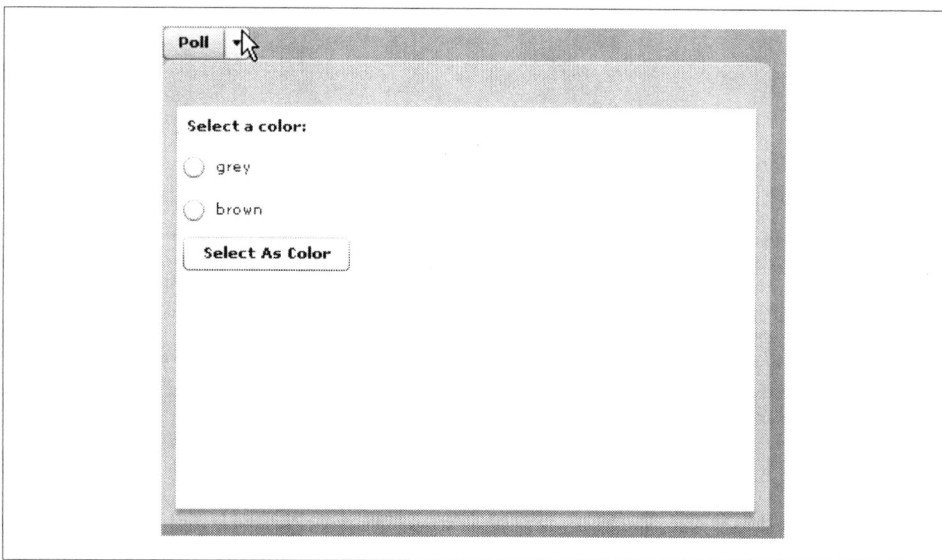

Figure 7-9. Using a PopUpButton to display a pop up

```
        </mx:VBox>
    </mx:TitleWindow>
```

Assuming we name the component `PollWindow` (and save it in the root directory), the code that allows the user to display the window using a pop-up button is as follows:

```
<?xml version="1.0" encoding="utf-8"?>
<mx:Application xmlns:mx="http://www.adobe.com/2006/mxml" layout="absolute">
    <mx:Script>
        <![CDATA[
            import com.oreilly.programmingflex.PollWindow;

            private var _poll:PollWindow = new PollWindow();

        ]]>
    </mx:Script>
    <mx:PopUpButton label="Poll" popUp="{_poll}" />
</mx:Application>
```

Using PopUpMenuButton

Flex supports a component called `Menu`, which allows Flex to display hierarchical menus as pop ups. Although you can use a `PopUpButton` to display a menu component, it is far easier to use the `PopUpMenuButton` component to display a menu. Before we can talk about `PopUpMenuButton`, we need to first talk about how to use a menu component.

Menus are an instance of `mx.controls.Menu`. Like tree controls, menu controls require hierarchical data providers. The following code creates a menu and populates it with an XMLListCollection data provider. It also sets the labelField property as you would when using a hierarchical data provider for a tree control.

```
var menu:Menu = new Menu();
var xmlList:XMLList = <items>
                        <item label="ActionScript">
                          <item label="Class" />
                          <item label="Interface" />
                        </item>
                        <item label="MXML">
                          <item label="Application" />
                          <item label="Component" />
                         </item>
                       </items>;
menu.dataProvider = new XMLListCollection(xmlList);
menu.labelField = "@label";
```

The PopUpMenuButton control simplifies associating a menu with a button by automatically creating the menu when assigning a data provider to the button, as illustrated in this example:

```
<mx:PopUpMenuButton labelField="@label">
    <mx:dataProvider>
        <mx:XMLListCollection>
            <mx:XMLList>
                <item label="ActionScript">
                    <item label="Class" />
                    <item label="Interface" />
                </item>
                <item label="MXML">
                    <item label="Application" />
                    <item label="Component" />
                </item>
            </mx:XMLList>
        </mx:XMLListCollection>
    </mx:dataProvider>
</mx:PopUpMenuButton>
```

Figure 7-10 shows what this example looks like.

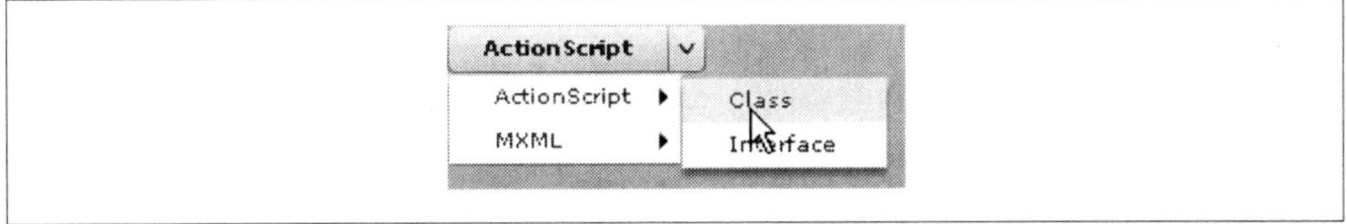

Figure 7-10. PopUpMenuButton

Listening to Menu Events

Menu controls dispatch itemClick events of type mx.events.MenuEvent every time the user selects a menu item. You can listen for the event directly from the menu using ActionScript and addEventListener. If you're using PopUpMenuButton, you can listen for the `itemClick` event directly from the button. You can even use MXML to listen for the event, as illustrated in this example that changes the button label each time the user selects a menu item:

```
<mx:PopUpMenuButton id="button" labelField="@label"
                    itemClick="button.label = event.label">
    <mx:dataProvider>
        <mx:XMLListCollection>
            <mx:XMLList>
                <item label="ActionScript">
                    <item label="Class" />
                    <item label="Interface" />
                </item>
                <item label="MXML">
                    <item label="Application" />
                    <item label="Component" />
                </item>
            </mx:XMLList>
        </mx:XMLListCollection>
    </mx:dataProvider>
</mx:PopUpMenuButton>
```

Navigators

Navigators are controls that allow users to navigate from screen to screen, page to page, section to section, or option to option within a Flex application. We can further categorize navigator controls as follows: accordion, divided boxes, option bars, and view stacks.

Accordion Controls

The accordion control consists of two or more collapsible containers. Only one element within an accordion can be visible at a time. The other elements in the accordion are collapsed so that only a title bar is visible. Accordions are often good for processes that require several steps and allow the user to return to previous steps. For example, an accordion is useful when a user input form contains many sections. Rather than trying to present all the sections at once, an accordion allows the user to view just one section at a time, making for a more manageable experience. Figure 7-11 shows an example of an accordion.

Creating accordions is quite simple. Accordions act just like all standard containers in that you can nest child elements in MXML, or use `addChild()` to add child elements using ActionScript. In the case of accordions, all child elements should be containers themselves, and you should add a `label` property to all accordion children. Accordions use the `label` properties of child elements for the title bar. Accordions also use the `icon` property of children to display icons when set. Here's an example:

```
<mx:Accordion>
    <mx:Form label="Name">
```

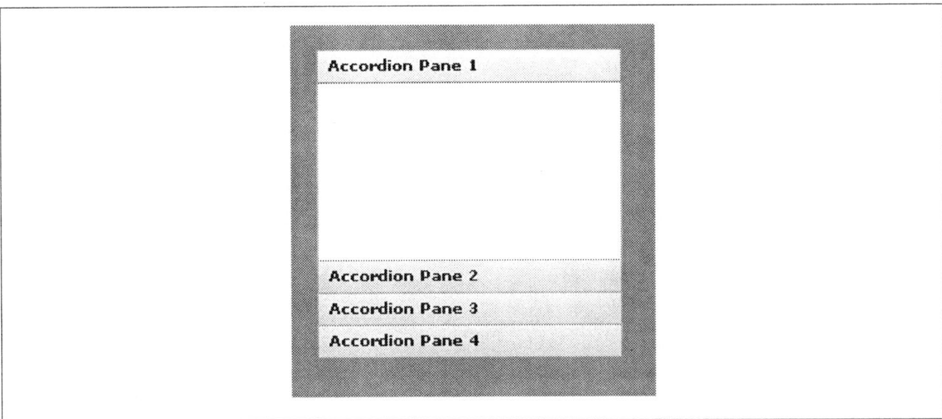

Figure 7-11. An accordion component

```
            <mx:FormItem label="First Name">
                <mx:TextInput id="first" />
            </mx:FormItem>
            <mx:FormItem label="Middle Name">
                <mx:TextInput id="middle" />
            </mx:FormItem>
            <mx:FormItem label="Last Name">
                <mx:TextInput id="last" />
            </mx:FormItem>
        </mx:Form>
        <mx:Form label="Comments">
            <mx:FormItem label="Comments">
                <mx:TextArea id="comments" />
            </mx:FormItem>
        </mx:Form>
    </mx:Accordion>
```

Option Bars

Option bars consist of the following: `ButtonBar`, `LinkBar`, `MenuBar`, and `ToggleButtonBar`. Each option bar type is similar in that they provide a convenient way in which to create groups of controls, whether buttons, link buttons, menus, and so on. Furthermore (and perhaps more important), you can use option bars in conjunction with view stacks, as discussed in the next section. Figure 7-12 shows examples of each option bar type.

Button bars, link bars, and toggle button bars are ways to create horizontal or vertical groups of buttons. These controls provide a convenient way to group buttons together. Furthermore, in the case of toggle button bars, you have the added behavior that only one of the toggle buttons can be selected at a time. All button, link, and toggle button bars use data providers. An example follows that creates a toggle button bar.

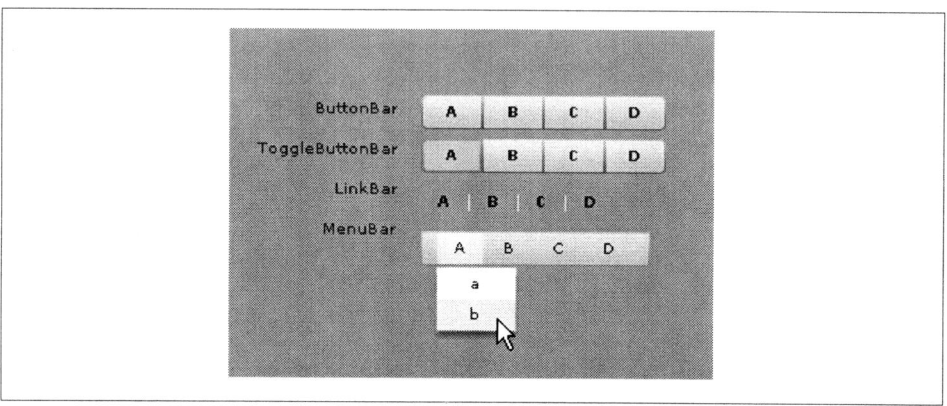

Figure 7-12. Option bars

```
<mx:ToggleButtonBar>
    <mx:ArrayCollection>
        <mx:Array>
            <mx:Object label="A" />
            <mx:Object label="B" />
            <mx:Object label="C" />
            <mx:Object label="D" />
        </mx:Array>
    </mx:ArrayCollection>
</mx:ToggleButtonBar>
```

Menu bars provide a convenient way to group together menus with a single data provider. Here's an example:

```
<mx:MenuBar labelField="@label">
    <mx:XMLListCollection>
        <mx:XMLList>
            <item label="File">
                <item label="New" />
                <item label="Open" />
                <item label="Close" />
                <item label="Properties" />
            </item>
            <item label="Edit">
                <item label="Select All" />
                <item label="Copy" />
                <item label="Cut" />
                <item label="Paste" />
            </item>
        </mx:XMLList>
    </mx:XMLListCollection>
</mx:MenuBar>
```

View Stacks

View stacks allow you to group together a set of containers and display just one at a time. This is useful when you want to use a page/screen/section metaphor. The easiest way to work with a view stack is to use the tab navigator control, which has view stack behavior built in. Here's an example of a tab navigator with nearly the same form contents used earlier in the accordion example:

```
<mx:TabNavigator>
    <mx:Form label="Name">
        <mx:FormItem label="First Name">
            <mx:TextInput id="first" />
        </mx:FormItem>
        <mx:FormItem label="Middle Name">
            <mx:TextInput id="middle" />
        </mx:FormItem>
        <mx:FormItem label="Last Name">
            <mx:TextInput id="last" />
        </mx:FormItem>
    </mx:Form>
    <mx:Form label="Comments">
        <mx:FormItem label="Comments">
            <mx:TextArea id="comments" />
        </mx:FormItem>
    </mx:Form>
</mx:TabNavigator>
```

As with the accordion, you can set label properties for the child containers of a tab navigator to determine what the tab labels should be. Figure 7-13 shows what this tab navigator looks like.

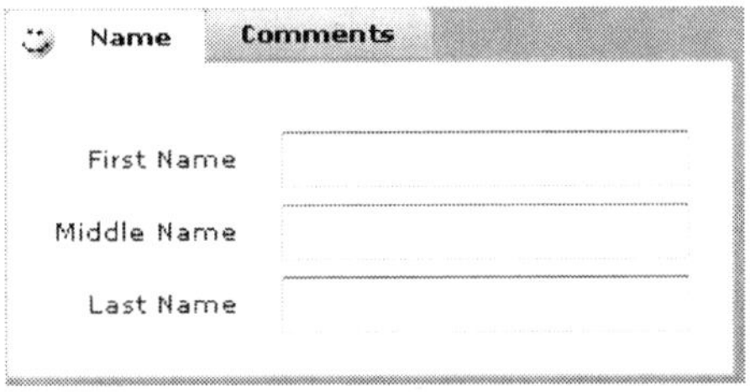

Figure 7-13. A tab navigator

You can use a view stack without having to use the tab navigator. It simply requires that you first create the view stack with the child containers. Then, assuming you use a button bar, link bar, or toggle button bar, you can simply assign the view stack as the data provider of the bar:

```
<mx:VBox>
    <mx:ToggleButtonBar dataProvider="{viewStack}" />
    <mx:ViewStack id="viewStack">
        <mx:Form label="Name">
```

```
            <mx:FormItem label="First Name">
                <mx:TextInput id="first" />
            </mx:FormItem>
            <mx:FormItem label="Middle Name">
                <mx:TextInput id="middle" />
            </mx:FormItem>
            <mx:FormItem label="Last Name">
                <mx:TextInput id="last" />
            </mx:FormItem>
        </mx:Form>
        <mx:Form label="Comments">
            <mx:FormItem label="Comments">
                <mx:TextArea id="comments" />
            </mx:FormItem>
        </mx:Form>
    </mx:ViewStack>
</mx:VBox>
```

Otherwise, you have to set the `selectedIndex` property of the view stack programmatically to change the view:

```
viewStack.selectedIndex = 1;
```

Control Bars

Control bars allow you to group together all the controls for a panel or title window. Application control bars are the application-wide analogs to control bars. Each allows you to group together all the controls for that container, even if the controls are of various types.

Control bars work with title window and panel components, and you should add them as the last child for a title window or panel. You can then place controls within the control bar. Here's an example:

```
<mx:Panel id="panel" width="250" height="200">
    <mx:TextArea id="textArea" width="80%" height="80%" text="Example" />
    <mx:ControlBar>
        <mx:Button label="Random Font Size"
            click="textArea.setStyle('fontSize', Math.random() * 20 + 8)" />
        <mx:ColorPicker id="color"
            change="panel.setStyle('backgroundColor', color.value)" />
    </mx:ControlBar>
</mx:Panel>
```

Figure 7-14 shows what this looks like. Clicking on the button changes the font size, and changing the value of the color selector changes the background of the panel.

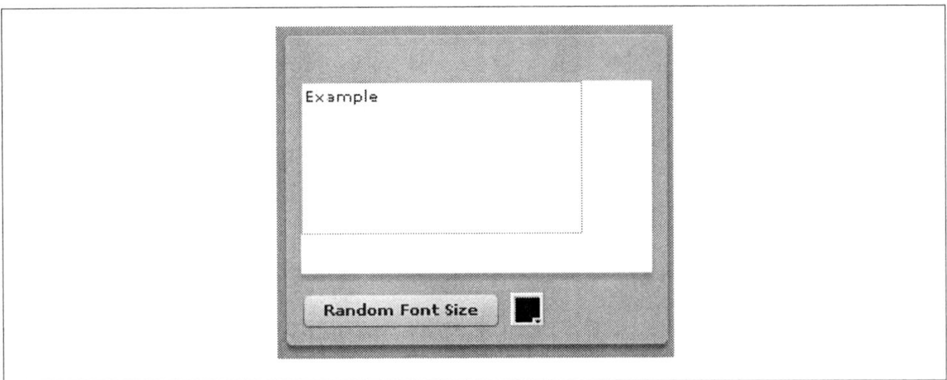

Figure 7-14. A panel with a control bar

The application control bar works similarly, but it is applied only to an application container. By default, the application control bar scrolls with the rest of the content. However, it is possible to set the dock property to true to dock the control panel such that it does not scroll. Here's how you would do that:

```
<?xml version="1.0"?>
<mx:Application xmlns:mx="http://www.adobe.com/2006/mxml" layout="absolute">
    <mx:Canvas x="0" y="0" width="200" height="2000" />
    <mx:ApplicationControlBar dock="true">
        <mx:Label text="Jump To Section:"/>
        <mx:ComboBox>
            <mx:dataProvider>
                <mx:ArrayCollection>
                    <mx:Array>
                        <mx:String>A</mx:String>
                        <mx:String>B</mx:String>
                        <mx:String>C</mx:String>
                        <mx:String>D</mx:String>
                    </mx:Array>
                </mx:ArrayCollection>
            </mx:dataProvider>
        </mx:ComboBox>
        <mx:VRule width="20" height="28"/>
        <mx:TextInput/>
        <mx:Button label="Search"/>
    </mx:ApplicationControlBar>
</mx:Application>
```

Figure 7-15 shows what this looks like.

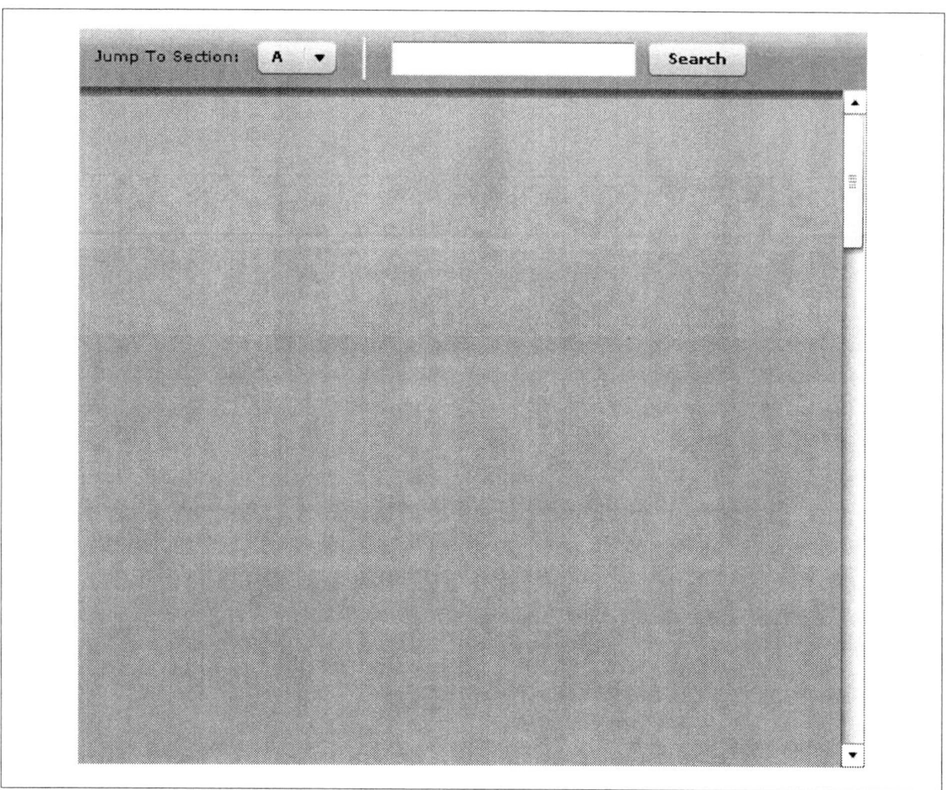

Figure 7-15. Application control bars docked so that they don't scroll with the rest of the content

Summary

In this chapter, you learned everything you need to know to start working with user interface controls in Flex 3. We discussed event handling with controls, and we provided an overview of all the major types of standard UI controls, from buttons to lists to control bars.

CHAPTER 8

Customizing Application Appearance

The Flex framework has a great deal of functionality built into it, making it relatively easy to start building applications. All of the user interface components and layout containers greatly simplify the process of creating a new application because you can utilize all the functionality of the components without having to write all the code to make them work. As great as that is, it would be nearly useless in most cases if you couldn't customize the appearance of the components. Yet, as we'll see in this chapter, customization of the appearance of Flex components is another built-in feature.

There are essentially two ways you can customize the appearance of components:

- Apply styles.
- Change skins.

Styles are settings such as color, font face, border settings, row height, and so on. These are settings that you can customize entirely programmatically both at compile time and at runtime. Styles allow you to customize a great deal of the appearance of components, yet they can go only so far. For example, if you want to change the background color of a button, you can do that using styles, but if you want to completely change the shape of a button (e.g., from a rounded rectangle to a trapezoid), you need to use a different technique in which you change the skins of the component. *Skins* can be graphical elements (e.g., PNG files) or programmatic elements (classes), and they allow you to not only customize the existing elements of a component, but also completely change which elements are used. Therefore, using custom skins allows you to alter the appearance of a component so completely that it is unrecognizable from its original default appearance. You can use both styles and skins at the same time (although oftentimes applying a skin will cancel out certain style settings).

In this chapter, we'll look more closely at all the techniques you can use to customize application appearance through the use of styles and skins. We'll also look at working with fonts, using Cascading Style Sheets (CSS), customizing an application preloader, and creating custom themes for styling.

Using Styles

Styles allow you to control a great many aspects of an application's appearance, including colors, fonts, spacing, animation settings, and more. You can define and apply styles in many ways, each with its own advantages and disadvantages. These can be categorized as follows:

- Instance styles
- Class selectors (stylesheets)
- Type selectors (stylesheets)
- Global styles

Because there are so many ways to apply styles, it is actually possible to apply different values for the same style to a component using different ways to apply that style. For example, you can set the color of a button component using an instance style as well as using a type selector. Because this is possible, it's necessary for Flex to have an order of precedence for the application of styles. That order (from greatest precedence to least) is the same as the list preceding this paragraph. That means that if Flex has to decide between an instance style and a type selector, it will use the value from the instance style.

Style Value Formats

There are lots of different styles, and each style has a required data type for its value. For example, the style used to set the font face (`fontFamily`) requires a string value specifying the name of the font to use, yet the style used to set the font size (`fontSize`) requires a numeric value. Behind the scenes, all styles accept values of one of these two data types: string and number. However, for convenience, some styles accept more than one type of value. For example, color styles should be specified using numeric values, but you can also specify one of the color strings, such as red or green. Those values are translated to number values behind the scenes. Also, some styles actually require number values of 0 or 1, but you can optionally specify a Boolean value of `true` or `false`. This next example sets the `dropShadowEnabled` property to `1`, but it could also use the value `true` to achieve the same effect:

```
<mx:Style>
    VBox {
        backgroundColor: green;
        borderStyle: solid;
        dropShadowEnabled: 1;
    }
</mx:Style>
<mx:VBox width="200" height="200" />
```

Some styles allow you to specify a unit of measurement. However, Flex ignores all units of measurement, using only the numeric portion of the value. For example, when you specify a font size, you can also specify a unit of measurement such as pixels or points, though the result will always be the same regardless of what unit of measurement is specified (or if none is specified). This allows you to use the same stylesheets for your Flex applications that you might use with HTML applications. The following example sets the `font-size` property of a class selector to `15px`, which is interpreted simply as 15 by Flex:

```
.example {
    font-size: 15px
}
```

The Flex Style Explorer allows you to see what styles are available for Flex components, and you can adjust those settings in real time and see the generated CSS to create the style settings. You can view the Flex Style Explorer at *http://examples.adobe.com/flex3/consulting/styleexplorer/Flex3StyleExplorer.html.*

Instance Styles

Instance styles are the styles set for a specific component instance. You can set instance styles using MXML or ActionScript. Setting instance styles using MXML is often referred to as setting an inline style, because you simply set the value for an attribute in the component tag. Here's an example of a button component for which we're setting the color style:

```
<mx:Button label="Example" color="red" />
```

You can set many inline styles at the same time. Here's the same button with additional styles set inline:

```
<mx:Button label="Example" color="red" borderColor="yellow"
    cornerRadius="10" fontStyle="italic" />
```

You can also set styles on an instance using ActionScript via the `setStyle()` method. The `setStyle()` method is defined by `UIComponent`, which means that you can call the method for all (visual) Flex components. The `setStyle()` method requires two parameters: the name of the style property as a string (e.g., color) and the value for the property. Here's an example that sets a button component's color style:

```
button.setStyle("color", "red");
```

If you want to set many styles for a component, you need to call `setStyle()` for each style. Here's an example that sets many styles for one component:

```
button.setStyle("color", "red");
button.setStyle("borderColor", "yellow");
button.setStyle("cornerRadius", 10);
button.setStyle("fontStyle", "italic");
```

If you apply styles using `setStyle()`, you can change styles at runtime. That means you can use `setStyle()` to change a style even if it was set inline. Example 8-1 sets the color style both inline and with ActionScript. Because `setStyle()` is called after the inline style was applied, the button label appears in red rather than green.

Example 8-1. Setting a style with setStyle()

```
<?xml version="1.0" encoding="utf-8"?>
<mx:Application xmlns:mx="http://www.adobe.com/2006/mxml"
    initialize="initializeHandler(event)">
    <mx:Script>
        <![CDATA[
            private function initializeHandler(event:Event):void {
                button.setStyle("color", "red");
            }
        ]]>
    </mx:Script>
    <mx:Button id="button" label="Example" color="green" />
</mx:Application>
```

The following shows an interactive version that demonstrates how `setStyle()` allows you to make changes at runtime:

```
<mx:Application xmlns:mx="http://www.adobe.com/2006/mxml">
    <mx:Script>
        <![CDATA[
            private function changeColor(color: String):void {
                button.setStyle("color", color);
            }
        ]]>
    </mx:Script>
    <mx:Button id="button" label="Change Color"
        color="green" toggle="true"
        click="changeColor(button.selected ? 'blue' : 'red')" />
</mx:Application>
```

If you want to retrieve the style value for a specific instance, you can use the `getStyle()` method. The `getStyle()` method requires a parameter specifying the name of the style. The method then returns the current value of the style. The following example retrieves the color style value for the button and displays it:

```
<mx:Button id="button" label="Example" color="red" />
<mx:TextInput text="{button.getStyle('color').toString(16)}" />
```

The use of `toString()` in the preceding code outputs the value using a radix of 16, effectively displaying the color in hexadecimal format.

Using CSS

Applying instance styles using inline style attributes is convenient. However, it has a major drawback in that it decentralizes style settings for the application, making it difficult to manage. Instead, you can use CSS to define styles for components. Although you can use CSS that gets loaded at runtime, this section deals only with CSS that is compiled into the Flex application. (We'll look at runtime CSS in "Runtime CSS" later in this chapter.)

CSS is a standard way for applying styles across platforms, languages, and frameworks. The syntax of CSS in Flex is identical to the syntax of CSS as it is used by HTML. For example, here's a sample class selector for a Flex application written in CSS:

```
.example {
    color: red;
}
```

Even though the syntax of CSS in Flex is identical to that used by HTML, some of the style properties available in HTML are not available in Flex.

When you define CSS for Flex applications, you have two basic options: external stylesheets and local style definitions. In both cases, the CSS is compiled into the Flex application, so they are functionally identical. However, there are advantages to each. External stylesheets enable you to more cleanly distinguish between layout (MXML) and style definitions (external CSS document). On the other hand, local style definitions are more convenient when you intend to use the style or styles in just one MXML file. For most applications external stylesheets are preferable.

An external stylesheet is a text file that you compile into a Flex application by using the `source` attribute of a `Style` MXML tag. The following code is an example of a `Style` tag that compiles in an external stylesheet defined in *styles.css*. The styles defined in the external document are then available within the MXML document within which the `Style` tag appears.

```
<mx:Style source="styles.css" />
```

If you want to define local style selector definitions, you can simply place the CSS between opening and closing `Style` tags, as in the following example:

```
<mx:Style>
    .example {
        color: red;
    }
</mx:Style>
```

Whether you're using external stylesheets or local style definitions, you can define the same sorts of style selectors: class selectors and type selectors. Class selector names are differentiated from type selector names because they use a dot (`.`), as in the preceding example. A selector can define one or more styles. The preceding example defines just one style for the selector. The following example defines two styles for the selector

```
.example {
    color: red;
```

```
    font-style: italic;
}
```

When you want to apply a class selector to a component, you must set the `styleName` property of the component. The `styleName` value should be the name of the class selector, but without the initial dot. The following example sets the `styleName` property of a button to the example style selector:

```
<mx:Button label="Example" styleName="example" />
```

If you want to set the `styleName` property of a component using ActionScript, you can do that using standard dot syntax, as follows:

```
button.styleName = "example";
```

The other kind of selector is called a type selector, and it automatically applies to all components of the type that match the name of the selector. For example, you can define a type selector called `Button`, and it will automatically get applied to all buttons:

```
Button {
    color: red;
}
```

Type selectors work with all component types, including custom components. That means you can define type selectors for standard Flex components such as `Button`, `Application`, `TileList`, and so forth, but you can also define type selectors for custom Flex components, whether those components are third-party components or components that you and your team have written.

You *cannot* combine type and class selectors by defining class selectors that are specific to a type as you would in HTML. Flex will not throw an error in this case, but it will simply ignore the type. The following example illustrates this:

```
<?xml version="1.0" encoding="utf-8"?>
<mx:Application xmlns:mx="http://www.adobe.com/2006/mxml">
    <mx:Style>
        Button.example {
            color: green;
        }
        Label.example {
            color: yellow;
        }
    </mx:Style>
    <mx:Button label="button" styleName="example" />
    <mx:Label text="label" styleName="example" />
</mx:Application>
```

In this example, you might expect that the button text would appear in green and the label text in yellow. However, both appear with yellow text. That is because Flex ignores the type selector portion of the selector names, and instead both selectors are defined simply as class selectors with the same name (`.green`) and the second overwriting the first. The result is that the text for both the button and the label is yellow.

With both type and class selectors you can use comma-delimited lists to define the same property values for several selectors. For example, the following sets the `color` for `Button` and `TextInput` components:

```
Button, TextInput {
    color: red;
}
```

You can also define properties for a selector in more than one property grouping. For example, the following defines the `color` as `red` for `Button` and `TextInput`, but then it also sets the `themeColor` for `Button`:

```
Button, TextInput {
    color: red;
}
Button {
    themeColor: black;
}
```

Type selectors always take precedence over class selectors. Example 8-2 defines a type selector and a class selector. In this case, the font style is italic because the type selector sets it. However, because the class selector defines the color as green, the button label is green rather than red.

Example 8-2. Selector precedence

```
<?xml version="1.0" encoding="utf-8"?>
<mx:Application xmlns:mx="http://www.adobe.com/2006/mxml">
    <mx:Style>
        Button {
            color: red;
            font-style: italic;
        }
        .example {
            color: green;
        }
    </mx:Style>
    <mx:Button label="Example" styleName="example" />
</mx:Application>
```

Neither local style definitions nor external stylesheets take precedence inherently. If you use both in one document, you will see that the order in which they appear in the document is what determines which takes precedence. Let's look at a complete example that illustrates this. Here's *styles.css*, an external stylesheet document. It contains just one style definition, a class selector called `example`:

```
.example {
    color: red;
    font-style: italic;
}
```

Example 8-3 is the MXML document that both uses this external stylesheet and has a local style definition for the same class selector. In this case, the button has a green and italicized label because the local style definition takes precedence over the external stylesheet, only because it appears after the external stylesheet included in the code.

Example 8-3. Order of style tags affects styles (part 1)

```
<?xml version="1.0" encoding="utf-8"?>
<mx:Application xmlns:mx="http://www.adobe.com/2006/mxml">
    <mx:Style source="styles.css" />
    <mx:Style>
        .example {
            color: green;
        }
    </mx:Style>
    <mx:Button label="Example" styleName="example" />
</mx:Application>
```

Yet, if you reverse the order of the two `Style` tags, as in Example 8-4, you'll see that the button label is now red. This is because when properties of the same name are defined for a selector multiple times, the last definition overrides previous definitions. In the case of this example, the latter definition is that which is imported into the document via the external *.css* file.

Example 8-4. Order of style tags affects styles (part 2)

```
<?xml version="1.0" encoding="utf-8"?>
<mx:Application xmlns:mx="http://www.adobe.com/2006/mxml">
    <mx:Style>
        .example {
            color: green;
        }
    </mx:Style>
    <mx:Style source="styles.css" />
    <mx:Button label="Example" styleName="example" />
</mx:Application>
```

Style Properties

In Flex, all style property names must be capable of being treated as variables. For this reason, it's necessary that all style property names follow the naming rules for variables, meaning they must consist of alphabetic and numeric characters. Notably, variable names cannot contain hyphens. However, traditional CSS style property names use hyphens (e.g., `font-family`), and for this reason, Flex supports both hyphenated and camel-case style property names in CSS. (Flex converts hyphenated style property names to the camel-case equivalent behind the scenes.) For example, if you want to set the font name, you can use the style property `font-family` or `fontFamily` when using CSS. However, you cannot use hyphenated style properties in ActionScript using `setStyle()` or with inline styles.

Using StyleManager

Behind the scenes, Flex converts all CSS to ActionScript instructions that are managed by a class called `mx.managers.StyleManager`. In most cases, it is not necessary to work directly with the `StyleManager` class. However, in the event that you want to have greater runtime control over styles applied as either class selectors or type selectors, you'll need to work with `StyleManager`.

The `StyleManager` class allows you to access and configure existing selectors that were created via CSS, and it allows you to add new selectors programmatically. To access an existing selector use the static method called `getStyleDeclaration()`. The method requires a string parameter specifying the name of the selector. The name of the selector should include the initial dot for class selectors. The method returns an `mx.styles.CSSStyleDeclaration` object representing the selector:

```
var selector:CSSStyleDeclaration =
StyleManager.getStyleDeclaration(".exampleSelector");
```

If you try to access a selector that does not exist, the Flex application will throw a runtime error.

You can use the `setStyle()` method for a `CSSStyleDeclaration` object to edit the styles for that object. The `setStyle()` method for `CSSStyleDeclaration` is identical to the method of the same name for `UIComponent`. You pass it the name of the style and the new value, as in the following example:

```
selector.setStyle("color", "red");
```

If you want to add a new selector at runtime that wasn't defined at compile time, you can do so by constructing a new `CSSStyleDeclaration` object and then adding it to the `StyleManager` using the `setStyleDeclaration()` method. The `setStyleDeclaration()` method allows you to specify the name of the selector (specifying `null` will cause the `StyleManager` to use the name of the selector from the `CSSStyleDeclaration` object), the `CSSStyleDeclaration` object, and a Boolean value indicating whether to immediately update the styles for affected components:

```
var selector:CSSStyleDeclaration = new CSSStyleDeclaration(".newSelector");
StyleManager.setStyleDeclaration(null, selector, true);
```

Setting a style declaration is a computationally expensive operation. If you are going to set more than one style declaration at a time, it is best to set the third parameter of the `setStyleDeclaration()` method to `false` for all but the last method call:

```
StyleManager.setStyleDeclaration(".newSelector1", selector1, false);
StyleManager.setStyleDeclaration(".newSelector2", selector2, false);
StyleManager.setStyleDeclaration(".newSelector3", selector3, false);
StyleManager.setStyleDeclaration(".newSelector4", selector4, true);
```

You should be careful when using `setStyleDeclaration()` that you don't mistakenly overwrite an existing selector. Most component types already have type selectors defined in the *defaults.css* document (found in the default theme used by Flex, as discussed in "Themes" later in this chapter) that is compiled into Flex applications by default. That means that even if you didn't define a `Button` type selector, your Flex application is probably using one that it compiled in from *defaults.css*. Therefore, if you replace the `Button` type selector with a call to `setStyleDeclaration()`, you will lose all the style settings that buttons have by default if you haven't explicitly given values to those styles in your new selector. The better option in most cases is to get a reference to the existing `CSSStyleDefinition` object and edit the style values for that object using `setStyle()`.

Global Styles

You can apply global styles using the `global` selector. You can set the `global` selector in external stylesheets, in local style definitions, or by using `StyleManager`. Global styles always have the lowest precedence. That means that a global style will be applied only if it's not overridden by a higher-priority setting such as a type selector, a class selector, or an instance style. Example 8-5 uses a `global` selector along with a class selector. In this example, the first button is green and italic, and the second button uses just the global style settings.

Example 8-5. Using a global selector with a class selector

```
<?xml version="1.0" encoding="utf-8"?>
<mx:Application xmlns:mx="http://www.adobe.com/2006/mxml" layout="vertical">
    <mx:Style>
        global {
            color: red;
            font-style: italic;
        }
        .example {
            color: green
        }
    </mx:Style>
    <mx:Button label="Example 1" styleName="example" />
    <mx:Button label="Example 2" />
</mx:Application>
```

Reviewing Style Precedence

Style precedence can be a little confusing at first because there are simply so many ways to set styles. For that reason, we'll now summarize the precedence. From highest precedence to lowest, here's the list:

- Instance style set with `setStyle()`
- Inline style
- Class selector set with `StyleManager`

- Class selector set in the stylesheet
- Type selector set with `StyleManager`
- Type selector set in the stylesheet
- Global styles

Working with Fonts

When you want to customize the font used by components within your Flex application, you'll need to know the specifics of how to work with font outlines. The first important thing to understand in regard to this topic is how Flex differentiates types of fonts. In terms of how Flex deals with fonts, there are three types of fonts:

System fonts
: These are the fonts that are installed on the user's system. Just as an HTML page can display text using a font installed on the user's system, so too can Flex applications.

Device fonts
: There are three device fonts: `_sans`, `_serif`, and `_typewriter`, which resolve to the most similar system font on the user's computer.

Embedded fonts
: Flex applications allow you to embed font outlines within the *.swf* file, so you can guarantee that all users will see the same font even if they don't have it installed on their system.

System fonts

When you use system fonts, you add no additional file size to the Flex application by embedding fonts. You can specify system fonts simply by specifying the name of the system font to use for the `fontFamily` (or `font-family`) style, as in the following example:

```
font-family: Verdana;
```

The problem with system fonts is that the user must have the font. Otherwise, the text will render using the default system font. For this reason, it's usually a good idea to specify system fonts as a fallback list. You can specify the value for `font-family` as a comma-delimited list of font names. The Flex application will try to use the first font on the list, and if it cannot find that system font, it will use the next font on the list.

```
font-family: Verdana, Arial, Helvetica;
```

Device fonts

Device fonts are not specific fonts, but rather names of font categories. Flex recognizes three device fonts: `_sans`, `_serif`, and `_typewriter`. These device fonts resolve to a system font that is in a general font category. For example, `_sans` usually resolves to Arial or Helvetica, `_serif` usually resolves to Times New Roman, and `_typewriter` usually resolves to Courier or Courier New. Using device fonts is a way to virtually guarantee that the text will appear in a general style (i.e., sans-serif, serif, or monotype). When you use a device font name in CSS, you must enclose the value in quotation marks:

```
font-family: "_sans";
```

Often when you use system fonts it is advisable to add a device font as the last font in the fallback list, as in the following example:

```
font-family: Verdana, Arial, Helvetica, "_sans";
```

Embedded fonts

Although there are use cases for system fonts and device fonts, the fonts most frequently used in Flex applications are embedded fonts. Embedded fonts compile the font outlines into the *.swf*, guaranteeing that all users will see the text in the same font. The potential downside of embedded fonts is that they increase the size of the *.swf* file. However, considering that Flex applications are rich Internet applications, the actual file size increase for an embedded font is usually insubstantial. The exception to that would be the use of extended characters and multibyte fonts, for use with languages such as Japanese and Chinese. Yet even in some of those cases, the file size increase can sometimes be mitigated by embedding only the outlines for the fonts required by the application.

There are other reasons to embed fonts besides wanting to guarantee consistent fonts for all users. Embedded fonts solve a few problems with system fonts. System fonts in Flex applications cannot be rotated, nor can you adjust the alpha of system fonts. If you attempt to rotate system fonts, the text disappears. If you attempt to adjust the alpha of a system font, you will not see an effect. However, if you embed the font, you can both rotate the text and adjust the alpha. Furthermore, system fonts are not anti-aliased. When you increase the size of system fonts the aliasing is more apparent, and it will look like the text has jagged edges. Embedded fonts are anti-aliased, meaning they look better at larger sizes. (Note that this is a double-edged sword because anti-aliased text is less legible at smaller font sizes. We'll look at the solution to this in "Using FlashType" later in this chapter.)

There are a handful of ways to embed fonts. First we'll look at how to embed fonts when you have the font file (a *.ttf* file). You can embed these fonts using the `Embed` metadata tag within ActionScript. To embed the font this way use the `source` attribute to specify the path to the *.ttf* file and the `fontName` attribute to specify the name of the font as you will want to reference it throughout your application. For the metadata tag to work, you must place it just before a variable declaration of type `Class`. You will not need to use the variable at all, but the compiler requires this.

Here's an example that embeds a font called Century Gothic from the *.ttf* file using the `fontName` of `gothicCentury`:

```
[Embed(source="GOTHIC.ttf", fontName="gothicCentury")]
private var _centuryGothic:Class;
```

Once you've embedded the font, you can use the `fontName` value to reference it just as you would any other font, as shown in Example 8-6.

Example 8-6. Embedding a font using the Embed metadata tag

```
<?xml version="1.0" encoding="utf-8"?>
<mx:Application xmlns:mx="http://www.adobe.com/2006/mxml">
    <mx:Style>
        global {
            fontFamily: gothicCentury;
        }
    </mx:Style>
    <mx:Script>
        <![CDATA[

            [Embed(source="GOTHIC.ttf", fontName="gothicCentury")]
            private var _centuryGothic:Class;

        ]]>
    </mx:Script>
    <mx:TextArea text="Example Text" />
</mx:Application>
```

When you embed a font, only one set of the font outlines is embedded. In Example 8-6, only the standard font outlines are embedded, not the bold or italic outlines. In Example 8-7, you can clearly see the effects of this when you try to add a button instance to the preceding example.

Example 8-7. Missing font outlines cause default fonts to appear

```
<?xml version="1.0" encoding="utf-8"?>
<mx:Application xmlns:mx="http://www.adobe.com/2006/mxml">
    <mx:Style>
        global {
            fontFamily: gothicCentury;
        }
    </mx:Style>
    <mx:Script>
        <![CDATA[

            [Embed(source="GOTHIC.ttf", fontName="gothicCentury")]
            private var _centuryGothic:Class;

        ]]>
    </mx:Script>
    <mx:TextArea text="Example Text" />
    <mx:Button label="Example" />
</mx:Application>
```

Because buttons default to using the bold version of a font, Example 8-7 will use the Century Gothic font for the text area, but it will use the default system font for the button label. To fix this, we must also embed the bold font outlines for the same font using the same `fontName` value. However, this time we need to set the `fontWeight` attribute to `bold`; see Example 8-8. (If you want to embed the italicized font outlines, you should set `fontStyle` to `italic`.)

Example 8-8. Embedding standard and bold font outlines

```
<?xml version="1.0" encoding="utf-8"?>
<mx:Application xmlns:mx="http://www.adobe.com/2006/mxml">
    <mx:Style>
        global {
            fontFamily: gothicCentury;
        }
    </mx:Style>
    <mx:Script>
        <![CDATA[

            [Embed(source="GOTHIC.ttf", fontName="gothicCentury")]
            private var _centuryGothic:Class;

            [Embed(source="GOTHICB.ttf", fontName="gothicCentury",
fontWeight="bold")]
            private var _centuryGothicBold:Class;

        ]]>
    </mx:Script>
    <mx:TextArea text="Example Text" />
    <mx:Button label="Example" />
</mx:Application>
```

You can also embed fonts from CSS using the `@font-face` directive. This is particularly useful when you use external stylesheets because then you can compile them to use as themes or as runtime CSS. However, it's also equally okay to use this technique for local style definitions simply because you prefer the syntax to the `Embed` metadata tag. In the following examples, we'll use local style definitions for the sake of simplicity and clarity.

The `@font-face` directive allows for all the same attributes/properties as the `Embed` metadata tag when embedding fonts. The exceptions are that the source attribute of the metadata tag is called `src` in the `@font-face` directive and `fontName` from the metadata tag is called `fontFamily` in the directive. Furthermore, the value of the `src` attribute should be wrapped in `url()`, as shown in the following example:

```
@font-face {
    src: url("GOTHIC.ttf");
    fontFamily: gothicCentury;
}
```

Example 8-9 is the earlier MXML example rewritten with `@font-face` directives.

Example 8-9. Using the @font-face directive

```
<?xml version="1.0" encoding="utf-8"?>
<mx:Application xmlns:mx="http://www.adobe.com/2006/mxml">
    <mx:Style>
        @font-face {
            src: url("GOTHIC.ttf");
            fontFamily: gothicCentury;
        }
        @font-face {
            src: url("GOTHICB.ttf");
            fontFamily: gothicCentury;
            fontWeight: bold;
        }
        global {
            fontFamily: gothicCentury;
        }
    </mx:Style>
    <mx:TextArea text="Example Text" />
    <mx:Button label="Example" />
</mx:Application>
```

Flex allows you to embed a font in a different manner as well. Rather than embedding the font by way of the *.ttf* file, you can use the font name as it's recognized by the computer system. When you want to do this, you can use the `Embed` metadata tag. Rather than using the `source` attribute, you should use the `systemFont` and specify the name of the font as it's known by the system. Additionally, when you specify a system font name, you must also specify the MIME type by using the `mimeType` attribute. The value should be either `application/x-font` or `application/x-font-truetype`. Example 8-10 uses system font names to embed fonts.

Example 8-10. Embedding fonts by system name

```
<?xml version="1.0" encoding="utf-8"?>
<mx:Application xmlns:mx="http://www.adobe.com/2006/mxml">
    <mx:Style>
        global {
            fontFamily: gothicCentury;
        }
    </mx:Style>
    <mx:Script>
        <![CDATA[

            [Embed(systemFont="Century Gothic", fontName="gothicCentury",
mimeType="application/x-font")]
            private var _centuryGothic:Class;

            [Embed(systemFont="Century Gothic", fontName="gothicCentury",
fontWeight="bold", mimeType="application/x-font")]
            private var _centuryGothicBold:Class;

        ]]>
    </mx:Script>
    <mx:TextArea text="Example Text" />
```

```
    <mx:Button label="Example" />
</mx:Application>
```

You can also embed fonts by name using CSS. To do so, you should wrap the `src` value using `local()` rather than `url()`. The following example illustrates how this works:

```
<?xml version="1.0" encoding="utf-8"?>
<mx:Application xmlns:mx="http://www.adobe.com/2006/mxml">
    <mx:Style>
        @font-face {
            src: local("Century Gothic");
            fontFamily: gothicCentury;
        }
        @font-face {
            src: local("Century Gothic");
            fontFamily: gothicCentury;
            fontWeight: bold;
        }
        global {
            fontFamily: gothicCentury;
        }
    </mx:Style>
    <mx:TextArea text="Example Text" />
    <mx:Button label="Example" />
</mx:Application>
```

Embedding font subsets

When you embed a font, by default all the outlines are embedded, regardless of what characters are used in the application. In some cases your application may not use all the font outlines, and in those cases it's unnecessary and wasteful to embed all the font outlines. For that reason, Flex lets you specify ranges of characters to embed using the `unicodeRange` attribute for `@font-face` or the `Embed` metadata tag. The `unicodeRange` attribute lets you specify one or more Unicode values or ranges of Unicode values. The Unicode values must be in the form `U+`*`code`*, such as `U+00A1`. You can specify ranges by placing a hyphen between two values, as in `U+00A1-U+00FF`. Specify more than one value or range by delimiting them with commas, as in Example 8-11.

Example 8-11. Embedding font subset ranges

```
<?xml version="1.0" encoding="utf-8"?>
<mx:Application xmlns:mx="http://www.adobe.com/2006/mxml">
    <mx:Style>
        @font-face {
            src: url("GOTHIC.ttf");
            fontFamily: gothicCentury;
            unicodeRange: U+0041-U+007F;
        }
        @font-face {
            src: url("GOTHICB.ttf");
            fontFamily: gothicCentury;
            fontWeight: bold;
            unicodeRange: U+0041-U+007F;
```

```
        }
        global {
            fontFamily: gothicCentury;
        }
    </mx:Style>
    <mx:TextArea text="++ Example Text ++" />
    <mx:Button label="Example" />
</mx:Application>
```

Example 8-11 embeds the range of standard Latin alphabet characters, but not the + character. That means the alphabetic characters in the components show up, but the + characters do not. Example 8-12 embeds the + character as well.

Example 8-12. Embedding lists of font subsets

```
<?xml version="1.0" encoding="utf-8"?>
<mx:Application xmlns:mx="http://www.adobe.com/2006/mxml">
    <mx:Style>
        @font-face {
            src: url("GOTHIC.ttf");
            fontFamily: gothicCentury;
            unicodeRange: U+0041-U+007F,U+002B;
        }
        @font-face {
            src: url("GOTHICB.ttf");
            fontFamily: gothicCentury;
            fontWeight: bold;
            unicodeRange: U+0041-U+007F,U+002B;
        }
        global {
            fontFamily: gothicCentury;
        }
    </mx:Style>
    <mx:TextArea text="++ Example Text ++" />
    <mx:Button label="Example" />
</mx:Application>
```

You can also use named ranges that you define in the compiler configuration file you specify using the `-load-config` attribute. If you want to add named ranges to the compiler configuration file, you must add the values in the following format:

```
<flex-config>
    <compiler>
        <fonts>
            <languages>
                <language-range>
                    <lang>Alpha And Plus</lang>
                    <range>U+0041-U+007F,U+002B</range>
                </language-range>
            </languages>
        </fonts>
    </compiler>
</flex-config>
```

If you want to add more than one named range, you can simply add more language-range tags nested within the languages tag.

You can then specify the named range as the value for the unicodeRange attribute. The name must appear in quotes, as in Example 8-13.

Example 8-13. Embedding fonts by named ranges

```
<?xml version="1.0" encoding="utf-8"?>
<mx:Application xmlns:mx="http://www.adobe.com/2006/mxml">
    <mx:Style>
        @font-face {
            src: url("GOTHIC.ttf");
            fontFamily: gothicCentury;
            unicodeRange: "Alpha And Plus";
        }
        @font-face {
            src: url("GOTHICB.ttf");
            fontFamily: gothicCentury;
            fontWeight: bold;
            unicodeRange: "Alpha And Plus";
        }
        global {
            fontFamily: gothicCentury;
        }
    </mx:Style>
    <mx:TextArea text="++ Example Text ++" />
    <mx:Button label="Example" />
</mx:Application>
```

To simplify things you can use predefined ranges. The predefined ranges are in the *flash-unicode-table.xml* document in the *frameworks* subdirectory of the *SDK* directory. If you want to use these predefined ranges, you can copy and paste the language-range tags from the *flash-unicode-table.xml* document to your configuration file.

Using advanced anti-aliasing

In Flex 3 it is possible to leverage greater control over embedded fonts using something called advanced anti-aliasing. Advanced anti-aliasing allows you to control text appearance with additional styles:

fontSharpness
: A value from -400 to 400 (the default value is 0) specifying how crisp the edges of the font appear. The higher the value is, the crisper the edges. Lowering the value for smaller fonts usually makes the fonts more legible.

`fontThickness`
: A value from –200 to 200 (the default value is 0) specifying how thick the edges of the font should be.

Advanced anti-aliasing also allows you to use the `fontAntiAliasType` and `fontGridFitType` styles, which are beyond the scope of this book. You can consult the Flex documentation for more details on these styles.

Example 8-14 uses two sliders that allow you to adjust the sharpness and thickness of the font in order to see the effects.

Example 8-14. Adjusting FlashType properties

```
<?xml version="1.0" encoding="utf-8"?>
<mx:Application xmlns:mx="http://www.adobe.com/2006/mxml">
    <mx:Style>
        global {
            fontFamily: gothicCentury;
            fontSize: 50;
        }
    </mx:Style>
    <mx:Script>
        <![CDATA[

            [Embed(systemFont="Century Gothic", fontName="gothicCentury",
mimeType="application/x-font")]
            private var _centuryGothic:Class;

            [Embed(systemFont="Century Gothic", fontName="gothicCentury",
fontWeight="bold", mimeType="application/x-font")]
            private var _centuryGothicBold:Class;

            private function sharpnessChangeHandler(event:Event):void {
                StyleManager.getStyleDeclaration("global").setStyle("fontSharpness",
sharpnessSlider.value);
            }

            private function thicknessChangeHandler(event:Event):void {
                StyleManager.getStyleDeclaration("global").setStyle("fontThickness",
thicknessSlider.value);
            }


        ]]>
    </mx:Script>
    <mx:Button label="Example" />
    <mx:HSlider id="sharpnessSlider" value="0" minimum="-400" maximum="400"
liveDragging="true" change="sharpnessChangeHandler(event)" />
    <mx:HSlider id="thicknessSlider" value="0" minimum="-200" maximum="200"
liveDragging="true" change="thicknessChangeHandler(event)" />
</mx:Application>
```

Advanced anti-aliasing is enabled for embedded fonts by default. Although there is no difference in runtime performance between advanced and nonadvanced anti-aliased fonts, there are compile-time performance hits when using advanced anti-aliasing. If you don't intend to use any of the styles enabled by advanced anti-aliasing and you are embedding a lot of fonts and notice compiler slowness, you can disable advanced anti-aliasing for the fonts using the `advancedAntiAliasing` attribute in the `@font-face` directive or `Embed` metadata tag:

```
@font-face {
    src: url("GOTHIC.ttf");
    fontFamily: gothicCentury;
    advancedAntiAliasing: false;
}
```

Skinning Components

Although styles are an excellent way to customize components, they can do only so much. If you want to change the color, font, or spacing settings for components, styles are perfect solutions. However, if you want to completely change the appearance of a component so that it uses a different shape, you'll need to use skins instead of (or in addition to) styles.

Component skins are graphics or classes that you can specify for states and/or parts of a component that will completely replace the standard appearance of the component. Every component type will have different skins that you can set. For example, buttons have skins such as `upSkin`, `overSkin`, and `downSkin` that determine the appearance of the button in the up, over, and down states. You can use embedded graphics such as *.jpg* files or *.png* files, or you can use programmatic skins. We'll discuss both options in the following sections.

Applying Skins

You can apply skins in the same ways as you apply styles: using inline skin settings, `setStyle()`, CSS, or `StyleManager`. Each component type has skin settings that are treated like styles. The skin styles for each component type vary. For example, buttons have skin styles such as `upSkin`, `overSkin`, and `downSkin` and text input components have skin styles such as `borderSkin`.

The values for skin styles must always reference a class. For graphical skins, the value should be a class created by an embedded image (see Chapter 11 for more information about embedding images). For programmatic skins, the value should be a reference to the skin class. We'll look at the details of both types in the following sections.

Graphical Skinning

Graphical skinning is often the fastest and simplest way to create highly customized component appearances. Graphical skins consist of embedded images or *.swf* content that is substituted for the default artwork for component states or parts of components. Typically the workflow is to create the artwork for each skin (determined by the available skin styles for the component you want to customize), output that artwork in an embeddable format (*.png*, *.jpg*, *.swf*, etc.), embed the artwork, and set the skin styles to point to the embedded artwork. The format of the artwork you want to embed often depends on what you are trying to achieve as well as the skill set of the designer creating the artwork. As a general rule, bitmap formats will contribute the most to file size and will pixelate when scaled, and vector artwork from *.svg* or *.swf* files will contribute the least to file size (assuming the vector artwork is relatively simple) and will scale without pixelating. Furthermore, within the bitmap category, *.gif* and *.png* (PNG24) are capable of supporting transparency, and vector formats also support transparency. This is an important consideration if the artwork you want to use for skins requires transparency (e.g., nonrectangular edges/corners).

You can set graphical skins in one of three ways: inline, using `setStyle()`, or using CSS.

Inline graphical skins

Inline graphical skins work just like inline styles, except that the value must be a reference to a class for an embedded graphical element. The most common way to achieve this is to add an `@Embed` directive within the inline value. The `@Embed` directive has the following syntax:

```
@Embed(source='path to asset')
```

Here's an example that sets the `upSkin`, `overSkin`, and `downSkin` of a button using this inline technique to embed the assets:

```
<mx:Button upSkin="@Embed('/assets/buttonUp.png')"
           overSkin="@Embed('/assets/buttonOver.png')"
           downSkin="@Embed('/assets/buttonDown.png')" />
```

Setting graphical skins with setStyle

When you use `setStyle()` to set a skin style, you must reference a class that points to the embedded asset. The way to achieve that is to embed the asset, point it to a variable of type `Class`, and then use that variable as the value for the `setStyle()` method. Here's an example:

```
[Embed(source="/assets/buttonUp.png")]
private var upSkin:Class;
[Embed(source="/assets/buttonOver.png")]
private var overSkin:Class;
[Embed(source="/assets/buttonDown.png")]
private var downSkin:Class;
```

```
private function initialize(event:Event):void {
    button.setStyle("upSkin", upSkin);
    button.setStyle("overSkin", overSkin);
    button.setStyle("downSkin", downSkin);
}
```

Using CSS to set graphical skins

You can use external stylesheets or local style definitions to assign skin styles for graphical skins. When using CSS for this purpose, you can add an `Embed` directive directly to the CSS, and Flex will automatically embed the asset and use that asset for the specified skin style. Here's an example:

```
.example {
    upSkin: Embed("/assets/buttonUp.png");
    overSkin: Embed("/assets/buttonOver.png");
    downSkin: Embed("/assets/buttonDown.png");
}
```

Using Scale-9

When you use graphical skins, it's important to consider whether the component will need to scale. If so, you'll frequently want to use Scale-9 (see Chapter 11 for more details). This is particularly important when the graphical skin has corners or edges that will distort when they scale. Figure 8-1 shows an example of such an image. In the following examples, we'll use this image as the background skin for a `VBox` to see the difference when Scale-9 is applied.

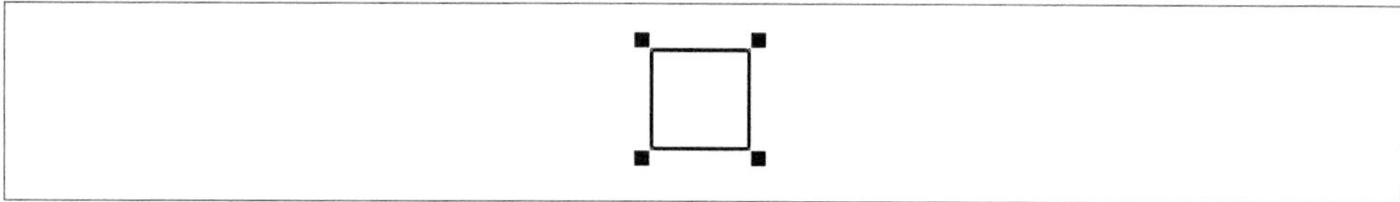

Figure 8-1. An image to be used as a skin for a VBox

First, Example 8-15 uses the image as the background image for a `VBox` without Scale-9.

Example 8-15. Embedding a skin without Scale-9

```
<?xml version="1.0" encoding="utf-8"?>
<mx:Application xmlns:mx="http://www.adobe.com/2006/mxml">
    <mx:Style>
        VBox {
            backgroundImage: Embed("vbox_background.png");
            backgroundSize: "100%";
        }
    </mx:Style>
    <mx:VBox height="200" width="200" />
</mx:Application>
```

Figure 8-2 shows the distortion caused by the preceding code.

Figure 8-2. Distorted version of image

Example 8-16 is the same code using Scale-9.

Example 8-16. Embedding a skin with Scale-9

```
<?xml version="1.0" encoding="utf-8"?>
<mx:Application xmlns:mx="http://www.adobe.com/2006/mxml">
    <mx:Style>
        VBox {
            backgroundImage: Embed("vbox_background.png",
scaleGridTop="5", scaleGridLeft="5", scaleGridBottom="29", scaleGridRight="29");
            backgroundSize: "100%";
        }
    </mx:Style>
    <mx:VBox height="200" width="200" />
</mx:Application>
```

With the preceding code, the image no longer distorts. Figure 8-3 shows the improvement.

Figure 8-3. Image that scales without distortion

Using Flash Library symbols

You can embed entire *.swf* files for use as graphical skins. For example, the following embeds three *.swf* files to use as button states:

```
<mx:Button upSkin="@Embed('/assets/buttonUp.swf')"
           overSkin="@Embed('/assets/buttonOver.swf')"
           downSkin="@Embed('/assets/buttonDown.swf')" />
```

However, you can embed individual symbols from the library of the *.swf* file by adding the `symbol` parameter to the directive. For this to work, you must have exported the *.swf* file from Flash authoring with the symbols set to export for ActionScript using linkage identifiers. The values of the `symbol` parameters should be equal to the linkage identifiers for the symbols you want to embed. The following code embeds the individual symbols from one *.swf* file:

```
<mx:Button upSkin="@Embed('buttonSkins.swf', symbol='buttonUp')"
           overSkin="@Embed('buttonSkins.swf', symbol='buttonOver')"
           downSkin="@Embed('buttonSkins.swf', symbol='buttonDown')" />
```

Programmatic Skinning

Programmatic skinning is far more complex than graphical skinning. However, programmatic skinning does provide advantages. Programmatic skinning allows greater control because you can respond to everything that occurs to the skin during runtime, such as state changes and scaling. Because programmatic skinning uses code rather than graphical assets, it has the potential to require a smaller file size than the graphical equivalent. Furthermore, programmatic skinning allows you to use low-level features such as display object filters (drop shadows, bevels, glows, etc.).

When you want to create a programmatic skin you should create a subclass of one of the following classes:

`mx.skins.ProgrammaticSkin`
: Most programmatic skins subclass `ProgrammaticSkin`, and this is an appropriate superclass for almost all skins.

`mx.skins.Border`
: The `Border` class is a subclass of `ProgrammaticSkin`, and it adds support for `borderMetrics` for skins that are borders.

`mx.skins.RectangularBorder`
: This class is a subclass of `Border`, and it adds support for `backgroundImage`.

All programmatic skins must implement the `updateDisplayList()` method. The `updateDisplayList()` method is a protected method that you must override. It expects two numeric parameters specifying the width and height of the skin, and the method return type should be `void`. The `updateDisplayList()` method gets called automatically every time the component needs to draw or redraw the skin. This is the method where you should place the code that does the drawing.

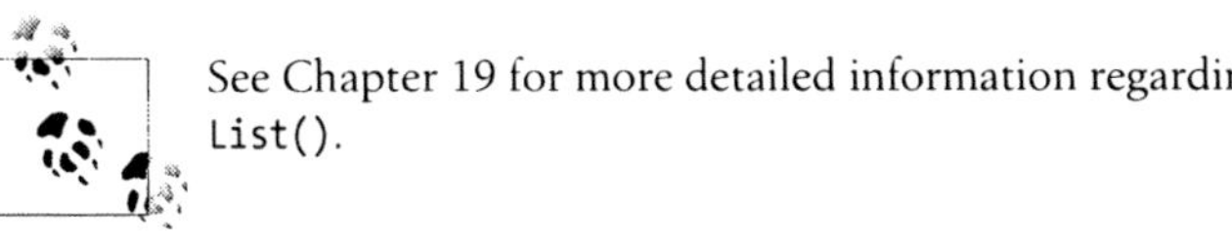

See Chapter 19 for more detailed information regarding `updateDisplayList()`.

Example 8-17 is a simple skin class. This version merely draws a white rectangle.

Example 8-17. A programmatic skin class

```
package com.oreilly.programmingflex.styles {
    import mx.skins.ProgrammaticSkin;

    public class ButtonSkin extends ProgrammaticSkin {

        public function ButtonSkin() {}

        override protected function updateDisplayList(unscaledWidth:Number,
unscaledHeight:Number):void {
            var backgroundColor:Number = 0xFFFFFF;
            graphics.clear();
            graphics.lineStyle(0, 0, 0);
            graphics.beginFill(backgroundColor, 1);
            graphics.drawRect(0, 0, unscaledWidth, unscaledHeight);
            graphics.endFill();
        }

    }
}
```

Once you've defined the programmatic skin class, you can assign that class as the skin using any of the techniques you can use for graphical skins: inline, `setStyle()`, or CSS. The difference, however, is that in each case you must specify a reference to the programmatic skin class (see Example 8-18).

Example 8-18. Using a programmatic skin class

```
<?xml version="1.0" encoding="utf-8"?>
<mx:Application xmlns:mx="http://www.adobe.com/2006/mxml">
    <mx:Script>
        <![CDATA[
            import com.oreilly.programmingflex.styles.ButtonSkin;
        ]]>
    </mx:Script>
    <mx:Button upSkin="{ButtonSkin}" overSkin="{ButtonSkin}" downSkin="{ButtonSkin}"
label="Example" />
</mx:Application>
```

Note that in Example 8-18, we use curly braces to evaluate the skin classes in the inline values. This is required if you want to import the class and reference the class by its shortened name (e.g., `ButtonSkin` rather than `com.oreilly.programmingflex.styles.ButtonSkin`). However, you can optionally specify the values as strings if you reference the fully qualified class name each time, as in Example 8-19.

Example 8-19. Using a programmatic skin class by fully qualified name

```
<?xml version="1.0" encoding="utf-8"?>
<mx:Application xmlns:mx="http://www.adobe.com/2006/mxml">
    <mx:Button upSkin="com.oreilly.programmingflex.styles.ButtonSkin"
               overSkin="com.oreilly.programmingflex.styles.ButtonSkin"
               downSkin="com.oreilly.programmingflex.styles.ButtonSkin"
               label="Example" />
</mx:Application>
```

Using `setStyle()`, you should simply pass a reference to the class as the second parameter, as in Example 8-20.

Example 8-20. Using a programmatic skin class using setStyle()

```
<?xml version="1.0" encoding="utf-8"?>
<mx:Application xmlns:mx="http://www.adobe.com/2006/mxml"
initialize="initializeHandler(event)">
    <mx:Script>
        <![CDATA[
            import com.oreilly.programmingflex.styles.ButtonSkin;

            private function initializeHandler(event:Event):void {
                button.setStyle("upSkin", ButtonSkin);
                button.setStyle("overSkin", ButtonSkin);
                button.setStyle("downSkin", ButtonSkin);
            }
        ]]>
    </mx:Script>
    <mx:Button id="button" label="Example" />
</mx:Application>
```

Using CSS, you must specify the fully qualified class name as a string wrapped by a `ClassReference` directive, as in Example 8-21.

Example 8-21. Using a programmatic skin class using CSS

```
<?xml version="1.0" encoding="utf-8"?>
<mx:Application xmlns:mx="http://www.adobe.com/2006/mxml">
    <mx:Style>
        Button {
            upSkin:
ClassReference("com.oreilly.programmingflex.styles.ButtonSkin");
            overSkin:
ClassReference("com.oreilly.programmingflex.styles.ButtonSkin");
            downSkin:
ClassReference("com.oreilly.programmingflex.styles.ButtonSkin");
        }
    </mx:Style>
    <mx:Button id="button" label="Example" />
</mx:Application>
```

You'll note that in the preceding examples, we set the skins for all the button states to the same class. Although this is not necessary, it is possible. Furthermore, it's possible to code the programmatic skin class so that it is able to detect the name of the skin to which it is applied. The ProgrammaticSkin class defines a name property that you can access from a subclass. The name property returns a string specifying the name of the skin. For instance, in the preceding examples, the possible values for the name property are upSkin, overSkin, and downSkin. Example 8-22 is a modification to the ButtonSkin class that uses different settings based on the skin name. This example also adds a drop-shadow filter to illustrate something you can achieve with programmatic skins.

Example 8-22. Detecting a programmatic skin name

```
package com.oreilly.programmingflex.styles {
    import mx.skins.ProgrammaticSkin;
    import flash.filters.DropShadowFilter;

    public class ButtonSkin extends ProgrammaticSkin {

        public function ButtonSkin() {}

        override protected function updateDisplayList(unscaledWidth:Number,
unscaledHeight:Number):void {
            var backgroundColor:Number = 0xFFFFFF;
            var distance:Number = 4;
            switch (name) {
                case "overSkin":
                    backgroundColor = 0xCCCCCC;
                    break;
                case "downSkin":
                    distance = 0;
                    backgroundColor = 0x7F7F7F;
            }
            graphics.clear();
            graphics.lineStyle(0, 0, 0);
            graphics.beginFill(backgroundColor, 1);
            graphics.drawRect(0, 0, unscaledWidth, unscaledHeight);
            graphics.endFill();
            var shadow:DropShadowFilter = new DropShadowFilter(distance);
            filters = [shadow];
        }

    }
}
```

Another thing that programmatic skins can do is respond to styles. Up to this point, the programmatic skin has used a hardcoded background color value. However, using styles we can enable greater flexibility with this button skin. Rather than the background always having to be white, we can allow the decision as to background color to be made for each button instance using styles. To accomplish this, we need only to retrieve the style value within the programmatic skin class using the getStyle() method. The getStyle() method requires the name of the style as a string parameter, and it returns the value. Example 8-23 is the new ButtonSkin class that accepts a background

Color style. Note that we also have to add a method that adjusts luminosity for the background color in the over and down states.

Example 8-23. Detecting style property values in a programmatic skin class

```
package com.oreilly.programmingflex.styles {
    import mx.skins.ProgrammaticSkin;
    import flash.filters.DropShadowFilter;

    public class ButtonSkin extends ProgrammaticSkin {

        public function ButtonSkin() {}

        override protected function updateDisplayList(unscaledWidth:Number,
unscaledHeight:Number):void {

              // If the backgroundColor style is defined then use that value.
              // Otherwise, default to 0xFFFFFF.
            var backgroundColor:Number = getStyle("backgroundColor")
? getStyle("backgroundColor") : 0xFFFFFF;
            var distance:Number = 4;
            switch (name) {
                case "overSkin":
                    backgroundColor = setLuminosity(backgroundColor, .8);
                    break;
                case "downSkin":
                    distance = 0;
                    backgroundColor = setLuminosity(backgroundColor, .5);
            }
            graphics.clear();
            graphics.lineStyle(0, 0, 0);
            graphics.beginFill(backgroundColor, 1);
            graphics.drawRect(0, 0, unscaledWidth, unscaledHeight);
            graphics.endFill();
            var shadow:DropShadowFilter = new DropShadowFilter(distance);
            filters = [shadow];
        }

         // The setLuminosity method takes a color value, splits it apart into
         // the red, green, and blue parts, multiplies each part by a value
         // (multiplier should be from 0 to 1), and recombines the parts to
         // make one RGB value. The result is an RGB value that is a luminosity
         // variant of the original color.
        private function setLuminosity(color:Number, percent:Number):Number {
            var red:Number = (color >> 16) * percent;
            var green:Number = (color >> 8 & 0xFF) * percent;
            var blue: Number = (color & 0xFF) * percent;
            return red << 16 | green << 8 | blue;
        }

    }
}
```

The MXML code in Example 8-24 illustrates how you could apply this style setting.

Example 8-24. Applying a style to a programmatic skin instance

```
<?xml version="1.0" encoding="utf-8"?>
<mx:Application xmlns:mx="http://www.adobe.com/2006/mxml">
    <mx:Style>
        Button {
            upSkin:
ClassReference("com.oreilly.programmingflex.styles.ButtonSkin");
            overSkin:
ClassReference("com.oreilly.programmingflex.styles.ButtonSkin");
            downSkin:
ClassReference("com.oreilly.programmingflex.styles.ButtonSkin");
            backgroundColor: red;
        }
    </mx:Style>
    <mx:Button id="button" label="Example" />
</mx:Application>
```

Skinning Application Backgrounds

Almost universally you'll want to customize the background of your Flex application. You can skin the application background using the `backgroundImage` skin style setting. You can use graphical skins or programmatic skins for application backgrounds. Here's an example that embeds a *.png* file to use as the application background:

```
<?xml version="1.0" encoding="utf-8"?>
<mx:Application xmlns:mx="http://www.adobe.com/2006/mxml"
    backgroundImage="@Embed('/assets/application_background.png')">
</mx:Application>
```

Skinning Tool Tips

You can skin tool tips as you would any other component—either graphically or programmatically. Simply set the value for the `ToolTip` type selector's `borderSkin` style. Example 8-25 is a programmatic skin for tool tips.

Example 8-25. An example tool tip skin class

```
package com.oreilly.programmingflex.styles {
    import mx.skins.ProgrammaticSkin;
    import flash.filters.DropShadowFilter;

    public class ToolTipSkin extends ProgrammaticSkin {

        public function ToolTipSkin() {}

        override protected function updateDisplayList(unscaledWidth:Number,
unscaledHeight:Number):void {
            graphics.clear();
            graphics.lineStyle(0, 0, 0);
            graphics.beginFill(0xFFFFFF, .8);
            graphics.drawRoundRectComplex(0, 0, unscaledWidth,
unscaledHeight, 0, 10, 10, 10);
```

```
            graphics.endFill();
            filters = [new DropShadowFilter()];
        }

    }
}
```

You can then apply the customized skin as shown in Example 8-26.

Example 8-26. Using a programmatic tool tip skin class

```
<?xml version="1.0" encoding="utf-8"?>
<mx:Application xmlns:mx="http://www.adobe.com/2006/mxml">
    <mx:Style>
        ToolTip {
            borderSkin:
ClassReference("com.oreilly.programmingflex.styles.ToolTipSkin");
        }
    </mx:Style>
    <mx:Button label="Example" toolTip="Example Tool Tip" />
</mx:Application>
```

Figure 8-4 shows what this customized tool tip looks like.

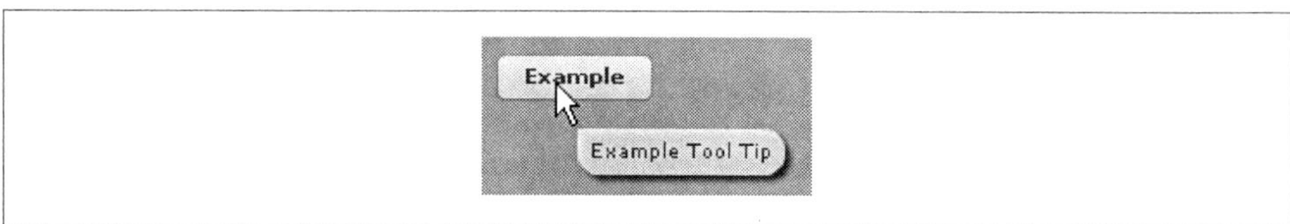

Figure 8-4. Customized tool tip

Customizing the Preloader

By default, all Flex applications use a standard preloader progress bar screen while the application itself is downloading. If you choose, you can create a custom preloader screen. This is possible and relatively simple to accomplish. There are two steps:

1. Create a class that subclasses `mx.preloaders.DownloadProgressBar` or subclasses `Sprite` and implements the `mx.preloaders.IPreloaderDisplay` interface.
2. Set the `preloader` property of the `Application` object to the path to the class from the preceding step.

The first of these two steps is the more complicated of the two, but it is still reasonably trivial. You have two options: either subclass `mx.preloaders.DownloadProgressBar` or create a `Sprite` subclass that also implements `mx.preloaders.IPreloader`. Let's look at the `DownloadProgressBar` subclass first.

Technically you can subclass `DownloadProgressBar` as an all-purpose solution. However, from an academic standpoint, it's better to subclass `DownloadProgressBar` only when you intend to customize the default preloader screen. When subclassing DownloadProgressBar you'll want to ensure that you always called the super constructor from the constructor of the subclass:

```
package com.oreilly.programmingflex.preloader {

    import mx.preloaders.DownloadProgressBar;

    public class CustomPreloaderSubclass extends DownloadProgressBar {

        public function CustomPreloaderSubclass() {
            super();
        }

    }
}
```

The super constructor ensures that the proper event handlers are configured for the class. Then you need only to override the event handler methods necessary for the particular subclass. If you consult the documentation for DownloadProgressBar you'll see that it has the following protected event handler methods that you can override: initProgressHandler, progressHandler, completeHandler, rslProgressHandler, rslCompleteHandler, and rslErrorHandler. Example 8-27 is a simple example that overrides just progressHandler. This example displays the bytes loaded and total bytes in the label field rather than the default value of Loading.

Example 8-27. Example custom preloader class

```
package com.oreilly.programmingflex.preloader {

    import mx.preloaders.DownloadProgressBar;
    import flash.events.ProgressEvent;

    public class CustomPreloaderSubclass extends DownloadProgressBar {

        public function CustomPreloaderSubclass() {
            super();
        }

        override protected function progressHandler(event:ProgressEvent):void {
            super.progressHandler(event);
            label = event.bytesLoaded + " of " + event.bytesTotal + " bytes";
        }

    }
}
```

Once you've created a custom preloader class, you can assign the class name to the preloader property of the Application tag for the project, as in Example 8-28.

Example 8-28. Setting the preloader for an application

```
<?xml version="1.0"?>
<mx:Application xmlns:mx="http://www.adobe.com/2006/mxml" layout="absolute"
preloader=" com.oreilly.programmingflex.preloader.CustomPreloaderSubclass">
<mx:Script>
    <![CDATA[

        // This example embeds a file so that there is a significant amount of data
         // to load and you will be able to see the preloader screen.
        [Embed(source="file.mp3")]
        private var _file:Class;

    ]]>
</mx:Script>
</mx:Application>
```

You may need to upload the application to a web server to see the preloader screen for more than just a second.

When you want to completely customize the preloader screen, you can still subclass `DownloadProgressBar` and simply not call the super constructor and/or override the `createChildren()` method. However, doing so misses the intent of subclassing. A subclass should use at least part of the implementation of the superclass. Therefore, it is better in such cases to write a class that instead subclasses `Sprite` and implements `IPreloaderDisplay`. If you view the documentation for `IPreloaderDisplay`, you'll see that an implementing class must define the public properties `backgroundAlpha`, `backgroundColor`, `backgroundImage`, `backgroundSize`, `preloader`, `stageWidth`, and `stageHeight`, as well as a method called `initialize`.

Example 8-29 is a simple customized preloader. This example uses a circle and animates a radial line moving around the axis as the application downloads.

Example 8-29. A preloader class subclassing Sprite

```
package com.oreilly.programmingflex.preloader {
    import mx.preloaders.IPreloaderDisplay;
    import flash.display.Sprite;
    import flash.display.Shape;
    import flash.events.Event;
    import flash.events.ProgressEvent;
    import mx.events.FlexEvent;
    import mx.preloaders.Preloader;

    public class CustomPreloaderScreen extends Sprite implements
IPreloaderDisplay {

        private var _progress:Shape;
        private var _preloader:Preloader;
        private var _backgroundAlpha:Number;
```

```
        private var _backgroundColor:uint;
        private var _backgroundImage:Object;
        private var _backgroundSize:String;
        private var _stageHeight:Number;
        private var _stageWidth:Number;

        public function set preloader(value:Sprite):void {
            _preloader = value as Preloader;
            value.addEventListener(ProgressEvent.PROGRESS, progressEventHandler);
            value.addEventListener(FlexEvent.INIT_COMPLETE,
initCompleteEventHandler);
        }

        public function set backgroundAlpha(value:Number):void {
            _backgroundAlpha = value;
        }

        public function get backgroundAlpha():Number {
            return _backgroundAlpha;
        }

        public function set backgroundColor(value:uint):void {
            _backgroundColor = value;
        }

        public function get backgroundColor():uint {
            return _backgroundColor;
        }

        public function set backgroundImage(value:Object):void {
            _backgroundImage = value;
        }

        public function get backgroundImage():Object {
            return _backgroundImage;
        }

        public function set backgroundSize(value:String):void {
            _backgroundSize = value;
        }

        public function get backgroundSize():String {
            return _backgroundSize;
        }

        public function set stageWidth(value:Number):void {
            _progress.x = value / 2;
            _stageWidth = value;
        }

        public function get stageWidth():Number {
            return _stageWidth;
        }

        public function set stageHeight(value:Number):void {
```

```
            _progress.y = value / 2;
            _stageHeight = value;
        }

        public function get stageHeight():Number {
            return _stageHeight;
        }

        public function CustomPreloaderScreen() {
            _progress = new Shape();
            addChild(_progress);
        }

        private function progressEventHandler(event:ProgressEvent):void {
            _progress.graphics.clear();
            _progress.graphics.lineStyle(0, 0, 1);
            _progress.graphics.drawCircle(0, 0, 20);
            _progress.graphics.moveTo(0, 0);
            _progress.graphics.lineTo(0, 20);
            _progress.graphics.moveTo(0, 0);
            var angle:Number = event.bytesLoaded / event.bytesTotal * Math.PI * 2;
            var newX:Number = Math.sin(angle) * 20;
            var newY:Number = Math.cos(angle) * 20;
            _progress.graphics.lineTo(newX, newY);
        }

        public function initialize():void {
            _progress.x = stage.stageWidth / 2;
            _progress.y = stage.stageHeight / 2;
        }

        private function initCompleteEventHandler(event:FlexEvent):void {
            dispatchEvent(new Event(Event.COMPLETE));
        }

    }
}
```

You can test this preloader in the same way as the earlier example. This time use the name CustomPreloaderScreen for the application's preloader property (see Example 8-30).

Example 8-30. Setting the preloader class for the application

```
<?xml version="1.0"?>
<mx:Application xmlns:mx="http://www.adobe.com/2006/mxml" layout="absolute"
preloader=" com.oreilly.programmingflex.preloader.CustomPreloaderScreen">
<mx:Script>
    <![CDATA[

        // This example embeds a file so there is a significant amount of data
         // to load and you will be able to see the preloader screen.
        [Embed(source="file.mp3")]
        private var _file:Class;
```

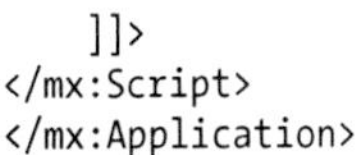

```
    ]]>
</mx:Script>
</mx:Application>
```

Figure 8-5 shows what the resulting preloader looks like.

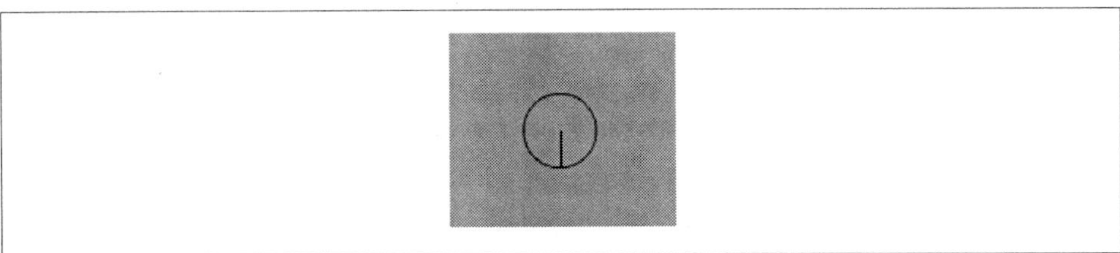

Figure 8-5. The custom preloader showing a circle with a line indicating progress

Themes

Themes provide a way to compile all *.css* files, graphical skin asset files, and programmatic skin classes in an *.swc* file that you can then tell the Flex compiler to use for your Flex application. This has two primary advantages:

- It allows you to precompile style and skin assets so that application compilation is faster.
- It allows you to more easily distribute and drop in preconfigured styles and skins for Flex applications.

Themes are fantastic when, say, you have a corporate style guide that you need to implement across many applications. Rather than having to distribute all the *.css* files, graphical elements, and programmatic skin classes, you can distribute just one *.swc* file.

Setting a Theme

Setting a theme for a Flex application is very simple. All that is necessary is to add a `-theme` compiler option to `mxmlc`. If you are compiling from the command line (or using Ant or another automatic build program), you will want to simply add `-theme` ***`themeFile`***`.swc` to the compiler options, as in this example:

```
mxmlc -theme corporate.swc Main.mxml
```

If you are using Flex Builder to build your application, you should open the project properties, select the Flex Compiler option, and add `-theme` ***`themeFile`***`.swc` to the additional compiler arguments field.

Creating a Theme

To use a theme, you clearly must have a theme first. A theme must contain at least one *.css* file, and likely contains additional assets such as image assets and/or a programmatic skin class. A theme file must be precompiled as an *.swc* file. You can compile an *.swc* file using `compc`, the command-line components compiler. When you compile a theme file, you should specify `-include-file` options for each *.css* and/or graphical skin asset file you want to add to the *.swc*. The `-include-file` option requires two parameters: the name by which you refer to the file in the *.css* and the path to the file. Here's an example:

```
compc -include-file corporate_styles.css ../assets/themes/corporate.css
-include-file background.jpg ../assets/themes/background.jpg -o corporate.swc
```

If you want to add programmatic skin classes to the theme *.swc* file, you can use the `-include-classes` option. The `-include-classes` option allows you to specify one or more fully qualified class names in a space-delimited list:

```
compc -include-file corporate_styles.css ../assets/themes/corporate.css
-include-classes com.company.styles.ButtonSkin com.company.styles.ToolTipSkin
```

As you can see, even with just two included files or classes, the command-line statement starts to get unwieldy, and adding more files just exacerbates the problem. A more elegant solution is to use the configuration file. The following is a sample configuration file called *example_theme.xml*:

```
<?xml version="1.0"?>
<flex-config xmlns="http://www.adobe.com/2006/flex-config">
    <output>corporate.swc</output>
    <include-file>
        <name>corporate.css</name>
        <path>../assets/themes/corporate.css</path>
    </include-file>
    <include-file>
        <name>background.jpg</name>
        <path>../assets/themes/background.jpg</path>
    </include-file>
    <include-classes>
        <class>com.company.styles.ButtonSkin</class>
        <class>com.company.styles.ToolTipSkin</class>
    </include-classes>
</flex-config>
```

You can then compile using the `-load-config` option of `compc` as follows:

```
compc -load-config example_theme.xml
```

Flex ships with sample themes in an uncompiled format. You can find the theme files in the *frameworks/themes* directory of the Flex SDK. (If you're using Flex Builder, the SDK is located in the *FlexSDK* directory of the Flex Builder installation.) To compile and use a theme, do the following:

1. Create a new Flex project with the main *.mxml* file code in Example 8-31.

   Example 8-31. Main MXML document

   ```
   <?xml version="1.0" encoding="utf-8"?>
   <mx:Application xmlns:mx="http://www.adobe.com/2006/mxml">
   ```

```
    <mx:ComboBox>
        <mx:dataProvider>
            <mx:ArrayCollection>
                <mx:String>a</mx:String>
                <mx:String>b</mx:String>
                <mx:String>c</mx:String>
                <mx:String>d</mx:String>
            </mx:ArrayCollection>
        </mx:dataProvider>
    </mx:ComboBox>
    <mx:Button label="Example" />
</mx:Application>
```

2. Navigate to the *themes* directory, and copy *Smoke.css* and *smoke_bg.jpg*.
3. Paste the copies of the Smoke theme files in the new Flex project.
4. In the new Flex project, create a new file called *smoke_config.xml*, and add the code in Example 8-32 to the file.

   Example 8-32. smoke_config.xml

```
<?xml version="1.0"?>
<flex-config xmlns="http://www.adobe.com/2006/flex-config">
    <output>smoke_theme.swc</output>
    <include-file>
        <name>Smoke.css</name>
        <path>Smoke.css</path>
    </include-file>
    <include-file>
        <name>smoke_bg.jpg</name>
        <path>smoke_bg.jpg</path>
    </include-file>
</flex-config>
```

5. From a command prompt, change to the directory with the *.xml* file, and run the following command which will compile the assets into an *.swc* file:

```
compc -load-config smoke_config.xml
```

6. You can delete the copies of *Smoke.css* and *smoke_bg.jpg* as well as *smoke_config.xml* just to verify that they are no longer necessary in order to use the theme now that the *.swc* file has been created.
7. Compile your Flex application with the `-theme` option set to *smoke_theme.swc*.

When you run the Flex application you'll see the Smoke theme applied, as shown in Figure 8-6.

Runtime CSS

In Flex 3 you can use runtime CSS. Thus far in the chapter, when we've talked about CSS we've talked exclusively about CSS that gets compiled into the Flex application.

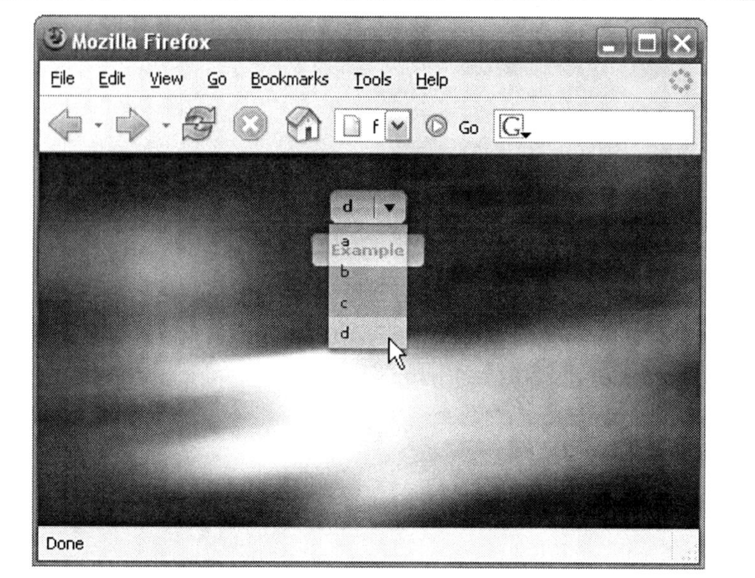

Figure 8-6. The Smoke theme

Now we'll look at how you can load and apply CSS at runtime, effectively restyling an application at runtime.

Because Flex styles often required embedded resources such as skin assets, classes, and fonts, Flex runtime CSS must be precompiled into *.swf* files. When using Flex 3, you can use the `mxmlc` compiler to compile a *.css* file into an *.swf* that includes all assets embedded by the *.css* file. To compile the *.css* file, simply pass the path to the file as the one compiler argument, as in the following example:

```
mxmlc styles.css
```

The preceding example will compile *styles.css* into a file called *styles.swf*. You can then load *styles.swf* into your Flex applications at runtime without having to include the *.css* or any of the embedded assets in the main Flex application. That means you can update the styles for an application without having to recompile and redeploy the application itself. All you have to do is update the styles file. Furthermore, you can have many styles files that the user can choose from at runtime.

To load CSS at runtime, you use the `StyleManager.loadStyleDeclarations()` method. The `loadStyleDeclarations()` method requires at least one parameter—the path to the *.swf* file containing the CSS:

```
StyleManager.loadStyleDeclarations("styles.swf");
```

If you're loading only one stylesheet, as soon as you've loaded the styles you'll want to apply them. By default, `loadStyleDeclarations()` behaves in this way. However, if you are loading several stylesheets (runtime stylesheets have the same cumulative potential as compile-time stylesheets), you likely don't want to apply the styles until after you've loaded the last stylesheet. This is because applying styles is a relatively expensive operation, and it is best to defer applying the styles until they have all loaded. You can achieve this by specifying `false` for the second parameter of all but the last `loadStyleDeclarations()` method call. Then specify a value of `true` (or do not specify a value because the default is true) for the last `loadStyleDeclarations()` method call.

```
StyleManager.loadStyleDeclarations("stylesA.swf", false);
StyleManager.loadStyleDeclarations("stylesB.swf", false);
StyleManager.loadStyleDeclarations("stylesC.swf", false);
StyleManager.loadStyleDeclarations("stylesD.swf", true);
```

The `loadStyleDeclarations()` method allows you to load stylesheets from the same domain as the Flex application or from different domains. However, if you load the stylesheet *.swf* file from a different domain, you'll need to specify `true` for the third (optional) parameter for `loadStyleDeclarations()`:

```
StyleManager.loadStyleDeclarations("http://www.differentdomain.com/styles.swf",
true, true);
```

Because styles are applied cumulatively, you need a mechanism for clearing loaded CSS. You can achieve that using the `StyleManager.unloadStyleDeclarations()` method. The `unloadStyleDeclarations()` method requires that you specify the path to the *.swf* file that was originally loaded, and you can optionally specify whether to immediately unload the styles or wait until you've unloaded other styles:

```
StyleManager.unloadStyleDeclarations("styles.swf");
```

To best understand runtime CSS, here's a simple exercise.

1. Create a file called *a.css* with the CSS in Example 8-33.

   Example 8-33. a.css

   ```
   @font-face {
       src: url("ARIAL.ttf");
       fontFamily: arial;
   }
   @font-face {
       src: url("ARIALBD.ttf");
       fontFamily: arial;
       fontWeight: bold;
   }
   global {
       fontFamily: arial;
   }
   Button {
       cornerRadius: 10;
   }
   ```

2. From a command prompt, compile *a.css* to *a.swf* using the following command (make sure you've added `mxmlc` to your path):

   ```
   mxmlc a.css
   ```

3. Create a file called *b.css* with the CSS in Example 8-34.

Example 8-34. b.css

```
@font-face {
    src: url("GOTHIC.ttf");
    fontFamily: gothicCentury;
}
@font-face {
    src: url("GOTHICB.ttf");
    fontFamily: gothicCentury;
    fontWeight: bold;
}
global {
    fontFamily: gothicCentury;
}
Application {
    themeColor: green;
}
Button {
    cornerRadius: 25;
}
ToolTip {
    borderSkin: ClassReference("com.oreilly.programmingflex.styles.ToolTipSkin");
}
```

You must ensure that `com.oreilly.programmingflex.styles.ToolTipSkin` is available in the source path for the project. You created this class earlier in the chapter.

4. From a command prompt, compile *b.css* to *b.swf* using the following command:

```
mxmlc b.css
```

5. Create a new document called *RuntimeCSS.mxml* with the code in Example 8-35.

Example 8-35. RuntimeCSS.mxml

```
<?xml version="1.0" encoding="utf-8"?>
<mx:Application xmlns:mx="http://www.adobe.com/2006/mxml"
initialize="initializeHandler(event)">
    <mx:Script>
        <![CDATA[

            private var _currentStyle:String;

            private function initializeHandler(event:Event):void {
                StyleManager.loadStyleDeclarations("a.swf");
                _currentStyle = "a.swf";
            }

            private function clickHandler(event:Event):void {
                StyleManager.unloadStyleDeclarations(_currentStyle);
                StyleManager.loadStyleDeclarations(stylesOptions.value.toString());
                _currentStyle = stylesOptions.value as String;
```

```
            }
        ]]>
    </mx:Script>
    <mx:ComboBox id="stylesOptions" toolTip="Select a Style Sheet">
        <mx:dataProvider>
            <mx:ArrayCollection>
                <mx:String>a.swf</mx:String>
                <mx:String>b.swf</mx:String>
            </mx:ArrayCollection>
        </mx:dataProvider>
    </mx:ComboBox>
    <mx:Button label="Change Style" click="clickHandler(event)" />
</mx:Application>
```

6. Compile and run *RuntimeCSS.mxml*.

When you run this test, you'll be able to switch between two runtime stylesheets and see the effects. Notice the difference if you comment the `unloadStyleDeclarations()` line.

Summary

In this chapter, you learned how to customize the appearance of a Flex application. This chapter discussed using styles and skins to change the appearance of components within the application. You also learned how to apply these settings using MXML, ActionScript, and CSS.

CHAPTER 9

Application Components

As the scope of your applications grows, sooner or later you will need a better way to organize all their different components. One principle that is known to be effective in this task is the component-based development principle.

This chapter focuses on application components. Application components are logically modular elements (not to be confused with Flex modules) within an application that you typically define using MXML and that behave in a manner similar to the components we have been exposed to throughout this book.

Component-based development allows a developer to divide an application into components. Doing so provides several benefits:

- It helps to promote many object-oriented design principles, including code reuse, loose coupling, encapsulation, and reduced bugs.
- It allows you to simplify a large problem into smaller ones.
- It allows different team members to focus on their own components, which allows teams to be more efficient.

Traditionally when developers think of components, they think of prepackaged components that have been developed by a third party. In component-based development, third-party components are important, but so are user-developed components. Instead of allowing application development using just third-party components, an effective component-based development platform should allow you to mix third-party and user-developed components. In earlier chapters, we discussed how Flex and MXML allow rapid application development using several components. In this chapter, we'll discuss the reasons application components are important and useful. We'll also discuss how to write application components.

The Importance of Application Components

To understand the importance of application components, let's examine where they would be helpful. In this example, we'll study a typical application: a contact manager. Figure 9-1 shows the completed contact manager application.

Figure 9-1. Contact manager application

This application is considered to be simple, but even a simple application can benefit from application components. If you were to build this application while making sure to separate your presentation code from your data communication and business logic, you would typically structure the application using many Flex components. The result would be one large MXML file, with many event handlers, associated UI code, and many ActionScript class files.

Although this book does not cover the popular Model-View-Controller (MVC) design pattern, it is assumed that you understand the benefits of separating the data access and business logic outside your presentation code. Flex allows you to rapidly develop applications using MXML. However, if application architecture is important, ideally you should use MXML mainly for the view, and use ActionScript for the model and controller. This does not mean that all applications should have such a structure, but if you are working on a large application, we recommend that you consider separating different parts of your application appropriately. We will touch upon some of these concepts in Chapter 22.

Although such a structure isn't bad, imagine if you were working on a team and one team member was responsible for the contact details area. Working on such an application would not be ideal because it would be built with one large MXML file that is difficult to manage. Taking this one step further, imagine if the contact details were used by other applications. You would ideally want to be able to write such code as a component once, and not have to rewrite it. The component would encompass the highlighted area in Figure 9-2.

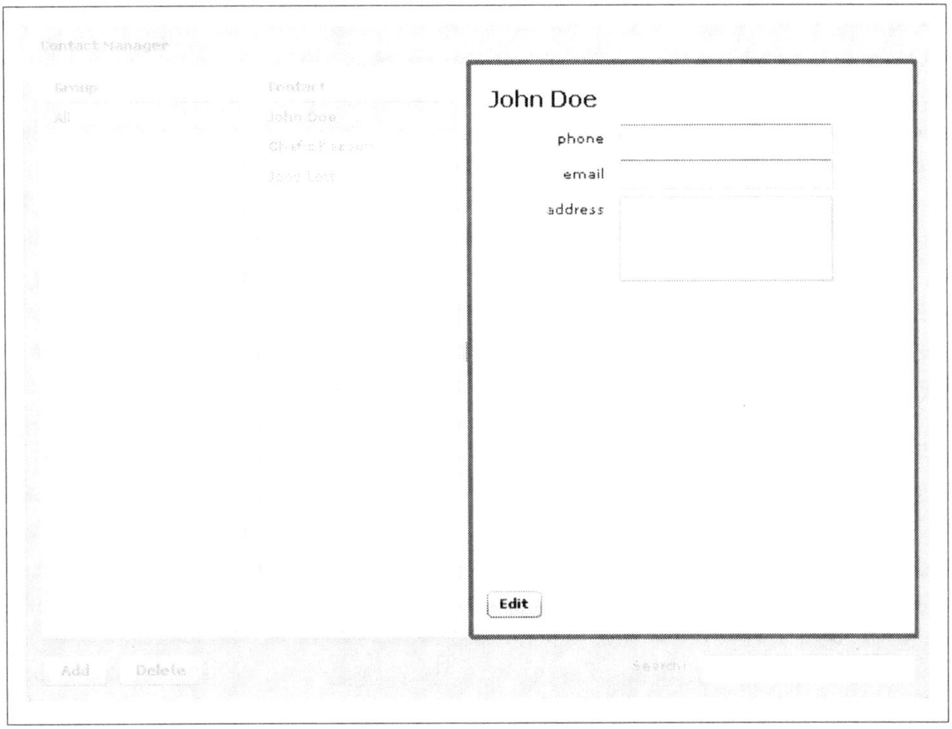

Figure 9-2. Contact details highlighted

There are even more benefits to creating an application out of many components. Imagine how large and unmanageable this single MXML file would become. You would have to have different event handlers for when a user selects a group, selects a contact, attempts to edit the user details, adds and deletes a user, and so on. This doesn't even include the complexity involved with nesting containers. It could easily become confusing to keep track of everything. Instead, this application would be simpler to manage if you could focus on the contact details alone as one component that almost lives in its own world. This is where application components come in.

You can develop application components in MXML or ActionScript. This chapter covers application component development with MXML because it's easier to build such components from existing components using MXML than it is using ActionScript. That does not mean you cannot develop application components in ActionScript. However, ActionScript-based components tend to be more advanced and more ideal for custom components, which we cover in Chapter 19, whereas MXML-based components are typically ideal for application components.

MXML Component Basics

To understand MXML components it helps to understand that MXML files are just classes behind the scenes. When an MXML file is compiled, the compiler translates the file to ActionScript and then compiles it into native Flash Player bytecode. This means that everything you can build in MXML you can also build in ActionScript. MXML code usually is shorter and easier to read than the equivalent ActionScript code. This makes MXML more convenient to work with than ActionScript in many cases. At the same time, because MXML is ultimately compiled to the same bytecode as ActionScript is, there is no loss in performance or features. This makes MXML ideal for application layout.

Now that you understand the benefits of working with MXML over ActionScript, let's discuss how to create a class, optimally implement its common features, and decouple application components written in MXML within an application.

Creating and Using a Component

To create a component in MXML, you create a new file with the root tag corresponding to the class you want to extend, and with a filename corresponding to the class name of the component. Typically when segmenting an application, the base class (root tag) will be a container component. In Figure 9-2, our contact details component example, the base class is the `Canvas` container. Example 9-1 provides the code for the `Canvas` container.

Example 9-1. ContactDetails.mxml

```
<?xml version="1.0" encoding="utf-8"?>
<mx:Canvas xmlns:mx="http://www.adobe.com/2006/mxml">
    <!--  Contact Details Implementation Details -->
</mx:Canvas>
```

The code in Example 9-1 should look very similar to a basic MXML application file, except that it uses the `Canvas` component as the root tag rather than the `Application` component. Also note that as each MXML file is a separate component, you need to reference the MXML namespace as you would in the application's root MXML file.

Although we do not cover it in this book, MXML components are also ideal for when you want to extend an existing component. By declaring your own MXML file that is based on an existing component and just adding your own additional logic where needed, you can customize the existing Flex framework components. Extending components requires an understanding of the underlying component framework and the component you want to extend. To learn more about the component framework, see Chapter 19, as well as the Flex SDK documentation.

Once the component is created, you can reference it using the filename used for the MXML file, as shown in Example 9-2.

Example 9-2. Main MXML application file

```
<?xml version="1.0" encoding="utf-8"?>
<mx:Application xmlns:mx="http://www.adobe.com/2006/mxml" xmlns:pf3="*">
    <pf3:ContactDetails/>
</mx:Application>
```

In Example 9-2, we declared an instance of the `ContactDetails` component as we would any other component. Notice the addition of the `pf3` namespace prefix. To inform the compiler of available components, you will need to reference the package, which in this case is just the root package, *.

In ActionScript, you would typically use the `package` keyword to declare the package of a class. In MXML, you declare a package simply via the directory structure. Because we placed the main MXML file and the MXML component in the same directory in Example 9-2, the compiler defaults to the top-level package. Although this is usable, you should specify a package for all your components. For example, to create the package `com.oreilly.programmingflex.contactmanager.views` you would just create the corresponding directory structure, *com/oreilly/programmingflex/contactmanager/views/*, and place the component's MXML file within the *views* directory. You can find more details on the source paths in Chapter 2.

Now, to update the main application file, we need to update the namespace reference to reflect the new package (see Example 9-3).

Example 9-3. Updating the namespace to reflect the new package

```
<?xml version="1.0" encoding="utf-8"?>
<mx:Application xmlns:mx="http://www.adobe.com/2006/mxml" xmlns:pf3="com.oreilly.
programmingflex.contactmanager.views.*">
    <pf3:ContactDetails/>
</mx:Application>
```

When dividing an application into several components, you will want to place many of the components together within the same folder (package). This allows you to create a single package for all your components. There is nothing wrong with having multiple packages; however, you will want to have a logical reason for doing so. One such reason could be to separate components created for use within the application you are developing versus shared components you develop to be shared across many applications.

Going back to the understanding that an MXML file is a class, you can also reference the newly created component in ActionScript classes as you would any class, as shown in the following code:

```
package com.oreilly.programmingflex.foo {
    //Import the ContactDetails component
    import com.oreilly.programmingflex.contactmanager.ContactDetails;

    public class SampleClass {
        //Instance variable of the ContactDetails type
        private var _contactDetails:ContactDetails;
        //Class code omitted for brevity
    }
}
```

As you can see, the basics of creating a new component are straightforward. The ability to quickly create components is one of the biggest benefits of Flex and MXML, and it helps support the component-based development nature of Flex.

Adding and Laying Out Controls

When creating an application component, typically you will base your component on an existing Flex container, and the new component will be composed of existing components. Adding and laying out components in an MXML component requires almost the same techniques we covered in Chapter 6 regarding the main MXML file.

In the `ContactDetails` component from Figure 9-2, we created a component based on the `Canvas` layout component. As we discussed in Chapter 6, the `Canvas` layout component allows you to place components using absolute positioning or constraint-based layout rules. Because this is the `Canvas` tag of the component rather than the `Application`, as you saw in the main application MXML file, we will use the layout rules for `Canvas` to lay out children that are added to the component.

Although not required, Flex Builder allows you to view the layout of a component in design mode, as well as visually lay out the component's contents in design mode. This can be helpful when working with application components, as there is no other mechanism to easily view a component's layout without needing to compile an application with your component.

Reviewing `ContactDetails` in Figure 9-2, you can see that the component is built from `Labels`, `TextInputs`, a `TextArea`, and a `Button`. You can add components using the same techniques we used previously. What follows is the earlier component, with the needed components added and positioned.

```
<?xml version="1.0" encoding="utf-8"?>
<mx:Canvas xmlns:mx="http://www.adobe.com/2006/mxml" width="100%" height="100%">
    <mx:Label id="heading" styleName="heading" x="10" y="10"/>
    <mx:Button id="edit" bottom="10" left="10" label="Edit" toggle="true"/>
    <mx:Label x="62" y="42" text="phone"/>
    <mx:Label x="53" y="94" text="address"/>
    <mx:Label x="66" y="68" text="email"/>
    <mx:TextArea x="110" y="93" editable="false" enabled="true" width="160" height=
"60" id="address"/>
    <mx:TextInput x="110" y="40" editable="false" id="phone"/>
    <mx:TextInput x="110" y="66" editable="false" id="email"/>
</mx:Canvas>
```

In the preceding code, we added the components and set their properties. We positioned the components using the properties for positioning (`x`, `y`, `left`, and `bottom`, in this example), as we would any child within a container. We set the root `Canvas` tag's width and height properties to `100%`. In the `ContactDetails` component, we positioned the children using absolute positioning relative to the edges of the parent. By setting the `Canvas` width and height properties to `100%`, we helped to ensure that the container would grow to the maximum space allowed for it. It is important to note that setting the values on the root tag of an MXML component doesn't disallow a parent from overriding the values. Because of this, the value set on the root MXML component is said to be the default value.

Understanding Interaction

When you create an MXML component, it lives isolated in its own world. When you build an application using one large MXML file, it is easy to reference component instances using the `id` attribute, data-bind directly to controls, and pretty much access anything within the same MXML file. When an application is split into multiple components, each component will be able to access its members, but it should not access another component's members, even though component instances in MXML are declared public by default. Although this may seem like a limitation, it helps to promote a key object-oriented programming principle: encapsulation.

Encapsulation is the process of hiding implementation details. With components, you can set properties and call methods, but a component should not access another component's internal workings.

With that said, when you are working with application components, you will need to communicate to and from each component instance. To communicate with a component, you interact with the interface it has defined—in other words, the methods and properties that are accessible. For example, in the following code, we are setting the `toolTip` property. We are able to do so because the `toolTip` property is defined by part of the ContactDetails API (in this case, it is inherited from the UIComponent class, which is part of the Flex framework).

```
<?xml version="1.0" encoding="utf-8"?>
<mx:Application xmlns:mx="http://www.adobe.com/2006/mxml" xmlns:pf3="com.oreilly.
programmingflex.contactmanager.views.*">
    <pf3:ContactDetails toolTip="Contact Details"/>
</mx:Application>
```

This code should look familiar to you in that you can work with the component in the same way you are used to working with the Flex component. In addition, because the ContactDetails component extends Canvas, its public API is inherited, including all methods, properties, events, and styles. This allows you to set the width and height properties even though you did not define them yourself. You also can use all the MXML features available with other components, including data binding.

When deciding on the component's interface, it is important to step back for a moment and think about the purpose of the component. The interface may initially be used for one specific purpose, but with time you will find that a good interface will improve reusability of your newly created component. A good interface also allows a developer to accomplish his goals without having to access the internals of the component.

Defining component properties

Component properties can aid in communicating to and from a component. You create properties by defining fields or getter/setter functions. You define properties in the same manner you would in ActionScript.

Although it's possible to define properties using *<mx:DataType>* syntax, it's generally recommended that you declare properties within the ActionScript <mx:Script> block. This will allow you to organize all public methods, properties, and getter and setter functions together. This chapter focuses on real-world usage rather than all possible methods of developing a component. You can review the Flex documentation for details on all possible methods of implementing component properties, methods, and metadata.

It is a good practice to not declare fields as public, but rather to declare getter/setter functions, as shown in the following code. This helps you to guarantee that if the implementation of the property changes in the future, the public interface will not change.

```
<?xml version="1.0" encoding="utf-8"?>
<mx:Canvas xmlns:mx="http://www.adobe.com/2006/mxml">
    <mx:Script>
        <![CDATA[

        private var _mode:String;

        [Bindable]
```

```
        public function set mode(value:String):void
        {
            _mode = value;
        }

        public function get mode():String
        {
            return _mode;
        }
        ]]>
    </mx:Script>
    <!-- contents omitted for brevity-->
</mx:Canvas>
```

In the preceding code, we declared a public property mode. You can use this property to set the mode property of the component from the parent. In the code, we declared the property as bindable using the `[Bindable]` metadata tag. It is a good idea to use `[Bindable]` whenever you declare a public property because it is likely that a developer will want to use the data-binding features of Flex with your new component. Finally, we declared a private `_mode` variable. It is a good practice to declare private properties with a preceding single underscore. This allows you to distinguish a public property from a private one, especially if you are exposing a private property via a public getter/setter function.

As you learned when adding ActionScript within MXML files in earlier chapters, you can add properties and methods using ActionScript within MXML as well, as within `<mx:Script/>`. This chapter covers inline ActionScript within a `Script` tag, but it is important to note that you can also use the other methods to add ActionScript to an MXML component just as you would reference an external ActionScript file via the `Script` tag's `source` property.

Once you've declared a property, you can access the property from the parent container as you would any other property. In the following code, we have set the property value from the parent container:

```
<?xml version="1.0" encoding="utf-8"?>
<mx:Application xmlns:mx="http://www.adobe.com/2006/mxml" initialize="init()"
xmlns:pf3="com.oreilly.programmingflex.contactmanager.views.*">
    <pf3:ContactDetails mode="view" />
    <!-- contents omitted for brevity -->
</mx:Application>
```

Most of the time, you will want a property to accept any value of a data type, and in such cases, this method works well. Sometimes, though, you will want to restrict the possible values. In the code we've been building on throughout this chapter, the mode value can accept only an enumeration of values. However, ActionScript does not support enumerations. It is a good practice, therefore, to provide the user with static variables. This reduces the possibility of user error and improves ease of use because static variables are a form of self-documentation for possible values. In addition to using static variables, we use the `Inspectable` metadata tag, which provides Flex Builder with hints on what data is accepted by the property. Adding both helps the developer and allows Flex Builder to provide code hinting for the possible values, but does not provide any sort of compile time or runtime type checking at this time. Example 9-4 is updated to make use of enumerations for the component, and Example 9-5 is the updated *Main.mxml*.

Example 9-4. Adding enumerations to a component

```
<?xml version="1.0" encoding="utf-8"?>
<mx:Canvas xmlns:mx="http://www.adobe.com/2006/mxml" width="100%"
backgroundColor="#f8f8f8" height="100%">
    <mx:Script>
        <![CDATA[

            public static const VIEW_MODE:String = "view";
            public static const EDIT_MODE:String = "edit";

            private var _mode:String;

            [Bindable]          [Inspectable(enumeration="{ContactDetails.VIEW_MODE},
{ContactDetails.EDIT_MODE}")]

            public function get mode():String
            {
                return _mode;
            }

            public function set mode(value:String):void
            {
                _mode = value;
            }
            ]]>
    </mx:Script>
    <!-- contents omitted for brevity -->
</mx:Canvas>
```

Example 9-5. Updated Main.mxml file referencing the enumeration value

```
<?xml version="1.0" encoding="utf-8"?>
<mx:Application xmlns:mx="http://www.adobe.com/2006/mxml" initialize="init()"
xmlns:pf3="com.oreilly.programmingflex.contactmanager.views.*">
    <pf3:ContactDetails mode="{ContactDetails.VIEW_MODE}"/>
</mx:Application>
```

So far in this section, we covered using properties to pass and retrieve values with a component. You also can use a property to pass an instance of an object with which you would like the component to communicate. For example, you could pass an instance of the root application to a component and have the component call methods directly on the root application. At first, this may seem like an appropriate method of communicating from child to parent, but it actually results in a tight coupling between the child and the passed object. This is not an absolute rule, but later in this chapter we will discuss how to use events to communicate with other objects. Although this requires more work, it will typically be the more appropriate method of communicating from a component as it helps promote loose coupling and reusability.

Tight coupling is where components are reliant on each other and cannot be separated without a fair amount of refactoring.

Defining component methods

In the same way you declare a property, you can declare a component method within part of a component. Although you do not have to add any methods with the `ContactDetails` component, Example 9-6 shows how you would add a `clear()` method.

Example 9-6. Adding a clear() method to ContactDetails

```
<?xml version="1.0" encoding="utf-8"?>
<mx:Canvas xmlns:mx="http://www.adobe.com/2006/mxml">
    <mx:Script>
        <![CDATA[
            public function clear():void
            {
                address.text = null;
                phone.text = null;
                email.text = null;
            }
        ]]>
    </mx:Script>
</mx:Canvas>
```

This method clears the text within the input components. Once you've defined a method with a proper accessor keyword, you can call the new method from the parent, as shown in Example 9-7.

Example 9-7. Calling the new method from the parent

```
<?xml version="1.0" encoding="utf-8"?>
<mx:Application xmlns:mx="http://www.adobe.com/2006/mxml" initialize=
"initializeHandler()" xmlns:pf3="com.oreilly.programmingflex.contactmanager.
views.*">
    <mx:Script>
        <![CDATA[
            private function initializeHandler():void
            {
                //In this example, calling clear is redundant
                contactDetails.clear();
            }
        ]]>
    </mx:Script>
```

```
    <pf3:ContactDetails id="contactDetails"/>
</mx:Application>
```

In Example 9-7, the composing object creates an instance of the component and calls the `clear()` method. The parent has no knowledge of the internal workings of the component; it only knows of the publicly accessible interface, and it trusts that the component knows how to do what it needs to do. This further helps to decouple the parent and child relationship between components built in an application.

Defining component events

When creating an MXML component, you will typically be composing other objects within the component, as you did in the `ContactDetails` component. These child components dispatch their own events, and the application will be interested in some of the events or a custom event that is specific to `ContactDetails`. Because the children reside within the component, their events won't be seen by the world outside the component. Actually, you wouldn't even want them to be seen. Doing so would allow any internal component to dispatch any event, and you would have no control over what events your component dispatches.

For this reason, and to be able to define custom events that do not depend on existing events, you will need to define your own events for your component. In the `ContactDetails` component, one event that would be useful to define is when a user clicks on the edit button. Although a lot can happen within the component, you are only interested in knowing when a user has changed the data or maybe when the user is about to change the data (in edit mode). For this reason, it would be ideal for this component to have an `EditChange` event, with a description of "begin" and "end," depending on whether the user has begun or finished editing the component.

All components in the Flex framework inherit from `EventDispatcher`, a class that implements the capability of an object to subscribe to and receive event notification. To add an event to a custom component, you need to define and dispatch the event.

To define an event, you first need to declare the event. You declare events using a metadata tag, and in MXML you do that using the `<mx:Metadata/>` tag, as shown in Example 9-8.

Example 9-8. ContactDetails with event metadata tag added

```
<?xml version="1.0" encoding="utf-8"?>
<mx:Canvas xmlns:mx="http://www.adobe.com/2006/mxml" width="100%" backgroundColor=
"#f8f8f8" height="100%">
    <mx:Metadata>
        [Event(name="editChange", type="com.oreilly.programmingflex.contactmanager.
events.EditChangeEvent")]
    </mx:Metadata>
    <!-- contents omitted for brevity -->
</mx:Canvas>
```

In Example 9-8, we added an event called editChange and the type EditChangeEvent. EditChangeEvent is the object type passed to the handler function when an event occurs. You could have used a generic event class here, but it is a good idea to create your own events for components. Doing so will allow you to provide added functionality that is specific to your component.

Let's create the EditChangeEvent class in the com.oreilly.programmingflex.contactmanager.events package. It's a good practice as usual to specify a package for a class and for events, and to place all events in an events package. This is consistent with the Flex framework and allows users to import a single package that will contain all events. Here is the definition of the EditChangeEvent class:

```
package com.oreilly.programmingflex.contactmanager.events
{
    import flash.events.Event;

    public class EditChangeEvent extends Event
    {
        public static const EDIT_CHANGE:String = "editChange";
        public var edit:Boolean;

        public function EditChangeEvent(edit:Boolean=false)
        {
            super(EDIT_CHANGE);
            this.edit = edit;
        }

        override public function clone():Event
        {
            return new EditChangeEvent(this.edit);
        }
    }
}
```

With the custom event type created, now you can dispatch the new event (see Example 9-9). We will incorporate the new event into the ContactDetails component later in this chapter.

Example 9-9. Dispatching EditChangeEvent

```
var eventEditing:EditChangeEvent = new EditChangeEvent(true);
dispatchEvent(eventEditing);
```

Component Styles

When you're working with an application component and styles, the application component can define its own style values for components within it. The easiest way to specify such styles is to define Cascading Style Sheets (CSS) within the application component as you would within an application (however, you will still have the limitation of not being able to specify CSS type selectors other than in ActionScript). When working with styles within a component, keep in mind why application components exist. They don't exist to be as fully featured and flexible as distributed components. They exist to allow you to build an application more efficiently. As such, you may find that defining styles within an application component is acceptable.

With application components, you can also define your own custom styles, as discussed in Chapter 19.

Also, as we saw in Chapter 8, styles in Flex support inheritance, which is also supported by application components. When defining a global style or CSS custom class, these styles are applied to all display items in Flex. This allows you the benefit of providing one master CSS file for an application. In the CSS file, you can define your custom style, and for any component in your application you can apply the style by setting the `styleName` property.

In this example, we first set the `styleName` property of the `Label` component:

```
<mx:Label id="contactName" styleName="heading" x="10" y="10" text="John Doe"/>
```

Once the `styleName` value is set, we can define style values anywhere within our application, including within the application component itself. Here a style definition is created in an `<mx:Style>` tag:

```
<mx:Style>
    .heading
    {
        font-size:16;
        font-weight:bold;
    }
</mx:Style>
```

Internal States

Application components can also define states internally. In the `ContactDetails` component, we want the ability to support two modes: an edit mode and a view mode. By default, the component will be in view mode, but with the public mode property defined earlier in this chapter, a user can change the state of the `ContactDetails` component easily.

First you define the states (we discuss this in more detail in Chapter 12):

```
<mx:states>
    <mx:State name="{VIEW_MODE}"/>
        <mx:State name="{EDIT_MODE}" basedOn="{VIEW_MODE}">
        <mx:SetProperty target="{address}" name="editable" value="true"/>
        <mx:SetProperty target="{email}" name="editable" value="true"/>
        <mx:SetProperty target="{phone}" name="editable" value="true"/>
```

```
    </mx:State>
</mx:states>
```

To set the default state of the component, you set the `currentState` property of the root node of the `ContactDetails` component:

```
<mx:Canvas xmlns:mx="http://www.adobe.com/2006/mxml" width="100%" backgroundColor=
"#f8f8f8" height="100%" currentState="view">
```

With the states defined, providing a mechanism to set the state is easy. We just need to update the mode setter to set the component's `currentState` property and the getter to return the value of the `currentState` property:

```
[Inspectable(enumeration="{ContactDetails.VIEW_MODE},{ContactDetails.EDIT_MODE}")]
public function set mode(value:String):void
{
    this.currentState = value;
}

[Bindable]
public function get mode():String
{
    return this.currentState;
}
```

Declaring your own public API to set the component's state isn't required, but it is a good practice. The `currentState` property is declared publicly, and defining your own setter with valid values reduces the likelihood of errors and is a form of documentation that can help others use a component.

Because we've been working on the code in snippets throughout the chapter, we thought it might help you to understand the utility of application components by providing you with the component code in its entirety:

```
<?xml version="1.0" encoding="utf-8"?>
<mx:Canvas xmlns:mx="http://www.adobe.com/2006/mxml" width="100%" backgroundColor=
"#f8f8f8" height="100%" currentState="view">
    <mx:Metadata>
    [Event(name="editChange", type="com.oreilly.programmingflex.contactmanager.events.
EditChangeEvent")]
    </mx:Metadata>
    <mx:Script>
        <![CDATA[
            import com.oreilly.programmingflex.contactmanager.events.EditChangeEvent;
            import mx.controls.Alert;
            import mx.states.State;

            public static const VIEW_MODE:String = "view";
            public static const EDIT_MODE:String = "edit";

            [Bindable]
            public function get mode():String
```

```
            {
                return this.currentState;
            }

            public function clear():void
            {
                address.text = null;
                phone.text = null;
                email.text = null;
            }
                                                [Inspectable(enumeration="
{ContactDetails.VIEW_MODE},{ContactDetails.EDIT_MODE}")]
            public function set mode(value:String):void
            {
                this.currentState = value;
            }

            private function clickHandler(e:Event):void
            {
                if(this.currentState == VIEW_MODE)
                {
                    this.mode = EDIT_MODE;
                    phone.setFocus();
                    var eventEditing:EditChangeEvent = new EditChangeEvent(true);
                    dispatchEvent(eventEditing);
                }
                else if(this.currentState == EDIT_MODE)
                {
                    this.mode = VIEW_MODE;
                    var eventDoneEditing:EditChangeEvent = new EditChangeEvent(false);
                    dispatchEvent(eventDoneEditing);
                }
            }
        ]]>
    </mx:Script>
    <mx:Style>
        .heading
        {
            font-size:16;
            font-weight:bold;
        }
    </mx:Style>
    <mx:states>
        <mx:State name="{VIEW_MODE}"/>
        <mx:State name="{EDIT_MODE}" basedOn="{VIEW_MODE}">
            <mx:SetProperty target="{address}" name="editable" value="true"/>
            <mx:SetProperty target="{email}" name="editable" value="true"/>
            <mx:SetProperty target="{phone}" name="editable" value="true"/>
        </mx:State>
    </mx:states>
    <mx:Label id="contactName" styleName="heading" x="10" y="10" text="John Doe"/>
    <mx:Button id="edit" bottom="10" left="10" label="Edit" width="41" height="20"
toggle="true" click="clickHandler(event)"/>
    <mx:Label x="62" y="42" text="phone"/>
    <mx:Label x="53" y="94" text="address"/>
```

```
    <mx:Label x="66" y="68" text="email"/>
    <mx:TextArea x="110" y="93" editable="false" enabled="true" width="160"
height="63" id="address"/>
    <mx:TextInput x="110" y="40" editable="false" id="phone"/>
    <mx:TextInput x="110" y="66" editable="false" id="email"/>
</mx:Canvas>
```

Summary

In this chapter, you learned how to build application components with a public API, events, and internal implementation details. Application components can greatly help to improve how you build and architect applications.

CHAPTER 10

Framework Utilities and Advanced Component Concepts

As you've already learned in earlier chapters, the Flex framework provides a large library of components, including layout containers and UI controls. However, in addition to the components themselves, the framework also provides libraries that offer you advanced features and functionality when working with those components. In this chapter, we'll look at the features and functionality these libraries provide. Specifically, we'll discuss tool tips, pop ups, cursor management, drag-and-drop, the ability to customize list-based items, and focus management and keyboard control.

Tool Tips

When an application contains graphics, it can often be helpful to users if you provide text-based descriptions to accompany the graphics. This is especially beneficial when the meaning of a particular UI element is not immediately obvious. It can also be useful for low-sighted and non-sighted users who rely on screen readers. Rather than cluttering the user interface with many text-based descriptions of graphics, however, many applications use *tool tips*, which are blocks of text that appear when the user moves the mouse over a visual element. In the following sections you'll learn how to work with Flex tool tips.

Adding Tool Tips

All components that inherit from `UIComponent` (which includes all UI controls and layout containers) implement a `toolTip` getter/setter property, which allows you to assign a string to the object that it will use to display tool tips. You can set the property inline using MXML, as in the following example:

```
<mx:Button id="button" label="Tool Tip Example" toolTip="Display Tool Tip" />
```

You can also set the toolTip property in ActionScript:

```
button.toolTip = "Example of Tool Tips";
```

By default, the toolTip property value for a component is null. When the value is null or an empty string, no tool tip appears. When you assign the property a non-null value, the tool tip appears after a short delay once the user moves the mouse over the object and keeps the mouse over the object. The tool tip then disappears after a delay (customizing the delay is discussed in the "Customizing Tool Tip Settings sections in this chapter) or after the user moves the mouse outside the object, whichever occurs first.

You can also use data binding to set the value of a tool tip for an object. The following example uses data binding to update the value of the tool tip text for a button based on the text input value:

```
<mx:VBox>
  <mx:Button id="button" label="Button" toolTip="{textInput.text}" />
  <mx:TextInput id="textInput" />
</mx:VBox>
```

There are rules that determine the tool tip behavior for containers and child components. The innermost component always takes highest precedence. If the innermost component has a valid tool tip text value, the tool tip for that component will be triggered. If not, the trigger bubbles up to the container until either a valid tool tip text value is found or no more containers exist. The following simple example illustrates this behavior. Because the button has a tool tip text value, moving the mouse over the button will trigger that component's tool tip. And because the text input has no tool tip text setting, the trigger will bubble up to the VBox container, displaying the container's tool tip.

```
<mx:VBox toolTip="This is the VBox tool tip.">
  <mx:Button id="button" label="Button" toolTip="This is the button tool tip." />
  <mx:TextInput id="textInput" />
</mx:VBox>
```

Navigator components such as accordions and tab navigators have a different default behavior in this regard. Whereas most container children will trigger the parent container tool tip, the children of navigator components do not. The only triggers for the container tool tips are the navigator elements corresponding to the containers. For example, in a tab navigator the tabs will trigger the tool tips for the corresponding containers. The following example illustrates this behavior. The accordion has two elements, each a VBox container. Each VBox specifies a toolTip value. Each VBox instance contains one button. The button within the first VBox does not specify a toolTip value, whereas the second does. If you test this code, you'll see that the tool tips for the VBox containers are never triggered by the child buttons.

```
<mx:Accordion height="200" width="200">
  <mx:VBox toolTip="A">
    <mx:Button label="Button 1" />
  </mx:VBox>
```

```
    <mx:VBox toolTip="B">
      <mx:Button label="Button 2" toolTip="Button" />
    </mx:VBox>
  </mx:Accordion>
```

Adding Tool Tips Programmatically

Although in most cases you will likely add tool tips using the `toolTip` property as described in the preceding section, you can also add tool tips programmatically using the `mx.managers.ToolTipManager` class. Using the static `createToolTip()` method you can add new tool tips. You need to specify three parameters: the text to display in the tool tip, the *x* coordinate for the tool tip, and the *y* coordinate for the tool tip. The coordinates are relative to the application itself, which means that values of 0 and 0 will place the tool tip in the upper left of the application. The following code adds a new tool tip to the application at 100, 100:

```
ToolTipManager.createToolTip("Example programmatic tool tip", 100, 100);
```

Clearly, using the `toolTip` property is simpler to implement, and therefore, in most cases it is preferable to use the `toolTip` property instead of the `createToolTip()` method. However, there are a few good reasons to use the `createToolTip()` method:

- Flex will display only one tool tip at a time of the tool tips defined by the `toolTip` property of components. Therefore, if you want to display two or more tool tips simultaneously, you must define all of them or all except one of them using the `createToolTip()` method.
- The `createToolTip()` method returns a reference to the new `ToolTip` object, which allows you to programmatically control that object.

Tool tips are instances of the `mx.controls.ToolTip` class, which is a `UIComponent` subclass. That means you can programmatically control `ToolTip` objects in much the same way as you can other sorts of components. The `createToolTip()` method returns a reference to the new tool tip, though the return type for `createToolTip()` is the interface `mx.core.IToolTip` rather than the concrete type of `ToolTip`.

If you programmatically create a tool tip, you will also need to programmatically remove it. You can remove tool tips using the `ToolTipManager.destroyToolTip()` method, which requires that you pass it the tool tip you want to remove. Typically you'll call `destroyToolTip()` after the user moves the mouse outside of the UI element. You can call the `destroyToolTip()` method immediately after the mouse moves outside the element, or you can use a Timer object to add a slight delay.

Controlling Tool Tip Width and Line Formatting

By default, tool tips have a maximum width of 300 pixels, and the text automatically wraps at that width. You can see the default behavior with the following example:

```
<mx:Button id="button" label="Tool Tip" toolTip="Lorem ipsum dolor sit amet,
consectetuer adipiscing elit. Integer commodo lacus sed dui. Pellentesque
est nisi, semper sit amet, feugiat eu, pellentesque id, erat." />
```

This example creates a button that has a tool tip with the default maximum width so that the text automatically wraps to form three lines.

You can control the maximum width of the tool tip using the static `mx.controls.ToolTip.maxWidth` property. The default value is `300`, which accounts for the default width of 300 pixels. If you set the value of the property, it affects the width of all tool tips within the application that are displayed from that point forward, unless and until you assign a new value to the property. There is no API for controlling the maximum width of an individual tool tip when using the `toolTip` property to create the tool tip. If you'd like to control the width of an individual tool tip, you must create it using `ToolTipManager.createToolTip()`. The following example uses a button with a tool tip. Initially, the maximum width of the tool tip is set to the default. However, when the user clicks on the button, it sets the maximum width to 500. Mousing over the button again will display the tool tip text on just two lines.

```
<mx:Button id="button" label="Tool Tip" toolTip="Lorem ipsum dolor sit amet,
consectetuer adipiscing elit. Integer commodo lacus sed dui. Pellentesque
est nisi, semper sit amet, feugiat eu, pellentesque id, erat."
click="mx.controls.ToolTip.maxWidth = 500" />
```

Tool tips use automatic word wrap to add soft line breaks when the text reaches the maximum width. If you want to add a hard line break, you can do so by inserting a newline character (`\n`), carriage return (`\r`), or form feed character (`\f`) in the tool tip text when assigning the text using ActionScript. When using an MXML attribute, you should use the `
` XML entity, as in the following example:

```
<mx:Button id="button" label="Tool Tip" toolTip="Lorem ipsum dolor sit amet,
consectetuer adipiscing elit.&#13;Integer commodo lacus sed dui.&#13;Pellentesque
est nisi, semper sit amet, feugiat eu, pellentesque id, erat." />
```

Applying Styles to Tool Tips

You can customize the look of tool tips using styles. The Flex framework doesn't provide a convenient way in which to set the styles of individual tool tips created using the `toolTip` property. You must set the tool tip style globally for all instances if you are going for convenience. You can do so by changing the `ToolTip` style definition. The following illustrates how to change the style definition using a `Style` tag:

```
<mx:Style>
  ToolTip {
    fontFamily: "_typewriter";
    backgroundColor: #FFFFFF;
```

```
    }
</mx:Style>
```

You can use ActionScript to set the style using the `StyleManager.getStyleDeclaration()` method to retrieve the `ToolTip` declaration. You can then use `setStyle()` to change individual styles:

```
var toolTipDeclaration:CSSStyleDeclaration =
    StyleManager.getStyleDeclaration("ToolTip");
toolTipDeclaration.setStyle("fontFamily", "_typewriter");
```

If you want to use a specific font, and you want to ensure that the user will be able to view the tool tip with that specific font, you can embed the font. Embedding the font for tool tips works just as it would for any other text for which you use styles. The following example embeds a font called *Georgia*:

```
<mx:Style>
  @font-face {
    src: local("Georgia");
    fontFamily: GeorgiaEmbedded;
  }
  ToolTip {
    fontFamily: GeorgiaEmbedded;
    backgroundColor: #FFFFFF;
  }
</mx:Style>
```

Although setting tool tip styles globally is the more convenient way to style tool tips, it has the drawback of not allowing you to customize the appearance of individual tool tips. If you want to customize individual tool tips you must create the instances using the `ToolTipManager.createToolTip()` method as described in the previous section. You can then apply styles to the instances as you would other components, using the `setStyle()` method or the `styleName` property.

Customizing Tool Tip Settings

You can customize several global tool tip settings using the `mx.managers.ToolTipManager` class. Using the static `enabled` property you can enable and disable tool tips globally. This can be useful if, for example, you want to temporarily disable tool tips while the application is awaiting a response to a remote procedure call. The default value of the `enabled` property is `true`, which means that if you want tool tips enabled, you don't have to do anything. If you want to disable tool tips, you can set the value to `false`:

```
ToolTipManager.enabled = false;
```

Of course, you'll need to set the property to `true` again if you want to reenable tool tips:

```
ToolTipManager.enabled = true;
```

The `showDelay`, `hideDelay`, and `scrubDelay` static properties allow you to control the amount of delay before showing and hiding tool tips. The `showDelay` property controls the amount of time before a tool tip displays after a user moves the mouse over the object. The value is specified in milliseconds. The default value is 500, which means the tool tip displays half a second after the user moves the mouse over the object. The following sets the delay to one second:

```
ToolTipManager.showDelay = 1000;
```

Tool tips disappear after the user moves the mouse off an object. However, they can also disappear after a delay even while the mouse is still over the object. The `hideDelay` property determines the number of milliseconds before the tool tip disappears. The default value is 10000, which means the tool tip disappears after 10 seconds. Setting the value to 0 is the same as telling the tool tips to disappear as soon as they appear, so they are never shown. You can use a value of `Infinity` (a global constant) if you want the tool tips to remain visible as long as the mouse is over the object:

```
ToolTipManager.hideDelay = Infinity;
```

The `scrubDelay` property allows you to specify the amount of allowable delay between mousing out of one object and mousing over another object to omit the show delay on the second object. This is especially important if there is a long show delay. For example, if you have a line of buttons, each with tool tips, you may want the user to be able to scroll across the buttons quickly and read the tool tips. Without the scrub delay setting, the user would have to pause over each button for the show delay duration before he could see the tool tip. The scrub delay setting says that if the amount of time between mousing out of one object and mousing over a second object is less than a specified number of milliseconds, the application should display the tool tip for the second object immediately. The default value for `scrubDelay` is 100. The greater the value for `scrubDelay`, the more likely it is that the user will have to delay before showing the tool tip on objects after mousing over them in succession.

The `ToolTipManager` class also allows you to use a custom class as a tool tip. This is a very rare use case, and for that reason we won't discuss it in detail. However, you can assign a `DisplayObject` class reference to the static `toolTipClass` property to use that class as the tool tip blueprint:

```
ToolTipManager.toolTipClass = CustomClass;
```

If you want to be able to use the custom class in the same way as a standard tool tip (e.g., set the tool tip text), the custom class must also implement `mx.core.IToolTip`. Because `IToolTip` extends `IUIComponent`, the most practical way to implement `IToolTip` is to first extend `mx.core.UIComponent` and then to implement just the specific interface defined by `IToolTip`.

Applying Effects

You can apply effects such as blurs, motion, and so on, to the showing and hiding of tool tips. You can use any effect that you can use with any Flex component. As with almost all other tool tip settings, using the most convenient and practical approach the effect settings apply globally to all tool tips. You can set the effect that gets applied when showing the tool tips by way of the `ToolTipManager.showEffect` property, and you can set the effect that gets applied when hiding the tool tips by way of the `ToolTipManager.hideEffect` property. Example 10-1 illustrates how this works, and it demonstrates that you can use not only single effects, but also composite effects.

Example 10-1. Applying composite effects

```
<?xml version="1.0" encoding="utf-8"?>
<mx:Application xmlns:mx="http://www.adobe.com/2006/mxml"
 initialize="initializeHandler(event)">

  <mx:Style>
  @font-face {
    src: local("Georgia");
    fontFamily: GeorgiaEmbedded;
  }
  ToolTip {
    fontSize: 16;
    fontFamily: GeorgiaEmbedded;
    backgroundColor: #FFFFFF;
  }
  </mx:Style>

  <mx:Script>
  <![CDATA[

    import mx.managers.ToolTipManager;

    private function initializeHandler(event:Event):void {
      ToolTipManager.showEffect = toolTipShowEffect;
      ToolTipManager.hideEffect = toolTipHideEffect;
    }

  ]]>
  </mx:Script>

  <mx:Parallel id="toolTipShowEffect">
    <mx:Fade alphaFrom="0" alphaTo="1" duration="1000" />
    <mx:Blur blurXFrom="10" blurYFrom="10" blurXTo="0"
             blurYTo="0" duration="1000" />
  </mx:Parallel>

  <mx:Parallel id="toolTipHideEffect">
    <mx:Fade alphaFrom="1" alphaTo="0" duration="1000" />
    <mx:Blur blurXFrom="0" blurYFrom="0" blurXTo="10"
             blurYTo="10" duration="1000" />
  </mx:Parallel>

  <mx:Button id="button" label="Tool Tip" toolTip="Tool Tip Effect Example" />

</mx:Application>
```

You'll notice that Example 10-1 embeds the font for the tool tips. This is because the font must be embedded to properly animate the alpha of the text. In this particular example, the blur portion of the effect causes the tool tips to be rendered as bitmap surfaces, lessening the need to embed the font. However, even with the bitmap surfaces enabled, the text can still quickly flash before fading in unless the font is embedded.

Although applying effects to tool tips globally is the most convenient approach, it is not the only way to apply effects. If you want to apply an effect to an individual tool tip, then you must construct the individual tool tip using the `ToolTipManager.createToolTip()` and apply the effect to the individual tool tip using the `setStyle()` method.

Pop Ups

The Flex framework has built-in support for pop-up windows and alerts. Pop ups can be useful for many reasons, including notifying the user of messages or news and displaying simple forms such as login forms or mailing-list sign-up forms. Unlike HTML pop ups, Flex pop ups do not open new browser windows. Flex application pop ups appear within the same Flash Player instance. This means that Flex application pop ups are never subject to the same restrictions as some types of HTML pop ups.

You can use two basic types of pop ups in Flex applications: alerts and custom pop-up windows. Alerts are quite similar to the pop ups that appear in HTML applications when using the JavaScript `alert()` function. They display text messages to the user in a modal window, and prompt the user to click a button. However, as we'll see in the next section, Flex alerts are more sophisticated than HTML alerts. Custom pop ups allow you to create more complex pop-up content. For example, using a custom pop up you can display a mailing list email form.

Using Alerts

Flex alerts are instances of the `mx.controls.Alert` component. Unlike many of the other Flex components, you cannot create an alert using MXML tags. You must use the static `show()` method of the `Alert` class. The `show()` method requires at least one parameter: a string specifying the message to display. The `show()` method returns a reference to the new `Alert` instance, which you can use to manipulate the `Alert` instance if needed. Example 10-2 displays an alert with a message and an OK button (the default behavior) when the user clicks a button.

Example 10-2. Using alerts

```
<?xml version="1.0" encoding="utf-8"?>
<mx:Application xmlns:mx="http://www.adobe.com/2006/mxml">

  <mx:Script>
  <![CDATA[

    import mx.controls.Alert;
```

```
    private function showAlert(event:Event):void {
      var alert:Alert = Alert.show("You have clicked a button to
display an alert.");
    }

  ]]>
  </mx:Script>

  <mx:Button id="button" label="Show Alert" click="showAlert(event)" />

</mx:Application>
```

The `show()` method also allows you to specify a value to display in a title bar, as in the following example:

```
var alert:Alert = Alert.show("You have clicked a button to display an alert.",
                             "Important Message");
```

As already noted, the default behavior for an alert is to display an OK button. However, alerts are capable of displaying from one to four buttons, including the following: OK, Cancel, Yes, and No. You can control which of the buttons is displayed by specifying a third parameter value using the `OK`, `CANCEL`, `YES`, and `NO` constants of the `Alert` class. The following displays a Cancel button rather than the default OK button:

```
var alert:Alert = Alert.show("You have clicked a button to display an alert.",
                             "Important Message",
                             Alert.CANCEL);
```

If you want to display several buttons, you can combine the constants using the bitwise `OR` operator (`|`). The following example displays both an OK and a Cancel button:

```
var alert:Alert = Alert.show("You have clicked a button to display an alert.",
                             "Important Message",
                             Alert.OK | Alert.CANCEL);
```

The next optional parameter allows you to specify the parent container of the alert. This determines what parts of the application are affected by the alert's modality, and it affects where the alert is centered. By default, the application container is used. In most cases, the application container is the appropriate parent, and you generally need to set the value only when passing additional parameters.

As with all modal windows in Flex, alerts display a modal overlay above the rest of the application. You can customize the modal overlay styles using the following global styles: `modalTransparencyBlur`, `modalTransparency`, `modalTransparencyColor`, and `modalTransparencyDuration`.

You may want to add listeners for click events dispatched by the alert. By default, alerts close when the user clicks a button. However, your application may still want to receive a notification that the user clicked a button. Furthermore, when an alert has several buttons, it is often particularly important to know which button the user clicked. You can add a listener to an alert by passing a listener function reference to the `show()` method as the fifth parameter. The listener will receive a parameter of type `mx.events.CloseEvent`. The detail property of that event object will have the value of the `Alert` constant corresponding to the button that the user clicked. Example 10-3 uses a listener to display which button the user clicked.

Example 10-3. Customizing alerts

```
<?xml version="1.0" encoding="utf-8"?>
<mx:Application xmlns:mx="http://www.adobe.com/2006/mxml">

  <mx:Script>
  <![CDATA[

    import mx.controls.Alert;
    import mx.events.CloseEvent;

    private function showAlert(event:Event):void {
      var alert:Alert = Alert.show("You have clicked a button to display
an alert.",
                                   "Important Message",
                                   Alert.OK | Alert.CANCEL,
                                   this,
                                   alertClickHandler);
    }

    private function alertClickHandler(event:CloseEvent):void {
      var buttonType:String;
      if(event.detail == Alert.OK) {
        buttonType = "OK";
      }
      else {
        buttonType = "Cancel";
      }
      textInput.text = buttonType;
    }

  ]]>
  </mx:Script>

  <mx:VBox>
    <mx:Button id="button" label="Show Alert" click="showAlert(event)" />
    <mx:TextInput id="textInput" />
  </mx:VBox>
</mx:Application>
```

You can use embedded images as icons within alerts as well. Alert icons always appear to the left of the message text. You can specify any valid embedded image resource (see Chapter 11 for information regarding embedding images) as the sixth parameter, as in the example that follows.

```
<?xml version="1.0" encoding="utf-8"?>
<mx:Application xmlns:mx="http://www.adobe.com/2006/mxml">

  <mx:Script>
  <![CDATA[

    import mx.controls.Alert;

    [Embed(source="icon.png")]
    private var sampleIcon:Class;

    private function showAlert(event:Event):void {
      var alert:Alert = Alert.show("You have clicked a button
to display an alert.",
                                   "Important Message",
                                   Alert.OK,
                                   this,
                                   null,
                                   sampleIcon);
    }

  ]]>
  </mx:Script>

  <mx:Button id="button" label="Show Alert" click="showAlert(event)" />

</mx:Application>
```

Creating a Pop-Up Window

Custom pop ups are different from alerts in a few important ways:

- Custom pop ups allow you to create many distinct types of content, from images to forms to audio and video players.
- Custom pop ups don't have built-in buttons and button event handling.
- Custom pop ups can be modal or non-modal.

You can create custom pop ups using the static method `mx.managers.PopUpManager.createPopUp()`. The `createPopUp()` method requires at least two parameters: the parent container for the pop up and the class from which to create the new pop up. The method returns a reference to the new pop-up instance. The return type for `createPopUp()` is `mx.core.IFlexDisplayObject`, which means in almost all cases you'll want to cast the return value to the correct type.

You can theoretically make a new pop up based on any sort of visual component, but most frequently you'll use a container (such as `mx.containers.TitleWindow` as in the following example) as the class for the new pop up. Example 10-4 uses a button to display a new window with a text area as a pop up.

Example 10-4. Using a pop-up window

```
<?xml version="1.0" encoding="utf-8"?>
<mx:Application xmlns:mx="http://www.adobe.com/2006/mxml">

  <mx:Script>
  <![CDATA[

    import mx.managers.PopUpManager
    import mx.containers.TitleWindow;
    import mx.controls.TextArea;

    private var _window:TitleWindow;

    private function showWindow(event:MouseEvent):void {
      var textArea:TextArea = new TextArea();
      textArea.text = "Lorem ipsum dolor sit amet, consectetuer adipiscing elit.
Sed eget massa iaculis metus interdum accumsan. Mauris pellentesque pulvinar
orci. Etiam suscipit tellus a nisl. Mauris elit risus, blandit non, varius vitae,
laoreet ac, ipsum. Fusce erat libero, imperdiet id, suscipit lacinia, nonummy
quis, metus. Ut sit amet est quis velit ullamcorper congue.Etiam in nunc id
mauris porta volutpat. Sed vitae metus. Integer lacinia. Maecenas a tortor.
Fusce mauris arcu, ullamcorper ac, sagittis id, condimentum in, dolor.
Praesent eros tortor, tincidunt in, blandit a, luctus quis, est.";
      textArea.height = 200;
      _window = TitleWindow(PopUpManager.createPopUp(this, TitleWindow));
      _window.addChild(textArea);
    }

  ]]>
  </mx:Script>

  <mx:Button id="button" label="Show Window" click="showWindow(event)" />

</mx:Application>
```

Removing a Pop-Up Window

You can remove a pop-up window using the `PopUpManager.removePopUp()` method. The method requires one parameter—the pop up you want to remove:

```
PopUpManager.removePopUp(_window);
```

Windows (`TitleWindow` instances) don't display close buttons by default. Nor do they handle close events automatically even when the close button is displayed. You can enable the close button by setting the `displayCloseButton` property to `true` for the window, and you can add a close event listener to handle the close button event, as shown in Example 10-5.

Example 10-5. Removing pop-up windows

```
<?xml version="1.0" encoding="utf-8"?>
<mx:Application xmlns:mx="http://www.adobe.com/2006/mxml">
```

```
  <mx:Script>
  <![CDATA[

    import mx.managers.PopUpManager
    import mx.containers.TitleWindow;
    import mx.controls.TextArea;
    import mx.events.CloseEvent;

    private var _window:TitleWindow;

    private function showWindow(event:Event):void {
      var textArea:TextArea = new TextArea();
      textArea.text = "Lorem ipsum dolor sit amet, consectetuer adipiscing elit.
Sed eget massa iaculis metus interdum accumsan. Mauris pellentesque pulvinar
orci. Etiam suscipit tellus a nisl. Mauris elit risus, blandit non, varius
vitae, laoreet ac, ipsum. Fusce erat libero, imperdiet id, suscipit lacinia,
nonummy quis, metus. Ut sit amet est quis velit ullamcorper congue.
Etiam in nunc id mauris porta volutpat. Sed vitae metus. Integer lacinia.
Maecenas a tortor. Fusce mauris arcu, ullamcorper ac, sagittis id,
condimentum in, dolor. Praesent eros tortor, tincidunt in, blandit a,
luctus quis, est.";
      textArea.height = 200;
      _window = TitleWindow(PopUpManager.createPopUp(this, TitleWindow));
      _window.addChild(textArea);
      _window.showCloseButton = true;
      _window.addEventListener(CloseEvent.CLOSE, closeHandler);
    }

    private function closeHandler(event:CloseEvent):void {
      PopUpManager.removePopUp(_window);
    }

  ]]>
  </mx:Script>

  <mx:Button id="button" label="Show Window" click="showWindow(event)" />

</mx:Application>
```

Custom Pop-Up Component Types

Although the preceding examples are valid use cases for a pop up, more often than not custom pop ups use custom components written in ActionScript or MXML. (See Chapter 9, and Chapter 19 for more information regarding how to create custom components.) For example, the following MXML component is a `TitleWindow` subclass with a text area that automatically handles the close event:

```
<?xml version="1.0" encoding="utf-8"?>
<mx:TitleWindow xmlns:mx="http://www.adobe.com/2006/mxml" showCloseButton="true"
close="closeWindow(event)">
  <mx:Script>
  <![CDATA[

    import mx.managers.PopUpManager;
```

```
        import mx.events.CloseEvent;

        private function closeWindow(event:CloseEvent):void {
          PopUpManager.removePopUp(this);
        }

      ]]>
      </mx:Script>
      <mx:TextArea height="200" width="200" text="Lorem ipsum dolor sit amet,
    consectetuer adipiscing elit. Sed eget massa iaculis metus interdum accumsan.
    Mauris pellentesque pulvinar orci. Etiam suscipit tellus a nisl.
    Mauris elit risus, blandit non, varius vitae, laoreet ac, ipsum. Fusce erat
    libero, imperdiet id, suscipit lacinia, nonummy quis, metus. Ut sit amet
    est quis velit ullamcorper congue. Etiam in nunc id mauris porta volutpat.
    Sed vitae metus. Integer lacinia. Maecenas a tortor. Fusce mauris arcu,
    ullamcorper ac, sagittis id, condimentum in, dolor. Praesent eros
    tortor, tincidunt in, blandit a, luctus quis, est." />
    </mx:TitleWindow>
```

You can then create pop ups based on this component using the following code. Assume that the preceding component is saved in a file called *TextAreaWindow.mxml*.

```
<?xml version="1.0" encoding="utf-8"?>
<mx:Application xmlns:mx="http://www.adobe.com/2006/mxml">

  <mx:Script>
  <![CDATA[

    import mx.managers.PopUpManager;

    private function showWindow(event:Event):void {
      PopUpManager.createPopUp(this, TextAreaWindow);
    }

  ]]>
  </mx:Script>

  <mx:Button id="button" label="Show Window" click="showWindow(event)" />

</mx:Application>
```

Adding Modality

Pop-up windows are not modal by default. However, you can easily make a pop up modal by passing a third parameter to the `createPopUp()` method. The default value is `false`, meaning the pop up should not be modal. If you specify a value of `true`, the new pop up will be modal, meaning nothing else within the parent container can receive focus as long as the pop up is visible.

```
PopUpManager.createPopUp(this, TextAreaWindow, true);
```

Cursor Management

By default, the Flex application cursor is an arrow, except when a selectable/editable text element has focus, at which point the cursor becomes a text selection cursor. Using the `mx.managers.CursorManager` class you can control the cursor that gets displayed in the application. This can be useful for giving the user a visual queue of the status of the application.

The `CursorManager` class has a handful of static methods that allow you to control the cursor by doing the following: showing and removing busy cursors and showing and removing custom cursors.

The Flex framework has just one built-in cursor apart from the default system cursors. The one built-in cursor is a busy cursor that displays a small clock face with a spinning hand to let the user know that something is being processed. The `CursorManager` class has two static methods for displaying and removing the busy cursor: `setBusyCursor()` and `removeBusyCursor()`. The following demonstrates a very simple example that sets and removes the busy cursor when the user clicks two buttons:

```
<?xml version="1.0" encoding="utf-8"?>
<mx:Application xmlns:mx="http://www.adobe.com/2006/mxml">

  <mx:Script>
  <![CDATA[

    import mx.managers.CursorManager;

  ]]>
  </mx:Script>

  <mx:VBox>
    <mx:Button label="Show Busy Cursor" click="CursorManager.setBusyCursor()" />
    <mx:Button label="Hide Busy Cursor" click="CursorManager.removeBusyCursor()"
/>
  </mx:VBox>

</mx:Application>
```

Typically, you would use the busy cursor for asynchronous operations such as remote procedure calls. You can use the `setBusyCursor()` method just prior to starting such an operation, and you can call `removeBusyCursor()` when the operation completes. To simplify things, several of the components have a built-in feature that automatically does this. The `SWFLoader`, `WebService`, `HttpService`, and `RemoteObject` components all allow you to set a `showBusyCursor` property. When the `showBusyCursor` property is set to `true` for any of these components, the component automatically displays the busy cursor when initiating the request, and it hides the busy cursor when the response is complete.

For customized cursors you can use any standard embedded graphic or SWF as a cursor using the `CursorManager.setCursor()` method. You can remove custom cursors using the `removeCursor()` method.

The `setCursor()` method requires at least one parameter: the `Class` object representing the embedded graphic. Example 10-6 uses a PNG as the cursor.

Example 10-6. Customizing the cursor

```
<?xml version="1.0" encoding="utf-8"?>
<mx:Application xmlns:mx="http://www.adobe.com/2006/mxml"
                initialize="initializeHandler(event)">

  <mx:Script>
  <![CDATA[

    import mx.managers.CursorManager;

    [Embed(source="cursor.png")]
    private var customCursor:Class;

    private function initializeHandler(event:Event):void {
      CursorManager.setCursor(customCursor);
    }

  ]]>
  </mx:Script>

</mx:Application>
```

The `setCursor()` method returns an integer ID, which you need in order to remove the cursor. You can pass the ID to the `removeCursor()` method, as the following example illustrates:

```
<?xml version="1.0" encoding="utf-8"?>
<mx:Application xmlns:mx="http://www.adobe.com/2006/mxml"
                initialize="initializeHandler(event)">

  <mx:Script>
  <![CDATA[

    import mx.managers.CursorManager;

    [Embed(source="cursor.png")]
    private var customCursor:Class;

    private var cursorId:int;

    private function initializeHandler(event:Event):void {
      cursorId = CursorManager.setCursor(customCursor);
    }

  ]]>
  </mx:Script>
```

```
    <mx:Button label="Reset Cursor" click="CursorManager.removeCursor(cursorId)" />

</mx:Application>
```

In this example, the custom cursor is applied when the application initializes using an initialize event handler. When the user clicks the button, it calls the `removeCursor()` method to remove the cursor. Note that the cursor ID returned by `setCursor()` is saved in a property so that it is accessible throughout the document.

Drag-and-Drop

Drag-and-drop is one of the many features that set Flex applications apart from other types of applications. As you'll see in the next few sections, it is extremely simple to enable drag-and-drop functionality for some standard components, and with a little additional work you can enable drag-and-drop functionality to any type of component.

Using Built-In Drag-and-Drop Features

The simplest way to implement drag-and-drop functionality is to use the built-in features of many of the components, including `List`, `Tree`, `DataGrid`, `Menu`, `HorizontalList`, `PrintDataGrid`, and `TileList`. Each of these components enables drag-and-drop in the same way. They each have a `dragEnabled` property and a `dropEnabled` property. The two properties are `false` by default. When you set the `dragEnabled` property to `true` for a component, the user can click and drag items. Of course, in most cases enabling a component so that a user can click and drag an item is not very useful until the user can also drop the item somewhere in the application. Typically, this is accomplished by setting the `dropEnabled` property of another component to `true`. When the `dropEnabled` property is set to `true` for a component, the user can drop an item on the component that he dragged from another component. This causes the data from that item to be added to the drop target component. Example 10-7 illustrates both a `dragEnabled` and a `dropEnabled` component working in conjunction. The first data grid contains data about the user's music collection. The user can drag items from the music collection to the second data grid to create a playlist.

Example 10-7. A simple drag-and-drop application

```
<?xml version="1.0"?>
<mx:Application xmlns:mx="http://www.adobe.com/2006/mxml">
  <mx:HBox width="100%">
    <mx:VBox height="100%">
      <mx:Label text="My Music"/>
      <mx:DataGrid dragEnabled="true">
        <mx:columns>
          <mx:DataGridColumn headerText="Song Title" dataField="title"/>
          <mx:DataGridColumn headerText="Artist" dataField="artist"/>
        </mx:columns>
        <mx:dataProvider>
```

```
        <mx:ArrayCollection>
          <mx:Object songId="0" title="Astronaut" artist="David Byrne" />
          <mx:Object songId="1" title="Rio" artist="Duran Duran" />
          <mx:Object songId="2" title="Enjoy the Silence" artist="Depeche
          Mode" />
          <mx:Object songId="3" title="Mesopotamia" artist="B-52s" />
        </mx:ArrayCollection>
      </mx:dataProvider>
    </mx:DataGrid>
  </mx:VBox>
  <mx:VBox height="100%">
    <mx:Label text="Playlist"/>
    <mx:DataGrid dropEnabled="true">
      <mx:columns>
        <mx:DataGridColumn headerText="Song Title" dataField="title"/>
        <mx:DataGridColumn headerText="Artist" dataField="artist"/>
      </mx:columns>
    </mx:DataGrid>
  </mx:VBox>
</mx:HBox>

</mx:Application>
```

When you test this you'll see two data grids side by side. You can click and drag an element in the My Music data grid, and you'll see that it creates a copy of that element that moves with the mouse. A small red circle with a white *X* appears next to the mouse cursor until the mouse is over a drop-enabled component, at which point the red circle becomes a green circle with a white +. If you drop the item anywhere in the application that is not drop-enabled, no further action occurs. However, if you drop the item on a drop-enabled component, the item is added to the drop target at the location where you dropped the object.

The default behavior for drag-enabled components is to allow the user to copy elements from the component. However, you can also allow the user to move elements rather than copy them by setting the `dragMoveEnabled` property to `true`. By itself, the `dragMoveEnabled` property will not have any effect. You must also ensure that `dragEnabled` is set to `true` for the component. Example 10-8 uses `dragMoveEnabled` to create a simple application that allows the user to move an email message from his inbox to the trash.

Example 10-8. A drag-and-drop example that moves items

```
<?xml version="1.0"?>
<mx:Application xmlns:mx="http://www.adobe.com/2006/mxml">
  <mx:HBox width="100%">
    <mx:VBox height="100%">
      <mx:Label text="Inbox"/>
      <mx:DataGrid dragEnabled="true" dragMoveEnabled="true">
        <mx:columns>
          <mx:DataGridColumn headerText="From" dataField="from"/>
          <mx:DataGridColumn headerText="To" dataField="to"/>
          <mx:DataGridColumn headerText="Subject" dataField="subject"/>
```

```
            <mx:DataGridColumn headerText="Date" dataField="date"/>
        </mx:columns>
        <mx:dataProvider>
          <mx:ArrayCollection>
            <mx:Object emailId="0" from="a@a.com" to="joey@person13.com"
                       subject="Important New Message" date="10/1/2010" />
            <mx:Object emailId="1" from="b@b.com" to="joey@person13.com"
                       subject="All Items On Sale" date="10/1/2010" />
            <mx:Object emailId="2" from="c@c.com" to="joey@person13.com"
                       subject="Amazing New Stock" date="10/1/2010" />
            <mx:Object emailId="3" from="d@d.com" to="joey@person13.com"
                       subject="Blatant Chain Letter" date="10/1/2010" />
          </mx:ArrayCollection>
        </mx:dataProvider>
      </mx:DataGrid>
    </mx:VBox>
    <mx:VBox height="100%">
      <mx:Label text="Trash"/>
      <mx:DataGrid dropEnabled="true">
        <mx:columns>
          <mx:DataGridColumn headerText="From" dataField="from"/>
          <mx:DataGridColumn headerText="To" dataField="to"/>
          <mx:DataGridColumn headerText="Subject" dataField="subject"/>
          <mx:DataGridColumn headerText="Date" dataField="date"/>
        </mx:columns>
      </mx:DataGrid>
    </mx:VBox>
  </mx:HBox>

</mx:Application>
```

In this example, you can move items only one way: from the inbox to the trash. In a real email application, you'd probably want to allow users to move messages back to the inbox from the trash if they wanted. In such a case, you can simply set `dragEnabled` and `dropEnabled` to `true` for both components.

When you set `dragMoveEnabled` to `true` for a component, it makes moving the default behavior. However, if the user holds down the Ctrl key while dragging and dropping, the item will be copied rather than moved. In some cases, that is acceptable behavior. In other cases, you want to ensure that the items always are moved rather than copied. You cannot make such a change via MXML. As we'll see in the next section, you can use ActionScript and event listeners to handle that behavior.

Understanding Drag-and-Drop Events

When using drag-and-drop functionality, the framework utilizes a handful of events behind the scenes. Understanding those events can be very helpful when you want to modify the default behavior or write completely customized drag-and-drop elements.

Table 10-1 lists all the events, the targets of the events, and what those events mean.

Table 10-1. Drag-and-drop events

Event	Target	Description
`mouseDown`	Drag initiator	This is usually the event that triggers the start of a drag-and-drop operation.
`mouseMove`	Drag initiator	In some cases, the drag-and-drop operation does not occur until a `mouseMove` event.
`dragEnter`	Drop target	The mouse has entered the drop target while still dragging an object.
`dragMove`	Drop target	The mouse is moving within the drop target. This is analogous to a `mouseMove` event, except that it is specific to the drop target while still dragging an object.
`dragExit`	Drop target	The mouse has moved outside the drop target while still dragging the object.
`dragDrop`	Drop target	The user has dropped an object on the target.
`dragComplete`	Drag initiator	This occurs anytime the user drops the object, whether over a drop target or not. You can use the `dragComplete` event to clean up whatever is necessary for the drag initiator.

The `mouseDown` and `mouseMove` events are standard Flash Player events of type `flash.events.MouseEvent`. The rest of the events are part of the Flex framework, and they are of type `mx.events.DragEvent`. `DragEvent` objects have a `dragInitiator` property, which references the component that originated the drag-and-drop behavior. They also have a `dragSource` property which is of type `mx.core.DragSource`, and it contains the data that was copied from the initiator.

`DragSource` objects have a `dataForFormat()` method, which requires a string parameter and returns the data that was stored for the format specified by the string parameter. We'll look at `DragSource` formats further in the next section. For now, all you need to know is that list-based drag initiators always create `DragSource` objects with one format called *items*, and the data returned for that format is an array of all the elements from the data provider of the drag initiator corresponding to the selected items. For example, if the user drags one element from a data grid, the `DragSource` object will contain an array with just one element.

`DragSource` objects also have an `action` property, which reports a value of `copy`, `move`, or `none`. You can use the `mx.managers.DragManager COPY`, `MOVE`, and `NONE` constants for comparison tests. The `action` property tells you what the expected action is for the drag-and-drop operation. This value is automatically set when using the built-in drag-and-drop behavior of list-based components.

In the preceding section, you saw how there's no simple MXML-based way to ensure that the user cannot copy elements rather than move them. Using events and ActionScript you can put such safeguards into place, as illustrated in Example 10-9.

Example 10-9. Using ActionScript for drag-and-drop behavior

```
<?xml version="1.0"?>
<mx:Application xmlns:mx="http://www.adobe.com/2006/mxml">
  <mx:Script>
    <![CDATA[
      import mx.collections.ArrayCollection;
      import mx.controls.DataGrid;
```

```
      import mx.events.DragEvent;
      import mx.managers.DragManager;

      private function dragCompleteHandler(event:DragEvent):void {
        if(event.action != DragManager.NONE) {
          var grid:DataGrid = event.dragInitiator as DataGrid;
          var data:ArrayCollection = grid.dataProvider as ArrayCollection;
          var item:Object = event.dragSource.dataForFormat("items")[0];
          data.removeItemAt(data.getItemIndex(item));
        }
      }

    ]]>
  </mx:Script>
  <mx:HBox width="100%">
    <mx:VBox height="100%">
      <mx:Label text="Inbox"/>
      <mx:DataGrid dropEnabled="true" dragEnabled="true"
 dragComplete="dragCompleteHandler(event)">
        <mx:columns>
          <mx:DataGridColumn headerText="From" dataField="from"/>
          <mx:DataGridColumn headerText="To" dataField="to"/>
          <mx:DataGridColumn headerText="Subject" dataField="subject"/>
          <mx:DataGridColumn headerText="Date" dataField="date"/>
        </mx:columns>
        <mx:dataProvider>
          <mx:ArrayCollection>
            <mx:Object emailId="0" from="a@a.com" to="joey@person13.com"
subject="Important New Message" date="10/1/2010" />
            <mx:Object emailId="1" from="b@b.com" to="joey@person13.com"
subject="All Items On Sale" date="10/1/2010" />
            <mx:Object emailId="2" from="c@c.com" to="joey@person13.com"
subject="Amazing New Stock" date="10/1/2010" />
            <mx:Object emailId="3" from="d@d.com" to="joey@person13.com"
subject="Blatant Chain Letter" date="10/1/2010" />
          </mx:ArrayCollection>
        </mx:dataProvider>
      </mx:DataGrid>
    </mx:VBox>
    <mx:VBox height="100%">
      <mx:Label text="Trash"/>
      <mx:DataGrid dropEnabled="true" dragEnabled="true" dragComplete=
"dragCompleteHandler(event)">
        <mx:columns>
          <mx:DataGridColumn headerText="From" dataField="from"/>
          <mx:DataGridColumn headerText="To" dataField="to"/>
          <mx:DataGridColumn headerText="Subject" dataField="subject"/>
          <mx:DataGridColumn headerText="Date" dataField="date"/>
        </mx:columns>
      </mx:DataGrid>
    </mx:VBox>
  </mx:HBox>

</mx:Application>
```

You'll notice that in this example, both data grids have dropEnabled and dragEnabled set to true. This in and of itself allows the user to copy contents from one data grid to the other. However, as we saw in Example 10-8, this does not ensure the type of behavior we require in this case. To achieve the move-only behavior each data grid also listens for dragComplete events. The dragCompleteHandler() method handles the events by either dismissing the event if the event action is set to none, or deleting the element from the drag initiator's data provider.

Custom Drag-and-Drop Operations

The built-in drag-and-drop functionality will work for many use cases. However, there are also many use cases in which you will want to employ drag-and-drop functionality not supported by the standard, built-in features of the handful of drag-and-drop-enabled components. For these cases, you can create custom drag-and-drop elements.

You can create custom drag-and-drop elements using the events discussed in the preceding section in conjunction with mx.managers.DragManager. The DragManager class has several static methods you can use to handle drag-and-drop functionality.

The doDrag() method allows you to start a drag-and-drop operation. The doDrag() method requires that you specify the following parameters: the drag initiator, a DragSource object specifying the data to copy from the initiator, and the mouse event used to start the drag operation. In addition, in most cases you'll need to pass it a reference to an object to use as the drag proxy image (the object that actually drags).

Before we can look at an example using doDrag(), we first have to discuss the details of working with DragSource. The DragSource object you pass to doDrag() is what is passed along to event handlers for drag events. This object contains data that you can use when copying, moving, or comparing data. That means you should generally store whatever data you want to pass along to the drag event handlers in the DragSource object. DragSource objects allow you to save many groups of data, each with a unique key (a string value), which is called a *format*. You can use the addData() method to add data to a DragSource object. The first parameter is the data to store, and the second parameter is the format, which is an arbitrary string:

```
var dragSource:DragSource = new DragSource();
dragSource.addData(initiator.dataProvider.getItemAt(index), "item");
```

The DragManager class also dictates the behavior of the drag proxy image when the user moves it over the drop target and when the user drops the object. Normally, the proxy indicates that it cannot be dropped successfully by displaying a small red circle with a white *X*. You can remove that icon by calling DragManager.acceptDragDrop() and passing it a reference to the drop target for which the user can drop the object. Typically, you call this method in response to a dragEnter event.

Example 10-10 illustrates how to create custom drag-and-drop elements. This simple application uses a column of colored canvases and a grid of canvases with the same colors. The canvases from the column are draggable. When the user drops one of the canvases over the canvas with the same color in the grid, the canvas is removed from the column and the canvas in the grid is lowered in opacity.

Example 10-10. A customized drag-and-drop application

```
<?xml version="1.0"?>
<mx:Application xmlns:mx="http://www.adobe.com/2006/mxml">
  <mx:Script>
    <![CDATA[
      import mx.core.DragSource;
      import mx.containers.Canvas;
      import mx.events.DragEvent;
      import mx.managers.DragManager;

      private function beginDragAndDrop(event:MouseEvent):void {
        var canvas:Canvas = event.currentTarget as Canvas;
        var dragSource:DragSource = new DragSource();
        var color:uint = canvas.getStyle("backgroundColor");

        // Add the color value to the drag source using the backgroundColor key
        dragSource.addData(color, "backgroundColor");

        // Create the (temporary) canvas that will be dragged
        var proxy:Canvas = new Canvas();
        proxy.width = 50;
        proxy.height = 50;
        proxy.setStyle("backgroundColor", color);

        DragManager.doDrag(canvas, dragSource, event, proxy);
      }

      private function dragEnterHandler(event:DragEvent):void {
        var target:Canvas = event.currentTarget as Canvas;
        var initiator:Canvas = event.dragInitiator as Canvas;

        // If the target and the initiator have the same color
        // then accept the drag drop operation
        if(matches(target, initiator)) {
          DragManager.acceptDragDrop(target);
        }
      }

      private function dragDropHandler(event:DragEvent):void {
        var target:Canvas = event.currentTarget as Canvas;
        var initiator:Canvas = event.dragInitiator as Canvas;

        // If the target and initiator have the same color then
        // remove the initiator and lower the alpha of the target
        if(matches(target, initiator)) {
          vbox.removeChild(initiator);
          target.alpha = .25;
        }
      }
```

```
        private function matches(a:Canvas, b:Canvas):Boolean {
          return a.getStyle("backgroundColor") == b.getStyle("backgroundColor");
        }

      ]]>
    </mx:Script>
    <mx:HBox width="100%">
      <mx:VBox id="vbox" height="100%">
        <mx:Canvas width="50" height="50" backgroundColor="#00ff80"
mouseDown="beginDragAndDrop(event)" />
        <mx:Canvas width="50" height="50" backgroundColor="#ff8040"
mouseDown="beginDragAndDrop(event)" />
        <mx:Canvas width="50" height="50" backgroundColor="#80ffff"
mouseDown="beginDragAndDrop(event)" />
        <mx:Canvas width="50" height="50" backgroundColor="#ffff80"
mouseDown="beginDragAndDrop(event)" />
      </mx:VBox>
      <mx:VRule height="213"/>
      <mx:Grid>
        <mx:GridRow width="100%" height="100%">
          <mx:GridItem width="100%" height="100%">
            <mx:Canvas width="50" height="50" backgroundColor="#00ff80"
dragEnter="dragEnterHandler(event)" dragDrop="dragDropHandler(event)" />
          </mx:GridItem>
          <mx:GridItem width="100%" height="100%">
            <mx:Canvas width="50" height="50" backgroundColor="#ff8040"
dragEnter="dragEnterHandler(event)" dragDrop="dragDropHandler(event)" />
          </mx:GridItem>
        </mx:GridRow>
        <mx:GridRow width="100%" height="100%">
          <mx:GridItem width="100%" height="100%">
            <mx:Canvas width="50" height="50" backgroundColor="#80ffff"
dragEnter="dragEnterHandler(event)" dragDrop="dragDropHandler(event)" />
          </mx:GridItem>
          <mx:GridItem width="100%" height="100%">
            <mx:Canvas width="50" height="50" backgroundColor="#ffff80"
dragEnter="dragEnterHandler(event)" dragDrop="dragDropHandler(event)" />
          </mx:GridItem>
        </mx:GridRow>
      </mx:Grid>
    </mx:HBox>


</mx:Application>
```

Customizing List-Based Controls

List-based controls such as lists, data grids, and trees have standard ways in which they display data. For example, a list displays one column of text, data grids display one or more columns of text, and trees display a hierarchical view of data. For many if not most applications, the default ways in which these controls display data are perfectly sufficient. However, there are cases in which you need to alter the displays in one way or another. For example, you may want to display a checkbox in a data grid column rather than standard text.

When you want to customize the way in which a list-based component displays elements, you can use what is called an *item renderer*. Item renderers allow you to specify what component to use in place of the standard text or text and icon that appear in the component, thus customizing the appearance of the elements in the component. The following components support custom item renderers: `List`, `HorizontalList`, `DataGrid`, `Menu`, `TileList`, and `Tree`.

There are two basic ways in which you can use custom item renderers:

Drop-in item renderers
: These are the simplest types of item renderers to implement. With a drop-in item renderer you simply specify a standard UI component to use in a particular column. For example, you can use a checkbox as a drop-in item renderer.

Inline item renderers
: These types of item renderers are still rather simple to implement, but they allow you to exert more control over the component. For example, with a drop-in item renderer you cannot specify the property settings for the component, but with an inline item renderer you can.

You can use standard or custom components as item renderers with either of these approaches.

Drop-In Item Renderers

Drop-in item renderers are extremely simple to implement. All you need to do is set the `itemRenderer` property of the component for which you want to customize the item views. The `itemRenderer` property should be a reference to a component class you want to use. For example, the following creates a list component that uses a date field component for each item:

```
<mx:Script>
<![CDATA[
  import mx.collections.ArrayCollection;
  [Bindable]
  private var dataSet:ArrayCollection =
          new ArrayCollection([new Date(2010, 1, 1), new Date(2010, 4, 15)]);
]]>
</mx:Script>

<mx:List itemRenderer="mx.controls.DateField" dataProvider="{dataSet}"
```

The results of this are shown in Figure 10-1.

All the list-based components that allow you to use item renderers allow you to set the `itemRenderer` property for the component itself, except in the case of the data grid,

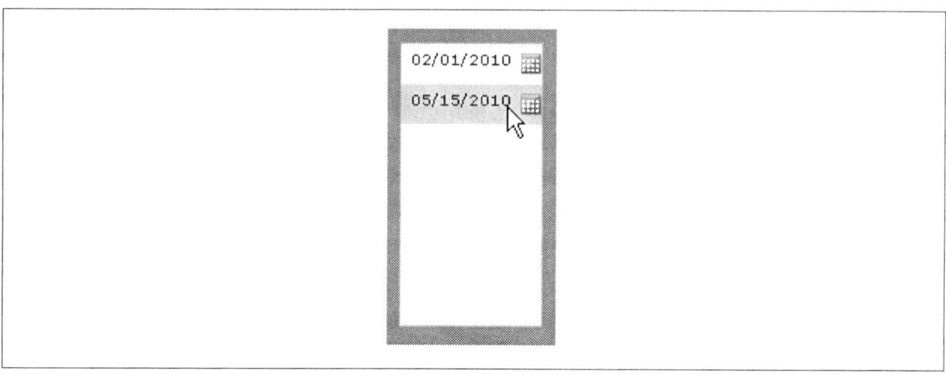

Figure 10-1. A date field used as an item renderer in a list component

which requires that you set the `itemRenderer` property at the column level. Example 10-11 sets one of the columns of a data grid to display a checkbox.

Example 10-11. Using a drop-in item renderer

```
<?xml version="1.0"?>
<mx:Application xmlns:mx="http://www.adobe.com/2006/mxml">
  <mx:VBox>
      <mx:DataGrid editable="false">
        <mx:columns>
          <mx:DataGridColumn headerText="Song Title" dataField="title"/>
          <mx:DataGridColumn headerText="Artist" dataField="artist"/>
          <mx:DataGridColumn headerText="In Favorites" dataField="inFavorites"
itemRenderer="mx.controls.CheckBox" />
        </mx:columns>
        <mx:dataProvider>
          <mx:ArrayCollection>
            <mx:Array>
              <mx:Object songId="0" title="Astronaut" artist="David Byrne"
rating="5" inFavorites="true" />
              <mx:Object songId="1" title="Rio" artist="Duran Duran"
rating="3" />
              <mx:Object songId="2" title="Enjoy the Silence"
artist="Depeche Mode" rating="4" />
              <mx:Object songId="3" title="Mesopotamia"
artist="B-52s" rating="5" inFavorites="true" />
            </mx:Array>
          </mx:ArrayCollection>
        </mx:dataProvider>
      </mx:DataGrid>
  </mx:VBox>

</mx:Application>
```

Drop-in item renderers are ideal when you want to use a simple type of item renderer. However, they have several major limitations.

- You can use only a handful of standard UI components as drop-in item renderers. Table 10-2 lists those components.
- The data value for an item always corresponds to one property of the item renderer. In other words, a list-based component is a view for the data model assigned to the `dataProvider` property. For example, the item value is always assigned to the value of a numeric stepper used as an item renderer. You cannot specify that the item value should be assigned to the maximum property of the numeric stepper.
- You can't customize the components used as item renderers.

Table 10-2. Drop-in components

Component	Property set by the item value
`Button`	`selected`
`CheckBox`	`selected`
`DateField`	`selectedDate`
`Image`	`source`
`Label`	`text`
`NumericStepper`	`value`
`Text`	`text`
`TextArea`	`text`
`TextInput`	`text`

Inline Item Renderers

Although drop-in item renderers are extremely simple to implement, they are also quite limited in terms of how you can configure them. For instance, in Example 10-11 you can display the checkbox in the data grid columns, but you cannot change any of the properties of the components used as item renderers.

Inline item renderers are a slight step up from drop-in item renderers in that you can configure the settings of the component used as the item renderer. For example, you can use an inline item renderer to set the `enabled` property of the checkbox to disable it so that the user cannot check or uncheck the box.

Inline item renderers require that you specify the `itemRenderer` value using nested MXML tags rather than attributes. You must then nest within the `itemRenderer` tag a `Component` tag with a nested tag to create the type of component you want to use as an item renderer. Example 10-12 specifies the checkbox item renderer as an inline item renderer. It also applies a label to the checkbox, and it disables the checkbox so that the user cannot select or deselect it.

Example 10-12. Using inline item renderers

```
<?xml version="1.0"?>
<mx:Application xmlns:mx="http://www.adobe.com/2006/mxml">
  <mx:VBox>
      <mx:DataGrid editable="false">
        <mx:columns>
          <mx:DataGridColumn headerText="Song Title" dataField="title"/>
          <mx:DataGridColumn headerText="Artist" dataField="artist"/>
          <mx:DataGridColumn headerText="In Favorites" dataField="inFavorites">
            <mx:itemRenderer>
              <mx:Component>
                 <mx:CheckBox label="Song in favorites" enabled="false" />
              </mx:Component>
            </mx:itemRenderer>
          </mx:DataGridColumn>
        </mx:columns>
        <mx:dataProvider>
          <mx:ArrayCollection>
            <mx:Array>
              <mx:Object songId="0" title="Astronaut" artist="David Byrne"
              rating="5" inFavorites="true" />
              <mx:Object songId="1" title="Rio" artist="Duran Duran" rating="3" />
              <mx:Object songId="2" title="Enjoy the Silence"
                         artist="Depeche Mode" rating="4" />
              <mx:Object songId="3" title="Mesopotamia"
                         artist="B-52s" rating="5" inFavorites="true" />
            </mx:Array>
          </mx:ArrayCollection>
        </mx:dataProvider>
      </mx:DataGrid>
  </mx:VBox>
</mx:Application>
```

The `Component` tag is a powerful MXML tag. It creates an entirely new scope within the MXML document. The code within the `Component` tag is essentially an MXML component, and the rules that apply to MXML components generally apply to the code within the `Component` tag. You can have just one root node, and within that root node you can use `Style`, `Script`, and all standard MXML tags you could use in an MXML component document. Because the `Component` tag creates its own scope, you don't have to worry about conflicts within the `Component` tag and the document within which the `Component` tag exists. However, this also means that you cannot reference data from the MXML document within the `Component` tag. For example, the following will cause a compile error:

```
<mx:Script>
<![CDATA[
  private var maximumCount:uint = 5;
]]>
</mx:Script>
<mx:List>
  <mx:itemRenderer>
    <mx:Component>
```

```
      <mx:NumericStepper maximum="{maximumCount}" />
    </mx:Component>
  </mx:itemRenderer>
</mx:List>
```

The error occurs because `maximumCount` is defined in the MXML document, but it is referenced within the `Component` tag, which has a different scope.

Although the `Component` tag is powerful, we strongly recommend that you use it only to the extent illustrated by Example 10-12 in which we set the `label` and `enabled` properties of the checkbox. If you need to create more sophisticated item renderers, it is far better to define them as MXML or ActionScript components. We'll look at how to do that next.

You can use a property called `outerDocument` within a `Component` tag to reference the MXML document containing the `Component` tag. You can then reference any public or internal properties, as in the following example:

```
<?xml version="1.0"?>
<mx:Application xmlns:mx="http://www.adobe.com/2006/mxml">

  <mx:Script>
  <![CDATA[
    internal var maximumCount:uint = 5;
  ]]>
  </mx:Script>
  <mx:List>
    <mx:itemRenderer>
      <mx:Component>
        <mx:NumericStepper maximum="{outerDocument.maximumCount}"/>
      </mx:Component>
    </mx:itemRenderer>
  </mx:List>

</mx:Application>
```

However, although this is possible, it is generally not recommended because it is much clearer to break out sophisticated item renderers into new custom components, as discussed in the next section.

Custom Components As Item Renderers

To exert the most control over item renderers you can use a custom component. Using a custom component (either MXML or ActionScript) you can create extremely sophisticated item renderers. For example, you could create an item renderer that displays a rating using colored shapes, as we'll do in this section.

A component must implement certain interfaces to work as an item renderer. There are three basic interfaces for item renderers: `IListItemRenderer`, `IDropInListItemRenderer`, and `IDataRenderer`. All item renderers must implement `IListItemRenderer` and `IDataRenderer`. Because `IListItemRenderer` extends `IDataRenderer`, you simply need to implement IListItemRenderer in most cases. The IListItemRen derer interface requires many getter/setter methods and public methods, and the best way to implement the interface is simply to extend a class that already implements the interface. The following classes already implement the interface: Button, ComboBox, Container, DataGridItemRenderer, DateField, Image, Label, ListBase, ListItemRen derer, MenuBarItem, MenuItemRenderer, NumericStepper, TextArea, TextInput, TileListI temRenderer, and TreeItemRenderer. Because Container implements the interface, you can extend any type of container.

The IDataRenderer interface requires that the implementing class defines a data getter and setter of type Object. The data setter is automatically called every time the data provider is updated and the item renderer needs to update. The data setter is always passed the data provider element corresponding to the item. For example, in a data grid the data is the object representing the row. Even though your custom item renderer component is likely to inherit the data implementation, you'll generally want to override that implementation.

Example 10-13 is saved in an MXML document called *Rating.mxml*, and it draws five squares using 10-by-10 canvases. The squares are blue by default, and they are colored red if they are activated by the value of the rating property from the data passed to the component. Notice that this component overrides the data getter and setter. The setter retrieves the rating value, and it draws the canvases with the appropriate colors based on the rating value.

Example 10-13. A custom component for use as an item renderer

```
<?xml version="1.0" encoding="utf-8"?>
<mx:HBox xmlns:mx="http://www.adobe.com/2006/mxml">

  <mx:Script>
    <![CDATA[

      import mx.containers.Canvas;

      private var _data:Object;

      override public function set data(value:Object):void {
        _data = value;
        var rating:uint = uint(value.rating);
        removeAllChildren();
        var canvas:Canvas;
        for(var i:uint = 0; i < 5; i++) {
          canvas = new Canvas();
          canvas.setStyle("backgroundColor", i < rating ? 0xFF0000 : 0x0000FF);
          canvas.width = 10;
          canvas.height = 10;
          addChild(canvas);
        }
      }

      override public function get data():Object {
```

```
        return _data;
    }

  ]]>
</mx:Script>

</mx:HBox>
```

The MXML application document in Example 10-14 uses the custom component as an item renderer in a data grid using drop-in syntax.

Example 10-14. Using a custom component as an item renderer

```
<?xml version="1.0"?>
<mx:Application xmlns:mx="http://www.adobe.com/2006/mxml">
  <mx:VBox>
      <mx:DataGrid editable="false">
        <mx:columns>
          <mx:DataGridColumn headerText="Song Title" dataField="title"/>
          <mx:DataGridColumn headerText="Artist" dataField="artist"/>
          <mx:DataGridColumn headerText="Rating" dataField="rating"
itemRenderer="Rating" />
        </mx:columns>
        <mx:dataProvider>
          <mx:ArrayCollection>
            <mx:Array>
              <mx:Object songId="0" title="Astronaut" artist="David Byrne"
rating="5" inFavorites="true" />
              <mx:Object songId="1" title="Rio" artist="Duran Duran" rating="3" />
              <mx:Object songId="2" title="Enjoy the Silence" artist="Depeche
Mode" rating="4" />
              <mx:Object songId="3" title="Mesopotamia" artist="B-52s" rating="5"
inFavorites="true" />
            </mx:Array>
          </mx:ArrayCollection>
        </mx:dataProvider>
      </mx:DataGrid>
  </mx:VBox>
</mx:Application>
```

If the item renderer MXML or ActionScript class is in a package, you would specify the fully qualified path to the MXML document or class in the `itemRenderer` property value.

The data grid with the custom item renderer is shown in Figure 10-2 on the following page.

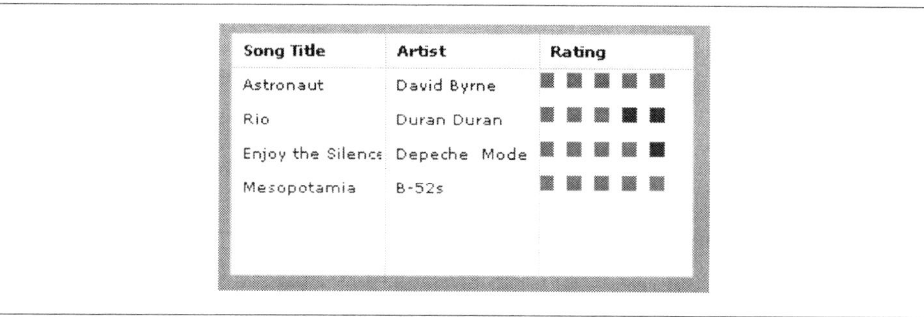

Figure 10-2. Using a custom item renderer in a data grid

Creating Item Editors

When components are editable, they utilize standard text inputs when the user is editing a value. For example, the following code creates a list with editable values simply by setting the `editable` property to `true`. But the user can edit the values only by using the standard text input when she clicks on an item.

```
<mx:List editable="true" width="200" labelField="rating">
  <mx:dataProvider>
    <mx:ArrayCollection>
      <mx:Array>
        <mx:Object songId="0" title="Astronaut" artist="David Byrne"
                   rating="5" inFavorites="true" />
        <mx:Object songId="1" title="Rio" artist="Duran Duran" rating="3" />
        <mx:Object songId="2" title="Enjoy the Silence" artist="Depeche Mode"
                   rating="4" />
        <mx:Object songId="3" title="Mesopotamia" artist="B-52s" rating="5"
                   inFavorites="true" />
      </mx:Array>
    </mx:ArrayCollection>
  </mx:dataProvider>
</mx:List>
```

You can customize the way in which a user can edit data using an item editor. You assign an item editor using the `itemEditor` property in exactly the same ways you can set an item renderer using the `itemRenderer` property. You must also specify a value for the `editorDataField` property that tells the component which property of the item renderer should be bound to the data provider. The following illustrates how to rewrite the `List` tag from the preceding example so that it uses a numeric stepper rather than a standard text input to edit the value. Note that it specifies `value` as the `editorDataField` because `value` is the name of the numeric stepper property that should be linked to the data provider.

```
<mx:List editable="true" width="200" labelField="rating"
        itemEditor="mx.controls.NumericStepper" editorDataField="value">
  <mx:dataProvider>
    <mx:ArrayCollection>
      <mx:Array>
        <mx:Object songId="0" title="Astronaut" artist="David Byrne" rating="5"
```

```
                inFavorites="true" />
        <mx:Object songId="1" title="Rio" artist="Duran Duran" rating="3" />
        <mx:Object songId="2" title="Enjoy the Silence" artist="Depeche Mode"
                rating="4" />
        <mx:Object songId="3" title="Mesopotamia" artist="B-52s" rating="5"
                inFavorites="true" />
      </mx:Array>
    </mx:ArrayCollection>
  </mx:dataProvider>
</mx:List>
```

One question that you might ask when working with the item editor is why you couldn't simply use an item renderer. For example, it's possible to list a numeric stepper as the item renderer in the preceding example. The user could update the numeric stepper value used as an item renderer. However, item renderers simply render the data. They do not create data binding with the data provider. Therefore, changing a value in a numeric stepper used as an item renderer will not affect the data provider whereas it will update the data provider when used as an item editor. However, you can tell a component to use the item renderer as the item editor by setting the `rendererIsEditor` property to `true`:

```
<mx:List editable="true" width="200" labelField="rating"
        itemRenderer="mx.controls.NumericStepper"
        rendererIsEditor="true" editorDataField="value">
  <mx:dataProvider>
    <mx:ArrayCollection>
      <mx:Array>
        <mx:Object songId="0" title="Astronaut" artist="David Byrne" rating="5"
                inFavorites="true" />
        <mx:Object songId="1" title="Rio" artist="Duran Duran" rating="3" />
        <mx:Object songId="2" title="Enjoy the Silence" artist="Depeche Mode"
                rating="4" />
        <mx:Object songId="3" title="Mesopotamia" artist="B-52s" rating="5"
                inFavorites="true" />
      </mx:Array>
    </mx:ArrayCollection>
  </mx:dataProvider>
</mx:List>
```

Any custom component you can use as an item renderer you can also use as an item editor. The only additional rule is that the component must set a public getter/setter method pair as bindable and you must specify that as the `editorDataField` value for the component using the custom editor. Example 10-15 modifies `Rating` so that it can be used as an editor. In this example we define *Rating.mxml* such that it has a bindable `data` getter and setter, and when the clicks on the canvases, we update the `rating` property of the data provided correspondingly.

Example 10-15. A custom item editor

```
<?xml version="1.0" encoding="utf-8"?>
<mx:HBox xmlns:mx="http://www.adobe.com/2006/mxml">
```

```
  <mx:Script>
    <![CDATA[

      import mx.containers.Canvas;
      import flash.events.MouseEvent;

      private var _data:Object;

      [Bindable(event="dataChanged")]
      override public function set data(value:Object):void {
        _data = value;
        draw();
        dispatchEvent(new Event("dataChanged"));
      }

      override public function get data():Object {
        return _data;
      }

      public function clickHandler(event:MouseEvent):void {
        _data.rating = uint(event.currentTarget.name);
        draw();
      }

      private function draw():void {
        var rating:uint = uint(_data.rating);
        removeAllChildren();
        var canvas:Canvas;
        for(var i:uint = 0; i < 5; i++) {
          canvas = new Canvas();
          canvas.setStyle("backgroundColor", i < rating ? 0xFF0000 : 0x0000FF);
          canvas.width = 10;
          canvas.height = 10;
          canvas.name = String(i + 1);
          canvas.addEventListener(MouseEvent.CLICK, clickHandler);
          addChild(canvas);
        }
      }

    ]]>
  </mx:Script>

</mx:HBox>
```

Example 10-16 uses `Rating` as both the item renderer and the item editor.

Example 10-16. Using a custom item editor

```
<?xml version="1.0"?>
<mx:Application xmlns:mx="http://www.adobe.com/2006/mxml">
  <mx:VBox>
      <mx:DataGrid editable="false">
        <mx:columns>
          <mx:DataGridColumn headerText="Song Title" dataField="title"/>
          <mx:DataGridColumn headerText="Artist" dataField="artist"/>
```

```
            <mx:DataGridColumn headerText="Rating" dataField="rating"
                               itemRenderer="Rating" rendererIsEditor="true"
                                editorDataField="data" />
          </mx:columns>
          <mx:dataProvider>
            <mx:ArrayCollection>
              <mx:Array>
                <mx:Object songId="0" title="Astronaut" artist="David Byrne"
                           rating="5" inFavorites="true" />
                <mx:Object songId="1" title="Rio" artist="Duran Duran" rating="3" />
                <mx:Object songId="2" title="Enjoy the Silence"
artist="Depeche Mode"
                           rating="4" />
                <mx:Object songId="3" title="Mesopotamia" artist="B-52s"
                           rating="5" inFavorites="true" />
              </mx:Array>
            </mx:ArrayCollection>
          </mx:dataProvider>
        </mx:DataGrid>
  </mx:VBox>
</mx:Application>
```

Focus Management and Keyboard Control

Focus management and keyboard control are two related topics in Flex. An object has *focus* when it can respond to keyboard events. For example, when a text input control has focus the user can enter text into the field. When a component has focus, it generally indicates that focus with a colored border. You can use the keyboard to control focus within a Flex application, and you can also respond to key presses. We'll look at all of these topics in the next few sections.

Controlling Tab Order

A standard convention of application usability is that pressing the Tab key advances the focus to the next element and Shift-Tab moves focus to the preceding element. This is true of most desktop applications. It is true of most HTML applications. And it is also true of Flex applications.

Many (though certainly not all) Flex components are capable of receiving focus. For example, text inputs, combo boxes, and buttons are all capable of receiving focus. Clearly, there are other types of components that cannot receive focus. For example, a `VBox` container, a label, or a spacer cannot receive focus because none of these components is capable of responding to keyboard input.

When several focus-enabled components exist on the screen at the same time, there exists a default order by which the user can move focus by pressing the Tab key. The default tab order follows the order in which components were initialized. The following code creates a form with three text inputs and a button. The first two text inputs are side by side on the same line, then the next text input follows on the next line, and that is followed by the button on the next line. In this example, if the user places focus in the `firstName` text input and then presses the Tab key, the focus will next move to the `lastName` text field. Another press of the Tab key and focus will shift to the `email` text input on the next line. Finally, one more Tab key press and focus will move to the button.

```
<mx:Form>
  <mx:FormItem label="Name">
    <mx:HBox>
      <mx:TextInput id="firstName" />
      <mx:TextInput id="lastName" />
    </mx:HBox>
  </mx:FormItem>
  <mx:FormItem label="Email">
    <mx:TextInput id="email" />
  </mx:FormItem>
  <mx:FormItem label="">
    <mx:Button label="Submit" />
  </mx:FormItem>
</mx:Form>
```

If the user presses Tab again with focus on the button, focus will return to the first item: the `firstName` text input. This is known as a *tab loop*, because pressing the Tab key shifts focus from component to component in a circular or looping fashion.

Although the default order of elements in a tab loop is generally what you would want and what a user of the application would expect, there are exceptions. For those exceptions you can control the order of the elements in a tab loop by specifying `tabIndex` property values. Every focus-enabled component has a `tabIndex` property. By default, the properties are `null`, and Flex applications use the default tab order. However, you can explicitly define the order of the elements in a tab loop by specifying incrementing integer values (starting with 1) for the `tabIndex` properties of all the components in a tab loop. The following example illustrates how this works with text inputs arranged in a grid. By default, the order would go from left to right, top to bottom. In this case, we're setting the `tabIndex` properties so that the order is from top to bottom, left to right.

```
<mx:Grid>
  <mx:GridRow width="100%" height="100%">
    <mx:GridItem width="100%" height="100%">
      <mx:TextInput id="a" tabIndex="1" />
    </mx:GridItem>
    <mx:GridItem width="100%" height="100%">
      <mx:TextInput id="c" tabIndex="3" />
    </mx:GridItem>
    <mx:GridItem width="100%" height="100%">
      <mx:TextInput id="e" tabIndex="5" />
    </mx:GridItem>
    <mx:GridItem width="100%" height="100%">
      <mx:TextInput id="g" tabIndex="7" />
    </mx:GridItem>
  </mx:GridRow>
```

```
    <mx:GridRow width="100%" height="100%">
      <mx:GridItem width="100%" height="100%">
        <mx:TextInput id="b" tabIndex="2" />
      </mx:GridItem>
      <mx:GridItem width="100%" height="100%">
        <mx:TextInput id="d" tabIndex="4" />
      </mx:GridItem>
      <mx:GridItem width="100%" height="100%">
        <mx:TextInput id="f" tabIndex="6" />
      </mx:GridItem>
      <mx:GridItem width="100%" height="100%">
        <mx:TextInput id="h" tabIndex="8" />
      </mx:GridItem>
    </mx:GridRow>
  </mx:Grid>
```

The behavior of the tab order can be unpredictable if you set one or more, but not all, of the `tabIndex` properties for the components in a tab loop. Generally, you should either use the default tab order or set the `tabIndex` for all the components in a tab loop.

Although focus-enabled components are included in the tab order by default, you can explicitly exclude them by setting their `tabEnabled` property to `false`. Setting `tabEnabled` to `false` does not mean the component cannot receive focus programmatically or when the user clicks on it with the mouse. However, it does mean that it will not be included in the tab loop.

If you want to exclude all the child components of a container from a tab loop, you can simply set the `tabChildren` property of the container to `false`. That has the same effect as setting `tabEnabled` to `false` for each of the child controls.

Programmatically Controlling Focus

You can control focus programmatically using an `mx.managers.FocusManager` instance. A `FocusManager` instance controls one tab loop, and at some point multiple tab loops may exist per application. This is so that some containers are capable of creating their own tab loops. For example, a pop-up window might have its own tab loop, distinct from the tab loop in a form behind the window. Because several tab loops might contain elements visible at the same time, a Flex application can have more than one `FocusManager` in use at any one time.

You never have to construct a new `FocusManager` instance. Every component has a `focusManager` property that references the `FocusManager` instance that controls the tab loop to which that component belongs.

You can programmatically retrieve the focused item using the `getFocus()` method of a `FocusManager` instance. The `getFocus()` method returns the component that currently has focus typed as `IFocusManagerComponent`. You should cast the return of `getFocus()`

when necessary. Unlike lower-level Flash Player APIs for focus management, the getFocus() method of a FocusManager instance always returns a reference to the actual component that has focus, not a raw child object of the component. For example, from a Flash Player perspective, when a text input control has focus, it is really the nested lower-level text field that has focus. Yet from a practical standpoint, you are usually interested in the component that has focus, not its subelements.

You can set focus using the setFocus() method of a FocusManager object. You can pass setFocus() a reference to any focus-enabled component. For example, the following code resets the values of the text input controls and then moves focus to the first text input when the user clicks the button:

```
<mx:Script>
  <![CDATA[

    private function reset(event:Event):void {
      a.text = "";
      b.text = "";
      c.text = "";
      d.text = "";
      focusManager.setFocus(a);
    }

  ]]>
</mx:Script>
<mx:VBox height="100%">
  <mx:Grid>
    <mx:GridRow width="100%" height="100%">
      <mx:GridItem width="100%" height="100%">
        <mx:TextInput id="a" tabIndex="1" />
      </mx:GridItem>
      <mx:GridItem width="100%" height="100%">
        <mx:TextInput id="c" tabIndex="3" />
      </mx:GridItem>
    </mx:GridRow>
    <mx:GridRow width="100%" height="100%">
      <mx:GridItem width="100%" height="100%">
        <mx:TextInput id="b" tabIndex="2" />
      </mx:GridItem>
      <mx:GridItem width="100%" height="100%">
        <mx:TextInput id="d" tabIndex="4" />
      </mx:GridItem>
    </mx:GridRow>
  </mx:Grid>
  <mx:Button label="Reset" click="reset(event)"/>
</mx:VBox>
```

Components also have a setFocus() method. In the preceding example, focusManager.setFocus(a) could be rewritten as a.setFocus() to achieve the same goal.

Components must be visible and enabled in order to receive focus. If a component is not visible or if it's disabled, it's taken out of the list of focus-enabled components for a FocusManager, and even if you explicitly call setFocus(), you can't apply the focus to that component until it's both enabled and visible.

Responding to Keyboard Events

You can listen for keyboard events like you listen for any other sort of event using inline MXML attributes and/or ActionScript. All display objects, including all controls, containers, and the stage itself, dispatch events of type flash.events.KeyboardEvent when the user presses a key on the keyboard. There are two distinct events with each key press: keyUp and keyDown, which are represented by the KeyboardEvent.KEY_UP and KeyboardEvent.KEY_DOWN constants.

The KeyboardEvent type defines several properties specific to the event. Among those properties are the keyCode property, which contains the code of the key that was pressed, and the charCode property, which contains the code of the specific character. The keyCode and charCode properties are the same for all alphanumeric keys when they are not Shifted, Ctrl'd, or Alt'd. For alphanumeric keys the key and character codes are the ASCII codes.

The flash.ui.Keyboard class defines constants that you can use for comparisons with key codes for non-alphanumeric keys. For example, Keyboard.ENTER and Keyboard.SHIFT contain the key code values for the Enter and Shift keys.

Components dispatch keyboard events only when they have focus. Example 10-17 uses this fact to create a simple context-based help system for a form in an application.

Example 10-17. A simple keyboard event example

```
<?xml version="1.0"?>
<mx:Application xmlns:mx="http://www.adobe.com/2006/mxml">

  <mx:Script>
    <![CDATA[
      import mx.controls.TextArea;
      import mx.managers.PopUpManager;
      import mx.containers.TitleWindow;
      import mx.events.CloseEvent;

      private var _helpWindow:TitleWindow;

      private function formKeyUpHandler(event:KeyboardEvent):void {
        if(_helpWindow != null) {
          return;
        }
        if(event.keyCode == Keyboard.F1) {
          _helpWindow = TitleWindow(PopUpManager.createPopUp(this,
          TitleWindow, true));
          _helpWindow.title = "Application Help";
          _helpWindow.width = 400;
```

```
            _helpWindow.height = 400;
            _helpWindow.showCloseButton = true;
            _helpWindow.addEventListener(CloseEvent.CLOSE, closeHandler);
            var textArea:TextArea = new TextArea();
            textArea.percentWidth = 100;
            textArea.percentHeight = 100;
            _helpWindow.addChild(textArea);
            if(event.currentTarget == firstName) {
              textArea.text = "Specify your first name, e.g. Bob";
            }
            else if(event.currentTarget == lastName) {
              textArea.text = "Specify your last name, e.g. Smith";
            }
            else if(event.currentTarget == email) {
              textArea.text = "Specify your email address, e.g. bob@yahoo.com";
            }
            else if(event.currentTarget == accountType) {
              textArea.text = "Select an account type from the drop-down";
            }
            else {
              textArea.text = "Generic application help";
            }
          }
        }

        private function closeHandler(event:CloseEvent):void {
          PopUpManager.removePopUp(_helpWindow);
          _helpWindow = null;
        }

      ]]>
    </mx:Script>

    <mx:Form>
      <mx:FormItem label="First Name">
        <mx:TextInput id="firstName" keyUp="formKeyUpHandler(event)" />
      </mx:FormItem>
      <mx:FormItem label="Last Name">
        <mx:TextInput id="lastName" keyUp="formKeyUpHandler(event)" />
      </mx:FormItem>
      <mx:FormItem label="Email">
        <mx:TextInput id="email" keyUp="formKeyUpHandler(event)" />
      </mx:FormItem>
      <mx:FormItem label="Account Type">
        <mx:ComboBox id="accountType" dataProvider="[bronze,silver,gold,platinum]"
keyUp="formKeyUpHandler(event)" ></mx:ComboBox>
      </mx:FormItem>
    </mx:Form>

</mx:Application>
```

In Example 10-17, the user can press F1, and a help window appears with help specific to the control that has focus.

The `KeyboardEvent` class also defines the Boolean properties `ctrlKey`, `altKey`, and `shiftKey`, which tell you whether the user is pressing the Ctrl key, the Alt key, or the Shift key. The following rewrite of the `if` statement in Example 10-17 causes the help to appear only when the user presses Ctrl-F1:

```
if(event.keyCode == Keyboard.F1 && event.ctrlKey) {
```

If you want to listen to events globally within an application, add listeners to the application container:

```
this.addEventListener(KeyboardEvent.KEY_DOWN, keyDownHandler);
```

Summary

In this chapter, we discussed a variety of topics spanning the gamut of framework utilities and advanced component concepts. These topics included working with Flex tool tips, adding pop ups, managing the cursor, adding drag-and-drop behavior, customizing list-based components, and focus management and keyboard control.

CHAPTER 11
Working with Media

A picture is worth ten thousand words, and with Flex you have the ability to add pictures as well as animation, audio, and video to your applications. Flash Player has its roots in graphics and animation, and over time it has grown into a strong development runtime for interactive custom user interfaces. Flash Player has a long history in handling rich media on the Web, and Flex can leverage that strength and provide a truly engaging user experience. Flash Player not only handles many of the bitmap graphics formats that traditional web browsers do, but it also has native support for vector-based graphics, animation, audio, and video.

This chapter covers loading and embedding assets, streaming media, supported media types, and working with the different media types.

Overview

You can incorporate media into an application in one of two ways: at runtime or at compile time. Adding media at compile time is called *embedding*, because the content is compiled into the SWF. Adding media at runtime is called *loading*, because the content exists as separate files from the application that must be loaded into the Flex application when they are requested.

One other method of loading media is called *streaming*. We'll discuss streaming in "Working with Audio and Video" later in this chapter, because streaming applies only to those media types.

There are benefits to both methods. Which one you choose is important, because each one can impact the loading time of your application, the file size of the resultant SWF, the ability to change the media after an application is compiled, and the ability to dynamically change the content.

It's beneficial to embed content within an SWF file; doing so makes the media asset available to the application as soon as it is initialized, since it is packaged within the

SWF file that is used to load the application. It is a good idea to embed small assets, such as button icons and application skins that often don't need to be redefined at runtime. You will typically want such graphics to be available immediately, as they can negatively impact the perceived performance of your application if each item requires a separate download.

> You also can embed assets using runtime shared libraries. Because runtime shared libraries are loaded when an application is initialized, they are treated in the same manner as embedding assets within the main application SWF. We covered working with shared libraries in Chapter 2.

It's beneficial to load content, because the content won't be embedded as a constant (resource) within your application. For example, when building an application to manage images, you cannot embed the images within your application; instead, you need to load the images because the content will change often as new images are added to the image repository. Also, not having to embed the content within the application SWF lets your application be downloaded quickly, and once it's initialized, the application can load the media that's needed on demand without having to reload the application SWF.

Embedding and loading assets are complementary and not competing approaches to working with media in a Flex application. As you work with media and Flex applications, you'll discover when to use which approach, but to start here are some guidelines.

Consider embedding assets when:

- The asset is mainly defined at compile time.
- The asset will always or almost always be needed by the user, such as component skins or application appearance items.
- You have few assets that are not large in terms of file size. Embedding items increases the file sizes proportionally.
- Flex supports the asset only at compile time.

Consider loading assets when:

- The assets are large. The definition of a large asset depends on where your application will be deployed. If your application is an internal intranet application that is always accessed from a high-bandwidth location, this may not be a factor. If your application will be public-facing, you will likely want to limit the total embedded assets to less than 200 KB.
- The assets are not defined at compile time. Instead, they are uploaded by a user or modified after the Flex application is compiled.
- The assets comprise video and most audio files, which typically are large in size.

Supported Media Types in Flex

Flash Player natively supports SWF, GIF, JPEG, PNG, MP3, and FLV media. As such, a Flex application can load all media supported by Flash Player.

Flex 3 requires Flash Player 9 or later. Our discussion of supported media and methods of dealing with media will assume that you are targeting Flash Player 9 or later. Although Flex 3 requires Flash Player 9, embedded and loaded SWF media do not have to be Flash Player 9 content.

In addition to the vast array of formats supported natively by the player, with the help of the Flex compiler you also can handle SVG content and Flash library items within SWF files. For example, Flash Player does not natively support SVG content, but it has the technical capability to render basic SVG content with the help of the Flex compiler. The Flex compiler achieves this by processing SVG files and embedding the converted graphics definition data within a compiled SWF as native Flash bytecode, including the vector data definition information. This means that at runtime, the developer cannot distinguish between SVG content and native Flash vector data but does get the benefit of using SVG content. Because SVG support is provided by the Flex compiler, SVG content cannot be loaded dynamically at runtime.

Table 11-1 lists Flex-supported media types.

Table 11-1. Flex-supported media types

Format	Media type	Loadable?	Notes
SWF	Graphics and animation	Yes	Flex 3 requires Flash Player 9, but it can load any SWF content. You will be limited by what type of interoperability you can have with the content based on the version of the SWF content. Flash Player 9 content that uses ActionScript 3.0 is the most compatible.
SWF library item	Graphics and animation	No	SWF files that contain a library of multiple graphics and animation files can be embedded. This requires the Flex compiler, and only the referenced library item will be embedded within the final SWF file.
GIF	Graphics	Yes	Standard GIF is supported, including transparency. Animated GIF files are not supported.
JPEG	Graphics	Yes	Baseline JPEG files as well as progressive JPEG files are supported.
PNG	Graphics	Yes	Both PNG8 and PNG24 are supported. Alpha transparency is fully supported as well.
SVG	Graphics	No	The Flex compiler supports the SVG 1.1 basic specifications. SMIL, animations, filters, pattern fills, advanced gradients, interactivity, and scripting are not supported.
MP3	Audio	Yes	MP3 files can be loaded, embedded, and streamed using a Real Time Messaging Protocol (RTMP) server.

Format	Media type	Loadable?	Notes
FLV	Video	Yes	FLV is Flash's video file format. Depending on the Flash Player version you will be targeting with your application, you can support traditional FLV video as well as H.264 encoded video. H.264 video support was added in Flash Player 9 Update 3. Files can be loaded, embedded, and streamed using an RTMP server. The file extensions of Flash video can be FLV as well as MP4. Flash Player does not actually care for the file extension. Instead, it inspects the binary data of the video being loaded to determine whether it is a valid video file.

Adding Media

As mentioned before, you can add media to an application by either loading it or embedding it. In this section, we will discuss the different syntax for loading and embedding media. This will serve as a good foundation for understanding the methods you have available to you when adding media to a Flex application. In the Flex framework, watch for component properties that accept a variable of type `Class`. These properties usually indicate the ability to accept a media type as a value.

If you have experience with developing Flash applications, you may be accustomed to creating classes for symbols such as images for when you want to access them in ActionScript. In Flex, this is no longer required as the compiler generates such classes for you automatically.

Loading Media

The easiest and most common way to load media at runtime is to use one of the MXML components specifically designed for that job. A variety of components are available for different types of media. You can use an `Image` component to load images, an `SWFLoader` component to load *.swf* files, or a `VideoDisplay` component to load video content. The `Image` component is the most commonly used of these components and the one we will focus on in this section.

Internally, Flex makes use of Flash Player's `Loader` class. You typically will not make use of the `Loader` class directly as the Flex framework abstracts away the details, but it is good to know that it exists and that if you ever need to implement the loading of custom file types not supported by Flex, you can easily do so.

Here is an example that uses an `Image` tag to load a *.jpg* file:

```
<?xml version="1.0" encoding="utf-8"?>
<mx:Application xmlns:mx="http://www.adobe.com/2006/mxml">
    <mx:Image source="assets/sun.jpg"/>
</mx:Application>
```

This simple code loads an image file called *sun.jpg* located in an *assets* directory relative to the *.swf* at runtime and displays it in an `Image` component. The JPEG file format is natively supported by Flash Player; as such, you are able to load it at runtime. Also important to note is that the application *.swf* does not contain the image; rather, it begins to load after the application is initialized. This behavior is very similar to how web browsers load images that are referenced in an HTML document.

Loaded assets are referenced at runtime based on the location of the *.swf* file by default. You can reference assets using both absolute and relative paths.

This example uses the `Image` component, which is a Flex component built to help you easily load images. The `Image` component loads the image provided by the source attribute and sizes it according to the `width` and `height` properties of the `Image` component instance, if any are provided. If no size is specified, the component expands to the dimensions of the image. Also, the `Image` component by default loads whatever you set in the `source` property. If you want to load the image based on user input or an event, you can call the `load()` method of the `Image` instance at runtime, or you can data-bind the `source` property to a variable that stores the image you would like to load. Here is an updated example of the preceding code that provides users with a button to load the image when they want to view it, with no explicit `width` or `height` properties set:

```
<?xml version="1.0" encoding="utf-8"?>
<mx:Application xmlns:mx="http://www.adobe.com/2006/mxml">
    <mx:Image id="sun"/>
    <mx:Button label="Load Image" click="sun.load('assets/sun.jpg')"/>
</mx:Application>
```

This version of the application does not automatically load the image, as before. The `Image` component instance exists, but it loads the image only after the application is initialized. Also, the `source` property has no value in this example. When you do not specify the `source` property for an `Image` instance, the component will not load an image automatically. When a user clicks on the button in the example, the `load()` method is called, along with the value of the image to load as a parameter.

The `Image` component along with the `SWFLoader` and `VideoDisplay` components dispatch events to indicate the status of the component. The `Image` component dispatches many events; the ones related to loading content are the `ioError`, `progress`, `open`, `httpStatus`, `securityError`, and `complete` events.

The Flex framework components use the underlying Flash Player API to load media. To learn the internal details about the underlying mechanism that Flex uses to load content, review the documentation on the `Loader` class in the `flash.display` package and the `LoaderInfo` class. An instance of the `LoaderInfo` class is exposed by all three components.

The events you'll be most interested in are `progress`, `complete`, and `ioError`. The `progress` event is dispatched while an asset is being loaded. This allows you to provide the user with a progress bar or some other indication that something is loading. This is especially useful when loading a lot of content or large content. The `complete` event allows you to determine when an asset has finished loading. This can be useful if you want to provide some sort of notification to the user, or have another process begin after the content is loaded. The `ioError` event is important when having to deal with content that may or may not exist, especially if the user is asked to enter his own URL, for example. The `ioError` event is dispatched when Flash Player is unable to find the referenced file, allowing you to provide the user with the option of reentering the URL. An error is usually reported immediately if the client receives a response from the server that shows an error such as File Not Found, but if you reference a server that can't be reached, the response won't be returned in a timely manner, if ever.

The code in Example 11-1 allows a user to enter a URL of an image to be loaded and notifies the user if he has entered an invalid URL.

Example 11-1. Notifying the user of an invalid URL

```
<?xml version="1.0" encoding="utf-8"?>
<mx:Application xmlns:mx="http://www.adobe.com/2006/mxml">
    <mx:Script>
        <![CDATA[
           import mx.controls.Alert;
           private function ioErrorHandler():void
           {
            Alert.show("There was an error loading: "+imageUrl.text+",
please enter a new URL");
           }
        ]]>
    </mx:Script>
    <mx:Image id="imageView" ioError="ioErrorHandler()"/>
    <!--when compiled and run locally, you can load remote images without security
    restrictions that are typically encountered with an application running in the
    browser sandbox -->
    <mx:TextInput id="imageUrl"
        text="http://www.google.com/intl/en/images/logo.gif"/>
    <mx:Button label="Load image" click="imageView.load(imageUrl.text)"/>
</mx:Application>
```

Embedding Media

When embedding media, you instruct the compiler to package the asset within the resultant *.swf* file rather than just referencing it externally, as you saw in the preceding section. In other platforms, such as Java and .NET, this is sometimes referred to as *compiling the asset as a resource*. You can embed media within the following types of content:

- MXML
- ActionScript
- CSS

You embed media by using any of these three variations of the `Embed()` directive. This directive accepts the `source`, `mimeType`, `scaleGridTop`, `scaleGridBottom`, `scaleGridLeft`, `scaleGridRight`, and `symbol` parameters. The parameter you will use most often—and the only parameter that is required—is `source`. This parameter identifies to the compiler the asset it needs to process and embed within the final *.swf* file.

Embedding media within MXML

The embed syntax when used in MXML begins with an `@Embed()` directive. The `@` character instructs the compiler that it will be receiving a directive in MXML—in this case, the `Embed()` directive.

Earlier you saw an example of how to load a *.jpg* asset at runtime. Now we'll look at how to embed the asset:

```
<?xml version="1.0" encoding="utf-8"?>
<mx:Application xmlns:mx="http://www.adobe.com/2006/mxml">
    <mx:Image source="@Embed(source='assets/sun.jpg')"/>
</mx:Application>
```

This example should look very similar to the earlier example, except for the additional syntax within the value of the `source` attribute. This syntax, when used within MXML, instructs the compiler to embed an asset rather than load it.

When embedding an asset, the compiler will not resize or recompress the media contained with the resultant SWF. It will embed the asset as is in its original form. If you intend to use an asset only at a specific size, you should match in the source the final size that will be used in the application.

Embedding media within ActionScript

Sometimes you will want to embed your assets in ActionScript. This allows you to reference them directly within ActionScript, or even reference the embedded asset from MXML. Embedding media in ActionScript has the same result as doing so in MXML, but can be more flexible, as we will see later in this chapter when we cover how to create an asset library; the only difference is that the compiler instructions for embedding are in ActionScript code. Example 11-2 shows the code from Example 11-1, but in ActionScript.

Example 11-2. Displaying an image using an Image component while embedding it in ActionScript

```
<?xml version="1.0" encoding="utf-8"?>
<mx:Application xmlns:mx="http://www.adobe.com/2006/mxml" initialize="init()">
```

```
    <mx:Script>
      <![CDATA[
            [Embed(source="assets/sun.jpg")]
            private var sunAsset:Class;
            //This method is called when the application is initialized
            private function init():void
            {
                sunImage.source = sunAsset;
            }
        ]]>
    </mx:Script>
    <mx:Image id="sunImage"/>
</mx:Application>
```

The main difference between Example 11-1 and Example 11-2 is that a change in the value of the `source` property for the `Image` instance is being set through ActionScript. When embedding content, you must assign data of type `Class` to the `source` property. You don't typically specify a class yourself; instead, the Flex compiler automatically generates such a type for you when you embed an asset. When embedding content, you will need to reference a variable declared with the `[Embed()]` metadata syntax. The contents of the `Embed()` directive in Example 11-2 are the same as in Example 11-1. In ActionScript, `Embed()` must be surrounded by `[]`. This is called a *metadata tag*, and it instructs the compiler that it needs special handling. The `Embed` metadata tag must precede the variable declaration, as shown in Example 11-2. Once done, the value of the variable will be the reference asset in the `Embed()` directive.

The declared variable of an asset must be of type `Class`. Placing an `Embed` metadata tag before the variable will cause the compiler to define the variable's class definition and allow you to instantiate it or reference it when you need to work with the asset. Although the variable is declared as a generic `Class` data type, each type of media asset maps to a more specific class definition, depending on the type of media embedded. All asset class types implement a common interface, `IFlexAsset`.

The different types of asset classes are as follows:

- `BitmapAsset`, which represents bitmap images (JPEG, GIF, and PNG).
- `MovieClipAsset`, which represents Flash library items within an SWF. Typically, such an asset is an animated graphic. For static (nonanimated) SWF library items, `SpriteClass` is used.
- `MovieClipLoaderAsset`, which represents SWF files.
- `SoundAsset`, which represents an embedded MP3 file.
- `SpriteClass`, which represents a static vector graphic from an SWF library item or SVG file.
- `ButtonAsset`, which is rarely used but is provided to ensure full compatibility with Flash authoring content.
- `TextFieldAsset`, which will never be produced by Flex, but is produced by other tools such as Flash authoring.

One of the strengths of using ActionScript for part of an application is the added flexibility it gives you when handling application logic at runtime. In that spirit, let's take a look at Example 11-3, which allows us to change an embedded image at runtime.

Example 11-3. Changing the embedded asset to be displayed at runtime

```
<?xml version="1.0" encoding="utf-8"?>
<mx:Application xmlns:mx="http://www.adobe.com/2006/mxml" initialize="init()">
    <mx:Script>
        <![CDATA[
            [Embed(source="assets/sun.jpg")]
            private var sunAsset:Class;
            [Embed(source="assets/moon.jpg")]
            private var moonAsset:Class;
            private function init():void
            {
                sunImage.source = sunAsset;
            }

            private function showMoon():void
            {
                sunImage.source = moonAsset;
            }
        ]]>
    </mx:Script>
    <mx:Image id="sunImage"/>
    <mx:Button label="Show the Moon!" click="showMoon()"/>
</mx:Application>
```

In Example 11-3, the sun image asset is initially displayed, and the user is presented with a button to display the moon image. The button's `click` event is set up to call the `showMoon()` function, which will set the `source` property of the `Image` instance to the `moonAsset` that contains the embedded image. When you declare an asset to be embedded, that asset is included within the final *.swf* file regardless of whether it is used. This means that when referencing different embedded assets, those assets will not need to be loaded.

Embedding media within CSS

Typically, you embed assets when stylizing and skinning components. So far, we have discussed using the `Image` component to load and embed images. The `Image` component is ideal for loading and displaying images and animations. With CSS, though, you can easily specify component skins.

Example 11-4 is an example of embedding assets to reskin a button component using CSS.

Example 11-4. Skinning a Button component by embedding in CSS

```
<?xml version="1.0" encoding="utf-8"?>
<mx:Application xmlns:mx="http://www.adobe.com/2006/mxml">
    <mx:Style>
```

```
    Button
    {
        down-skin:Embed(source="assets/btnDown.PNG");
        over-skin:Embed(source="assets/btnOver.PNG");
        up-skin:Embed(source="assets/btnUp.PNG");
    }
    </mx:Style>
    <mx:Button label="Hello World!"/>
</mx:Application>
```

Example 11-4 showcases the power of Flex in terms of handling CSS and embedding assets. In this example, we redefined the base skin for all instances of the `Button` component within three lines (you can find more information on skinning components in Chapter 8). We did this by setting the values of the CSS properties to images that we embedded. The syntax is similar to that used in Example 11-3 and Example 11-2. In CSS, though, you don't need to use identifier characters as you do with the other two forms of syntax. In CSS, you just use the `Embed()` directive directly inline.

Working with the Different Media Types

So far, we have explored how to load media and the different syntax used for embedding media. Although the general approach is very similar across the different media types, there are some subtle differences that you need to be aware of to best use media in your Flex applications.

Working with Graphics

Graphics are static images, either bitmap or vector, and are typically the most used media asset of all. You will use such assets to skin a UI control, to load pictures, and pretty much whenever you want to display a graphic that you do not want to reproduce using ActionScript or CSS. Graphics are an important part of Flex. You can't completely maximize the strength of using such a rich UI framework as Flex without including custom user interfaces and engaging interaction.

Vector graphics differ from bitmap graphics in that they are represented through polygon shape definition rather than pixels. Because they're represented via polygon data rather than pixels, vector graphics have higher resolutions and smaller file sizes than bitmap graphics do. Flash Player also exposes vector drawing capability through the ActionScript drawing API.

Adding graphics

The Flex framework simplifies working with graphics. One way to work with graphics in Flex is via the `Image` component. All Flex components that use graphics work in a similar manner, but each serves its own purpose. The `Button` component, for example, has an `icon` property. This property, like the `source` property of an `Image` component, can accept an embedded or loaded graphic. Becoming familiar with the component you are working with, and its capability to work with graphics, can help you maximize how effectively you use the Flex framework.

So far, we have looked at using JPEG and PNG files. The Flex framework also supports GIF, SVG, and SWF graphics files. When loading a media asset, the component takes care of loading the asset and displaying it. This traditionally requires writing code to load the asset, and then displaying it and sizing it appropriately.

Static graphics are implemented in the same manner. When adding such content, though, it is good to understand the goals and benefits of each file format:

GIF
: This lossless image format is for simple, nonphoto bitmaps. Flash Player can handle transparent GIF files but not animated GIF files. Thus, if animation is important, you will need to use an SWF file instead.

JPEG
: The JPEG file format is a lossy graphics format that is ideal for photo-like content. This file format does not support any type of animation.

PNG
: This lossless bitmap graphics file format supports multiple levels of transparency. It is ideal when you need high-quality bitmap graphics. Usually, PNG files produce a file size comparable to GIF and JPEG files, although often PNG files are larger. You should compare the output quality and file size of the three different bitmap formats when trying to decide which format to use.

SVG
: SVG is a vector-based format that is supported only at compile time. This format can be useful in cases where vector data can be obtained in only this format.

SWF
: This is the ideal vector graphics format. Many existing tools produce SWF files that can be easily integrated into Flex applications.

Here is an example that uses an SWF file as a button icon:

```
<?xml version="1.0"?>
<mx:Application xmlns:mx="http://www.adobe.com/2006/mxml">
    <mx:Button label="Logout" icon="@Embed(assets/logoutIcon.swf)"/>
</mx:Application>
```

This example sets the `icon` property of the `Button` instance to the embedded asset. As you can see, the asset here functions similarly to the way it was used with the `Image` component.

So far, you've set the value of a component property to a media asset. Although this is a common usage, sometimes you might want to display an arbitrary number of images. Without Flex, the only way to do this is to manually write ActionScript code to load, position, size, and display the images. With Flex, though, you can easily display a set of images that are stored in an array using a Repeater component. Here is an example of using the Repeater component with loaded images:

```
<?xml version="1.0" encoding="utf-8"?>
<mx:Application xmlns:mx="http://www.adobe.com/2006/mxml">
    <mx:Repeater id="images"
        dataProvider="['assets/image1.png','assets/image2.png']">
        <mx:Image source="{images.currentItem}"/>
    </mx:Repeater>
</mx:Application>
```

This example uses the same Image component, but this time you are using a Repeater component to instantiate an arbitrary number of Image component instances depending on how many images need to be displayed. You do this by setting the Repeater component's dataProvider property to an array of images (in this example, it is specified inline, but it could have been a list from a server), and through data binding you set the source property of the Image component to the current item that needs to be rendered.

Scaling Graphics Using a Scaling Grid (Scale-9)

Another unique capability of Flash Player is the Scale-9 feature, which helps to scale graphics so that the corners don't stretch. It's common to use Scale-9 when working with graphics that need to scale while keeping the corners properly sized. Figure 11-1 and Figure 11-2 show a graphical asset before and after it is scaled using the default model.

Figure 11-1. Original graphic

Figure 11-2. Traditional scaling of the graphic in Figure 11-1

Notice that in Figure 11-2 the graphic was scaled, including the rounded corners. Although this is sometimes the desired result, more often you will be interested in scaling both the width and the height of the graphic while keeping the corner radius consistent, as shown in Figure 11-3.

Figure 11-3. Graphic in Figure 11-2 scaled, with corners remaining consistent

This is particularly important in regard to skinning components, and here Scale-9 becomes indispensable. It allows you to divide a graphic into a 3-by-3 grid, resulting in a nine-region grid with the four corner squares remaining consistent in size while the other squares scale to fill the needed area. Figure 11-4 shows the original graphic from Figure 11-1, but with the grid drawn on top of it.

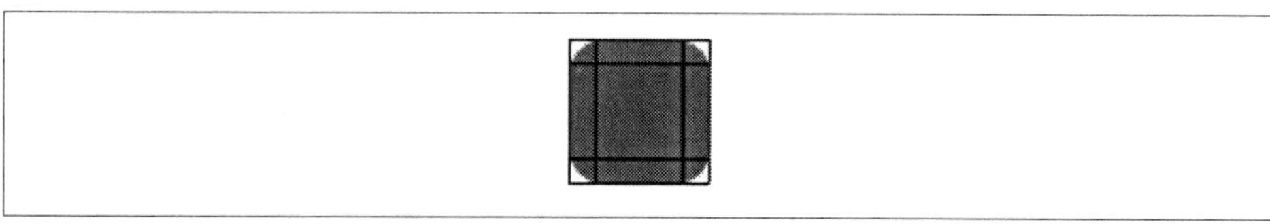

Figure 11-4. Graphic from Figure 11-1, but with Scale-9 guides drawn

Now when the graphic from Figure 11-1 is scaled, it will maintain the corner radius graphics, as seen in Figure 11-5, without scaling the corners.

Figure 11-5. Graphic from Figure 11-4, scaled with Scale-9 guides drawn

To use Scale-9, you have to define the coordinates of the scaling grid. You can define grid coordinates in several ways. The simplest and most common way is to specify them within the `Embed()` directive.

The `Embed()` directive, when used with a graphic, supports the special parameters **`scaleGridTop`**, **`scaleGridBottom`**, **`scaleGridLeft`**, and **`scaleGridRight`** for just this purpose. These parameters take an integer value, and their registration point is the top left of the graphic. As an example, the following code of an embedded graphic has the Scale-9 grid defined:

```
<?xml version="1.0" encoding="utf-8"?>
<mx:Application xmlns:mx="http://www.adobe.com/2006/mxml">
    <mx:Image width="100" height="100" source="@Embed(source='assets/cube.GIF',
scaleGridTop='10',scaleGridLeft='10',
scaleGridBottom='90',scaleGridRight='90')"/>
</mx:Application>
```

This example uses the same graphic shown in Figure 11-4 and defines the properties within MXML, but you can achieve the same result in ActionScript and CSS. The box has an original **`width`** and **`height`** of 100 pixels. In this example, we are defining the guides 10 pixels away from each edge. Notice that `scaleGridBottom` and `scaleGridRight` are not set to 10, but are set to 100 minus 10 because the registration point of where Flash Player calculates things is the top left. Also, the distance from each edge does not need to be equal, but all values need to be defined. If you forget to define one of the scale grid properties, you will receive a compiler error. Also, although commonly you will define the Scale-9 grid at compile time, it is possible to do so at runtime using ActionScript. For more information on the ActionScript API, review the `scale9Grid` property of the `DisplayObject` class.

Scale-9 with embedded content can also be implemented outside Flex within an SWF graphic from tools that produce the needed data within the resultant SWF. Adobe Flash Professional is one such tool, and when a graphic is compiled into an SWF with Scale-9 grid data embedded, Flex automatically uses the already defined data with the SWF. If you define values within both an `Embed()` directive and an SWF that already includes the grid data, the SWF file data will be used. Defining the grid in an SWF file is useful when a designer wants to configure the grid as part of the material he provides to a development team.

Working with SWF libraries

If you're working on a team that plans to produce graphical assets in Adobe Flash Professional, which supports creating SWF libraries, creating such libraries may be an ideal choice because it allows you to provide a single file that contains many, if not all, of the assets needed for an application. This also allows a designer to update a single file throughout the development process, in a single step.

In the following code, an SWF library item with a linkage identifier of `circleAnimation` is used as a button icon:

```
<?xml version="1.0" encoding="utf-8"?>
<mx:Application xmlns:mx="http://www.adobe.com/2006/mxml">
    <mx:Button label="Click me" source="@Embed(source='assets/library.SWF',
symbol='circleAnimation')"/>
</mx:Application>
```

In this example, the `circleAnimation` symbol within the *library.swf* file is being embedded. The syntax for doing so is the same as that used to embed other content, except for the addition of the `symbol` parameter for the `Embed()` directive. The `symbol` parameter is a special parameter supported only with SWF libraries. If the referenced symbol is not valid, the Flex compiler returns an error.

If an SWF library contains many library items, but only some of the items are referenced in an application, only those library items are embedded within the final *.swf*. Finally, you may have noticed that you didn't have to specify the type of asset. If it was a bitmap graphic, video, or animation, the Flex compiler automatically embeds it for you. If the type of symbol with the SWF library changes—for example, from a vector graphic to

Flash video—you don't need to change anything within your code to handle the embedding process differently. However, if your code relies on a specific type for an asset, you may need to update it to reflect the new asset type.

Building an asset library using a static class in Flex

Another way to improve asset management is to define ActionScript classes that are dedicated to defining all the assets in an application. This allows you to centrally store the definition of all your assets and easily reference the assets throughout an application by referencing the asset class members.

To begin, you define the class that contains all the embedded assets. The asset will contain public static constant properties, which you can reference within your application. In the following example, the class is small, and you have a single class. In a large application, the class will likely be larger and with many assets, and you may have several asset classes defined if you feel the need to split different types of assets.

```
package com.oreilly.programmingflex.assets
{
    public class Images
    {
        [Embed(source="/assets/btnOver.png")]
        public static const LOGO:Class;
        [Embed(source="/assets/sun.jpg")]
        public static const LOGOUT_ICON:Class;
    }
}
```

Now that you've defined the class that will contain the embedded assets, you can reference the embedded resources within MXML or ActionScript. Here is an example in MXML:

```
<?xml version="1.0" encoding="utf-8"?>
<mx:Application xmlns:mx="http://www.adobe.com/2006/mxml">
    <mx:Script>
        <![CDATA[
          import com.oreilly.programmingflex.assets.Images;
        ]]>
    </mx:Script>
    <mx:Image source="{Images.LOGO}"/>
    <mx:Button label="Logout" icon="{Images.LOGOUT_ICON}"/>
</mx:Application>
```

This method lets you centralize all your assets and keep a manageable list of what assets are included within the application, which is generally a good practice when building an application. When adding and redefining assets, you need to edit only the class. This also allows you to reference the same asset throughout your application, be it from MXML or ActionScript, in one place.

Working with SWF animations

The Flash platform began its life as an animation tool for the Web, and as such, it only makes sense that Flex would be able to take advantage of that strength. Flex allows any Flash content to be embedded or loaded, including animated content. Usually such content is produced by a graphic designer or animator using animation software and the result is an SWF file that doesn't contain any code but does contain a Flash animation.

For example, say you wanted to include an animated character to guide users through an application. You could reproduce the character in ActionScript, but that would take a lot of time, and chances are a developer would not be interested in producing such content. Tools such as Adobe Flash Professional or any 3D animation package that produces *.swf* files are better suited for this purpose. For the purposes of our discussion, we won't be covering how to use such tools. Instead, we will focus on how such content is incorporated.

Here are some important items to keep in mind when working with SWF animations:

Frame rate
: The frame rate of an animation is not the frame rate that is ultimately used during playback. When content is added to a Flex application, the frame rate of the application is used (the main SWF) rather than the content's frame rate. The default frame rate used in Flex is 24 frames per second. It is a good idea to develop animated content to match that frame rate. Also, although it's not advisable (unless you're careful), you could change the frame rate of your application to match the SWF content by setting the `-default-frame-rate` compiler flag to match that of the SWF content you plan to embed.

Transparency
: SWF files support full transparency. Content loaded into a Flex application typically has no background; instead, the items below the animation on the Z index within Flash Player are used. Alpha transparency is also possible.

Animation size
: Sometimes referred to as *canvas* or *movie* size, animated content size is dictated by the bounding box of the animation. If you attempt to retrieve the width and height of the content, the currently used area is returned. This means that when an animation that is playing causes the size of the bounding box to change, the value returned by the `width` and `height` properties changes as well.

Embedding versus loading
: As with SWF graphics files, SWF animations can be loaded or embedded. If the animation exists within an SWF library, embedding is the only option. You will have to decide what approach to take based on the file size of the SWF animation and the need for immediately availability.

ActionScript communication
: If the SWF animation is loaded and contains ActionScript code, you can communicate between your Flex application and the ActionScript code. If the SWF is compiled for Flash Player 9 with ActionScript 3.0 code, you will have more power to control the asset. If you are loading an SWF with an older version of ActionScript, you will have to implement the `LocalConnection` interface on both the loaded SWF and the main application to bridge the communication as older ActionScript bytecode is executed in a separate runtime engine within Flash Player.

  If an SWF is embedded and not loaded, the ActionScript code within the SWF is removed, and the only interactivity you'll be able to perform is to control the playback of the animation as you would any other `MovieClip` instance.

Working with Audio and Video

You can add audio and video to a Flex application through embedding, loading, and streaming. In practice, though, because audio and video content tends to produce large files, you will load or stream such media rather than embed it. Loading audio and video is the same as loading graphics, except you have some additional capabilities, such as controlling playback. Streaming is similar to loading because it can occur anytime after an application is initialized. With streaming, you rely on a server to continuously return to the client the media data, broken up into smaller parts. This allows the user to seek to the middle of the content without having to download the entire file.

Adding a sound effect

The Flex framework provides the `SoundEffect` component for handling sound effects in an application when an effect event occurs. The `SoundEffect` component makes it easy to play back a sound that is tied to a Flex effect. For more information on effects, see Chapter 13.

When an effect event occurs, the audio can be played back using `SoundEffect`. The `SoundEffect` component is not used for just any audio playback; it is used only when tied to a Flex effect event. For example, the following code causes a sound effect to play when a user clicks on the button labeled "Click me":

```
<?xml version="1.0" encoding="utf-8"?>
<mx:Application xmlns:mx="http://www.adobe.com/2006/mxml">
    <mx:SoundEffect id="clickSound" source="assets/click.MP3"/>
    <mx:Button label="Click me" mouseDownEffect="{clickSound}"/>
</mx:Application>
```

In this example, when a user clicks the "Click me" button, the *click.mp3* file is loaded and played. By default, the `SoundEffect` class plays up to 500 milliseconds of an audio file. You can change the duration by setting the `duration` property, or if you want the entire audio file to play through no matter the duration, you can set `useDuration` to `false`.

Advanced sound control

The SoundEffect component is great when you want to add an audio effect that doesn't need to be controlled and when it ties in nicely to the Flex framework effects system. In other instances, when you may want to play an audio file and provide full audio controls, Flash Player exposes the low-level flash.media package that contains classes that provide granular control over media playback and handling. The most important classes to become familiar with are the Sound, SoundChannel, and SoundTransform classes. Together these classes enable you to load an MP3 file, control playback and volume, and retrieve meta information from the file.

The Sound class is a factory object used to create an instance of an MP3 file and play it back. The play() instance method of the Sound class returns a SoundChannel instance that lets you work directly with the playing instance. At first it may seem counterintuitive to have this extra step, but when you want to play multiple channels of the same audio, this separation is needed. SoundChannel also provides a reference to the Sound Transform instance that allows you to control the channel's audio level and panning.

The code in Example 11-5 includes a reusable SoundPlayer class for loading an MP3 file, starting playback, and allowing the user to stop and pause playback.

Example 11-5. A class to play and control sound

```
package com.oreilly.programmingflex
{
    import flash.media.SoundChannel;
    import flash.media.Sound;
    import flash.net.URLStream;
    import flash.events.Event;
    import flash.media.ID3Info;
    import flash.net.URLRequest;
    import flash.events.EventDispatcher;

    public class SoundPlayer extends EventDispatcher
    {
        [Bindable]
        public var songName:String = "Loading";

        private var _sound:Sound;
        private var _soundChannel:SoundChannel;
        private var _currentPosition:Number;

        public function SoundPlayer(url:String)
        {
            _sound = new Sound(new URLRequest(url));
            //Subscribe to the ID3 event so that we can retrieve the songName
            _sound.addEventListener(Event.ID3,id3Handler);
            play();
        }

        public function stop():void
        {
```

```
            _soundChannel.stop();
            //reset the position so that play() starts from the beginning
            _currentPosition = 0;
        }

        public function pause():void
        {
            //store the position so that we can resume playback
            _currentPosition = _soundChannel.position;
            _soundChannel.stop();
        }

        public function play():void
        {
            //If it is already playing, stop playback
            if(_soundChannel != null)
            {
                _soundChannel.stop();
            }
            //Store a reference to the playing channel
            _soundChannel = _sound.play(_currentPosition);
            //Set the volume, valid values are from 0 to 1
            _soundChannel.soundTransform.volume = .7;
        }

        private function id3Handler(id3Event:Event):void
        {
            songName = _sound.id3.songName;
            dispatchEvent(new Event("songNameChanged"));
        }
    }
}
```

Example 11-6 is an example of using the SoundPlayer class.

Example 11-6. A simple application that uses the SoundPlayer class

```
<?xml version="1.0" encoding="utf-8"?>
<mx:Application xmlns:mx="http://www.adobe.com/2006/mxml">
    <mx:Script>
        <![CDATA[
           import com.oreilly.programmingflex.SoundPlayer;
           //Initialize the soundPlayer as soon as the application starts
           public var soundPlayer:SoundPlayer = new SoundPlayer("assets/sound.MP3");
        ]]>
    </mx:Script>
    <mx:VBox>
        <mx:Text text="{soundPlayer.songName}" id="songName" width="100%"/>
        <mx:HBox width="100%">
            <mx:Button label="Play" click="soundPlayer.play()"/>
            <mx:Button label="Stop" click="soundPlayer.stop()"/>
            <mx:Button label="Pause" click="soundPlayer.pause()"/>
        </mx:HBox>
    </mx:VBox>
</mx:Application>
```

Although Example 11-6 is a simple MP3 player, it demonstrates much of what is needed to have deeper control over audio.

The SoundPlayer class does not require any Flex framework functionality. As such, you can reuse it within both a Flex application and a pure ActionScript application.

Working with video

Flex also supports the ability to display full-motion video. Flash Player supports four video codecs: H.264, On2 VP6, Sorenson Spark, and Screen. Unless you have existing encoded Flash video, the H.264 codec will be optimal as it currently has the best support for high-quality video playback; however, the On2 VP6, Spark, and Screen codecs have their own benefits as well. For instance, the Sorenson Spark codec is ideal for low-latency real-time video broadcast and for low CPU usage needs, such as for playback on handheld devices. It is the only codec currently available for client-to-server transmission and capturing, which allows you to capture an end-user's web camera. The Screen codec, meanwhile, is ideal for screen capturing, which typically is useful for video screen captures.

Codecs are compression algorithms that are used when digitally encoding video. There tend to be some trade-offs among the different codecs available today. Some of the trade-offs include faster encoding speed for lower latency in real-time applications, higher quality and resolution, the ability to better handle specific use cases such as screen capturing, and wider adoption. When beginning to work on an application that will use a lot of video, it is a good idea to compare the different codecs to determine which best meets your needs.

As you can with audio, you can load, embed, and stream Flash video. You probably won't want to embed video within your application; typically, you will be loading video or streaming it because video files can be very large.

For working with video, the Flex framework provides the `VideoDisplay` component, which allows you to load and display video. Example 11-7 is an example of the `VideoDisplay` component with the playback and volume controls of a loaded video.

Example 11-7. A simple video player

```
<?xml version="1.0" encoding="utf-8"?>
<mx:Application xmlns:mx="http://www.adobe.com/2006/mxml">
    <mx:Panel title="Video Viewer">
        <mx:VideoDisplay id="videoViewer" source="assets/video.flv"
volume="{volumeControl.value}"/>
        <mx:ControlBar>
            <mx:Label text="{videoViewer.playheadTime.toPrecision(2)}"/>
```

```
            <mx:Button label="Play" click="videoViewer.play()"/>
            <mx:Button label="Pause" click="videoViewer.pause()"/>
            <mx:Button label="Stop" click="vi-deoViewer.stop()"/>
            <mx:HSlider id="volumeControl" maximum="1"/>
        </mx:ControlBar>
    </mx:Panel>
</mx:Application>
```

Even with such a short example, we have a fully functioning video player. The `VideoDisplay` component loads the video once it is initialized. The control bar contains a label displaying the time as the playback progresses; the buttons allow the user to pause, play, and stop playback; and the slider allows the user to control the volume. The playback is controlled through the `VideoDisplay` methods `play()`, `pause()`, and `stop()`. The volume is controlled by data-binding the `volume` property of the `VideoDisplay` component to the `value` property of the slider. The valid volume range is between 0 and 1, with 1 being the maximum.

Although the `VideoDisplay` component is useful, it may not provide the functionality you require. For such cases, you will need to write your own video player to suit your needs.

Streaming media

Streaming is similar to loading, except that streaming allows the user to seek to any point of a media file without having to download the entire file, and it allows the user to download only a small portion of the file rather than the entire file, before being able to play it. It does this by segmenting the media file into chunks that are sent to the player, which in turn buffers enough chunks to begin playback with the ability to keep adding to the buffer as playback continues. This can be beneficial when bandwidth consumption is a concern or when serving large files that users will often want to seek within, rather than just starting from the beginning of the file.

Flash Player supports streaming through the Real Time Messaging Protocol (RTMP). RTMP was developed by Macromedia (now Adobe) and is a part of Adobe's Flash Media Server product (*http://www.adobe.com/products/flashmediaserver/*).

Assuming you have an FLV file hosted on a local RTMP server with the URL *rtmp://localhost/pf/video/video.flv*, here is code that uses the `VideoDisplay` component to display a streamed video:

```
<?xml version="1.0" encoding="utf-8"?>
<mx:Application xmlns:mx="http://www.adobe.com/2006/mxml">
    <mx:Panel title="Video Viewer">
        <mx:VideoDisplay bufferTime="3" id="videoViewer"
source="rtmp://localhost/pf2/video/video.flv" volume="{volumeControl.value}"/>
        <mx:ControlBar>
            <mx:Label text="{videoViewer.playheadTime.toPrecision(2)}"/>
           <mx:Button label="Play" click="videoViewer.play()"/>
```

```
            <mx:Button label="Pause" click="videoViewer.pause()"/>
            <mx:Button label="Stop" click="videoViewer.stop()"/>
            <mx:HSlider id="volumeControl" maximum="1" width="80"/>
        </mx:ControlBar>
    </mx:Panel>
</mx:Application>
```

Notice how this example is almost identical to the previous one, except for the addition of the `bufferTime` property and a change to the value of the `source` property. The `source` property accepts a reference to an RTMP video stream, and it takes care of communicating with the streaming server. `bufferTime` is a property of the `VideoDisplay` component that affects only streamed video. In the example, `bufferTime` is set to three seconds, which means the player will buffer for three seconds before playing back the stream to ensure that playback in not interrupted. You may not need to set this value very often, but if you find that your video is having difficulty playing continuously, typically because of network performance, you may want to compensate by raising the value of `bufferTime`.

Summary

Throughout this chapter, you have seen how Flex can easily allow developers to harness the power of Flash Player in adding images, animations, video, and audio. The different types of media can be embedded, loaded, and in some cases, streamed.

CHAPTER 12

Managing State

In Flex terminology, a *state* is a collection of changes (called *overrides*) to a view. The overrides can comprise additions or removals of components as well as changes to their properties and behaviors. Every Flex application (and every Flex component) has at least one state, referred to as its *base state*. Flex states enable you to more easily change the view for an application, whether at a macro or a micro level. For example, you can define two states that act as screens in an application (e.g., a login screen and a menu screen). Using states for screens is an example of a macro-level use. At the micro level, you can use states to manage cascading forms and even different views for components (e.g., rollover changes).

The Flex framework provides an entire library for states and state management. You can create and manage states from MXML or ActionScript. Furthermore, you can use states in conjunction with other Flex features, such as transitions and history management, to create robust, responsive, and engaging applications and user interfaces with relative ease. In this chapter, you'll learn how to work with Flex states.

Creating States

You can create states for an application, and you can create states for components. The process for creating states for either is identical (remember that applications and components both inherit from `UIComponent`, which is what defines the ability to work with states). You can create states using ActionScript or using MXML. Practically speaking, it is usually much easier to create states using MXML whenever possible. You'll probably find that you define states using ActionScript relatively infrequently. However, creating states with ActionScript provides you with a level of runtime flexibility you couldn't otherwise achieve. Therefore, we'll look at how to create states with both MXML and ActionScript. Initially we'll focus primarily on using MXML because that is the most common way to work with states, but later in the chapter we'll look at using ActionScript.

Every application and component has a `states` property that allows you to define an array of states. From MXML you can use the following syntax to populate the `states` array:

```
<mx:states>
    <!-- State elements -->
</mx:states>
```

The states themselves are instances of the `mx.states.State` class, and you can create a new state using the `<mx:State>` tag in MXML. When you create a new state, you should —at a minimum—specify a `name`. The `name` for a state is the identifier by which you can reference it. The following MXML creates a new state with a name of `exampleState`:

```
<mx:State name="exampleState"></mx:State>
```

Within the opening and closing `<mx:State>` tags, you can specify the state definition. A state definition consists of override elements that do the following:

- Add or remove components
- Set properties of components/objects
- Set styles of components
- Set event handlers for objects
- Perform custom overrides (meaning custom code to handle behaviors not handled by standard overrides)

The next several sections discuss each element type in more detail.

Applying States

By default, the base state is applied to an application or component. You can define many states for each application and component, but you can apply only one state at any one time. You can apply a state using the `currentState` property. Example 12-1 defines a state that adds a checkbox (see "Adding and Removing Components" later in this chapter for details on adding components to states). The state is applied when the user clicks the button in the base state.

Example 12-1. Applying a state

```
<?xml version="1.0" encoding="utf-8"?>
<mx:Application xmlns:mx="http://www.adobe.com/2006/mxml" layout="absolute">

    <mx:VBox id="vbox">
        <mx:Button label="Add Checkbox" click="currentState='newCheckbox';" />
    </mx:VBox>

    <mx:states>
        <mx:State name="newCheckbox">
            <mx:AddChild relativeTo="{vbox}">
                <mx:CheckBox id="checkbox" label="New Checkbox" />
            </mx:AddChild>
```

```
        </mx:State>
    </mx:states>

</mx:Application>
```

Note that the value of the currentState property is a string specifying the name of the state to apply. In the preceding example, when the user clicks the button, the value of newCheckbox is assigned to the currentState property of the application. The Flex framework then looks for a state with a name attribute of newCheckbox and applies that state. In the preceding example, the state with the name of newCheckbox uses an <mx:AddChild> tag to add a new checkbox to the VBox instance. If you want to return to the base state, you can assign a null value or an empty string to the currentState property. Example 12-2 demonstrates how this works by adding a second button that returns the application to the base state.

Example 12-2. Returning to the base state

```
<?xml version="1.0" encoding="utf-8"?>
<mx:Application xmlns:mx="http://www.adobe.com/2006/mxml" layout="absolute">

    <mx:VBox id="vbox">
        <mx:Button label="Return to Base State" click="currentState='';" />
        <mx:Button label="Add Checkbox" click="currentState='newCheckbox';" />
    </mx:VBox>

    <mx:states>
        <mx:State name="newCheckbox">
            <mx:AddChild relativeTo="{vbox}">
                <mx:CheckBox id="checkbox" label="New Checkbox" />
            </mx:AddChild>
        </mx:State>
    </mx:states>

</mx:Application>
```

Figure 12-1 and Figure 12-2 show the two states created from Example 12-2.

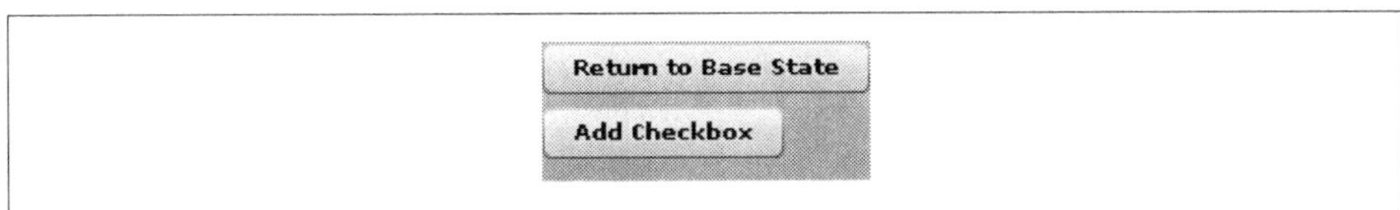

Figure 12-1. The base state

Figure 12-2. The newCheckbox state

The currentState property is a property inherited from the UIComponent class. That means each application and each component has its own currentState property, and you can set the states of each independently. Another way to say this is that setting the currentState property for component A changes the state for component A only, and setting the currentState property for component B changes the state for component B only.

Defining States Based on Existing States

By default, all states are based on the base state. For example, the new checkbox in Example 12-1 and Example 12-2 from the preceding section is added to the VBox. When the new state is applied, the VBox and nested button from the base state continue to exist. However, note that states are not applied cumulatively. For instance, Example 12-3 defines two states in addition to the base state. The base state has two buttons. Each button applies one of the states. When applying the newCheckbox state, a new checkbox is added. When applying the newTextArea state, a new text area is added, but if the checkbox had been previously added, it is removed.

Example 12-3. Defining a state that is not based on an existing state

```
<?xml version="1.0" encoding="utf-8"?>
<mx:Application xmlns:mx="http://www.adobe.com/2006/mxml" layout="absolute">

    <mx:VBox id="vbox">
        <mx:Button label="Add Checkbox" click="currentState='newCheckbox';" />
        <mx:Button label="Add Text Area" click="currentState='newTextArea';" />
    </mx:VBox>

    <mx:states>
        <mx:State name="newCheckbox">
            <mx:AddChild relativeTo="{vbox}">
                <mx:CheckBox id="checkbox" label="New Checkbox" />
            </mx:AddChild>
        </mx:State>
        <mx:State name="newTextArea">
            <mx:AddChild relativeTo="{vbox}">
                <mx:TextArea id="textarea" />
            </mx:AddChild>
        </mx:State>
    </mx:states>

</mx:Application>
```

When components are removed by changing states, the components are still stored in memory. Once a component has been created, moving away from the state in which it is created is the equivalent of calling the removeChild() method in ActionScript: the component is removed from the display list, but it still exists in memory.

Figure 12-3 and Figure 12-4 show what these two states look like. You'll notice that only one of the components (checkbox or text area) gets added at a time.

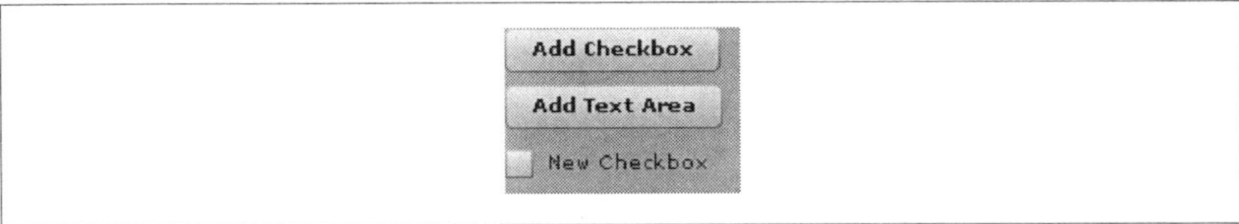

Figure 12-3. The newCheckbox state displaying a checkbox, but not the text area

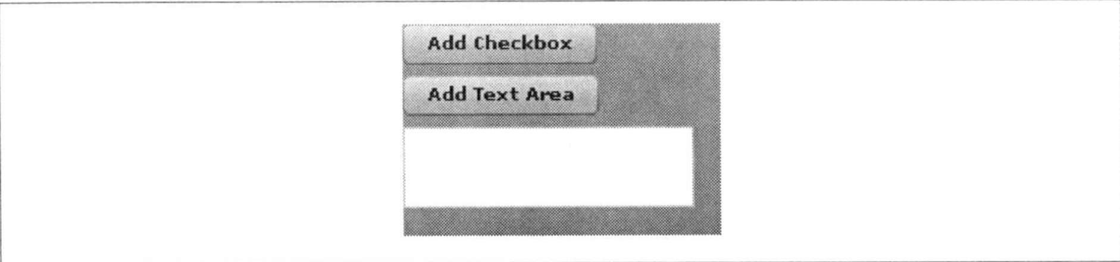

Figure 12-4. The newTextArea state displaying a text area, but not a checkbox

If you want to define a state so that it's based on a state other than the base state, use the `basedOn` attribute of the `<mx:State>` tag. You can assign the name of a state to the `basedOn` attribute of a different state, and the state with the `basedOn` value automatically inherits the state's overrides, specified in the `basedOn` attribute. For example, rewrite the `newTextArea` state definition so that the `<mx:State>` tag appears as follows:

```
<mx:State name="newTextArea" basedOn="newCheckbox">
```

When the `newTextArea` state is rewritten with the `basedOn` attribute (as in the preceding line of code), the `newTextArea` state adds both a checkbox and a text area. Figure 12-5 shows the `newTextArea` state now that it's based on `newCheckbox`.

Figure 12-5. The newTextArea state includes the checkbox when based on newCheckbox

Adding and Removing Components

One of the most common uses of states is adding and removing components. You can use the `<mx:AddChild>` tag to add a component or components. Example 12-4 defines a state named `newTextInput` that adds a text input component instance.

Example 12-4. Basic addition of a component using a state

```
<?xml version="1.0" encoding="utf-8"?>
<mx:Application xmlns:mx="http://www.adobe.com/2006/mxml" layout="vertical">

    <mx:Button id="button" label="Add Text Input"
        click="currentState='newTextInput';" />

    <mx:states>
        <mx:State name="newTextInput">
            <mx:AddChild>
                <mx:TextInput id="textinput" />
            </mx:AddChild>
        </mx:State>
    </mx:states>

</mx:Application>
```

The default behavior of the `<mx:AddChild>` tag is to add the component or components to the application container or component for which the state is defined. However, if you want to define an explicit target to the component (or components) you added, use the `relativeTo` attribute. Example 12-5 adds the new text input as a child of the `VBox` instance with an `id` of `vbox`.

Example 12-5. Adding one component relative to another

```
<?xml version="1.0" encoding="utf-8"?>
<mx:Application xmlns:mx="http://www.adobe.com/2006/mxml" layout="vertical">

    <mx:VBox id="vbox">
        <mx:CheckBox id="checkbox1" label="One" />
        <mx:CheckBox id="checkbox2" label="Two" />
        <mx:Button id="button" label="Add Text Input"
            click="currentState='newTextInput';" />
    </mx:VBox>

    <mx:states>
        <mx:State name="newTextInput">
            <mx:AddChild relativeTo="{vbox}">
                <mx:TextInput id="textinput" />
            </mx:AddChild>
        </mx:State>
    </mx:states>

</mx:Application>
```

When adding child components, the new instance is added as the last child of the target by default. For instance, in the preceding example, the new text input is added below the two checkboxes and button in the base state, as you can see in Figure 12-6. However, you can control where the new instances are added using the `position` attribute. The default value is `lastChild`, but you can optionally specify `firstChild` to add the new instance(s) to the beginning of the target container.

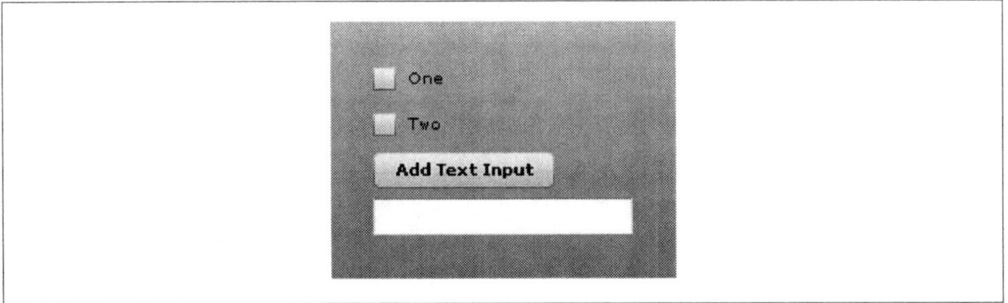

Figure 12-6. By default, new components are added as the last child of the container

When you use `lastChild` or `firstChild` as the position value, the target value is interpreted as the container to which you want to add the child component(s). When you use a value of `before` or `after` for the `position` attribute, the target is interpreted as a sibling of the component(s) you are adding. If you want to add the child component(s) immediately before or after an existing component, you can specify the sibling component as the target and then use the value of `before` or `after` for the `position` attribute. Example 12-6 adds the new text input immediately after the first checkbox in the base state.

Example 12-6. Adding a component using the position property

```
<?xml version="1.0" encoding="utf-8"?>
<mx:Application xmlns:mx="http://www.adobe.com/2006/mxml" layout="absolute">

    <mx:VBox id="vbox">
        <mx:CheckBox id="checkbox1" label="One" />
        <mx:CheckBox id="checkbox2" label="Two" />
        <mx:Button id="button" label="Add Text Input"
            click="currentState='newTextInput';" />
    </mx:VBox>

    <mx:states>
        <mx:State name="newTextInput">
            <mx:AddChild relativeTo="{checkbox1}" position="after">
                <mx:TextInput id="textinput" />
            </mx:AddChild>
        </mx:State>
    </mx:states>

</mx:Application>
```

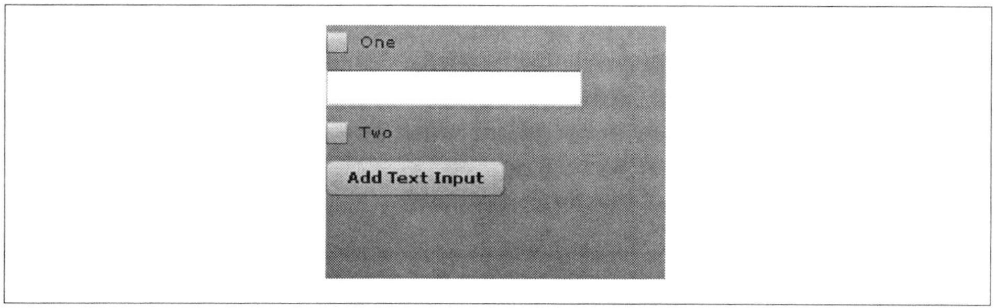

Figure 12-7. Adding a component as a sibling

As you can see in Figure 12-7, the text input is now between the two checkboxes.

You remove components with the `<mx:RemoveChild>` tag, and the process generally is simpler than adding components. The `<mx:RemoveChild>` tag requires just one attribute, called `target`. The `target` attribute allows you to specify a reference to a component you want to remove. Example 12-7 has two checkboxes in the base state. The `noCheckboxes` state uses the `<mx:RemoveChild>` tag to remove both checkboxes.

Example 12-7. Removing a component

```
<?xml version="1.0" encoding="utf-8"?>
<mx:Application xmlns:mx="http://www.adobe.com/2006/mxml" layout="absolute">

    <mx:VBox id="vbox">
        <mx:CheckBox id="checkbox1" label="One" />
        <mx:CheckBox id="checkbox2" label="Two" />
        <mx:Button id="button" label="Remove Checkboxes"
            click="currentState='noCheckboxes';" />
    </mx:VBox>

    <mx:states>
        <mx:State name="noCheckboxes">
            <mx:RemoveChild target="{checkbox1}" />
            <mx:RemoveChild target="{checkbox2}" />
        </mx:State>
    </mx:states>

</mx:Application>
```

Setting Properties

Using the `<mx:SetProperty>` tag you can set the property value for any component existing within the state. For example, you can set the text for a label, toggle the `enabled` property for a text input, change the *x* and *y* coordinates for a box, or even apply a filter, such as a blur effect. The `<mx:SetProperty>` tag requires `target`, `name`, and `value` attributes. The `target` attribute value needs to be a reference to the object to which you want to apply the new property value. The `name` attribute lets you specify the name of the property you want to set. The `value` attribute allows you to specify the value you want to assign to the property. Example 12-8 uses two buttons to toggle between the base state and a state that enables a text input.

Example 12-8. Setting properties

```
<?xml version="1.0" encoding="utf-8"?>
<mx:Application xmlns:mx="http://www.adobe.com/2006/mxml" layout="absolute">

    <mx:HBox id="hbox">
        <mx:Button id="enableButton" label="Enable"
            click="currentState='enabled';" />
        <mx:Button id="disableButton" label="Disable" click="currentState='';" />
        <mx:TextInput id="textinput" enabled="false" text="example text" />
    </mx:HBox>

    <mx:states>
        <mx:State name="enabled">
            <mx:SetProperty target="{textinput}" name="enabled" value="{true}" />
        </mx:State>
    </mx:states>

</mx:Application>
```

Setting Styles

Use the `<mx:SetStyle>` tag to set styles for components when defining states. You set styles when you want to change the appearance (such as the color or font) of a component when its state changes. The `<mx:SetStyle>` tag has the same attributes as the `<mx:SetProperty>` tag. The `target` property allows you to reference the component to which you want to apply the style, the `name` attribute allows you to specify the style you want to set, and the `value` attribute allows you to set the value of the style.

Example 12-9 uses three buttons to toggle among three states. Each state sets the color styles of checkboxes to highlight groups of transportation types (land, air, and water). For example, when the user clicks the Land button, the car, train, and motorcycle checkbox labels are displayed using a red font.

Example 12-9. Setting styles

```
<?xml version="1.0" encoding="utf-8"?>
<mx:Application xmlns:mx="http://www.adobe.com/2006/mxml" layout="absolute">

    <mx:VBox id="vbox">
        <mx:HBox>
            <mx:Button id="land" label="Land" click="currentState='landState';" />
            <mx:Button id="air" label="Air" click="currentState='airState';" />
            <mx:Button id="water" label="Water" click="currentState='waterState';" />
        </mx:HBox>
        <mx:CheckBox id="helicopter" label="Helicopter" />
        <mx:CheckBox id="motorcycle" label="Motorcycle" />
        <mx:CheckBox id="car" label="Car" />
        <mx:CheckBox id="airplane" label="Airplane" />
```

```
        <mx:CheckBox id="train" label="Train" />
        <mx:CheckBox id="boat" label="Boat" />
        <mx:CheckBox id="submarine" label="Submarine" />
    </mx:VBox>

    <mx:states>
        <mx:State name="landState">
            <mx:SetStyle target="{car}" name="color" value="0xFF0000" />
            <mx:SetStyle target="{train}" name="color" value="0xFF0000" />
            <mx:SetStyle target="{motorcycle}" name="color" value="0xFF0000" />
        </mx:State>
        <mx:State name="airState">
            <mx:SetStyle target="{helicopter}" name="color" value="0xFF0000" />
            <mx:SetStyle target="{airplane}" name="color" value="0xFF0000" />
        </mx:State>
        <mx:State name="waterState">
            <mx:SetStyle target="{boat}" name="color" value="0xFF0000" />
            <mx:SetStyle target="{submarine}" name="color" value="0xFF0000" />
        </mx:State>
    </mx:states>

</mx:Application>
```

Also remember that a best practice is to use CSS selectors (and external stylesheets) wherever possible. Although there's nothing wrong with setting individual style properties using the `SetStyle` override, you can also change the class selector for a component using the `SetProperty` override to change the value of a component's `styleName` property.

Setting Event Handlers

Use the `<mx:SetEventHandler>` tag to add or change an event handler for a component. The tag requires that you specify values for `target`, `name`, and `handler` attributes. The `target` attribute value needs to be a reference to the component for which you want to add or change an event handler. The `name` attribute value needs to be the name of the event. The `handler` attribute specifies the new event handler.

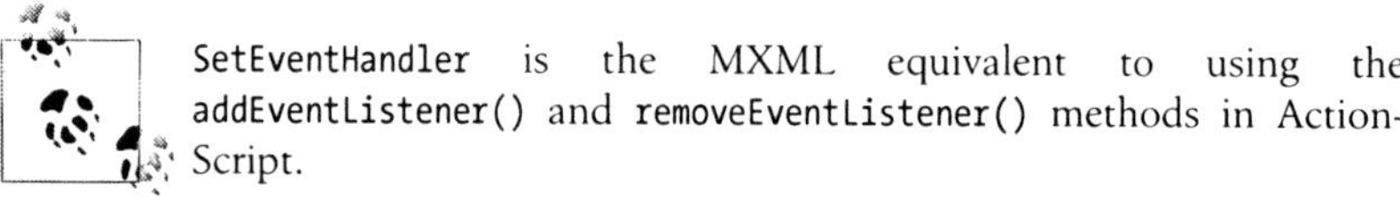

`SetEventHandler` is the MXML equivalent to using the `addEventListener()` and `removeEventListener()` methods in ActionScript.

Example 12-10 modifies Example 12-8 so that it uses one button rather than two to toggle the enabled state of a text input. It does this by changing the event handler for the button (as well as the label) when it is clicked.

Example 12-10. Setting event handlers

```
<?xml version="1.0" encoding="utf-8"?>
<mx:Application xmlns:mx="http://www.adobe.com/2006/mxml" layout="absolute">

    <mx:HBox id="hbox">
        <mx:Button id="button" label="Enable" click="currentState='enabled';" />
        <mx:TextInput id="textinput" enabled="false" text="example text" />
    </mx:HBox>

    <mx:states>
        <mx:State name="enabled">
            <mx:SetProperty target="{textinput}" name="enabled" value="{true}" />
            <mx:SetEventHandler target="{button}" name="click"
                handler="currentState='';" />
            <mx:SetProperty target="{button}" name="label" value="Disable" />
        </mx:State>
    </mx:states>

</mx:Application>
```

Using ActionScript to Define States

In most cases, it's more appropriate to use MXML than ActionScript to define states. However, sometimes you want to define states dynamically (in which case you must use ActionScript). One such example is when you want to define a multipage form based on data loaded at runtime. Creating the form dynamically is advantageous because you can change the form without recompiling and republishing the SWF. However, because form elements aren't known at compile time, you cannot use MXML to define the states.

The ActionScript used to work with states corresponds to the MXML. In the following sections, you'll learn about the ActionScript equivalents to the MXML you learned about earlier.

Defining States

When defining states using ActionScript, you use the `mx.states.State` class. You can use the constructor as part of a new statement to define a new `State` instance:

```
var stateA:State = new State();
```

You can assign a name to a state using the `name` property, in much the same way as you'd use the `name` attribute of the `<mx:State>` tag:

```
stateA.name = "exampleStateA";
```

And just as you can use the `basedOn` attribute of the `<mx:State>` tag to define state inheritance, you can use the `basedOn` property of the `State` class. The following code defines a new state that is based on the state constructed in the previous two code snippets. Note that the `basedOn` property expects a string specifying the `name` of the state upon which you want to base the new state; you cannot assign it a reference to the State object.

```
var stateB:State = new State();
stateB.name = "exampleStateB";
stateB.basedOn = "exampleStateA";
```

Adding States

With MXML, you use the <mx:states> tag to define an array of states for an application or component. With ActionScript, you use the states property. The states property is defined in UIComponent, and it is inherited by all applications and components. The data type of states is Array, and by default the value is an empty array. If you want to add states to an application or component using only ActionScript, you need only add states to the array:

```
states.push(stateA);
states.push(stateB);
```

Adding Overrides

As you'll read in the next few sections, you can define overrides (e.g., AddChild and SetProperty) using ActionScript. However, in addition to defining the overrides, you also must add the overrides to a state. Using MXML, you simply nest the override tags within the <mx:State> tag. With ActionScript, you must use the overrides property of the State class.

The overrides property is defined as an array data type. By default, the overrides property value of a State object is an empty array and can add overrides to the array:

```
stateA.overrides.push(exampleAddChild);
```

Adding and Removing Child Elements

You can add and remove child elements in MXML using the <mx:AddChild> and <mx:RemoveChild> tags. The corresponding ActionScript classes are mx.states.AddChild and mx.states.RemoveChild.

When you want to add child elements using the AddChild class, you must first construct a new instance:

```
var addChild:AddChild = new AddChild();
```

When using MXML, nest the component tag within the <mx:AddChild> tag. When using ActionScript, you must assign a component reference to the target property of the AddChild object:

```
var button:Button = new Button();
button.label = "Example";
addChild.target = button;
```

If you want to specify a parent, you can use the relativeTo property. Simply assign a reference to the relativeTo component:

```
addChild.relativeTo = vbox;
```

Also, just as you can specify where you want to add the child element using the position attribute of the <mx:AddChild> tag, you can use the position property of the AddChild class. The property accepts the same values (firstChild, lastChild, before, and after) as the corresponding attribute. The values have the same effects as when working with MXML. When you specify a value of firstChild or lastChild, the child element is added as a child of the target. When you specify a value of before or after, the child element is added as a sibling of the target. If you don't specify any value or you assign a value of null, the default behavior is that the component is added as the last child of the target:

```
addChild.position = "firstChild";
```

When you want to remove a child element, use the RemoveChild object and specify the child using the target property:

```
var removeChild:RemoveChild = new RemoveChild();
removeChild.target = button;
```

Setting Properties and Styles

To set properties and styles with ActionScript you use the mx.states.SetProperty and mx.states.SetStyle classes. Each class has properties that correspond exactly to the attributes of the <mx:SetProperty> and <mx:SetStyle> tags. Both classes define target, name, and value properties. To simplify things you can also pass the target, name, and value to the constructors. The following example illustrates how to use the SetProp erty and SetStyle classes:

```
var setProperty:SetProperty = new SetProperty(button, "width", 200);
var setStyle:SetStyle = new SetStyle(button, "color", 0xFF00FF);
```

Setting Event Handlers

The mx.states.SetEventHandler class corresponds to the <mx:SetEventHandler> tag for setting event handlers. The class defines target and name properties that correspond to the target and name attributes of the <mx:SetEventHandler> tag. To make things even simpler, the SetEventHandler constructor allows you to pass the target and name parameters:

```
var setEventHandler:SetEventHandler = new SetEventHandler(button, "click");
```

When you use the <mx:SetEventHandler> tag, you use the handler attribute to specify the ActionScript to call when the event occurs. However, when working with a SetEventHandler object, you use the handlerFunction property. The handlerFunction property requires a reference to a function/method. Flash Player then calls that function/method when the event occurs. The following instructs Flash Player to call a function named `clickHandler` when the user clicks the button:

```
setEventHandler.handlerFunction = clickHandler;
```

Using Dynamic States

To better understand how to use ActionScript's dynamic states created at runtime, let's look at an example. Example 12-11 builds a multipage form from XML data and loads it at runtime. The form is composed of states for each page.

For the purposes of this example, the following XML data is used and saved in a file called *forms.xml*.

Example 12-11. forms.xml

```
<forms>
    <form id="1" label="Name">
        <item type="textinput" name="firstName" label="First Name" />
        <item type="textinput" name="lastName" label="Last Name" />
    </form>
    <form id="2" label="Address">
        <item type="textinput" name="address" label="Street Address" />
        <item type="textinput" name="city" label="City" />
        <item type="textinput" name="state" label="State" />
        <item type="textinput" name="postalCode" label="Postal Code" />
    </form>
    <form id="3" label="Phone and Email">
        <item type="textinput" name="phone" label="Phone Number" />
        <item type="textinput" name="email" label="Email" />
    </form>
    <form id="4" label="Address">
        <item type="textarea" name="agreement" label="">
        Example Corporation reserves all rights.
        </item>
        <item type="checkbox" itemName="city" label="I agree" />
    </form>
</forms>
```

To work with the data, you can define several classes: `CustomFormItem`, `CustomForm`, and `CustomFormManager`.

The `CustomFormItem` class can be used to represent an item from the form. An item can consist of a `label` and a form control such as a text input, text area, or checkbox. Example 12-12 defines the `CustomFormItem` class.

Example 12-12. CustomFormItem.as

```
package com.oreilly.programmingflex.states {

    public class CustomFormItem {

        private var _type:String;
```

```
        private var _label:String;
        private var _name:String;
        private var _value:String;

        public function get type():String {
            return _type;
        }

        public function get label():String {
            return _label;
        }

        public function get name():String {
            return _name;
        }

        public function get value():String {
            return _value;
        }

        public function CustomFormItem(type:String, label:String,
                                       name:String, value:String) {
            _type = type;
            _label = label;
            _name = name;
            _value = value;
        }

        public static function parseFromXML(xml:XML):CustomFormItem {
            var type:String = xml.@type;
            var label:String = xml.@label;
            var name:String = xml.@itemName;
            var value:String = null;
            if(type == "textarea") {
                value = xml.children()[0].toString();
            }
            return new CustomFormItem(type, label, name, value);
        }

    }
}
```

The `CustomForm` class (Example 12-13) is essentially a collection of form items with the addition of a method that constructs a new state based on the form.

Example 12-13. CustomForm.as

```
package com.oreilly.programmingflex.states {

    import mx.states.State;
    import mx.containers.GridRow;
    import mx.containers.GridItem;
    import mx.controls.Label;
    import mx.core.UIComponent;
    import mx.controls.TextInput;
```

```
import mx.controls.CheckBox;
import mx.controls.TextArea;
import mx.states.AddChild;
import com.oreilly.programmingflex.states.CustomFormItem;
import mx.containers.Grid;

public class CustomForm {

    private var _label:String;
    private var _items:Array;

    public function CustomForm(label:String, items:Array) {
        _label = label;
        _items = items;
    }

    public function getLabel():String {
        return _label;
    }

    public function getItems():Array {
        return _items.concat();
    }

    public function toState(parent:Grid):State {
        var state:State = new State();
        state.overrides = new Array();
        var gridRow:GridRow;
        var gridItem:GridItem;
        var count:uint = _items.length;
        var i:uint;
        var type:String;
        var label:Label;
        var component:UIComponent;
        var item:com.oreilly.programmingflex.states.CustomFormItem;
        var addChild:AddChild;
        for(i = 0; i < count; i++) {
            item = _items[i];
            gridRow = new GridRow();
            type = item.type;
            if(type != "checkbox" && item. label.length > 0) {
                label = new Label();
                label.text = item.label;
                gridItem = new GridItem();
                gridItem.addChild(label);
                gridRow.addChild(gridItem);
            }
            if(type == "textinput") {
                component = new TextInput();
            }
            else if(type == "checkbox") {
                component = new CheckBox();
                CheckBox(component).label = item.label;
            }
            else if(type == "textarea") {
```

```
                component = new TextArea();
                component.width = 200;
                TextArea(component).text = _items[i]. value;
            }
            component.id = "component";
            gridItem = new GridItem();
            gridItem.addChild(component);
            gridRow.addChild(gridItem);
            addChild = new AddChild();
            addChild.relativeTo = parent;
            addChild.target = gridRow;
            state.overrides.push(addChild);
        }
        return state;
    }

    public static function parseFromXML(xml:XML):CustomForm {
        var label:String = xml.@label;
        var items:Array = new Array();
        var i:uint;
        for(i = 0; i < xml.children().length(); i++) {
            items.push(CustomFormItem.parseFromXML(xml.children()[i]));
        }
        return new CustomForm(label, items);
    }

  }
}
```

The CustomFormManager class (Example 12-14) is a Singleton class that loads the XML data and provides an interface to a collection of forms.

Example 12-14. CustomFormManager.as

```
package com.oreilly.programmingflex.states {

    import flash.events.Event;
    import flash.events.ProgressEvent;
    import flash.events.IOErrorEvent;
    import flash.net.URLRequest;
    import flash.net.URLLoader;
    import flash.events.EventDispatcher;
    import com.oreilly.programmingflex.states;

    public class CustomFormManager extends EventDispatcher {

        private static var _instance:CustomFormManager;

        private var _forms:Array;
        private var _index:uint;

        public function CustomFormManager(enforcer:SingletonEnforcer) {
        }

        public static function getInstance():CustomFormManager {
```

```
            if(_instance == null) {
                _instance = new CustomFormManager(new SingletonEnforcer());
            }
            return _instance;
        }

        public function load(url:String):void {
            var request:URLRequest = new URLRequest(url);
            var loader:URLLoader = new URLLoader();
            loader.load(request);
            loader.addEventListener(Event.COMPLETE, dataHandler);
        }

        public function hasNextForm():Boolean {
            return _index < _forms.length;
        }

        public function getNextForm():CustomForm {
            if(_index >= _forms.length) {
                return null;
            }
            return _forms[_index++];
        }

        public function hasPreviousForm():Boolean {
            return _index > 0;
        }

        public function getPreviousForm():CustomForm {
            if(_index < 0) {
                return null;
            }
            return _forms[_index--];
        }

        private function dataHandler(event:Event):void {
            _index = 0;
            _forms = new Array();
            var xml:XML = new XML(event.target.data);
            var forms:XMLList = xml.children();
            var i:uint;
            var form:CustomForm;
            for(i = 0; i < forms.length(); i++) {
                form = CustomForm.parseFromXML(forms[i]);
                _forms.push(form);
            }
            dispatchEvent(new Event(Event.COMPLETE));
        }

    }
}
class SingletonEnforcer {}
```

The MXML (with embedded ActionScript) in Example 12-15 illustrates how to use the preceding code to construct dynamic states based on XML data.

Example 12-15. Dynamic states

```
<?xml version="1.0" encoding="utf-8"?>
<mx:Application xmlns:mx="http://www.adobe.com/2006/mxml" layout="absolute"
initialize="initializeHandler(event)">
    <mx:Script>
        <![CDATA[
            import mx.states.SetProperty;
            import mx.states.SetEventHandler;
            import mx.states.State;
            import com.oreilly.programmingflex.states.CustomForm;

            import com.oreilly.programmingflex.states.CustomFormManager;

            private var _stateIndex:uint;
            private var _stateCount:uint;

            private function initializeHandler(event:Event):void {
                var formManager:CustomFormManager = CustomFormManager.getInstance();
                formManager.load("forms.xml");
                formManager.addEventListener(Event.COMPLETE, dataHandler);
            }

            private function dataHandler(event:Event):void {
                _stateIndex = 1;
                _stateCount = 0;
                var formManager:CustomFormManager = CustomFormManager.getInstance();
                var form:CustomForm;
                states = new Array();
                var state:State;
                var index:uint = 1;
                var setProperty:SetProperty;
                var hasPreviousForm:Boolean;
                while(formManager.hasNextForm()) {
                    hasPreviousForm = formManager.hasPreviousForm();
                    _stateCount++;
                    form = formManager.getNextForm();
                    state = form.toState(grid);
                    setProperty = new SetProperty(next, "visible",
                      formManager.hasNextForm());
                    state.overrides.push(setProperty);
                    setProperty = new SetProperty(previous, "visible",
                      hasPreviousForm);
                    state.overrides.push(setProperty);
                    state.name = "form" + index++;
                    states.push(state);
                }
                currentState = "form1";
            }

            private function nextForm():void {
                currentState = "form" + ++_stateIndex;
            }

            private function previousForm():void {
                currentState = "form" + --_stateIndex;
```

```
            }
        ]]>
    </mx:Script>
    <mx:VBox id="vbox">
        <mx:Label id="formLabel" />
        <mx:HBox>
            <mx:Button id="previous" label="Previous" visible="false"
                click="previousForm()" />
            <mx:Button id="next" label="Next" click="nextForm()" />
        </mx:HBox>
        <mx:Grid id="grid">
        </mx:Grid>
    </mx:VBox>
</mx:Application>
```

Figure 12-8 through Figure 12-11 show what the states look like.

Figure 12-8. The first form state

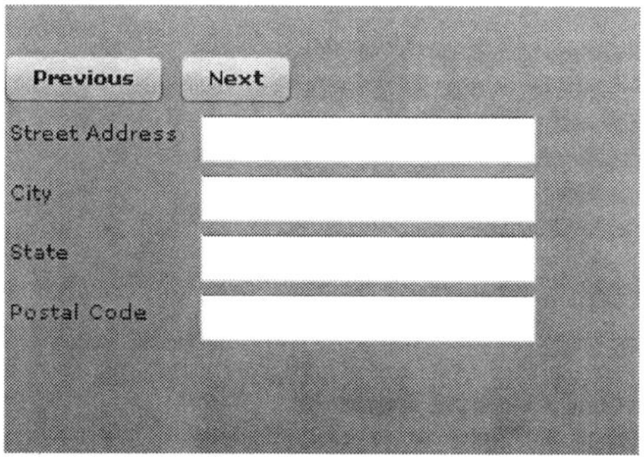

Figure 12-9. The second form state

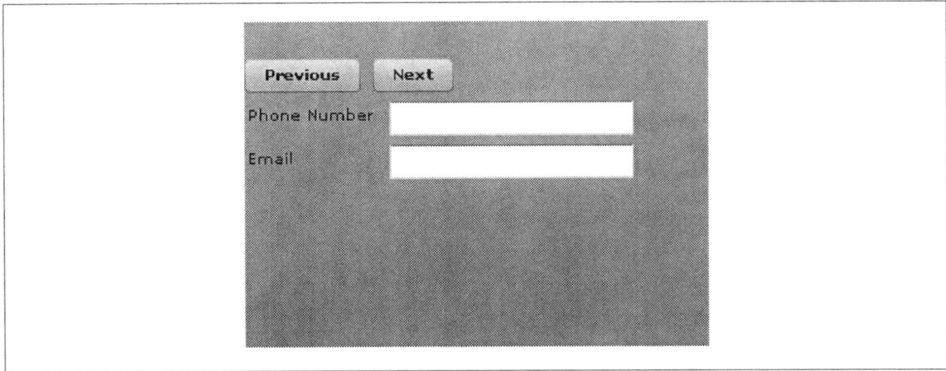

Figure 12-10. The third form state

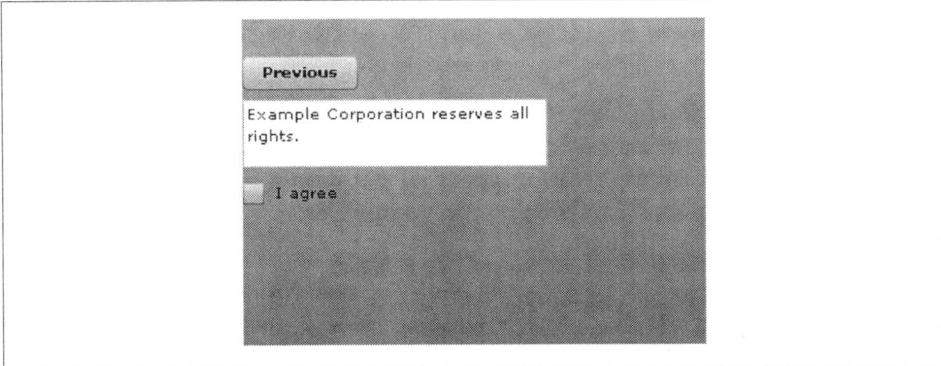

Figure 12-11. The fourth form state

Managing Object Creation Policies (Preloading Objects)

By default, components added by nonbase states aren't instantiated until the state is first requested. The MXML in Example 12-16 illustrates this. The `trace()` statement outputs `null` because `button` is not yet defined when the application first starts.

Example 12-16. Understanding object creation policies: Default policy

```
<?xml version="1.0" encoding="utf-8"?>
<mx:Application xmlns:mx="http://www.adobe.com/2006/mxml" layout="absolute"
initialize="initializeHandler(event)">

    <mx:Script>
        <![CDATA[

            private function initializeHandler(event:Event):void {
                trace(button);
            }
```

```
        ]]>
    </mx:Script>

    <mx:states>
        <mx:State name="example">
            <mx:AddChild>
                <mx:Button id="button" label="Example" />
            </mx:AddChild>
        </mx:State>
    </mx:states>

</mx:Application>
```

However, you can manage when components added by states are instantiated using a creation policy. The default creation policy setting is auto, which means the component is instantiated when the state is first requested. You can set creation policies for each added component using the creationPolicy attribute of the <mx:AddChild> tag, or the creationPolicy property of the AddChild class. The possible values are auto (default), all, and none.

When you set the creation policy of an added component to all, the component is instantiated when the application first starts. The MXML in Example 12-17 illustrates how that works. Because the creation policy of the button is now set to all, the trace() statement outputs the reference to the component.

Example 12-17. Understanding object creation policies: Policy all

```
<?xml version="1.0" encoding="utf-8"?>
<mx:Application xmlns:mx="http://www.adobe.com/2006/mxml" layout="absolute"
initialize="initializeHandler(event)">

    <mx:Script>
        <![CDATA[

            private function initializeHandler(event:Event):void {
                trace(button);
            }

        ]]>
    </mx:Script>

    <mx:states>
        <mx:State name="example">
            <mx:AddChild creationPolicy="all">
                <mx:Button id="button" label="Example" />
            </mx:AddChild>
        </mx:State>
    </mx:states>

</mx:Application>
```

When the creation policy is set to none, the component isn't instantiated until you explicitly call the createInstance() method of the AddChild object. If you're defining the AddChild object using the <mx:AddChild> tag, you must assign an id. Example 12-18 illustrates how the none creation policy works. The first trace() statement outputs null because the component hasn't been instantiated. The second trace() statement outputs the reference to the component because it is called immediately following the call to createInstance().

Example 12-18. Understanding object creation policy: Policy none

```
<?xml version="1.0" encoding="utf-8"?>
<mx:Application xmlns:mx="http://www.adobe.com/2006/mxml" layout="absolute"
initialize="initializeHandler(event)">
    <mx:Script>
        <![CDATA[

            private function initializeHandler(event:Event):void {
                trace(button);
                 exampleAddChild.createInstance();
                 trace(button);
            }

        ]]>
    </mx:Script>

    <mx:states>
        <mx:State name="example">
            <mx:AddChild creationPolicy="none" id="exampleAddChild"
>

                <mx:Button id="button" label="Example" />
            </mx:AddChild>
        </mx:State>
    </mx:states>

</mx:Application>
```

In most applications, the default (auto) creation policy is the correct setting. However, there are several reasons you might want to select a different creation policy. The all policy, for example, is useful in at least two scenarios:

The added component requires a long time to initialize
: If the component isn't initialized until the state is requested, the user might experience a delay. By setting the policy to all, the component is initialized when the application first starts; that should mitigate any issues related to component initialization times and delays when changing states.

You want to reference the added component before first requesting the state
: For example, when you create a component with several states, you might want to reference added components via an accessor method.

The none policy may not seem immediately useful; however, consider that the auto and all policies are very black and white:

- When you select auto, components aren't instantiated until the state is requested.

- When you select `all`, components are instantiated when the application initializes.

There are reasons you might want to ensure that a component initializes before a state is requested, but you don't want to force the component to instantiate when the application initializes. For example, a complex application might contain many states, each having components that take a long time to initialize. If you set the creation policy of all the `AddChild` objects to `all`, the user might have to wait a long time before the application initializes. However, it might be a better user experience if the application starts right away while the components for the rest of the states initialize in the background. Using the `none` creation policy allows you to do just that. Simply call the `createInstance()` method of the `AddChild` object to instantiate the child component.

Handling State Events

Four events are associated with state changes:

- When a state change is requested, the application or component containing the state dispatches a `currentStateChanging` event. The event occurs before the state actually changes.
- Once the state has changed, the application or component dispatches a `currentStateChanged` event. Both events are of type `mx.events.StateChangeEvent` (use the constants `CURRENT_STATE_CHANGING` and `CURRENT_STATE_CHANGED` to add listeners). Neither event is cancelable, which means you cannot prevent a state change from occurring by canceling a `currentStateChanging` event, for example. Rather, both events are used primarily by the transitions framework to detect when a transition should occur.
- The `enterState` and `exitState` events occur when the state starts and stops:
    - The `enterState` event occurs as soon as the state has started but before it is applied to the view.
    - The `exitState` event occurs as soon as the state is about to stop.

    Both events are of type `mx.events.FlexEvent` (use the constants `ENTER_STATE` and `EXIT_STATE` to add listeners).
- The `enterState` event is dispatched by a `State` object when the state starts, and by an application or component when returning to the base state. The `exitState` event is dispatched by a `State` object when the state stops, and by an application or component when exiting the base state.

Understanding State Life Cycles

One aspect of states that initially can be confusing is the life cycle of the components within a state. As you learned in "Managing Object Creation Policies (Preloading Objects)" earlier in this chapter, by using states you can manage the creation policy for components within the state. By default, all the components in a state are not created until the state is first requested. You also learned that you can control the creation policy such that components are created when the application starts up regardless of whether they belong to the base state, or you can manually create the components in a state. That covers the possibilities for how and when components in states can get created. Next, we need to look at what happens to components once they have been created, because this point can cause a fair amount of confusion if misunderstood.

When a state is set to the current state one of two possible things can happen. If the components in the state have already been created they are immediately added to the display list; if the components haven't yet been created they are first created and then added to the display list. On the other end of things, when a state is replaced as the current state only one thing can happen: the components that are part of that state are removed from the display list. Once the components in a state have been created, they are not destroyed. Replacing a state as the current state does not destroy the components it contains. This has subtle repercussions.

We'll start by considering a relatively simple scenario to see the implications of how components are managed by states. In this scenario, we'll create an application with two states: each is a simple form. We'll assume that for business or legal reasons it is critical that if the user wants to return to one of the forms to change something, she must fill out the entire form again. To start, Example 12-19 shows the initial MXML code that creates the two forms, two states, and two buttons for switching between them.

Example 12-19. Creating two states, two forms, and two buttons

```
<?xml version="1.0" encoding="utf-8"?>
<mx:Application xmlns:mx="http://www.adobe.com/2006/mxml" layout="vertical">
    <mx:HBox>
        <mx:Button label="Form A" click="currentState='formA';" />
        <mx:Button label="Form B" click="currentState='formB';" />
    </mx:HBox>
    <mx:states>
        <mx:State name="formA">
            <mx:AddChild>
                <mx:VBox>
                    <mx:Label text="Select from the following list" />
                    <mx:CheckBox id="cars" label="Cars" />
                    <mx:CheckBox id="boats" label="Boats" />
                    <mx:CheckBox id="airplanes" label="Airplanes" />
                    <mx:CheckBox id="trains" label="Trains" />
                </mx:VBox>
            </mx:AddChild>
        </mx:State>
        <mx:State name="formB">
            <mx:AddChild>
                <mx:Form>
                    <mx:FormItem label="Name">
                        <mx:TextInput id="contactName" />
                    </mx:FormItem>
```

```
                <mx:FormItem label="Email">
                    <mx:TextInput id="contactEmail" />
                </mx:FormItem>
            </mx:Form>
        </mx:AddChild>
    </mx:State>
</mx:states>
</mx:Application>
```

If you test this application, fill out the forms, and switch back and forth between them, you'll see that the form values are retained even as you switch states. In most cases, this is quite a good thing. However, in the scenario that we've created, we want to make sure the forms are always reset to the starting point when the user returns to them. Using the enterState event that we discussed in the preceding section, we can do just that. Use the enterState event to trigger ActionScript that resets the forms, as shown in Example 12-20.

Example 12-20. Resetting forms using the enterState event

```
<?xml version="1.0" encoding="utf-8"?>
<mx:Application xmlns:mx="http://www.adobe.com/2006/mxml" layout="vertical">

    <mx:Script>
        <![CDATA[

            private function resetFormA():void {
                cars.selected = false;
                boats.selected = false;
                airplanes.selected = false;
                trains.selected = false;
            }

            private function resetFormB():void {
                contactName.text = "";
                contactEmail.text = "";
            }

        ]]>
    </mx:Script>

    <mx:HBox>
        <mx:Button label="Form A" click="currentState='formA';" />
        <mx:Button label="Form B" click="currentState='formB';" />
    </mx:HBox>
    <mx:states>
        <mx:State name="formA" enterState="resetFormA();">
            <mx:AddChild>
                <mx:VBox>
                    <mx:Label text="Select from the following list" />
                    <mx:CheckBox id="cars" label="Cars" />
                    <mx:CheckBox id="boats" label="Boats" />
                    <mx:CheckBox id="airplanes" label="Airplanes" />
                    <mx:CheckBox id="trains" label="Trains" />
                </mx:VBox>
```

```
            </mx:AddChild>
        </mx:State>
        <mx:State name="formB" enterState="resetFormB();">
            <mx:AddChild>
                <mx:Form>
                    <mx:FormItem label="Name">
                        <mx:TextInput id="contactName" />
                    </mx:FormItem>
                    <mx:FormItem label="Email">
                        <mx:TextInput id="contactEmail" />
                    </mx:FormItem>
                </mx:Form>
            </mx:AddChild>
        </mx:State>
    </mx:states>
</mx:Application>
```

It's likely that you'll frequently use states to add and remove custom application components. For example, if you were to write an application such as the one shown in Example 12-19 and Example 12-20, you'd probably convert the forms to components. If you were to do that, the basic strategy for resetting the form values would be similar, but there would be slight changes. To better understand this we'll first look at the code for the componentized version of the application. Example 12-21 and Example 12-22 show the MXML components for the two forms.

Example 12-21. FormA.mxml

```
<?xml version="1.0" encoding="utf-8"?>
<mx:VBox xmlns:mx="http://www.adobe.com/2006/mxml">
    <mx:Label text="Select from the following list" />
    <mx:CheckBox id="cars" label="Cars" />
    <mx:CheckBox id="boats" label="Boats" />
    <mx:CheckBox id="airplanes" label="Airplanes" />
    <mx:CheckBox id="trains" label="Trains" />
</mx:VBox>
```

Example 12-22. FormB.mxml

```
<?xml version="1.0" encoding="utf-8"?>
<mx:Form xmlns:mx="http://www.adobe.com/2006/mxml">
    <mx:FormItem label="Name">
        <mx:TextInput id="contactName" />
    </mx:FormItem>
    <mx:FormItem label="Email">
        <mx:TextInput id="contactEmail" />
    </mx:FormItem>
</mx:Form>
```

Next, in Example 12-23, you can see what the revised application MXML looks like. We've removed the Script block from this code because it is no longer relevant.

Example 12-23. Using custom application components for the forms

```
<?xml version="1.0" encoding="utf-8"?>
<mx:Application xmlns:mx="http://www.adobe.com/2006/mxml"
    layout="vertical" xmlns:local="*">
    <mx:HBox>
        <mx:Button label="Form A" click="currentState='formA';" />
        <mx:Button label="Form B" click="currentState='formB';" />
    </mx:HBox>
    <mx:states>
        <mx:State name="formA">
            <mx:AddChild>
                <local:FormA id="formA" />
            </mx:AddChild>
        </mx:State>
        <mx:State name="formB">
            <mx:AddChild>
                <local:FormB id="formB" />
            </mx:AddChild>
        </mx:State>
    </mx:states>
</mx:Application>
```

At this point, we're back to where we were when we started because the forms still don't clear out when the user returns to them. We had to remove the ActionScript code we used before because it was trying to reference components that don't exist now that we've converted the forms to components. We'll use the same basic strategy we used before, but now we'll encapsulate it. Example 12-24 and Example 12-25 show what the MXML components look like when we add `reset()` methods to them. Notice that the `reset()` methods are merely the old `resetFormA()` and `resetFormB()` methods.

Example 12-24. FormA.mxml with the reset() method

```
<?xml version="1.0" encoding="utf-8"?>
<mx:VBox xmlns:mx="http://www.adobe.com/2006/mxml">
    <mx:Script>
        <![CDATA[

            public function reset():void {
                cars.selected = false;
                boats.selected = false;
                airplanes.selected = false;
                trains.selected = false;
            }

        ]]>
    </mx:Script>

    <mx:Label text="Select from the following list" />
    <mx:CheckBox id="cars" label="Cars" />
    <mx:CheckBox id="boats" label="Boats" />
    <mx:CheckBox id="airplanes" label="Airplanes" />
    <mx:CheckBox id="trains" label="Trains" />
</mx:VBox>
```

Example 12-25. FormB.mxml with the reset() method

```
<?xml version="1.0" encoding="utf-8"?>
<mx:Form xmlns:mx="http://www.adobe.com/2006/mxml">
    <mx:Script>
        <![CDATA[

            public function reset():void {
                contactName.text = "";
                contactEmail.text = "";
            }

        ]]>
    </mx:Script>

    <mx:FormItem label="Name">
        <mx:TextInput id="contactName" />
    </mx:FormItem>
    <mx:FormItem label="Email">
        <mx:TextInput id="contactEmail" />
    </mx:FormItem>
</mx:Form>
```

Now all we need to do is call the `reset()` method of the corresponding component on the `enterState` event handlers within the application code, as shown in Example 12-26.

Example 12-26. The application using the enterState event to trigger calls to the reset() method

```
<?xml version="1.0" encoding="utf-8"?>
<mx:Application xmlns:mx="http://www.adobe.com/2006/mxml" layout="vertical"
xmlns:local="*">
    <mx:HBox>
        <mx:Button label="Form A" click="currentState='formA';" />
        <mx:Button label="Form B" click="currentState='formB';" />
    </mx:HBox>
    <mx:states>
        <mx:State name="formA" enterState="formA.reset();">
            <mx:AddChild>
                <local:FormA id="formA" />
            </mx:AddChild>
        </mx:State>
        <mx:State name="formB" enterState="formB.reset();">
            <mx:AddChild>
                <local:FormB id="formB" />
            </mx:AddChild>
        </mx:State>
    </mx:states>
</mx:Application>
```

It's easy enough to become accustomed to using `creationComplete` and/or `initialize` event handlers to control actions that you want to occur when a custom MXML component appears on the display list, because in many cases all of these events coincide. However, when a component is added and removed from the display list using states, the `creationComplete` and `initialize` events will occur only the first time the state with the component is set to the current state (assuming that the creation policy is set to `auto`). Do not rely on these events for things that need to occur each time the component is added again as a result of a state change. See Chapter 19 for more information about component phases.

When to Use States

States are a powerful and extremely useful feature of the Flex framework. You can accomplish many things using states. In fact, you can use states for so many things that it's possible to use them in ways for which they are not really designed. States are very closely associated with the view, so they should be used for things that affect the view or changes in behavior associated with the view (in the case of setting event handlers). Although you could easily use states to change data models, for example, it's not an appropriate use. To better understand the most appropriate use of states, consider the following guidelines for when to use them:

For applying a transition effect
: If you want to use a transition, you ought to use states.

For changing or replacing all or part of a screen
: If you're adding or removing components, states are usually the most appropriate choice.

There are some gray areas that make states an unlikely choice. For example, you might have a form with a text input control that is disabled until the user selects a checkbox. You *could* use states for that, but unless you want to apply a transition, it is probably much more appropriate to simply use ActionScript triggered by the `click` event of the checkbox.

Summary

In this chapter, you learned about Flex view states—what they are and how to create them. States consist of overrides, which are the parts of a state that specify how the state differs from another state. Overrides frequently consist of things like adding and removing components as well as setting styles, properties, and event listeners.

CHAPTER 13

Using Effects and Transitions

Flex applications always consist of one or more user interface and/or container components. At a minimum, a Flex application has an application container, but usually it has many additional components. Although the default behavior for components is fairly static, you can liven up an application with the use of effects. An *effect* is an action that takes place, such as moving, fading, or zooming into or out of a component. An effect can even be a nonvisual behavior, such as playing a sound. Using effects, you can create applications that are more visually (and audibly) interesting. Perhaps more importantly, you can use effects to direct focus and help users better understand how to use applications.

Another way in which you can use effects is to create transitions between states. In Chapter 12, you learned about creating state views. However, so far you've learned how to create only sudden state changes. Using effects as transitions, you can create more interesting and seamless changes between states. For example, rather than an added component suddenly appearing, it can fade in. Not only does this generally create a more visually engaging user experience, but also effects can be used to show emphasis and to highlight change.

In this chapter, we'll look at how to work with effects and transitions. We'll discuss how to trigger effects, how to programmatically control effects, and even how to create custom effects. We'll also discuss how to use an effect as a transition between states, as well as how to create custom transition types.

Using Effects

Effects are actions that you can apply to components. Common examples of effects are fades, moves, and zooms. The Flex framework includes many standard effects, as you'll see later in Table 13-1. However, you are not limited to using those effects exclusively. You can also create composite effects both in sequence (e.g., fade, then move) and in parallel (e.g., fade and move). You can also write custom effects using ActionScript. These custom effects can then be used in exactly the same ways as standard effects.

Working with Effects

To use an effect you must first create an instance of the effect. There are two basic ways to create an effect instance: using MXML or using ActionScript. We'll look at each technique.

MXML is arguably the most common way to create an effect instance. You need merely to add a tag of the appropriate type and give it an ID. You should place the tag as a child of the root document element. For example, you can place the tag as a child of an `Application` tag. The tag should never be nested within other tags (i.e., within other child components). The following example creates a new move effect instance:

```
<mx:Move id="moveEffect" />
```

Table 13-1 lists all the standard effects.

Table 13-1. Standard effects

Effect	Description
Blur	Animate a blur.
Move	Animate the motion of a component in the x and/or y direction.
Fade	Animate the alpha value of a component.
Dissolve	Animate the alpha value of a rectangular overlay.
Glow	Apply a glow to a component, and animate the appearance/disappearance of the glow.
Resize	Animate the width and height of a component.
Rotate	Rotate a component.
Zoom	Animate the x and y scales of a component.
WipeLeft, WipeRight, WipeUp, WipeDown	Apply a mask that moves to reveal or hide a component.
Iris	Apply a mask that scales to hide or reveal a component.
AnimateProperty	Animate any numeric property of a component.

Each effect in Table 13-1 has a different set of properties that you can set to customize the effect. For example, by default a move effect moves both to and from the component's current location. The result is that the effect doesn't seem to do anything. However, you can specify the `xFrom`, `xTo`, `yFrom`, and/or `yTo` property to affect how the component will move. The following example creates an effect that moves the component along the *x*-axis from –100 to the current x coordinate value:

```
<mx:Move id="moveEffect" xFrom="-100" />
```

You can also construct effects using the appropriate constructor as part of a `new` statement. For example, the following code creates a new `Move` instance:

```
private var moveEffect:Move = new Move();
```

Regardless of how you construct the effect instance, you can always set the properties using ActionScript:

```
moveEffect.xFrom = -100;
```

If you've created an effect using MXML, you'll typically set the properties using MXML. However, setting the properties using ActionScript allows you to change the values at runtime. For example, you could create a blur effect using MXML, but based on different things the user does during runtime you could use ActionScript to change the properties.

Playing Effects

There are two ways in which you can play effects: using the `play()` method or using a trigger. We'll look at the `play()` method first because it is the most straightforward way to use an effect. Then we'll look at using triggers.

Manually playing effects

You can use the `play()` method of an effect to manually play the effect. For an effect to play, it must have a target to which it applies the settings. For example, if you have created a move effect instance that is supposed to move a component from -100 to its current location, you must tell it what component to use as the target. You can accomplish that using the `target` attribute or property. The following sets the target attribute of an effect using MXML:

```
<mx:Move id="moveEffect" target='{textInput1}" xFrom="-100" />
```

Once you've created an effect and assigned it a target, you can play it by calling the `play()` method using ActionScript:

```
moveEffect.play();
```

Example 13-1 shows an example of an effect applied in this manner. In this example, there are four text input controls and four move effects. Each move effect uses one of the text inputs as its target. Each text input is wired up such that when its `creationComplete` event occurs, the system tells the corresponding move effect to play.

Example 13-1. Creating and playing effects

```
<?xml version="1.0" encoding="utf-8"?>
<mx:Application xmlns:mx="http://www.adobe.com/2006/mxml" layout="absolute">
    <mx:Script>
        <![CDATA[

            private function applyEffect1(event:Event):void {
                moveEffect1.play();
            }

            private function applyEffect2(event:Event):void {
                moveEffect2.play();
```

```
        }

        private function applyEffect3(event:Event):void {
            moveEffect3.play();
        }

        private function applyEffect4(event:Event):void {
            moveEffect4.play();
        }

    ]]>
</mx:Script>

<mx:VBox>
    <mx:TextInput id="textInput1" creationComplete="applyEffect1(event)" />
    <mx:TextInput id="textInput2" creationComplete="applyEffect2(event)" />
    <mx:TextInput id="textInput3" creationComplete="applyEffect3(event)" />
    <mx:TextInput id="textInput4" creationComplete="applyEffect4(event)" />
</mx:VBox>

<mx:Move id="moveEffect1" target="{textInput1}" xFrom="-100" />
<mx:Move id="moveEffect2" target="{textInput2}" xFrom="-100" />
<mx:Move id="moveEffect3" target="{textInput3}" xFrom="-100" />
<mx:Move id="moveEffect4" target="{textInput4}" xFrom="-100" />

</mx:Application>
```

The result of the preceding code is that the four text inputs appear to slide into place from the left once they are created. As nice as that may be, it doesn't yet demonstrate the full flexibility of working with effects. The preceding example is really quite clumsy because it has a lot of redundancy. It works, but we can improve upon it vastly using just a bit of ActionScript.

You've seen how to set the target of an effect using MXML. You can achieve the same result using ActionScript by assigning an object to the target property of the effect. The following example illustrates how you could assign a button as the target for a move effect:

```
moveEffect.target = button;
```

By assigning the target of an effect using ActionScript, it is possible to use one effect for more than one target. This is very useful in situations such as the one from Example 13-1 in which you have one type of effect with the same settings that you'd like to apply to more than one component. Example 13-2 shows how we can greatly simplify the code in Example 13-1 by using ActionScript to set the target.

Example 13-2. Setting the target using ActionScript

```
<?xml version="1.0" encoding="utf-8"?>
<mx:Application xmlns:mx="http://www.adobe.com/2006/mxml" layout="absolute">
    <mx:Script>
        <![CDATA[
```

```
            private function applyEffect(event:Event):void {
              moveEffect.target = event.target;
              moveEffect.play();
            }

        ]]>
    </mx:Script>

    <mx:VBox>
        <mx:TextInput id="textInput1" creationComplete="applyEffect(event)" />
        <mx:TextInput id="textInput2" creationComplete="applyEffect(event)" />
        <mx:TextInput id="textInput3" creationComplete="applyEffect(event)" />
        <mx:TextInput id="textInput4" creationComplete="applyEffect(event)" />
    </mx:VBox>

    <mx:Move id="moveEffect" xFrom="-100" />

</mx:Application>
```

In Example 13-2, you can see that we've removed the redundancy by simplifying to just one effect (`moveEffect`) and one method (`applyEffect()`). Instead of setting the target of the effect using MXML, we're setting the target at runtime using ActionScript. The result of this code is the same as that of the previous code, except this code is more elegant.

You can also specify more than one target at one time for an effect, using the **`targets`** attribute or property. With **`targets`**, you can specify an array of references to objects to which the effect should be applied. In Example 13-3, the result is visually identical to the preceding two examples, but this time the effect is played just once rather than four times.

Example 13-3. Applying an effect using targets

```
<?xml version="1.0" encoding="utf-8"?>
<mx:Application xmlns:mx="http://www.adobe.com/2006/mxml" layout="absolute">
    <mx:Script>
        <![CDATA[

            private function applyEffect(event:Event):void {
                moveEffect.play();
            }

        ]]>
    </mx:Script>

    <mx:VBox creationComplete="applyEffect(event);">
        <mx:TextInput id="textInput1" />
        <mx:TextInput id="textInput2" />
        <mx:TextInput id="textInput3" />
        <mx:TextInput id="textInput4" />
    </mx:VBox>

    <mx:Move id="moveEffect"
```

```
        targets="{[textInput1, textInput2, textInput3, textInput4]}"
        xFrom="-100" />

</mx:Application>
```

In this example, we set the targets using MXML. You could just as easily use ActionScript to set the targets. Although there would be no real advantage to doing that in this example, in a situation in which you'd like to apply an effect to several groups of components at different times such an approach would be advantageous.

It's also worth noting that you can apply an effect to a container. In the case of the move effect applied in the preceding examples, it would be much simpler to apply the effect to the `VBox` instance, as shown in Example 13-4.

Example 13-4. Applying an effect to a container

```
<?xml version="1.0" encoding="utf-8"?>
<mx:Application xmlns:mx="http://www.adobe.com/2006/mxml" layout="absolute">
    <mx:Script>
        <![CDATA[

            private function applyEffect(event:Event):void {
                moveEffect.play();
            }

        ]]>
    </mx:Script>

    <mx:VBox id="vbox" creationComplete="applyEffect(event)">
        <mx:TextInput id="textInput1" />
        <mx:TextInput id="textInput2" />
        <mx:TextInput id="textInput3" />
        <mx:TextInput id="textInput4" />
    </mx:VBox>

    <mx:Move id="moveEffect" target="{vbox}" xFrom="-100" />

</mx:Application>
```

However, note that this works only when the result of the effect is the same when applied to the container as when applied to the child components. The preceding examples have the same visual result because the effect (move) works identically if applied to the container or the child components. This is not true for all effects; for example, a rotate effect will have a different result if applied to a container than it would if applied to the child components. The code in Example 13-5 applies a rotate effect to the individual child components.

Example 13-5. Applying a rotate effect to individual components

```
<?xml version="1.0" encoding="utf-8"?>
<mx:Application xmlns:mx="http://www.adobe.com/2006/mxml" layout="absolute">
    <mx:Script>
        <![CDATA[
```

```
            private function applyEffect(event:Event):void {
                rotateEffect.target = event.currentTarget;
                rotateEffect.originX = event.currentTarget.width / 2;
                rotateEffect.originY = event.currentTarget.height / 2;
                rotateEffect.play();
            }

        ]]>
    </mx:Script>

    <!-- Set clipContent to false so that the components aren't masked
         while rotating -->
    <mx:VBox id="vbox" x="400" y="400" clipContent="false">
        <mx:TextInput id="textInput1" creationComplete="applyEffect(event)" />
        <mx:TextInput id="textInput2" creationComplete="applyEffect(event)" />
        <mx:TextInput id="textInput3" creationComplete="applyEffect(event)" />
        <mx:TextInput id="textInput4" creationComplete="applyEffect(event)" />
    </mx:VBox>

    <mx:Rotate id="rotateEffect" />

</mx:Application>
```

When applied this way, the individual text inputs rotate independently, each around their own center point. In Example 13-6, we'll use the same effect, but we'll apply it to the VBox instance instead.

Example 13-6. Applying a rotate effect to a container

```
<?xml version="1.0" encoding="utf-8"?>
<mx:Application xmlns:mx="http://www.adobe.com/2006/mxml" layout="absolute">
    <mx:Script>
        <![CDATA[

            private function applyEffect(event:Event):void {
                rotateEffect.originX = event.currentTarget.width / 2;
                rotateEffect.originY = event.currentTarget.height / 2;
                rotateEffect.play();
            }

        ]]>
    </mx:Script>

    <mx:VBox id="vbox" x="400" y="400"
clipContent="false" creationComplete="applyEffect(event)">
        <mx:TextInput id="textInput1" />
        <mx:TextInput id="textInput2" />
        <mx:TextInput id="textInput3" />
        <mx:TextInput id="textInput4" />
    </mx:VBox>

    <mx:Rotate id="rotateEffect" target="{vbox}" />

</mx:Application>
```

This change causes the entire container to rotate, rather than each child component rotating independently.

Using triggers

Triggers occur within a Flex application to start an effect. Using triggers allows you to create and apply effects entirely with MXML. This is not necessarily better or worse than using the `play()` method. It is just a different way of applying effects. The biggest advantage of triggers is that they allow you to apply effects with less code and in a simpler manner than if you were applying the effects using ActionScript. Triggers give you less control, but if you don't need too much control over an effect in a particular scenario, using a trigger is usually easier than using ActionScript.

In Flex terminology, a trigger combined with an effect is called a *behavior*.

Standard triggers are available to all components. Table 13-2 lists these common triggers.

Table 13-2. Standard triggers

Trigger	Description
`addedEffect`	The component has been added to the display list.
`removedEffect`	The component has been removed from the display list.
`creationCompleteEffect`	The component has been created and initialized.
`focusInEffect`	The component has received focus.
`focusOutEffect`	The focus has moved from the component.
`hideEffect`	The component has been hidden (made not visible).
`showEffect`	The component has been shown (made visible).
`rollOverEffect`	The user has moved the mouse over the component.
`rollOutEffect`	The user has moved the mouse out of the component.
`mouseDownEffect`	The user has pressed the mouse button over the component.
`mouseUpEffect`	The user has released the mouse button over the component.
`moveEffect`	The x and/or y property of the component has changed.
`resizeEffect`	The width and/or height of the component has changed.

You can assign an effect instance to the trigger for a component, and the effect will be applied automatically when that trigger occurs. When you use triggers, you do not have to set a target for the effect. Instead, the target is automatically set when the effect is triggered. Example 13-7 uses triggers to apply a move effect to each of four text input controls as they are created.

Example 13-7. Using triggers to play effects

```
<?xml version="1.0" encoding="utf-8"?>
<mx:Application xmlns:mx="http://www.adobe.com/2006/mxml" layout="absolute">

    <mx:VBox>
        <mx:TextInput id="textInput1" creationCompleteEffect="{moveEffect}" />
        <mx:TextInput id="textInput2" creationCompleteEffect="{moveEffect}" />
        <mx:TextInput id="textInput3" creationCompleteEffect="{moveEffect}" />
        <mx:TextInput id="textInput4" creationCompleteEffect="{moveEffect}" />
    </mx:VBox>

    <mx:Move id="moveEffect" xFrom="-100" />

</mx:Application>
```

Of course, you can apply effects to containers using triggers as well. Example 13-8 applies the move effect to the container rather than the child components.

Example 13-8. Using triggers to play an effect on a container

```
<?xml version="1.0" encoding="utf-8"?>
<mx:Application xmlns:mx="http://www.adobe.com/2006/mxml" layout="absolute">

    <mx:VBox creationCompleteEffect="{moveEffect}">
        <mx:TextInput id="textInput1" />
        <mx:TextInput id="textInput2" />
        <mx:TextInput id="textInput3" />
        <mx:TextInput id="textInput4" />
    </mx:VBox>

    <mx:Move id="moveEffect" xFrom="-100" />

</mx:Application>
```

Oftentimes, triggers are the simplest way to apply an effect. As you can see, you typically need fewer lines of code to apply an effect using a trigger than you would need if you were using ActionScript. However, triggers typically work best for simple uses of effects. When you need to customize how the effect is applied, it can get more difficult to use triggers, and in those cases, it is typically better to use ActionScript.

Effect Events

All effects dispatch events that notify listeners when the effects start and when they end. Those events are called `effectStart` and `effectEnd`. The effect events are of type `mx.events.EffectEvent`. Example 13-9 illustrates how to use the `effectEnd` event to set the alpha of a container after it has moved from the left.

Example 13-9. Listening for an effectEnd event

```
<?xml version="1.0" encoding="utf-8"?>
<mx:Application xmlns:mx="http://www.adobe.com/2006/mxml" layout="absolute">

    <mx:Script>
        <![CDATA[
            import mx.events.EffectEvent;

            private function effectEndHandler(event:EffectEvent):void {
                // The initial alpha is .5. Once the effect is complete set the
alpha to 1.
                vbox.alpha = 1;
            }

        ]]>
    </mx:Script>

    <mx:VBox id="vbox" alpha=".5" creationCompleteEffect="{moveEffect}">
        <mx:TextInput id="textInput1" />
        <mx:TextInput id="textInput2" />
        <mx:TextInput id="textInput3" />
        <mx:TextInput id="textInput4" />
    </mx:VBox>

    <mx:Move id="moveEffect" xFrom="-100" effectEnd="effectEndHandler(event)" />

</mx:Application>
```

The `EffectEvent` type inherits the standard event properties such as `target` and `currentTarget`. However, effects use factories to create the effect instances, and the `target` property of an `EffectEvent` object references the factory used to create the effect, not the effect instance. A factory is a programming construct that is responsible for creating objects. In this case, a `Move` object (or any other effect type) is a factory that creates the actual instances of the effect that get applied to components. If you need to retrieve a reference to the actual effect instance (rather than the factory), you can use the `effectInstance` property. Example 13-10 illustrates this by reversing a move effect once it has played.

Example 13-10. Reversing an effect

```
<?xml version="1.0" encoding="utf-8"?>
<mx:Application xmlns:mx="http://www.adobe.com/2006/mxml" layout="absolute">

    <mx:Script>
        <![CDATA[
            import mx.events.EffectEvent;

            private function effectEndHandler(event:EffectEvent):void {
                event.effectInstance.reverse()
                event.effectInstance.play();
            }
```

```
    ]]>
</mx:Script>

<mx:VBox creationCompleteEffect="{moveEffect}">
    <mx:TextInput id="textInput1" />
    <mx:TextInput id="textInput2" />
    <mx:TextInput id="textInput3" />
    <mx:TextInput id="textInput4" />
</mx:VBox>

<mx:Move id="moveEffect" xFrom="-100" effectEnd="effectEndHandler(event)" />

</mx:Application>
```

The preceding examples illustrate how to add a handler for an event using an attribute. Of course, you can also add a handler using ActionScript. With ActionScript you use `addEventListener` as you would normally when registering any listener for any event. In that case, you can use the `EffectEvent.EFFECT_START` and `EffectEvent.EFFECT_END` constants, as shown here:

```
moveEffect.addEventListener(EffectEvent.EFFECT_START, effectStartHandler);
moveEffect.addEventListener(EffectEvent.EFFECT_END, effectEndHandler);
```

All effects dispatch `effectStart` and `effectEnd` events. Most, though not all, also dispatch `tweenStart`, `tweenUpdate`, and `tweenEnd` events. The `tween` events are inherited by all subclasses of `TweenEffect` and `MaskEffect`, which include all the effects listed in Table 13-1. The only effects that don't dispatch `tween` events are composite effects (which are discussed in the next section).

Tween is a word carried over from Flash. Tween is short for *in between*, which refers to an animation technique in which starting and ending values are given, and the intermediate values are automatically calculated. The result is that an animation (such as a translation, scale, or rotation) can be achieved quite simply by providing just the starting and ending values along with duration.

`Tween` events are of type `mx.events.TweenEvent`. The `tweenStart` event occurs as a tween begins, which is immediately after the `effectStart` event in most cases. The `tweenUpdate` event occurs for each change to the tweened property or properties. That means that there might be many `tweenUpdate` events. Then, once a tween effect has completed, it dispatches a `tweenEnd` event. The `tweenEnd` event always follows the last `tweenUpdate` event and precedes the `effectEnd` event.

The `TweenEvent` class defines a `value` property in addition to the inherited event properties. The `value` property contains the current value of the property or properties being changed over time. For example, for a rotate effect, the `TweenEvent` object's `value` property is a number corresponding to the current `rotation` property of the component being rotated. Yet if the effect affects more than one property, the `value` property of the

TweenEvent object is an array of the values of the affected properties. For example, a move effect animates the x and y properties of a component. The TweenEvent dispatched by a move effect has a value property that is an array with two elements corresponding to the x and y values.

Composite Effects

Not only can you create simple effects using the standard effect types, but you also can create composite effects by combining them. There are two ways you can combine effects: in sequence and in parallel.

The Sequence component allows you to group together effects that you want to occur one after the other. For example, you can use a Sequence component to first apply a fade effect and then apply a move effect. From MXML, you can simply nest the effects you want to sequence within a Sequence tag, as follows:

```
<mx:Sequence id="sequenceEffect">
  <mx:Fade />
  <mx:Move xTo="100" />
</mx:Sequence>
```

Note that in the preceding example, the Sequence instance has the id attribute, indicating that you will only need to refer to the Sequence instance rather than the nested, sequenced effects:

```
<mx:TextInput creationCompleteEffect="{sequenceEffect}" />
```

You can add a pause between sequenced effects using a pause effect. You can affect the length of the pause by specifying a value (in milliseconds) for the duration property. The following example fades a target, pauses for 1,000 milliseconds, and then moves the target:

```
<mx:Sequence id="sequenceEffect">
  <mx:Fade />
  <mx:Pause duration="1000" />
  <mx:Move xTo="100" />
</mx:Sequence>
```

The Parallel component allows you to group together effects that you want to play at the same time. For example, if you want to fade and move a component at the same time, you can use the following parallel effect:

```
<mx:Parallel id="parallelEffect">
  <mx:Fade />
  <mx:Move xFrom="-100" />
</mx:Parallel>
```

You can also nest composite effects within other composite effects. For example, the following will fade and move a target at the same time, pause for 1,000 milliseconds, and then rotate 360 degrees.

```
<mx:Sequence id="sequenceEffect">
  <mx:Parallel>
    <mx:Fade />
    <mx:Move xFrom="-100" />
  </mx:Parallel>
  <mx:Pause duration="1000" />
  <mx:Rotate />
</mx:Sequence>
```

You can also create composite effects using ActionScript. All the same rules apply to creating composite effects via ActionScript as when creating standard effects using ActionScript. The only difference is that you need a way to programmatically group effects within the composite effect. To accomplish that, use the `addChild()` method for the `Parallel` or `Sequence` object:

```
var sequenceEffect:Sequence = new Sequence();
sequenceEffect.addChild(rotateEffect);
```

Note that although effects and display objects both have `addChild()` methods, you cannot add an effect to the display list, nor can you add a display object to an effect.

Pausing, Resuming, and Reversing Effects

By default, an effect plays straight through. However, you can pause, resume, and even reverse an effect. All effects have `pause()` and `resume()` methods that pause and resume the playback of an effect, respectively.

You can reverse the playback of an effect using the `reverse()` method as you saw in Example 13-10. If you call the `reverse()` method while an effect is currently playing, it will reverse from that point and play back to the start. If the effect is not playing, calling the `reverse()` method will not play the effect, but it will configure the effect so that the next time it is triggered or played, it will play in reverse.

Delaying and Repeating Effects

When you want to delay an effect, you have several options depending on what you are trying to accomplish. If you want to wait to start an effect until a user or system event occurs, you should associate the effect with the correct trigger or you should call the effect's `play()` method in response to an event. If you want to add a timed delay before an effect starts after it's been triggered or played, you can specify a value for the `startDelay` property of the effect. The `startDelay` property allows you to specify how many milliseconds the effect will pause before playback starts. The default value is `0`, which means there is no delay. The following example creates a fade effect that adds a 1,000-millisecond delay:

```
<mx:Fade id="fadeEffect" startDelay="1000" />
```

The `repeatCount` property allows you to repeat the effect. The default value is `1`, which means the effect plays exactly once. If you specify a value greater than 1, the effect will repeat the specified number of times. For example, the following plays the fade effect twice:

```
<mx:Fade id="fadeEffect" repeatCount="2" />
```

If you specify a value of `0`, the effect repeats until you explicitly call the `end()` method.

You can add a delay between repeats using the `repeatDelay` property. The default value is `0`. The value is interpreted as milliseconds.

Customizing Animation Easing

For all tween effects (blur, move, fade, glow, etc.), you can control the *easing* that gets applied to the effect. Easing refers to the rate at which the effect is applied over time. The default easing type is linear, meaning the effect is applied at a fixed rate from start to end. However, you may want to apply effects in a nonlinear fashion. You can apply custom easing to effects using the `easingFunction` property.

The `easingFunction` property allows you to assign a reference to a function that accepts four numeric parameters (playback time, initial value, total change in value, and duration of effect) and returns the new value to use. The effect then calls that function automatically every time it needs to update the value of a property for the target component. Although you can certainly create custom easing functions, you may find it more convenient to try one of the many easing functions that are included in the Flex framework's `mx.effects.easing` package.

The `mx.effects.easing` package includes an assortment of classes such as `Cubic`, `Elastic`, `Exponential`, `Quadratic`, and so on. Each class has static methods called `easeIn`, `easeOut`, and `easeInOut`. You can reference these functions for use with effects. Here's an example that applies an elastic `easeOut` to a fade effect:

```
<mx:Fade id="fadeEffect" easingFunction="{mx.effects.easing.Elastic.easeOut}" />
```

Using Effects and Fonts

You can use effects with any UI component. However, if the component contains text (e.g., labels, text inputs, etc.), the fade and rotate effects will not work as intended unless you embed the font. By default, all text in UI controls uses system fonts rather than embedded fonts. Flash Player does not properly render text for system fonts if the font in the `alpha` property is set to anything other than 1 or if the `rotation` property is not 0. Because the fade effect changes the `alpha` property and the rotate effect changes the `rotation` property, these effects will not work properly unless you embed the font. In the case of a fade effect, the text portion of the control will always be opaque. In the case of a rotate effect, the text will not be visible, except when the rotation is set to 0.

See Chapter 8 for more information about embedding fonts.

Using Effects with Lists

List-based components have built-in support for effects when the data provider changes. For example, when removing an item from a list, you may want to fade that item out from the list, or when adding an item, you may want to fade that item in. First, consider the following example, which uses a list component with the default settings such that no effects are applied:

```
<?xml version="1.0" encoding="utf-8"?>
<mx:Application xmlns:mx="http://www.adobe.com/2006/mxml" layout="vertical"
creationComplete="creationCompleteHandler();">
    <mx:Script>
        <![CDATA[
            import mx.collections.ArrayCollection;
            import mx.effects.DefaultListEffect;

            [Bindable]
            private var _data:ArrayCollection;

            private function creationCompleteHandler():void {
                _data = new ArrayCollection([1, 2, 3, 4]);
            }

            private function removeSelected():void {
                var indices:Array = list.selectedIndices;
                var count:int = indices.length;
                for(var i:Number = 0; i < count; i++) {
                    _data.removeItemAt(indices[i]);
                }
            }

            private function addToList():void {
                _data.addItemAt(_data.length,
Math.floor(Math.random() * _data.length));
            }

        ]]>
    </mx:Script>
    <mx:List id="list" dataProvider="{_data}" width="100%"
        allowMultipleSelection="true" />
    <mx:Button label="Remove" click="removeSelected();" />
    <mx:Button label="Add" click="addToList();" />
</mx:Application>
```

The list in this example allows for multiple selections. When the user clicks on the button, the code removes all the selected elements from the list. If you were to run this code, select one or more elements from the list, and click the Remove button, you'd see that the removal of the items is instant and sudden. Likewise, if you were to click the Add button, you'd see that the addition of items is also sudden and instant. To make the whole thing a little clearer and easier to see we can add a custom item renderer to the picture. The custom item renderer we'll use is 100 pixels high and has a random color background, making it easy to see and differentiate each item in the list. The code for the item renderer we'll use is as follows. We'll call this *ExampleItemRenderer.mxml*.

```
<?xml version="1.0" encoding="utf-8"?>
<mx:Canvas xmlns:mx="http://www.adobe.com/2006/mxml" width="200" height="100"
creationComplete="creationCompleteHandler();">
    <mx:Script>
        <![CDATA[

            private function creationCompleteHandler():void {
                var randomColor:Number = Math.random() * 0xFFFFFF;
                setStyle("backgroundColor", randomColor);
            }

        ]]>
    </mx:Script>
    <mx:Label text="{data}" />
</mx:Canvas>
```

We can use the item renderer in the list by adding an `itemRenderer` attribute to the tag as follows.

```
<mx:List id="list" dataProvider="{_data}" width="100%" allowMultipleSelection="true"
itemRenderer="ExampleItemRenderer" />
```

Although not strictly necessary in this example, the custom item renderer makes the contrast between the default behavior (with no effects) and the use of effects much greater.

It's very easy to add an effect to a list that will affect the addition and removal of items. All you need to do is assign a reference to the effect to the `itemsChangeEffect` attribute. Flex has a built-in effect that is configured especially for this purpose, and it is called `DefaultListEffect`. The following code shows how to apply this default list effect:

```
<?xml version="1.0" encoding="utf-8"?>
<mx:Application xmlns:mx="http://www.adobe.com/2006/mxml" layout="vertical"
creationComplete="creationCompleteHandler();">
    <mx:Script>
        <![CDATA[
            import mx.collections.ArrayCollection;
            import mx.effects.DefaultListEffect;

            [Bindable]
            private var _data:ArrayCollection;

            private function creationCompleteHandler():void {
                _data = new ArrayCollection([1, 2, 3, 4]);
            }

            private function removeSelected():void {
                var indices:Array = list.selectedIndices;
                var count:int = indices.length;
                for(var i:Number = 0; i < count; i++) {
                    _data.removeItemAt(indices[i]);
```

```
                }
            }

            private function addToList():void {
                _data.addItemAt(_data.length,
Math.floor(Math.random() * _data.length));
            }

        ]]>
    </mx:Script>
    <mx:List id="list" dataProvider="{_data}" width="100%"
        allowMultipleSelection="true"
        itemRenderer="ExampleItemRenderer"
        itemsChangeEffect="{defaultEffect}" />
    <mx:Button label="Remove" click="removeSelected();" />
    <mx:Button label="Add" click="addToList();" />
    <mx:DefaultListEffect id="defaultEffect" />
</mx:Application>
```

The default list effect will cause the following behavior:

- When an item is added the space for the new item expands and then the item fades in.
- When an item is removed the item fades and then the space where the item was collapses.

If you were to run the preceding code, you'd likely notice that the spaces for the items don't seem to open or collapse very smoothly in the list when adding or removing items. That's because for a list to properly handle resizing of items you must set the list's `variableRowHeight` property to `true`. If we change the list tag as follows, we'll see a big difference in how the effect works:

```
<mx:List id="list" dataProvider="{_data}"
    width="100%" allowMultipleSelection="true"
    itemRenderer="ExampleItemRenderer"
    itemsChangeEffect="{defaultEffect}"
    variableRowHeight="true" />
```

You can also customize some of the settings on the effect using the following properties:

`fadeInDuration` *and* `fadeOutDuration`
: These properties allow you to control the amount of time (in milliseconds) that it takes for added items to fade in and removed items to fade out. The default value for both is 300 milliseconds.

`color`
: This property allows you to control the color from which and to which items fade. The default value is white.

`growDuration` *and* `shrinkDuration`
: These properties allow you to specify the amount of time (in milliseconds) that it takes for added items to grow and removed items to shrink. The default value for both is 300 milliseconds.

`removedElementOffset`
: This property has an effect only when removing more than one element at a time. In such cases, the `removedElementOffset` property determines the amount of time (in milliseconds) used to stagger the removal of the elements. The default value is 100 milliseconds. That means that by default, 100 milliseconds elapse after the first element is faded out for removal before the second element begins to fade out for removal, and so forth.

The following example creates an effect in which the elements take five seconds to fade in and out, and there's a two-second delay between the start of the fadeout of each element when more than one element is removed at the same time:

```
<mx:DefaultListEffect id="defaultEffect" fadeInDuration="5000" fadeOutDuration="5000"
removedElementOffset="2000" />
```

The default list effect allows you to customize to a point, as you've seen. However, if you want to create a completely custom effect, you can do that as well. If you decide to create a custom effect, you need to package the effect in a sequence, and you should assign filters to the effect. You can assign filters using the `filter` attribute for each effect. A filter determines when an effect is applied and when it is not applied. There are two filter names used by the `itemsChangeEffect` for a list control: `addItem` and `removeItem`. The following is an example of a custom effect that we can apply to a list. This effect uses easing to create a bounce effect as the items open or collapse.

```
<mx:Sequence id="customEffect">
    <mx:Sequence filter="removeItem">
        <mx:Fade alphaFrom="1" alphaTo="0" duration="2000" />
        <mx:Resize heightTo="0" duration="2000"
easingFunction="{mx.effects.easing.Bounce.easeOut}" />
    </mx:Sequence>
    <mx:Sequence filter="addItem">
        <mx:Resize heightFrom="0" duration="2000"
easingFunction="{mx.effects.easing.Bounce.easeIn}" />
        <mx:Fade alphaFrom="0" alphaTo="1" duration="2000" />
    </mx:Sequence>
</mx:Sequence>
```

Tile lists also support the `itemsChangeEffect` attribute. Tile lists work almost identically to lists in this regard. However, there are a few minor differences:

- You cannot use the `DefaultListEffect` with tile lists. Instead, you must use `DefaultTileListEffect`.
- When you use an effect with a tile list, you should set the `offscreenExtraRowsOrColumns` to `2` to achieve the smoothest effects.

Creating Custom Effects

Although you can use standard effects and composite effects to solve most of an application's effects requirements, sometimes these off-the-shelf solutions won't achieve the intended result. For those cases, the Flex framework allows you to create your own custom effects that you can use exactly as you would use other standard effects.

Creating custom effects requires a more thorough understanding of the effect framework structure. Because working with effects is so simple, it's not necessary to look at the inner workings of the effect framework until you want to write a custom effect.

The effect framework consists of two basic types of classes: *effect factories* and *effect instances*. When you create a new effect object using MXML or ActionScript, you are working with an effect factory class. However, when the effect is applied to a component, the actual object utilized is an effect instance (one that is created automatically behind the scenes). The effect objects that you create using MXML and/or ActionScript using classes such as `Move` or `Resize` utilize a design pattern called the *Factory Method*. The Factory Method pattern means that the factory class is responsible for creating the effect instances, which are what are applied to the components.

Next we'll look at how to define factory and instance classes.

Defining an Effect Instance Class

The effect instance class is the one used as the blueprint for the actual objects that apply the effect to the components. You don't directly create instances of this class normally. That is handled by the factory class. For example, when you use a move effect, the actual effect object that is applied to a component is of type `MoveInstance`. You don't typically create a `MoveInstance` object directly. Rather, that instance is automatically created by the `Move` factory object. We'll look at how to create factories in the next section. First, let's look at how to create an effect instance class.

All effect instance classes must inherit from `mx.effects.EffectInstance`, and at a minimum, all `EffectInstance` subclasses must override the `play()` method, and the overridden `play()` method must also call the `super.play()` method. Additionally, all effect instance classes should have constructors that accept one parameter typed as `Object`. The parameter is the target for the effect instance that is automatically passed to the constructor when it is called by the factory. The constructor should call `super()` and pass it the parameter. Example 13-11 is a simple example that merely places a red dot in the upper-right corner of a component.

Example 13-11. FlagInstance class as an example of a custom effect instance

```
package com.oreilly.programmingflex.effects {

    import mx.effects.EffectInstance;
    import flash.display.Shape;
    // The class must extend EffectInstance.
    public class FlagInstance extends EffectInstance {

        // Allow for configuration of the color.
        private var _color:Number;
```

```
        public function set color(value:Number):void {
            _color = value;
        }

        public function get color():Number {
            return _color;
        }

        // The constructor must accept a parameter and pass that
        // along to the super constructor.
        public function FlagInstance(newTarget:Object) {
            super(newTarget);
        }

        // All effect instances must override play().
        override public function play():void {

            // Call the super.play() method.
            super.play();

            // Create a shape with a red dot.
            var shape:Shape = new Shape();
            shape.graphics.lineStyle(0, 0, 0);
            shape.graphics.beginFill(_color, 1);
            shape.graphics.drawCircle(0, 0, 5);
            shape.graphics.endFill();

            // Move the shape to the upper-right corner of the component.
            shape.x = target.x + target.width;
            shape.y = target.y;

            // Add the shape to the display list.
            target.parent.rawChildren.addChild(shape);
        }

    }
}
```

Defining an Effect Factory Class

All effect factory classes must extend the `mx.effects.Effect` class. When you subclass `Effect`, you must override the `getAffectedProperties()` and `initInstance()` methods, and you must assign a reference to the `instanceClass` property.

The `getAffectedProperties()` method should return an array of all the names of the properties affected. If the effect doesn't affect any properties, the method should return an empty array.

The `initInstance()` method should accept one parameter of type `IEffectInstance`. It should always call `super.initInstance()`, and then it should set any necessary properties of the instance. For example, if you want to pass through any settings from the factory to the instance, you should do so in the `initInstance()` method.

The instanceClass property is a property inherited from Effect that determines what class is used by the factory to create instances. You must set the instanceClass property. Typically, you should do this in the constructor.

Example 13-12 is a simple factory class corresponding to the FlagInstance class from the preceding section.

Example 13-12. Flag class as an example of an effect

```
package com.oreilly.programmingflex.effects {
    import mx.effects.Effect;
    import mx.effects.IEffectInstance;

    // All factory classes must inherit from Effect.
    public class Flag extends Effect {

        // Allow for the configuration of the color. Use a default of red.
        private var _color:Number = 0xFF0000;

        public function set color(value:Number):void {
            _color = value;
        }

        public function get color():Number {
            return _color;
        }

        // The constructor must call the super constructor, and it should also
        // assign the instance class reference to instanceClass.
        public function Flag(newTarget:Object = null) {
            super(newTarget);
            instanceClass = FlagInstance;
        }

        // In this example there are no affected properties for the target.
        override public function getAffectedProperties():Array {
            return [];
        }

        override protected function initInstance(instance:IEffectInstance):void {
            super.initInstance(instance);

            // Since instance is typed as EffectInstance you must cast as FlagInstance
            // to set the color property.
            FlagInstance(instance).color = _color;
        }

    }
}
```

Using Custom Effects

Once you've created a custom effect, you can use it just as you would use a standard effect. The following example illustrates this by applying the flag effect to text input controls as the user moves focus:

```
<?xml version="1.0" encoding="utf-8"?>
<mx:Application xmlns:mx="http://www.adobe.com/2006/mxml" layout="absolute"
xmlns:pf="com.oreilly.programmingflex.effects.*">

    <mx:VBox x="164" y="187">
        <mx:TextInput focusOutEffect="{flagEffect}" />
        <mx:TextInput focusOutEffect="{flagEffect}" />
        <mx:TextInput focusOutEffect="{flagEffect}" />
        <mx:TextInput focusOutEffect="{flagEffect}" />
    </mx:VBox>
    <pf:Flag id="flagEffect" color="0xFFFFFF" />

</mx:Application>
```

Creating Tween Effects

Thus far, you've seen how to create a custom effect that essentially has two states: off and on. For example, the flag effect that you saw in the previous sections is either not applied or applied, but there's no transition between these two states. Yet sometimes an effect should take place over a period of time. For example, the standard Flex move effect takes place over time by changing the `x` and `y` properties of the target incrementally, until the target has reached the destination over the allotted duration. When you want to create effects that cause changes over time, you should create a tween effect. Tween effect classes extend `TweenEffect` and `TweenEffectInstance` rather than `Effect` and `EffectInstance`. We'll talk more about that in just a moment. First, we'll look at how to use the `mx.effects.Tween` class to create animated changes.

The `Tween` class constructor requires that you pass it four parameters: a callback object, a starting value, an ending value, and duration in milliseconds. For example, the following creates a `Tween` object that automatically sends notifications at intervals for 5,000 milliseconds. Each notification includes a value from 0 to 100. The progression of values is a linear change from 0 to 100. The notifications are sent to the `this` object.

```
new Tween(this, 0, 100, 5000);
```

Unlike most of the Flex framework, the `Tween` class does not use the normal event model. Instead, it uses a callback model in which the callback object must define methods with specific names. Those methods are then called in response to specific events. In the case of the `Tween` class, the callback object can define the `onTweenUpdate()` and `onTweenEnd()` methods. The `onTweenUpdate()` method receives notifications as the value changes over time. The `onTweenEnd()` method receives notifications when the tween has completed.

Once you construct a Tween object, it automatically starts to run. It calls the methods on the callback method at the appropriate intervals, sending the current value of the range over which it is changing over time. For example, on the first onTweenUpdate() method call, the Tween object passes it a value of 0 based on the preceding example, but the second call to onTweenUpdate() will be a value slightly larger than 0, with each successive call passing the method a larger value. Once the value reaches the maximum value in the range (100 in our example), the Tween object calls onTweenEnd().

Most of the standard effects, such as move, rotate, and blur, are tween effects. Because TweenEffect and TweenEffectInstance extend Effect and EffectInstance, respectively, implementing a concrete subclass of each of these types is very similar to implementing classes that directly extend Effect and EffectInstance. In fact, all the rules discussed in the preceding sections are applicable to tween effects as well. Apart from extending TweenEffect, all tween effect factory classes have the same rules as nontween effects. Tween effect instance classes, however, must follow several rules.

TweenEffectInstance subclasses should construct a Tween object in the play() method, and the Tween object should use the this object as the callback object. Furthermore, the subclass must override the onTweenUpdate() method at a minimum. The onTweenUpdate() method should accept one parameter typed as Object. And the onTweenUpdate() method should be responsible for updating the property or properties of the target.

In Example 13-13, WobbleInstance is a TweenEffectInstance subclass that uses Tween objects to cause the target to appear to wobble a specified number of times.

Example 13-13. WobbleInstance class as an example of a tween effect instance

```
package com.oreilly.programmingflex.effects {

    import mx.effects.effectClasses.TweenEffectInstance;
    import mx.effects.Tween;

    // The class must extend TweenEffectInstance.
    public class WobbleInstance extends TweenEffectInstance {

        // The _wobbleRepeat property determines how many times the target should
        // wobble. The _wobbleCount property counts how many wobbles have occurred.
        private var _wobbleRepeat:uint;
        private var _wobbleCount:uint;

        public function set wobbleRepeat(value:uint):void {
            _wobbleRepeat = value;
        }

        public function get wobbleRepeat():uint {
            return _wobbleRepeat;
        }

        // The constructor looks very much like a regular Effect subclass.
        public function WobbleInstance(newTarget:Object) {
```

```
            super(newTarget);
        }

        // The play() method calls super.play(). Then it creates a new Tween object.
        // In this case the Tween object changes from 0 to 2 over the course of 100
        // milliseconds.
        override public function play():void {
            super.play();
            _wobbleCount = 0;
            new Tween(this, 0, 2, 100);
        }

        // The onTweenUpdate() method is required. In this case onTweenUpdate() simply
        // sets the rotation property of the target.
        override public function onTweenUpdate(value:Object):void {
            super.onTweenUpdate(value);
            target.rotation = value;
        }

        // The onTweenEnd() method is not strictly required. However, in this case we
        // need to override it so that it can create new Tween objects for as long as
        // the target is supposed to wobble.
        override public function onTweenEnd(value:Object):void {
            super.onTweenEnd(value);
            if(_wobbleCount < _wobbleRepeat) {
                new Tween(this, value, value == 2 ? -2 : 2, 200);
            }
            else if(_wobbleCount == _wobbleRepeat) {
                new Tween(this, value, 0, 100);
            }
            _wobbleCount++;
        }

    }
}
```

Example 13-14 shows the `Wobble` factory class. Notice that it looks very similar to a regular effect factory class.

Example 13-14. Wobble class as an example tween effect factory

```
package com.oreilly.programmingflex.effects {
    import mx.effects.TweenEffect;
    import mx.effects.IEffectInstance;

    public class Wobble extends TweenEffect {

        private var _wobbleRepeat:uint = 2;

        public function set wobbleRepeat(value:uint):void {
            _wobbleRepeat = value;
        }

        public function get wobbleRepeat():uint {
            return _wobbleRepeat;
```

```
        }

        public function Wobble(newTarget:Object = null) {
            super(newTarget);
            instanceClass = WobbleInstance;
        }

        override public function getAffectedProperties():Array {
            return ["rotation"];
        }

        override protected function initInstance(instance:IEffectInstance):void {
            super.initInstance(instance);
            WobbleInstance(instance).wobbleRepeat = _wobbleRepeat;
        }

    }
}
```

Example 13-15 shows the effect applied to components.

Example 13-15. Applying a custom tween effect

```
<?xml version="1.0" encoding="utf-8"?>
<mx:Application xmlns:mx="http://www.adobe.com/2006/mxml" layout="absolute"
xmlns:pf="com.oreilly.programmingflex.effects.*">

    <mx:VBox x="164" y="187">
        <mx:TextInput focusOutEffect="{wobbleEffect}" />
        <mx:TextInput focusOutEffect="{wobbleEffect}" />
        <mx:TextInput focusOutEffect="{wobbleEffect}" />
        <mx:TextInput focusOutEffect="{wobbleEffect}" />
    </mx:VBox>

    <pf:Wobble id="wobbleEffect" wobbleRepeat="10" />

</mx:Application>
```

Using Transitions

Transitions allow you to apply effects to state view changes. Utilizing transitions is very simple. The prerequisite for transitions is that you have two or more states between which you want to apply the transition. Once you have the states defined, you next create the transitions you want to use.

You can create transitions using MXML or ActionScript. First we'll look at how to create transitions using MXML. Then we'll look at how to accomplish the same thing using ActionScript.

Creating Transitions with MXML

As shown in Chapter 12, all applications and components have a `states` property that you can use to define all the states they use. Likewise, all applications and components have a `transitions` property that is an array of all the transitions you want to use. In MXML, you can define the `transitions` property value using the following code within an application or component root tag:

```
<mx:transitions>
  <!-- All transitions appear here. -->
</mx:transitions>
```

All the elements of the `transitions` array must be `Transition` objects. In MXML, you create `Transition` instances using the `Transition` tag. All `Transition` objects must define `fromState` and `toState` properties, and these properties should be the names of the states from and to which the transition should apply. For example, the following code creates a transition from a state called A to a state called B:

```
<mx:Transition fromState="A" toState="B" />
```

If you want to use a transition for all changes to or from a particular state, you can use the asterisk (*) as a wildcard that means "all states." The following example creates a transition from all states to a state named B:

```
<mx:Transition fromState="*" toState="B" />
```

Transition objects have an effect property that determines what effect is applied during the state change. The effect property is the default property when you create the `Transition` object using MXML, which means you can simply nest an effect tag within a `Transition` tag, as in the following example:

```
<mx:Transition fromState="*" toState="B">
  <mx:Move target="{vbox}" />
</mx:Transition>
```

Notice that in this example, the effect specifies a target. In most cases, the effect must specify a target or targets when used as a transition. If you want to specify more than one target, you can use the `targets` property of an effect and specify an array of targets, as in the following example:

```
<mx:Transition fromState="*" toState="B">
  <mx:Move targets="{[textInput1, textInput2, textInput3, textInput4]}" />
</mx:Transition>
```

In many cases, you don't need to set the effect properties specifying things such as alphas or x and y coordinates. When effects are applied as transitions, the `to` and `from` properties are automatically set to the values of the targets' properties in the from and to states. For example, when you apply a move effect as a transition, the `xFrom` and `yFrom` properties are automatically set to the `x` and `y` property values of the target in the from state, and the `xTo` and `yTo` properties are automatically set to the `x` and `y` property values of the target in the to state. However, if you want to set the effect properties explicitly, you can do that as you would for any normal effect, and those settings will override any automatic settings. For instance, the following example creates a transition that uses a rotate effect with explicit settings for `angleFrom` and `angleTo`:

```
<mx:Transition fromState="*" toState="B">
  <mx:Rotate target="{vbox}" angleFrom="0" angleTo="360" />
</mx:Transition>
```

Now that we've had the opportunity to discuss all the fundamentals of working with transitions, let's look at a working example. Example 13-16 creates four title windows and four states—each state featuring one of the windows larger than the others. This example uses a transition that animates all the state changes so that the windows move and resize.

Example 13-16. Applying transitions between states

```
<?xml version="1.0" encoding="utf-8"?>
<mx:Application xmlns:mx="http://www.adobe.com/2006/mxml" layout="absolute">

    <mx:TitleWindow x="23" y="19" width="250" height="200"
        layout="absolute" title="A" id="windowA" click="currentState='A'" />
    <mx:TitleWindow x="309" y="19" width="250" height="200"
        layout="absolute" title="B" id="windowB" click="currentState='B'" />
    <mx:TitleWindow x="23" y="260" width="250" height="200"
        layout="absolute" title="C" id="windowC" click="currentState='C'" />
    <mx:TitleWindow x="309" y="260" width="250" height="200"
        layout="absolute" title="D" id="windowD" click="currentState='D'" />

    <mx:states>
        <mx:State name="A">
            <mx:SetProperty target="{windowA}" name="width" value="500"/>
            <mx:SetProperty target="{windowA}" name="height" value="300"/>
            <mx:SetProperty target="{windowC}" name="width" value="150"/>
            <mx:SetProperty target="{windowC}" name="height" value="150"/>
            <mx:SetProperty target="{windowC}" name="y" value="333"/>
            <mx:SetProperty target="{windowD}" name="x" value="373"/>
            <mx:SetProperty target="{windowD}" name="width" value="150"/>
            <mx:SetProperty target="{windowD}" name="height" value="150"/>
            <mx:SetProperty target="{windowD}" name="y" value="333"/>
            <mx:SetProperty target="{windowB}" name="x" value="23"/>
            <mx:SetProperty target="{windowB}" name="y" value="333"/>
            <mx:SetProperty target="{windowB}" name="width" value="150"/>
            <mx:SetProperty target="{windowB}" name="height" value="150"/>
            <mx:SetProperty target="{windowC}" name="x" value="200"/>
        </mx:State>
        <mx:State name="B">
            <mx:SetProperty target="{windowD}" name="width" value="150"/>
            <mx:SetProperty target="{windowD}" name="height" value="150"/>
            <mx:SetProperty target="{windowC}" name="width" value="150"/>
            <mx:SetProperty target="{windowC}" name="height" value="150"/>
            <mx:SetProperty target="{windowA}" name="width" value="150"/>
            <mx:SetProperty target="{windowA}" name="height" value="150"/>
            <mx:SetProperty target="{windowB}" name="width" value="500"/>
            <mx:SetProperty target="{windowB}" name="height" value="300"/>
```

```
            <mx:SetProperty target="{windowA}" name="y" value="333"/>
            <mx:SetProperty target="{windowC}" name="x" value="200"/>
            <mx:SetProperty target="{windowC}" name="y" value="333"/>
            <mx:SetProperty target="{windowB}" name="x" value="23"/>
            <mx:SetProperty target="{windowD}" name="x" value="373"/>
            <mx:SetProperty target="{windowD}" name="y" value="333"/>
        </mx:State>
        <mx:State name="C">
            <mx:SetProperty target="{windowD}" name="width" value="150"/>
            <mx:SetProperty target="{windowD}" name="height" value="150"/>
            <mx:SetProperty target="{windowB}" name="width" value="150"/>
            <mx:SetProperty target="{windowB}" name="height" value="150"/>
            <mx:SetProperty target="{windowA}" name="width" value="150"/>
            <mx:SetProperty target="{windowA}" name="height" value="150"/>
            <mx:SetProperty target="{windowC}" name="width" value="500"/>
            <mx:SetProperty target="{windowC}" name="height" value="300"/>
            <mx:SetProperty target="{windowA}" name="y" value="333"/>
            <mx:SetProperty target="{windowB}" name="x" value="200"/>
            <mx:SetProperty target="{windowB}" name="y" value="333"/>
            <mx:SetProperty target="{windowC}" name="x" value="23"/>
            <mx:SetProperty target="{windowC}" name="y" value="19"/>
            <mx:SetProperty target="{windowD}" name="x" value="373"/>
            <mx:SetProperty target="{windowD}" name="y" value="333"/>
        </mx:State>
        <mx:State name="D">
            <mx:SetProperty target="{windowC}" name="width" value="150"/>
            <mx:SetProperty target="{windowC}" name="height" value="150"/>
            <mx:SetProperty target="{windowB}" name="width" value="150"/>
            <mx:SetProperty target="{windowB}" name="height" value="150"/>
            <mx:SetProperty target="{windowA}" name="width" value="150"/>
            <mx:SetProperty target="{windowA}" name="height" value="150"/>
            <mx:SetProperty target="{windowD}" name="width" value="500"/>
            <mx:SetProperty target="{windowD}" name="height" value="300"/>
            <mx:SetProperty target="{windowA}" name="y" value="333"/>
            <mx:SetProperty target="{windowB}" name="x" value="200"/>
            <mx:SetProperty target="{windowB}" name="y" value="333"/>
            <mx:SetProperty target="{windowD}" name="x" value="23"/>
            <mx:SetProperty target="{windowD}" name="y" value="19"/>
            <mx:SetProperty target="{windowC}" name="x" value="373"/>
            <mx:SetProperty target="{windowC}" name="y" value="333"/>
        </mx:State>
    </mx:states>

    <mx:transitions>
        <mx:Transition fromState="*" toState="*">
            <mx:Parallel targets="{[windowA, windowB, windowC, windowD]}">
                <mx:Move />
                <mx:Resize />
            </mx:Parallel>
        </mx:Transition>
    </mx:transitions>

</mx:Application>
```

Creating Transitions with ActionScript

Transitions work much the same way in both MXML and ActionScript inasmuch as you must set the same properties and all the properties work in the same way regardless of whether you're using MXML or ActionScript.

You can construct a new `mx.states.Transition` instance using the constructor:

```
var transition:Transition = new Transition();
```

You can then set the `fromState` and `toState` properties:

```
transition.fromState = "*";
transition.toState = "*";
```

Now you can assign an effect to the `effect` property:

```
var move:Move = new Move();
move.targets = [textInput1, textInput2];
transition.effect = move;
```

Finally, you simply need to add the transition to the `transitions` property of the application or component:

```
transitions = [transition];
```

There's no real advantage to using transitions from ActionScript or MXML. You determine which to use based on the type of document for which you are trying to define the states. If you are adding transitions to an MXML document, you should use MXML to define the transitions, and if you are adding transitions to an ActionScript class, you should use ActionScript for the transitions.

Using Transition Filters

When you apply transitions, the effects are applied to all targets all the time. Often that is the correct behavior. However, sometimes you want to make the application of some effects conditional for some targets based on what changes are taking place for the targets. For instance, consider Example 13-17, which is a rewrite of the transition in Example 13-16.

Example 13-17. Adding a blur to the transition

```
<mx:transitions>
        <mx:Transition fromState="*" toState="*">
            <mx:Sequence targets="{[windowA, windowB, windowC, windowD]}">
                <mx:Blur bluryFrom="0" bluryTo="10" duration="100" />
                <mx:Parallel>
                    <mx:Move />
                    <mx:Resize />
                </mx:Parallel>
                <mx:Blur bluryFrom="10" bluryTo="0" duration="100" />
            </mx:Sequence>
        </mx:Transition>
    </mx:transitions>
```

In this example, first a blur is applied to all the targets, then the move and resize effects are applied, and then the blur is applied again in reverse (essentially removing the blur). This creates a nice effect that depicts a motion blur when the windows are moving. However, there is one problem with this transition: the blur is always applied to all targets even when the target isn't actually going to move. This is a good case for using *transition effect filters*.

A filter on a transition effect allows you to make the application of the effect conditional. Table 13-3 shows all the filter values.

Table 13-3. Transition effect filter values

Filter value	Description
`add`	The target was added using `AddChild`.
`remove`	The target was removed using `RemoveChild`.
`show`	The target was made visible using `SetProperty` to set the visible property to `true`.
`hide`	The target was made nonvisible using `SetProperty` to set the visible property to `false`.
`move`	The target's x and y properties change during the transition.
`resize`	The target's width and height properties change during the transition.

Example 13-18 is a rewrite of the transition from the preceding example and corrects the blur problem by applying the blur only to the targets that are moving during the transition.

Example 13-18. Adding filters to the transition

```
<mx:transitions>
        <mx:Transition fromState="*" toState="*">
            <mx:Sequence targets="{[windowA, windowB, windowC, windowD]}">
                <mx:Blur blurYFrom="0" blurYTo="10" duration="100" filter="move" />
                <mx:Parallel>
                    <mx:Move />
                    <mx:Resize />
                </mx:Parallel>
                <mx:Blur blurYFrom="10" blurYTo="0" duration="100" filter="move" />
            </mx:Sequence>
        </mx:Transition>
    </mx:transitions>
```

Creating Custom Transitions

As you've already seen, transitions use effects. That means you can create custom transitions the same way you create custom effects. The only difference when creating custom transitions is that the effect instance class needs to handle the fallback rules for automatically determining the starting and ending property values. For example, we've seen that if you don't explicitly set the `xFrom`, `yFrom`, `xTo`, and `yTo` properties for an effect used as a transition, the values are automatically retrieved from the target in the from and to states. When you create an effect instance class that you intend to use as a transition, you should include the ability to automatically detect these default property values.

`EffectInstance` subclasses automatically inherit a property called `propertyChanges`, which is of type `mx.effects.effectClasses.PropertyChanges`. The `propertyChanges` property has two properties: `start` and `end`. These properties are associative arrays containing the affected property values of the target in the from and to states.

Summary

In this chapter, you learned about working with effects and transitions in Flex. You learned that effects are frequently paired with a trigger to create what is known as a behavior. You also learned that effects can be applied declaratively using MXML tags or through ActionScript and that transitions allow you to apply animated changes between Flex component states.

CHAPTER 14

Working with Data

Although some Flex applications use data more extensively than others, nearly all use data to some extent. The Flex SDK is a robust set of tools for working with data. This chapter examines how to work with data on the client side without an extensive discussion of client/server data communication, which is covered in Chapter 16. Rather, this chapter focuses primarily on the following topics: modeling data and data binding.

When working with data, you generally want to store it in some sort of data repository within memory. These repositories are known as *data models*. In the first section of this chapter, we'll look at each of the three basic ways to store data in data models.

You can use ActionScript for all your data management needs, but then you're not really using the power of the Flex framework. To simplify linking data from a data model to a control or from one control to another control or component you can use a powerful feature called *data binding*.

Once you know the basics of working with data in a Flex application, you'll have a foundation for sending and receiving data. That topic is discussed further in Chapter 16.

Using Data Models

You can work with data in many ways in Flex applications, including as low-level ActionScript solutions and high-level MXML solutions; this section looks at both techniques. You can use these data models as a repository for data retrieved from a remote procedure call (RPC) such as a web service method call. You can also use a data model to store user input data before sending it to the server. You can even use a data model simply as a mechanism for populating form input, such as a combo box.

Using the Model Tag

The `<mx:Model>` tag allows you to create an object that represents a data structure using MXML. To use the tag practically, you must always specify an `id` attribute:

```
<mx:Model id="example" />
```

Once you've created a model this way, you can do one of two things:

- Create a data structure using tags.
- Specify a source attribute to populate the model from a file.

Creating tag-based model structures

If you want to populate a model object within your MXML document, you can specify the structure using *tags*. Tags are useful when you want to use the data model for storing user input or data you retrieve from an RPC. The tags are arbitrary XML tags that you select to represent the data structure. The data model must contain only one root node. The following example uses a data model to represent a user:

```
<mx:Model id="userData">
    <user>
        <email></email>
        <phone></phone>
        <address>
            <city></city>
            <state></state>
        </address>
    </user>
</mx:Model>
```

Of course, you can populate the data model with real data, as in the next example:

```
<mx:Model id="userData">
    <user>
        <email>example@example.com</email>
        <phone>123 555-1212</phone>
        <address>
            <city>Exampleville</city>
            <state>CA</state>
        </address>
    </user>
</mx:Model>
```

However, in most cases when you want to initialize a data model with data, you should use an external file, as described in the next section. When you create the structure of a data model in the MXML document in this fashion, you won't initialize the object with data. Instead, you'll use it with data binding (discussed in the "Data Binding" section later in this chapter) to store data from user input or data retrieved with RPCs.

Populating a model from a file

If you want to use a data model to store static data, often the best approach is to load that data from a file rather than defining the structure and initializing the object data, all from the MXML document. For example, consider a data model in which you want to store all the U.S. state names. If you define the structure and initialize it within the MXML document, your MXML document becomes cluttered with lots of lines that are not used to define the user interface or the business logic, but rather are used just to populate a data model. It is better to place that data in a separate file and simply reference it in the MXML document. The `<mx:Model>` tag makes that an easy task.

If you specify a source attribute for an `<mx:Model>` tag, the object looks to the file you specify, and it loads the data from that file at compile time, not at runtime. Specifying the `source` attribute achieves exactly the same effect as placing the contents of the source file within the `<mx:Model>` tag, but it allows you to place the data in a separate file to clean up the MXML. Once the *.swf* is compiled, you won't need to distribute the data source file with the *.swf* file as all the data is compiled into the *.swf*. This is also a potential downside since it also increases the file size of the *.swf* file.

Note that while using `<mx:Model>` tags may seem like a solution for application-wide data sources, you'll likely find that it is preferable to use ActionScript data model classes for that purpose. You can read about using ActionScript data model classes in the "Using ActionScript Classes" section of this chapter.

Consider the following XML document called *states.xml*, an XML file that contains the names of all 50 U.S. states (to save space, this example has been shortened, but you can assume the actual file contains all 50 states):

```
<states>
    <state>Alabama</state>
    <state>Alaska</state>
    <state>Arizona</state>
    <state>Arkansas</state>
    <state>California</state>
    <state>Colorado</state>
    <state>Connecticut</state>
    <state>Delaware</state>
    <state>Florida</state>
    <state>Georgia</state>
    <state>Hawaii</state>
    <state>Idaho</state>
    <state>Illinois</state>
    <!-- additional states... -->
</states>
```

You can populate a model with that data by adding the `source` attribute to the `<mx:Model>` tag, as shown in the following example:

```
<mx:Model id="statesModel" source="states.xml" />
```

Note that the preceding assumes that *states.xml* is in the same directory as the main MXML file for the application.

Referencing model data

Having a data model doesn't do you much good unless you can reference the data stored within it—either to update it or to retrieve it. In many, if not most cases, you will use something called data binding to reference model data. (The details of data binding are discussed later in this chapter, in the "Data Binding" section.) You can also reference a model using ActionScript. You'll see how the same concepts apply when using data binding later in this chapter.

To understand how to reference data in a data model it's important to understand how an `<mx:Model>` tag translates into ActionScript. Unlike many MXML tags, the `<mx:Model>` tag does not correspond to an ActionScript class by the same name. There is no `Model` class. Rather, an object created using the `<mx:Model>` tag is an instance of the `ObjectProxy` class. An `ObjectProxy` object is essentially a wrapper for an `Object` instance. In practical terms, you can treat an `ObjectProxy` object exactly as you would an `Object` instance. The primary purpose of `ObjectProxy` is to enable data binding, which would not be available for a simple `Object` instance.

The fact that an object created with `<mx:Model>` is an `ObjectProxy` object in ActionScript immediately tells you that you can access the data using standard ActionScript dot syntax. The only thing you need to now know about these objects is how the tag-based data structure translates to ActionScript. As we've discussed, a model created with `<mx:Model>` can have only one root node. That root node is always synonymous with the model object itself. The child nodes of the root node become properties of the `ObjectProxy` object, and the child nodes of the child nodes become properties of the properties of the object.

The following example defines a simple data model and a button. When the user clicks the button, it calls `trace()` and displays the value of the `email` property of the data model. Because the root node of the data model (`user`) is synonymous with the data model object (`userData`), you do not need to (nor can you) treat the root node as a child of the data model; to retrieve the email value, `userData.email` is used, not `userData.user.email`:

```
<mx:Model id="userData">
    <user>
        <email>example@example.com</email>
        <phone>123 555-1212</phone>
        <address>
            <city>Exampleville</city>
            <state>CA</state>
        </address>
    </user>
</mx:Model>
<mx:Button click="trace(userData.email)" />
```

You can also assign values to the data model properties using standard ActionScript expressions. The following example uses the same data model as the preceding example, but with two buttons—one that updates the city value by appending a random number, and one that traces the value:

```
<mx:VBox>
    <mx:Button click="userData.address.city = 'Exampleville' +
                    Math.round(Math.random() * 10)" label="Update City" />
    <mx:Button click="trace(userData.address.city)" label="Trace" />
</mx:VBox>
```

There is one conversion that takes place that might not be intuitive. When a data model structure consists of two or more sibling nodes with the same name, they are converted into an array. Consider the states example again:

```
<states>
    <state>Alabama</state>
    <state>Alaska</state>
    <state>Arizona</state>
    <state>Arkansas</state>
    <state>California</state>
    <state>Colorado</state>
    <state>Connecticut</state>
    <state>Delaware</state>
    <state>Florida</state>
    <state>Georgia</state>
    <state>Hawaii</state>
    <state>Idaho</state>
    <state>Illinois</state>
    <!-- additional states... -->
</states>
```

The states data is loaded into a data model using the source attribute, as follows:

```
<mx:Model id="statesModel" source="states.xml" />
```

Here, statesModel.state is an array that contains the name of each state as an element. The following traces true when the user clicks the button because statesModel.state is an array:

```
<mx:Button click="trace(statesModel.state is Array)" />
```

The following example uses an ActionScript function to loop through all the elements of the array and display them in a text area:

```
<mx:Script>
    <![CDATA[

        private function displayStates():void {
            for(var i:uint = 0; i < statesModel.state.length; i++) {
                statesTextArea.text += statesModel.state[i] + "\n";
            }
        }

    ]]>
</mx:Script>
<mx:Model id="statesModel" source="states.xml" />
<mx:VBox>
```

```
        <mx:Button click="displayStates()" />
        <mx:TextArea id="statesTextArea" height="500" />
    </mx:VBox>
```

Using XML

The <mx:Model> tag is useful when you want to work with data stored in traditional types such as objects, strings, and arrays. If you want to work with XML-formatted data, you can use the <mx:XML> tag to create an XML-based data model (that you can access using E4X).

The <mx:Model> and <mx:XML> tags are structurally very similar. As with <mx:Model>, you should always specify an id attribute when creating an <mx:XML> tag:

```
<mx:XML id="example" />
```

Also, as with <mx:Model>, there are two basic ways to create the structure and/or initialize an <mx:XML> data model:

- Create a data structure using tags.
- Specify a source attribute to populate the model from a file.

Specifying an XML structure with tags

You can specify an XML structure using tags in the MXML document much as you would for an ObjectProxy-based model created with <mx:Model>. The following defines the structure for an <mx:XML> tag:

```
<mx:XML id="chaptersXml" xmlns="">
    <chapters label="Chapters">
        <chapter label="Chapter 1">
            <file label="File 1.1" />
        </chapter>
        <chapter label="Chapter 2">
            <file label="File 2.1" />
        </chapter>
    </chapters>
</mx:XML>
```

As with <mx:Model>, the structure for <mx:XML> must have only one root node.

The MXML parser uses namespaces extensively, and it is important that the XML tag has a unique namespace from the default namespace of the containing MXML document. For this reason, Flex Builder adds xmlns="", as in the preceding example.

Loading XML from a file

You can load the XML data for an <mx:XML> tag using the source attribute just as you would with <mx:Model>. When you use the source attribute, that data is loaded at compile time, and it is compiled into the *.swf*. That means you do not need to distribute the source file with the *.swf*, and it means the data is static. The following loads the data from *chapters.xml*:

```
<mx:XML id=chaptersXml" source="chapters.xml" />
```

Referencing XML data

When you use an <mx:XML> tag, it creates an XML object in ActionScript. By default, the XML object is a top-level E4X XML object. However, you can use the format attribute to specify whether to use an E4X XML object or a legacy flash.xml.XMLNode object. The default value for the format attribute is e4x. Setting the value to xml creates an XMLNode object instead. For all the examples in this book, E4X XML data models are used unless otherwise noted.

When you want to reference the data from a model created using <mx:XML>, the root node of the data is synonymous with the data model object. The following uses E4X syntax to trace the label attribute of the first <chapter> child node:

```
<mx:XML id="chaptersXml">
    <chapters label="Chapters">
        <chapter label="Chapter 1">
            <file label="File 1.1" />
        </chapter>
        <chapter label="Chapter 2">
            <file label="File 2.1" />
        </chapter>
    </chapters>
</mx:XML>
<mx:Button click="trace(chaptersXml.chapter[0].@label)" />
```

The following example assigns the data model as the data provider for a tree component:

```
<mx:XML id="chaptersXml">
    <chapters label="Chapters">
        <chapter label="Chapter 1">
            <file label="File 1.1" />
        </chapter>
        <chapter label="Chapter 2">
            <file label="File 2.1" />
        </chapter>
    </chapters>
</mx:XML>
<mx:VBox>
    <mx:Button click="chapters.dataProvider = chaptersXml" />
    <mx:Tree id="chapters" width="200" labelField="@label" />
</mx:VBox>
```

Using ActionScript Classes

Although the `<mx:Model>` and `<mx:XML>` data models provide a simple and convenient way to work with data, they are not the ideal solution in most cases. Even though they work well for simple, static data (such as a list of U.S. state names), they are not well suited for complex data, dynamic data, or data that has rules applied to it. In those cases, it is better to use a custom ActionScript class as the data model. Although there's nothing wrong with using the `<mx:Model>` and `<mx:XML>` tags, it is best to be very sparse in your use of them. Remember that MXML is primarily intended for creating user interfaces and layout. ActionScript, on the other hand, is ideal for managing and working with data. Here are a few of the advantages of using a custom ActionScript class:

Strong typing
: With `<mx:Model>` and `<mx:XML>` you cannot enforce data types, but with ActionScript classes you can (i.e., a string must be a `String`, and an int must be an `int`).

Data testing/consistency
: You cannot verify that a value assigned to an object created using `<mx:Model>` or `<mx:XML>` is a valid value. For example, if a particular property can have values only in the range from 1 to 10, you can't verify that when assigning values to `<mx:Model>` or `<mx:XML>`. However, an ActionScript class setter method can test for valid values. If a value is invalid, the class can discard the new assignment, convert the value to a value in the valid range, or throw an error.

Business logic
: When you assign a value to a property of an instance created from `<mx:Model>` or `<mx:XML>`, you're simply assigning a value without the ability to run any business logic. However, with an ActionScript class you can run any ActionScript operations you want when getting or setting values.

Design patterns
: You cannot employ sophisticated design patterns with `<mx:Model>` and `<mx:XML>`, yet you can with an ActionScript class. For example, you may need to have a single, managed instance of a data model such as a user account data model. That way, it is accessible throughout the application. With an ActionScript class you can employ the Singleton design pattern to accomplish this goal.

It's worth noting that the main application class is a type of Singleton class in that there is only one instance per application, and that one instance is globally accessible (via `mx.core.Application.application`). You could, theoretically, add a data model instance to the main class and access it globally through the main class. Although that would accomplish the goal, the architectural soundness of that decision is questionable. It is generally advisable to use an ActionScript class as the data model.

Writing an ActionScript class as a data model is quite simple. You merely need to define a new class with public accessor methods for all the properties. The class in Example 14-1 defines a data model for a user. Note that all the getters and setters are strongly typed and several of the setters use data testing.

Example 14-1. User class

```
package com.oreilly.programmingflex.data {

    public class User {

        private var _nameFirst:String;
        private var _nameLast:String;
        private var _email:String;
        private var _lastLogin:Date;
        private var _userType:uint;

        public function get nameFirst():String {
            return _nameFirst;
        }

        public function set nameFirst(value:String):void {
            _nameFirst = value;
        }

        public function get nameLast():String {
            return _nameLast;
        }

        public function set nameLast(value:String):void {
            _nameLast = value;
        }

        public function get email():String {
            return _email;
        }

        public function set email(value:String):void {
            var expression:RegExp = /\b[A-Z0-9._%-]+@[A-Z0-9.-]+\.[A-Z]{2,4}\b/i;
            if(expression.test(value)) {
                _email = value;
            }
            else {
                _email = "invalid email";
            }
        }

        public function get lastLogin():Date {
            return _lastLogin;
        }

        public function set lastLogin(value:Date):void {
            _lastLogin = value;
        }
```

```
        public function get userType():uint {
            return _userType;
        }

        public function set userType(value:uint):void {
            if(userType <= 2) {
                _userType = value;
            }
        }

        public function User() {}

    }
}
```

You can then create an instance of the model class using MXML or ActionScript. With MXML you have to define the namespace, then use `<namespace:Class>` to create the instance:

```
<?xml version="1.0" encoding="utf-8"?>
<mx:Application xmlns:mx="http://www.adobe.com/2006/mxml"
xmlns:data="com.oreilly.programmingflex.data.*" layout="absolute">

    <data:User id="user" email="example@example.com" lastLogin="{new Date()}"
               nameFirst="Abigail" nameLast="Smith" userType="1" />

</mx:Application>
```

With ActionScript you need to import the class, and then use the constructor as part of a new statement:

```
import com.oreilly.programmingflex.data.User;
private var user:User;

private function initializeHandler(event:Event):void {
    user = new User();
    user.email = "example@example.com';
    // etc.
}
```

In the next section, we'll look at data binding. If you want to enable the data binding feature for a custom ActionScript-based data model, you must use the `[Bindable]` metadata tag when declaring the class:

```
[Bindable]
public class User {
```

If you create the instance using MXML, the instance is automatically enabled for data binding, assuming the class uses the `[Bindable]` metadata tag. However, if you create the instance using ActionScript, you must also use the `[Bindable]` tag when declaring the variable you use to store the reference:

```
[Bindable]
private var user:User;
```

We'll talk more about data binding and the [Bindable] metadata tag in the "Data Binding" section later in this chapter.

Working with Collections

Another way that you can work with data is to use a collection. In this case, we're using the word *collection* to refer to a class that implements the mx.collections.ICollectionView interface. Two of the primary such collection classes are mx.collections.ArrayCollection and mx.collections.XMLListCollection.

In some cases, collections can be substitutes for the other techniques we described earlier. For example, you can use a collection in place of a Model tag if you intend to use the data as a data provider for a list component. However, when you are using an ActionScript class to model data, a collection isn't necessarily a substitute, but rather a complement. The primary value of a collection in such a case is that it provides a data-bindable way to store data.

You can use an ArrayCollection instead of an Array when you'd like to use data binding (see the next section for more information about data binding). This is because an Array does not allow for data binding. A change to an element in an array will not trigger changes in other components. However, ArrayCollection instances are data-bindable, and if you add or remove an element from the collection, it triggers binding changes. As with many things in Flex, you can create an ArrayCollection instance using ActionScript or MXML. First we'll look at an example using MXML. In the following code, we create an ArrayCollection instance using an ArrayCollection tag. We are assigning the collection to the dataProvider property of a combo box component. You'll notice that nested in the ArrayCollection tag is an Array tag. That's because an ArrayCollection object is a data-bindable wrapper for an array.

```
<?xml version="1.0" encoding="utf-8"?>
<mx:Application xmlns:mx="http://www.adobe.com/2006/mxml" layout="vertical">
    <mx:ComboBox>
        <mx:dataProvider>
            <mx:ArrayCollection id="letters">
                <mx:Array>
                    <mx:String>A</mx:String>
                    <mx:String>B</mx:String>
                    <mx:String>C</mx:String>
                    <mx:String>D</mx:String>
                </mx:Array>
            </mx:ArrayCollection>
        </mx:dataProvider>
    </mx:ComboBox>
</mx:Application>
```

You can omit the <mx:Array> tag in the preceding example and it will still work. When you nest values inside an <mx:ArrayCollection> tag, the Flex compiler assumes they're elements of an array. Therefore, you may sometimes see code where the <mx:Array> tag is absent. Either way works. In this case, we are opting for the explicit use of the <mx:Array> tag for clarity.

Once we've created an `ArrayCollection` instance we can update it using various methods. We can use the `addItem()` method to add elements to the collection. We can use the `removeItemAt()` method to remove elements at specific indexes. We can use the `getItemAt()` method to retrieve elements at specific indexes. Adding and removing elements using these methods triggers data binding changes, as you can see in the next example. In this code, we add a button that adds a random letter to the collection when the user clicks it. Because the update triggers data binding, the following code will result in the combo box redrawing itself, and it will display a new item in the drop-down list.

```
<?xml version="1.0" encoding="utf-8"?>
<mx:Application xmlns:mx="http://www.adobe.com/2006/mxml" layout="vertical">
    <mx:ComboBox>
        <mx:dataProvider>
            <mx:ArrayCollection id="letters">
                <mx:Array>
                    <mx:String>A</mx:String>
                    <mx:String>B</mx:String>
                    <mx:String>C</mx:String>
                    <mx:String>D</mx:String>
                </mx:Array>
            </mx:ArrayCollection>
        </mx:dataProvider>
    </mx:ComboBox>
    <mx:Button label="Change"
     click="letters.addItem(String.fromCharCode
(Math.round(Math.random() * 26) + 65))" />
</mx:Application>
```

As we said earlier, we can also create `ArrayCollection` instances using ActionScript. When we create `ArrayCollection` instances in this way, we can create the empty instance and add elements programmatically using the `addItem()` method, or we can initialize the collection by passing an array to the constructor, as in the following example.

```
<?xml version="1.0" encoding="utf-8"?>
<mx:Application xmlns:mx="http://www.adobe.com/2006/mxml" layout="vertical">
    <mx:Script>
        <![CDATA[
            import mx.collections.ArrayCollection;

            [Bindable]
            private var letters:ArrayCollection =
new ArrayCollection(["A", "B", "C", "D"]);
```

```
        ]]>
    </mx:Script>
    <mx:ComboBox dataProvider="{letters}" />
    <mx:Button label="Change"
     click="letters.addItem(String.fromCharCode
(Math.round(Math.random() * 26) + 65))" />
</mx:Application>
```

The XMLListCollection class is to XMLList objects what the ArrayCollection is to arrays. XMLListCollection instances wrap XMLList objects. XMLListCollection provides the same API for adding, retrieving, and removing elements as the ArrayCollection class does. However, when you call these methods, you use XML elements instead of non-hierarchical values, as you would with ArrayCollection. The following code illustrates how you can create an XMLListCollection using MXML:

```
<?xml version="1.0" encoding="utf-8"?>
<mx:Application xmlns:mx="http://www.adobe.com/2006/mxml" layout="vertical">
    <mx:Script>
        <![CDATA[

            private function addNewItem():void {
                var item:XML = <element label="Numbers">
                                    <element label="1" />
                                    <element label="2" />
                               </element>
                collection.addItem(item);
            }

        ]]>
    </mx:Script>
    <mx:Tree labelField="@label" width="200">
        <mx:dataProvider>
            <mx:XMLListCollection id="collection">
                <mx:XMLList xmlns="">
                    <element label="Letters">
                        <element label="A" />
                        <element label="B" />
                    </element>
                </mx:XMLList>
            </mx:XMLListCollection>
        </mx:dataProvider>
    </mx:Tree>
    <mx:Button label="Change" click="addNewItem();" />
</mx:Application>
```

In this example, we create an XMLListCollection with an ID of collection, and we assign it as the dataProvider for a tree component. The XMLListCollection instance wraps an XMLList object with one element called Letters. When the user clicks the button we use the addItem() method to add a second element to the XMLListCollection. Because XMLListCollection updates data binding, the changes are reflected in the UI immediately.

You can also create an XMLListCollection object using ActionScript. The following example illustrates how to do this. This code results in the same behavior as the preceding example, but it uses ActionScript to create the XMLListCollection instance.

```
<?xml version="1.0" encoding="utf-8"?>
<mx:Application xmlns:mx="http://www.adobe.com/2006/mxml" layout="vertical">
    <mx:Script>
        <![CDATA[
            import mx.collections.XMLListCollection;

            private var xmlList:XMLList = new XMLList(<element label="Letters">
                                                        <element label="A" />
                                                        <element label="B" />
                                                    </element>);

            [Bindable]
            private var collection:XMLListCollection =
new XMLListCollection(xmlList);

            private function addNewItem():void {
                var item:XML = <element label='Numbers'>
                                    <element label="1" />
                                    <element label="2" />
                                </element>
                collection.addItem(item);
            }

        ]]>
    </mx:Script>
    <mx:Tree labelField="@label" width="200" dataProvider="{collection}" />
    <mx:Button label="Change" click="addNewItem();" />
</mx:Application>
```

Data Binding

Flex applications typically utilize lots of data retrieved from both RPCs (server-side method calls) and user input collected in forms. One of the ways in which you can work with data is to use extensive ActionScript. ActionScript provides you with low-level access to all the data in your Flex application. Yet the ActionScript code can be redundant, and it can be time-consuming to write. Although extensive ActionScript may be necessary in some cases, the Flex framework provides a feature called *data binding* that simplifies working with data in most cases.

Data binding lets you associate data from one object with data from another object. There are lots of ways to use data binding. The following examples list a few of the most common uses for data binding:

- Link form input controls (text inputs, checkboxes, etc.) with data models.
- Link two or more controls (e.g., display a slider value in a text component).

In the following sections, we'll look at the rules of data binding as well as examples of different ways to use data binding.

Understanding Data Binding Syntax

There are three basic ways to apply data binding:

- Curly brace ({}) syntax
- `<mx:Binding>`
- `BindingUtils`

Each of these techniques for applying data binding has advantages and disadvantages, which we'll discuss in the next few sections.

Curly braces

Using curly braces to apply data binding is the simplest and fastest technique. Throughout the early part of this book, you've seen quite a few examples of curly brace syntax. Placing curly braces around any expression causes it to be evaluated. Consider the following example with a combo box and a text input control:

```
<mx:HBox>
    <mx:ComboBox id="level">
        <mx:Array>
            <mx:Object label="A" data="1" />
            <mx:Object label="B" data="2" />
            <mx:Object label="C" data="3" />
            <mx:Object label="D" data="4" />
        </mx:Array>
    </mx:ComboBox>

    <mx:TextInput id="selectedLevel" text="level.value" />
</mx:HBox>
```

In this example, the `text` attribute of the text input is set to `level.value`. In that format, the value is interpreted literally, so the string `level.value` displays in the text input. Changing the text input tag to the following makes a big difference:

```
<mx:TextInput id="selectedLevel" text="{level.value}" />
```

With this change the text input now selects the data corresponding to the selected combo box item. As the user selects a different combo box item, the value in the text input also updates. This is because the text `level.value` is now placed within curly braces, so it is treated as an expression rather than as literal text.

More than just evaluating the expression, the curly braces attempt to make a data binding association. If the association is successful, as the value of the target (in the example, the target is `level.value`) changes, the listening property (the text property of the text input in this example) also updates. The preceding example illustrates this because as the combo box value changes, so does the value displayed in the text input. For a more dramatic example, consider the following:

```
<mx:Panel id="panel" width="{panelWidth.value}" height="{panelHeight.value}">
    <mx:NumericStepper id="panelWidth"  value="200" minimum="200"
                       maximum="400" stepSize="10" height="22"/>
    <mx:NumericStepper id="panelHeight"  value="200" minimum="200"
                       maximum="400" stepSize="10" height="22"/>
</mx:Panel>
```

In this example, the panel contains two nested numeric steppers. The panel uses data binding to link the `width` property to the value of the first numeric stepper and the `height` property to the value of the second stepper. So as the user changes the values of the numeric steppers, the `width` and `height` of the panel change accordingly.

There are many scenarios in which you can use curly brace syntax for data binding. As you've seen in the preceding example, you can use the syntax to directly associate a target property with a property of a form control such as a text input. You can also link a value from a control to a data model, as the following example illustrates:

```
<mx:Model id="dataModel">
    <userData>
        <email>{email.text}</email>
        <phone>{phone.text}</phone>
        <city>{city.text}</city>
        <state>{state.value}</state>
    </userData>
</mx:Model>

<mx:VBox>
    <mx:Label text="Email" />
    <mx:TextInput id="email" />
    <mx:Label text="Phone" />
    <mx:TextInput id="phone" />
    <mx:Label text="City" />
    <mx:TextInput id="city" />
    <mx:Label text="State" />
    <mx:ComboBox id="state">
        <mx:Array>
            <mx:Object label="CA" />
            <mx:Object label="MA" />
        </mx:Array>
    </mx:ComboBox>
</mx:VBox>
```

The preceding code uses data binding to link the values from form controls to a data model. You can use data binding both to assign values to a data model, as in the preceding example, and to retrieve data from a data model and display it. And you can even use data binding in both directions at the same time. The following code, used in conjunction with the preceding example, formats and displays the text from the data model in a text area, updating as the user changes the values in the controls bound to the model.

```
<mx:TextArea width="200" height="200" text="{'Contact Information\nEmail: ' +
            dataModel.email + '\nPhone: ' + dataModel.phone + '\nLocation: ' +
            dataModel.city + ', ' + dataModel.state}" />
```

Perhaps an even more useful example is one in which you use data binding to link data either directly from controls or from a data model to an RPC component such as a `RemoteObject` component. Using data binding in this way allows you to make RPCs without having to write much, if any, ActionScript. The following example uses data binding to link the data from the data model in the preceding example to a `RemoteObject` instance as the parameters for a method call:

```
<mx:RemoteObject id="example" destination="exampleService">
    <mx:method name="saveContactInformation">
        <mx:arguments>
            <email>{dataModel.email}</email>
            <phone>{dataModel.phone}</phone>
            <city>{dataModel.city}</city>
            <state>{dataModel.state}</state>
        </mx:arguments>
    </mx:method>
</mx:RemoteObject>
```

As the values in the data model update via data binding, so, too, will the values in the `RemoteObject` method arguments update. This allows you to call the method by simply calling a `send()` method with no parameters, as in the following example:

```
<mx:Button label="Save" click="example.saveContactInformation.send()" />
```

This is a very simple example of working with `RemoteObject`. The same principles are true when working with `HTTPService` and `WebService`. We discuss all of these RPC techniques in more detail in Chapter 17.

Because curly brace syntax allows you to evaluate any ActionScript expression, you can also use data binding with E4X expressions. That means you can use data binding not only to link XML data with control values, but also to link controls and RPC components to XML values using E4X expressions. For instance, instead of using a `Model` object, as in the earlier example, you can use an XML object as follows:

```
<mx:XML id="xmlData">
    <userData email="{email.text}" phone="{phone.text}"
            city="{city.text}" state="{state.value}" />
</mx:XML>
```

You can then use E4X expressions to link the text area value to values from the XML object:

```
<mx:TextArea width="200" height="200" text="{'Contact Information\nEmail: ' +
            xmlData.@email + '\nPhone: ' + xmlData.@phone + '\nLocation: ' +
            xmlData.@city + ', ' + xmlData.@state}" />
```

<mx:Binding>

The `<mx:Binding>` tag allows you to do exactly the same things as curly brace syntax, but with MXML tags rather than inline expressions. The `<mx:Binding>` tag requires the following attributes:

`source`
: The origin of the data you want to link

`destination`
: The point which you want notified when the value changes from the source

For the following example, the same basic premise is used as in the first example of the curly brace discussion: we'll link the value from a combo box to a text input so that when the user changes the value in the combo box, the value in the text input also changes. First we'll add the controls:

```
<mx:HBox>
    <mx:ComboBox id="level">
        <mx:Array>
            <mx:Object label="A" data="1" />
            <mx:Object label="B" data="2" />
            <mx:Object label="C" data="3" />
            <mx:Object label="D" data="4" />
        </mx:Array>
    </mx:ComboBox>

    <mx:TextInput id="selectedLevel" />
</mx:HBox>
```

Notice that we're not setting the text property of the text input. With curly brace syntax we'd set the text property inline. With the `<mx:Binding>` tag we'll use a separate tag to achieve the goal of data binding. To link the source (`level.value`) and the destination (`selectedLevel.text`), you can add the following tag to your code (note that the tag must appear outside any layout container tags):

```
<mx:Binding source="level.selectedItem.data" destination="selectedLevel.text" />
```

This code works identically to how the curly brace example worked, yet it uses a different mechanism to achieve that goal.

You can use `<mx:Binding>` with data models and RPC components as well. We can rewrite the earlier data model example to illustrate this point. First, add the data model, the `RemoteObject`, and the controls. Note that in this example, the data model and the remote method arguments do not define any values inline:

```
<mx:Model id="dataModel">
    <userData>
        <email></email>
        <phone></phone>
        <city></city>
        <state></state>
    </userData>
</mx:Model>
```

```
<mx:RemoteObject id="example" destination="exampleService">
    <mx:method name="saveContactInformation">
        <mx:arguments>
            <email></email>
            <phone></phone>
            <city></city>
            <state></state>
        </mx:arguments>
    </mx:method>
</mx:RemoteObject>

<mx:VBox>
    <mx:Label text="Email" />
    <mx:TextInput id="email" />
    <mx:Label text="Phone" />
    <mx:TextInput id="phone" />
    <mx:Label text="City" />
    <mx:TextInput id="city" />
    <mx:Label text="State" />
    <mx:ComboBox id="state">
        <mx:Array>
            <mx:Object label="CA" />
            <mx:Object label="MA" />
        </mx:Array>
    </mx:ComboBox>
    <mx:TextArea id="summary" width="200" height="200" />
</mx:VBox>
```

Next, we need to define the data bindings using the `<mx:Binding>` tag:

```
<mx:Binding source="email.text" destination="dataModel.email" />
<mx:Binding source="phone.text" destination="dataModel.phone" />
<mx:Binding source="city.text" destination="dataModel.city" />
<mx:Binding source="state.value" destination="dataModel.state" />
<mx:Binding source="'Contact Information\nEmail: ' + dataModel.email +
    '\nPhone: ' + dataModel.phone + '\nLocation: ' + dataModel.city + ', ' +
    dataModel.state" destination="summary.text" />
<mx:Binding source="dataModel.email"
            destination="example.saveContactInformation.arguments.email" />
<mx:Binding source="dataModel.phone"
            destination="example.saveContactInformation.arguments.phone" />
<mx:Binding source="dataModel.city"
            destination="example.saveContactInformation.arguments.city" />
<mx:Binding source="dataModel.state"
            destination="example.saveContactInformation.arguments.state" />
```

You can also use E4X expressions with the `<mx:Binding>` tag. Assume you change the data model from a `Model` object to an `XML` object as follows:

```
<mx:XML id="xmlData">
    <userData email="{email.text}" phone="{phone.text}"
              city="{city.text}" state="{state.value}" />
</mx:XML>
```

You can then change the <mx:Binding> tags as follows:

```
<mx:Binding source="email.text" destination="xmlData.@email" />
<mx:Binding source="phone.text" destination="xmlData.@phone" />
<mx:Binding source="city.text" destination="xmlData.@city" />
<mx:Binding source="state.value" destination="xmlData.@state" />
<mx:Binding source="'Contact Information\nEmail: ' + xmlData.@email + '\nPhone: ' +
            xmlData.@phone + '\nLocation: ' + xmlData.@city + ', ' +
            xmlData.@state" destination="summary.text" />
<mx:Binding source="xmlData.@email"
            destination="example.saveContactInformation.arguments.email" />
<mx:Binding source="xmlData.@phone"
            destination="example.saveContactInformation.arguments.phone" />
<mx:Binding source="xmlData.@city"
            destination="example.saveContactInformation.arguments.city" />
<mx:Binding source="xmlData.@state"
            destination="example.saveContactInformation.arguments.state" />
```

The `<mx:Binding>` tag requires more code than the curly brace syntax. Curly brace syntax can appear inline within existing tags, whereas `<mx:Binding>` syntax requires that you add additional tags to your code. This may seem like a disadvantage at first; however, in the long run it is advantageous to use `<mx:Binding>` in most cases because it allows you to create a cleaner separation between the UI layout and the data used. Using the `<mx:Binding>` tag is a cleaner implementation of data binding, yet it does not allow any greater functionality than curly brace syntax. If you need more functionality (such as dynamically changing data binding endpoints at runtime), you can use `BindingUtils`, discussed in the next section.

Although using `<mx:Binding>` may have its advantages (as mentioned in the preceding paragraph), the disadvantage is that it requires more code to accomplish the same thing as simply using curly braces within component tags. This is a trade-off that you must evaluate for yourself.

BindingUtils

In most cases, you should use curly brace or `<mx:Binding>` syntax for data binding. However, neither of those techniques let you dynamically configure data binding at runtime. The `mx.binding.utils.BindingUtils` class has a static method called `bindProperty()` that lets you configure data binding from ActionScript. This ActionScript solution provides the most flexibility and the lowest-level access to data binding of all the techniques. As such, the `BindingUtils.bindProperty()` method can be a useful resource in those special cases in which you require more flexibility than the other techniques afford you.

The syntax for the `bindProperty()` method is as follows:

```
BindingUtils.bindProperty(destinationObject, destinationProperty,
                          sourceObject, sourceProperty);
```

The destination and source object parameters are object references and the property parameters are strings. The following example links the value from a combo box so that it displays in a text input:

```
BindingUtils.bindProperty(textInput, "text", comboBox, "value");
```

Because `BindingUtils` is ActionScript, you can place the code anywhere that you can place ActionScript code. The following example uses a button to enable data binding between a combo box and a text input when the user clicks the button:

```
<mx:Script>
    <![CDATA[
        import mx.binding.utils.BindingUtils;
    ]]>
</mx:Script>

<mx:VBox>
  <mx:ComboBox id="comboBox">
    <mx:Array>
      <mx:Object label="1" />
      <mx:Object label="2" />
      <mx:Object label="3" />
      <mx:Object label="4" />
    </mx:Array>
  </mx:ComboBox>
  <mx:TextInput id="textInput" />
  <mx:Button label="enable data binding"
   click="BindingUtils.bindProperty(textInput, 'text', comboBox, 'value')" />
</mx:VBox>
```

In the preceding example, the combo box and the text input are not initially linked. However, when the user clicks on the button, it calls the `bindProperty()` method, which links the controls such that the combo box value is displayed in the text input, and the display changes as the value changes. To use `BindingUtils`, you must add an `import` statement, as in the example.

The `bindProperty()` method returns a reference to a new `mx.binding.utils.ChangeWatcher` object. The `ChangeWatcher` class defines a class of objects that represents the actual data binding link between a source and a destination. Using `bindProperty()` by itself allows you to enable data binding at runtime, but if you want to further modify that data binding, you'll have to work with a `ChangeWatcher` object. Using a `ChangeWatcher` object, you can disable data binding or change the source point.

The `ChangeWatcher` object returned by a `bindProperty()` method call represents that data binding association, and if you want to change that association or stop it, you must use the `ChangeWatcher` object. You can stop a data binding association between two points by calling the `unwatch()` method of the `ChangeWatcher` object:

```
changeWatcher.unwatch();
```

You can retrieve the current source value using the `getValue()` method:

```
changeWatcher.getValue();
```

You can change the source object using the reset() method. The reset() method accepts one parameter specifying the new source object:

```
changeWatcher.reset(newSourceObject);
```

The reset() method does not allow you to change the property of the source object. If you want to change the property, you must call unwatch() to stop the current data binding association. Then you can start a new association using BindingUtils.bindProperty():

```
changeWatcher.unwatch();
changeWatcher = BindingUtils.bindProperty(newSource, newProperty, destination,
destinationProperty);
```

Example 14-2 uses BindingUtils and ChangeWatcher to toggle the source object between two combo boxes. The example uses two combo boxes, a text input, and a button. When the application initializes, it calls the initializeHandler() method as that is assigned to the Application initialize handler. The initializeHandler() method sets data binding between the level combo box and the selectedLevel text input. When the user clicks the button, the data binding system calls the toggleDataBinding() method, which uses the reset() method of the ChangeWatcher object to change the source object.

Example 14-2. Working with BindingUtils

```
<?xml version="1.0" encoding="utf-8"?>
<mx:Application xmlns:mx="http://www.adobe.com/2006/mxml" layout="absolute"
 initialize="initializeHandler(event)">

  <mx:Script>
    <![CDATA[

        import mx.binding.utils.BindingUtils;
        import mx.binding.utils.ChangeWatcher;

        private var _changeWatcher:ChangeWatcher;
        private var _currentHost:ComboBox;

        private function initializeHandler(event:Event):void {
            // Set the initial data binding, and assign the ChangeWatcher
            // object to the _changeWatcher property.
            _changeWatcher = BindingUtils.bindProperty(selectedLevel, "text",
                                                  level, "value");

            // Save a reference to the current source object.
            _currentHost = level;
        }

        private function toggleDataBinding(event:Event):void {

            // Determine the new source object. If the current source
            // object is level, set the new source to subLevel. If the
            // current source object is subLevel then set the new
            // source to level.
```

```
            _currentHost = _currentHost == level ? subLevel : level;

            // Use the reset() method to change the source object.
            _changeWatcher.reset(_currentHost);

            // Calling reset() changes the source for the data binding, but it does
            // not immediately update the destination. For that, you need to
            // manually update the destination value by retrieving the source value
            // using the getValue() method of the ChangeWatcher object.
            selectedLevel.text = _changeWatcher.getValue().toString();
        }

    ]]>
  </mx:Script>

  <mx:VBox>
    <mx:ComboBox id="level">
        <mx:Array>
            <mx:Object label="A" data="1" />
            <mx:Object label="B" data="2" />
            <mx:Object label="C" data="3" />
            <mx:Object label="D" data="4" />
        </mx:Array>
    </mx:ComboBox>

    <mx:ComboBox id="subLevel">
        <mx:Array>
            <mx:Object label="A" data="1.1" />
            <mx:Object label="B" data="1.2" />
            <mx:Object label="C" data="1.3" />
            <mx:Object label="D" data="1.4" />
        </mx:Array>
    </mx:ComboBox>

    <mx:TextInput id="selectedLevel" />

    <mx:Button label="toggle data binding" click="toggleDataBinding(event)" />

  </mx:VBox>
</mx:Application>
```

Enabling Data Binding for Custom Classes

Data binding is enabled for some types of objects by default, but to make it work for custom classes, enable data binding with the [Bindable] metadata tag which tells the Flex compiler to configure whatever it precedes. Use [Bindable] with:

- A class
- A property
- An implicit getter method
- An implicit setter method

For data binding to work when using implicit getters and setters, you need a getter and a setter for every property that you want to use data binding.

When you use the `[Bindable]` metadata tag before a class declaration, it marks all the public properties and all the getter and setter pairs as data-binding-enabled:

```
[Bindable]
public class Example {
```

When you use `[Bindable]` before a property declaration, it sets just that property as data-binding-enabled:

```
[Bindable]
private var _exampleProperty:String;
```

When you use `[Bindable]` before a getter and/or setter method, that method becomes data-binding-enabled. If a getter and setter have the same name, you must place the `[Bindable]` metadata tag before only one of them. If you have only a getter method, the method works only as the source for data binding. If you have only a setter method, the method works only as the destination for data binding:

```
[Bindable]
public function get exampleGetter():String {
    return "example";
}
```

Always enable both the contents of a custom class and an instance of the class (if instantiated using ActionScript) to use the instance for data binding. Consider the simple class in Example 14-3.

Example 14-3. Basic data binding class example

```
package com.oreilly.programmingflex.binding {

    [Bindable]
    public class DataBindableExample {

        private var _example:String;

        public function get example():String {
            return _example;
        }

        public function set example(value:String):void {
            _example = value;
        }

        public function DataBindableExample() {
            _example = "example";
        }
    }
}
```

The class in Example 14-4 uses [Bindable] to enable the entire class. But if you want to use an instance of the class in an MXML document as either the source or the destination for data binding, you must declare the instance using the [Bindable] tag as well.

Example 14-4. Implementation of basic data binding

```
<?xml version="1.0" encoding="utf-8"?>
<mx:Application xmlns:mx="http://www.adobe.com/2006/mxml" layout="absolute"
initialize="initializeHandler(event)">

    <mx:Script>
        <![CDATA[

            import com.oreilly.programmingflex.binding.DataBindableExample;

            [Bindable]
            private var _dataBindableExample:DataBindableExample;

            private function initializeHandler(event:Event):void {
                _dataBindableExample = new DataBindableExample();
            }

        ]]>
    </mx:Script>
    <mx:VBox>
        <mx:TextInput id="input" />
        <mx:TextInput id="output" />
    </mx:VBox>

    <mx:Binding source="input.text" destination="_dataBindableExample.example" />
    <mx:Binding source="_dataBindableExample.example" destination="output.text" />
</mx:Application>
```

The preceding example uses the DataBindableExample instance as an intermediary between the two text inputs. This particular example does not demonstrate a useful use case, but it does illustrate a simple working example that shows which elements are necessary to build a custom class that works with data binding. We'll look at more practical, more complex examples later in this chapter, when we talk about building proxies for endpoints that wouldn't otherwise be data-binding-enabled.

Customizing Data Binding

Data binding works by dispatching events using the standard Flash Player event model. If you were to look at the generated ActionScript for an application that uses data binding, you would see that classes with bindable properties dispatch events, and where MXML uses data binding syntax, the generated ActionScript class registers event listeners. When you use the [Bindable] tag, the default event type that gets dispatched is propertyChange. In many cases, this is perfectly workable. However, it can introduce inefficiencies when one class has several properties using data binding, because anytime any of the properties changes, all listeners for all changes in all bindable properties for the object instance will receive a notification. It's more efficient if each property dispatches a unique event name. You get this by adding an event setting for the `[Bindable]` tag.

```
[Bindable(event="customEvent")]
```

In cases where you customize the event name, you also manually dispatch the event.

```
dispatchEvent(new Event("customEvent"));
```

Obviously, when you customize the event name, you must add a `[Bindable]` tag before each property (or getter/setter), rather than using one tag just prior to the class declaration. Example 14-5 uses custom event names.

Example 14-5. Customized data binding

```
package com.oreilly.programmingflex.binding {

    import flash.events.Event;
    import flash.events.EventDispatcher;

    public class CustomizedDataBindableExample extends EventDispatcher {

        static public const A_CHANGE:String = "aChange";
        static public const B_CHANGE:String = "bChange";

        private var _a:String;
        private var _b:String;

        [Bindable(event="aChange")]
        public function get a():String {
            return _a;
        }

        public function set a(value:String):void {
            _a = value;
            dispatchEvent(new Event(A_CHANGE));
        }

        [Bindable(event="bChange")]
        public function get b():String {
            return _b;
        }

        public function set b(value:String):void {
            _b = value;
            dispatchEvent(new Event(B_CHANGE));
        }

        public function CustomizedDataBindableExample() {
            _a = "a";
            _b = "b";
        }
    }
}
```

You'll also notice that the class in the preceding example extends `EventDispatcher`. When using the `Bindable` tag without an `event` attribute, the Flex compiler automatically takes care of configuring the class to dispatch events, even if the class doesn't explicitly extend `EventDispatcher`. (Remember that the Flex compiler always compiles in several steps, and that during the first step the compiler converts MXML and ActionScript classes to an intermediate ActionScript stage in which it translates things such as metadata tags into concrete ActionScript implementations.) However, when you specify an event attribute for the `Bindable` metadata tag, you must dispatch events explicitly. Therefore, if you do not extend `EventDispatcher` explicitly (or use composition to include an `EventDispatcher` instance), you'll receive a compiler error because there will be no such method as `dispatchEvent()`. Therefore, when you use the `event` attribute, you must account for this either by extending `EventDispatcher` (as in the preceding example) or by using composition to include an `EventDispatcher` object and dispatch the events using that object.

Data Binding Examples

In the next few sections, we'll look at examples using data binding to achieve a variety of goals.

Controlling Images

Example 14-6 uses data binding to work with images. Using a combo box, the user can select an image to view. Using data binding, the value of the combo box is linked to the `source` property of an image component. Additionally, the example uses three slider controls to control the alpha, width, and height of the image, all of which are linked using data binding.

Example 14-6. Data binding example

```
<?xml version="1.0" encoding="utf-8"?>
<mx:Application xmlns:mx="http://www.adobe.com/2006/mxml" layout="absolute">

    <mx:VBox x="0" y="0" height="100%" horizontalAlign="center">

        <!-- Add a combo box with several options. Each option has a label
             and then a data property that contains a URL to an image. -->
        <mx:ComboBox id="imageUrl">
            <mx:Array>
                <mx:Object label="Water Lilies" data="example1.jpg" />
                <mx:Object label="Sunset" data="example2.jpg" />
            </mx:Array>
        </mx:ComboBox>

        <!-- Place the image within a canvas with a fixed size so that when the
             image resizes it won't cause the rest of the layout to change -->
        <mx:Canvas width="160" height="120">
            <!-- Make sure maintainAspectRatio is set to false so you can change
```

```
            the width and height independently. -->
        <mx:Image id="image" width="160" height="120" alpha="0"
            maintainAspectRatio="false" />
    </mx:Canvas>

    <!-- Add three labels and sliders. -->
    <mx:Label text="Alpha"/>
    <mx:HSlider id="imageAlpha" minimum="0" maximum="1" value="1"
        liveDragging="true" />
    <mx:Label text="Width"/>
    <mx:HSlider id="imageWidth" minimum="0" maximum="160" value="160"
        liveDragging="true" />
    <mx:Label text="Height"/>
    <mx:HSlider id="imageHeight" minimum="0" maximum="120" value="120"
        liveDragging="true" />
</mx:VBox>

<!-- Define the data binding between the components. The image alpha,
     width, and height properties are linked to the slider values.
     The image source is linked to the combo box value. -->
<mx:Binding source="imageAlpha.value" destination="image.alpha" />
<mx:Binding source="imageWidth.value" destination="image.width" />
<mx:Binding source="imageHeight.value" destination="image.height" />
<mx:Binding source="imageUrl.value" destination="image.source" />
</mx:Application>
```

Working with Web Services

In this example, we build a simple application that calls web service methods. In the first part, we'll use data binding to link the result of a web service method call to text input controls. In the second part, we'll link the values from numeric steppers to the parameters for a web service method.

This section uses the WebService component to access a SOAP Web service. If you are unfamiliar with web services and the WebService component, you can consult Chapter 17 for more information. However, you can complete this example without necessarily having a detailed understanding of those concepts.

First we'll add the `WebService` object and define the first operation. Web Services Description Language (WSDL) is at *http://www.rightactionscript.com/webservices/FlashSurvey.php?wsdl*. The operation's called `getAverages` and doesn't need parameters. This method returns an object with two properties indicating number of years using Flash and ActionScript.

```
<?xml version="1.0" encoding="utf-8"?>
<mx:Application xmlns:mx="http://www.adobe.com/2006/mxml" layout="absolute">

    <mx:WebService id="survey"
wsdl="http://www.rightactionscript.com/webservices/FlashSurvey.php?wsdl">
```

```
        <mx:operation name="getAverages" resultFormat="object" />
    </mx:WebService>

</mx:Application>
```

We'll next add controls to call the method and display the results. Note the click event handler for the button calls the send() method of the web service operation:

```
<?xml version="1.0" encoding="utf-8"?>
<mx:Application xmlns:mx="http://www.adobe.com/2006/mxml" layout="absolute">

    <mx:WebService id="survey"
wsdl="http://www.rightactionscript.com/webservices/FlashSurvey.php?wsdl">
        <mx:operation name="getAverages" resultFormat="object" />
    </mx:WebService>

    <mx:HBox>
        <mx:VBox>
            <mx:Button id="getAveragesButton" label="Get Averages"
click="survey.getAverages.send()" />
            <mx:TextInput id="resultFlash" enabled="false" />
            <mx:TextInput id="resultActionScript" enabled="false" />
        </mx:VBox>
    </mx:HBox>

</mx:Application>
```

Now we can use data binding to link the results to the text input controls. The getAverages web service method for this web service returns an object with two properties: flash and actionscript. The return value is stored in the lastResult property of the operation object. That means we can use survey.getAverages.lastResult.flash and survey.getAverages.lastResult.actionscript as the sources for the bindings:

```
<?xml version="1.0" encoding="utf-8"?>
<mx:Application xmlns:mx="http://www.adobe.com/2006/mxml" layout="absolute">

    <!-- Existing application code -->

    <mx:Binding source="survey.getAverages.lastResult.flash"
                destination="resultFlash.text" />
    <mx:Binding source="survey.getAverages.lastResult.actionscript"
destination="resultActionScript.text" />

</mx:Application>
```

When you test this application and click the button, you'll see the averages returned and displayed (assuming you have a working Internet connection).

Now we'll add one more operation, called takeSurvey. The takeSurvey method requires two parameters, called years_flash and years_actionscript:

```
<?xml version="1.0" encoding="utf-8"?>
<mx:Application xmlns:mx="http://www.adobe.com/2006/mxml" layout="absolute">

    <mx:WebService id="survey"
```

```
wsdl="http://www.rightactionscript.com/webservices/FlashSurvey.php?wsdl">
        <mx:operation name="getAverages" resultFormat="object" />
        <mx:operation name="takeSurvey">
            <mx:request>
                <years_flash></years_flash>
                <years_actionscript></years_actionscript>
            </mx:request>
        </mx:operation>
    </mx:WebService>

    <!-- Existing application code -->

</mx:Application>
```

Now that the operation is defined, you can add the controls to allow the user to select the values for the parameters and call the method. For that purpose, add two numeric steppers and a button with a click handler:

```
<?xml version="1.0" encoding="utf-8"?>
<mx:Application xmlns:mx="http://www.adobe.com/2006/mxml" layout="absolute">

    <!-- Existing application code -->

    <mx:HBox>
        <!-- Existing application code -->
        <mx:VBox>
            <mx:Button id="sendValuesButton" label="Take Survey"
                click="survey.takeSurvey.send()" />
            <mx:NumericStepper id="flashValue" />
            <mx:NumericStepper id="actionScriptValue" />
        </mx:VBox>
    </mx:HBox>

    <!-- Existing application code -->

</mx:Application>
```

The remaining step is to define the data binding for the numeric steppers and the operation request parameters:

```
<?xml version="1.0" encoding="utf-8"?>
<mx:Application xmlns:mx="http://www.adobe.com/2006/mxml" layout="absolute">

    <!-- Existing application code -->
    <mx:Binding source="flashValue.value"
        destination="survey.takeSurvey.request.years_flash" />
    <mx:Binding source="actionScriptValue.value"
destination="survey.takeSurvey.request.years_actionscript" />

</mx:Application>
```

Now you can run the application, select values from the numeric steppers, and click the button to take the survey. If you click the button to get the averages, you'll notice that the numbers have changed from the previous time you viewed the values.

Building Data Binding Proxies

Some types of objects and some elements in Flex applications cannot use data binding directly. For example, you cannot use data binding directly with component styles. Yet you can build an elegant solution that uses something called *delegation*. Delegation is what occurs when a class called a *proxy* wraps an object, and it passes along requests to the object it wraps. The goal of delegation may be different in different scenarios, but in this case, the goal is to provide a layer of indirection so that the data-binding-enabled proxy can accept requests in place of the object that cannot accept those requests.

A proxy class generally uses the following structure:

```
package {

    public class ProxyClass {

        private var _object:Object;

        public function ProxyClass(object:Object) {
            _object = object;
        }

        public function method():void {
            _object.method();
        }

    }

}
```

Obviously, the preceding format is overly simplified, and each proxy class may vary the format slightly. We'll look at two specific implementations of proxy classes designed to facilitate data binding in the next two subsections. Hopefully you'll then be able to generalize this solution so that you can apply it to similar scenarios when you need to enable data binding for an object that doesn't natively support data binding.

Using Data Binding with a Shared Object

You cannot use data binding with shared objects. Yet you can use a proxy to enable data binding. For this example, we'll use a very simple case in which you want to store one user preference in a local shared object. That one preference is a Boolean value indicating whether to show a form in the application. Of course, you could accomplish this task through ActionScript, yet you could also enable data binding with a proxy class that wraps the shared object. For this example, here's our proxy class definition:

```
package com.oreilly.programmingflex.binding.proxies {
    import flash.net.SharedObject;

    [Bindable]
```

```
    public class UserPreferences {

        private var _sharedObject:SharedObject;

        // Retrieve the value from the shared object.
        public function get showForm():Boolean {
            return _sharedObject.data.showForm;
        }

        // Assign the value to the shared object, and call flush()
        // to ensure that it writes to disk immediately.
        public function set showForm(value:Boolean):void {
            _sharedObject.data.showForm = value;
            _sharedObject.flush();
        }

        // The class wraps a shared object. Pass the reference to the constructor,
        // and assign that reference to a private property.
        public function UserPreferences(sharedObject:SharedObject):void {
            _sharedObject = sharedObject;
        }

    }
}
```

Then, you can use the following MXML to demonstrate how the proxy works:

```
<?xml version="1.0" encoding="utf-8"?>
<mx:Application xmlns:mx="http://www.adobe.com/2006/mxml" layout="absolute"
initialize="initializeHandler(event)">

    <mx:Script>
        <![CDATA[
            import com.oreilly.programmingflex.binding.proxies.UserPreferences;
            import flash.net.SharedObject;

            // Declare a variable for the instance of the UserPreferences
            // class. Make the variable data-binding-enabled with the
            // [Bindable] metadata tag.
            [Bindable]
            private var _userPreferences:UserPreferences;

            // When the application starts construct the UserPreferences object,
            // passing it a reference to a local shared object.
            private function initializeHandler(event:Event):void {
                _userPreferences =
new UserPreferences(SharedObject.getLocal("userPreferences"));
            }

            // This is the function we call via data binding when the
            // shared object's showForm property changes. Toggle the
            // current state.
            private function set toggleForm(value:Boolean):void {
                currentState = value ? null : "hideForm";
            }
```

```
    ]]>
</mx:Script>

<!-- Define a state that removes the form -->
<mx:states>
    <mx:State name="hideForm">
        <mx:RemoveChild target="{form}" />
    </mx:State>
</mx:states>

<!-- Define a form and a checkbox -->
<mx:VBox id="vbox">
    <mx:Form id="form">
        <mx:FormHeading label="Form"/>
        <mx:FormItem label="First Name">
            <mx:TextInput id="firstName"/>
        </mx:FormItem>
        <mx:FormItem label="Last Name">
            <mx:TextInput id="lastName"/>
        </mx:FormItem>
    </mx:Form>
    <mx:CheckBox id="showForm" label="Show Form" />
</mx:VBox>

<!-- Define data bindings between the checkbox and proxy object as well
     as between the proxy object and the toggleForm() function. -->
<mx:Binding source="_userPreferences.showForm"
    destination="showForm.selected" />
<mx:Binding source="showForm.selected"
    destination="_userPreferences.showForm" />
<mx:Binding source="_userPreferences.showForm" destination="toggleForm" />

</mx:Application>
```

This example toggles the state, and it remembers the state every time you return to the application because it's storing the data in the shared object.

Summary

In this chapter, you learned about the basics of working with data. You read about using data models, both the Flex framework tag-based data models and the preferred ActionScript class-based data models. You also learned about using data binding to link data to components and ensure that the data is always in sync.

CHAPTER 15

Validating and Formatting Data

When working with data, you'll frequently need to ensure that the data adheres to certain rules. When the data is from user input, this is called *validation*. When the data is being displayed or needs to be in a particular form before storing it or sending it to a service method, this is called *formatting*. The Flex framework provides mechanisms for both of these types of operations. In this chapter, we will look at both validating and formatting data.

Validating User Input

When you work with user input, you frequently may want to validate that input before submitting it for some sort of course of action, either client-side or server-side. For example, if you want to submit form data to a server script that inserts the data to a database, you may need to verify that the values are in the correct format so that you can insert them (e.g., a numeric value needs to be a number and a date needs to be formatted in a way that your script can parse it into the format you require for the database). Often it is advisable to add both client-side *and* server-side validation. The server-side validation ensures that no strange or incorrect values were inserted at the time the request was made, and the client-side validation makes sure the data is valid before even making a request. Only client-side validation is within the scope of Flex coding, and therefore we will look at how to validate data client-side using Flex.

You can write your own validation procedures for this purpose. Yet most validations require rewriting the same basic code time after time. All that redundancy leads to a lot of time spent rewriting the same basic code rather than focusing on new tasks. For this reason, the Flex framework ships with a type of component called a *validator*, which you can use to assist with validating user input. There are a handful of standard validator types, including `StringValidator`, `NumberValidator`, `DateValidator`, `PhoneValidator`, and `ZipCodeValidator`. The next few sections discuss how to work with each of the standard validators and show you how to build custom validator types.

Using Validators

There are two ways you can work with validators: with MXML or with ActionScript. For many use cases, MXML is sufficient for your validation needs. Although it is common to work with validators in MXML, there are many cases in which you'll work with validators both in MXML *and* in ActionScript for the same project—creating the validators using MXML, and adding extra functionality with ActionScript. In a few cases, you'll work with validators entirely in ActionScript. Those are special cases in which you need to be able to build the validators dynamically at runtime because the exact user input controls and validation needs are not known at compile time.

Validator basics

All validator types inherit from a base type called `mx.validators.Validator`. Although you'll work with subtypes more frequently (e.g., `StringValidator`), you can work with `Validator` for very basic validation requirements, and all the validator types inherit the basic functionality and properties of the `Validator` type.

When you create a validator, you must specify at least two properties, called `source` and `property`. The `source` is a reference to the object containing the data you want to validate, and the `property` is the property of that object that contains the data. You can create a validator using MXML using the following structure:

```
<mx:Validator source="{sourceObject}" property="sourceProperty" />
```

By default, the behavior of a validator is simply to validate that the user has specified a value. All validators have a property called `required` that defaults to `true`. The following achieves exactly the same thing as the preceding code example:

```
<mx:Validator source="{sourceObject}" property="sourceProperty" required="true" />
```

The default trigger for a validator is a `valueCommit` event. All input controls dispatch `valueCommit` events when the value is changed programmatically, or when the focus shifts away from the control. Example 15-1 illustrates a very basic validator use. The application consists of a form with a text input and a button. The validator uses the text input as the source, and it validates that the user has input at least one character. The validator runs when the user moves focus away from the text input. That means you must first move focus to the text input (by clicking in it) and then shift focus away either by clicking on the button or by pressing the Tab key.

Example 15-1. Basic form validation

```
<?xml version="1.0" encoding="utf-8"?>
<mx:Application xmlns:mx="http://www.adobe.com/2006/mxml" layout="absolute">

    <mx:Form>
        <mx:FormHeading label="Sample Form"/>
        <mx:FormItem label="Name">
            <mx:TextInput id="username"/>
        </mx:FormItem>
```

```
        <mx:FormItem>
            <mx:Button id="button" label="Submit"/>
        </mx:FormItem>
    </mx:Form>

    <mx:Validator source="{username}" property="text" />

</mx:Application>
```

When a validator runs, there are two possible outcomes: either it will validate the data successfully or it won't. If it validates the data, the default behavior is to do nothing. If it does not successfully validate the data, the default behavior for a validator is to apply a red outline to the input control and display a message when the user moves the mouse over the control.

As mentioned earlier, it is more common to create validators using MXML than ActionScript. Yet there are valid use cases that require you to create the validators using ActionScript. For example, if you create a form at runtime based on XML data, you must also create the validators at runtime, and that requires ActionScript. To create a validator at runtime, use a standard `new` statement with the constructor for the validator type. For example, the following creates a `Validator` object:

```
_validator = new Validator();
```

You must always set both the `source` and the `property` properties as well:

```
_validator.source = sourceObject;
_validator.property = "sourceProperty";
```

Example 15-2 achieves exactly the same thing as Example 15-1, but in this case, the validator is created using ActionScript.

Example 15-2. ActionScript-based validator

```
<?xml version="1.0" encoding="utf-8"?>
<mx:Application xmlns:mx="http://www.adobe.com/2006/mxml" layout="absolute"
initialize="initializeHandler(event)">
    <mx:Script>
        <![CDATA[
            import mx.validators.Validator;

            private var _validator:Validator;

            private function initializeHandler(event:Event):void {
                _validator = new Validator();
                _validator.source = username;
                _validator.property = "text";
            }

        ]]>
    </mx:Script>

    <mx:Form>
        <mx:FormHeading label="Sample Form"/>
```

```
        <mx:FormItem label="Name">
            <mx:TextInput id="username"/>
        </mx:FormItem>
        <mx:FormItem>
            <mx:Button id="button" label="Submit"/>
        </mx:FormItem>
    </mx:Form>

</mx:Application>
```

Unless stated otherwise, properties of validators are set using MXML or ActionScript.

Customizing validator messages

When a validator runs and fails to successfully validate the data, it displays a message by default. The message type depends on the type of validator as well as the way in which the validator failed. The `Validator` class defines just one type of message that appears when a required field contains no data. The default message is "This field is required." That message may be appropriate in most cases, but if your application requires a custom message, you can change the value using the `requiredFieldError` property:

```
<mx:Validator source="{sourceObject}" property="sourceProperty"
requiredFieldError="Hey, fill out this item" />
```

All validator types inherit the `required` and `requiredFieldError` properties, and so you can set a custom `requiredFieldError` message for any validator type. However, many validator types may fail for reasons other than the field simply being required. For example, a `PhoneNumberValidator` can fail if the data contains an invalid character. Each validator type also defines properties allowing you to customize the error messages for each type of possible error. For example, the following customizes the error message when the user specifies an invalid character for a phone number:

```
<mx:PhoneNumberValidator source="{sourceObject}" property="sourceProperty"
    invalidCharError="You really ought to use the proper characters" />
```

We'll look at all the possible errors for each validator type later in this chapter.

Handling validator events

Validators dispatch two basic types of events: valid and invalid. When a validator runs successfully, it dispatches a valid event; when it doesn't, it dispatches an invalid event. By default, the source control receives and handles the events. All input controls are configured to respond to valid and invalid events, typically by applying a red outline and displaying a message. For this reason, it's not a necessity that you explicitly handle the validator events. However, if you want to modify the default behavior, you'll need to listen for and handle the validator events.

You can handle the events in one of two ways.

- Specify values for the valid and invalid attributes of the MXML tag used to create the validator:

```
<mx:Validator source="{sourceObject}" property="sourceProperty"
    valid="validHandler(event)" invalid="invalidHandler(event)" />
```

- Use `addEventListener()` to register listeners for the events via ActionScript. Use the `mx.events.ValidationResultEvent.VALID` and the `mx.events.ValidationResultEvent.INVALID` constants:

```
validator.addEventListener(ValidationResultEvent.VALID, validHandler);
validator.addEventListener(ValidationResultEvent.INVALID, invalidHandler);
```

Example 15-3 handles the valid and invalid events such that in addition to the default behavior, the form item label also changes.

Example 15-3. Handling validator events

```
<?xml version="1.0" encoding="utf-8"?>
<mx:Application xmlns:mx="http://www.adobe.com/2006/mxml" layout="absolute">
    <mx:Script>
        <![CDATA[

            import mx.events.ValidationResultEvent;

            private function invalidHandler(event:ValidationResultEvent):void {
                usernameItem.setStyle("color", 0xFF0000);
                usernameItem.label = "*Name";
            }

            private function validHandler(event:ValidationResultEvent):void {
                usernameItem.setStyle("color", 0x000000);
                usernameItem.label = "Name";
            }

        ]]>
    </mx:Script>

    <mx:Form>
        <mx:FormHeading label="Sample Form"/>
        <mx:FormItem id="usernameItem" label="Name">
            <mx:TextInput id="username"/>
        </mx:FormItem>
        <mx:FormItem>
            <mx:Button id="button" label="Submit" />
        </mx:FormItem>
    </mx:Form>

    <mx:Validator id="validator" source="{username}" property="text"
invalid="invalidHandler(event)" valid="validHandler(event)" />

</mx:Application>
```

Every validator can have a listener that is automatically configured to listen to validator events. By default, the listener is the source object. As mentioned, all user input controls are able to listen for the validator events and respond to them in a default manner. If you want to specify a different, nondefault listener for a validator, you can use the `listener` property to assign a reference to a new object. The listener object must be an object that implements the `IValidatorListener` interface. The `UIComponent` class implements `IValidatorListener`, so you can assign any `UIComponent` instance (including any user input control) as the listener. Although slightly convoluted, the following example illustrates how the `listener` property can work. In this example, the validator is applied to a data model rather than a control. The data model value is assigned via data binding from a text input:

```
<?xml version="1.0" encoding="utf-8"?>
<mx:Application xmlns:mx="http://www.adobe.com/2006/mxml" layout="absolute">

    <mx:Model id="userData">
        <userData>
            <username></username>
        </userData>
    </mx:Model>

    <mx:Form>
        <mx:FormHeading label="Sample Form"/>
        <mx:FormItem id="usernameItem" label="Name">
            <mx:TextInput id="username"/>
        </mx:FormItem>
        <mx:FormItem>
            <mx:Button id="button" label="Submit" />
        </mx:FormItem>
    </mx:Form>

    <mx:Binding source="username.text" destination="userData.username" />

    <mx:Validator id="validator" source="{userData}" property="username" />

</mx:Application>
```

Although the validator is applied to the data model field, it does not actually do anything useful. This is for two reasons, the first of which is that the normal trigger for the validator won't work because data models don't dispatch `valueCommit` events. We'll talk more about alternative ways of triggering validators in the next section, but for now you can simply define the validator's `trigger` property so that it's a reference to the input control. That tells the validator to listen for `valueCommit` events from the input control rather than the data model:

```
<mx:Validator id="validator" source="{userData}" property="username"
    trigger="{username}" />
```

However, even with the preceding change, the application won't display any sort of notification when the validation fails. That's due to the second reason, which is that a validator's default listener is the `source` object, which is a data model in this case. However, a data model does not know how to handle those events. Instead, if you want a listener object to handle the events, you must override the default listener value by setting the `listener` property for the validator. With the following change to the validator, it uses the input control as the `listener`:

```
<mx:Validator id="validator" source="{userData}" property="username"
    trigger="{username}" listener="{username}" />
```

This example isn't very practical, though. There is no reason in this case for you to validate data in a data model rather than in the text input. However, it does illustrate the basics of how a listener works. Now let's look at two more useful examples, the first of which is extremely simple.

As you saw earlier in this section, you can explicitly handle valid and invalid events. However, when doing so, you might have noticed that the default listener behavior (the red outline and message applied to the source control) is still applied. If you want to use explicit event handlers for the valid and invalid events without the default listener behavior, you must override the default `listener` setting by using a value of an empty object. You can use the {} literal notation to create an object, or you can use the `Object` constructor as part of a new statement. Example 15-4 uses an empty object for the `listener` along with explicit event handlers. In this example, the `label` changes when validator events occur, but the default listener behavior does not. As already stated, by default validators will display outlines around components with invalid values. However, in this example, we're short-circuiting the default behavior.

Example 15-4. Overriding default validator behavior

```
<?xml version="1.0" encoding="utf-8"?>
<mx:Application xmlns:mx="http://www.adobe.com/2006/mxml" layout="absolute">
    <mx:Script>
        <![CDATA[

            import mx.events.ValidationResultEvent;

            private function invalidHandler(event:ValidationResultEvent):void {
                usernameItem.setStyle("color", 0xFF0000);
                usernameItem.label = "*Name";
            }

            private function validHandler(event:ValidationResultEvent):void {
                usernameItem.setStyle("color", 0x000000);
                usernameItem.label = "Name";
            }

        ]]>
    </mx:Script>

    <mx:Form>
        <mx:FormHeading label="Sample Form"/>
        <mx:FormItem id="usernameItem" label="Name">
            <mx:TextInput id="username"/>
        </mx:FormItem>
        <mx:FormItem>
            <mx:Button id="button" label="Submit" />
```

```
        </mx:FormItem>
    </mx:Form>

    <mx:Validator id="validator" source="{username}" property="text"
invalid="invalidHandler(event)" valid="validHandler(event)"
listener="{new Object()}" />

</mx:Application>
```

You can also assign a non-default listener when you want to use a customized listener. The customized listener might do any number of things, such as auto-correcting a value. To register a custom listener, the class must implement the `mx.validators.IValidatorListener` interface, which requires public properties (or getters/setters) called `errorString` and `validationSubField` as well as a public method called `validationResultHandler()`, which accepts a parameter of type `mx.events.ValidationResultEvent`. Example 15-5 is an example of a simple class that implements the interface. This class allows you to pass it any control with a text property, and it attempts to auto-correct the field. In this example, the auto-correction is very limited in scope: it auto-corrects only the string `abc` and makes it `abcd`.

Example 15-5. Customized validator listener (AutoCorrectTextListener.as)

```
package com.oreilly.programmingflex.validation.listeners {

    import mx.events.ValidationResultEvent;
    import mx.validators.IValidatorListener;
    import mx.core.UIComponent;

    public class AutoCorrectTextListener implements IValidatorListener {

        private var _errorString:String;
        private var _validationSubField:String;
        private var _control:Object;
        private var _passThroughEvent:Boolean;

        // Implement the errorString and validationSubField getters and setters.
        // They simply act as accessor methods for corresponding private properties.
        public function get errorString():String {
            return _errorString;
        }

        public function set errorString(value:String):void {
            _errorString = value;
        }

        public function get validationSubField():String {
            return _validationSubField;
        }

        public function set validationSubField(value:String):void {
            _validationSubField = value;
        }
```

```
        // The constructor accepts two parameters: the control with a text
        // property you want to target, and an optional parameter specifying
        // whether or not to pass through the event to the control if it
        // cannot auto-correct.
        public function AutoCorrectTextListener(control:Object,
                                         passThroughEvent:Boolean = true) {
            _control = control;
            _passThroughEvent = passThroughEvent;
        }

        // This method gets called when the validator dispatches an event. The code
        // auto-corrects the text if possible (in this case it only auto-corrects
        // one case). If it cannot auto-correct, it passes the event (if
        // applicable) to the control.
        public function validationResultHandler(event:ValidationResultEvent):void {
            if(_control.text == "abc" || _control.text == "abcd") {
                _control.text = "abcd";
            }
            else {
                if(_passThroughEvent) {
                    _control.validationResultHandler(event);
                }
            }
        }

    }
}
```

The MXML in Example 15-6 uses this custom listener.

Example 15-6. Using a customized validator listener

```
<?xml version="1.0" encoding="utf-8"?>
<mx:Application xmlns:mx="http://www.adobe.com/2006/mxml" layout="absolute"
initialize="initializeHandler(event)">
    <mx:Script>
        <![CDATA[

            import com.oreilly.programmingflex.validation.listeners.
AutoCorrectTextListener;

            private var _listener:AutoCorrectTextListener;

            private function initializeHandler(event:Event):void {

                // Create a new listener that targets the text input control.
                _listener = new AutoCorrectTextListener(username);

                // Register the listener with the validator. The validator is
                // created via MXML later in the document. The MXML id attribute
                // is set to validator, which is the reason you can reference the
                // object by that name here.
                validator.listener = _listener;
            }
```

```
        ]]>
    </mx:Script>

    <mx:Form>
        <mx:FormHeading label="Sample Form"/>
        <mx:FormItem id="usernameItem" label="Name">
            <mx:TextInput id="username"/>
        </mx:FormItem>
        <mx:FormItem>
            <mx:Button id="button" label="Submit" />
        </mx:FormItem>
    </mx:Form>

    <mx:Validator id="validator" source="{username}" property="text" />

</mx:Application>
```

When you test this application, you can try using any text other than abc or abcd, and the event will be passed to the control with the standard behavior following it. If you use the text abc, it auto-corrects to abcd.

Triggering validators

To run, a validator must first be *triggered*. As you've already seen, the default trigger for a validator is the valueCommit event, which is dispatched by the source object. In many cases, that is appropriate because the valueCommit event occurs for all input controls when the value is set programmatically or when the focus shifts from the control. However, there are reasons you may want to change the default trigger for a validator. For example, although the most common use case for validators is to use a user input control as the source, you could theoretically use any object and any property. If the object type you use as the source does not dispatch a valueCommit event, the default trigger will never occur. Another, more common scenario for changing the default trigger is one in which you want a different object to trigger the validator. For example, rather than triggering a validator when the user moves focus from a text input, you might want to trigger the validator when the user clicks on a button.

The two properties you can use with a validator to change the trigger are trigger and triggerEvent. The trigger property requires a reference to an object (which must be an event dispatcher) that you want to use as the trigger. The triggerEvent property requires the name of the event you want to use to trigger the validator. The following example uses the click event for the button to trigger the validator:

```
<?xml version="1.0" encoding="utf-8"?>
<mx:Application xmlns:mx="http://www.adobe.com/2006/mxml" layout="absolute">

    <mx:Form>
        <mx:FormHeading label="Sample Form"/>
        <mx:FormItem label="Name">
            <mx:TextInput id="username"/>
        </mx:FormItem>
        <mx:FormItem>
```

```
            <mx:Button id="button" label="Submit" />
        </mx:FormItem>
    </mx:Form>

    <mx:Validator source="{username}" property="text" trigger="{button}"
        triggerEvent="click" />

</mx:Application>
```

You can have even further control over how and when validators run by using ActionScript to run the validators. All validators have a **validate()** method that you can call to run the validator. If you want to call the **validate()** method for a validator, you must ensure that the object can be referenced via ActionScript, regardless of whether you set the **id** property when creating the validator via MXML or you assign the validator to a variable when creating it with ActionScript. The following example sets the **trigger** property of a validator to a new **EventDispatcher** object so that the default trigger does not work:

```
<?xml version="1.0" encoding="utf-8"?>
<mx:Application xmlns:mx="http://www.adobe.com/2006/mxml" layout="absolute">

    <mx:Form>
        <mx:FormHeading label="Sample Form"/>
        <mx:FormItem label="Name">
            <mx:TextInput id="username"/>
        </mx:FormItem>
        <mx:FormItem>
            <mx:Button id="button" label="Submit" />
        </mx:FormItem>
    </mx:Form>

    <mx:Validator id="validator" source="{username}" property="text"
        trigger="{new EventDispatcher()}" />

</mx:Application>
```

If you were to test the preceding code, you'd find that the validator does not run automatically because the **trigger** is a new **EventDispatcher** object. Now you can add an event listener to the button so that it calls a function when clicked by the user. The **validate()** method of the validator can be called with the function, as shown here:

```
<?xml version="1.0" encoding="utf-8"?>
<mx:Application xmlns:mx="http://www.adobe.com/2006/mxml" layout="absolute">

    <mx:Script>
        <![CDATA[

            private function runValidator(event:MouseEvent):void {
                validator.validate();
            }

        ]]>
    </mx:Script>
```

```
    <mx:Form>
        <mx:FormHeading label="Sample Form"/>
        <mx:FormItem label="Name">
            <mx:TextInput id="username"/>
        </mx:FormItem>
        <mx:FormItem>
            <mx:Button id="button" label="Submit" click="runValidator(event)" />
        </mx:FormItem>
    </mx:Form>

    <mx:Validator id="validator" source="{username}" property="text"
        trigger="{new EventDispatcher()}" />

</mx:Application>
```

If you wanted to achieve the same result as with the standard trigger, it is far simpler to use the default behavior rather than writing all the extra code (as in the preceding example). However, the `validate()` method allows you greater control over how the application behaves.

The `validate()` method not only runs the validator, but it also returns a `ValidationResultEvent` object, which tells you whether the validation succeeded. The `type` property of the object is either valid or invalid (for which you can use the `ValidationResultEvent.VALID` and `ValidationResultEvent.INVALID` constants, respectively). Example 15-7 uses `validate()` to display an alert when the user clicks on the button but doesn't properly fill in a required field.

Note that in this example we're calling `validate()` with two optional parameters. The first parameter specifies the value to validate. A value of null indicates to use the default value, which is retrieved from the source of the validator. The second parameter indicates whether or not to suppress validation events.

Example 15-7. Running validation with ActionScript

```
<?xml version="1.0" encoding="utf-8"?>
<mx:Application xmlns:mx="http://www.adobe.com/2006/mxml" layout="absolute">
    <mx:Script>
        <![CDATA[
            import mx.events.ValidationResultEvent;
            import mx.controls.Alert;

            private function runValidators(event:Event):void {
                // Run the validate() method and assign the result to a variable.
                var validationResultEvent:ValidationResultEvent =
validator.validate(null, true);
                // If the result of the validate() method call is invalid then
                // display an alert.
                if(validationResultEvent.type == ValidationResultEvent.INVALID) {
                    Alert.show("You must specify a value");
                }
```

```
            }

        ]]>
    </mx:Script>

    <mx:Form>
        <mx:FormHeading label="Sample Form"/>
        <mx:FormItem id="usernameItem" label="Name">
            <mx:TextInput id="username"/>
        </mx:FormItem>
        <mx:FormItem>
            <mx:Button id="button" label="Submit" click="runValidators(event)" />
        </mx:FormItem>
    </mx:Form>

    <mx:Validator id="validator" source="{username}" property="text"
        trigger="{null}" />

</mx:Application>
```

When you're working with more than one validator and you want to call the `validate()` method of each, you can explicitly call the method of each, or you can use a static `Validator` class method, called `validateAll()`. The `validateAll()` method requires an array parameter for which every element is a validator object. The `validateAll()` method then returns an array with all the `ValidationResultEvent` objects for every validator that returned an invalid response. If all the validations passed, the return array is empty. Example 15-8 uses four validators (each of these are standard validator types discussed in more detail in the next section). When the user clicks the button, the button dispatches an event that calls a function that runs `validateAll()`, and it displays an alert notifying the user if any of the fields did not validate properly.

Example 15-8. Using validateAll()

```
<?xml version="1.0" encoding="utf-8"?>
<mx:Application xmlns:mx="http://www.adobe.com/2006/mxml" layout="absolute"
initialize="initializeHandler(event)">
    <mx:Script>
        <![CDATA[
            import mx.events.ValidationResultEvent;
            import mx.controls.Alert;
            import mx.validators.Validator;

            private var _validators:Array;

            private function initializeHandler(event:Event):void {
                // Create an array with the validators.
                _validators = [usernameValidator, phoneValidator, emailValidator,
zipCodeValidator];
            }

            private function runValidators(event:Event):void {
                // Run all the validators.
                var results:Array = Validator.validateAll(_validators);
```

```
            // If the results array is empty then everything passed. If it's not
            // empty then at least one validator didn't pass.
            if(results.length > 0) {
                var message:String = "The following fields are incorrect:\n";

                // Loop through all the results, and retrieve the id of the
                // source for the corresponding validator.
                for(var i:uint = 0; i < results.length; i++) {
                    message += results[i].target.source.id + "\n";
                }
                Alert.show(message);
            }
        }

    ]]>
</mx:Script>

<mx:Form>
    <mx:FormHeading label="Sample Form"/>
    <mx:FormItem id="usernameItem" label="Name">
        <mx:TextInput id="username"/>
    </mx:FormItem>
    <mx:FormItem label="Phone">
        <mx:TextInput id="phone"/>
    </mx:FormItem>
    <mx:FormItem label="Email">
        <mx:TextInput id="email"/>
    </mx:FormItem>
    <mx:FormItem label="Zip Code">
        <mx:TextInput id="zipcode"/>
    </mx:FormItem>
    <mx:FormItem>
        <mx:Button id="button" label="Submit" click="runValidators(event)" />
    </mx:FormItem>
</mx:Form>

<mx:Validator id="usernameValidator" source="{username}" property="text" />
<mx:PhoneNumberValidator id="phoneValidator" source="{phone}" property="text" />
<mx:EmailValidator id="emailValidator" source="{email}" property="text" />
<mx:ZipCodeValidator id="zipCodeValidator" source="{zipcode}" property="text" />

</mx:Application>
```

Using Standard Framework Validators

The Flex framework includes not only the base validator, `Validator`, but also many validators for common sorts of data formats. The framework ships with the following validators:

- `StringValidator`
- `NumberValidator`
- `DateValidator`

- EmailValidator
- PhoneNumberValidator
- ZipCodeValidator
- CreditCardValidator
- CurrencyValidator
- SocialSecurityValidator
- RegExpValidator

All the validator types are subtypes of `Validator`, and they inherit all the same properties and methods. But each of these subtypes implements specialized validation behaviors. We discuss each of these validator types in greater detail in the next few sections.

StringValidator

The `StringValidator` allows you to verify that a string value length is within a specific range. You can define `minLength` and `maxLength` property values for `StringValidators`, as in the following example:

```
<mx:StringValidator source="{sourceObject}" property="sourceProperty"
    minLength="5" maxLength="10" />
```

You can also specify custom error messages, just in case the validation fails, using the `tooShortError` and `tooLongError` properties. These error messages are displayed when the value length is less than the `minLength` and greater than the `maxLength`, respectively.

```
<mx:StringValidator source="{sourceObject}" property="sourceProperty"
    minLength="5" maxLength="10" tooShortError="You gotta use a
longer number, buddy" tooLongError="Whoa! Shorter numbers, please" />
```

NumberValidator

The `NumberValidator` allows you to validate all sorts of number values. You can specify a range of allowable values using the `minValue` and `maxValue` properties:

```
<mx:NumberValidator source="{sourceObject}" property="sourceProperty"
    minValue="-5" maxValue="5" />
```

The default value for `minValue` and `maxValue` is `NaN` (not a number), which means that no limit is placed on the range. If you set a value for either property and you later want to remove the limit, just assign a value of `NaN` to the validator, as shown here:

```
numberValidator.minValue = NaN;
```

If you want to allow or disallow negative numbers, you can use the `allowNegative` property. The default value is `true`, but setting it to `false` disallows use of negative numbers:

```
<mx:NumberValidator source="{sourceObject}" property="sourceProperty"
    allowNegative="false" />
```

By default, a `NumberValidator` allows any number type, but you can explicitly specify whether you want to accept all number types (`real`) or just integers (`int`) using the `domain` property. The default value is `real`, but the following example allows only integers:

```
<mx:NumberValidator source="{sourceObject}" property="sourceProperty"
    domain="int" />
```

When allowing real numbers you can also control the allowable precision. The precision is the measure of the number of decimal places. The `precision` property controls this setting, and it has a default value of `-1`, which allows all precisions. A value of `0` effectively accomplishes the same thing as setting `domain` to `int` (meaning all values must be integers). Positive integer values for `precision` limit the number of allowable decimal places. The following allows up to only four decimal places:

```
<mx:NumberValidator source="{sourceObject}" property="sourceProperty"
    precision="4" />
```

By default, a `NumberValidator` validates using the thousands place marker and decimal marker characters used in the United States: the comma for thousands and the dot for a decimal place. However, if you need to validate using different marker characters, you can specify those values using the `thousandsSeparator` and `decimalSeparator` properties, respectively. The only rules for these properties are that they must not be digits and they cannot each have the same value. The following example uses the characters used by many European countries:

```
<mx:NumberValidator source="{sourceObject}" property="sourceProperty"
    thousandsSeparator="." decimalSeparator="," />
```

You can also specify many custom errors using the properties of a `NumberValidator`, including the following: `decimalPointCountError`, `exceedsMaxError`, `integerError`, `invalidCharError`, `invalidFormatCharsError`, `lowerThanMinError`, `negativeError`, `precisionError`, and `separationError`. Each of these properties is documented at *http://livedocs.macromedia.com/flex/3/langref/mx/validators/NumberValidator.html*.

DateValidator

`DateValidator` allows you to validate values as dates. There are several basic properties you can configure to customize this type of validator, and there are advanced properties that allow you to use the validator with several inputs at once.

The basic properties you can use with a `DateValidator` are `allowedFormatChars` and `inputFormat`. The `allowedFormatChars` property allows you to specify which characters are allowable as delimiters between year, month, and date. The default value is `/\-.,` which means any of the following are valid:

```
1/20/2010
1 20 2010
1.20.2010
1-20-2010
1\20\2010
```

The following allows only the asterisk character as a delimiter:

```
<mx:DateValidator source="{sourceObject}" property="sourceProperty"
    allowedFormatChars="*" />
```

The `inputFormat` property determines the order of the year, month, and date parts. You can use the strings YYYY, MM, and DD to represent each of those parts. You can use any of the default delimiter characters as delimiters in the `inputFormat` string. The default value is MM/DD/YYYY. The following example requires that the date appear with the year followed by the month followed by the date:

```
<mx:DateValidator source="{sourceObject}" property="sourceProperty"
    inputFormat="YYYY/MM/DD" />
```

Unlike most of the validators, the `DateValidator` allows you to use one validator to validate more than one input. This is because date inputs frequently may span three inputs: one for the year, one for the month, and one for the date. When you specify a `source` property value for a `DateValidator`, it assumes you want to validate just one input. However, you have the option to specify three different sources and properties using the `yearSource`, `monthSource`, `daySource`, `yearProperty`, `monthProperty`, and `dayProperty` properties:

```
<?xml version="1.0" encoding="utf-8"?>
<mx:Application xmlns:mx="http://www.adobe.com/2006/mxml" layout="absolute">

    <mx:HBox>
        <mx:VBox>
            <mx:TextInput id="year" width="40" />
            <mx:Label text="Year" />
        </mx:VBox>
        <mx:VBox>
            <mx:TextInput id="month" width="40" />
            <mx:Label text="Month" />
        </mx:VBox>
        <mx:VBox>
            <mx:TextInput id="day" width="40" />
            <mx:Label text="Day" />
        </mx:VBox>
        <mx:Button click="trace(validator.validate())" label="Validate" />
    </mx:HBox>
    <mx:DateValidator id="validator" yearSource="{year}" yearProperty="text"
        monthSource="{month}" monthProperty="text" daySource="{day}"
        dayProperty="text" inputFormat="YYYY/MM/DD" />

</mx:Application>
```

EmailValidator

The `EmailValidator` is easy to implement, as it doesn't require any additional properties aside from the standard `source` and `property`. It simply validates the `source` value as a valid email address:

```
<mx:EmailValidator source="{sourceObject}" property="sourceProperty" />
```

PhoneNumberValidator

The PhoneNumberValidator lets you validate that a value is in a valid format for a phone number. According to the PhoneNumberValidator rules, a valid phone number consists of at least 10 numeric characters as well as possible additional formatting characters. You can use just one property to customize the rules a PhoneNumberValidator uses. The allowedFormatChars property lets you specify the valid non-numeric characters that are allowable in a phone number value. The default set of allowable characters consists of (,), -, ., +, and a space. The following code allows for phone number values in which the only valid formatting characters are dots:

```
<mx:PhoneNumberValidator source="{sourceObject}" property="sourceProperty"
    allowedFormatChars="." />
```

ZipCodeValidator

The ZipCodeValidator validates that the value is in the format of a valid U.S. zip code or a Canadian postal code. You can specify what type of code it validates using the domain property. The default value is set to the ZipCodeValidatorDomainType.US_ONLY value, which means the validator won't validate Canadian-style postal codes. Optionally, you can use the ZipCodeValidatorDomainType.US_OR_CANADA constant to recognize Canadian postal codes, as shown here:

```
<mx:ZipCodeValidator source="{sourceObject}"
property="sourceProperty" domain="{ZipCodeValidatorDomainType.US_OR_CANADA}" />
```

You can also use the allowedFormatChars property to specify a set of allowable formatting characters consisting of nonalphanumeric characters; the default set consists of a space or a hyphen (-).

CreditCardValidator

The CreditCardValidator allows you to validate that a number is in the proper format and follows the basic rules for credit card numbers. Although it cannot verify that the number is a valid credit card number, it can provide a simple test to ensure that no user error caused an incorrect number of digits or the wrong prefix for a card type. The CreditCardValidator can test for American Express, Diners Club, Discover, MasterCard, and Visa number formats. This validator type requires two input sources: one for the card type (usually a radio button group or a combo box) and one for the card number (usually a text input). Here's an example:

```
<?xml version="1.0" encoding="utf-8"?>
<mx:Application xmlns:mx="http://www.adobe.com/2006/mxml" layout="absolute">

    <mx:VBox>
        <mx:ComboBox id="cardType">
            <mx:dataProvider>
                <mx:ArrayCollection>
                    <mx:Array>
                        <mx:String>American Express</mx:String>
```

```
                    <mx:String>Diners Club</mx:String>
                    <mx:String>Discover</mx:String>
                    <mx:String>MasterCard</mx:String>
                    <mx:String>Visa</mx:String>
                </mx:Array>
            </mx:ArrayCollection>
        </mx:dataProvider>
    </mx:ComboBox>
    <mx:TextInput id="cardNumber" />
    <mx:Button click="trace(validator.validate())" label="Validate" />
  </mx:VBox>
  <mx:CreditCardValidator id="validator" cardNumberSource="{cardNumber}"
cardNumberProperty="text" cardTypeSource="{cardType}" cardTypeProperty="value" />

</mx:Application>
```

CurrencyValidator

The `CurrencyValidator` validates currency values, such as dollar amounts. Obviously, currency formatting and numeric formatting have much in common, and for that reason there are many similarities between `CurrencyValidator` and `NumberValidator`. For example, `CurrencyValidator`'s `minValue`, `maxValue`, `precision`, `allowNegative`, `decimalSeparator`, and `thousandsSeparator` properties work exactly as they do for a `NumberValidator`. In addition, a `CurrencyValidator` lets you specify `currencySymbol` and `alignSymbol` properties. The default value for `currencySymbol` is the U.S. dollar sign (`$`). You can use the `alignSymbol` property to specify where the currency symbol must appear relative to the numeric value. The valid values are `CurrencyValidatorAlignSymbol.LEFT`, `CurrencyValidatorAlignSymbol.RIGHT`, and `CurrencyValidatorAlignSymbol.ANY`. *`CurrencyValidatorAlignSymbol.LEFT`* is the default value.

SocialSecurityValidator

The `SocialSecurityValidator` validates a value that adheres to the rules for a U.S. Social Security number (###-##-####). This validator allows you to customize the validation rules by specifying the allowable formatting characters via the `allowedFormatChars` property; the default value is a space or a hyphen (-).

RegExpValidator

The `RegExpValidator` allows you to use regular expressions to validate values. You can use the `RegExpValidator` for any type of validation that isn't covered by the other standard validators. The `RegExpValidator` requires that you set at least one property, `expression`, which is the regular expression you want to use to validate the data. In addition, you can optionally specify a value for the `flags` property, which can use any combination of the valid regular expression flags: `i`, `g`, `m`, `s`, and `x`.

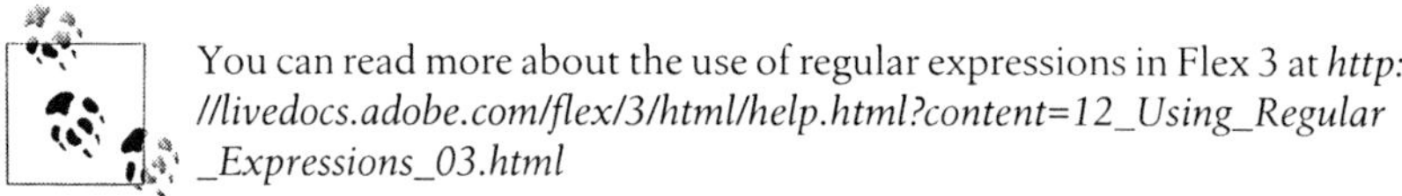

You can read more about the use of regular expressions in Flex 3 at *http://livedocs.adobe.com/flex/3/html/help.html?content=12_Using_Regular_Expressions_03.html*

The following example validates a text area to ensure that it contains at least 5 words:

```
<mx:RegExpValidator expression="(\b\w+\b\W*)\{5,\}" flags="ig"
    source="{comments}" property="text" />
```

Writing Custom Validators

If one of the standard validators doesn't run the sort of validation you require, you can write a custom validator. To write a custom validator, you must write an ActionScript class that extends `mx.validators.Validator`, and the class must override the `doValidation()` method. The `doValidation()` method is protected; it requires an `Object` parameter and returns an array. If the validation does not succeed, the method returns an array of `ValidationResult` objects. If the validation does succeed, the method returns an empty array. The `WordCountValidator` in Example 15-9 is a simple example that validates a value based on minimum word count.

Example 15-9. Custom validator

```
package com.oreilly.programmingflex.validators {

    import mx.validators.Validator;
    import mx.validators.ValidationResult;

    public class WordCountValidator extends Validator {

        private var _count:int;

        public function get count():int {
            return _count;
        }

        public function set count(value:int):void {
            _count = value;
        }

        public function WordCountValidator() {
            super();
            _count = -1;
        }

        override protected function doValidation(value:Object):Array {
            var results:Array = new Array();
            results = super.doValidation(value);
            if(results.length > 0) {
                return results;
            }
            if(_count > -1) {
```

```
                var expression:RegExp = /\b\w+\b\W*/ig;
                var matches:Array = String(value).match(expression);
                if(matches.length < _count) {
                    results.push(new ValidationResult(true, null, "tooFewWords",
"You must enter at least " + _count + " words."));
                }
            }
            return results;
        }

    }
}
```

The MXML in Example 15-10 illustrates how you might use `WordCountValidator`. In this case the `count` property is set to 5, indicating that the comments text area must contain at least 5 words.

Example 15-10. Using the WordCountValidator custom validator

```
<?xml version="1.0" encoding="utf-8"?>
<mx:Application xmlns:mx="http://www.adobe.com/2006/mxml"
xmlns:validators="com.oreilly.programmingflex.validators.*" layout="absolute">

    <mx:Form>
        <mx:FormHeading label="Sample Form"/>
        <mx:FormItem label="Comments">
            <mx:TextArea id="comments" />
        </mx:FormItem>
        <mx:FormItem>
            <mx:Button id="button" label="Submit"/>
        </mx:FormItem>
    </mx:Form>

    <validators:WordCountValidator source="{comments}" property="text" count="5" />

</mx:Application>
```

Formatting Data

The Flex framework provides a group of components that allow you to format values. You can use these formatters to format data for any reason, though they're most useful for displaying data.

Flex ships with a handful of formatters, such as `NumberFormatter` and `PhoneFormatter`, and you can even build custom formatters based on the same framework. Each formatter uses different properties, but all the formatters work in the same basic manner. First you must create the formatter either with MXML or with ActionScript, assigning property values as necessary. Then you can call the `format()` method of the formatter, passing it the value you want to format. The `format()` method returns a string. If the formatter can't format a string, it dispatches an error event.

You can create a formatter using MXML with the corresponding MXML tag. For example, the following creates a NumberFormatter instance. This example uses all the default property values, though you could also set the property values in the MXML. Note that you should always assign an id value to formatters because you'll need to reference them with ActionScript.

```
<mx:NumberFormatter id="numberFormatter" />
```

You can optionally create a formatter with ActionScript using the constructor, as shown here:

```
var numberFormatter:NumberFormatter = new NumberFormatter();
```

Once you've created a formatter object, you must call the format() method to apply the formatting. The format() method requires that you pass it the value you want to format. The method does not change the original value, but it returns a new string formatted according to the rules set by the formatter and its properties:

```
var formattedValue:String = numberFormatter.format(userInput.text);
```

NumberFormatter

The NumberFormatter allows you to format (as a string) any number or value that can be converted to a number. You can see the default formatting using the following code:

```
<mx:TextInput text="{numberFormatter.format('1234.56789')}" />
<mx:NumberFormatter id="numberFormatter" />
```

The preceding example displays 1,234.56789. The default formatting doesn't affect the precision of the number; it merely adds a thousands place marker.

With a NumberFormatter you can control whether and how a number is rounded with the rounding property. The default value is none, although you can optionally specify a value of up, down, or nearest. The following example displays 1,235, as it rounds up to the nearest whole number:

```
<mx:TextInput text="{numberFormatter.format('1234.56789')}" />
<mx:NumberFormatter id="numberFormatter" rounding="nearest" />
```

You can also control the precision of the formatted output using the precision property. The default value is -1, which doesn't enforce any precision constraints. A non-negative integer value for the precision property rounds the decimal places to that many, if necessary. The rounding property value is used to determine how to round for precision, if necessary. The following displays 1,234.56:

```
<mx:TextInput text="{numberFormatter.format('1234.56789')}" />
<mx:NumberFormatter id="numberFormatter" precision="2" />
```

If the input value uses decimal and/or thousands place markers, the formatter needs to know how to interpret them. NumberFormatter uses the decimalSeparatorFrom and thousandsSeparatorFrom properties for this purpose. The default values are the dot (.) and the comma (,); however, you can specify different values. The following example uses the delimiting characters as they are used in many European countries (the formatted text is 1,234.56789):

```
<mx:TextInput text="{numberFormatter.format('1.234,56789')}" />
<mx:NumberFormatter id="numberFormatter" decimalSeparatorFrom=","
    thousandsSeparatorFrom="." />
```

You can also specify the delimiting characters to use in the formatted output by way of the `decimalSeparatorTo` and `thousandsSeparatorTo` properties. The following example displays `1.234,56789`:

```
<mx:TextInput text="{numberFormatter.format('1,234.56789')}" />
<mx:NumberFormatter id="numberFormatter" decimalSeparatorTo=","
    thousandsSeparatorTo="." />
```

You can also specify whether to use the thousands delimiter at all with the `useThousandsSeparator` property; the default value is `true`. A value of `false` won't display the thousands place delimiter.

The `useNegativeSign` property lets you specify how negative numbers are formatted. The default value is `true`, and it results in a number preceded by a negative sign (e.g., `-1`). If the property is set to `false`, the number is surrounded by parentheses (e.g., `(1)`).

DateFormatter

The `DateFormatter` allows you to format the data from a `Date` object as a string. There is one configurable property that you can use with a `DateFormatter`. That property, called `formatString`, allows you to specify the way in which the elements of a `Date` object (year, month, day, hours, etc.) should be formatted in the output string. The default value is MM/DD/YYYY, which is the month followed by the day of the month followed by the four-digit year. The following characters have special meaning in the `formatString` value:

- Y: year
- M: month
- D: day of month
- E: day of week
- A: AM/PM
- J: hour (0–23)
- H: hour (1–24)
- K: hour (0–11 for use with AM/PM)
- L: hour (1–12 for use with AM/PM)
- N: minute
- S: second

Y, M, D, and E yield different results when used in different groupings. For example, YY results in a two-digit year, whereas YYYY results in a four-digit year. This same pattern is generally true for each of these characters. For example, M/D/YYYY displays 1/2/2010 for January 2, 2010, but MM/DD/YYYY displays 01/02/2010. M and E also result in abbreviations and full names of the months and days of the week when used in groups of three and four. For example, MMM can display Jan., and MMMM displays January.

You can use any other characters in a `formatString` value, and they are interpreted literally. The following example displays January 2, 2010 at 4:25:10 PM:

```
<mx:TextInput text="{dateFormatter.format(new Date(2010, 0, 2, 16, 25, 10))}" />
<mx:DateFormatter id="dateFormatter" formatString="MMMM D, YYYY at L:N:S A" />
```

CurrencyFormatter

The `CurrencyFormatter` works very much like the `NumberFormatter` except that it adds a currency symbol in addition to formatting a number value. `CurrencyFormatter` uses all the same properties as `NumberFormatter`, but it adds two additional properties: `currencySymbol` and `alignSymbol`. The default value for `currencySymbol` is the U.S. dollar sign (`$`). The default value for `alignSymbol` is `left`; the other possible value is `right`.

PhoneFormatter

The `PhoneFormatter` takes any number or string that can be converted to a number, and it formats that as a phone number. The `PhoneFormatter` allows you to configure the format of the output using the `formatString` property. The default value of the `formatString` property is `(###) ###-####`, in which the `#` is a placeholder for a digit. The following example outputs `123.456.7890`:

```
<mx:TextInput text="{phoneFormatter.format(1234567890)}" />
<mx:PhoneFormatter id="phoneFormatter" formatString="###.###.####" />
```

By default, the `formatString` property allows only a specific set of characters. That set of characters is dictated by the `validPatternChars` property, which has a default value set consisting of `+`, `(`, `)`, `#`, `-`, `.`, and a space. You can customize the allowable characters in the pattern if you want. The following example outputs `123*456*7890`:

```
<mx:TextInput text="{phoneFormatter.format(1234567890)}" />
<mx:PhoneFormatter id="phoneFormatter" formatString="###*###*####"
    validPatternChars="#*" />
```

You can also specify the area code using an `areaCode` property. The `areaCode` property defaults to -1, which means that no area code is prepended to the formatted string. However, if you specify a non-negative integer value for the `areaCode` property, it gets prepended to the phone number. For example, the following displays `(123) 456-7890`:

```
<mx:TextInput text="{phoneFormatter.format(4567890)}" />
<mx:PhoneFormatter id="phoneFormatter" formatString="###-####" areaCode="123 " />
```

If you want to specify the pattern for the area code, you can use the `areaCodeFormat` property. The default value is `(###)`. The following example displays `123 456-7890`:

```
<mx:TextInput text="{phoneFormatter.format(4567890)}" />
<mx:PhoneFormatter id="phoneFormatter" formatString="###-####"
    areaCode="123" areaCodeFormat="### " />
```

Note that when you use a specific value for the `areaCode` property, the formatter will not place a space between the area code and the formatted number. Therefore, in the preceding example, we added a space as the last character of the `areaCodeFormat` property.

ZipCodeFormatter

The `ZipCodeFormatter` lets you format a number or string as a zip or postal code in U.S. or Canadian format. You can configure the formatter via the `formatString` property. The default value is `#####`, which formats a value as a U.S. zip code. The only other possible `formatString` property values are `#####-####` (U.S. zip+4 format), `##### ####` (U.S. zip+4 format with a space), `###-###` (Canadian format), and `### ###` (Canadian format with a space). The following formats the number in U.S. zip+4 format:

```
<mx:TextInput text="{zipCodeFormatter.format(123456789)}" />
<mx:ZipCodeFormatter id="zipCodeFormatter" formatString="#####-####" />
```

Writing Custom Formatters

If one of the standard formatters does not assist you in a particular formatting requirement, you can write a custom formatter. To write a custom formatter, you must write an ActionScript class that extends `mx.formatters.Formatter`. The class must override the `format()` method. Example 15-11 applies zero-fill to numbers.

Zero-fill refers to placing leading zeros to the left of digits to form a new string. For example, 15 with zero-fill to four characters is 0015.

Example 15-11. Creating a custom formatter

```
package com.oreilly.programmingflex.formatters {
    import mx.formatters.Formatter;

    public class ZeroFillFormatter extends Formatter {

        private var _count:int;

        // The count getter/setter allows the user of the formatter
        // to set the number of total characters up to which the value
        // may require zero-fill.
```

```
        public function set count(value:int):void {
            _count = value;
        }

        public function get count():int {
            return _count;
        }

        // Call the superclass constructor, and set _count to -1, which is
        // used as the value to indicate no zero-fill should be applied.
        public function ZeroFillFormatter() {
            super();
            _count = -1;
        }

        // The format() method signature must match that of Formatter.
        override public function format(value:Object):String {

            // If necessary, convert the parameter to a string. Otherwise,
            // cast to a string.
            var stringValue:String;
            if(!(value is String)) {
                stringValue = value.toString();
            }
            else {
                stringValue = String(value);
            }

            // If the length of the string value is less than _count,
            // prepend zeros.
            while(_count > stringValue.length) {
                stringValue = "0" + stringValue;
            }
            return stringValue;
        }

    }
}
```

Example 15-12 illustrates how to use this custom formatter.

Example 15-12. Using a custom formatter

```
<?xml version="1.0" encoding="utf-8"?>
<mx:Application xmlns:mx="http://www.adobe.com/2006/mxml"
xmlns:formatters="com.oreilly.programmingflex.formatters.*" layout="absolute">

    <mx:TextInput text="{zeroFillFormatter.format(123456789)}" />
    <formatters:ZeroFillFormatter id="zeroFillFormatter" count="15" />

</mx:Application>
```

The preceding example displays 000000123456789 in the text input control.

Summary

In this chapter, you learned about additional ways to work with data. This chapter covered two main topics: validating and formatting. Validating data means ensuring that the data meets certain rules prior to submitting it for some course of action. This is useful when you want to verify that user input data is in the correct form. Formatting data typically means displaying data to the user in a particular way, such as adding hyphens, parentheses, decimal place separators, and so on.

CHAPTER 16

Client Data Communication

Flex applications are capable of many types of data communication, from the simple to the complex. Often when we think of data communication in Flex applications we think of client/server communications such as remote procedure calls (RPCs). However, some types of data communication occur entirely on the client side, and these types are the subject of this chapter.

At a minimum, all Flex applications require a client-side element in the form of a *.swf* file running in Flash Player. Some Flex applications even use several *.swf* files running in one or more instances of Flash Player on the client machine. The client-side portion of a Flex application is capable of several types of client data communication intended for a variety of purposes.

There are three main ways in which a Flex application can run data communications on the client:

Local connections
: A local connection allows two *.swf* files to communicate as long as they are running on the same client machine at the same time. The *.swf* files can be running in two different instances of Flash Player. They can even be running in different host environments. For example, one *.swf* can be running in a web browser while another is running embedded within an executable running on the desktop. The *.swf* files can even communicate while served from different domains if configured correctly.

Shared objects
: Local shared objects allow the application to store and retrieve persistent data on the client machine. For example, a user can save preferences that the application can retrieve automatically the next time the application runs.

External interface
: The external interface is a mechanism by which a Flex application can communicate with the host environment. This allows the Flex application to run as an integrated part of a larger application. In practical terms, this means communicating with JavaScript in the containing HTML page.

The Flex framework does not provide special behaviors for working with client data communications. Rather, all of the topics in this book utilize low-level Flash Player API ActionScript.

Local Connections

Local connections are a way in which two *.swf* files can communicate even if they are running in two different Flash Player instances. Local connections allow you to create integrated applications composed of two or more *.swf* files running in separate Flash Player instances, such as several pods or modules that are part of a complex rich Internet application (RIA) that uses both Flex elements and HTML elements. Furthermore, local connections allow you to communicate between Flash 9 content (Flex applications) and older, legacy Flash content (Flash 8 or earlier).

Local connections use Action Messaging Format (AMF), a binary messaging format, as the protocol for local connection data packets. A local connection request uses one AMF packet, and the maximum size for a local connection AMF packet is 40 KB. Local connections exclusively use a form of AMF called AMF0. This is in contrast with other ActionScript classes (such as `flash.net.NetConnection`), which can use AMF0 as well as AMF3, a newer form of AMF. AMF0 is compatible with older Flash content, making local connections a compatible way to communicate from Flex applications to older Flash content.

Basic Local Connection Communication

Typically when implementing local connections, at least two *.swf* files are needed: one that sends the requests and one that receives the requests. You cannot establish a local connection with a *.swf* without its explicit consent, because the receiving *.swf* must have the necessary code to listen for the specific requests.

Technically it is possible to use a local connection to send and receive requests all within one *.swf*. However, in all practical cases, you will use two *.swf* files.

Both the sending and receiving *.swf* files use the `flash.net.LocalConnection` object. The `LocalConnection` object communicates over a named connection channel. The name of the channel is arbitrary and is a string value, but for the communication to work, the sending and receiving *.swf* files must send and receive over a channel with the same name.

The sending *.swf* uses the `send()` method of a `LocalConnection` object to send the request. The `send()` method requires at least two parameters specifying the name of the channel and the name of the method to call on the receiving *.swf*. The following example creates a new `LocalConnection` instance and calls the `send()` method:

```
var localConnection:LocalConnection = new LocalConnection();
localConnection.send("channel", "exampleMethod");
```

If the method in the receiving *.swf* expects parameters, you can pass them to the `send()` method following the name of the method to call. For instance, the following example calls `exampleMethod` on the receiving *.swf* and passes it integer parameters:

```
localConnection.send("channel", "exampleMethod", 10, 25);
```

The receiving *.swf* must listen for requests on the same channel as the sending *.swf* sends them. You can instruct a `LocalConnection` object to listen for requests by calling the `connect()` method, passing it the name of the channel to which to listen:

```
var receivingLocalConnection:LocalConnection = new LocalConnection();
receivingLocalConnection.connect("channel");
```

If you do not call the `connect()` method, the *.swf* will have no way of knowing that it should be listening for requests. In such a case, a sending *.swf* will throw errors if it cannot find the connection over which to send requests.

You must also tell the `LocalConnection` object where to direct the requests. For instance, when the sending *.swf* makes a request for `exampleMethod`, the receiving `LocalConnection` object needs to know where it can find `exampleMethod`. You can tell it where to find the method by assigning a reference to the appropriate object to the client property of the `LocalConnection` object. For example, the following tells the `LocalConnection` object on the receiver application where it can find the requested methods as methods of this class:

```
receivingLocalConnection.client = this;
```

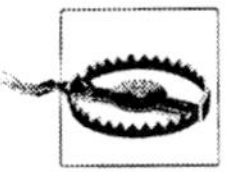

The methods that you expose via a local connection must be declared as `public`. Otherwise, the application will throw an error. Methods must be defined for the object specified as the client of the receiving `LocalConnection` object.

This step of setting the client is essential. Without setting the `client` property, the `LocalConnection` object will throw errors when it receives requests.

Example 16-1 requires two MXML files compiled into two *.swf* files. The first MXML file creates the sending *.swf*. It contains a text area and a button. When the user clicks the button, the event handler sends a local connection request to call a method named `displayMessage` with a parameter equal to the value of the text area text.

Example 16-1. Local connection send example

```
<?xml version="1.0" encoding="utf-8"?>
<mx:Application xmlns:mx="http://www.adobe.com/2006/mxml">

    <mx:Script>
        <![CDATA[

            import flash.net.LocalConnection;

            private var _localConnection:LocalConnection = new LocalConnection();

            private function sendMessage(event:MouseEvent):void {
                _localConnection.send("dataChannel", "displayMessage", message.text);
            }

        ]]>
    </mx:Script>

    <mx:VBox id="vbox">
        <mx:TextArea id="message" />
        <mx:Button label="Send" click="sendMessage(event)" />
    </mx:VBox>

</mx:Application>
```

For the preceding example to clearly work, you must enter text into the text area before clicking the Send button.

The second MXML document defines the receiving *.swf*. This file (Example 16-2) contains a text area.

Example 16-2. Local connection receive example

```
<?xml version="1.0" encoding="utf-8"?>
<mx:Application xmlns:mx="http://www.adobe.com/2006/mxml" layout="absolute"
initialize="initializeHandler(event)">

    <mx:Script>
        <![CDATA[

            import flash.net.LocalConnection;

            private var _localConnection:LocalConnection;

            private function initializeHandler(event:Event):void {
                _localConnection = new LocalConnection();
                _localConnection.connect("dataChannel");
                _localConnection.client = this;
            }

              // Note that this method is declared as public because it is
```

```
            // exposed as a method to a local connection.
            public function displayMessage(message:String):void {
                output.text += message + "\n";
            }

        ]]>
    </mx:Script>

    <mx:TextArea id="output"  width="539" height="589"/>

</mx:Application>
```

The `initializeHandler()` method runs when the application initializes because it is set to handle the application initialize event, and it creates the `LocalConnection` object, connects to the channel to listen for requests, and designates this as the client for the requests, meaning that the requests get routed to methods of the same name defined for the MXML document. Notice that `displayMessage()` is declared as `public`. Methods called via a local connection must be declared as `public`.

Legacy Communication

One nonobvious use for local connections is to allow inter-*.swf* communication between Flash 9 (Flex) applications and content published to Flash 8 or earlier. Flex applications can load any sort of *.swf*, whether it was published from Flex or any version of Flash authoring. However, because Flash 9 applications use a fundamentally different virtual machine than older Flash content, it's not possible for a Flash 9 application to communicate directly with a *.swf* published from Flash 8 or earlier. If a Flash 9 application loads a Flash 9 *.swf*, they can communicate directly by calling methods on the loaded *.swf*. However, that's not possible when a Flash 9 application loads a Flash 8 or earlier *.swf*. That's because Flash 9 and later content uses a completely separate ActionScript virtual machine (AVM) from that used by older content.

Local connection communication is a solution for interoperability, as it is supported by both older Flash content as well as Flash 9 applications. You can create a local connection API in the legacy content that the Flex application can call once it loads the *.swf*.

Cross-Domain Communication

In our discussion of local connection communication, we have thus far assumed that all communicating *.swf* files are in the same domain. By default, Flash Player disallows local connection communication when the *.swf* files are being loaded from different domains. However, you can explicitly allow cross-domain communication for a specific receiving *.swf*.

There are two basic types of cross-domain local connection communication: *known domains communication* and *unknown domains communication*. Known domains communication occurs when both the sending and receiving applications know about one another and the domains from which they are hosted. However, there are many cases in which the domains are not necessarily known at compile time. For example, you may use a local connection to create a plug-in-style application that can interact with many different applications. In such a case, you don't necessarily know what all the possible domains are ahead of time.

The technique for unknown domains will work for both unknown and known domains, but it is also more lax. Therefore, it is recommended that you use the known domains technique whenever possible. If you must enable cross-domain communication but you do not know the domains from which the *.swf* files will be hosted, you can use the unknown domains technique.

To allow cross-domain local connection communication for known domains you must do two things: explicitly tell the receiving `LocalConnection` object to allow requests from the sending domain, and prefix the sending request channel name with the domain of the receiving *.swf*. Use the `allowDomain()` method to specify a list of all the domains to allow.

For the next example assume that the sending *.swf* is hosted at www.a.com (*http://www.a.com*) and the receiving *.swf* is hosted at www.b.com. (*http://www.b.com.*) The following illustrates the code to send a request:

```
var localConnection:LocalConnection = new LocalConnection();
localConnection.send("www.b.com:channel", "exampleMethod");
```

The following illustrates the code necessary to receive the request with an application hosted at www.a.com (*http://www.a.com*):

```
var receivingLocalConnection:LocalConnection = new LocalConnection();
receivingLocalConnection.allowDomain("www.a.com");
receivingLocalConnection.connect("channel");
receivingLocalConnection.client = this;
```

When the domains are unknown, you can use the wildcard character (*) when calling `allowDomain()`, and rather than prefixing the channel with the receiving domain, you can name the channel with an initial underscore:

```
// Sending .swf
var localConnection:LocalConnection = new LocalConnection();
localConnection.send("_channel", "exampleMethod");

// Receiving .swf
var receivingLocalConnection:LocalConnection = new LocalConnection();
receivingLocalConnection.allowDomain("*");
receivingLocalConnection.connect("channel");
receivingLocalConnection.client = this;
```

When testing cross-domain communication, it's useful to run the application using the debugger, which will notify you if there is a problem.

Persistent Data

Many applications need to store persistent data on the client computer, and Flex applications are no exception. For example, a Flex application may display a "start page" for new users, yet the application may give the user the option to hide the start page on subsequent visits. Though you could store that preference remotely, a more common way to accomplish that is to store the preference on the client side.

Flash Player security is a top priority at Adobe, and for this reason Flash Player does not have the capability to write to arbitrary files on the client computer. However, Flash Player does have a designated area on the client computer where it can write to very specific files that are controlled and managed entirely by Flash Player. These files are called *local shared objects*, and you can use ActionScript to write to and read from these files.

Flash Player uses the `flash.net.SharedObject` class to manage access to local shared object data. Although the data is stored in files on the client machine, the access to those files is controlled exclusively through the `SharedObject` interface. This both simplifies working with shared objects and improves security to protect Flex application users from malicious programmers.

The `SharedObject` class also allows you to work with *remote* shared objects. For this reason, you may notice that the `SharedObject` class API includes many properties and methods not discussed in this chapter. Remote shared objects allow real-time data synchronization across many clients, but they also require server software such as Flash Media Server. In this book, we discuss local shared objects, not remote shared objects.

Creating Shared Objects

Unlike many ActionScript classes, the `SharedObject` constructor is never used directly, and you cannot meaningfully create a new instance using the constructor. Rather, the `SharedObject` class defines a static, lazy instantiation factory method called `getLocal()`. The `getLocal()` method returns a `SharedObject` instance that acts as a proxy to a local shared object file on the client computer. There can obviously be many local shared objects on a client computer, so you must specify the specific shared object you want to reference by passing a string parameter to `getLocal()`. If the file does not yet exist, Flash Player first creates the file and then opens it for reading and writing. If the file already exists, Flash Player simply opens it for reading and writing. The following code retrieves a reference to a shared object called example:

```
var sharedObject:SharedObject = SharedObject.getLocal("example");
```

Reading and Writing to Shared Objects

Once you've retrieved the reference to the shared object, you can read and write to it using the data property of the object, which is essentially an associative array. You must write all data that you want to persist to disk to the data property. You can use dot syntax or array-access notation to read and write arbitrary keys and values. In general, dot syntax is marginally optimal because it yields slightly faster performance. The following writes a value of true to the shared object for a key called hideStartScreen:

```
sharedObject.data.hideStartScreen = true;
```

You should use array-access notation when you want to read or write using a key that uses characters that are not valid for use in variable/property names. For example, if you want to use a key that contains spaces, you can use array-access notation:

```
sharedObject.data["First Name"] = "Bob";
```

Data is not written to disk as you write it to the SharedObject instance. By default, Flash Player will attempt to write the data to disk when the *.swf* closes. However, this can fail silently for several reasons. For example, the user might not have allocated enough space, or the user might have disallowed writing to shared objects entirely. In these cases, the shared object data will not write to disk, and the Flex application will have no notification. For this reason, it is far better to explicitly write the data to disk.

You can explicitly write data to disk using the flush() method. The flush() method serializes all the data and writes it to disk. If the user has disallowed local data storage for Flash Player for the domain, flush() will throw an error:

```
try {
  sharedObject.flush();
}
catch {
  Alert.show("An error occurred. This could be because
you have disallowed local data storage.");
}
```

The flush() method also returns a string value corresponding to either the PENDING or the FLUSHED constants of flash.net.SharedObjectFlushStatus. If the return value is FLUSHED, the data was successfully saved to disk. If the return value is PENDING, it means that the user has not allocated enough disk space for the amount of data the shared object is trying to write to disk, and Flash Player is displaying a settings dialog to the user, prompting her to allow the necessary allocation. When the user selects either to allow or disallow the allocation, the shared object will dispatch a netStatus event. You can listen for the event using the flash.events.NetStatusEvent.NET_STATUS constant:

```
sharedObject.addEventListener(NetStatusEvent.NET_STATUS, flushStatusHandler);
```

The `NetStatusEvent` type defines a property called `info` that contains a property called `code`. The `code` property will have a string value of either `SharedObject.Flush.Success` or `SharedObject.Flush.Failed`. Example 16-3 tries to write to disk. If the user has disallowed local data storage or does not allocate the space when prompted, the application displays an alert.

Example 16-3. Shared object example

```
<?xml version="1.0" encoding="utf-8"?>
<mx:Application xmlns:mx="http://www.adobe.com/2006/mxml" layout="absolute"
initialize="initializeHandler(event)">

    <mx:Script>
        <![CDATA[

            import flash.net.SharedObject;
            import mx.controls.Alert;

            private var _sharedObject:SharedObject;

            private function initializeHandler(event:Event):void {
                _sharedObject = SharedObject.getLocal("example");
                if(_sharedObject.data.count == null) {
                    _sharedObject.data.count = 20;
                    try {
                        var status:String = _sharedObject.flush();
                        if(status == SharedObjectFlushStatus.PENDING) {
                            _sharedObject.addEventListener(
NetStatusEvent.NET_STATUS, flushStatusHandler);
                        }
                    }
                    catch (error:Error) {
                        Alert.show("An error has occurred. This may be
because you have disallowed local data storage.");
                    }
                }
                else {
                    Alert.show("Shared object data: " + _sharedObject.data.count);
                }
            }

            private function flushStatusHandler(event:NetStatusEvent):void {
                event.target.removeEventListener(NetStatusEvent.NET_STATUS,
                                                 flushStatusHandler);
                if(event.info.code == "SharedObject.Flush.Failed") {
                    Alert.show("You must allow local data storage.");
                }
            }

        ]]>
    </mx:Script>

</mx:Application>
```

By default, Flash Player attempts to allocate enough space for the shared object data. If the shared object is likely to grow over time, Flash Player might prompt the user to allocate more space with each incremental increase. If you know that a shared object will require more disk space in the future, you can preallocate space by calling `flush()` with the number of bytes you want to allocate. For example, the following attempts to allocate 512,000 bytes:

```
sharedObject.flush(512000);
```

The default allocation is 100 KB. Unless the user has changed his Flash Player settings you can generally assume that you can store up to 100 KB of data in a local shared object without prompting the user.

Controlling Scope

By default, every shared object is specific to the *.swf* from which it originates. However, you can allow several *.swf* files to access the same shared object(s) by specifying a path when calling `getLocal()`. The default path is the path to the *.swf*. For example, if the *.swf* is at *http://www.example.com/flex/client/a.swf*, the path is */flex/client/a.swf*, which means only *a.swf* can access the shared object. For this example, we'll assume that *a.swf* retrieves a reference to a shared object called `example` as follows:

```
var sharedObject:SharedObject = SharedObject.getLocal("example");
```

If *b.swf* is in the same directory as *a.swf* and *b.swf* also tries to retrieve a reference to a shared object called `example` using the exact same code as appears in *a.swf*, *b.swf* will retrieve a reference to a different shared object—one that is scoped specifically to the path */flex/client/b.swf*. If you want *a.swf* and *b.swf* to be able to access the same shared object, you must specify a path parameter using a common path that they both share, such as */flex/client*:

```
var sharedObject:SharedObject = SharedObject.getLocal("example", "/flex/client");
```

For *.swf* files to have access to the same shared objects they must specify a path that they have in common. For example, both *a.swf* and *b.swf* have */flex/client* in common. They also share the paths */flex* and */*. If *http://www.example.com/main.swf* wants to use the same shared object as *a.swf* and *b.swf*, all three *.swf* files must specify a path of / for the shared object because that is the only path they have in common.

Shared objects can be shared by all *.swf* files within a domain. However, *.swf* files in two different domains cannot access the same local shared object.

Using Local Shared Objects

Thus far, we've talked about local shared objects in theory. In this section, we'll build a simple application that utilizes a shared object in a practical way. This example displays a log-in form in a pop up. However, the user has the option to set a preference so that the application will remember her.

This example application uses an MXML component that displays the log-in window. It also uses a User Singleton class that allows the user to authenticate. Note that in this example, the application uses hardcoded values against which it authenticates. In a real application the authentication would be against data from a database, LDAP, or some similar data store. The `UserAuthenticator` class looks like Example 16-4.

Example 16-4. UserAuthenticator class for shared object example

```
package com.oreilly.programmingflex.lso {

    import flash.events.EventDispatcher;
    import flash.events.Event;

    public class UserAuthenticator extends EventDispatcher {

        // The managed instance.
        private static var _instance:UserAuthenticator;

        // Declare two constants to use for event names.
        public static const AUTHENTICATE_SUCCESS:String = "success";
        public static const AUTHENTICATE_FAIL:String = "fail";

        public function UserAuthenticator () {}

        // The Singleton accessor method.
        public static function getInstance():UserAuthenticator {
            if(_instance == null) {
                _instance = new UserAuthenticator();
            }
            return _instance;
        }

        // The authenticate() method tests if the username and password are valid.
        // If so it dispatches an AUTHENTICATE_SUCCESS event. If not it dispatches
        // an AUTHENTICATE_FAIL event.
        public function authenticate(username:String, password:String):void {
            if(username == "user" && password == "pass") {
                dispatchEvent(new Event(AUTHENTICATE_SUCCESS));
            }
            else {
                dispatchEvent(new Event(AUTHENTICATE_FAIL));
            }
        }

    }
}
```

The log-in form component looks like Example 16-5 (name the file *LogInForm.mxml* and save it in the *com/oreilly/programmingflex/lso/ui* directory for the project).

Example 16-5. LogInForm.mxml

```
<?xml version="1.0" encoding="utf-8"?>
<mx:TitleWindow xmlns:mx="http://www.adobe.com/2006/mxml">
    <mx:Script>
        <![CDATA[

            import mx.managers.PopUpManager;
            import com.oreilly.programmingflex.lso.UserAuthenticator;

            // This method handles click events from the button.
            private function onClick(event:MouseEvent):void {
                // If the user selected the remember me checkbox then save the
                // username and password to the local shared object.
                if(rememberMe.selected) {
                    var sharedObject:SharedObject =
SharedObject.getLocal("userData");
                    sharedObject.data.user = {username: username.text,
password: password.text};
                    sharedObject.flush();
                }
                // Authenticate the user.
                UserAuthenticator.getInstance().authenticate(username.text,
                                                             password.text);
            }

        ]]>
    </mx:Script>
    <mx:Form>
        <mx:FormHeading label="Log In" />
        <mx:FormItem label="Username">
            <mx:TextInput id="username" />
        </mx:FormItem>
        <mx:FormItem label="Password">
            <mx:TextInput id="password" displayAsPassword="true" />
        </mx:FormItem>
        <mx:FormItem>
            <mx:Button id="submit" label="Log In" click="onClick(event)" />
        </mx:FormItem>
        <mx:FormItem>
            <mx:CheckBox id="rememberMe" label="Remember Me" />
        </mx:FormItem>
    </mx:Form>
</mx:TitleWindow>
```

The application MXML file itself is shown in Example 16-6.

Example 16-6. Main MXML file for shared object example

```
<?xml version="1.0" encoding="utf-8"?>
<mx:Application xmlns:mx="http://www.adobe.com/2006/mxml" layout="absolute"
initialize="initializeHandler(event)">
```

```
    <mx:Script>
        <![CDATA[
            import mx.containers.Form;
            import mx.managers.PopUpManager;
            import com.oreilly.programmingflex.lso.UserAuthenticator;
            import com.oreilly.programmingflex.lso.ui.LogInForm;

            private var _logInForm:LogInForm;

            private function initializeHandler(event:Event):void {

                // Retrieve the same shared object used to store the data from the
                // log-in form component.
                var sharedObject:SharedObject = SharedObject.getLocal("userData");

                // Listen for events from the UserAuthenticator instance.

                UserAuthenticator.getInstance().addEventListener
(UserAuthenticator.AUTHENTICATE_SUCCESS, removeLogInForm);

                UserAuthenticator.getInstance().addEventListener
(UserAuthenicator.AUTHENTICATE_FAIL, displayLogInForm);

                // If the shared object doesn't contain any user data then
                // display the log-in form. Otherwise, authenticate the
                // user with the data retrieved from the local shared object.
                if(sharedObject.data.user == null) {
                    displayLogInForm();
                }
                else {
                    UserAuthenticator.getInstance().authenticate
(sharedObject.data.user.username, sharedObject.data.user.password);
                }
            }

            private function displayLogInForm(event:Event = null):void {
                if(_logInForm == null) {
                    _logInForm = new LogInForm();
                    PopUpManager.addPopUp(_logInForm, this, true);
                }
            }

            private function removeLogInForm(event:Event = null):void {
                if(_logInForm != null) {
                    PopUpManager.removePopUp(_logInForm);
                    _logInForm = null;
                }
            }

        ]]>
    </mx:Script>
    <mx:TextArea x="10" y="10" text="Application"/>

</mx:Application>
```

This simple application illustrates a practical use of local shared objects. When you test this example, use the username user and the password pass.

Customizing Serialization

Many built-in types are automatically serialized and deserialized. For example, strings, numbers, Boolean values, Date objects, and arrays are all automatically serialized and deserialized. That means that even though shared object data is ultimately saved to a flat file, when you read a Date object or an array from a shared object, it's automatically recognized as the correct type. Flash Player automatically serializes all public properties (including public getters/setters) for custom types as well. However, Flash Player does not automatically store the class type. That means that when you retrieve data of a custom type from a shared object, it doesn't deserialize to the custom type by default. For instance, consider the class shown in Example 16-7.

Example 16-7. The Account class

```
package com.oreilly.programmingflex.serialization {
    public class Account {

        private var _firstName:String;
        private var _lastName:String;

        public function get firstName():String {
            return _firstName;
        }

        public function set firstName(value:String):void {
            _firstName = value;
        }

        public function get lastName():String {
            return _lastName;
        }

        public function set lastName(value:String):void {
            _lastName = value;
        }

        public function Account() {}

        public function getFullName():String {
            return _firstName + " " + _lastName;
        }

    }
}
```

If you try to write an object of this type to a shared object, it correctly serializes the firstName and lastName properties (getters/setters). That means that when you read the data back from the shared object, it displays those values properly. However, it throws an error if you attempt to call `getFullName()` because the deserialized object won't be of type `Account`. To test this we'll use two MXML applications called A and B. A is defined as shown in Example 16-8, and it sets the shared object data.

Example 16-8. Application A

```
<?xml version="1.0" encoding="utf-8"?>
<mx:Application xmlns:mx="http://www.adobe.com/2006/mxml" layout="absolute"
initialize="initializeHandler(event)">

    <mx:Script>
        <![CDATA[

            import flash.net.SharedObject;
            import mx.controls.Alert;
            import com.oreilly.programmingflex.serialization.Account;

            private var _sharedObject:SharedObject;

            private function initializeHandler(event:Event):void {
                _sharedObject = SharedObject.getLocal("test", "/");
                var account:Account = new Account();
                account.firstName = "Joey";
                account.lastName = "Lott";
                _sharedObject.data.account= account;
                try {
                    var status:String = _sharedObject.flush();
                    if(status == SharedObjectFlushStatus.PENDING) {
                        _sharedObject.addEventListener(NetStatusEvent.NET_STATUS,
flushStatusHandler);
                    }
                }
                catch (error:Error) {
                    Alert.show("You must allow local data storage.");
                }
            }

            private function flushStatusHandler(event:NetStatusEvent):void {
                event.target.removeEventListener(NetStatusEvent.NET_STATUS,
flushStatusHandler);
                if(event.info.code == "SharedObject.Flush.Failed") {
                    Alert.show("You must allow local data storage.");
                }
            }

        ]]>
    </mx:Script>

</mx:Application>
```

Application B, shown in Example 16-9, reads the shared object data and attempts to display the data in alert pop ups. Note that it will correctly display `firstName` and `lastName`, but it will throw an error on `getFullName()`.

Example 16-9. Application B

```
<?xml version="1.0" encoding="utf-8"?>
<mx:Application xmlns:mx="http://www.adobe.com/2006/mxml" layout="absolute"
initialize="initializeHandler(event)">

    <mx:Script>
        <![CDATA[

            import flash.net.SharedObject;
            import flash.utils.describeType;
            import com.oreilly.programmingflex.serialization.Account;
            import mx.controls.Alert;

            private var _sharedObject:SharedObject;

            private function initializeHandler(event:Event):void {
                _sharedObject = SharedObject.getLocal("test", "/");
                try {
                    var account:Account = _sharedObject.data.account as Account;
                    Alert.show(account.firstName + " " + account.lastName);
                    Alert.show(account.getFullName());
                }
                catch (error:Error) {
                    Alert.show(error.toString());
                }
            }

        ]]>
    </mx:Script>

</mx:Application>
```

If you want to store the type in the serialized data, you can use either of two approaches: the `flash.net.registerClassAlias()` function or the `RemoteClass` metadata tag. The `registerClassAlias()` function and `RemoteClass` tag do the same thing by allowing you to map the class to an alias. The alias is written to the serialized data. When the data is deserialized, Flash Player automatically instantiates the object as the specified type. The following revisions to applications A and B will cause the `Account` data to deserialize as an `Account` object. Although you can use either the `registerClassAlias()` function or the `RemoteClass` metadata tag, the latter is simpler and is specific to Flex. Therefore, we'll look at how to use the `RemoteClass` metadata tag to achieve the goal in this section.

Example 16-10 shows the new `Account` class. Because the code now registers the class to the alias, `Account`, it will store the alias in the serialized data as well.

Example 16-10. Application A registering a class alias

```
package com.oreilly.programmingflex.serialization {

   [RemoteClass(alias="Account")]
   public class Account {
```

```
        private var _firstName:String;
        private var _lastName:String;

        public function get firstName():String {
            return _firstName;
        }

        public function set firstName(value:String):void {
            _firstName = value;
        }

        public function get lastName():String {
            return _lastName;
        }

        public function set lastName(value:String):void {
            _lastName = value;
        }

        public function Account() {}

        public function getFullName():String {
            return _firstName + " " + _lastName;
        }

    }
}
```

You'll notice that the `RemoteClass` metadata tag appears just prior to the class declaration. It requires one attribute called **`alias`** to which you must assign the alias to use for the class.

When you register a class, it must not have any required parameters in the constructor. If it does, Flash Player throws an error when trying to deserialize the data.

The default serialization and deserialization for custom classes work well for standard value object-style data model types. However, if you want to serialize and deserialize any nonpublic state settings, you must implement `flash.utils.IExternalizable`. When a class implements `IExternalizable`, Flash Player automatically uses the custom serialization and deserialization you define rather than the standard. That allows you much more control over what the objects will store and how they will store it.

The `IExternalizable` interface requires two methods, called `writeExternal()` and `readExternal()`. The `writeExternal()` method requires a `flash.utils.IDataOutput` parameter, and the `readExternal()` method requires a `flash.utils.IDataInput` parameter. Both `IDataInput` and `IDataOutput` provide interfaces for working with binary data. `IDataInput` lets you read data using methods such as `readByte()`, `readUTF()`, and `readObject()`. `IDataOutput` lets you write data using methods like `writeByte()`, `writeUTF()`, and `writeObject()`. The `writeExternal()` method is called when the object needs to be serialized. You must write all data to the `IDataOutput` parameter that you want to store. The `readExternal()` method is called when the object is deserialized. You must read all the data from the IDataInput parameter. The data you read from the IDataInput parameter is in the same order as the data you write to the IDataOutput parameter. Example 16-11 rewrites Account using IExternalizable. There's no setter method for firstName or lastName, which proves the data is set via the customized deserialization.

Example 16-11. Account rewritten to implement IExternalizable

```
package com.oreilly.programmingflex.serialization {
    import flash.utils.IExternalizable;
    import flash.utils.IDataInput;
    import flash.utils.IDataOutput;

    public class Account implements IExternalizable {

        private var _firstName:String;
        private var _lastName:String;

        public function get firstName():String {
            return _firstName;
        }

        public function get lastName():String {
            return _lastName;
        }

        public function Account(first:String = "", last:String = "") {
            _firstName = first;
            _lastName = last;
        }

        public function getFullName():String {
            return _firstName + " " + _lastName;
        }

        public function readExternal(input:IDataInput):void {
            _firstName = input.readUTF();
            _lastName = input.readUTF();
        }

        public function writeExternal(output:IDataOutput):void {
            // Verify that _firstName is not null because this method may get called
            // when the data is null. Only serialize when the object is non-null.
            if(_firstName != null) {
                output.writeUTF(_firstName);
                output.writeUTF(_lastName);
            }
        }

    }
}
```

Communicating with the Host Application

Flex applications require the Flash Player runtime environment to work. For this reason, it is common to think of Flex applications as being confined to Flash Player. However, it is entirely possible for a Flex application to communicate with the host application. For example, if a Flex application is running within a web browser, the application can interact with the browser. If a Flex application is running within a desktop executable, it can interact with that executable. This lets you create integrated applications that span beyond the Flash Player context.

Flex application/host application communication takes place via a Flash Player class called `flash.external.ExternalInterface`. `ExternalInterface` allows you to make synchronous calls to host application methods from the Flex application, and from the host application to Flex application methods. `ExternalInterface` is quite simple to work with, and in most cases it is quite appropriate.

Working with ExternalInterface

The `flash.external.ExternalInterface` class defines two static methods, named `call()` and `addCallback()`, enabling Flex-to-host-application communication and host-application-to-Flex communication, respectively.

The `call()` method allows you to call a method of the host application by passing it the name of the method. If the host application method expects parameters, you can pass those parameters to the `call()` method following the name of the host application method. For example, the following will call the `alert()` JavaScript method when the Flex application is run in a web browser:

```
ExternalInterface.call("alert", "Test message from Flex");
```

The `call()` method works synchronously. For example, the JavaScript `confirm()` function creates a new dialog with OK and Cancel buttons. The confirm dialog pauses the application until the user clicks on a button, at which time it returns either `True` (OK) or `False` (Cancel).

```
var option:Boolean = ExternalInterface.call("confirm",
                     "Do you really want to close the application?");
```

Of course, the host application functions can be custom functions as well.

If you want to call a Flex method from the host application, you must register the method within the Flex application using `ExternalInterface.addCallback()`. The `addCallback()` method lets you register a particular function or method with an alias by which the method or function may be called from the host application. For example, the following registers `Alert.show` as `showAlert`:

```
ExternalInterface.addCallback("showAlert", Alert.show);
```

You can then call the `Alert.show` method by way of the `showAlert` alias from the host application.

Within the host application you must retrieve a reference to the Flash Player instance that is running the *.swf*. You can then call the method by its alias directly from the reference. For example, if `getFlexApplicationReference()` is a function within the host application that returns a reference to the Flash Player instance, the following would launch an alert:

```
getFlexApplicationReference().showAlert("Alert message from host application");
```

In JavaScript, the Flash Player reference is different depending on the type of browser (IE or non-IE). In IE you can retrieve a reference to the Flash Player instance by `window.`*`id`*, where *`id`* is the value of the `id` parameter of the `<object>` tag, and in non-IE browsers the reference is `document.`*`name`*, where *`name`* is the value of the `name` attribute of the `<embed>` tag. The following JavaScript function determines the browser type and returns the correct reference where both the `id` parameter and the `name` attribute are `Example`:

```
function getFlexApplicationReference() {
  if (navigator.appName.indexOf("Microsoft") != -1) {
    return window.Example;
  } else {
    return document.Example;
  }
}
```

Setting the Web Browser Status

`ExternalInterface` might seem a little confusing until you see an example or two. In this section and the next, we'll look at a few simple examples that should clarify how `ExternalInterface` works. This first application simply allows a Flex application to call to JavaScript in a hosting web browser so that it sets the status bar message as the user moves the mouse over Flex buttons.

Firefox disables JavaScript access to `window.status` by default, and therefore this example might not work with the default Firefox configuration.

This application uses one simple MXML document and one HTML page. The MXML document should contain the code shown in Example 16-12.

Example 16-12. ExternalInterfaceExample.mxml

```
<?xml version="1.0" encoding="utf-8"?>
<mx:Application xmlns:mx="http://www.adobe.com/2006/mxml" layout="absolute">

    <mx:Script>
```

```
    <![CDATA[

        private function rollOverHandler(event:MouseEvent):void {
            ExternalInterface.call("setStatus", event.currentTarget.label);
        }

    ]]>
</mx:Script>
<mx:VBox>
    <mx:Button label="A" rollOver="rollOverHandler(event)" />
    <mx:Button label="B" rollOver="rollOverHandler(event)" />
    <mx:Button label="C" rollOver="rollOverHandler(event)" />
    <mx:Button label="D" rollOver="rollOverHandler(event)" />
</mx:VBox>

</mx:Application>
```

This MXML document creates four buttons. Each button has a different label. Using event handlers for the `rollOver` event each button notifies the `rollOverHandler()` method when the user has moved the mouse over the button. The `rollOverHandler()` method uses `ExternalInterface.call()` to call the `setStatus` method that is defined using JavaScript in the HTML page within which the application is to be embedded. The label for the corresponding button gets passed to the `setStatus` function.

The HTML page should contain the standard HTML template for embedding Flex content. In addition, it must define the `setStatus()` JavaScript function as follows:

```
<script language="JavaScript" type="text/javascript">
<!--

  function setStatus(value) {
    window.status = value;
  }

// -->
</script>
```

When you test this application, the browser status bar message changes as you move the mouse over the Flex buttons.

Integrating HTML and Flex Forms

There are cases where you may want to display the majority of a form in HTML, but you want to utilize Flex components for one or more of the form elements. For example, you may want to use sliders, color pickers, or, as in this example, date choosers.

In this simple example, we'll create a basic HTML form with a checkbox and a small embedded Flex application. The Flex application consists of one date chooser component. The checkbox simply enables and disables the date chooser. Additionally, to highlight the synchronous nature of `ExternalInterface` the Flex application makes a request to the HTML page for an array of disabled dates, which it uses to disable those dates in the date chooser.

For this application, we'll first create the HTML page as shown in Example 16-13. Note that this example uses SWFObject, which is a JavaScript library described in Chapter 21.

Example 16-13. ExternalInterface example HTML page

```
<!DOCTYPE html PUBLIC "-//W3C//DTD XHTML 1.0 Strict//EN"
"http://www.w3.org/TR/xhtml1/DTD/xhtml1-strict.dtd">
<html xmlns="http://www.w3.org/1999/xhtml" lang="en" xml:lang="en">
    <head>
        <title>Flex Example</title>
        <meta http-equiv="Content-Type" content="text/html; charset=iso-8859-1" />
        <script type="text/javascript" src="swfobject.js"></script>
        <script type="text/javascript">
            swfobject.registerObject("flexApplication", "9.0.0");
function getDisallowedDates() {
                return [new Date()]
            }
        </script>
    </head>
    <body>
        <input name="checkbox" type="checkbox" onChange="swfobject.
getObjectById('flexApplication').setEnabled(this.checked)" />
        <div>
            <object classid="clsid:D27CDB6E-AE6D-11cf-96B8-444553540000"
                    width="175" height="180" id="flexApplication">
                <param name="movie" value="Flex3.swf" />
                <!--[if !IE]>-->
                <object type="application/x-shockwave-flash" data="Flex3.swf"
                        width="175" height="180">
                <!--<![endif]-->
                    <p>This site is best viewed as a Flex application, which requires
                       Flash Player 9. For users who prefer not to use Flash Player
                       we have provided a <a href='textVersion.html'>text-only
                       version of the site</a/>.</p>
                <!--[if !IE]>-->
                </object>
                <!--<![endif]-->
            </object>
        </div>
    </body>
</html>
```

In the preceding HTML code, we've highlighted a few of the key things to notice. You'll see that the checkbox uses an `onChange` handler to call the `setEnabled()` method of the Flex application, passing it the checked value of the checkbox. This means that the Flex application must map a method to the `setEnabled()` name as a valid `ExternalInterface` callback. You'll also see that the code defines a JavaScript method called `getDisallowedDates()`. This is callable from the Flex application to retrieve an array of `Date` objects.

The Flex application consists of just one MXML document, as shown in Example 16-14.

Example 16-14. ExternalInterface example MXML Flex3.mxml

```
<?xml version="1.0" encoding="utf-8"?>
<mx:Application xmlns:mx="http://www.adobe.com/2006/mxml" layout="absolute"
initialize="initializeHandler(event)" width="175" height="180">

    <mx:Script>
        <![CDATA[

            private function initializeHandler(event:Event):void {
                var disallowedDates:Array =
ExternalInterface.call("getDisallowedDates");
                calendar.disabledRanges = disallowedDates;
                ExternalInterface.addCallback("setEnabled", setEnabled);
            }

            public function setEnabled(value:Boolean):void {
                calendar.enabled = value;
            }

        ]]>
    </mx:Script>
    <mx:DateChooser id="calendar" enabled="false" />

</mx:Application>
```

In this code, you'll notice that when the application initializes, it calls the `getDisallowedDates()` JavaScript function in a synchronous fashion, retrieving the returned value immediately. It then uses that value—an array of `Date` objects—to specify the disabled ranges for the date chooser instance. Because `ExternalInterface` automatically serializes and deserializes arrays and `Date` objects, this code works without having to further convert the returned values.

When the application initializes, it also registers `setEnabled()` as an `ExternalInterface` callback. That is what allows the JavaScript-to-Flex communication.

The `setEnabled()` method takes the parameter and assigns it to the `enabled` property of the date chooser. Again, because Boolean values are automatically serialized and deserialized, the code works as is.

Summary

In this chapter, we looked at the three basic ways in which you can enable data communication that occurs entirely on the client. These mechanisms enable different types of behavior:

- Local connections allow communication between two or more *.swf* files running on the same computer.
- Local shared objects allow persistent data storage and retrieval on the client computer.
- `ExternalInterface` allows Flash and Flex applications to communicate with the application that hosts Flash Player.

CHAPTER 17

Remote Data Communication

Remote data communication occurs at runtime. It does not reside strictly in the client, but requires network connections to send and receive data between the client and the server. Flex applications support a variety of remote data communication techniques built on standards. There are three basic categories of Flex application remote data communication:

HTTP request/response-style communication
: This category consists of several overlapping techniques. Utilizing the Flex framework `HTTPService` component or the Flash Player API `URLLoader` class, you can send and load uncompressed data such as text blocks, URL encoded data, and XML packets. You can also send and receive SOAP packets using the Flex framework `WebService` component. And you can use a technology called *Remoting* to send and receive AMF packets, which use a binary protocol that is similar to SOAP (but is considerably smaller). Each technique achieves the similar goal of sending requests and receiving responses using HTTP or HTTPS. See *http://www.jamesward.org/census* for a comparison of various methods for loading data at runtime over HTTP.

Real-time communication
: This category consists of persistent socket connections. Flash Player supports several types of general socket connections: those that require a specific format for packets (`XMLSocket`) and those that allow raw socket connections (`Socket`). In both cases, the socket connection is persistent between the client and the server, allowing the server to push data to the client—something that is not possible using standard HTTP request/response-style techniques. Flash Player also supports a real-time communication protocol called Real Time Messaging Protocol (RTMP). RTMP is used by a variety of server-side products, including Flash Media Server, Red5, FluorineFx, some versions of WebORB, and Wowza.

File upload/download communication
: This category consists of the `FileReference` API, which is native to Flash Player and allows file upload and download directly within Flex applications.

Of these three generalized categories, it is fairly easy to distinguish between file upload/download communication and the other two types. Clearly, file upload/download communication applies only to cases in which the application requires file uploading and downloading. However, the distinction between HTTP request/response and real-time communication is not always as obvious.

HTTP request/response is far more common than real-time data communication. Although real-time data communication is necessary for some low-latency applications, it adds network overhead to the application because it requires a persistent socket connection for each user. In contrast, HTTP request/response communication is always initiated by the client in the form of a request. The server returns a response to the client, and then the connection is closed again until the client makes another request. In most cases, the request/response model is more efficient. Furthermore, request/response over HTTP is generally less of a challenge to existing security models than real-time communication over persistent socket connections.

In this chapter, we'll focus primarily on two forms of remote data communication: request/response and file upload/download. We'll focus primarily on asynchronous (request/response) communication techniques because they make up the majority of remote data communication you'll use for Flex applications. We'll also discuss the basics of file upload and download.

Understanding Strategies for Data Communication

When you build Flex applications that utilize data communication, it's important to understand the strategies available for managing those communications and how to select the right strategy for an application. If you're new to working with Flash platform applications, it's important that you take the time to learn how data communication works within Flash Player and how that compares and contrasts with what you already know about developing for other platforms. For example, some of what you might know from working with HTML-based applications or Ajax applications may be useful, but you should never assume that Flex applications behave in the same way as applications built on other platforms.

As you already know by this time, all Flex applications run in Flash Player. With the exception of some Flex applications created using Flex Data Services, almost all Flex applications are composed of precompiled *.swf* files that are loaded in Flash Player on the client. The *.swf* files are initially requested from the server, but they run on the client. This means dynamic data (any data not statically compiled into the *.swf*) must be requested at runtime from the client to a server in most cases.

Because Flex applications are stateful and self-contained, they don't require new page requests and wholesale screen refreshes to make data requests and handle responses. This behavior is something Flex applications have in common with Ajax. Rather than being page-driven, Flex applications are event-driven. Even as the view within a Flex application might not change, it can be making requests and receiving responses.

Therefore, Flex data communication clearly requires different strategies from those employed by page-driven applications.

The Flex framework provides components for working with data communication using standard HTTP requests as well as SOAP requests. These components are useful when using the first of the common strategies for data communication: placing the code (the component) that makes a request within the class or MXML document that utilizes the data. This is often the most obvious strategy, and it is often the strategy that scales the least. This strategy decentralizes data communication, which causes several problems:

- Managing data communication is difficult when the code is decentralized, simply because it makes it difficult to locate the code at times.
- When data communication is tightly coupled with a particular view that uses the data, that data is not readily accessible to other parts of the application. This may not seem like a problem until you consider that many applications use the same data in many places, and if you place the data communication code within the views that use the data, you make it difficult to synchronize the data and you may require many requests for the same data.
- Decentralizing data communication code makes the application fragile because changing anything about the data communication process (protocols, APIs, etc.) can break the application in many places. In contrast, when data communication code is centralized, it's relatively easier to adapt the application when something in the data communication process changes.

Although the first strategy has these significant pitfalls associated with it, we still include discussions of the components within this chapter because the strategy is not completely without merit. The components often provide a much faster way to assemble data-communication-ready applications. This is useful in cases of rapid prototypes, test applications, and small-scale (nonenterprise) applications with less demanding technical requirements.

The second strategy requires centralizing data communication using *remote proxy objects*. Remote proxies are objects that reside within the client tier where they can stand in for remote services. The remote proxy objects may even have the same APIs as the remote services. Remote proxies provide a centralized location for data communication code, and they hide the details of how data communication takes places from the rest of the application. Even if the implementation changes, the rest of the application can still continue to make calls on the remote proxy objects.

The second strategy is much more scalable than the first. Furthermore, because data communication code is centralized, this strategy is not susceptible to the same problems as the first strategy, such as duplication of data requests, synchronization problems, and adaptability issues. For these reasons, we strongly prefer the use of remote proxies for enterprise applications.

Working with Request/Response Data Communication

You can work with request/response data communication in three basic ways: via simple HTTP services (including REST services and services using JSON), SOAP web services, and Remoting. Each achieves the same basic goal of sending a request and receiving a response, and as such you can use them for the same purposes within Flex applications. Which method you choose depends primarily on what type of service you have available. For example, if you want to load XML data from an XML document you should use simple HTTP service communication. However, if you want to call a web service method, you should use web services communication.

Simple HTTP Services

The most basic type of HTTP request/response communication uses what we call *simple HTTP services*. These services include things such as text and XML resources, either in static documents or dynamically generated by something such as a ColdFusion page, a servlet, or an ASP.NET page. Simple HTTP services might also include pages that run scripts when called in order to do things such as insert data into or update databases or send email. You can use simple HTTP services to execute these sorts of server behaviors, to load data, or to do both.

Flex provides two basic ways in which you can call simple HTTP services: using `HTTPService`, a Flex framework component; and using the Flash Player class `flash.net.URLLoader`.

HTTPService

`HTTPService` is a component that allows you to make requests to simple HTTP services such as text files, XML files, or scripts and pages that return dynamic (or static) data. You must always define a value for the `url` property of an `HTTPService` object. The `url` property tells the object where it can find the resource to which it should make the request. The value can be either a relative URL or an absolute URL. The following example uses MXML to create an `HTTPService` object that loads text from a file called *data.txt* saved in the same directory as the compiled *.swf* file:

```
<mx:HTTPService id="textService" url="data.txt" />
```

Now that you know how to create a new `HTTPService` instance, let's discuss how to send requests, handle results, and pass parameters.

Sending requests

Creating an `HTTPService` object does not automatically make the request to load the data. To make the request, you must call the `send()` method. You can call the `send()` method in response to any framework or user event. For example, if you want to make the request as soon as the application initializes, you can call `send()` in response to the initialize event. If you want to load the data when the user clicks a button, you can call the `send()` method in response to a click event:

```
textService.send();
```

Handling responses

The `send()` method makes the request, but a response is not likely to be returned instantaneously. Instead, the application must wait for a result event. The result event occurs when the entire response has been returned. The following example displays an alert when the data loads:

```
<mx:HTTPService id="textService" url="data.txt"
    result="Alert.show('Data loaded')" />
```

Of course, normally you would want to do something more useful than display an alert when the data loads. More commonly, you will want to use the data in some way. You can retrieve the response data (i.e., the data that has loaded) using the `lastResult` property. Plain text is always loaded as string data. However, the `HTTPService` component is capable of automatically converting serialized data into associative arrays. For this reason, the `lastResult` property is typed as `Object`. If you want to treat it as a string, you must cast it. Example 17-1 loads text from a file and then displays it in a text area.

Example 17-1. Loading text with HTTPService

```
<?xml version="1.0" encoding="utf-8"?>
<mx:Application xmlns:mx="http://www.adobe.com/2006/mxml" xmlns:remoting="
com.oreilly.programmingflex.rpc.*" layout="absolute"
initialize="initializeHandler(event)">

    <mx:Script>
        <![CDATA[

            private function initializeHandler(event:Event):void {
                textService.send();
            }

            private function resultHandler(event:Event):void {
                textArea.text = String(textService.lastResult);
            }

        ]]>
    </mx:Script>

    <mx:HTTPService id="textService" url="data.txt" result="resultHandler(event)" />

    <mx:TextArea id="textArea" />

</mx:Application>
```

Although you can explicitly handle the result event, it is far more common to use data binding. Example 17-2 accomplishes the same thing as Example 17-1, but it uses data binding.

Example 17-2. Using data binding with HTTPService

```
<?xml version="1.0" encoding="utf-8"?>
<mx:Application xmlns:mx="http://www.adobe.com/2006/mxml" xmlns:remoting="
com.oreilly.programmingflex.rpc.*" layout="absolute"
initialize="initializeHandler(event)">

    <mx:Script>
        <![CDATA[

            private function initializeHandler(event:Event):void {
                textService.send();
            }

        ]]>
    </mx:Script>

    <mx:HTTPService id="textService" url="data.txt" />

    <mx:TextArea id="textArea" text="{textService.lastResult}" />

</mx:Application>
```

When possible, HTTPService will deserialize data it loads in much the same way as it would interpret data placed in a Model tag. For example, consider the following data:

```
<countries>
  <country>Select One</country>
  <country>Canada</country>
  <country>U.S.</country>
</countries>
```

If you attempt to load this data using HTTPService, it will be parsed into an object named countries that contains an array named country, each element of which corresponds to the <country> elements. Example 17-3 illustrates this using a live XML file that contains the XML data shown in the preceding code block. It uses data binding to populate the combo box with the data.

Example 17-3. Loading XML with HTTPService

```
<?xml version="1.0" encoding="utf-8"?>
<mx:Application xmlns:mx="http://www.adobe.com/2006/mxml" layout="absolute"
initialize="initializeHandler(event)">

    <mx:Script>
        <![CDATA[

            private function initializeHandler(event:Event):void {
                countriesService.send();
            }

        ]]>
    </mx:Script>

    <mx:HTTPService id="countriesService"
```

```
url="http://www.rightactionscript.com/states/xml/countries.xml" />

    <mx:VBox>
        <mx:ComboBox id="country"
            dataProvider="{countriesService.lastResult.countries.country}"  />
    </mx:VBox>

</mx:Application>
```

As we've already seen, by default `HTTPService` results are interpreted as text if they are blocks of text, and if the results are XML data, they're parsed into an object. However, that's merely the default behavior. You can explicitly dictate the way in which the results are handled using the `resultFormat` property of the `HTTPService` object. The default value is `object`, which yields the default behavior you've already seen. You can optionally specify any of the following values:

`text`
: The data is not parsed at all, but is treated as raw text.

`flashvars`
: The data is assumed to be in URL-encoded format, and it will be parsed into an object with properties corresponding to the name/value pairs.

`array`
: The data is assumed to be in XML format, and it is parsed into objects much the same as with the object settings. However, in this case, the result is always an array. If the returned data does not automatically parse into an array, the parsed data is placed into an array.

`xml`
: The data is assumed to be in XML format, and it is interpreted as XML using the legacy `XMLNode` ActionScript class.

`e4x`
: The data is assumed to be in XML format, and it is interpreted as XML using the ActionScript 3.0 `XML` class (E4X).

Sending parameters

When you want to pass parameters to the service, you can use the `request` property of the `HTTPService` instance. The `request` property requires an `Object` value. By default, the name/value pairs of the object are converted to URL-encoded format and are sent to the service using HTTP `GET`. You can assign an object using ActionScript, as in the following:

```
var parameters:Object = new Object();
parameters.a = "one";
parameters.b = "two";
service.request = parameters;
```

However, when creating an HTTPService object using MXML, it's often convenient to declare the parameters using MXML as well:

```
<mx:HTTPService id="service" url="script.php">
  <mx:request>
    <a>one</a>
    <b>two</b>
  </mx:request>
</mx:HTTPService>
```

Declaring the request in this way also allows you to use data binding with the parameters. To illustrate this with a working example, consider the code in Example 17-4, which builds on Example 17-3 by using a second HTTPService object to retrieve state names based on the selected country.

Example 17-4. Using HTTPService with input parameters

```
<?xml version="1.0" encoding="utf-8"?>
<mx:Application xmlns:mx="http://www.adobe.com/2006/mxml" layout="absolute"
initialize="initializeHandler(event)">

    <mx:Script>
        <![CDATA[

            private function initializeHandler(event:Event):void {
                countriesService.send();
            }

            private function changeHandler(event:Event):void {
                statesService.send();
            }

        ]]>
    </mx:Script>

    <mx:HTTPService id="countriesService"
url="http://www.rightactionscript.com/states/xml/countries.xml" />

    <mx:HTTPService id="statesService"
url="http://www.rightactionscript.com/states/xml/states.php">
        <mx:request>
            <country>
                {country.value}
            </country>
        </mx:request>
    </mx:HTTPService>

    <mx:VBox>
        <mx:ComboBox id="country"
            dataProvider="{countriesService.lastResult.countries.country}"
            change="changeHandler(event)" />
        <mx:ComboBox dataProvider="{statesService.lastResult.states.state}" />
    </mx:VBox>

</mx:Application>
```

In the preceding example, the first combo box is populated with a list of countries. When the user selects a country from the combo box, it sends a request to the second service, a PHP script, sending the selected country as a parameter. The return value is in the following format:

```
<states>
  <state>Alabama</state>
  <state>Alaska</state>
  <!-- etc. -->
</states>
```

As noted, by default, parameters are sent in URL-encoded format using HTTP GET. However, you can adjust those settings. The contentType property of the HTTPService object determines the format in which the content is sent. The default value is application/x-www-form-urlencoded, which sends the values in URL-encoded format. You can specify application/xml to send the data as XML if the service expects raw XML data:

```
<mx:HTTPService id="service" url="script.php" contentType="application/xml">
  <mx:request>
    <parameters>
      <a>one</a>
      <b>two</b>
    </parameters>
  </mx:request>
</mx:HTTPService>
```

The method property determines what transport method is used. The default is GET, but you can also specify a value of POST, HEAD, OPTIONS, PUT, TRACE, or DELETE, though Flash Player supports only GET and POST when running in a browser (AIR applications support all methods).

Using HTTPService with ActionScript

Although the simplest and quickest way to use an HTTPService object is to primarily use MXML, this technique is best-suited to nonenterprise applications in which the data communication scenarios are quite simple. However, for more complex data communication requirements, it is advisable to use remote proxies, as discussed earlier in this chapter. Because HTTPService components provide significant data conversion advantages (such as automatic serialization of data), it is still frequently a good idea to use an HTTPService object within a remote proxy. However, it is generally necessary to then work with the HTTPService component entirely with ActionScript, including constructing the object and handling the responses.

When working with HTTPService objects entirely with ActionScript, you'll want to import the mx.rpc.http.HTTPService class. You can then construct an instance with a standard new statement:

```
var httpRequest:HTTPRequest = new HTTPRequest();
```

You should then set the url property:

```
httpRequest.url = "data.txt";
```

Just as you would listen for any event from any object, you need to add listeners to HTTPService objects using addEventListener(). HTTPService objects dispatch events of type ResultEvent when a response is returned, and they dispatch events of type FaultEvent when an error is returned from the server. The ResultEvent and FaultE vent classes are in the mx.rpc.events package:

```
httpRequest.addEventListener(ResultEvent.RESULT, resultHandler);
```

Example 17-5 is a simple working example that uses the recommended remote proxy approach in conjunction with HTTPService. This example accomplishes the same basic thing as previous MXML-based examples—displaying countries and states in combo boxes. However, this example uses several classes to accomplish this. The first class we'll look at is a simple data model class called ApplicationDataModel. Here's the code.

Example 17-5. ApplicationDataModel.as

```
package com.oreilly.programmingflex.remotedata {
    import mx.collections.ListCollectionView;

    public class ApplicationDataModel {

        private static var _instance:ApplicationDataModel;

        private var _countryNames:ListCollectionView;
        private var _statesNames:ListCollectionView;

        [Bindable]
        public function set countryNames(value:ListCollectionView):void {
            _countryNames = value;
        }

        public function get countryNames():ListCollectionView {
            return _countryNames;
        }

        [Bindable]
        public function set statesNames(value:ListCollectionView):void {
            _statesNames = value;
        }

        public function get statesNames():ListCollectionView {
            return _statesNames;
        }

        public function ApplicationDataModel() {}

        public static function getInstance():ApplicationDataModel {
            if(_instance == null) {
                _instance = new ApplicationDataModel();
            }
```

```
            return _instance;
        }
    }
}
```

In Example 17-6, we'll define StatesService, the remote proxy that loads XML data using HTTPService. The class defines two service methods: getCountries() and getStates(). When the results are returned for the service method calls, they're assigned to the data model.

Example 17-6. StatesService.as

```
package com.oreilly.programmingflex.remotedata {
    import mx.rpc.http.HTTPService;
    import mx.rpc.events.ResultEvent;
    import mx.collections.XMLListCollection;
    import com.oreilly.programmingflex.remotedata.ApplicationDataModel;

    public class StatesService {

        private var _service:HTTPService;

        public function StatesService() {
            _service = new HTTPService();
            _service.resultFormat = "e4x";
        }

        public function getCountries():void {
            _service.addEventListener(ResultEvent.RESULT, countriesResultHandler);
            _service.url = "http://rightactionscript.com/states/xml/countries.xml";
            _service.send();
        }

        public function getStates(country:String):void {
            _service.addEventListener(ResultEvent.RESULT, statesResultHandler);
            _service.url = "http://rightactionscript.com/states/xml/
states.php?country=" + country;
            _service.send();
        }

        private function countriesResultHandler(event:ResultEvent):void {
            _service.removeEventListener(ResultEvent.RESULT, countriesResultHandler);
            ApplicationDataModel.getInstance().countryNames = new
XMLListCollection(_service.lastResult.children() as XMLList);
        }

        private function statesResultHandler(event:ResultEvent):void {
            _service.removeEventListener(ResultEvent.RESULT, statesResultHandler);
            ApplicationDataModel.getInstance().statesNames = new
XMLListCollection(_service.lastResult.children() as XMLList);
        }
    }
}
```

Example 17-7 is the MXML application that utilizes both of these classes.

Example 17-7. Using the states service proxy and application data model

```
<?xml version="1.0" encoding="utf-8"?>
<mx:Application xmlns:mx="http://www.adobe.com/2006/mxml" layout="absolute"
creationComplete="creationCompleteHandler(event)">
    <mx:Script>
        <![CDATA[
            import mx.rpc.http.HTTPService;
            import mx.rpc.events.ResultEvent;
            import com.oreilly.programmingflex.remotedata.StatesService;
            import com.oreilly.programmingflex.remotedata.ApplicationDataModel;

            private var _statesService:StatesService;
            private function creationCompleteHandler(event:Event):void {
                _statesService = new StatesService();
                _statesService.getCountries();
            }
        ]]>
    </mx:Script>
    <mx:VBox>
        <mx:ComboBox id="countryMenu"
dataProvider="{ApplicationDataModel.getInstance().countryNames}"
change="_statesService.getStates(countryMenu.selectedLabel)" />
        <mx:ComboBox
         dataProvider="{ApplicationDataModel.getInstance().statesNames}" />
    </mx:VBox>
</mx:Application>
```

In this example, the `StatesService` instance is created, and `getCountries()` is called immediately. The first combo box is data-bound to the `countryNames` property of the data model. As the user selects a value from the first combo box, it calls `getStates()`, passing it the selected country. The second combo box is data-bound to the `states Names` property of the data model.

URLLoader

`HTTPService` allows you to use requests and handle responses to and from simple HTTP services. You can optionally use the Flash Player class called `flash.net.URLLoader` to accomplish the same tasks entirely with ActionScript, but at a slightly lower level. Practically speaking, there is little to no difference between using `URLLoader` and `HTTPService`. However, because many developers building pure ActionScript 3 libraries will rely on `URLLoader` (and you may rely on their code), you will likely find it useful to be familiar with how to use `URLLoader`.

The first step when working with a `URLLoader` object is always to construct the object using the constructor method, as follows:

```
var loader:URLLoader = new URLLoader();
```

Once you've constructed the object, you can do the following:

- Send requests.
- Handle responses.
- Send parameters.

Sending requests

You can send requests using the `load()` method of a `URLLoader` object. The `load()` method requires that you pass it a `flash.net.URLRequest` object specifying at a minimum what URL to use when making the request. The following makes a request to a text file called *data.txt*:

```
loader.load(new URLRequest("data.txt"));
```

Handling responses

`URLLoader` objects dispatch complete events when a response has been returned. Any return value is stored in the `data` property of the `URLLoader` object. Example 17-8 loads XML data from a URL and handles the response.

Example 17-8. Loading XML using URLLoader

```
<?xml version="1.0" encoding="utf-8"?>
<mx:Application xmlns:mx="http://www.adobe.com/2006/mxml" layout="absolute"
initialize="initializeHandler(event)">

    <mx:Script>
        <![CDATA[

            private var _countriesService:URLLoader;

            private function initializeHandler(event:Event):void {
                _countriesService = new URLLoader();
                _countriesService.addEventListener(Event.COMPLETE,
countriesCompleteHandler);
                _countriesService.load(new
URLRequest("http://www.rightactionscript.com/states/xml/countries.xml"));
                XML.ignoreWhitespace = true;
            }

            private function countriesCompleteHandler(event:Event):void {
                var xml:XML = new XML(_countriesService.data);
                country.dataProvider = xml.children();
            }

        ]]>
    </mx:Script>

    <mx:VBox>
        <mx:ComboBox id="country" />
    </mx:VBox>

</mx:Application>
```

When data is returned to a URLLoader object, it's interpreted as a string by default. In the preceding example, you can see that this is so because the data must be converted to an XML object.

It is possible to receive binary data and URL-encoded data in response to a URLLoader request. If you want to handle a binary response, you must set the dataFormat property of the URLLoader object to flash.net.URLLoaderDataFormat.BINARY. Binary data will then be interpreted as a ByteArray. If the returned data is in URL-encoded format, you can set the dataFormat property to flash.net.URLLoaderDataFormat.VARIABLES and the returned data will be interpreted as a flash.net.URLVariables object. URLVariables objects contain properties corresponding to the name/value pairs in the returned value. For example, if a URLLoader object is set to handle URL-encoded return data, a return value of a=one&b=two will create a URLVariables object with a and b properties accessible, as in the following:

```
trace(loader.data.a + " " + loader.data.b);
```

Sending parameters

You can send parameters using URLLoader as well. To send parameters, you assign a value to the data property of the URLRequest object used to make the request. The URLRequest object can send binary data or string data. If you assign a ByteArray to the data property it's sent as binary. If you assign a URLVariables object to the data property, the data is sent in URL-encoded format. Otherwise, the data is converted to a string. Example 17-9 builds on Example 17-8 to send a parameter when requesting state data.

Example 17-9. Sending parameters with URLLoader

```
<?xml version="1.0" encoding="utf-8"?>
<mx:Application xmlns:mx="http://www.adobe.com/2006/mxml" layout="absolute"
initialize="initializeHandler(event)">

    <mx:Script>
        <![CDATA[

            private var _countriesService:URLLoader;
            private var _statesService:URLLoader;

            private function initializeHandler(event:Event):void {
                _countriesService = new URLLoader();
                _countriesService.addEventListener(Event.COMPLETE,
countriesCompleteHandler);
                _countriesService.load(new
URLRequest("http://www.rightactionscript.com/states/xml/countries.xml"));
                _statesService = new URLLoader();
                _statesService.addEventListener(Event.COMPLETE,
statesCompleteHandler);
                XML.ignoreWhitespace = true;
            }

            private function countriesCompleteHandler(event:Event):void {
```

```
                var xml:XML = new XML(_countriesService.data);
                country.dataProvider = xml.children();
            }

            private function statesCompleteHandler(event:Event):void {
                var xml:XML = new XML(_statesService.data);
                state.dataProvider = xml.children();
            }

            private function changeHandler(event:Event):void {
                var request:URLRequest = new
URLRequest("http://www.rightactionscript.com/states/xml/states.php");
                var parameters:URLVariables = new URLVariables();
                parameters.country = country.value;
                request.data = parameters;
                _statesService.load(request);
            }

        ]]>
    </mx:Script>

    <mx:VBox>
        <mx:ComboBox id="country" change="changeHandler(event)" />
        <mx:ComboBox id="state" />
    </mx:VBox>

</mx:Application>
```

You can use the `method` property to specify how the data should be sent. Possible values are `flash.net.URLRequestMethod.POST` and `flash.net.URLRequestMethod.GET`.

Using URLLoader in a remote proxy

Now that we've had a chance to see the basics of working with `URLLoader`, here's an example that uses `URLLoader` in context. In "Using HTTPService with ActionScript" you saw a complete working example. You can use the same MXML document and data model class and make a few minor edits to the remote proxy class to use `URLLoader` instead of `HTTPService`. Example 17-10 is the new remote proxy class.

Example 17-10. The new StatesService.as

```
package com.oreilly.programmingflex.remotedata {
    import flash.net.URLLoader;
    import flash.net.URLRequest;
    import flash.events.Event;
    import flash.net.URLVariables;
    import mx.collections.XMLListCollection;
    import com.oreilly.programmingflex.remotedata.ApplicationDataModel

    public class StatesService {

        private var _service:URLLoader;

        public function StatesService() {
```

```
            _service = new URLLoader();
        }

        public function getCountries():void {
            _service.addEventListener(Event.COMPLETE, countriesResultHandler);
            var request:URLRequest = new
URLRequest("http://rightactionscript.com/states/xml/countries.xml");
            _service.load(request);
        }

        public function getStates(country:String):void {
            _service.addEventListener(Event.COMPLETE, statesResultHandler);
            var request:URLRequest = new
URLRequest("http://rightactionscript.com/states/xml/states.php");
            var parameters:URLVariables = new URLVariables();
            parameters.country = country;
            request.data = parameters;
            _service.load(request);
        }

        private function countriesResultHandler(event:Event):void {
            _service.removeEventListener(Event.COMPLETE, countriesResultHandler);
            ApplicationDataModel.getInstance().countryNames =
new XMLListCollection(new XML(_service.data).children() as XMLList);
        }

        private function statesResultHandler(event:Event):void {
            _service.removeEventListener(Event.COMPLETE, statesResultHandler);
            ApplicationDataModel.getInstance().statesNames =
new XMLListCollection(new XML(_service.data).children() as XMLList);
        }


    }
}
```

You can test this new `StatesService` class using the same MXML document and `ApplicationDataModel` class from earlier in the chapter.

Web Services

Flash Player has no built-in support for SOAP web services. However, Flex provides a `WebService` component that uses built-in HTTP request/response support as well as XML support to enable you to work with SOAP-based web services. There are two ways you can work with the `WebService` components: using MXML and using ActionScript.

Using WebService Components with MXML

You can create a `WebService` component instance using MXML. When you do, you should specify an `id` and a value for the `wsdl` property, as in the example that follows.

```
<mx:WebService id="statesService"
wsdl="http://www.rightactionscript.com/states/webservice/StatesService.php?wsdl" />
```

Web services define one or more methods or operations. You must define the `WebService` instance so that it knows about the operations using nested operation tags. The operation tag requires that you specify the name at a minimum. The following example defines an operation called `getCountries`. This means that the WSDL document must also define a `getCountries` operation.

```
<mx:WebService id="statesService"
wsdl="http://www.rightactionscript.com/states/webservice/StatesService.php?wsdl">
  <mx:operation name="getCountries" />
</mx:WebService>
```

Once you've defined the `WebService` instance and an operation, you need to be able to call the method and handle the response, which we'll look at in the next few sections.

Calling web service methods

All operations that you define for a `WebService` component instance are accessible as properties of the instance. For example, in the preceding section we created a `WebService` instance called `statesService` with an operation called `getCountries`. That means you can use ActionScript to reference the operation as `statesService.getCountries`.

You can then call `getCountries` just as though it were a method of `statesService`:

```
statesService.getCountries();
```

Optionally, you can call the `send()` method of `getCountries`:

```
statesService.getCountries.send();
```

Each of these ways of calling the operation is equivalent in many cases. The only time you must use one instead of the other is when you want to declaratively define operation parameters using MXML. In such cases, you must use the `send()` method.

Handling responses

When a web service operation returns a result, you can handle it in one of two ways: explicitly handle the result event or use data binding. Then, once a result is returned, you can retrieve the result value from the `lastResult` property of the operation.

All web service operations dispatch a result event when the result is returned. The following code tells the application to call `trace()` when the result is returned:

```
<mx:WebService id="statesService"
wsdl="http://www.rightactionscript.com/states/webservice/StatesService.php?wsdl">
  <mx:operation name="getCountries" result="trace('result returned')" />
</mx:WebService>
```

Here we're using the same code, except we're tracing the result of the operation using `statesService.getCountries.lastResult`:

```
<mx:WebService id="statesService"
wsdl="http://www.rightactionscript.com/states/webservice/StatesService.php?wsdl">
  <mx:operation name="getCountries"
      result="trace(statesService.getCountries.lastResult)" />
</mx:WebService>
```

Example 17-11 is a simple example that loads an array of countries and uses data binding to populate a combo box.

Example 17-11. Using a WebService to load data

```
<?xml version="1.0" encoding="utf-8"?>
<mx:Application xmlns:mx="http://www.adobe.com/2006/mxml" layout="absolute"
initialize="initializeHandler(event)">

    <mx:Script>
        <![CDATA[

            private function initializeHandler(event:Event):void {
                statesService.getCountries.send();
            }

        ]]>
    </mx:Script>

    <mx:WebService id="statesService" wsdl="http://www.rightactionscript.com/
states/webservice/StatesService.php?wsdl">
        <mx:operation name="getCountries" />
    </mx:WebService>

    <mx:VBox>
        <mx:ComboBox id="country"
dataProvider="{statesService.getCountries.lastResult}" />
    </mx:VBox>

</mx:Application>
```

In Example 17-11 and the two short code snippets preceding it, the result returned by the operation is an array.

Sending parameters

You can send parameters to a web service method using the `WebService` component. When you want to send parameters, you have two basic options: you can pass the parameters when calling the method, or you can declare the parameters when declaring the operation.

First we'll look at passing parameters to a web service method when calling it. When you want to pass parameters in this way, you must call the operation as a method of the `WebService` instance. You can then pass parameters to the method in the function call operator just as you would any standard method:

```
service.exampleOperation("a", "b");
```

If you want to pass parameters with dynamic values obtained from user input, you can use expressions, just as you would for any method. For example, the following assumes that `textInput1` and `textInput2` are text input controls:

```
service.exampleOperation(textInput1.text, textInput2.text);
```

Example 17-12 adds another operation, `getStates`, and calls the method passing it the selected country value.

Example 17-12. Calling a WebService method with parameters

```
<?xml version="1.0" encoding="utf-8"?>
<mx:Application xmlns:mx="http://www.adobe.com/2006/mxml" layout="absolute"
initialize="initializeHandler(event)">

    <mx:Script>
        <![CDATA[

            private function initializeHandler(event:Event):void {
                statesService.getCountries();
            }

            private function changeHandler(event:Event):void {
                statesService.getStates(country.value);
            }

        ]]>
    </mx:Script>

    <mx:WebService id="statesService" wsdl="http://www.rightactionscript.com/
states/webservice/StatesService.php?wsdl">
        <mx:operation name="getCountries" />
        <mx:operation name="getStates" />
    </mx:WebService>

    <mx:VBox>
        <mx:ComboBox id="country"
dataProvider="{statesService.getCountries.lastResult}" change="changeHandler(event)"
/>
        <mx:ComboBox dataProvider="{statesService.getStates.lastResult}" />
    </mx:VBox>

</mx:Application>
```

You can optionally use the `send()` method to call the operation. When you want to send parameters using the `send()` method, you simply pass the parameters to the `send()` method:

```
statesService.getStates.send(country.value);
```

Another option when passing parameters to a web service method is to declare them when declaring the operation. You can do that by nesting a request tag in the operation tag. Then, within the request tag, you can create a structure of the parameters. You should use the names of the parameters as they are expected by the web service method (as defined in the WSDL). For example, the following code declares an operation that expects two parameters, called `a` and `b`:

```
<mx:WebService id="exampleService" wsdl="http://www.example.com/service.wsdl ">
  <mx:operation name="exampleOperation">
    <mx:request>
      <a>1</a>
      <b>2</b>
    </mx:request>
  </mx:operation>
</mx:WebService>
```

When you use this form of declarative parameter, you must call the operation using the `send()` method. You don't need to pass any parameters to the `send()` method.

```
exampleService.exampleOperation.send();
```

Note that you can use data binding to bind to parameters as well, as in Example 17-13.

Example 17-13. Using the send() method

```
<?xml version="1.0" encoding="utf-8"?>
<mx:Application xmlns:mx="http://www.adobe.com/2006/mxml" layout="absolute"
initialize="initializeHandler(event)">

    <mx:Script>
        <![CDATA[

            private function initializeHandler(event:Event):void {
                statesService.getCountries.send();
            }

            private function changeHandler(event:Event):void {
                statesService.getStates.send();
            }

        ]]>
    </mx:Script>

    <mx:WebService id="statesService" wsdl="http://www.rightactionscript.com/
states/webservice/StatesService.php?wsdl">
        <mx:operation name="getCountries" />
        <mx:operation name="getStates">
            <mx:request>
                <country>
                    {country.value}
                </country>
            </mx:request>
        </mx:operation>
    </mx:WebService>
```

```
    <mx:VBox>
        <mx:ComboBox id="country"
dataProvider="{statesService.getCountries.lastResult}"
change="changeHandler(event)" />
        <mx:ComboBox dataProvider="{statesService.getStates.lastResult}" />
    </mx:VBox>

</mx:Application>
```

This example first populates the list of states. Then it uses parameter binding to link the selection from the country combo box to the parameter sent to the `getStates` *operation.*

Using WebService Components with ActionScript

You can use a `WebService` component using ActionScript instead of MXML. This is useful in cases where you want to fully separate the view from the controller and the model, such as in the recommended remote proxy approach. The MXML version of the `WebService` component is an instance of `mx.rpc.soap.mxml.WebService`, which is a subclass of `mx.rpc.soap.WebService`. When you use the component directly from ActionScript, you should instantiate `mx.rpc.soap.WebService` directly:

```
// Assume the code already has an import statement for mx.rpc.soap.WebService.
var exampleService:WebService = new WebService();
```

Once you have created a `WebService` instance, you need to specify the WSDL URL using the `wsdl` property:

```
exampleService.wsdl = "http://www.example.com/Service.wsdl";
```

Next, you must call a method called `loadWSDL()`. You must call the method prior to calling any of the web service operations. Assuming you set the `wsdl` property, you don't need to pass any parameters to `loadWSDL()`:

```
exampleService.loadWSDL();
```

Sending requests

Once you've called the `loadWSDL()` method, you can call any operations defined by the web service. You can call the operations either as methods of the `WebService` object or by using the `send()` method:

```
// The following lines of code accomplish the same thing.
exampleService.testOperation();
exampleService.testOperation.send();
```

Sending parameters

If you want to pass parameters to an operation, you can pass them when calling the operation as a method, or you can pass them to the `send()` method.

```
// The following lines of code accomplish the same thing.
exampleService.testOperation(parameter);
exampleService.textOperation.send(parameter);
```

Handling responses

You can handle the results of a web service operation either by listening for events or by way of data binding. If you want to use events, you can register listeners for result and error events dispatched by the operation(s). The result events are of type `mx.rpc.events.ResultEvent`, and the error events are of type `mx.rpc.events.FaultEvent`. The following example registers listeners for result and error events:

```
exampleService.testOperation.addEventListener(ResultEvent.RESULT, onResult);
exampleService.testOperation.addEventListener(FaultEvent.FAULT, onError);
```

If you want to use data binding, you must declare the `WebService` instance as bindable, as in Example 17-14.

Example 17-14. Using data binding with WebService

```
<?xml version="1.0" encoding="utf-8"?>
<mx:Application xmlns:mx="http://www.adobe.com/2006/mxml" layout="absolute"
initialize="initializeHandler(event)">

    <mx:Script>
        <![CDATA[
            import mx.rpc.soap.WebService;

            [Bindable]
            private var _statesService:WebService;

            private function initializeHandler(event:Event):void {
                _statesService = new WebService();
                _statesService.wsdl =
"http://www.rightactionscript.com/states/webservice/StatesService.php?wsdl";
                _statesService.loadWSDL();
                _statesService.getCountries.send();
            }

            private function changeHandler(event:Event):void {
                _statesService.getStates.send(country.value);
            }

        ]]>
    </mx:Script>

    <mx:VBox>
        <mx:ComboBox id="country"
dataProvider="{_statesService.getCountries.lastResult}" change="changeHandler(event)"
 />
        <mx:ComboBox dataProvider="{_statesService.getStates.lastResult}" />
    </mx:VBox>

</mx:Application>
```

Using WebService with a remote proxy

In keeping with the previous sections, let's now look at how to use a `WebService` instance as part of a remote proxy class. Example 17-15 uses the same MXML document and data model class as Example 17-6, in "Using HTTPService with ActionScript." The only changes are to the remote proxy class shown here.

Example 17-15. StatesService.as with changes to the remote proxy class

```
package com.oreilly.programmingflex.remotedata {
    import mx.rpc.soap.WebService;
    import mx.rpc.events.ResultEvent;
    import mx.collections.ArrayCollection;
    import com.oreilly.programmingflex.remotedata.ApplicationDataModel;

    public class StatesService {

        private var _service:WebService;

        public function StatesService() {
            _service = new WebService();
            _service.wsdl = "http://www.rightactionscript.com/states/webservice/
StatesService.php?wsdl";
            _service.loadWSDL();
        }

        public function getCountries():void {
            _service.getCountries.addEventListener(ResultEvent.RESULT,
                                                   countriesResultHandler);
            _service.getCountries();
        }

        public function getStates(country:String):void {
            _service.getStates.addEventListener(ResultEvent.RESULT,
                                                statesResultHandler);
            _service.getStates(country);
        }

        private function countriesResultHandler(event:ResultEvent):void {
            _service.getCountries.removeEventListener(ResultEvent.RESULT,
                                                      countriesResultHandler);
            ApplicationDataModel.getInstance().countryNames =
_service.getCountries.lastResult;
        }

        private function statesResultHandler(event:ResultEvent):void {
            _service.getStates.removeEventListener(ResultEvent.RESULT,
                                                   statesResultHandler);
            ApplicationDataModel.getInstance().statesNames =
_service.getStates.lastResult;
        }


    }
}
```

Data Type Conversion

One of the advantages of using web services is that the result packets specify not only the return value, but also the type. For example, the result packets for the `getCountries()` and `getStates()` operations of the web service used in the preceding sections specify that the return value is an array. The result packet can specify that the return data is an integer, a floating-point number, an array, a string, a date, a Boolean value, or any number of custom data types. The Flex framework `WebService` class automatically converts the result to the appropriate ActionScript type. Table 17-1 describes common types and how they are converted to ActionScript.

Table 17-1. Common types and how they are converted to ActionScript

Data type name	SOAP type	ActionScript type
String	`xsd:string`	`String`
Integer	`xsd:int`	`Int`
Floating-point number	`xsd:float`	`Number`
Boolean	`xsd:boolean`	`Boolean`
Date	`xsd:date`	`Date`
Array	`xsd:string[]`, etc.	`mx.collections.ArrayCollection`

Not only does the `WebService` component automatically map standard SOAP types to ActionScript objects, but with a little additional work you can also map custom SOAP types to custom ActionScript types using the `mx.rpc.xml.SchemaTypeRegistry` class. The `SchemaTypeRegistry` class has a `registerClass()` method that allows you to specify a `QName` object and an ActionScript class to which to map the type. When you construct a `QName` object, you must provide two parameters: the namespace and the name of the element. The `QName` object should correspond to the SOAP type that you'd like to map. The following is an example that maps a custom SOAP type of `Account` (with a namespace of *http://www.oreilly.com/soap*) to an `Account` ActionScript class. Note that this is a fictional example, but it illustrates how `SchemaTypeRegistry` works. Also note that `SchemaTypeRegistry` uses the Singleton design pattern, and you can access the one instance using the `getInstance()` method.

```
SchemaTypeRegistry.getInstance().registerClass(new QName("http://www.oreilly.com/
soap", "Account"), Account);
```

Remoting

Remoting is a technology for HTTP-based request/response data communication. Remoting has many advantages, including the following:

- Data serialization and deserialization are handled automatically. That means when you send a `Date` object from a Flex application, it's automatically converted to the correct corresponding type on the server (and vice versa). This is also possible for custom data types.

- Remoting uses AMF, which is a binary messaging protocol, ensuring the smallest packet size of almost any option for data communication.
- AMF is a native messaging format understood by Flash Player, meaning that the data serialization and deserialization on the client are not only automatic, but also fast.
- Because a gateway receives requests on the server and delegates them to the correct services, the actual services can be standard classes on the server. This means little to no adaptation is required to utilize existing services with Remoting.

Remoting is supported natively by Flash Player, so no additional special libraries are necessary for the client-side implementation of Remoting service calls. However, on the server you'll need a gateway product capable of receiving and sending AMF packets over HTTP (port 80) or HTTPS (port 443), serializing and deserializing AMF, and delegating requests to the appropriate services.

Because this book focuses on Flex, our discussion focuses on how to implement Remoting service method calls from Flex applications rather than how to configure the server-side elements. However, the basic configuration is generally quite simple, and you can read more about the specifics based on the gateway product you select. You'll also find that most of the products provide examples to help get you started. Here's a list of popular Remoting gateway products:

- AMFPHP (PHP, *http://www.amfphp.org*)
- FluorineFx (.NET, *http://www.fluorinefx.com*)
- Cinnamon (Java, *http://www.spicefactory.org/cinnamon*)
- WebORB (.NET, Java, Ruby on Rails, *http://www.themidnightcoders.com*)
- BlazeDS (Java, *http://opensource.adobe.com/wiki/display/blazeds/BlazeDS*)
- PyAMF (Python, *http://www.pyamf.org*)
- RubyAMF (Ruby, *http://www.rubyamf.org*)
- ColdFusion (the Remoting gateway is part of a standard ColdFusion installation)

Several of the Remoting gateway products have added support for a Flex data component called `RemoteObject`. However, because we have found no practical use for `RemoteObject`, we are omitting any discussion of `RemoteObject` in this chapter.

Creating Remoting connections

All Remoting service calls are made using a native Flash Player class called `flash.net.NetConnection`. The first step is always to construct a new `NetConnection` instance.

```
var netConnection:NetConnection = new NetConnection();
```

Next, you must specify the location of the Remoting gateway. You can accomplish this by calling the `connect()` method, passing it the URL to the gateway:

```
netConnection.connect("http://www.server.com/flashremoting/gateway");
```

Calling Remoting methods

You can call Remoting methods using the `call()` method of a `NetConnection` object. The `call()` method requires, at a minimum, that you pass it two parameters: the name of the service method to call and a `flash.net.Responder` object that specifies what listeners should handle the response.

The name of the service method should include the full name of the service and the method name, delimited by dots. The name of the service is always the name by which the service is known to the gateway. Generally, this is the fully qualified class name or an alias. For example, if the service is a Java class called `com.oreilly.Example`, the service name would be `com.oreilly.Example`. If the service method is named `testMethod`, the full name of the service method (as specified in the first parameter of the `call()` method) should be `com.oreilly.Example.testMethod`.

The `Responder` class allows you to specify the listeners that handle responses from the service method call. The `Responder` constructor requires at least one parameter referencing the listener method to handle the result response. Optionally, you can specify a second parameter referencing the listener method to handle a fault response. Here's an example that calls a service method and specifies a result handler:

```
netConnection.call("com.oreilly.Example.testMethod", new Responder(resultHandler));
```

Passing parameters to Remoting methods

When a service method expects parameters you can pass those parameters via the `call()` method. Any parameters passed to the `call()` method beyond the two required parameters are passed to the service method as parameters. Here's an example that passes a string and a number to the service method:

```
netConnection.call("com.oreilly.Example.testMethod",
                   new Responder(resultHandler), "a", 1);
```

Using Remoting remote proxies

You can (and generally should) use Remoting in the context of a remote proxy class. Example 17-16 is based on the example from "Using HTTPService with Action-Script." This example uses the same MXML document and data model class, but the remote proxy class needs to be changed to use Remoting. Here's the new remote proxy class.

Example 17-16. The new proxy class

```
package com.oreilly.programmingflex.remotedata {

    import flash.net.NetConnection;
    import flash.net.Responder;
    import mx.collections.ArrayCollection;
    import com.oreilly.programmingflex.remotedata.ApplicationDataModel;

    public class StatesService {

        private var _service:NetConnection;

        public function StatesService() {
            _service = new NetConnection();
            _service.connect("http://www.rightactionscript.com/states/flashremoting/
gateway.php");
        }

        public function getCountries():void {
            _service.call("StatesService.getCountries",
                          new Responder(countriesResultHandler));
        }

        public function getStates(country:String):void {
            _service.call("StatesService.getStates",
new Responder(statesResultHandler), country);
        }

        private function countriesResultHandler(countries:Array):void {
            ApplicationDataModel.getInstance().countryNames =
new ArrayCollection(countries);
        }

        private function statesResultHandler(states:Array):void {
            ApplicationDataModel.getInstance().statesNames =
new ArrayCollection(states);
        }


    }
}
```

Real-Time/Socket Connection

Flash Player supports lower-level, persistent socket connections, allowing you to create low-latency, real-time applications. Furthermore, with the use of binary sockets you can create Flex applications that communicate directly with services not otherwise directly accessible to Flash Player. For example, binary socket connections allow for the creation of mail clients, Virtual Network Computing (VNC) clients, and more.

Essentially, three types of socket connections are available from Flex applications.

XML sockets
Socket connections that require a specific communication protocol.

Binary sockets
Raw binary sockets.

RTMP
Real Time Messaging Protocol is used not only for media (video, audio, etc.), but also for real-time data communication. RTMP is supported by Flex Data Services, Flash Media Server, and other third-party applications.

Each of these persistent socket connection options is quite specialized and nonspecific to Flex applications. Entire books can be (and have been) written about these topics. Therefore, our goal in this chapter is simply to make you aware of their existence rather than to detail their use. You can learn more about using ActionScript to communicate using socket connections in the *ActionScript 3.0 Cookbook* (O'Reilly).

File Upload/Download

Flex applications support file upload and download using the Flash Player `flash.net.FileReference` class. You can enable the user to download one file at a time, as well as select and upload one or more files at the same time.

Downloading Files

Use the `download()` method of a `FileReference` object to download a file. The `download()` method requires at least one parameter: a `URLRequest` object. The `URLRequest` object should point to the URL from which you want to download the file. Here's an example that downloads a file called *test.txt*:

```
var fileReference:FileReference = new FileReference();
fileReference.download(new URLRequest("test.txt"));
```

As soon as the `download()` method is called, Flash Player will open a dialog prompting the user to accept the file. The user has complete control over whether to save the file, where to save the file, and what to name the file. However, by default, the filename field in the dialog will be filled out with the name of the file as it exists on the server. If you want to customize the default filename in the dialog, you can do so with a second parameter in the `download()` method. This is particularly useful when the URL from which the file is requested is a script that generates the file or proxies the request to the file. For example, if the URL from which you request the file is **`test.cgi`**, a script that outputs a text file, you likely will want to use a custom filename rather than allow it to default to **`test.cgi`**. Here's an example:

```
fileReference,download(new URLRequest("test.cgi"), "test.txt");
```

The `download()` method can potentially throw errors. The two most common error types are `IllegalOperationError` and `SecurityError`. An `IllegalOperationError` occurs when a save dialog is already open (because only one can be open at a time). The SecurityError type occurs when the *.swf* is untrusted in the domain to which it is trying to make the request.

As a file downloads, you can optionally monitor progress from within the Flex application. The FileReference object downloading the file dispatches progress events as the file downloads and then a complete event once the file has downloaded.

Uploading Files

The FileReference.browse() method allows you to enable the user to browse his files and select one for upload. Optionally, you can use FileReferenceList.browse() to allow the user to select one or more files at a time.

In either case (FileReference or FileReferenceList) the browse dialog has two buttons allowing the user to close the dialog: Open and Cancel. The FileReference or FileReferenceList object dispatches different events depending on which button the user clicks. If the user clicks the Cancel button, it dispatches a cancel event (Event.CANCEL). If the user clicks the Open button, it dispatches a select event (Event.SELECT).

When the user has selected a file or files (the select event has been dispatched), you can start to upload the file or files using the upload() method. The method requires that you pass it a URLRequest object specifying the URL to which to upload the file:

```
fileReference.upload(new URLRequest("upload.php"));
```

If you're using a FileReferenceList object, you must call the upload() method of each instance stored within the fileList property:

```
var request:URLRequest = new URLRequest("upload.php");
for(var i:int = 0; i < fileReferenceList.fileList.length; i++) {
    fileReferenceList.fileList[i].upload(request);
}
```

To upload files from Flash Player, you must have a script on the server that is capable of receiving the requests. When a file upload request is made to the server-side script, it's made in exactly the same way as a standard request from an HTML form submit request with a file field: using POST with a content type of multipart/form-data. The Content-Disposition header value is Filedata by default. If you need to customize this setting, you can specify a Content-Disposition header value using the second parameter in the upload() method:

```
fileReference.upload(request, "UploadFile");
```

Because file uploading is usually not instantaneous, it can be useful to monitor the progress of the upload. As with file downloads, the FileReference object dispatches events as a file is uploading. It will dispatch progress events as each piece of the file is uploaded, and when the file has completely uploaded, it will dispatch a complete event.

Summary

In this chapter, you learned how to work with remote data communication. Remote data communication consists of HTTP requests/responses, sockets, and file upload/download. The HTTP request/response category can be further broken down into the different messaging formats, such as plain text, XML, SOAP, and AMF, each of which you learned about in this chapter.

CHAPTER 18

Application Debugging

One of the strengths of Flex is its modern debugging capabilities. Debugging client-side code in web applications has traditionally been cumbersome. The Flash Debug Player, provided with Flex, allows developers the ability to debug applications in the same way they have been accustomed to with other modern development platforms.

In this chapter, we will cover runtime errors, debugging applications using FDB, debugging applications using the Flex Builder debugger, remote debugging, and tracing and logging.

The Flash Debug Player

The Flash Debug Player is at the core of the debugging capabilities provided to Flex. The Debug Player provides several benefits specific to developers and is required for most types of debugging you will need to do. The browser plug-in and standalone editions of the Debug Player are included in the free SDK in the */runtimes/player* folder, and in the *<Path to Flex Builder 3>/Player* folder if you are using Flex Builder 3. Also, if you installed Flex Builder, the Debug Player browser plug-in is typically installed during the install process. You can always check to ensure that you have the latest edition of the Debug Player by visiting *http://www.adobe.com/support/flashplayer/downloads.html*.

If you are unsure whether you have the Debug Player installed within a browser, you can build a simple application to check the version of the player installed. Here's an example:

```
<?xml version="1.0" encoding="utf-8"?>
<mx:Application xmlns:mx="http://www.adobe.com/2006/mxml">
 <mx:Label text="Flash Player Version: {flash.system.Capabilities.version},
Debug Player: {flash.system.Capabilities.isDebugger}"/>
</mx:Application>
```

When you open the application in your browser, you should be presented with the version of Flash Player and whether it is the debug edition. `flash.system.Capabilities` is a class that Flash Player provides that allows you to retrieve information about the runtime environment in which an application is executing. In this example, we are checking the `isDebugger` property, which should return `true` if you have the Debug Player installed. You can also use this property to enable additional debugging type features of an application only when they are running within a Debug Player.

The Debug Player provides several additional capabilities on top of the traditional player, as we'll see in the next section. This functionality allows a developer access to the runtime behavior of a running application and is required for some debugging tools, including the command-line debugger and the Flex Builder debugger.

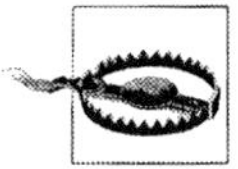

Running an application in the Debug Player, especially when it is being debugged, will impact runtime performance and can even impact application behavior. You should install the Debug Player only for debugging purposes and never in a production environment.

Runtime Errors

Flash Player 9 supports runtime type checking and exceptions capabilities that developers have become accustomed to in any modern runtime. Runtime errors when identified during the development process can help a great deal when debugging applications. Runtime errors are not presented to users with the non-Debug Player installed, but for development and testing purposes, you should have the Flash Debug Player installed (as should any team members who are involved in application testing). The Debug Player will display runtime errors by presenting you with a dialog as errors occur in your application. You may wonder why such errors are not presented to the user with the regular Flash Player. This is because Adobe silently hides such errors from regular users to minimize their impact on the application experience. The runtime errors still occur, but rather than interrupt the user with a dialog and halt the applications, Flash Player attempts to silently continue code execution. This does not guarantee that an application will always continue to run; some exceptions are fatal and will cause an application to halt. Because of this, it is not advisable to deploy any application that contains runtime exceptions that are not handled. This also does not guarantee that an application will respond as expected when a nonfatal exception occurs. In general, it is a good practice to properly handle exceptions to prevent unexpected results.

A good practice on a team is to have all testers and developers install the Flash Debug Player. Doing so will allow you to catch runtime errors earlier in your development process.

If you execute this code in the Debug Player, you will receive a runtime error:

```
<?xml version="1.0" encoding="utf-8"?>
<mx:Application xmlns:mx="http://www.adobe.com/2006/mxml" initialize=
"initializeHandler()">
    <mx:Script>
```

```
        <![CDATA[
            private function initializeHandler():void
            {
                var loader:Loader = new Loader();
                loader.load(new URLRequest("foo"));
            }
        ]]>
    </mx:Script>
</mx:Application>
```

The runtime error you'll receive is `IOErrorEvent`, as the example doesn't handle such an exception. Figure 18-1 shows the dialog that results when running Debug Player.

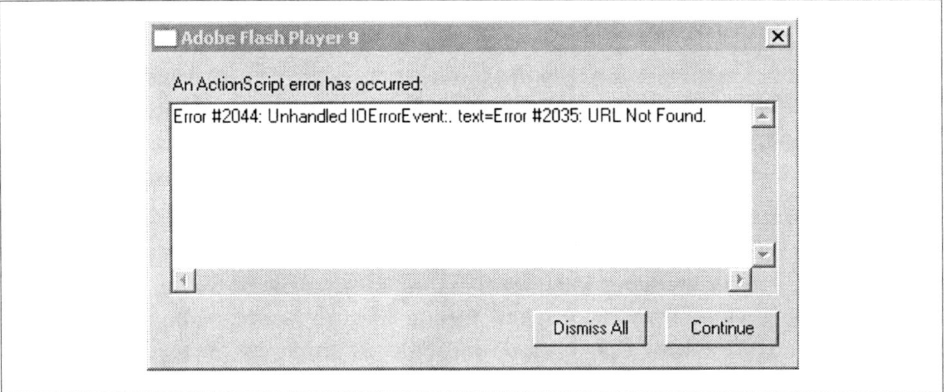

Figure 18-1. Flash Debug Player error dialog

You can find a list of runtime error codes, along with descriptions, in the Flex Language Reference documentation, under Appendixes→Run-Time Errors.

The Debugging API

Although runtime errors are useful, often you will require more than just runtime errors to identify bugs. For such cases, the Flash Debug Player exposes an API for debuggers to interact with an application at runtime. This includes the ability to set breakpoints, step through code, set and retrieve variables at runtime, as well as other debugging-related tasks. Adobe provides two debuggers. One is the free FDB command-line debugger provided by the Flex SDK, and the other is the integrated GUI debugger that is part of Flex Builder. The debuggers communicate with the Flash Debug Player through a TCP socket connection. Typically, this happens on the same machine, but it is possible to also do remote debugging whereby one machine is the client and the other is running the debugger.

To allow the Debug Player to initiate a debug session, the application must be compiled with the debug data included within the SWF.

To do this, you need to set the `-debug` `mxmlc` compiler flag to `true`.

```
mxmlc -debug=true main.mxml
```

This flag generates a debug-enabled SWF. Although you may not experience any side effects from using a debug-enabled SWF for production, this is strongly discouraged because the `-debug` compiler flag produces larger SWF files and exposes the internals of an application. If a user has the Debug Player installed, he could inspect the internals of your application and even change client-side variable values. Later in this chapter, we will discuss how to use debug-enabled SWF files using various debuggers available today.

Using Show Redraw Regions

Even with modern hardware, you can run into rendering performance bottlenecks with graphics-intensive applications. Isolating such bottlenecks can be challenging, especially considering all the variables involved in how Flash Player renders content. For this reason, the Debug Player exposes an option called Show Redraw Regions.

When this option is enabled, the player will highlight areas of a running application that are being redrawn, which can help you in identifying graphical regions of an application that may be drawing inefficiently. You enable this option by selecting the Show Redraw Regions option from the Debug Player's context menu or through ActionScript. To enable this option through ActionScript you can call the `showRedrawRegions()` method of the `flash.profiler` package. This method works only with the Debug Player and doesn't require a debug-enabled SWF. Here's a simple example that will allow you to experiment with how this feature works:

```
<?xml version="1.0" encoding="utf-8"?>
<mx:Application xmlns:mx="http://www.adobe.com/2006/mxml"
initialize="flash.profiler.showRedrawRegions(true)">
    <mx:HSlider width="100%"/>
</mx:Application>
```

Compile and run this example in the Debug Player. Drag the slider to see how the Debug Player highlights what areas are being redrawn. This is especially helpful with Flex applications because the Flex framework provides a lot of functionality that you don't need to implement and often may not even know how it is implemented. Using the Show Redraw Regions feature can help you identify rendering bottlenecks in Flash Player.

By default, the `showRedrawRegions()` method will highlight regions by drawing a blue rectangle outline around the regions being redrawn and the player context menu will use a red outline. However, sometimes you might find the default color difficult to identify. If so, you can specify your own color values by passing in a color value for the second parameter of the `showRedrawRegions()` method.

Using FDB

As part of the Flex SDK, Adobe includes FDB, a free command-line debugger. This debugger is fully featured, although usually you will opt to use the Flex Builder debugger if available. With that said, it is great to have access to a free debugging tool included as part of the SDK. This allows developers who do not want to purchase Flex Builder access to a fully featured debugger. We won't be covering FDB in depth, but we will discuss the basics and some of the possible benefits it has to offer.

You launch FDB from the command line as you would any other command-line application. Once it is started, you will be prompted with the FDB prompt (`fdb`). You can type **`help`** at the prompt for a list of available commands.

The starting point for a debug session with FDB is to launch an *.swf* compiled with debugging enabled in the Debug Player and establish a connection with FDB. You do this by first executing the `run` command at the FDB prompt. Once the command is executed, FDB will confirm that it is waiting for the player to connect. To connect Flash Player to FDB, open a debug-enabled *.swf* with the Debug Player. When a debug-enabled *.swf* is opened, the player will attempt to auto-connect to the local debugger, if available. If you open an application without the debugger listening for a connection from the player, the Flash Debug Player will prompt you to select the debugger you want to use. Although typically a user will be running the application and the debugger on the same machine, which means you may never receive the prompt requesting you to select the debugger, it is possible to initiate a *remote debugging* session. Remote debugging allows you to execute an application on a machine that is separate from the debugger, allowing you to debug problems that are reproducible on only certain machines, or even debug across platforms wherein a Mac OS X machine executes an application with the debugger running on a Windows machine. For this purpose, all debugging communication occurs through TCP on port 7935. We cover remote debugging later in this chapter.

Once a connection is established, you can set breakpoints or instruct the debugger to continue execution of the application. To continue execution you can issue the `continue` command. Application trace messages are shown in the debugger as they are encountered.

Breakpoints can be set using several methods. The most typical method of setting a breakpoint is to specify the class and line number for the breakpoint, which you can achieve by issuing the `break` command. For example, if you wanted to insert a breakpoint in line 56 of the class `MainApp`, you would input the command `break MainApp.mxml:56`. If you want a breakpoint when a button is pressed but you are not sure of the method that will be called when the event occurs, you could enter **`break button`**. This will return a list of methods that begin with the word *button*. From the list, you should see `buttonPressed` and the location of the method. With that information, you could set the breakpoint by calling `break buttonPressed`. Once you do that, you will need to call the command `continue`, which will tell the debugger to allow the player to continue executing the application. There are other methods of setting breakpoints with FDB, which you can find by issuing the command `help breakpoint`.

When an application is executing, the debugger will inform you when it encounters a breakpoint. Once a breakpoint is encountered, you have several options. You can issue the `continue` command, which will continue execution of the application, step through the application using the `step` command, and set the value of a variable using the `set` command. When done debugging, you can exit FDB to end the debugging session, which will automatically end the active connection with the Debug Player, or you can execute the `kill` command.

As discussed, FDB makes it easy to search for methods on which you want to set breakpoints. Some of the other nice features of FDB that Flex Builder's debugger doesn't support are the ability to set conditional breakpoints using the `condition` command, and the ability to review a list of all the loaded types and functions with the `info functions` command.

FDB can be a powerful tool and is worth exploring, but as you will see in the next section, Flex Builder provides a more practical method of application debugging, which you will likely opt for over FDB.

Debugging with Flex Builder

One of the best selling points of Flex Builder is the integrated GUI debugger. FDB is free, but for day-to-day debugging, Flex Builder's debugger makes it much easier to debug applications.

A default Flex Builder installation (see Figure 18-2) will configure the tasks needed to get you up and running for debugging applications. To debug an application you are working on, you just need to select Run→Debug from the main menu (or press F11). This will compile the application if it is not already compiled, launch it within the browser, and connect the application to the debugger. The first time you debug an application you will be prompted to switch perspectives to the debugging perspective in Flex Builder, which usually is recommended.

When in the debugging perspective, you will have access to the currently running application. Often you will set a breakpoint to stop the application at a point during the execution process in which you are interested. You can set breakpoints by double-clicking the left margin of a source line or by using the keyboard shortcut Ctrl-Shift-B. You can do this during a debug session or even before a session is started in the development perspective. You can navigate through a list of breakpoints by using the Breakpoints panel (see Figure 18-3). The Breakpoints panel contains a list of all breakpoints currently set and lets you navigate directly to a breakpoint or disable a breakpoint. This panel can also be very useful if you aren't sure what breakpoints you have set in your application as it allows you to view all breakpoints and manage them from one central location.

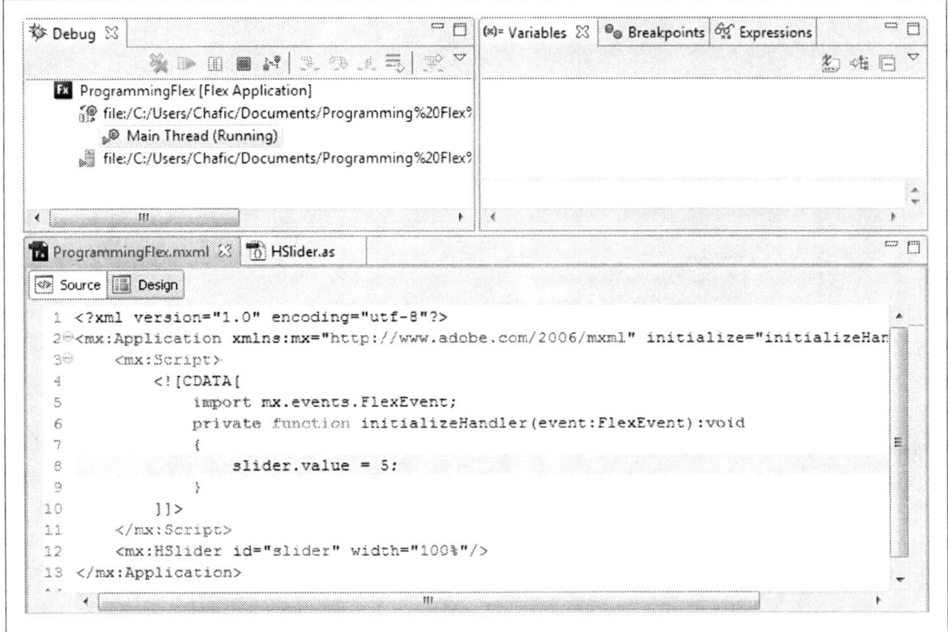

Figure 18-2. Default debugging perspective

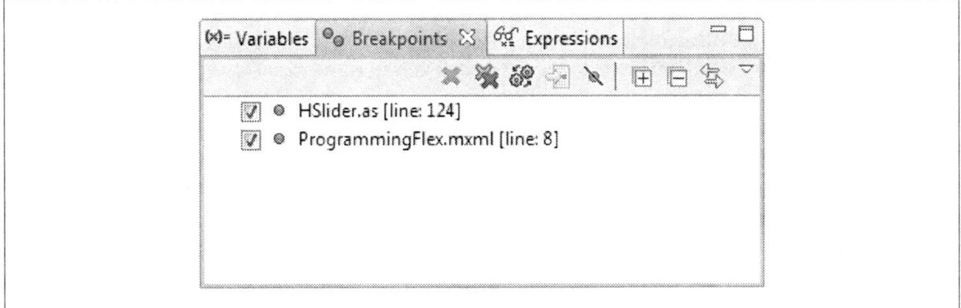

Figure 18-3. The Breakpoints panel

When Flash Player encounters a breakpoint, as in Figure 18-4, execution will halt, the debugger will gain focus, and the call stack will be displayed. You then will have the option of having the application continue execution, step through code, set variables, or evaluate expressions.

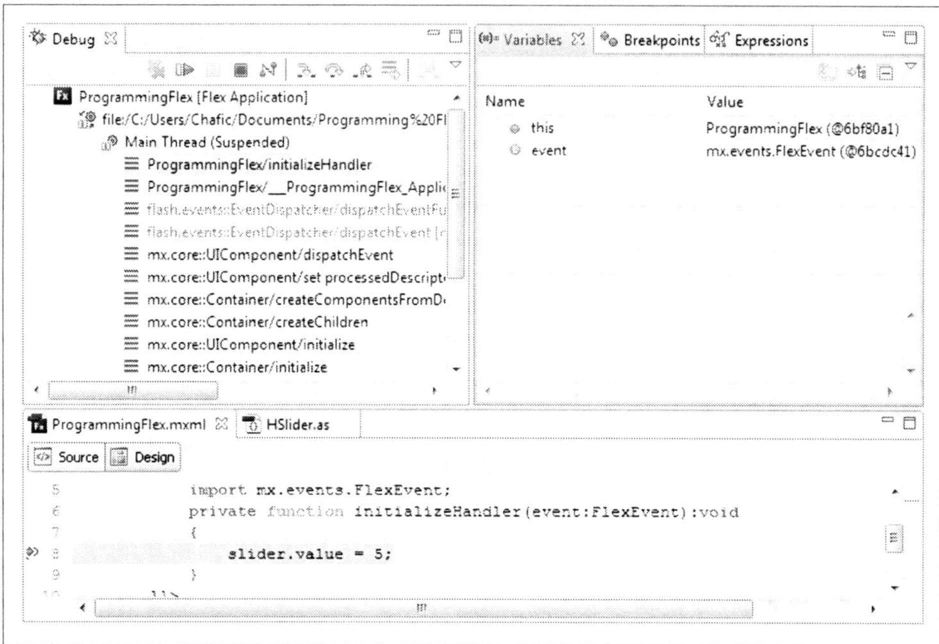

Figure 18-4. Debugging view when a breakpoint is reached

Breakpoints can be set on both ActionScript and MXML code. Breakpoints on MXML code are valid only when ActionScript event handlers exist. In cases where you set a breakpoint on an invalid MXML line, Flex Builder will attempt to find the nearest valid breakpoint. It does so by scanning the next 10 lines of execution for points where a breakpoint would be valid, and automatically moving the breakpoint to that location.

To help speed up the debugging process, Flex Builder offers the following default keyboard shortcuts for stepping through code:

- Stepping into (F5)
- Stepping over (F6)
- Step return (F7)
- Resume execution (F8)

While stepping through code, the debugger will have control over the player. At times, this may cause the player and browser to seem unresponsive. This is normal as you step through code. To suspend the debugger from having control until the next breakpoint, you have to tell the debugger to resume execution by clicking on the Play button or by using the F8 keyboard shortcut.

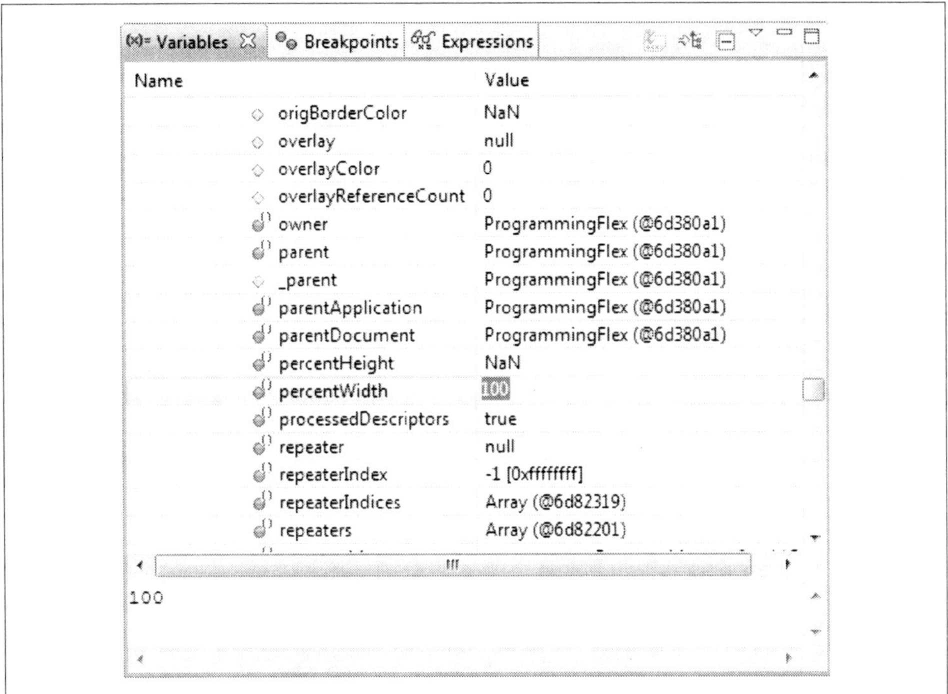

Figure 18-5. Changing a value in the Variables panel

While debugging, you also have the ability to review values of variables. The Variables panel (see Figure 18-5) will list all object instances as well as their child properties and values. You can also review the values of variables right within the code editor by hovering above a variable within the code. This will display a tool tip with the current value of the variable. To change a value, click the Value column for the field that you wish to change, as shown in Figure 18-6, or right-click the property you wish to change and select Change Value.

Changing variables will often result in other variables changing as well. To give you insight into the changes that occur as a result of changing a variable, the Variables panel will highlight in yellow the affected variables in the panel.

When debugging an application, you also have the ability to set breakpoints in and step through Flex framework code. Stepping through Flex framework code will happen automatically when encountered. To set breakpoints within the framework, you will need to open the class file. An easy way to do this is to use the shortcut Ctrl-Shift-T within Flex Builder and select the appropriate type. Once the class file is opened, you can set breakpoints as you would normally.

To end a debug session you can either close Flash Player or your browser, or click the red square within the Debug panel. Caution should be taken when closing an active debug session by closing the browser when it is executing within a browser, as sessions that are in a halted state can cause a web browser to close unexpectedly.

This book does not fully cover all the functionality possible with the debugger within Flex Builder. For full coverage, you can review the documentation provided with Flex Builder.

Remote Debugging

When attempting to isolate a bug in an application, it is possible that you will encounter a case where a bug is reproducible on only a specific machine. For such a case, you can use the Flash Debug Player's remote debugging feature. This feature can also be useful if you would want to use the Flex Builder debugger on a Windows or Mac-based machine while the application is executed under Linux, which does not have a native version of Flex Builder available.

As mentioned earlier, debugging occurs over a TCP connection on port 7935. Such a connection is typically established on the same machine transparently, but with remote debugging it is established from one machine to another. One machine will typically be running the debugger and can be referred to as the *server*, while the other will be running the application and can be referred to as the *client machine*. Once a connection is established between the client and the server, all of the features of using a debugger function in the same manner. It's important to remember that in a typical workstation, the client machine may not be configured properly for remote debugging. Remember that the Flash Debug Player is required for a debug session, so you will need to ensure that it is installed on the client machine. It is also important to keep in mind that the client machine will need to be executing a debug-enabled SWF in the same manner as we discussed earlier in the chapter.

To initiate a debug session, follow these steps:

1. Initialize the debugger on the server machine.
    a. With FDB: one benefit of using FDB when initializing a remote debugging session is that the steps for initializing FDB are exactly the same as those for initializing a local session. You initialize FDB by launching FDB and executing the `run` command.
    b. With Flex Builder's Debugger: initializing a remote debugging session with Flex Builder is more involved. Flex Builder's debugger doesn't formally support remote debugging, although it is possible. We will cover remote debugging with Flex Builder in the next section.
2. Initialize the debug-enabled SWF on the client machine and ensure that the Debug Player is installed.

3. Once initialized, the player will prompt you for a debugger, because the debugger is not running on the client machine. Input the IP address of the server running the debugger and select Connect.
4. If the server is running the debugger and listening for a connection, the client and server will connect. Note here that you will also need to ensure that the server is not blocking port 7935.

Once a connection has been established, debugging can be performed in the manner discussed earlier in this chapter.

Establishing a Remote Debugging Session with the Flex Builder Debugger

As mentioned earlier, debugging sessions—both local and remote—are established over a TCP connection on port 7935. Flex Builder uses the same connection to establish debug sessions. Although by default Flex Builder does not expose remote debugging capabilities, it still is possible to do so.

To initiate a remote debug session with Flex Builder, follow these steps:

1. Compiled a debug-enabled *.swf*.
2. Copy the debug-enabled *.swf* to the remote client machine.
3. On the machine that will run the Flex Builder debugger (server), create an empty HTML file (typically within your project's *bin-debug* folder). Since no content exists in an empty file, the Flex Builder debugger will launch a session that is empty and just wait for a remote connection.
4. Ensure that no firewall is actively blocking port 7935 on the client machine.
5. Edit the debug configuration within Flex Builder (select Run→Run).
6. Select the target debug configuration.
7. Uncheck the "Use defaults" checkbox.
8. Click the Browse button for the debug file path.
9. Select the blank HTML page created in step 3.
10. Click Debug in Flex Builder. You should see "Launching {application name}" and a progress bar in the bottom status bar of Flex Builder (at this point, Flex Builder is waiting for a remote connection, in the same manner FDB does).
11. Open the debug-enabled *.swf* on the remote machine and, when prompted for a remote host address, input the host address of the machine with the Flex Builder debugger.

Logging Using trace() Within an Application

Although not an advanced debugging technique, at one time or another a developer will find a need to trace (also referred to as *log*) messages from within an application.

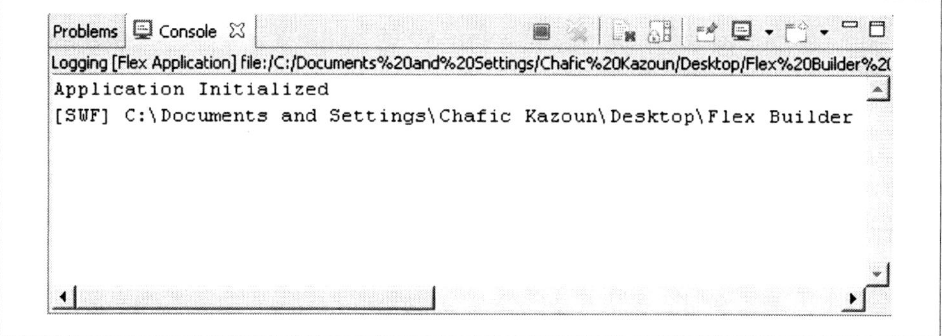

Figure 18-6. Flex Builder Debugger Console panel

For this purpose, Flash Player exposes a global `trace()` method. You can log messages from anywhere within an application simply by calling the `trace()` method and passing any parameter of type `string`:

```
trace("application initialized");
```

Trace messages are typically displayed by attaching the debugger to an application. With an active FDB debug session, trace messages will be displayed in the console. With Flex Builder, launching a debug session will automatically do this and trace messages will be shown in the Console panel in the debugging perspective (see Figure 18-6).

One of the great benefits of using the trace statement in this manner is the ability to receive the messages in real time while an application is running. The `trace()` method also supports passing in arrays or multiple arguments (rest-style arguments). This can be very useful in dumping data for informational purposes—for example, if you wanted to be able to easily track what children are currently in the Display Child list.

Example 18-1 contains two children. When you click the `buttonOne` button, the `clickHandler()` function is called and an array of children is displayed in the output window.

Example 18-1. Calling the clickHandler() function

```
<?xml version="1.0" encoding="utf-8"?>
<mx:Application xmlns:mx="http://www.adobe.com/2006/mxml">
    <mx:Script>
        <![CDATA[

            private function clickHandler():void
            {
                trace("Childrent: "+this.getChildren());
            }

        ]]>
    </mx:Script>
    <mx:Button id="buttonOne" click="clickHandler()" label="Dump Data"/>
    <mx:Label id="labelTwo"/>
</mx:Application>
```

As with other debugging methods we have seen thus far, using the `trace()` function requires the Flash Debug Player. Although often you will just use the Flex Builder Debugger to output trace messages, with the debug version of the player you have the option of outputting the trace messages to a file. You may want to use this feature if you are having a hard time isolating user-reported bugs by having the user configure his machine to log all trace calls to a file and allow you to review the logfiles at a later time for clues on what sequence of events may have caused the bug. This also is useful for when a tester isolates a bug in an application and provides corresponding log information.

By default, installing the Debug Player does not enable trace logging. You will need to configure the player to enable logging. The configuration filename is *mm.cfg*. Under Windows XP it is located at *C:\Documents and Settings\<user_name>*, on Windows Vista it is located at *c:\users\<user_name>*, on Linux it is located at */home/<user_name>*, and under Mac OS X it is located at */Library/Application Support/Macromedia/*. For other operating systems and a full list, consult the Flash Player documentation.

As of this writing, the Flash Player documentation relating to debugger configuration was available at *http://livedocs.adobe.com/flex/3/html/help.html?content=logging_04.html*. The paths to both *mm.cfg* and *flashlog.txt* can change with different versions of Flash Player. It is advisable that you review the latest documentation on where such files are located according to the player version you are using if you are having difficulty making the examples in this section work.

First review your operating-system-specific path for an existing *mm.cfg*. If none already exists, you will need to create one in the location appropriate for your operating system. The configuration file is a plain-text file that supports several options. Most important, you will be interested in the `ErrorReportingEnable`, `MaxWarnings`, and `TraceOutputFileEnable` configuration properties.

A basic *mm.cfg* file that enables the trace output includes the following:

```
TraceOutputFileEnable=1
```

Once the configuration file is updated and saved to the proper location with the filename *mm.cfg*, the Flash Debug Player will log trace messages to *flashlog.txt* in the folder specific to your operating system. Under Windows XP, it will be located at *C:\Documents and Settings<\username>\Application Data\Macromedia\Flash Player\Logs*, under Windows Vista it is at *C:\Users\<username>\AppData\Roaming\Macromedia\Flash Player\Logs*, under Mac OS X it is at */Users/<username>/Library/Preferences/Macromedia/Flash Player/Logs/*, and under Linux it is at */home/<username>/.macromedia/Flash_Player/Logs/*.

Along with enabling trace logging, the Debug Flash Player can also log all runtime errors to the same logfile. You can enable error reporting using `ErrorReportingEnable`:

```
TraceOutputFileEnable=1
ErrorReportingEnable=1
```

The Logging Framework

The `trace()` statement can be a powerful method of logging, but if you have been exposed to logging in the past, you likely used some sort of logging framework or built your own. Flex includes a logging framework that offers several benefits over using the `trace()` statement alone.

The logging framework consists of two main components: the logger and the target. The logger is used by an application to configure the logging framework and to send messages that are output via a target.

A target is used to specify where log messages are output. They can be output to any mechanism that Flash Player supports. The logging framework includes a `TraceTarget`, which inherits from `LineFormattedTarget` and `AbstractTarget` and implements the `ILoggingTarget` interface.

`TraceTarget` internally sends messages via the global `trace()` function. This will often be the target you use. Here's an example using the logging framework with `TraceTarget`:

```
<?xml version="1.0" encoding="utf-8"?>
<mx:Application xmlns:mx="http://www.adobe.com/2006/mxml"
initialize="initializeHandler()">
        <mx:Script>
        <![CDATA[
            import mx.logging.Log;
            import mx.logging.targets.TraceTarget;

            private var _target:TraceTarget;

            private function initializeHandler():void
            {
                _target = new TraceTarget();
                _target.includeTime = true;
                _target.includeLevel = true;
                _target.includeCategory = true;
                Log.addTarget(_target);
            }

            private function sendToLog():void
            {
                Log.getLogger("com.oreilly.programmingflex.MainClass").info("Log
Message");
            }
        ]]>
    </mx:Script>
```

```
    <mx:Button click="sendToLog()" label="Log Message"/>
</mx:Application>
```

In this example, clicking on a button will send a message in the same manner as calling `trace()` would. The main distinction to just using `trace()` is the ability to configure the target to include extra information, define a category for a message, and have different levels of errors.

> The Flex framework internally uses the logging framework within the `mx.rpc.*` package with the `WebService`, `RemoteObject`, and `HTTPService` components. This allows you to retrieve details of the communication between the Flex client and the server. We will cover debugging remote data communication later in this chapter.

A target can support extra functionality. In the preceding example, the date, category, and level were enabled. This will instruct the target to include the time, category of message, and level with the messages. The built-in targets support other properties that you may want to explore.

Specifying the Logging Options

A log message must define two values: the level of the message, which we discussed, and the category. The category is required to define the origins of a message and, in return, allow you to filter what is displayed by the logging framework. In the preceding example, the category was `com.oreilly.programmingflex.MainClass`. It is a good idea to specify a category based on the package and class, as this will allow you to easily filter and identify the origins of logged messages.

The built-in targets support the ability to filter the messages so that only messages you are interested in are displayed. This is useful in cases where you're interested only in log messages that are within a certain package, and it's achieved via the `filters` property of the target. The `filters` property accepts an array of categories. A category filter can be any text value, but it is recommended that you follow package-naming conventions. You may also specify an * (wildcard) filter—for example, the following category filter of `com.oreilly.*` will instruct the target to output all messages in the `com.oreilly` package and within its subpackages:

```
_target.filters = ["com.oreilly.*"];
```

You also can define multiple filters as well as redefine the filters at any time. Setting the level is achieved in a similar manner.

The default logging level is `ALL`, but you can define another level by setting the `level` property:

```
_target.level = LogEventLevel.FATAL;
```

The logger supports sending several levels of messages with the debug(), info(), warn(), error(), and fatal() methods. Alternatively, you can call the log() method of the logger and pass in a log level. You can find the different levels with the constant values LogEventLevel.FATAL, LogEventLevel.ERROR, LogEventLevel.WARN, LogEventLevel.INFO, and LogEventLevel.DEBUG. This can be useful if you want to output all messages during development and debugging, but limit what is output in a production environment. When you set a log level, all messages in that level and above are logged. For example, setting the level to WARN will log all messages with that level as well as messages with a FATAL or ERROR level.

Defining a Custom Target

If the built-in targets are not sufficient, you can define your own. To define your own target you need to implement the ILoggingTarget interface. For convenience, the logging framework includes the AbstractTarget class, which already implements a default set of behaviors that you can easily subclass to define your own target. Example 18-2 is a custom target that will send a message to a remote server via the Socket class rather than via trace().

Example 18-2. Custom target sending a message to a remote server via the Socket class

```
package com.oreilly.programmingflex.logging.targets
{
    import flash.net.Socket;
    import mx.logging.LogEvent;
    import mx.logging.AbstractTarget;

    public class SocketTarget extends AbstractTarget
    {
        private var _host:String;
        private var _port:int;
        private var _socket:Socket;

        public function SocketTarget(host:String = "localhost",port:int = 18080)
        {
            _host = host;
            _port = port;
            //This example omits the error handling. For production you will
            //need to handle errors when creating the socket and when sending
            //messages
            _socket = new Socket(host,port);
            super();
        }

        override public function logEvent(event:LogEvent):void
        {
            _socket.writeUTF(event.message);
            _socket.flush();
        }
    }
}
```

Example 18-3 is updated to use the new SocketTarget.

Example 18-3. Example 18-2 updated to use the new SocketTarget

```
<?xml version="1.0" encoding="utf-8"?>
<mx:Application xmlns:mx="http://www.adobe.com/2006/mxml"
initialize="initializeHandler()">
    <mx:Script>
        <![CDATA[
            import com.oreilly.programmingflex.logging.targets.SocketTarget;
            import mx.logging.Log;

            private var _target:SocketTarget;

            private function initializeHandler():void
            {
                _target = new SocketTarget();
                Log.addTarget(_target);
            }

            private function sendToLog():void
            {
                Log.getLogger("com.oreilly.programmingflex.MainClass").info("Log
Message");
            }
        ]]>
    </mx:Script>
    <mx:Button click="sendToLog()" label="Log Message"/>
</mx:Application>
```

With Flex's built-in logging framework, you will be able to log messages, easily change options so that you can more easily debug an application, and integrate the framework within your application.

Debugging Remote Data

Although you can use the debugger to inspect data after Flex has received it and before Flex sends it, you may want to find out more details regarding what data is being sent and received. You can achieve this by using the logging framework or a data inspector.

Debugging with the Flex Logging Framework

The WebService, HTTPService, and RemoteObject components use the Flex logging framework, which can greatly assist debugging applications. Messages are automatically logged to the Flex logging framework, so you won't need to enable the components to explicitly begin logging. Messages that are logged are within the mx.messaging.* filter. Example 18-4 is an HTTPService call with a TraceTarget that will show only log messages related to the server calls.

Example 18-4. HTTPService call with a TraceTarget that shows log messages related to server calls

```
<?xml version="1.0" encoding="utf-8"?>
<mx:Application xmlns:mx="http://www.adobe.com/2006/mxml"
initialize="initializeHandler()">
        <mx:Script>
        <![CDATA[
            import mx.logging.Log;
            import mx.logging.targets.TraceTarget;

            private var _target:TraceTarget;

            private function initializeHandler():void
            {
                _target = new TraceTarget();
                _target.includeTime = true;
                _target.includeLevel = true;
                _target.includeCategory = true;
                _target.filters = ["mx.messaging.*"];
                Log.addTarget(_target);
            }

            private function sendToLog():void
            {
                Log.getLogger("com.oreilly.programmingflex.Logging").
info("Log Message");
            }
        ]]>
    </mx:Script>
    <mx:Button click="sendToLog()" label="Log Message"/>
    <mx:Button click="service.send();" label="Send HTTPService"/>
    <mx:HTTPService id="service" url="http://www.w3c.org"/>
</mx:Application>
```

This example will log messages from the HTTPService but not from the button click handler, which can be very useful when you are working with a larger application and you are interested in viewing only the log information from the mx.rpc components. The server component logs useful information on both the data that is being sent and received, as well as the information that can be used for profiling messaging performance. For the WebService component, this can be especially useful in gauging Flex's performance in terms of serializing and deserializing SOAP messages.

Debugging Using a Data Inspector

When debugging network programming code, using a data inspector (packet sniffing tools or a proxy) is invaluable. With Flex, these tools can also be very useful. Adobe does not provide such a built-in tool, but many tools exist that work with Flex. If you are already comfortable with a tool, you can continue to use that tool.

Some common network debugging tools include the following:

Charles
: This cross-platform proxy tool for debugging RPC communication also supports AMF3 (*http://www.charlesproxy.com/*).

ServiceCapture
: This cross-platform proxy tool for debugging RPC communication supports AMF3 as well (*http://kevinlangdon.com/serviceCapture*).

Wireshark (similar to Ethereal)
: This is a feature-complete packet sniffer that is capable of inspecting all traffic for both real-time applications as well as RPC (*http://www.wireshark.org*).

Fiddler
: This is a quick HTTP proxy debugger that is free. It supports RPC debugging, but does not support AMF3 (*http://www.fiddlertool.com*).

Summary

In many ways, a development platform is only as good as the debugging capabilities available to the developer. In this chapter, we covered many of the methods you can use to debug Flex applications.

CHAPTER 19

Building Custom Components

At some point, you may want to build advanced components. For instance, you may want to create a truly custom component or a commercial-grade distributed component, or you may just want a much deeper understanding of and level of control over the underlying framework. Although Flex allows you to build components rapidly, as we saw in Chapter 9, developing advanced components requires a deeper understanding of the component framework and methodology.

In this chapter, you will learn about the component framework life cycle and will develop an understanding of what it has to offer. You will do so through theory as well as by developing a custom component. You will also learn about ways to implement functionality within the component framework.

Component Framework Overview

Understanding what the component framework implements, as well as how and where it does so, is key to building good components. Flex contains a sophisticated framework that aims to abstract many of the underlying details of Flash Player and add many features not supported natively by Flash Player. A majority of the framework is built to support a rich set of features for the UI components that the Flex components use. This framework allows components to share a common set of APIs, and it allows components to function in a predictable manner based on the needs of the Flex framework. Using this framework will allow you to develop your own custom components that also behave and operate in a consistent manner with other Flex components.

As with developing components for any platform, it is important to do some initial planning. This book doesn't cover the theories and methodologies of designing components, but it is important to note that when developing custom components, it is highly recommended that you define requirements and the public interface and that you plan things more carefully before writing any code. This is not as important with application components (discussed in Chapter 9), but it is critical when developing custom components that others will consume. Also keep in mind that when developing custom components, there is always a chance that a user may extend your component.

The Flex component framework contains many classes, most of which we won't be covering in detail here. Instead, we will focus on the most important classes for developing custom components: the `UIComponent` and `Container` classes. Figure 19-1 shows those classes and their inheritance chain.

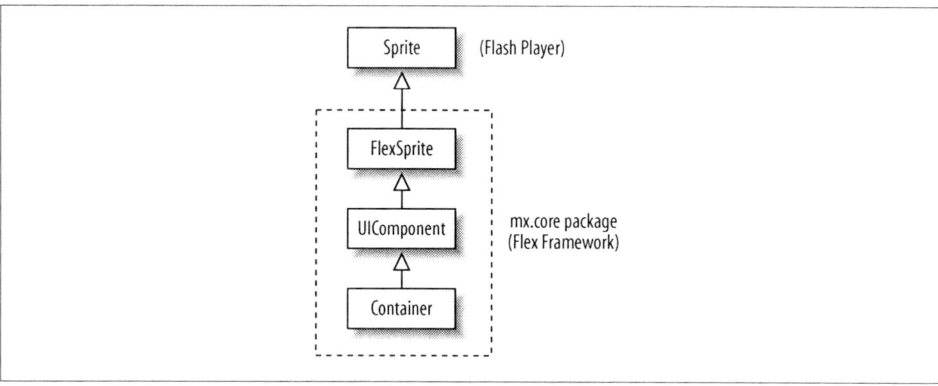

Figure 19-1. Component framework classes

All interface components in Flex inherit from `UIComponent`, which itself inherits from many classes, including `Sprite`. When developing a custom component, you will have to decide which of the following two classes to use: the `UIComponent` class or the `Container` class. Generally speaking, you will use the `UIComponent` class unless you are developing your own container (e.g., if you need scrolling and clipping support built in). The `UIComponent` class is essentially an abstract class that implements the core functionality the Flex framework requires from components. It also implements most of the common sets of behaviors, leaving you to implement the parts that are pertinent to your component.

You could also use an existing component as the base class. In such a case, you would be extending the existing component rather than developing a completely custom component. We will not cover the specifics of how to extend components in this chapter, but many of the lessons you will learn in this chapter apply to extending components as well.

`UIComponent` has several requirements that you will need to understand; we will cover those requirements later in the chapter. For now, it's important to note that `UIComponent` implements what your component needs in order to participate in the Flex framework and behave appropriately. It also provides you with a predefined component life cycle, as well as event handling, sizing, skinning, styling, invalidation, and rendering techniques.

Component Life Cycle

The life cycle that the component framework provides is an important aspect of the Flex framework. By understanding the component life cycle, you will be able to build better components more quickly.

Most of the Flex framework—and the built-in component in particular—is based on the same component life cycle discussed in this chapter. As such, not only is it helpful to learn the component life cycle for building custom components, but it is also helpful for understanding the Flex framework as a whole for building applications.

The component life cycle comprises three phases: initialization, update, and destruction. The initialization phase consists of three main steps: construction, attachment, and initialization (the latter is not to be confused with the initialization phase of which it is a part). The initialization step is composed of its own steps. For instance, during the initialization step, the component dispatches the `preinitialize` event, calls the `createChildren()` method, dispatches the `initialize` event, goes through a full invalidation and validation, and finally dispatches the `creationComplete` event. At this point, the component has completed the initialization step. Figure 19-2 outlines the initialization phase and its steps.

The update phase comprises everything that occurs between the initialization and destruction phases, and it is the phase during which the component responds to changes. The update phase begins right after the initialization phase and goes through a repeated set of steps to keep the component updated. Typically in the update phase, the component is initially in the waiting step, during which it awaits a request to change. If a component is initialized and never changes, it will stay in the waiting step. If the component receives a request to change—for example, if it receives a request to set a new

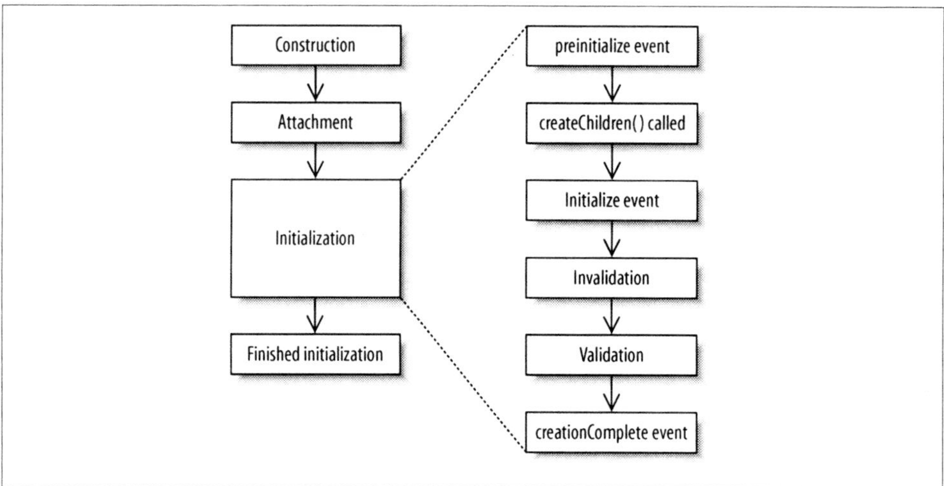

Figure 19-2. Component life cycle during the initialization phase

value for `Button.label`—it goes through an invalidation step, then through validation, and finally back to the waiting step.

Flash Player renders on a frame-by-frame basis. Because of this, it is important to merge the rendering updates together rather than process them immediately.

The invalidation and validation steps in the update phase are the same steps as those in the initialize phase. Also important to note is that a component can go through an update phase many times throughout its lifetime. If many updates to a component are requested at different times, the component will go through the same cycle each time and return to the waiting step. That is why, for performance considerations, you will need to ensure that the validation step is optimized to handle many calls, and you will need to reduce the processing required to satisfy this step. Figure 19-3 outlines the update phase and the repeated cycle of validation. In the next section, you will learn more about the details of each step in the life cycle of a component.

Construction

In this step of the life cycle, the component is instantiated, the constructor is called, and the component begins its life cycle. The component is instantiated either by being declared in MXML or through the `new` operator in ActionScript. The component constructor typically does not contain any implementation other than calling `super()`, and sometimes it adds event listeners to application events that your component needs to be aware of. Typically you will want to do very little during this step because it is early

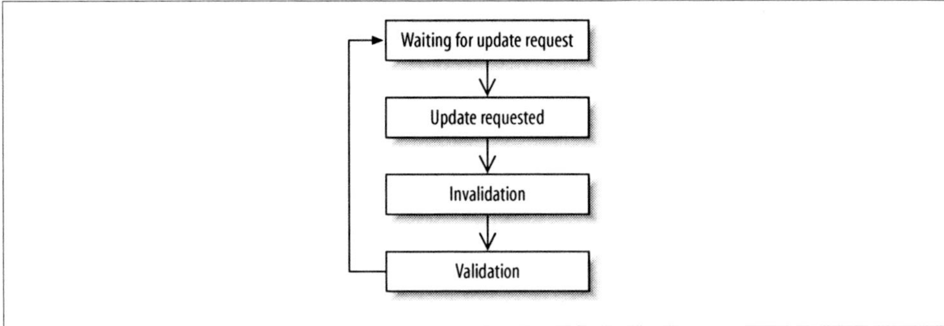

Figure 19-3. The steps during the update phase

in the component's life, and most parts of the component are not ready yet. Instead, you will perform the other functions in other methods, as we will see later.

Configuration

During this step, which occurs only during the initialization phase, component properties are set internally to be processed later in the component's life cycle. The values are set using the setter functions of the defined component. We will cover how to handle setter functions within components later in this chapter.

Attachment

When a component is instantiated, it does not automatically complete the entire initialization phase until it's added to the display list, and it has a parent. Once a component is attached using `addChild` or `addChildAt`, or is declared via MXML (which internally calls `addChild` automatically), this step of the cycle begins and the internal `initialize()` function of the component is called.

Initialization

This step occurs after attachment. In this step, the `preinitialize` event is dispatched, the `createChildren()` method is called, the `initialize` event is dispatched, invalidation and validation occur, and finally the `creationComplete` event is fired. After this step, the component has finished the initialization phase and will enter the update phase.

Invalidation

This step occurs both the first time a component is initialized and during the update phase. Invalidation is a key concept in the component framework. Invalidation is a mechanism by which changes made to a component are queued and processed simultaneously. Flash Player internally renders on a frame-by-frame basis. Therefore, there is no benefit to immediately updating values that will affect the rendered view of a component. With invalidation, all changes are noted within the component, and the component is marked for validation. In the validation step, the values that were noted are actually rendered. This occurs when the next frame is reached in Flash Player.

When a component is first initialized, it is automatically marked for full validation. But after a component is initialized, it is marked for validation during the update phase by calling the `invalidateProperties()`, `invalidateSize()`, or `invalidateDisplayList()` method. Later in this chapter, we will examine the role these methods play and how to implement proper invalidation.

Validation

When a component is being initialized, the last step before the `creationComplete` event is dispatched is the validation step. This step also occurs when a component is invalidated using one of the invalidate methods. The validation phase is where the `commitProperties()`, `measure()`, or `updateDisplayList()` method of the component is called. During initialization all three methods are called. We will cover how to implement the validation methods properly later in this chapter.

Destruction

The destruction phase (also sometimes referred to as the detachment phase) occurs when a component is removed from the display list. At this point, the component no longer participates in the layout events, and if it is no longer referenced anywhere, it will be garbage-collected and removed from memory.

Component Implementation

Now that you have a good understanding of the component life cycle, we will discuss how to implement a component.

Throughout this chapter, you will develop a custom instant messenger status icon component (`StatusIcon`) that uses many of the features of the component framework. Figure 19-4 shows the finished component.

Figure 19-4. Finished StatusIcon component

`StatusIcon` allows the user to set a name, status (available, busy, idle), and font color. It also should automatically resize to display the entire name and let the user data-bind to the value of the username, dispatch an event when the status is changed, and set icons for the different statuses.

Implementing the Constructor

The first step in building a component is to decide on the base class and constructor. For this component, we will use `UIComponent`. The `UIComponent` class gives us a basic implementation for writing a custom component and allows us to build on top of it as we please. Here are the beginnings of the component:

```
package com.oreilly.programmingflex.controls
{
    import mx.core.UIComponent;

    public class StatusIcon extends UIComponent
    {
        public function StatusIcon()
        {
            super();
        }
    }
}
```

In this chapter, you'll develope custom components using ActionScript. Although it's possible to build the same components in MXML, you will find that for custom components, you'll often opt to use ActionScript.

In this example, we have created the component's main class, `StatusIcon`, which contains the basic implementation for the constructor. The constructor calls `super()` and nothing else. Also important to note is the fact that the constructor in a component should not have any required parameters because when used in MXML, there would be no way to pass such parameters to the constructor.

Although at this point the component doesn't perform any useful function, it already has inherited many capabilities from the component framework, including the component life cycle. For every custom component, the constructor will be the starting point on which to build. The constructor is also the first thing to be called when a component is instantiated. Because of this, many things may not be ready for you to work with. For this reason, it is advisable that you do very little within the constructor and instead save most of the implementation for other steps in the component's life cycle.

In addition to the constructor, every component overrides some or all four of the following methods: `createChildren()`, `commitProperties()`, `measure()`, and `updateDisplayList()`, which well cover shortly. These methods are called in that order during initialization, as shown in Figure 19-5.

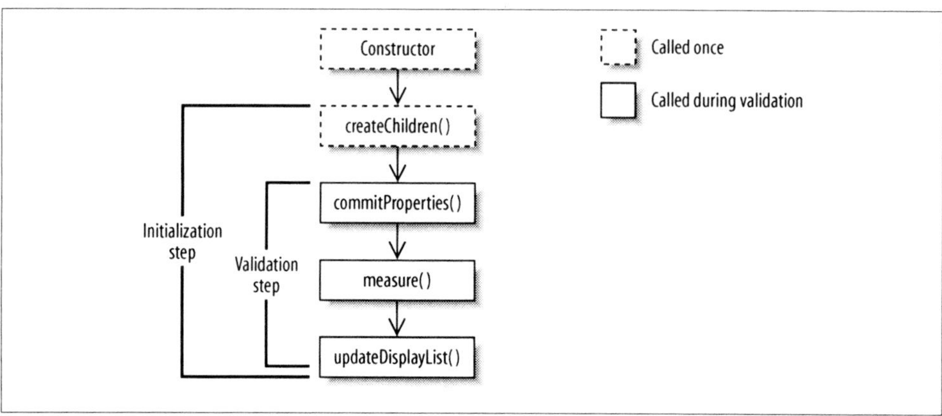

Figure 19-5. UIComponent required methods, and their order

The initialization step includes the call to the constructor as well as the `createChildren()`, `commitProperties()`, `measure()`, and `updateDisplayList()` methods. Within the initialization step, a validation step occurs. This validation step includes where the calls to the `commitProperties()`, `measure()`, and `updateDisplayList()` methods occur. This same validation step is used in the update phase as well, which occurs several times during the life of a component. The only difference between the validation step in the initialization and the update is that in the initialization step, all the methods are called. In the update phase, the methods that get called depend on many factors, which we will cover throughout different parts of this chapter.

Implementing createChildren()

The `createChildren()` method is called during the initialization phase. Its purpose is to attach subobjects to your component at the beginning of the life of the component. Unlike containers and components in Flex, in which a child needs to be a `UIComponent` (or needs to implement the `IUIComponent` interface), children of a custom component can be any type of Flash Player display object.

As you can see in Figure 19-5, `createChildren()` is called only once throughout a component's life cycle. Because this method is typically called only once, it is ideal for adding children that are required through the life of a component, as instantiating new objects is one of the most intensive operations in Flash Player. The `createChildren()` method doesn't have many rules. First you should call `super.createChildren()`. Then all you have to do is decide what children you would like to create early in the life of the component; typically these would include the children that will be needed throughout the life of the component, or at least at the beginning of the component's life. Then you simply set their initial states, checking to ensure that the children have not been instantiated already (in cases where your component has been subclassed). Our `StatusIcon` component has two child objects: the status icon and the user's label. In the `createChildren()` method, we will need to add both children to the display list because they are required at all times. To implement the `createChildren()` method, you override the `UIComponent` base class implementation. Here is the code to implement the `createChildren()` method:

```
[Embed(source="/images/available.gif")]
private var IconAvailable:Class;
[Embed(source="/images/busy.gif")]
private var IconBusy:Class;
[Embed(source="/images/idle.gif")]
private var IconIdle:Class;

private var currentIcon:DisplayObject;
private var displayNameLabel:Label;

override protected function createChildren():void
{
    super.createChildren();

    if(currentIcon == null)
    {
        currentIcon = new IconAvailable();
    }
    addChild(currentIcon);

    if(displayNameLabel == null)
    {
        displayNameLabel = new Label();
    }
    addChild(displayNameLabel);
}
```

In the `createChildren()` body, you call `super.createChildren()`, then instantiate both children and add them to the display list using `addChild()` while ensuring that the children have not already been instantiated. Notice that for the icon we referenced the `IconAvailable` bitmap class, and for the display name we used an existing Flex component, the `Label` component.

Understanding Invalidation

In addition to the initialization phase, during which a component automatically goes through a full validation, a component also goes through validation via update requests. An update request can occur when a user interacts with a component and triggers an event, when methods and properties are set, and when the application or parent it is a part of can interact with a component. To handle such interaction efficiently, the Flex component framework implements an invalidation routine.

Invalidation routines can handle several constraints and assumptions for you. For example, invalidation routines assume that when a component needs to be redrawn, only parts of it may need to be redrawn, not the entire component. Because of this, the component framework divides the view update routines into three types: those that update subobject properties, those that update component sizing, and those that update drawing.

To understand this better, let's take the example of a component that is a child of another component. At some point within the component's lifetime, its parent may ask to resize it. When that occurs, the component may not have to change any values or do any redrawing; instead, it may require only that a component measure its size. For this purpose, a specific invalidation method, `invalidateSize()`, and a corresponding validation method, `measure()`, are available. Figure 19-6 shows the invalidation methods and their corresponding validation methods.

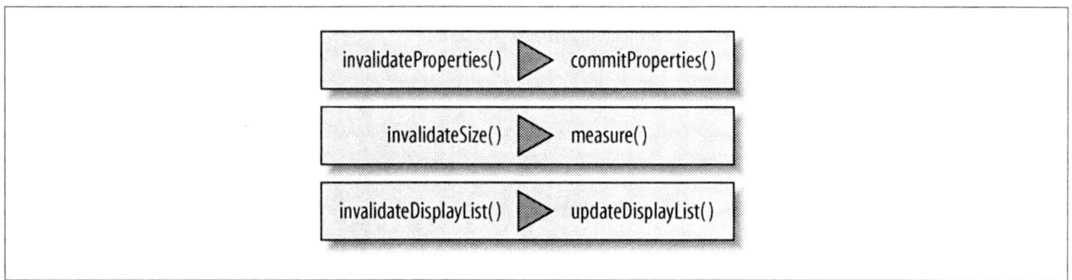

Figure 19-6. Invalidation methods and their corresponding validation methods

You may be wondering why you need an invalidation method if you can call the validation method directly. The reason concerns another key aspect of invalidation, and it relates to Flash Player behavior.

Flash Player renders on a frame-by-frame basis. Thus, if a value is changed in the middle of a frame several times, although the value is set several times, only the last value set is rendered to the user in the next frame. For this reason, it is a waste to call a validation more than once per frame. Thus, the invalidation routines (also sometimes referred to as marking the component as *dirty*) have the job of merging changes needed together into a single frame that the component renders in the next frame during validation (the validation step). With this process, an invalidation method may be called several times during a single frame, and the corresponding validation method will be called only once in the next frame.

For this process to work properly, you will need to cache data changes and allow the validation methods to make the actual change. For component properties, you should follow the pattern of defining a private variable for every public property that will hold the new value until the validation methods are called. For the `StatusIcon` component, a property label is used to set the username by updating the values of the `_displayNameLabel.text` property. Rather than setting the `_displayNameLabel.text` property directly, however, we will store the new value in a private property, `_label`.

Another reason to have setter functions store values in a temporary property is that setter functions could be called before children are instantiated. If you attempt to set the value of the child immediately before the child is instantiated, this could cause an error.

Here are the label setter and getter functions for `StatusComponent`:

```
private var _label:String;

public function set label(value:String):void
{
    _label = value;
    invalidateProperties();
    invalidateSize();
}
```

In the label setter function, we set the `private _label` property with the new value and then call the invalidation methods `invalidateProperties()` and `invalidateSize()`. Although we haven't looked at how to implement the validation methods, it's easy to understand that when the label value is changed, the value of the internal label component needs to change as well. Thus, when you call the `invalidateProperties()` method, the size of the component may change because of the new values of the label, so you call the `invalidateSize()` method. Although it may not be clear when to call which invalidation method, after reviewing how to implement the three invalidation methods, keeping in mind Figure 19-6 and what invalidation methods cause a call to what validation method, and gaining some experience, you will have a clear understanding when building your own component.

Implementing commitProperties()

The validation method that corresponds to calling the `invalidateProperties()` invalidation method, and the first validation method to be called during initialization, is `commitProperties()`. This method's purpose is to commit any values typically set by using a setter function. Often the `commitProperties()` method is as simple as calling `super.commitProperties()` and setting the cached values:

```
override protected function commitProperties():void
{
    super.commitProperties();
    displayNameLabel.text = _label;
}
```

If your component contains many public properties, you may find that your `commitProperties()` method becomes inefficient as it attempts to set values for every value even though only a single value was changed. To work around this, it is recommended that you not only store the new value of the set data in a temporary property, but also track what has changed. You do so by declaring a Boolean property (also referred to as a *dirty flag*) for each public property that serves as a flag for the `commit`

Properties() method to help it know how to conditionally set values. Here are the updated setter and the commitProperties() method which adds this optimization:

```
private var _label:String;
private var labelChanged:Boolean = false;

public function set label(value:String):void
{
    _label = value;
    labelChanged = true;
    invalidateProperties();
    invalidateSize();
}
```

And here is the updated implementation of commitProperties():

```
override protected function commitProperties():void
{
    super.commitProperties();
    if(labelChanged)
    {
        //reset to false as the value is being commited
        labelChanged = false;
        displayNameLabel.text = _label;
    }
}
```

Sometimes when a component value is changed, it may require that new children be created or that existing children be removed. In addition to updating the values of existing children, the commitProperties() method also serves to add and remove children. Keep in mind that if a child is going to be required through the entire life of a component, it should be instantiated and added to the display list in the createChildren() method. In the StatusIcon component, this isn't required, but if, for example, you wanted to display a label only if it contained a value, and that use case was the norm, you would add logic to handle such a case in the commitProperties() method.

Implementing measure()

When the invalidateSize() invalidation method is called, the corresponding validation method, measure(), will be called, and as with other validation methods, measure() is always called during the initialization phase of a component as well. The purpose of this method is to perform measurement calculation and define sizing information for the framework. Flex provides a sophisticated set of layout containers whose underlying implementation requires that each component perform appropriate size measurements. Specifically, the framework requires that a component specify the optimal size of the component and, optionally, the minimum size. In Chapter 6, we covered how to use containers to lay out components. With containers and components, you can specify the width and height of components explicitly, by percentage, or not at all, and the framework will automatically do its best to decide on the sizing for you. This is why the `measure()` method exists. If your component is used, and its size is not defined or is defined using constraint-based layout logic, your component will need to tell the layout containers what it would like its size to be (the default size). Also, when the layout logic is attempting to size a component, it will need to tell its container how small the component can be sized. Because of this, the `measure()` method also has a mechanism for defining the minimum size of the component.

Both the default and minimum sizes of the component are set to a width and height of zero. You may find that having a minimum width and height of zero is acceptable, but typically you will at least want to define the default width and height yourself. Defining the default and minimum values in the `measure()` method requires that you set the values of the `measuredWidth`, `measuredHeight`, and optionally, `measuredMinWidth` and `measuredMinHeight` properties:

`measuredWidth`, `measuredHeight`
: These are the component's default width and height. You should set these values to the width and height that your component requires.

`measuredMinWidth`, `measuredMinHeight`
: These are the component's minimum width and height. You will often set their values to the same as the measured value.

Here is the `measure()` method implemented for the `StatusIcon` component:

```
override protected function measure():void
{
    super.measure();
    measuredHeight = measuredMinHeight = currentIcon.height;
    measuredWidth = measuredMinWidth = currentIcon.width + displayNameLabel.
getExplicitOrMeasuredWidth();
}
```

In this `measure()` implementation, we override the existing implementation and call `super.measure()`. This is typically how most `measure()` implementations will begin. We also set `measuredHeight`, `measuredMinHeight`, `measuredWidth`, and `measuredMinWidth`. `measuredHeight` and `measuredMinHeight` are set to the height of the icon image, and `measuredWidth` and `measuredMinWidth` are set to the total width of the children within the component (icon and label).

When performing measurement in order to decide on sizing, you will often need to retrieve the size of the children along with any chrome/padding that needs to be taken into account. As a general rule, you will typically use the children's `width` and `height` properties to retrieve the size values of children that do not inherit from `UIComponent`. For children that do inherit from `UIComponent`, you will want to use the `getExplicitOrMeasuredWidth()` and `getExplicitOrMeasuredHeight()` methods.

Implementing updateDisplayList()

The last validation method is `updateDisplayList()`. This validation method is called as a result of calling the `invalidateDisplayList()` invalidation method, and by the Flex framework internally (typically the `LayoutManager` class). The purpose of this validation method is to lay out the contents of the component and perform any needed drawing and redrawing. Typically this method contains a lot of the implementation of a component.

In `StatusComponent`, we will implement the basic `updateDisplayList()` method. The method will position the `displayNameLabel` and then set its size:

```
override protected function updateDisplayList(unscaledWidth:Number,
unscaledHeight:Number):void
{
    super.updateDisplayList(unscaledWidth,unscaledHeight);
    displayNameLabel.move(currentIcon.x + currentIcon.width,0);
    displayNameLabel.setActualSize(unscaledWidth-currentIcon.width,
unscaledHeight);
}
```

The `updateDisplayList()` method is implemented by overriding the existing implementation. Notice that this method receives two arguments: `unscaledWidth` and `unscaledHeight`. You begin by calling `super.updateDisplayList()`, passing in the two arguments. Then typically you will perform any drawing API rendering before measuring and positioning children.

The `updateDisplayList()` method can get very long, especially when you need to handle many children and styles. For this reason, you may want to break up parts of the method into smaller functions.

In the `measure()` validation method we retrieved the size, and in the `updateDisplayList()` method we will set the size and position the children. When positioning and sizing children, if a child does not inherit from `UIComponent`, you'll want to use the `x` and `y` properties for positioning and the `width` and `height` properties for sizing. If a child does inherit from `UIComponent`, you should use the `setActualSize(width,height)` method for sizing and the `move(x,y)` method for positioning.

Adding Custom Properties and Events

When creating components, you will often want to declare some sort of public API. It is typically advisable that you create properties rather than methods with components. Doing so will allow component properties to be set more naturally within MXML as attributes, because methods are not declaratively called within MXML.

You create a public property in a custom component by creating a getter/setter. For the `StatusIcon` component, one feature you might want to have is the ability to set the status of the component. The status could be a public property that you can set and whose value you could retrieve. Also, the property should be bindable. To create the property you first declare the getter/setter function and make it bindable via `[Bindable]` metadata:

```
public static const STATUS_AVAILABLE:String = "available";
public static const STATUS_BUSY:String = "busy";
public static const STATUS_IDLE:String = "idle";

private var _status:String;
private var statusChanged:Boolean = false;

[Bindable]
public function set status(value:String):void
{
    _status = value;
    statusChanged = true;
    invalidateProperties();
}

public function get status():String
{
    return _status;
}
```

Next, you will need to update the `commitProperties()` method to support the new property. You first declare public constant values for the different values that the setter supports. Although ActionScript 3 does not support enumerations, declaring public properties for valid values is a good practice when a setter can accept only a limited set of values. Then you should check for a change in the `statusChanged` value. If the value evaluates to `true`, you handle the new status as follows:

```
override protected function commitProperties():void
{
    //code omitted for brevity

    if(statusChanged)
    {
        statusChanged = false;
        removeChild(currentIcon);

        switch (_status)
        {
            case STATUS_AVAILABLE:
                currentIcon = new IconAvailable();
                break;
            case STATUS_BUSY:
                currentIcon = new IconBusy();
                break;
            case STATUS_IDLE:
                currentIcon = new IconIdle();
```

```
                break;
            }
            addChild(currentIcon);
        }
    }
```

With the property added and set to `bindable`, users can manipulate the value and data-bind to the new property easily.

One other common need may be to dispatch an event whenever the status is changed. You can dispatch events within components using the same techniques we discussed throughout this book. Remember that `UIComponent` inherits from `EventDispatcher`, which implements the event system.

A custom event class is not always required. If you are dispatching an event that already exists within the Flex framework or another component, you may opt to reuse the existing event object rather than create your own.

To create an event, you first should create a custom event class:

```
package com.oreilly.programmingflex.events
{
    import flash.events.Event;

    public class StatusChangeEvent extends Event
    {
        public static const STATUS_CHANGE:String = "statusChange";
        public var status:String;

        public function StatusChangeEvent(status:String,bubbles:Boolean = false,
cancelable:Boolean = false)
        {
            super(STATUS_CHANGE,bubbles,cancelable);
            this.status = status;
        }

        public override function clone():Event
        {
            return new StatusChangeEvent(status, bubbles, cancelable );
        }
    }
}
```

Next, you can dispatch the new event for when the status value is set. Here is the updated status setter function:

```
[Bindable(event="statusChanged")]
public function set status(value:String):void
{
    _status = value;
    statusChanged = true;
    invalidateProperties();
```

```
        dispatchEvent(new StatusChangeEvent(value))
    }
```

When developing custom components, it is a good practice to create events that you think your users may find useful. This helps to promote good application design principles and helps to decouple a component from an application.

Adding Styling Support

One of the key features of Flex that Flash Player does not inherently support is styles. As we discussed earlier in the book, styles in Flex are a robust mechanism for defining component styles on an instance, class, or global basis, within MXML, ActionScript, and CSS. Styling support is built into the Flex framework and is exposed to custom components that inherit from `UIComponent`. Because of this, the complexity for integrating styling support for our components is greatly reduced.

To add support for styles, you need to add a style metadata tag and override the `styleChanged()` method. After you do that, you can use the `getStyle()` utility method from within your component to retrieve the value of the style. In this section, we will build the code to add a `horizontalGap` style that will control the space between the icon and the label in our instant messenger status icon component.

First, you need to define the style metadata tag by preceding the class declaration, specifying the style's name and type, and usually disable inheritance:

```
[Style(name="horizontalGap",type="int", inheriting="false")]
public class StatusIcon extends UIComponent
{
```

Next, you need to implement the `styleChanged()` method:

```
override public  function styleChanged(styleProp:String):void
{
    super.styleChanged(styleProp);
    if(styleProp == "horizontalGap")
    {
        invalidateSize();
        invalidateDisplayList();
    }
}
```

In `styleChanged()`, we first call `super.styleChanged()`, passing it the `styleProp` value. Then we check for the changed value. Because `styleChanged()` is called whenever a style is changed, you need to check what style has changed and handle each type of style change separately. If you do not conditionally check for this you will likely run into performance issues, as the framework calls `styleChanged()` at different times throughout the application life cycle.

In the implementation of `styleChanged()`, after you check for the properly styled property, you call the invalidate methods. Although you could handle the required style changes with styleChanged(), typically it is best to call the proper invalidation methods and have the component redraw what it needs to. In this case, the component needs to recalculate its size and perform the drawing and layout functions.

With basic implementation of styling added to the StatusIcon, now we can update the rest of the component to support the new style. The simplest way to retrieve the style value from within our validation methods is to call the getStyle() function. The getStyle() function retrieves the value of a particular style. For example, it will automatically handle instance- versus class-based style values for you. However, if getStyle() cannot find a value for a style you request, it will return undefined. You should make sure that you handle such cases by providing a default value of your own if none exists. A common way to do this is to define a private getter function for the style. In our example, the getter should be called horizontalGapDefault. Here is the getter function that attempts to retrieve a valid value from getStyle(). If it does not find a valid value, it will return a default value of 5.

```
private function get horizontalGapDefault():int
{
    var horizontalGap:Number = getStyle("horizontalGap");
    return  (horizontalGap == undefined ? 5 : horizontalGap);
}
```

Now that we have a convenient method of retrieving the style, let's update the validation methods to support the new style:

```
override protected function measure():void
{
    super.measure();
    measuredHeight = measuredMinHeight = currentIcon.height;
    measuredWidth = measuredMinWidth = currentIcon.width+horizontalGapDefault
+displayNameLabel.getExplicitOrMeasuredWidth
();
}

override protected function updateDisplayList(unscaledWidth:Number,
unscaledHeight:Number):void
{
    super.updateDisplayList(unscaledWidth,unscaledHeight);
    displayNameLabel.move(currentIcon.x + currentIcon.width +
horizontalGapDefault,0);
    displayNameLabel.setActualSize(unscaledWidth-currentIcon.width -
horizontalGapDefault,unscaledHeight);
}
```

When child components exist that contain their own styles, you will often want to allow the child styles to be set as well. For example, it would be convenient if our status icon component supported styling of the label component's font type and font size. There are two methods you can use to achieve this. You can have the label component inherit the same style values from its parent, or you can define a custom style that only that child will use.

To allow children to inherit directly from their parents, you only need to add a metadata tag, like so:

```
[Style(name="fontSize", type="Number", format="Length", inherit="yes")]
```

This method is very useful when a component does not contain many types of children. In the status icon component, this method works well because only one component uses the `fontSize` value. If there were many children, you might run into a situation where you want some children to have different styles than others. For such a case, you can define a custom style for a child. For our status icon component, the name of the style would be `labelFontSize`. The naming convention is to prefix the style with the component type. To add support for this style, you will first need to define the style metadata tags in the same way you did the other methods:

```
[Style(name="labelFontSize", type="Number", format="Length", inherit="no")]
```

Next, you need to manually handle this new style and set the style of the child. Here is the updated code:

```
private var labelFontSizeChanged:Boolean = false;

override protected function commitProperties():void
{
        //code omitted for brevity

        if(labelFontSizeChanged)
        {
            displayNameLabel.setStyle("fontSize",labelFontSizeDefault);
            labelFontSizeChanged = false;
        }
    }
}

private function get labelFontSizeDefault():Number
{
    return (getStyle("labelFontSize") == undefined ? 12 :
getStyle("labelFontSize"));
}

override public  function styleChanged(styleProp:String):void
{
    super.styleChanged(styleProp);
    if(styleProp == "horizontalGap")
    {
        invalidateSize();
        invalidateDisplayList();
    }

    if(styleProp=="labelFontSize")
    {
        labelFontSizeChanged = true;
        invalidateProperties();
    }
}
```

Summary

The Flex framework greatly simplifies the task of developing custom components. In this chapter, you learned the basics of custom components—the component life cycle, validation mechanisms, adding styles, and adding events. Although these are some of the key topics when it comes to developing components, developing custom components is a vast subject that takes time to master. You can learn more about this subject in the "Custom Component Development" topic in the Flex documentation.

CHAPTER 20

Embedding Flex Applications in a Web Browser

Although it is possible to build Flex applications to deploy on the desktop (see Chapter 22), the vast majority of Flex applications today are deployed on the Web. To deploy a Flex application on the Web you should embed it in an HTML page. Although this may seem like a fantastically simple task (and it can be), it has larger implications. In this chapter, we'll look at these implications and the options available to you for embedding a Flex application in HTML and how a Flex application can interact with the web browser environment.

Embedding a Flex Application in HTML

By now, you should be aware that Flex applications get compiled to *.swf* files. When you deploy a Flex application to the Web, you must place the *.swf* file for the Flex application on the web server. At a minimum, this one file is always required. However, in almost all cases you will need to provide at least one additional file: an HTML file that embeds the *.swf*. Although it is possible for users to access an *.swf* file directly in a web browser, such an approach is inadvisable. Keep in mind that when users access a Flex application in a browser, you will still want the browser to display basic information such as a title, information that only an HTML page can provide. Furthermore, by using an HTML page, it is possible to do much more with a Flex application than if the user was accessing the application's *.swf* file directly in the browser. For example, using an HTML page you can utilize JavaScript. And by embedding a Flex application in HTML, you can place the application alongside other non-Flex content. Not only that, but by using JavaScript and HTML, you can detect whether the user even has Flash Player installed. Therefore, embedding Flex applications in HTML is a fundamental skill for creating Flex applications. In the next few sections, we will look at various ways in which you can embed Flex content in HTML pages.

Any technology that writes HTML to a browser can be used interchangeably with HTML files, as we describe in this chapter. For example, you can use the same principles described in this chapter with PHP, .NET, and Ruby to embed a Flex application.

Using HTML Tags to Embed Flex Content

Flex applications are *.swf* files that must be run by an ActiveX control or a browser plug-in. Therefore, you embed Flex applications in HTML pages in much the same way that you can embed other types of applications or media that requires an ActiveX control or a browser plug-in.

Flash Player runs as an ActiveX control in Internet Explorer and as a plug-in for Firefox and other browsers.

Two tags allow you to embed content in an HTML page: `object` and `embed`. There is much debate among developers as to which is better and how they should and shouldn't be used. For instance, the `embed` tag is supported in all modern browsers, and that might sound like a good enough reason to use it exclusively. However, there are drawbacks to using the `embed` tag. For one, the `embed` tag is not standards-compliant; it is not the W3C-recommended way in which to embed content. This is because the `embed` tag is proprietary and is covered by patents. Furthermore, there is the issue of alternative content. Although some popular search engines (notably Google) are capable to some degree of indexing Flash and Flex content, it is still customary (and recommended) that you provide alternative content whenever you have a Flex application. This allows you to create content that will be visible not only to users who do not have Flash Player, but also to search engines, allowing you greater control over how search engines index the site. The `embed` tag simply doesn't allow this to happen. Although the `embed` tag does allow alternative content using a `noembed` tag, only users using a browser that doesn't support the `embed` tag can view the alternative content, and this doesn't include search engines. For these reasons, we recommend that you use only the `object` tag, which is the W3C recommendation. Also, the `object` tag allows you to specify alternative content that is indexable.

Although there is one W3C recommendation for how to embed such content using an `object` tag, as we'll see not all browsers are designed to work according to the same specification. One of the strengths of Flex is that it shields application developers from the majority of browser inconsistencies. However, the only time you'll have to deal with these issues is when you embed the Flex application in an HTML page.

All browsers are consistent in that when you use the `object` tag, you must specify `width` and `height` attributes, indicating the dimensions (in pixels) of the content to embed in the page. However, beyond that they differ on two important points:

- How the `object` tag determines which control or plug-in to use
- How the `object` tag determines which *.swf* to load into the control or plug-in

Microsoft Internet Explorer determines the control to use by way of an attribute called `classid`. The `classid` value for Flash Player is a long value that you are unlikely to memorize. Instead, you'll simply want to copy and paste it from one document to another. Therefore, an `object` tag that will embed a Flash Player control in a page for Internet Explorer (at 400 by 400 pixels) looks like the following:

```
<object classid="clsid:d27cdb6e-ae6d-11cf-96b8-444553540000"
        width="400" height="400">
</object>
```

The `classid` value is case-insensitive.

Internet Explorer relies on a nested `param` tag with a name of `movie` to specify the *.swf* that should be loaded into the control. The following example will load an *.swf* file called *example.swf*:

```
<object classid="clsid:d27cdb6e-ae6d-11cf-96b8-444553540000"
        width="400" height="400">
    <param name="movie" value="example.swf">
</object>
```

You can also specify a `codebase` attribute for Internet Explorer to tell the browser where it can go to download the control if it's not already installed. This is generally not advised because it interferes with alternative content and there are better ways to allow users to install Flash Player. The HTML templates that ship with the Flex SDK (and Flex Builder) use the `codebase` attribute. However, as you'll read later in this chapter, we advise against using the Flex HTML templates for this and other reasons.

Internet Explorer is alone in its answers to these questions. All other major browsers take a different approach and have standardized on specifying the plug-in to use via the MIME type as indicated by the value of a type attribute. They also have standardized on specifying the content to load into the plug-in via an attribute called `data`.

The following is an example of an `object` tag that accomplishes the same thing as the preceding example, except that it works for all browsers excluding Internet Explorer:

```
<object type="application/x-shockwave-flash" data="example.swf"
width="400" height="400" />
```

The obvious question is how can you support all browsers at the same time if different browsers require different implementations? One of the preferred answers to this question is to nest the `object` tags with the Internet Explorer version on the outside. Browsers that don't use the `classid` attribute will ignore the outer `object` tag, using only the inner tag. Internet Explorer has a bug with nested `object` tags, but to resolve this you can use Internet Explorer conditional statements to effectively hide the inner tag. The result looks like the following:

```
<object classid="clsid:d27cdb6e-ae6d-11cf-96b8-444553540000"
        width="400" height="400">
    <param name="movie" value="example.swf">
    <!--[if !IE]>-->
    <object type="application/x-shockwave-flash" data="example.swf"
width="400" height="400" />
    <!--<![endif]-->
</object>
```

You can improve this further by adding alternative content, as in the following example:

```
<object classid="clsid:d27cdb6e-ae6d-11cf-96b8-444553540000"
        width="400" height="400">
    <param name="movie" value="example.swf">
    <!--[if !IE]>-->
    <object type="application/x-shockwave-flash" data="example.swf"
width="400" height="400">
    <!--<![endif]-->
        <p>Alternative Content</p>
    <!--[if !IE]>-->
    </object>
    <!--<![endif]-->
</object>
```

Any additional parameters that you'd like to pass to the `object` tag you should place inside the nested `object` tag but outside the conditional statements, right next to the alternative content. When using the `object` tag to embed Flex content, you can specify a lot of different parameters, all of which are listed at the Adobe web site (*http://livedocs.adobe.com/flex/3/html/help.html?content=wrapper_13.html*). You'll see an example of how to use one such parameter in the next section.

The Flex HTML templates use an `object` tag for Internet Explorer and a nested `embed` tag for all other browsers. Although that approach does work, it is not ideal because the `embed` tag is a proprietary tag that is not part of the W3C recommendation for standards.

Passing Values to Flex Applications from HTML

In earlier chapters, you learned the various ways in which a Flex application loads data. For example, you learned how to use the `WebService` component to load data from web services. However, a Flex application can acquire data at runtime in yet another way: you can pass values to the Flex application from HTML. Just as web services have their uses and purposes, this technique of passing values from HTML to Flex has its uses and purposes, which are generally different from those of web services (or any other remote procedure call [RPC] techniques). Typically, you will want to pass only small amounts of data to a Flex application from HTML, and the data is typically *environment-specific*. For example, you may pass values to a Flex application telling it where the web services can be found on a specific environment (i.e., testing versus production).

One major advantage to passing data to the Flex application from HTML over other techniques is that the data is available immediately when the application starts.

This technique of passing values to a Flex application from HTML is sometimes referred to as *using flashvars* because the `object` tag parameter used to pass the values to the Flex application is called `flashvars`. Values passed to a Flex application using the `flashvars` parameter must be in URL-encoded name-value pairs delimited by equals signs and ampersands exactly as they would be in a URL query string. For example, the following code embeds a Flex *.swf* file and uses `flashvars` to pass in two variables called `variable1` and `variable2`:

```
<object classid="clsid:d27cdb6e-ae6d-11cf-96b8-444553540000"
        width="400" height="400">
    <param name="movie" value="example.swf">
    <!--[if !IE]>-->
    <object type="application/x-shockwave-flash" data="example.swf"
width="400" height="400">
    <!--<![endif]-->
        <param name="flashvars" value="variable1=a&variable2=b" />
        <p>Alternative Content</p>
    <!--[if !IE]>-->
    </object>
    <!--<![endif]-->
</object>
```

When values are passed to a Flex application via `flashvars`, they are available via ActionScript using the `parameters` property of the `Application` instance. You can access this property from anywhere in a Flex application using `Application.application.parameters`. The `parameters` property is an associative array where the keys correspond to the names of the variables passed in through `flashvars`.

For example, you could use the following code to output the values passed in via the preceding HTML example:

```
trace(Application.application.parameters.variable1);
trace(Application.application.parameters.variable2);
```

Detecting Flash Player

Flex applications require that the user has Flash Player installed if he is to use the application. Not only do Flex applications require that the user has Flash Player in general, but they specifically require that the user has Flash Player 9 or later. Therefore, it is important that you account for users who might not have Flash Player installed (according to Adobe's studies, this accounts for just around 1% of users) as well as users who might have Flash Player installed, but don't have the necessary version (i.e., they need to update their Flash Player to Version 9 or later). Additionally, for users connecting via devices that don't support Flash Player (e.g., some mobile devices), you can display alternative content.

You can detect Flash Player and/or the Flash Player version in a variety of ways, ranging from client-side JavaScript to server-side scripting to ActionScript. Adobe has a Flash Player Detection Kit (*http://www.adobe.com/products/flashplayer/download/detection_kit*) that is available as a free download (all the necessary files are also included in the Flex SDK with the HTML templates, as you'll read in "Using the Standard Templates" later in this chapter). The Flash Player Detection Kit is Adobe's current official solution to Flash Player detection, and it is worth downloading the kit just to read the documentation that is included because it provides a helpful context and a fair amount of useful information. However, plenty of criticisms have been leveled at the Flash Player Detection Kit, most of which are warranted. The key criticisms are as follows:

- The kit relies on non-standards-compliant markup code because it uses both the `object` and the `embed` tags.
- It requires that you define alternative content twice instead of once, and in two different ways.
- It is difficult to customize the code.

There is nothing necessarily wrong with using the Flash Player Detection Kit. However, for the reasons just mentioned, we do not recommend it as the best solution. Instead, we recommend using SWFObject, which we describe in "Using SWFObject" later in this chapter.

Although we don't recommend its use outright, the Flash Player Detection Kit is not without value. It contains one component that highlights an important feature of Flash Player, called Express Install. Express Install is available in Flash Player 6.0.65 and later, and it allows Flash Player to download and install the latest version of itself. That means that if a user has Flash Player 6.0.65 or later installed but she doesn't have the latest version required by your Flex application, it is possible to allow the user to download and install the latest version from within your site. The user will never have to leave the site, and once the installation is complete, the browser will restart and open to the same page the user was just on (the page with the Flex application).

Technically, Express Install is a feature of Flash Player, and it doesn't require the Flash Player Detection Kit. However, practically speaking, the detection kit provides an Express Install *.swf* file that you can use to trigger Express Install if necessary. You'd need the Flash IDE to create a custom Express Install *.swf* file, and for most purposes the version that is included in the detection kit is all you need.

The general process for using Express Install is as follows:

1. Use a detection method (client-side, server-side, or Flash-based) to detect whether the user has Flash Player installed. If the user has no version of Flash Player or a version prior to 6.0.65, direct the user to alternative content.
2. If the user has the version of Flash Player required by your Flex application, simply display the application. However, if the user has a version that is earlier than what your application requires, load the Express Install *.swf* file into Flash Player. This will automatically prompt the user to download and install the latest version of Flash Player right from within the browser.
3. Once the installation is complete, the browser will restart and will open to the page that was open prior to installation. This time the detection method will detect that the user has the necessary version of Flash Player.

In the *templates* directory of the Flex 3 SDK or in the Flash Player Detection Kit, the Express Install *.swf* is called *playerProductInstall.swf*.

Using the Standard Templates

Flex ships with a variety of standard templates that you can use. The templates are located in the *templates* directory of the SDK. These templates include the following:

- No player detection
- Client-side detection
- Express Installation
- No player detection with history
- Client-side detection with history
- Express Installation with history

All of these templates use the same JavaScript file and the same markup as the Flash Player Detection Kit, which puts the templates in the same boat with the detection kit as far as the previously mentioned criticisms are concerned. Therefore, we do not recommend using the templates, except perhaps in the early stages of application development, while testing applications locally using Flex Builder.

By default, when you run or debug an application in Flex Builder, you are using the templates.

Using SWFObject

SWFObject is a method for embedding Flash and Flex content in an HTML page. It uses JavaScript for Flash Player detection and for a variety of other features. SWFObject is the unofficial standard for embedding Flash and Flex content, and it is the method we recommend in this book. SWFObject is easy to use, and it uses standards-compliant markup and unobtrusive JavaScript. You can download SWFObject from *http://code.google.com/p/swfobject*.

The SWFObject documentation is excellent at explaining both how and why to use SWFObject, and we won't attempt to repeat too much of that here in this book. However, we'll give you a brief introduction that will provide you with enough information to get started, and you can consult the documentation for further details.

SWFObject 2.0 (the current version as of this writing) provides two ways for you to embed content: static publishing and dynamic publishing. *Static publishing* uses markup directly in the HTML, and it uses JavaScript to resolve issues that cannot be dealt with by markup (such as player detection). The biggest advantage of static publishing is that because it doesn't rely on JavaScript to embed the content, your Flex application will be available to browsers that don't support JavaScript or that have JavaScript disabled; devices that have poor JavaScript support; and automated tools. *Dynamic publishing*, on the other hand, uses JavaScript to write the Flex application to the page. The advantage to this is that it sidesteps click-to-activate issues related to the Eolas patent (note that this primarily affected Internet Explorer, and Microsoft has since reversed this change) and it allows for easier integration with scripted applications. Dynamic publishing works only if enough JavaScript support is available. Otherwise, the user will see only alternative content.

The Eolas patent is a patent awarded in 1998 to Eolas Technologies, a U.S. company. The patent ostensibly covers embedding content (such as Flash Player content) in HTML pages. Eolas sued Microsoft for infringement on the patent because Microsoft didn't license its embedding technology from Eolas.

Clearly, sometimes dynamic publishing is advantageous, and we encourage you to learn more about it by reading the SWFObject documentation. However, for most purposes static publishing is a better option, and it is the option we will look at in more detail in this chapter.

To use static publishing follow these steps:

1. Place the *swfobject.js* file in the same directory as your HTML page and *.swf* file.
2. Use the nested `object` tag markup discussed earlier in this chapter to embed the Flex application.

   Your HTML page might look like the following:

```
<!DOCTYPE html PUBLIC "-//W3C//DTD XHTML 1.0 Strict//EN"
"http://www.w3.org/TR/xhtml1/DTD/xhtml1-strict.dtd">
<html xmlns="http://www.w3.org/1999/xhtml" lang="en" xml:lang="en">
    <head>
        <title>Flex Example</title>
        <meta http-equiv="Content-Type" content="text/html; charset=iso-8859-1" />
    </head>
    <body>
        <div>
            <object classid="clsid:D27CDB6E-AE6D-11cf-96B8-444553540000"
                    width="400" height="400">
                <param name="movie" value="Example.swf" />
                <!--[if !IE]>-->
                <object type="application/x-shockwave-flash" data="Example.swf"
                        width="400" height="400">
                <!--<![endif]-->
                    <p>This site is best viewed as a Flex application, which requires
                       Flash Player 9. For users who prefer not to use Flash Player
                       we have provided a <a href='textVersion.html'>text-only
                       version of the site</a/>.</p>
                <!--[if !IE]>-->
                </object>
                <!--<![endif]-->
            </object>
        </div>
    </body>
</html>
```

3. Next, you must set an `id` attribute for the outer `object` tag:

```
<!DOCTYPE html PUBLIC "-//W3C//DTD XHTML 1.0 Strict//EN"
"http://www.w3.org/TR/xhtml1/DTD/xhtml1-strict.dtd">
<html xmlns="http://www.w3.org/1999/xhtml" lang="en" xml:lang="en">
    <head>
        <title>Flex Example</title>
        <meta http-equiv="Content-Type" content="text/html; charset=iso-8859-1" />
    </head>
    <body>
        <div>
            <object classid="clsid:D27CDB6E-AE6D-11cf-96B8-444553540000"
                    width="400" height="400" id="flexApplication">
                <param name="movie" value="Example.swf" />
                <!--[if !IE]>-->
                <object type="application/x-shockwave-flash" data="Example.swf"
                        width="400" height="400">
                <!--<![endif]-->
                    <p>This site is best viewed as a Flex application, which requires
                       Flash Player 9. For users who prefer not to use Flash Player
```

```
                we have provided a <a href='textVersion.html'>text-only
                version of the site</a/>.</p>
            <!--[if !IE]>-->
            </object>
            <!--<![endif]-->
        </object>
    </div>
  </body>
</html>
```

4. Add a `script` tag to the head of the document. The `script` tag should include the SWFObject JavaScript file, as in the following code:

```
<!DOCTYPE html PUBLIC "-//W3C//DTD XHTML 1.0 Strict//EN"
"http://www.w3.org/TR/xhtml1/DTD/xhtml1-strict.dtd">
<html xmlns="http://www.w3.org/1999/xhtml" lang="en" xml:lang="en">
  <head>
    <title>Flex Example</title>
    <meta http-equiv="Content-Type" content="text/html; charset=iso-8859-1" />
    <script type="text/javascript" src="swfobject.js"></script>
  </head>
  <body>
    <div>
        <object classid="clsid:D27CDB6E-AE6D-11cf-96B8-444553540000"
                width="400" height="400" id="flexApplication">
            <param name="movie" value="Example.swf" />
            <!--[if !IE]>-->
            <object type="application/x-shockwave-flash" data="Example.swf"
                    width="400" height="400">
            <!--<![endif]-->
              <p>This site is best viewed as a Flex application, which requires
                Flash Player 9. For users who prefer not to use Flash Player
                we have provided a <a href='textVersion.html'>text-only
                version of the site</a/>.</p>
            <!--[if !IE]>-->
            </object>
            <!--<![endif]-->
        </object>
    </div>
  </body>
</html>
```

5. Add a second `script` tag following the first, and inside this `script` tag add a line of code that calls `swfobject.registerObject()`. This method requires that you specify at least two parameters: the ID of the outer `object` tag and the minimum required Flash Player version in the form of *major.minor.release*. For example, if your application requires Flash Player 9 and it does not require any later releases, you can use the string `9.0.0`:

```
<!DOCTYPE html PUBLIC "-//W3C//DTD XHTML 1.0 Strict//EN"
"http://www.w3.org/TR/xhtml1/DTD/xhtml1-strict.dtd">
<html xmlns="http://www.w3.org/1999/xhtml" lang="en" xml:lang="en">
  <head>
    <title>Flex Example</title>
    <meta http-equiv="Content-Type" content="text/html; charset=iso-8859-1" />
```

```
        <script type="text/javascript" src="swfobject.js"></script>
        <script type="text/javascript">
            swfobject.registerObject("flexApplication", "9.0.0");
        </script>
    </head>
    <body>
        <div>
            <object classid="clsid:D27CDB6E-AE6D-11cf-96B8-444553540000"
                    width="400" height="400" id="flexApplication">
                <param name="movie" value="Example.swf" />
                <!--[if !IE]>-->
                <object type="application/x-shockwave-flash" data="Example.swf"
                        width="400" height="400">
                <!--<![endif]-->
                    <p>This site is best viewed as a Flex application, which requires
                       Flash Player 9. For users who prefer not to use Flash Player
                       we have provided a <a href='textVersion.html'>text-only
                       version of the site</a/>.</p>
                <!--[if !IE]>-->
                </object>
                <!--<![endif]-->
            </object>
        </div>
    </body>
</html>
```

6. You can also optionally use Express Install with SWFObject. If you want to use Express Install, you will need to specify a third parameter for `registerObject()`, indicating the location of the *.swf* to use. You can use *playerProductInstall.swf* from the Flex SDK, or you can use the *expressinstall.swf* file that is included with SWFObject.

Managing New Flex Application Builds

It is important to remember that when you embed Flex applications in HTML pages, web browsers will likely cache the *.swf* files. That is both advantageous and disadvantageous. The upside is that because a Flex application gets cached, users will not have to download the *.swf* file upon subsequent visits to a site. However, the downside is that when you deploy updates to the Flex application, it is possible that users will still see cached versions instead of the new version.

One of the simplest and most effective ways to deal with this caching issue is to append a variable to the name of the *.swf* file that you are embedding and increment that variable value with each new build. This simple strategy will ensure that users can use cached versions of the application until you deploy a new version, and at that point they will be forced to download the new version when they next visit the site. To add a variable to the *.swf* file reference you should add a question mark (?) and a name-value pair following the name of the *.swf* file. For example, if you normally reference a file as `example.swf`, you could instead reference the same file as `example.swf?build=1`. When you deploy a new build, you need only update the build variable such that the reference is now `example.swf?build=2`. This way, you don't have to change the name of the *.swf* file (simplifying build scripts and versioning), but you still can address the caching issue.

Integrating with Browser Buttons and Deep Linking

Web browsers are designed primarily to render HTML content. Traditionally, web sites and web applications were built around the page metaphor whereby each page was a unique HTML file. The implications of this are important because the way in which browsers are designed to navigate the Web is built around the page metaphor. For example, browsers have Back buttons that allow users to navigate to the page they were viewing previously. Additionally, browsers inherently support a concept known as *deep linking*, which is simply a matter of allowing a user to navigate directly to a URL such as *http://www.adobe.com/go/flex*. The deep part of the deep link is the path following the domain name (`/go/flex`).

Users are accustomed to using the Back button and deep linking. These features are such an important part of the web experience that you may even wonder why we're mentioning them in this chapter. After all, you may think these features are incredibly obvious. However, the new generation of web applications, including Flash, Ajax, and Flex applications, breaks these features. The result is that users of these applications can feel frustrated when they habitually use the Back button or copy and paste a link and these actions don't work as expected.

Exactly how do these behaviors break in Flex applications? First, consider how the Back button works. The browser maintains a history of pages the user has viewed. When the user clicks the Back button, the browser simply goes to the previous page in the history. Flex applications don't use pages, though they may have many distinct screens or states. When the user navigates through the sections of the Flex application, she may feel that clicking the browser's Back button should move her back through the sections of the Flex application. However, because the Flex application resides in one HTML page, the default behavior of the Back button will be to simply take the user back to the previous HTML page she had viewed, and it will not navigate through sections of the Flex application.

The same issues affect deep linking as well. When a user navigates through a Flex application, she may get to a section she'd like to bookmark or email to a friend. Most users are accustomed to being able to simply add a bookmark or copy and paste the URL from the browser's address bar. Yet, as a user navigates through a Flex application, the URL in the address bar doesn't change. That means distinct sections of the Flex application don't have distinct URLs that can be bookmarked or emailed. The result is that returning to a Flex application's URL means returning to the starting point of that Flex application, not to a specific section.

The solution to the Back button and deep linking dilemmas is to use a bit of JavaScript to update the URL as the user navigates the Flex application. Every time the URL changes, the browser will register a new element in the history, which enables the Back button functionality. This also helps to provide unique URLs corresponding to different sections of the Flex application, which allows deep linking.

Normally, when you change the URL in a browser a new page loads. However, there is an exception to that rule. Changing the anchors will not cause a new page to load. An *anchor* in a URL is indicated by a pound sign (#). For example, consider that your Flex application is at *http://www.example.com/index.html*. If you update the URL with JavaScript to *http://www.example.com/index.html#a*, the page will not reload, but the Back button will be enabled and you also will have created a distinct, new URL that you can use to access the same Flex application.

Flex 3 includes an `mx.managers.BrowserManager` class that is intended to create a simple solution both for Back button integration and deep linking using the aforementioned technique. The `BrowserManager` solution is not as elegant as it could be, but it does work, and in the next section we'll look at how you can use it.

Working with BrowserManager

The `BrowserManager` class is a Singleton class for which the `getInstance()` method return type is set to `mx.managers.IBrowserManager`, an interface. That means that when you want to work with `BrowserManager` you should declare a variable of type `IBrowserManager` and assign `BrowserManager.getInstance()` to that variable.

The `BrowserManager` instance does the following things, which are of interest in this section:

- It allows you to set the new URL fragment (the value following a # sign) using a `setFragment()` method.
- It allows you to retrieve the URL fragment using the `fragment` property.
- It allows you to set the title of the HTML page using the `setTitle()` method.
- It allows you to set a default fragment and title using the `init()` method.
- It dispatches events to notify the application when the URL has changed.

Initializing BrowserManager

When working with `BrowserManager`, you must always initialize the instance by calling the `init()` method. The `init()` method requires two parameters: a fragment value and a page title. The application uses the first parameter (the fragment) when the user clicks the Back button to return to a point at which the URL has no fragment. In that sense, the first parameter defines the default fragment value, though it has an effect only when the user is clicking the Back button. The second parameter sets the title of the web page in the browser. In addition, the `init()` method also sets the historyManagementEnabled property of the application to false, which is necessary for the correct history management and deep linking to work correctly.

It may seem strange that historyManagementEnabled must be set to false for history management to work correctly. That is because historyManagementEnabled is wired to the older HistoryManager, not to BrowserManager. BrowserManager supersedes HistoryManager, and setting historyManagementEnabled to true can interfere with BrowserManager.

The following is an example of how you can use the init() method. In this example, the init() method is being called on creationComplete, which is appropriate because this method must be called before you run any other BrowserManager code.

```
<?xml version="1.0" encoding="utf-8"?>
<mx:Application xmlns:mx="http://www.adobe.com/2006/mxml" layout="absolute"
creationComplete="creationCompleteHandler();">

    <mx:Script>
        <![CDATA[

            import mx.managers.IBrowserManager;
            import mx.managers.BrowserManager;

            private var _browserManager:IBrowserManager =
BrowserManager.getInstance();

            private function creationCompleteHandler():void {
                // When the user clicks the Back button to the point
                // where there is no fragment, the application will use
                // the default fragment value of example.
                _browserManager.init("example", "Example Page");
            }

        ]]>
    </mx:Script>
</mx:Application>
```

Setting and retrieving a URL fragment

In BrowserManager lingo, a *fragment* is the portion of the URL that follows the # sign. For example, in the URL *http://www.example.com/#flex/page2*, the fragment is flex/page2. You can set the fragment using the setFragment() method. The following example will set the fragment to exampleTwo as soon as the application starts:

```
<?xml version="1.0" encoding="utf-8"?>
<mx:Application xmlns:mx="http://www.adobe.com/2006/mxml" layout="absolute"
creationComplete="creationCompleteHandler();" historyManagementEnabled="false">

    <mx:Script>
        <![CDATA[
```

```
            import mx.managers.IBrowserManager;
            import mx.managers.BrowserManager;

            private var _browserManager:IBrowserManager =
BrowserManager.getInstance();

            private function creationCompleteHandler():void {
                _browserManager.init("example", "Example Page");
                _browserManager.setFragment("exampleTwo");
            }

        ]]>
    </mx:Script>
</mx:Application>
```

On the flip side, you often will want to retrieve the current fragment value. The `fragment` property of `BrowserManager` returns that value.

Setting the page title

You already saw how to set the page title for the browser using the `init()` method. However, the `init()` method is designed to be called just once, when the application starts. Normally, you'll want to change the page title as the user interacts with the application. You can change the page title at any time using the `setTitle()` method by simply passing it the title as a parameter.

Handling BrowserManager events

When working with `BrowserManager`, two events are of interest: `applicationUrlChange` and `browserUrlChange`. The `applicationUrlChange` event occurs when the URL changes programmatically, such as when it is changed via the `setFragment()` method. Otherwise, when the URL changes because the user clicks the Back or Forward button or because the user changes the URL in the address bar, `BrowserManager` dispatches the `browserUrlChange` event. Both events are of type `mx.events.BrowserChangeEvent`. Typically, you'll handle both events using the same method because most applications should behave identically in all cases regardless of how the URL changes.

The `browserUrlChange` event does not occur when testing applications locally using Internet Explorer. However, when run from a web server, the event does get dispatched. That means that if you test your application locally using Internet Explorer while developing the application, you will not be able to use the Back and Forward buttons or deep linking features, but it will work when deployed on a web server. Consider testing using another browser, such as Firefox.

Building a Sample BrowserManager Application

In this section, we'll look at a simple example application that uses `BrowserManager` to enable deep linking and integration with the browser's Back and Forward buttons. The application merely consists of four simple MXML application components corresponding to four screens or pages within the application, and a navigational button bar for navigating between the screens. The four screens are called Home, Books, Authors, and Events.

We'll create these four components first. Three of the four components will consist of nothing more than a label component. One of them will contain an accordion component, and we'll later see how to integrate that into `BrowserManager` as well. You should define the Home screen component in *HomeScreen.mxml* using the code shown in Example 20-1.

Example 20-1. HomeScreen.mxml

```
<?xml version="1.0" encoding="utf-8"?>
<mx:Canvas xmlns:mx="http://www.adobe.com/2006/mxml">
    <mx:Label text="Thank you for visiting O'Reilly's Flex site" />
</mx:Canvas>
```

Next, you can define the Books screen in *BooksScreen.mxml*, as shown in Example 20-2.

Example 20-2. BooksScreen.mxml

```
<?xml version="1.0" encoding="utf-8"?>
<mx:Canvas xmlns:mx="http://www.adobe.com/2006/mxml">
    <mx:Label text="O'Reilly books catalog" />
</mx:Canvas>
```

The Authors screen is defined in *AuthorsScreen.mxml*, as shown in Example 20-3. This is the screen with the accordion.

Example 20-3. AuthorsScreen.mxml

```
<?xml version="1.0" encoding="utf-8"?>
<mx:Canvas xmlns:mx="http://www.adobe.com/2006/mxml">
    <mx:Accordion id="authorsAccordion" width="400" height="400">
        <mx:VBox label="Joey Lott" />
        <mx:VBox label="Chafic Kazoun" />
    </mx:Accordion>
</mx:Canvas>
```

The Events screen is defined in *EventsScreen.mxml*, as shown in Example 20-4.

Example 20-4. EventsScreen.mxml

```
<?xml version="1.0" encoding="utf-8"?>
<mx:Canvas xmlns:mx="http://www.adobe.com/2006/mxml">
    <mx:Label text="Events this month" />
</mx:Canvas>
```

Now we can assemble all the screens in the main application MXML file with a navigational button bar, as shown in Example 20-5.

Example 20-5. Main.mxml

```
<?xml version="1.0" encoding="utf-8"?>
<mx:Application xmlns:mx="http://www.adobe.com/2006/mxml" layout="absolute"
creationComplete="creationCompleteHandler();" xmlns:local="*" currentState="Home">

    <mx:Script>
        <![CDATA[
            import mx.core.UIComponent;
            import mx.collections.ArrayCollection;
            import mx.managers.IBrowserManager;
            import mx.managers.BrowserManager;
            import mx.events.BrowserChangeEvent;
            import mx.events.ItemClickEvent;

            private var _browserManager:IBrowserManager =
BrowserManager.getInstance();
            private var _navigationData:ArrayCollection;

            private function creationCompleteHandler():void {
                _navigationData = new ArrayCollection();
                _navigationData.addItem({section: "Home",
title: "O'Reilly Publishing", component: "homeScreen"});
                _navigationData.addItem({section: "Books",
title: "O'Reilly Publishing - Our Catalog", component: "booksScreen"});
                _navigationData.addItem({section: "Authors",
title: "O'Reilly Publishing - Meet the Authors", component: "authorsScreen"});
                _navigationData.addItem({section: "Events",
title: "O'Reilly Publishing - Current Events", component: "eventsScreen"});
                navigation.dataProvider = _navigationData;
                _browserManager.init("Home", _navigationData.getItemAt(0).title);
            }

            private function itemClickHandler(event:ItemClickEvent):void {
            }

        ]]>
    </mx:Script>

    <mx:VBox>
        <mx:ToggleButtonBar id="navigation" labelField="section"
itemClick="itemClickHandler(event);" />
        <mx:Canvas id="sections" />
    </mx:VBox>

    <mx:states>
        <mx:State name="Home">
            <mx:AddChild relativeTo="{sections}">
                <local:HomeScreen id="homeScreen" />
            </mx:AddChild>
        </mx:State>
        <mx:State name="Books">
```

```
            <mx:AddChild relativeTo="{sections}">
                <local:BooksScreen id="booksScreen" />
            </mx:AddChild>
        </mx:State>
        <mx:State name="Authors">
            <mx:AddChild relativeTo="{sections}">
                <local:AuthorsScreen id="authorsScreen" />
            </mx:AddChild>
        </mx:State>
        <mx:State name="Events">
            <mx:AddChild relativeTo="{sections}">
                <local:EventsScreen id="eventsScreen" />
            </mx:AddChild>
        </mx:State>
    </mx:states>

</mx:Application>
```

In this code, we define an ArrayCollection called _navigationData, and we add four elements to it. Each element corresponds to a screen in the application. Each element has three properties: section, title, and component. The section corresponds to the name of the state for the screen, the title is the page title, and the component is the ID of the screen component instance. Then we assign the _navigationData collection to the dataProvider property of the ToggleButtonBar instance. This will create four buttons corresponding to the four screens.

At this point, nothing happens when you click the buttons because we haven't defined the behavior. Typically, if you wanted to change the state when the user clicked on a button, you would simply set the currentState property. However, in this case we want to route all requests for state changes through BrowserManager. That means we need to call setFragment() instead. And that means the new, revised itemClickHandler() method now looks like the following:

```
private function itemClickHandler(event:ItemClickEvent):void {
    _browserManager.setFragment(event.item.section);
}
```

This code sets the fragment to the value of the section property of the dataProvider element corresponding to the button. The result is that the fragment will be one of the following: Home, Books, Authors, or Events, which just happen to also correspond to the names of the states.

If you were to test the application at this point, you'd see that the fragment does indeed update when you click the buttons, but the application state doesn't change. To change the application state we need to handle the applicationUrlChange event. We can do that by first registering a listener for the event in the creationCompleteHandler() method with the following code:

```
_browserManager.addEventListener(BrowserChangeEvent.APPLICATION_URL_CHANGE,
urlChangeHandler);
```

Then we need only to define the urlChangeHandler() method. This new method looks like the following:

```
private function urlChangeHandler(event:BrowserChangeEvent):void {
    var fragment:String = _browserManager.fragment;
    var item:Object;
    for(var i:int = 0; i < _navigationData.length; i++) {
        if(_navigationData.getItemAt(i).section == fragment) {
            item  = _navigationData.getItemAt(i);
            navigation.selectedIndex = i;
        }
    }
    _browserManager.setTitle(item.title);
    currentState = item.section;
}
```

This code loops through the elements in the _navigationData collection to find the one that corresponds to the fragment. It then sets the page title and the current state for the application.

Remember that with some browsers you will see the correct behavior only when running the application from a web server.

At this point, the application will allow you to click the buttons to navigate to different sections. However, if you try to use deep linking or the browser's Back button, you will find that neither one works. That is because the application is handling only the applicationUrlChange event. To enable the Back button and deep linking features all you need to do is handle the browserUrlChange event in the same way you handled the applicationUrlChange event. Therefore, you need to add only one line of code to the creationCompleteHandler() method:

```
_browserManager.addEventListener(BrowserChangeEvent.BROWSER_URL_CHANGE,
urlChangeHandler);
```

Enabling BrowserManager to Manage Granular States

In the preceding section, you saw how to build an application in which BrowserManager mediated all state changes at the application level. However, you might want to build an application that has state changes occurring within screens, not just between them. In this section, we'll continue the example application from the previous section. We'll enable state changes in the accordion component on the Authors screen to be managed by BrowserManager.

The first change we'll make is to change the URL fragment when the user clicks on an accordion section. Example 20-6 shows these changes to *AuthorsScreen.mxml*.

Example 20-6. AuthorsScreen.mxml

```
<?xml version="1.0" encoding="utf-8"?>
<mx:Canvas xmlns:mx="http://www.adobe.com/2006/mxml">
    <mx:Script>
        <![CDATA[
            import mx.events.BrowserChangeEvent;
            import mx.managers.IBrowserManager;
            import mx.managers.BrowserManager;

            private var _browserManager:IBrowserManager =
BrowserManager.getInstance();

            private function changeAuthorHandler(event:Event):void {
                _browserManager.setFragment("Authors/" +
authorsAccordion.selectedIndex);
            }

        ]]>
    </mx:Script>
    <mx:Accordion id="authorsAccordion" width="400" height="400"
change="changeAuthorHandler(event);">
        <mx:VBox label="Joey Lott" />
        <mx:VBox label="Chafic Kazoun" />
    </mx:Accordion>
</mx:Canvas>
```

You can see that when the user clicks on an accordion section the URL fragment updates to `Authors/0` or `Authors/1` depending on which section the user clicks.

If you run the application now, you'll see that clicking on one of the accordion sections actually causes an error. That's because `Authors/0` and `Authors/1` cannot be found in the navigational data at the application level. Therefore, we need to make a change to the `urlChangeHandler()` method in the application MXML file. Instead of simply using the fragment as is, we'll extract each piece using the slash as the delimiter. Example 20-7 shows the changes.

Example 20-7. Updated urlChangeHandler()

```
private function urlChangeHandler(event:BrowserChangeEvent):void {
    var fragment:Array = _browserManager.fragment.split("/");
    var item:Object;
    for(var i:int = 0; i < _navigationData.length; i++) {
        if(_navigationData.getItemAt(i).section == fragment[0]) {
            item = _navigationData.getItemAt(i);
            navigation.selectedIndex = i;
        }
    }
    _browserManager.setTitle(item.title);
    currentState = item.section;
}
```

Now the application works again without error. However, it still doesn't handle state changes within the Authors screen correctly when the user clicks the Back or Forward button or uses deep linking. There are lots of strategies for how to handle setting state in these cases. We'll tackle the issue by defining an interface called `IScreen` that will allow fragment data to be passed to screens from the application level. Example 20-8 shows `IScreen`.

Example 20-8. IScreen.as

```
package {
    public interface IScreen {

        function setScreenFragment(value:String):void;

    }
}
```

Next we'll update *AuthorsScreen.mxml* to implement `IScreen`. Example 20-9 shows the new *AuthorsScreen.mxml*.

Example 20-9. AuthorsScreen.mxml implementing IScreen

```
<?xml version="1.0" encoding="utf-8"?>
<mx:Canvas xmlns:mx="http://www.adobe.com/2006/mxml" implements="IScreen">
    <mx:Script>
        <![CDATA[
            import mx.events.BrowserChangeEvent;
            import mx.managers.IBrowserManager;
            import mx.managers.BrowserManager;

            [Bindable]
            private var _accordionIndex:int;

            private var _browserManager:IBrowserManager =
BrowserManager.getInstance();

            public function setScreenFragment(value:String):void {
                if(value == "") {
                    _accordionIndex = 0;
                }
                else {
                    _accordionIndex = parseInt(value);
                }
            }

            private function changeAuthorHandler(event:Event):void {
                _browserManager.setFragment("Authors/" +
authorsAccordion.selectedIndex);
            }

        ]]>
    </mx:Script>
    <mx:Accordion id="authorsAccordion" width="400" height="400"
change="changeAuthorHandler(event);" selectedIndex="{_accordionIndex}">
        <mx:VBox label="Joey Lott" />
        <mx:VBox label="Chafic Kazoun" />
```

```
    </mx:Accordion>
</mx:Canvas>
```

All we did was implement `IScreen`, and in the `setScreenFragment()` method we parsed the index value and assigned it to a bindable `_accordionIndex` property, which will set the accordion's `selectedIndex` correctly.

Next we need to update the `urlChangeHandler()` method of the application again. This time we'll test whether the selected screen implements `IScreen`, and if it does we'll pass along the fragment. Example 20-10 shows this new code.

Example 20-10. Updated urlChangeHandler()

```
private function urlChangeHandler(event:BrowserChangeEvent):void {
    var fragment:Array = _browserManager.fragment.split("/");
    var item:Object;
    for(var i:int = 0; i < _navigationData.length; i++) {
        if(_navigationData.getItemAt(i).section == fragment[0]) {
            item  = _navigationData.getItemAt(i);
            navigation.selectedIndex = i;
        }
    }
    _browserManager.setTitle(item.title);
    currentState = item.section;
    var screen:UIComponent = this[item.component];
    if(screen is IScreen) {
        (screen as IScreen).setScreenFragment(fragment[1]);
    }
}
```

If you test the application, you'll see that you can navigate between the accordion sections using the Back and Forward browser buttons.

Deploying BrowserManager Flex Applications

One of the big drawbacks of `BrowserManager` is that Adobe has tied `BrowserManager` to the Flex HTML templates. Therefore, if you use `BrowserManager`, the easiest way to deploy the application is to use the Flex HTML template. As we stated earlier in this chapter, the Flex HTML templates are not ideal, and we generally advise that you not use them, if possible. However, in this case, using the Flex templates is the simplest solution. You need to use one of the templates with history management enabled. Then, when you deploy the application, you need to deploy the HTML file, the *.swf* file, and the *history* directory containing *history.js*, *history.css*, and *historyFrame.html*. If you omit any of those files, the application will not work correctly.

Because we think that SWFObject is a far better way to embed Flex applications, we think it's important to explain how to use `BrowserManager` applications with SWFObject as well. Although it is possible, it does require that you make a few edits to the *history.js* JavaScript code provided by Adobe. This is not due to any failure on the part of SWFObject, but rather because of oversights in the *history.js* code.

When embedding a `BrowserManager` application using SWFObject, you should embed the application normally. In addition to the normal HTML and JavaScript code, you'll need to include *history.css* and *history.js*. An example that does this follows:

```
<!DOCTYPE html PUBLIC "-//W3C//DTD XHTML 1.0 Strict//EN"
"http://www.w3.org/TR/xhtml1/DTD/xhtml1-strict.dtd">
<html xmlns="http://www.w3.org/1999/xhtml" lang="en" xml:lang="en">
    <head>
        <title>Flex Example</title>
        <meta http-equiv="Content-Type" content="text/html; charset=iso-8859-1" />
        <script type="text/javascript" src="swfobject.js"></script>
        <link rel="stylesheet" type="text/css" href="history/history.css"/>
        <script src="history/history.js" language="javascript"></script>
        <script type="text/javascript">
            swfobject.registerObject("flexApplication", "9.0.0");
        </script>
    </head>
    <body>
        <div>
            <object classid="clsid:D27CDB6E-AE6D-11cf-96B8-444553540000"
                    width="400" height="400" id="flexApplication">
                <param name="movie" value="Example.swf" />
                <!--[if !IE]>-->
                <object type="application/x-shockwave-flash" data="Example.swf"
                        width="400" height="400">
                <!--<![endif]-->
                    <param name="allowScriptAccess" value="always" />
                    <p>This site is best viewed as a Flex application, which requires
                       Flash Player 9. For users who prefer not to use Flash Player
                       we have provided a <a href='textVersion.html'>text-only
                       version of the site</a/>.</p>
                <!--[if !IE]>-->
                </object>
                <!--<![endif]-->
            </object>
        </div>
    </body>
</html>
```

As we already mentioned, the *history.js* file code is shortsighted in the way it works, and because of this you'll need to edit it for it to work with SWFObject-embedded applications. The primary error is that *history.js* assumes that all applications are embedded using `object` tags for Internet Explorer and `embed` tags for other browsers. That assumption doesn't work for SWFObject-embedded applications that use nested `object` tags. Therefore, you need to adapt the *history.js* code to be able to find applications embedded using nested `object` tags. The authors of this book don't claim to be JavaScript experts, and we don't claim that our solution is the best or most elegant, but it does work and it is simple. All you need to do is edit *history.js* and add a few lines of code to the `getPlayer()` method, as shown in Example 20-11. This code returns `BrowserHistory.flexApplication` if it is defined. We'll set this property in the HTML file using SWFObject to retrieve the reference.

Example 20-11. Changes to getPlayer() in history.js

```
function getPlayer(objectId) {
         if(BrowserHistory.flexApplication != null) {
             return BrowserHistory.flexApplication;
         }
        var objectId = objectId || null;
        var player = null;
        if (browser.ie && objectId != null) {
            player = document.getElementById(objectId);
        }
        if (player == null) {
            player = document.getElementsByTagName('object')[0];
        }

        if (player == null || player.object == null) {
            player = document.getElementsByTagName('embed')[0];
        }

        return player;
    }
```

Next, in the HTML, we need to set `BrowserHistory.flexApplication` to reference the Flex application instance. We need to use SWFObject's `getObjectById()` method to retrieve the reference. We'll also use the `addLoadEvent()` method of SWFObject to ensure that we assign the reference once the application is defined in the page. Example 20-12 shows the new code.

Example 20-12. Setting BrowserHistory.flexApplication in the HTML file

```
<script type="text/javascript">
            swfobject.registerObject("flexApplication", "9.0.0");
            swfobject.addLoadEvent(loadEventHandler);
            function loadEventHandler() {
                BrowserHistory.flexApplication =
swfobject.getObjectById("flexApplication");
            }
        </script>
```

With these changes, SWFObject will work with `BrowserManager`. You need to make sure that when you deploy the application, you deploy the *.swf* file, the HTML file, *swfobject.js*, and the *history* directory with *history.js*, *history.css*, and *historyFrame.html*.

Flash Player Security

Flash Player enforces security rules for what and how applications can access data, and you'll notice this especially when embedding a Flex application in an HTML page. Flex applications can typically access all data resources in the same domain as the *.swf*. For example, if the *.swf* is deployed to www.example.com (*http://www.example.com*), it can access a web service that is also deployed at www.example.com (*http://www.exam ple.com*). However, access to data resources at different domains is disallowed by Flash

Player unless that domain explicitly gives permission. The Flash Player security rules disallow access to data resources unless the domains match exactly, including subdomains, even if the domain names resolve to the same physical address. That means an *.swf* deployed at www.example.com (*http://www.example.com*) cannot access data from test.example.com (*http://test.example.com*) or even example.com (*http://example.com*) unless the server explicitly allows access. The domain can give permission by way of a cross-domain policy file.

When working with the socket class and loading data through sockets rather than through request/response mechanisms, Flash Player 9,0,115,0 and later introduce an additional socket policy file requirement. Since Flash Player security is continually evolving, we recommend that you review the latest articles at *http://www.adobe.com/devnet/flashplayer/* for any changes that may impact your application.

A *cross-domain policy file* is an XML file that resides on the server that hosts the data resources. The format for a cross-domain policy file is as follows:

```
<?xml version="1.0"?>
<!DOCTYPE cross-domain-policy SYSTEM
        "http://www.adobe.com/xml/dtds/cross-domain-policy.dtd">
<cross-domain-policy>
   <allow-access-from domain="www.example.com" />
</cross-domain-policy>
```

The root `<cross-domain-policy>` node can contain one or more `<allow-access-from>` elements. The `<allow-access-from>` elements specify the domains that can access the resources on the server. You can use an * wildcard in place of the subdomain, which means that any subdomain can access the data resources. For example, the following policy allows access from www.example.com (*http://www.example.com*), beta.example.com (*http://beta.example.com*), test.example.com (*http://test.example.com*), etc.:

```
<?xml version="1.0"?>
<!DOCTYPE cross-domain-policy SYSTEM
        "http://www.adobe.com/xml/dtds/cross-domain-policy.dtd">
<cross-domain-policy>
   <allow-access-from domain="*.example.com" />
</cross-domain-policy>
```

You can also use the * wildcard in place of the entire domain to allow access from all domains:

```
<?xml version="1.0"?>
<!DOCTYPE cross-domain-policy SYSTEM
        "http://www.adobe.com/xml/dtds/cross-domain-policy.dtd">
<cross-domain-policy>
   <allow-access-from domain="*" />
</cross-domain-policy>
```

If the server uses HTTPS and wants to allow access to *.swf* files deployed on nonsecure domains, it must specify a value for the secure attribute. The following allows access to *.swf* files deployed at www.example.com (*http://www.example.com*):

```
<?xml version="1.0"?>
<!DOCTYPE cross-domain-policy SYSTEM
        "http://www.adobe.com/xml/dtds/cross-domain-policy.dtd">
<cross-domain-policy>
   <allow-access-from domain="www.example.com" secure="false" />
</cross-domain-policy>
```

By default, Flash Player looks for a policy file named *crossdomain.xml* at the root of the web server from which it is requesting the data resources. If Flash Player attempts to load an XML document from *http://www.example.com/data/xml/data.xml*, it will look for *http://www.example.com/crossdomain.xml*. If you want to set different permissions for different resources on a server, you can optionally deploy different policy files in different locations on the server. For example, a policy file located at *http://www.example.com/data/xml* would apply only to the resources in that directory. However, when you place policy files in nondefault locations, you must use ActionScript to load the policy file in your Flex application. The ActionScript code uses the static `loadPolicyFile()` method of the `flash.system.Security` class. The following loads a policy file:

```
Security.loadPolicyFile("http://www.example.com/data/xml/policy.xml");
```

Deploying a cross-domain policy file presupposes that you have access to the server with the data resources—or that you can persuade those with the server to deploy the policy file. In the few cases where you cannot deploy a policy file on a server whose data resources you need to utilize, you have the option of deploying a *proxy file* on your server. A proxy file is a file that exists on your server (a *.jsp*, an ASP.NET page, a ColdFusion page, a PHP page, etc.) to which your Flex application can make requests. The proxy file then makes the requests to the remote resource and relays the data back to Flash Player.

Using Runtime Shared Libraries

Runtime shared libraries are a way to share assets and libraries among multiple *.swf* files on the same domain. This is useful when you have several *.swf* files that comprise an application or that span several applications deployed in the same domain in which each *.swf* file utilizes many common assets and/or libraries. For example, if *a.swf* and *b.swf* both utilize the same subset of 25 classes and embedded images that add up to 100 KB, the user has to download the same 100 KB twice, once for each *.swf*.

The theory behind runtime shared libraries involves a concept called *linking*. All *.swf* files employ one or both forms of linking: static and dynamic. By default, all linking is static. When an asset or source file is statically linked with an *.swf*, it is compiled into the *.swf*. Dynamic linking means that the asset or source file is not compiled into the *.swf*, but the *.swf* has a reference to an *.swf* into which it has been compiled. Through dynamic linking, you can specify certain elements that should not be compiled into an *.swf* to reduce the total file size of the *.swf*. The *.swf* is then linked to another *.swf* where the elements have been compiled. This allows you to extract common elements from two or more *.swf* files and place them into another *.swf* to which all the *.swf* files are linked dynamically. This new *.swf* is called a *runtime shared library*.

We can understand the benefit of runtime shared libraries by looking at the *a.swf* and *b.swf* example in more detail. In this example, *a.swf* is 200 KB and *b.swf* is 400 KB. Both *.swf* files are deployed on the same domain. The two *.swf* files happen to use 100 KB of common elements. That means that if a user uses both *a.swf* and *b.swf*, she downloads 600 KB, of which 100 KB is duplicate content. Using a runtime shared library, you can introduce a new *.swf*, *library.swf*, which contains the 100 KB of common content. Although there's some overhead in creating a runtime shared library for our purposes, we'll keep the numbers simple: *a.swf* will now be 100 KB and *b.swf* will now be 300 KB. Each will be dynamically linked to *library.swf*, which also has to download. However, the second time the user requests *library.swf* it will be retrieved from client cache rather than from the server, effectively saving 100 KB.

The underlying manner in which you create and use runtime shared libraries is always the same. However, if you are working with the compiler from a command line or from a custom build script using Ant, the workflow is different from using Flex Builder, which automates a lot of the work involved with runtime shared libraries.

Creating Runtime Shared Libraries with the Command-Line Compilers

When you want to create a runtime shared library with the command-line compilers, you need to use both the `mxmlc` application compiler and the `compc` component compiler. First you must use the `compc` compiler to compile all the common elements into an *.swc* file. An *.swc* is an archive format, and in the case of a runtime shared library it contains two files: *library.swf* and *catalog.xml*. The *.swf* file contained within the *.swc* is the runtime shared library file. You then use the `mxmlc` compiler to compile the application as usual, but this time you notify the compiler to dynamically link to the runtime shared libraries.

Creating runtime shared libraries is an advanced feature. You may want to return to this section only after you're comfortable creating Flex applications and you want to optimize an application or applications that would benefit from runtime shared libraries.

Using compc

Like the `mxmlc` compiler, the `compc` compiler has options that you can use to determine what gets compiled and how. The first option you'll need to specify is `source-path`, which tells the compiler where to look for the files you want to compile. If you are compiling classes in packages, the `source-path` should be the root directory of the packages. If you want to use the current directory you must still specify a value, using a dot. If you want to use more than one directory, you can list the directories delimited by spaces.

You must compile one or more classes into a runtime shared library. You have to list each class using the `include-classes` option. There is no option to simply include all the classes in a directory. You must list each class individually. You must list each class using the fully qualified class name, and you can list multiple classes by separating them with spaces.

You must also specify an output file when calling `compc`. Use the `output` option, and specify the path to an *.swc* file that you want to export. The following example compiles the class `com.oreilly.programmingflex.A` into an *.swc* file called *example.swc*:

```
compc -source-path . -include-classes com.oreilly.programmingflex.A
-output example.swc
```

Compiling many classes into a runtime shared library can result in a very long command. To simplify this you can use either configuration files or manifest files.

Like `mxmlc`, you can use configuration files with `compc` by specifying a `load-config` option. Also like `mxmlc`, the `compc` compiler automatically loads a default configuration file called *flex-config.xml*, and unless you want to duplicate all the contents of *flex-config.xml* (much of which is required), it generally is better to specify a configuration file in addition to the default by using the `+=` operator, as in the following example:

```
compc -load-config+=configuration.xml
```

The following example configuration file is the equivalent of the earlier command, which specified the source path and output, and included classes from the command line:

```
<flex-config>
  <compiler>
    <source-path>
      <path-element>.</path-element>
    </source-path>
  </compiler>
  <output>example.swc</output>
  <include-classes>
    <class>com.oreilly.programmingflex.A</class>
  </include-classes>
</flex-config>
```

If you want to include many classes, you can simply add more `<class>` nodes, as in the following example:

```
<flex-config>
  <compiler>
    <source-path>
      <path-element>.</path-element>
    </source-path>
  </compiler>
```

```
  <output>example.swc</output>
  <include-classes>
    <class>com.oreilly.programmingflex.A</class>
    <class>com.oreilly.programmingflex.B</class>
    <class>com.oreilly.programmingflex.C</class>
    <class>com.oreilly.programmingflex.D</class>
  </include-classes>
</flex-config>
```

You can use manifest files to achieve the same result of simplifying the compiler command. However, manifest files also have an added benefit in that they allow you to create a namespace for components that you compile into the runtime shared library. This is more useful when the runtime shared library contains user interface components that you want to be able to add to an application using MXML tags. However, using a manifest file is not hurtful in any case, because it lets you simplify the compiler command.

A manifest file is an XML file in the following format:

```
<?xml version="1.0"?>
<componentPackage>
    <component id="Identifier" class="ClassName"/>
</componentPackage>
```

The following example will tell the compiler to add classes `A`, `B`, `C`, and `D` to the library:

```
<?xml version="1.0"?>
<componentPackage>
    <component id="A" class="com.oreilly.programmingflex.A"/>
    <component id="B" class="com.oreilly.programmingflex.B"/>
    <component id="C" class="com.oreilly.programmingflex.C"/>
    <component id="D" class="com.oreilly.programmingflex.D"/>
</componentPackage>
```

Once you've defined a manifest file, you need to tell the compiler to use the file. You can achieve that with the `namespace` and `include-namespaces` options. A *namespace* is an identifier that you can use within your MXML documents that will map to the manifest file contents. The `namespace` option requires that you specify two values: first the namespace identifier and then the manifest file to which the identifier corresponds. The `include-namespaces` option requires that you list all the identifiers for which you want to compile the contents into the *.swc* file. The following example compiles the classes specified in *manifest.xml* into the *.swc*:

```
compc -namespace http://oreilly.com/programmingflex manifest.xml
-include-namespaces http://oreilly.com/programmingflex -output example.swc
```

You can also combine the use of a manifest file with a configuration file. The following configuration file uses the manifest file:

```
<flex-config xmlns="http://www.adobe.com/2006/flex-config">
  <compiler>
    <source-path>
      <path-element>.</path-element>
    </source-path>
```

```
    <namespaces>
      <namespace>
        <uri>http://oreilly.com/programmingflex</uri>
        <manifest>manifest.xml</manifest>
      </namespace>
    </namespaces>
  </compiler>
  <output>example.swc</output>
  <include-namespaces>
    <uri>http://oreilly.com/programmingflex</uri>
  </include-namespaces>
</flex-config>
```

When you use a runtime shared library, you'll need two files: the *.swc* and the library *.swf* file contained within the *.swc* file. You need the *.swc* file because the `mxmlc` compiler uses the *.swc* file to determine which classes to dynamically link. You need the *.swf* file because it's the file you deploy with the application and from which the application loads the libraries. The SWC format is an archive format—essentially a ZIP format. You can use any standard unzip utility to extract the *.swf* file from the *.swc*. The *.swc* always contains a file called *library.swf* that you should extract and place in the deploy directory for the application. If you plan to use several runtime shared libraries with an application, you need to either place the *library.swf* files in different subdirectories or rename the files.

Compiling an application using a runtime shared library

Once you've compiled an *.swc* file containing a runtime shared library and extracted the *.swf* file, you next need to compile the application that uses the library. To accomplish that you'll use `mxmlc` in much the same way as you'd compile an application that uses only static linking. However, when you use a runtime shared library, you need to dynamically link the relevant classes in the main application and tell the application where to find the runtime shared library *.swf* file at runtime. The `external-library-path` option specifies the *.swc* file or files that tell the compiler which classes to dynamically link. Use the `runtime-shared-libraries` option to tell the compiler where it can find the runtime shared library file(s) at runtime. The following tells the compiler to compile the application using *example.swc* for dynamic linking and *example.swf* as the URL for the shared library:

```
mxmlc -external-library-path=example.swc
-runtime-shared-libraries=example.swf Example.mxml
```

You can use configuration files for these purposes as well. The following configuration file achieves the same result as the preceding command:

```
<flex-config>
  <compiler>
    <external-library-path>
      <path-element>example.swc</path-element>
    </external-library-path>
  </compiler>
  <file-specs>
```

```
    <path-element>RSLClientTest.mxml</path-element>
  </file-specs>
  <runtime-shared-libraries>
    <url>example.swf</url>
  </runtime-shared-libraries>
</flex-config>
```

When you deploy the application, you must also deploy the runtime shared library *.swf* file. You do not need to deploy the *.swc* file along with the rest of your application.

Using Ant to build runtime shared library applications

As you've seen, building an application that uses a runtime shared library requires quite a few steps. To summarize:

1. Compile the *.swc*.
2. Extract the *.swf*.
3. Move the *.swf*.
4. Compile the application.

Using Ant can simplify things because you can write just one script that will run all the tasks. The following is an example of such a script:

```
<?xml version="1.0"?>
<project name="RSLExample" basedir="./">

  <property name="mxmlc" value="C:\FlexSDK\bin\mxmlc.exe"/>
  <property name="compc" value="C:\FlexSDK\bin\compc.exe"/>

  <target name="compileRSL">
    <exec executable="${compc}">
      <arg line="-load-config+=rsl/configuration.xml" />
    </exec>
    <mkdir dir="application/rsl" />
    <move file="example.swc" todir="application/rsl" />
    <unzip src="application/rsl/example.swc" dest="application/rsl/" />
  </target>

  <target name="compileApplication">
    <exec executable="${mxmlc}">
      <arg line="-load-config+=application/configuration.xml" />
    </exec>
  </target>

  <target name="compileAll" depends="compileRSL,compileApplication">
  </target>

</project>
```

Using Flex Builder to Build Runtime Shared Libraries

Flex Builder automates a lot of the tasks and provides dialog boxes for steps to create and use runtime shared libraries. Working with runtime shared libraries in Flex Builder comprises two basic steps: creating a Flex Library Project and linking your main application to the library project.

Creating a Flex Library Project

The first step in creating a Flex Library Project is to create the project by selecting File→New→Flex Library Project. Every Flex Library Project needs to have at least one element—generally a class. You can add classes to the project as you would any standard Flex project. Once you've defined all the files for the project, you'll next need to tell Flex Builder which of those classes to compile into the *.swc* file. You can do that by way of the project properties. You can access the properties by selecting Project→Properties. Then select the Flex Library Build Path option from the menu on the left of the dialog. In the Classes tab you should select every class that you want to compile into the library. This is all that is necessary to create a Flex Library Project.

Linking an application to a library

When you want to use a library from a Flex application, you need to tell Flex Builder to link to the corresponding Flex Library Project. You can accomplish this by selecting Project→Properties for the Flex project. Then select the Flex Build Path option from the menu in the dialog, and select the "Library path" tab. Within the "Library path" tab you click the Add Project button. This opens a new dialog that prompts you to select the Flex Library Project you want to link to your application. When you select the library project and click OK, the project will show up in the "Library path" tab list. By default, libraries are statically linked rather than dynamically linked. You must tell Flex Builder to dynamically link the library by expanding the library project icon in the list, selecting the Link Type option and then selecting the Runtime Shared Library (RSL) option from the menu.

When you add a library project to the library path for a Flex project, the application can use any of the classes defined in the library project.

Adding Nonclass Assets to Runtime Shared Libraries

Runtime shared libraries do not directly allow you to dynamically link anything other than classes. That means you cannot directly add a dynamic link to an asset such as an image, a sound, or a font. However, if you can embed an asset in an ActionScript class, you can add indirect dynamic linking. (See Chapter 11 for more details on general embedding.) The following example embeds an image using a class constant:

```
package com.oreilly.programmingflex {
  public class Images {
```

```
        [Embed(source="image.jpg")]
        public static const IMAGE_A:Class;

    }
}
```

You can compile such a class into a runtime shared library, and the asset (an image in this case) is also embedded into the runtime shared library. The following example illustrates how you could use the dynamically linked image from an application:

```
<?xml version="1.0" encoding="utf-8"?>
<mx:Application xmlns:mx="http://www.adobe.com/2006/mxml" layout="absolute">

  <mx:Script>
    <![CDATA[

      import com.oreilly.programmingflex.Images;

    ]]>
  </mx:Script>
  <mx:VBox>
    <mx:Image source="{Images.IMAGE_A}" scaleContent="true"
              width="100" height="100" />
  </mx:VBox>
</mx:Application>
```

Summary

In this chapter, you learned how to embed Flex applications in HTML pages. You learned how to use the industry-standard SWFObject to embed Flex applications using the static publishing method employing standards-compliant nested `object` tags. You also learned how to enable deep linking within Flex applications and how to integrate an application with the browser's Back and Forward buttons using `BrowserManager`. Furthermore, you learned how to work with cross-domain loading issues, and you learned about creating runtime shared libraries to improve loading times on applications sharing common libraries and assets.

CHAPTER 21

Building AIR Applications

Up to this point in the book, we've looked at how to use Flex to build web applications. However, Flex 3 allows you to build more than web applications. It also allows you to build AIR applications for the desktop. In this chapter, you'll learn about Adobe AIR and how to use Flex to build AIR applications.

Understanding AIR

Adobe AIR allows developers to use Flash, Flex, and/or HTML/Ajax to create desktop applications. As this is a book about Flex, we'll only look at using Flex to build AIR applications in this chapter.

AIR is a platform consisting of a runtime environment and developer tools for creating AIR applications. The runtime environment, called the AIR runtime, is a free download from Adobe that users must have installed on their computers to run AIR applications. Conceptually, this runtime environment is very similar to other common runtime environments such as the .NET runtime and the Java runtime. The basic concept is that developers can build applications that run in the runtime environment, allowing for a simple way to create cross-platform applications.

Building an AIR application with Flex is remarkably easy. You can build a basic AIR application using what you learned in the other chapters in this book, together with just a few workflow and technical changes that you'll read about in the next section. However, you can do more in an AIR application than merely run a standard Flex application in the AIR runtime instead of in a web browser. The AIR runtime enables an AIR-only feature set, which includes the following:

- Working with the local filesystem (e.g., writing files)
- Creating and accessing local SQL databases
- Creating and managing application windows
- Working with system clipboards (including interapplication drag and drop and copy and paste)

- Rendering HTML within the Flex application and supporting all HTTP verbs (GET, POST, PUT, and DELETE)

Throughout this chapter, you'll learn how to configure, compile, and deploy AIR applications, and you'll learn how to work with all the features from the preceding list. However, we should note that this chapter is not intended to be a comprehensive guide to building AIR applications. That would require an entire book. Instead, the goal of this chapter is to provide you with the basic information you'll need to start building AIR applications using Flex. We recommend that you read the AIR document at Adobe's web site (*http://www.adobe.com/go/learn_air_flex3*) as well as the Flex language reference (*http://www.adobe.com/go/learn_flex3_aslr*) for more detail.

Building AIR Applications

Building desktop applications usually is not a simple task. Building desktop applications with elegant user interfaces, animated transitions, and all that Flex provides is typically even more challenging. Therefore, in a relative way building AIR applications is extraordinarily simple. There are a few minor differences between building AIR applications and building web applications using Flex. The workflow for building AIR applications using Flex is as follows:

1. Create a new Flex project. If you are using the SDK, there is nothing different about how you configure a Flex AIR project versus a Flex web project. If you are using Flex Builder, you should select the "Desktop application" option from the "Application type" section of the first screen of the New Flex Project Wizard.
2. Write a Flex application using MXML and ActionScript just as you would for a web application. However, instead of using `Application` as the root tag for the application MXML document you must use the `WindowedApplication` tag. Also, because AIR allows for features beyond what web applications allow, you can also use the AIR-specific APIs and components.
3. In addition to the normal application files (MXML, ActionScript, embedded assets, CSS files, etc.), you also need to define a *descriptor file*. A descriptor file is an XML file that contains information about the application, such as the names of files to include in the application, the name of the application, and various other pieces of information, some required and some optional.
4. Compile the AIR application as an *.swf* file using the `amxmlc` compiler from the command line or from an Ant script (if you are using the SDK), or by using Flex Builder. Note that if you are using Flex Builder, the application will compile automatically if Build Automatically is selected; otherwise, it will compile when you run the application. The `amxmlc` compiler is really just a shortcut to the standard `mxmlc` compiler, automatically setting the flag that tells the compiler to compile for AIR instead of for the Web.

5. Test the AIR application by running the *.swf* using the AIR debug launcher. If you are using the SDK, you need to run the debug launcher, which is called `adl`. If you are using Flex Builder, running or debugging the application will launch the application using the debug launcher.
6. Once you have a complete application to distribute, you need to create an *.air* file, which contains the *.swf*, the descriptor, and any additional files you'd like to include in the application (database files, image files, audio or video files, text files, etc.). You can use the AIR developer tool for this step. The developer tool is called `adt`, and you'll need to run it from the command line or from an Ant script if you're using the SDK. Otherwise, if you are using Flex Builder, you can use the Project→Export Release Builder option. Creating an *.air* file requires that you digitally sign it by providing a certificate. If you don't already have a certificate, you'll need to either acquire one or create one during this step.
7. Now you can distribute the AIR application. You can achieve this by simply emailing the *.air* file or making it available for download. You can also use the seamless install feature, which allows users to install the application from the Web using what's called a *badge*, a simple Flash application that runs in the browser.

Next, we'll look in more detail at creating a new Flex AIR project, defining descriptor files, compiling AIR applications, and testing AIR applications. We'll look at creating and distributing *.air* files later in the chapter.

Creating a New Flex AIR Project

As we already mentioned, you create and organize a Flex AIR project the same way you would a Flex web application if you are using the Flex SDK. If you are using Flex Builder, the only difference is that you must specify that the new application is a desktop application. You can do that by selecting the "Desktop application" option in the "Application type" section of the New Flex Project dialog.

Once you've created a new Flex AIR project, you need to do one more thing to differentiate it from a Flex web application. Instead of defining the main application document's root tag as `Application`, you must define it as `WindowedApplication`. That means an empty main application file for an AIR application looks like this:

```
<?xml version="1.0" encoding="utf-8"?>
<mx:WindowedApplication xmlns:mx="http://www.adobe.com/2006/mxml" layout="absolute">
</mx:WindowedApplication>
```

`WindowedApplication` is a subclass of `Application`, which means everything that applies to `Application` also applies to `WindowedApplication`. However, in addition to the properties, methods, and events in the `Application` class, the `WindowedApplication` class also defines an API that is specific to AIR. For example, `WindowedApplication` objects have a `title` property, which allows you to set the text that appears in the title bar of the application window. If you look at the documentation for `WindowedApplication` (*http://livedocs.adobe.com/flex/3/langref/mx/core/WindowedApplication.html*), you'll see that many of the properties (e.g., `systemChrome`, `maximizable`, `minimizable`, `transparent`, etc.) are read-only. Many of these properties can be set only from the application descriptor file, which you can read about in the next section.

Defining Descriptor Files

Descriptor files are XML files that AIR applications require to determine what to run and how to run it, as well as how the *.air* file gets packaged and installed. For example, a descriptor file tells the AIR runtime what *.swf* file to run in the main window, and it can specify various settings for the main window, such as title and transparency.

The descriptor file allows you to configure a lot of settings. However, at a minimum, AIR requires that you define the following settings: application ID, name of the AIR file, version number, and content for the main (initial) window. Here is an example of a basic descriptor file:

```
<?xml version="1.0" encoding="UTF-8"?>
<application xmlns="http://ns.adobe.com/air/application/1.0">
    <id>Example</id>
    <filename>Example</filename>
    <version>1.0</version>
    <initialWindow>
        <content>Main.swf</content>
    </initialWindow>
</application>
```

Many of the additional settings apply to the `initialWindow` tag, within which you can nest additional elements for those settings. For example, you can add `x` and `y` elements to set the initial x and y coordinates of the main window.

You can read about all the descriptor file settings at *http://livedocs.adobe.com/flex/3/html/help.html?content=File_formats_1.html#1043413*.

If you are using Flex Builder, when you create a new desktop application project, Flex Builder will automatically create a descriptor file for you. The descriptor file will be placed alongside the main MXML file, and it will be named *<ProjectName>-app.xml* where *<ProjectName>* is the name of the Flex project.

If you're using the Flex SDK, you must create the descriptor file yourself. The file should be a UTF-8-encoded XML file. You do not have to use a specific name for the file.

Compiling and Testing AIR Applications

Compiling and testing AIR applications is extraordinarily simple if you are using Flex Builder. In fact, all you need to do is run the application as you would for any Flex application, and Flex Builder will take care of compiling for AIR and running the application in the debug launcher. Therefore, if you are using Flex Builder, you can skip the remainder of this section and jump to "Working with AIR Features."

If you are using the Flex SDK, compiling and testing AIR applications is not difficult, but it is a little more involved than compiling and testing using Flex Builder. To compile an AIR application using the SDK you must run the standard Flex compiler (`mxmlc`) using the additional `+configname=air` parameter. Optionally, you can use the `amxmlc` compiler instead, which is a shortcut that automatically adds the `+configname=air` parameter. For the examples in this section, we'll use `amxmlc`.

At a minimum, the compiler requires a main MXML file. In the simplest format, the following command will compile *Main.mxml* into an AIR *.swf*:

```
amxmlc Main.mxml
```

When you compile an AIR application, the compiler options are identical to those you use when compiling a web application. You can refer back to Chapter 2 for more information about these options.

Working with AIR Features

As mentioned previously, AIR allows additional features beyond those of a Flex web application. In the following sections, you'll learn about working with these features.

Accessing the Local Filesystem

Arguably, one of the most significant features of AIR applications is that they can access the local filesystem. That means that with Flex AIR applications, you can read, write, create, move, and delete files and directories.

Referencing files and directories

As far as AIR is concerned, all files and directories are similar enough that AIR defines just one type of object for both: the `flash.filesystem.File` class. Instances of the `File` class reference files or directories. When you want to get a reference to an existing file or directory, the ideal way to do so is to use a relative reference. Using relative references helps to avoid absolute references that might be platform- or system-specific, thereby allowing applications to run across many computers and many operating systems. To facilitate retrieving relative references, AIR defines a handful of built-in references to common directories. These include the following:

`File.applicationDirectory`
: The directory in which the AIR application is installed.

`File.applicationStorageDirectory`
: The directory in which the AIR application can store files. This directory is unique to the AIR application, but it is also a different directory than the directory in which the application is installed.

`File.desktopDirectory`
: The desktop directory for the current user.

`File.documentsDirectory`
: The documents directory for the current user.

`File.userDirectory`
: The current user's directory.

These static properties of the `File` class automatically map to correct directories for a given system and user. Each property is a `File` object. Once you have a `File` object that references a directory, you can retrieve relative references using the `resolvePath()` method. The `resolvePath()` method will return a new `File` object that references a file or directory relative to the `File` object from which the method is called. The method requires one parameter specifying the relative path. For example, the following code creates a `File` object that references a file called *example.jpg* on the desktop:

```
var image:File = File.desktopDirectory.resolvePath("example.jpg");
```

You can use forward slashes as a delimiter between directories, and you can use two consecutive dots (`..`) to indicate the parent directory. For example, the following will reference a file called *example.txt* in the parent directory of the AIR application install directory:

```
var textFile:File = File.applicationDirectory.resolvePath("../example.txt");
```

Although relative paths are recommended, you can also create `File` objects that reference files or directories using absolute paths by using the constructor and passing it an absolute path as a parameter. For example, the following creates a `File` object that references the *C:* drive (presumably for a Windows machine):

```
var cDrive:File = new File("C:/");
```

Retrieving a directory listing

You can retrieve a listing of a directory by calling the `getDirectoryListingAsync()` method on a `File` object that references a directory. The `getDirectoryListingAsync()` method, as the name implies, is asynchronous. That means you'll have to listen for a `directoryListing` event (use the `flash.events.FileListEvent.DIRECTORY_LISTING` constant) before you can work with the directory listing.

There is a synchronous `getDirectoryListing()` method as well. However, we recommend that you always use asynchronous methods when there are both asynchronous and synchronous versions. This is because asynchronous methods are not likely to cause an AIR application to lock up, as are synchronous methods.

When the `directoryListing` event is handled, the parameter passed to the listener method will be of type `FileListEvent`, which has a `files` property containing an array of `File` objects (the files and directories contained within the directory).

All `File` objects have many properties that may be of use when retrieving a directory listing. Here are a few key properties in this context:

`Name`
: The name of the file or directory.

`modificationDate`
: The date when the file or directory was last modified.

`size`
: The size of the file or directory in bytes.

`isDirectory`
: A Boolean value indicating whether the object references a directory (if `false`, the object references a file). This is useful for determining whether you can run file- or directory-specific operations.

Example 21-1 retrieves all the files and directories from the desktop and displays them in a text area component.

Example 21-1. Displaying files and directories on the desktop

```
<?xml version="1.0" encoding="utf-8"?>
<mx:WindowedApplication xmlns:mx="http://www.adobe.com/2006/mxml"
layout="absolute" creationComplete="creationCompleteHandler();">
    <mx:Script>
        <![CDATA[

            private function creationCompleteHandler():void {
                var desktop:File = File.desktopDirectory;
                desktop.addEventListener(FileListEvent.DIRECTORY_LISTING,
directoryListingHandler);
                desktop.getDirectoryListingAsync();
            }

            private function directoryListingHandler(event:FileListEvent):void {
                var count:int = event.files.length;
                var file:File;
                for(var i:int = 0; i < count; i++) {
                    file = event.files[i] as File;
                    textArea.text += file.name + " | " +
                                     file.modificationDate + " | " +
                                     file.size + " | " + file.isDirectory + "\n";
                }
            }

        ]]>
    </mx:Script>
    <mx:TextArea id="textArea" width="100%" height="100%" />
</mx:WindowedApplication>
```

Creating directories

Typically, you create a directory on the filesystem with a specific path and a specific name. For example, you may want to programmatically create a *mediaFiles* directory in the application storage directory for the purpose of storing video and audio files that the AIR application downloads. When you want to create a directory in this fashion, you need to do the following:

1. Create a `File` object that references the nonexistent directory.
2. Call the `createDirectory()` method on that object.

For example, the following creates a *mediaFiles* directory in the application storage directory:

```
var mediaFilesDirectory:File = File.applicationStorageDirectory.resolvePath
("mediaFiles");
mediaFilesDirectory.createDirectory();
```

If the directory already exists, no action takes place. If the directory doesn't yet exist, it is created. Furthermore, if parent directories of that directory don't exist, they are created as well.

You can create a new temporary directory using the static `File.createTempDirectory()` method, which returns a reference to the new directory. The directory is created in the system's temporary directory path. The directory is not deleted automatically.

Reading and writing files

Reading and writing files requires use of a `File` object and a `flash.filesystem.FileStream` object. You can use a `FileStream` object to open a file (`File` object) and then use a variety of methods to read and write bytes.

As we already mentioned, the first step when reading or writing a file is to open the file using a `FileStream` object. The `openAsync()` method of a `FileStream` object requires two parameters: a reference to the `File` object and the mode in which you want to open the file. You can open a file in the following modes: read, write, append, or update. You can use the `READ`, `WRITE`, `APPEND`, and `UPDATE` constants of the `flash.filesystem.FileMode` class to indicate which mode you want to use. The read mode simply allows for reading. The write, append, and update modes allow for writing to the file, but they are each subtly different. The write mode always truncates the file, which means you'll overwrite any existing data. The update and append modes retain existing data, but the append mode automatically begins to write at the end of the file. Any of the writing modes will create the file if it doesn't already exist.

You can also open a file for reading and writing in a synchronous fashion using the `open()` method. However, as previously noted, we'll be looking only at asynchronous methods in detail in this chapter.

Once you've opened a file, you can read or write (depending on the mode) using the various read and write methods of the `FileStream` class. The `FileStream` class implements both the `flash.utils.IDataInput` and `flash.utils.IDataOutput` interfaces, which are also implemented by ActionScript classes such as `ByteArray`, `Socket`, and `URLStream`. Because these interfaces aren't specific to Flex or AIR, we will not discuss them in great detail in this chapter. You can read more about the interfaces on the Adobe website at *http://livedocs.adobe.com/flex/3/langref/flash/utils/IDataOutput.html* and *http://livedocs.adobe.com/flex/3/langref/flash/utils/IDataInput.html*. The basic premise is that using methods such as `writeBytes()`, `writeUTFBytes()`, `writeInt()`, and `writeObject()`, you can write data to a file, and using methods such as `readBytes()`, `readUTFBytes()`, `readInt()`, and `readObject()`, you can read data from a file. The data is always read and written as bytes, but the read and write methods automatically convert the data to more developer-friendly formats such as strings, integers, and so on.

Because you can read and write bytes, you can even go so far as to write a compression utility. An example of such a project is available at *http://code.google.com/p/ascompress*.

The `openAsync()` method opens a file for reading or writing asynchronously. This has no effect on how you need to structure code for writing data. You can call the write methods immediately after you call `openAsync()`. However, reading data requires that the data is available in the `FileStream` buffer before you can use it (e.g., display it in a component). When you call `openAsync()` using the read file mode, two events indicate when data is available: `progress` and `complete`. The `progress` event (which is of type `ProgressEvent`) notifies you each time more bytes are available in the buffer. The `complete` event notifies you when all the bytes have been read from the file into the buffer.

Example 21-2 shows how to read and write text to a file.

Example 21-2. Reading and writing a text file

```
<?xml version="1.0" encoding="utf-8"?>
<mx:WindowedApplication xmlns:mx="http://www.adobe.com/2006/mxml">
    <mx:Script>
        <![CDATA[

            // Create a file reference to a file on the desktop.
            private var _file:File = File.desktopDirectory.
resolvePath("example.txt");

            private function saveFile():void {
```

```
                var stream:FileStream = new FileStream();

                // Open the file for writing.
                stream.openAsync(_file, FileMode.WRITE);

                // Write the contents of the text area plus a timestamp.
                stream.writeUTFBytes(textArea.text + "\n\n[this file saved on " +
(new Date()) + "]");
            }

            private function readFile():void {

                // Test if the file exists. If it does then open it for reading.
                // Otherwise, display a message to the user.
                if(_file.exists) {
                    var stream:FileStream = new FileStream();

                    // Listen for the complete event before trying to use the
                    // data.
                    stream.addEventListener(Event.COMPLETE, readCompleteHandler)
                    stream.openAsync(_file, FileMode.READ);
                }
                else {
                    textArea.text = "You must save the file before reading it";
                }
            }

            // Display the data in the text area.
            private function readCompleteHandler(event:Event):void {
                var stream:FileStream = event.target as FileStream;
                textArea.text = stream.readUTFBytes(stream.bytesAvailable);
            }
        ]]>
    </mx:Script>
    <mx:TextArea id="textArea" width="100%" height="80%" />
    <mx:Button label="Read" click="readFile();" />
    <mx:Button label="Save" click="saveFile();" />
</mx:WindowedApplication>
```

Although this example illustrates reading and writing text, you can use the same basic principles to read and write any sort of data, including binary data such as images and video.

AIR will automatically serialize and deserialize custom data types when you write to a file and then read from a file if you have added the `[RemoteClass]` metadata tag to the custom data type class. Then you only need to write an instance of the class to the file using the `writeObject()` method of the file stream, and you can read the object from a file stream using `readObject()`.

Using Local SQL Databases

AIR includes a SQLite database engine, which allows AIR applications to create and work with databases using Structured Query Language (SQL). Databases are exceptionally useful for AIR applications for a variety of reasons, including the following:

- Creating sometimes-connected applications that have offline data storage that allows the application to be used even when the user is not connected to the Internet
- Storing persistent application data for offline applications

AIR SQLite databases allow for a tremendous amount of functionality. In this chapter, we'll focus exclusively on the basics, such as creating databases and database connections and running SQL statements. To learn more about all of the details of working with SQLite databases with AIR, visit the Adobe web site at *http://livedocs.adobe.com/air/1/devappsflash/SQL_01.html*.

You can use SQLite Admin for AIR, written by Christophe Coenraets, to administrate SQLite databases on your computer. This program is available at *http://coenraets.org/blog/2008/02/sqlite-admin-for-air-10*.

Creating a database connection

When you want to work with a local database using AIR, you must first create a connection to the database using an instance of `flash.data.SQLConnection`. SQLite databases are written to disk as files. Therefore, when you create a `SQLConnection` object, you must tell it what file to use. You can do that using the `openAsync()` method, as in the following code:

```
var databaseFile:File = File.applicationStorageDirectory.resolveFile("example.db");
var sqlConnection:SQLConnection = new SQLConnection();
sqlConnection.openAsync(databaseFile);
```

If a database file doesn't yet exist, the default behavior of the `openAsync()` method is to create the file. You can optionally specify a second parameter that indicates the mode in which to open the database. You can use the `flash.data.SQLMode` constants of `CREATE` (the default), `READ`, and `UPDATE` for this purpose. If you use the read or update mode and the file does not exist, the `SQLConnection` object will dispatch an error event.

Typically, an AIR application will need to run SQL statements as soon as the connection is opened. For example, an AIR application may need to create tables or read data from existing tables when the application starts. Because the `openAsync()` method opens a connection asynchronously, you must listen for the open event before executing any SQL statements. Therefore, the preceding code would typically include adding an event listener for the open event, as in the following code example on the next page.

```
var databaseFile:File = File.applicationStorageDirectory.resolveFile("example.db");
var sqlConnection:SQLConnection = new SQLConnection();
sqlConnection.addEventListener(Event.OPEN, openHandler);
sqlConnection.openAsync(databaseFile);
```

Running SQL statements

Once you've established a connection to a database, you can execute SQL statements. The SQLite engine used by AIR supports most standard SQL statements, including `CREATE TABLE`, `INSERT`, `UPDATE`, `DELETE`, and `SELECT`, among others. Regardless of what SQL statements you want to run, the steps are the same:

1. Create a `flash.data.SQLStatement` object.
2. Set the `sqlConnection` property of the statement object to the `SQLConnection` object.
3. Assign the SQL text to the `text` property of the statement object.
4. Call the `execute()` method.

Example 21-3 creates a connection to a database when the application starts and then runs a `CREATE TABLE` SQL statement to create a table if it doesn't yet exist.

Example 21-3. Running a basic SQL statement

```
<?xml version="1.0" encoding="utf-8"?>
<mx:WindowedApplication xmlns:mx="http://www.adobe.com/2006/mxml"
    creationComplete="creationCompleteHandler();">
    <mx:Script>
        <![CDATA[
            private var _sqlConnection:SQLConnection;

            private function creationCompleteHandler():void {
                var file:File = File.applicationStorageDirectory.
resolvePath("example.db");
                _sqlConnection = new SQLConnection();
                _sqlConnection.addEventListener(Event.OPEN, openHandler);
                _sqlConnection.openAsync(file);
            }

            private function openHandler(event:Event):void {
                var statement:SQLStatement = new SQLStatement();
                statement.sqlConnection = _sqlConnection;
                statement.text = "CREATE TABLE IF NOT EXISTS inventory(" +
                                 "id INTEGER PRIMARY KEY AUTOINCREMENT, " +
                                 "title TEXT, isbn TEXT, count INTEGER)";
                statement.execute();
            }

        ]]>
    </mx:Script>
</mx:WindowedApplication>
```

In Example 21-3, the columns of the table are declared as `INTEGER` and `TEXT`. These are called *storage classes*. SQLite supports the following storage classes: `NULL`, `INTEGER`, `REAL`, `TEXT`, and `BLOB`. Other types used by other database engines, such as `VARCHAR`, are automatically mapped to the corresponding SQLite storage classes (`TEXT` in the case of `VARCHAR`).

When a SQL statement successfully finishes executing, the `SQLStatement` object dispatches a `result` event of type `flash.events.SQLEvent`. This can be useful for making sure one dependent statement doesn't run before the previous one is complete. Example 21-4 builds on Example 21-3 by listening for the result event for the `CREATE TABLE` statement and then running a `SELECT` statement. This example also adds a data grid and an `ArrayCollection` data provider for displaying the results of the `SELECT` statement.

Example 21-4. Retrieving table data

```
<?xml version="1.0" encoding="utf-8"?>
<mx:WindowedApplication xmlns:mx="http://www.adobe.com/2006/mxml"
    creationComplete="creationCompleteHandler();">
    <mx:Script>
        <![CDATA[
            import mx.collections.ArrayCollection;

            private var _sqlConnection:SQLConnection;

            [Bindable]
            private var _tableData:ArrayCollection = new ArrayCollection();

            private function creationCompleteHandler():void {
                var file:File = File.applicationStorageDirectory.
resolvePath("example.db");

                _sqlConnection = new SQLConnection();
                _sqlConnection.addEventListener(Event.OPEN, openHandler);
                _sqlConnection.openAsync(file);
            }

            private function openHandler(event:Event):void {
                var statement:SQLStatement = new SQLStatement();
                statement.sqlConnection = _sqlConnection;
                statement.addEventListener(SQLEvent.RESULT, createHandler);
                statement.text = "CREATE TABLE IF NOT EXISTS inventory(" +
                                 "id INTEGER PRIMARY KEY AUTOINCREMENT, " +
                                 "title TEXT, isbn TEXT, count INTEGER)";
                statement.execute();
            }

            private function createHandler(event:Event):void {
                retrieveData();
            }

            private function retrieveData(event:Event = null):void {
                var statement:SQLStatement = new SQLStatement();
```

```
                statement.sqlConnection = _sqlConnection;
                statement.addEventListener(SQLEvent.RESULT, retrieveDataHandler);
                statement.text = "SELECT id, title, isbn, count FROM inventory";
                statement.execute();
            }

            private function retrieveDataHandler(event:SQLEvent):void {
            }

        ]]>
    </mx:Script>
    <mx:DataGrid id="tableData" dataProvider="{_tableData}"
        width="100%" height="50%" />
</mx:WindowedApplication>
```

At this point, the preceding example handles the result event of the SELECT statement, but it doesn't actually retrieve the results. That requires an additional step, which we'll look at in "Retrieving results later in the chapter. However, before retrieving results, the database must have data, which requires that we insert data. We'll look at how to insert data next.

Using parameters to insert data

Inserting data into a local database is as simple as using a standard INSERT statement. You can also update existing records by using UPDATE statements. However, in both cases it is important to ensure that data that is written to the database is free of malicious SQL added by a user. Therefore, any parameters should be provided by way of a built-in parameterization mechanism of the SQLStatement class.

When you want to use a parameter with an INERT or UPDATE statement, you can use a named placeholder in the SQL text by preceding the placeholder with an at sign (@) or a colon (:). For example, the following creates two placeholders called @a and @b:

```
statementObject.text = "INERT INTO exampleTable(column1, column2) VALUES(@a, @b)";
```

When you use named placeholders, you must define the values using the parameters property of the statement object. The parameters property is an associative array in which you must add entries for each placeholder where the placeholders are used as keys. For example, the following defines @a and @b as the values from text input components:

```
statementObject.parameters["@a"] = textInputA.text;
statementObject.parameters["@b"] = textInputB.text;
```

When you define parameters in this way, you are making sure the user cannot intentionally or accidentally insert values that would be problematic. Example 21-5 shows statement parameterization in context. This example builds on Example 21-4, allowing the user to add a new record to the table via a form.

Example 21-5. Adding new records

```
<?xml version="1.0" encoding="utf-8"?>
<mx:WindowedApplication xmlns:mx="http://www.adobe.com/2006/mxml"
    creationComplete="creationCompleteHandler();">
    <mx:Script>
        <![CDATA[
            import mx.collections.ArrayCollection;

            private var _sqlConnection:SQLConnection;

            [Bindable]
            private var _tableData:ArrayCollection = new ArrayCollection();

            private function creationCompleteHandler():void {
                var file:File = File.applicationStorageDirectory.
resolvePath("example.db");

                _sqlConnection = new SQLConnection();
                _sqlConnection.addEventListener(Event.OPEN, openHandler);
                _sqlConnection.openAsync(file);
            }

            private function openHandler(event:Event):void {
                var statement:SQLStatement = new SQLStatement();
                statement.sqlConnection = _sqlConnection;
                statement.addEventListener(SQLEvent.RESULT, createHandler);
                statement.text = "CREATE TABLE IF NOT EXISTS inventory(" +
                                 "id INTEGER PRIMARY KEY AUTOINCREMENT, " +
                                 "title TEXT, isbn TEXT, count INTEGER)";
                statement.execute();
            }

            private function createHandler(event:Event):void {
                retrieveData();
            }

            private function retrieveData(event:Event = null):void {
                var statement:SQLStatement = new SQLStatement();
                statement.sqlConnection = _sqlConnection;
                statement.addEventListener(SQLEvent.RESULT, retrieveDataHandler);
                statement.text = "SELECT id, title, isbn, count FROM inventory";
                statement.execute();
            }

            private function retrieveDataHandler(event:SQLEvent):void {
            }

            private function addBook():void {
                var statement:SQLStatement = new SQLStatement();
                statement.sqlConnection = _sqlConnection;

                // When the value is inserted run retrieveData() to query for the
                // latest table data.
                statement.addEventListener(SQLEvent.RESULT, retrieveData);
                statement.text = "INSERT INTO inventory(title, isbn, count)" +
```

```
                                   "VALUES(@title, @isbn, @count)";

                // Parameterize the statement using the values from the
                // text input controls
                statement.parameters["@title"] = bookTitle.text;
                statement.parameters["@isbn"] = bookIsbn.text;
                statement.parameters["@count"] = bookCount.text;
                bookTitle.text = "";
                bookIsbn.text = "";
                bookCount.text = "";
                statement.execute();
            }

        ]]>
    </mx:Script>
    <mx:DataGrid id="tableData" dataProvider="{_tableData}"
        width="100%" height="50%" />
    <mx:Form>
        <mx:FormItem label="title">
            <mx:TextInput id="bookTitle" />
        </mx:FormItem>
        <mx:FormItem label="isbn">
            <mx:TextInput id="bookIsbn" />
        </mx:FormItem>
        <mx:FormItem label="count">
            <mx:TextInput id="bookCount" restrict="0-9" />
        </mx:FormItem>
    </mx:Form>
    <mx:Button label="Add Book" click="addBook();" />
</mx:WindowedApplication>
```

Retrieving results

As you learned earlier, all SQL statements dispatch result events when they complete. This is true for all SQL statements regardless of whether they return a value or not. However, for some SQL statements this is particularly important. For example, when you run a SELECT statement you typically expect the statement to return a result set for use in the application. If you want to retrieve the result of a SQL statement you must handle the result event and then call the getResult() method of the SQLStatement object. The getResult() method returns a SQLResult object, which has a data property that is an array of the records returned. Example 21-6 shows this in context. This example builds on Example 21-5 by displaying the results in a data grid component.

Example 21-6. Displaying results in a data grid

```
<?xml version="1.0" encoding="utf-8"?>
<mx:WindowedApplication xmlns:mx="http://www.adobe.com/2006/mxml"
    creationComplete="creationCompleteHandler();">
    <mx:Script>
        <![CDATA[
            import mx.collections.ArrayCollection;

            private var _sqlConnection:SQLConnection;
```

```
            [Bindable]
            private var _tableData:ArrayCollection = new ArrayCollection();

            private function creationCompleteHandler():void {
                var file:File = File.applicationStorageDirectory.
resolvePath("example.db");

                _sqlConnection = new SQLConnection();
                _sqlConnection.addEventListener(Event.OPEN, openHandler);
                _sqlConnection.openAsync(file);
            }

            private function openHandler(event:Event):void {
                var statement:SQLStatement = new SQLStatement();
                statement.sqlConnection = _sqlConnection;
                statement.addEventListener(SQLEvent.RESULT, createHandler);
                statement.text = "CREATE TABLE IF NOT EXISTS inventory(" +
                                 "id INTEGER PRIMARY KEY AUTOINCREMENT, " +
                                 "title TEXT, isbn TEXT, count INTEGER)";
                statement.execute();
            }

            private function createHandler(event:Event):void {
                retrieveData();
            }

            private function retrieveData(event:Event = null):void {
                var statement:SQLStatement = new SQLStatement();
                statement.sqlConnection = _sqlConnection;
                statement.addEventListener(SQLEvent.RESULT, retrieveDataHandler);
                statement.text = "SELECT id, title, isbn, count FROM inventory";
                statement.execute();
            }

            private function retrieveDataHandler(event:SQLEvent):void {
                var result:SQLResult = event.target.getResult();
                _tableData = new ArrayCollection(result.data);
            }

            private function addBook():void {
                var statement:SQLStatement = new SQLStatement();
                statement.sqlConnection = _sqlConnection;
                statement.addEventListener(SQLEvent.RESULT, retrieveData);
                statement.text = "INSERT INTO inventory(title, isbn, count)" +
                                 "VALUES(@title, @isbn, @count)";
                statement.parameters["@title"] = bookTitle.text;
                statement.parameters["@isbn"] = bookIsbn.text;
                statement.parameters["@count"] = bookCount.text;
                bookTitle.text = "";
                bookIsbn.text = "";
                bookCount.text = "";
                statement.execute();
            }
```

```
        ]]>
    </mx:Script>
    <mx:DataGrid id="tableData" dataProvider="{_tableData}"
        width="100%" height="50%" />
    <mx:Form>
        <mx:FormItem label="title">
            <mx:TextInput id="bookTitle" />
        </mx:FormItem>
        <mx:FormItem label="isbn">
            <mx:TextInput id="bookIsbn" />
        </mx:FormItem>
        <mx:FormItem label="count">
            <mx:TextInput id="bookCount" restrict="0-9" />
        </mx:FormItem>
    </mx:Form>
    <mx:Button label="Add Book" click="addBook();" />
</mx:WindowedApplication>
```

Managing Windows

As you've already read (and likely seen if you've tested any of the examples in this chapter), AIR applications run outside the web browser. That means AIR applications are responsible for managing their own windows. All AIR applications have at least one window, but they can also have more than one window. In the next few sections, we'll look at a variety of topics related to AIR windows.

Creating a window

All AIR windows are instances of `flash.display.NativeWindow`. However, when building AIR applications using Flex it is far simpler to create windows using the `Window` component, which hides much of the complexity of working directly with `NativeWindow` objects. Therefore, when you want to create a window, you should create a new MXML document with a `Window` tag as the root tag, as in the following example:

```
<?xml version="1.0" encoding="utf-8"?>
<mx:Window xmlns:mx="http://www.adobe.com/2006/mxml">
</mx:Window>
```

When creating new windows, it's important to consider what type of window you want to create. You'll use two types of windows on a consistent basis: normal and utility. *Normal windows* use the full system chrome, and they appear in the Windows task bar and OS X window menu. *Utility windows*, on the other hand, use a system chrome without a title or icon, and they do not appear in the task bar or window menu. The main application window is typically a normal window, and usually you'll want to use the normal type of window when creating new windows that are conceptually new instances of something within the application (e.g., new photos in a photo editing application) if you want those instances to show up on the task bar or window menu. Utility windows are usually best suited for palettes or other parts of an application that shouldn't be accessible via the task bar or window menu.

You can specify the window type using the `type` property of the `Window` object. You cannot change the type of a window once it has been opened. The default type is `normal`. The following sets the type of a window using MXML:

```
<?xml version="1.0" encoding="utf-8"?>
<mx:Window xmlns:mx="http://www.adobe.com/2006/mxml" type="utility">
</mx:Window>
```

Windows also have a handful of properties you can set to affect the window appearance, such as the title bar and the status bar. Use the `status` property to customize the text that appears in the status bar and use the `title` property and the `titleIcon` property to customize the text and icon that appear in the title bar.

You can place any MXML or ActionScript code within a window document just as you would an application document or a component document.

Opening and closing windows

The first thing you must do if you want to open a window is create an instance of the window. You should use ActionScript to create the instance of the window, and not MXML. Example 21-7 creates an instance of a window (`ExampleWindow`) when the user clicks a button.

Example 21-7. Creating a new window

```
<?xml version="1.0" encoding="utf-8"?>
<mx:WindowedApplication xmlns:mx="http://www.adobe.com/2006/mxml">
    <mx:Script>
        <![CDATA[

            private function newWindow():void {
                var window:ExampleWindow = new ExampleWindow();
            }

        ]]>
    </mx:Script>
    <mx:Button label="New Window" click="newWindow();" />
</mx:WindowedApplication>
```

Once you have created an instance of a window, you can open it by calling the `open()` method, as in Example 21-8.

Example 21-8. Displaying a window

```
<?xml version="1.0" encoding="utf-8"?>
<mx:WindowedApplication xmlns:mx="http://www.adobe.com/2006/mxml">
    <mx:Script>
        <![CDATA[

            private function newWindow():void {
                var window:ExampleWindow = new ExampleWindow();
                window.open();
            }
```

```
        ]]>
    </mx:Script>
    <mx:Button label="New Window" click="newWindow();" />
</mx:WindowedApplication>
```

You can close a window using the `close()` method. However, closing a window in this fashion prevents the window from being reopened, so you should use the `close()` method only when you're certain that you really want to close the window. In contrast, if you want to hide a window (but be able to reopen it later), you should merely set the `visible` property to `false`.

Users can also close windows by clicking on the window's Close button, which has the same effect as calling the `close()` method. If you want to merely hide the window when the user clicks the Close button, you must do the following:

1. Listen for the closing event for the window.
2. When the closing event occurs cancel the event.
3. Set the `visible` property of the window to `false`.

Example 21-9 illustrates how this works.

Example 21-9. Hiding a window instead of closing it

```
<?xml version="1.0" encoding="utf-8"?>
<mx:Window xmlns:mx="http://www.adobe.com/2006/mxml"
    width="200" height="200" closing="closingHandler(event);">
    <mx:Script>
        <![CDATA[

            private function closingHandler(event:Event):void {
                event.preventDefault();
                visible = false;
            }

        ]]>
    </mx:Script>
    <mx:Label text="New Window" />
</mx:Window>
```

Managing opened windows

An AIR application keeps references to all opened windows. This is important and useful for a variety of reasons. One common example of when this is useful is when the user closes the main application window and you want the entire application to close. By default, all opened windows remain open, even if the main application window closes. To close opened windows when the main window closes you must call the `close()` method of all the opened windows.

To retrieve references to all the opened windows you have to work with lower-level (ActionScript, not Flex component) types, such as `flash.desktop.NativeApplication` and flash.display.NativeWindow. Although Flex shelters you from working with these types directly in most cases, this is one instance in which you have to. All AIR applications have just one instance of NativeApplication, and that one instance is accessible via the nativeApplication property of the WindowedApplication instance. The NativeApplication instance has a property called openedWindows, which is an array of NativeWindow objects. Note that every Window component manages exactly one NativeWindow instance, and it is the NativeWindow instance that is stored in the openedWindows array, not the Window component. However, many of the Window and NativeWindow APIs overlap. For example, both have close() methods, allowing you to close all opened windows, as in the following example. In this example, when the user clicks the Close button for the main window, the application loops through all the opened windows and closes them:

```
<?xml version="1.0" encoding="utf-8"?>
<mx:WindowedApplication xmlns:mx="http://www.adobe.com/2006/mxml"
closing="closingHandler(event);">
    <mx:Script>
        <![CDATA[

            private function closingHandler(event:Event):void {
                var windows:Array = nativeApplication.openedWindows;
                for(var i:int = 0; i < windows.length; i++) {
                    windows[i].close();
                }
            }

            private function newWindow():void {
                var window:ExampleWindow = new ExampleWindow();
                window.open();
            }

        ]]>
    </mx:Script>
    <mx:Button label="New Window" click="newWindow();" />
</mx:WindowedApplication>
```

Working with Clipboards

AIR applications can utilize copy and paste as well as drag and drop behaviors, not only within the application itself but also between AIR applications and even between the AIR application and non-AIR applications or the operating system. For example, a user of an AIR application can drag and drop an image from the AIR application onto the desktop where it can be saved as an image file, and a user can copy an image from a web page and paste it into an AIR application.

Both the copy and paste and drag and drop behaviors use clipboards, and they both use similar operations. However, they are different enough that we'll look at each independently.

Copy and paste

Copy and paste operations clearly have two poles: copying and pasting, each of which you'll need to know how to handle in an AIR application. Both copying and pasting use the system clipboard, which is accessible via a static `generalClipboard` property of the `flash.system.Clipboard` class. The `generalClipboard` property is a reference to a `Clipboard` object that maps to the system clipboard that the computer system uses for storing and retrieving data for copy and paste operations. For example, if the user copies text from a text editor or a web page, that text gets written to the system clipboard and you can access it in an AIR application via the `Clipboard.generalClipboard` object.

To copy data from an AIR application to the system clipboard you use the `setData()` method. The `setData()` method requires that you specify two pieces of information: the format in which to write the data and the data to write to the clipboard. AIR recognizes four formats: text, bitmap, URL, and file list. These formats correspond to the `TEXT_FORMAT`, `BITMAP_FORMAT`, `URL_FORMAT`, and `FILE_LIST_FORMAT` constants of the `flash.system.ClipboardFormats` class, and they also correspond to four different MIME types that the system clipboard typically uses. Example 21-10 takes a screenshot of the AIR application contents when the user clicks on the button, and it writes the bitmap to the system clipboard. You can then paste the image into another application that accepts data of that format (such as Microsoft Word).

Example 21-10. Copying a snapshot to the system clipboard

```
<?xml version="1.0" encoding="utf-8"?>
<mx:WindowedApplication xmlns:mx="http://www.adobe.com/2006/mxml">
    <mx:Script>
        <![CDATA[

            private function takeSnapshot():void {
                var bitmapData:BitmapData = new BitmapData(width, height);
                bitmapData.draw(this);
                var clipboard:Clipboard = Clipboard.generalClipboard;
                clipboard.clear();
                clipboard.setData(ClipboardFormats.BITMAP_FORMAT, bitmapData);
            }

        ]]>
    </mx:Script>
    <mx:FileSystemDataGrid />
    <mx:Button label="Take Snapshot" click="takeSnapshot();" />
</mx:WindowedApplication>
```

In Example 21-10, we call the `clear()` method on the clipboard before writing data to it. The `clear()` method removes all data in all formats from the clipboard. This is generally a good idea when working with the system clipboard because it ensures that other data in other formats will not be pasted into another application by mistake.

Pasting from the system clipboard into an AIR application is simply a matter of retrieving the data using the `getData()` method of the system clipboard. This requires that you know the format of the data you want to retrieve. The formats for retrieving data are the same as those for writing data to the system clipboard. Example 21-11 allows the user to paste an image into the application either by way of copying an image from an application (such as a web browser) or by copying a path (such as a URL) to an image.

Example 21-11. Pasting an image from a clipboard

```
<?xml version="1.0" encoding="utf-8"?>
<mx:WindowedApplication xmlns:mx="http://www.adobe.com/2006/mxml">
    <mx:Script>
        <![CDATA[

            var _bitmap:Bitmap;

            private function pasteImage():void {
                var clipboard:Clipboard = Clipboard.generalClipboard;
                if(clipboard.hasFormat(ClipboardFormats.BITMAP_FORMAT)) {
                    if(_bitmap == null) {
                        _bitmap = new Bitmap();
                        imageCanvas.rawChildren.addChild(_bitmap);
                    }
                    _bitmap.bitmapData = clipboard.getData(
ClipboardFormats.BITMAP_FORMAT) as BitmapData;
                    _bitmap.visible = true;
                    image.visible = false;
                    imageCanvas.width = _bitmap.bitmapData.width;
                    imageCanvas.height = _bitmap.bitmapData.height;
                }
                else if(clipboard.hasFormat(ClipboardFormats.TEXT_FORMAT)) {
                    image.source = clipboard.getData(
ClipboardFormats.TEXT_FORMAT) as String;
                    image.visible = true;
                    _bitmap.visible = false;
                }
            }

        ]]>
    </mx:Script>
    <mx:Canvas id="imageCanvas">
        <mx:Image id="image" />
    </mx:Canvas>
    <mx:Button label="Paste Image" click="pasteImage();" />
</mx:WindowedApplication>
```

You'll notice in Example 21-11 that we cast the value retrieved from the `getData()` method. Because any data can be written to the clipboard, it is necessary to cast the return value appropriately if assigning it to a typed variable or property.

Drag and drop

Drag and drop operations use the same basic clipboard principles as copy and paste. However, instead of using the system clipboard, drag and drop operations require a nonsystem instance of the `Clipboard` class. That means you must construct an instance of the `Clipboard` class using a `new` statement. You can then write data to the clipboard and read data from the clipboard.

There are two aspects to a drag and drop operation: the drag initiation and the drop. Both rely on the `flash.desktop.NativeDragManager` class. For initiating a drag operation you can call the static `doDrag()` method, which requires that you pass it a display object that is triggering the drag operation and the clipboard to use. Example 21-12 allows a user to drag an image from the AIR application to another application that accepts bitmap data (such as Word).

Example 21-12. Dragging an image from an AIR application

```
<?xml version="1.0" encoding="utf-8"?>
<mx:WindowedApplication xmlns:mx="http://www.adobe.com/2006/mxml">
    <mx:Script>
        <![CDATA[

            private function imageMouseDownHandler():void {
                var bitmapData:BitmapData = new BitmapData(image.width,
image.height);
                bitmapData.draw(image);
                var clipboard:Clipboard = new Clipboard();
                clipboard.setData(ClipboardFormats.BITMAP_FORMAT, bitmapData);
                NativeDragManager.doDrag(image, clipboard);
            }

        ]]>
    </mx:Script>
    <mx:Image id="image"
        source="http://www.rightactionscript.com/samplefiles/image2.jpg"
        mouseDown="imageMouseDownHandler();" />
</mx:WindowedApplication>
```

You'll notice that in Example 21-12 the `doDrag()` method is called in the event handler for a `mouseDown` event. The `doDrag()` method will work only when called in an event handler for a `mouseDown` event or a `mouseMove` event with the mouse button down.

When you want to handle the drop aspect of a drag and drop operation, you need to listen for two primary events: `nativeDragEnter` and `nativeDragDrop`. The `nativeDragEnter` event occurs when the user drags something over an interactive object. At that point, you must determine whether that interactive object should accept drops for the data being dragged over the object. This is possible by calling the `NativeDrag`

Manager.acceptDragDrop() method and passing it a reference to the interactive object. Only then will the object be capable of receiving notifications when the user actually drops anything on it, thus causing a nativeDragDrop event. Both nativeDragEnter and nativeDragDrop events are of type flash.events.NativeDragEvent, which has a clipboard property that references a Clipboard object that contains the data for the operation. Example 21-13 allows the user to drag an image (from a web page, for example) or a URL into the AIR application and drop it on the canvas.

Example 21-13. Dropping an image into an AIR application

```
<?xml version="1.0" encoding="utf-8"?>
<mx:WindowedApplication xmlns:mx="http://www.adobe.com/2006/mxml">
    <mx:Script>
        <![CDATA[

            private var _bitmap:Bitmap;

            private function nativeDragEnterHandler(event:NativeDragEvent):void {
                var clipboard:Clipboard = event.clipboard;
                if(clipboard.hasFormat(ClipboardFormats.BITMAP_FORMAT)) {
                    NativeDragManager.acceptDragDrop(imageCanvas);
                }
            }

            private function nativeDragDropHandler(event:NativeDragEvent):void {
                var clipboard:Clipboard = event.clipboard;
                if(clipboard.hasFormat(ClipboardFormats.BITMAP_FORMAT)) {
                    if(_bitmap == null) {
                        _bitmap = new Bitmap();
                        imageCanvas.rawChildren.addChild(_bitmap);
                    }
                    _bitmap.bitmapData = clipboard.getData(
ClipboardFormats.BITMAP_FORMAT) as BitmapData;
                    _bitmap.visible = true;
                    image.visible = false;
                    imageCanvas.width = _bitmap.bitmapData.width;
                    imageCanvas.height = _bitmap.bitmapData.height;
                }
                else if(clipboard.hasFormat(ClipboardFormats.TEXT_FORMAT)) {
                    image.source = clipboard.getData(
ClipboardFormats.TEXT_FORMAT) as String;
                    image.visible = true;
                    _bitmap.visible = false;
                }
            }

        ]]>
    </mx:Script>
    <mx:Canvas id="imageCanvas" backgroundColor="#FFFFFF" width="100%" height="100%"
        nativeDragEnter="nativeDragEnterHandler(event);"
        nativeDragDrop="nativeDragDropHandler(event);">
        <mx:Image id="image" />
    </mx:Canvas>
</mx:WindowedApplication>
```

Using HTML

Arguably one of the "coolest" features of AIR applications for Flex developers is the ability to render HTML content in Flex components. AIR includes the WebKit engine, the same HTML engine used by the Safari web browser, and this engine allows AIR applications to render HTML. Not only can you load and render HTML, but because it renders inside a Flex component, you can treat the component just as you would any other component, applying transforms, filters (blurs, etc.), and effects to the HTML.

All you need to do to render HTML in a Flex-based AIR application is to use the `HTML` component. You can set the URL to load and render for an `HTML` component by setting the `location` property. The following example loads the O'Reilly web site into an `HTML` component:

```
<?xml version="1.0" encoding="utf-8"?>
<mx:WindowedApplication xmlns:mx="http://www.adobe.com/2006/mxml">
    <mx:HTML id="html" location="http://www.oreilly.com" width="100%" height="80%" />
</mx:WindowedApplication>
```

This example illustrates that you can apply a filter to an `HTML` component:

```
<?xml version="1.0" encoding="utf-8"?>
<mx:WindowedApplication xmlns:mx="http://www.adobe.com/2006/mxml">
    <mx:Script>
        <![CDATA[

            private function toggleBlur():void {
                if(html. filters.length > 0) {
                    html. filters = [];
                }
                else {
                    html. filters = [new BlurFilter()];
                }
            }

        ]]>
    </mx:Script>
    <mx:HTML id="html" location="http://www.oreilly.com" width="100%" height="80%" />
    <mx:Button toggle="true" label="Toggle Blur" click="toggleBlur();" />
</mx:WindowedApplication>
```

If you test this example, you might notice that the filter is applied to the entire `HTML` component, including the scroll bars. If you prefer to access just the rendered HTML, you can access the lower-level `HTMLLoader` object nested within the `HTML` component via the `htmlLoader` property. The following rewrite of the preceding example applies the filter only to the HTML and not to the scroll bars:

```
<?xml version="1.0" encoding="utf-8"?>
<mx:WindowedApplication xmlns:mx="http://www.adobe.com/2006/mxml">
    <mx:Script>
        <![CDATA[

            private function toggleBlur():void {
```

```
                if(html.htmlLoader.filters.length > 0) {
                    html.htmlLoader.filters = [];
                }
                else {
                    html.htmlLoader.filters = [new BlurFilter()];
                }
            }

        ]]>
    </mx:Script>
    <mx:HTML id="html" location="http://www.oreilly.com" width="100%" height="80%" />
    <mx:Button toggle="true" label="Toggle Blur" click="toggleBlur();" />
</mx:WindowedApplication>
```

You can navigate through the browsing history of an `HTML` component using the following properties and methods: `historyLength`, `historyPosition`, `historyBack()`, `historyForward()`, and `historyGo()`. The following example adds back and forward buttons:

```
<?xml version="1.0" encoding="utf-8"?>
<mx:WindowedApplication xmlns:mx="http://www.adobe.com/2006/mxml">
    <mx:Script>
        <![CDATA[

            private function back():void {
                if(html.historyPosition > 0) {
                    html.historyBack();
                }
            }

            private function forward():void {
                if(html.historyPosition < html.historyLength - 1) {
                    html.historyForward();
                }
            }

        ]]>
    </mx:Script>
    <mx:HBox>
        <mx:Button label="Back" click="back();" />
        <mx:Button label="Forward" click="forward();" />
    </mx:HBox>
    <mx:HTML id="html" location="http://www.oreilly.com" width="100%" height="80%" />
</mx:WindowedApplication>
```

Distributing AIR Applications

Distributing AIR applications involves the following basic aspects:

- Creating *.air* files
- Allowing users to install the application

In the following sections, we'll look at each of these topics in more detail.

Creating Installers

AIR application installers are *.air* files, which contain all the files necessary to run the AIR application. All installers must be digitally signed, which ensures the integrity of the installation file (meaning a user will know the installation file has not been altered since it was published). You can digitally sign an installer using a certificate. Certificates can be of two types: a self-signed certificate or a certificate from a certificate authority (CA) such as VeriSign. When you sign an installer using a self-signed certificate, the installer will display the publisher as unknown. But, if you use a certificate from a CA, the installer will display the identity of the publisher contained in the certificate.

If you want to use a certificate from a CA, you must purchase the certificate. If you want to use a self-signed certificate, you can create the certificate yourself using the Flex SDK, which we'll look at in the following section.

Creating a self-signed certificate

You can create a self-signed certificate using the Flex SDK. If you are using Flex Builder, you can create a certificate while exporting the installer using the Create Self-Signed Digital Certificate dialog described in the following section. Otherwise, if you're not using Flex Builder, you'll need to run a command from the command line.

To create a certificate from the command line, use `adt` with the `certificate` option. The syntax is as follows:

```
adt -certificate -cn certificateName keyType pfxFile password
```

The certificate name is simply an arbitrary name you assign to the certificate. For self-signing certificates created using `adt` the key type should always be either 1024-RSA or 2048-RSA. Certificates created using `adt` are stored in *.pfx* files, and you must specify the file to which to save the certificate. Furthermore, certificates must have passwords. The following line of code creates a certificate:

```
adt -certificate -cn Example 1024-RSA certificate.pfx r5t6b3
```

Creating an .air file using Flex Builder

Flex Builder has a wizard that walks you through the steps of creating an *.air* file for an AIR application. You can select the Project→Export Release Build option from the application menus to open the Export Release Build window. The wizard has three steps:

Step 1: Project settings
: In this step, you must select the Flex project to export and the name of the *.air* file to export.

Step 2: Digital signature
: In this step, you must select a certificate to use, and you must specify the password for the certificate. If you don't have a certificate, you can click the Create button to create a new self-signed certificate.

Step 3: Files to include
: In this step, you select the files to include in the *.air* file. Remember that an *.air* file is the installer, and it must include all the files necessary to run the application. At a minimum, this will require the main *.swf* file and the descriptor XML file. However, depending on what else your application requires you may need to include additional files.

Creating an .air file using the SDK

When you want to create an *.air* file using the Flex SDK, you can use `adt` from the command line. In this case, you use `adt` with the `package` option. The syntax is as follows:

```
adt -package SIGNING_OPTIONS airFile descriptor FILES_TO_INCLUDE
```

The signing options vary depending on the type of keystore used for the certificate, and we'll see one example of this in a minute. The output of running `adt` in this way is an *.air* file, and you must specify the name of the *.air* file to output. To create an *.air* file you must specify a descriptor file. You can also specify the files to include in the installer; those files will always include at least one file: the main *.swf*.

The signing options are different based on the types of keystores used, and the various options are too numerous to list in detail in this chapter. You can read more about signing options at the website *http://livedocs.adobe.com/flex/3/html/CommandLineTools_5.html*. For the purposes of this chapter, we'll look at just one specific example, which is the case of a self-signed certificate created using `adt`. In that case, the signing options are as follows:

```
-storetype pkcs12 -keystore pfxFile
```

The `storetype` in this case tells `adt` that the certificate is of type `pkcs12`, and the `keystore` tells `adt` where to find the file in which the certificate is stored.

Therefore, the following command will create an *.air* file called *Example.air* using a self-signed certificate called *certificate.pfx*:

```
adt -package -storetype pkcs12 -keystore certificate.pfx Example.air
Example-descriptor.xml Main.swf
```

Once you run the preceding command, you will be prompted for the password for the certificate.

Creating a Badge

After you've created an *.air* file, you can distribute it to anyone with the AIR runtime, and he can install the AIR application simply by double-clicking on the *.air* file. That means one strategy for deploying applications is to email an *.air* file or make the *.air* file available for download. However, if the user does not already have the AIR runtime installed, his system will not know what to do with the *.air* file. Therefore, you may prefer to use the seamless install feature.

The seamless install feature allows users to click a badge on a web page to install an AIR application. A *badge* is merely a web-based *.swf* that does the following:

1. It detects whether the user has the AIR runtime installed.
2. If the user does not have the AIR runtime installed, he is presented an option to install the runtime from the badge.
3. Once it is determined that the user has the AIR runtime, the AIR application is installed.

You can create a custom badge *.swf* file. The steps are as follows:

1. Create a standard Flex web project.
2. Use a `flash.display.Loader` object to load a *.swf* file from *http://airdownload.adobe.com/air/browserapi/air.swf*, and load the *.swf* into `ApplicationDomain.currentDomain`.
3. Use a UI mechanism (such as a button click) to trigger the installation sequence.
4. Call the `installApplication()` method of the content property of the loader.

The *air.swf* file on the Adobe.com (*http://Adobe.com*) server contains a few methods you can use to create a seamless install badge, the most important of which is the `installApplication()` method. To use this and the other methods on the server you must load the *.swf* into the current application domain. You can then call the methods from the content property of the loader. The `installApplication()` method requires two parameters: the path to the *.air* file and the required AIR runtime version (as a string). Example 21-14 is an example of a badge.

Example 21-14. A basic AIR badge

```
<?xml version="1.0" encoding="utf-8"?>
<mx:Application xmlns:mx="http://www.adobe.com/2006/mxml" layout="absolute"
creationComplete="creationCompleteHandler();">
    <mx:Script>
        <![CDATA[

            private var _loader:Loader;

            private function creationCompleteHandler():void {
                _loader = new Loader();
                var context:LoaderContext = new LoaderContext();
                context.applicationDomain = ApplicationDomain.currentDomain;
                _loader.contentLoaderInfo.addEventListener(Event.INIT, initHandler);
                _loader.load(new URLRequest("http://airdownload.adobe.com/
air/browserapi/air.swf"));
            }
```

```
            private function initHandler(event:Event):void {
                button.enabled = true;
            }

            private function install():void {
                (_loader.content as Object).installApplication("Example.air", "1.0");
            }

        ]]>
    </mx:Script>
    <mx:Button id="button" label="Install" enabled="false" click="install();" />
</mx:Application>
```

Summary

In this chapter, you learned about Adobe AIR, a technology that allows you to leverage your Flex knowledge to create applications that run on the desktop. These applications have access to all the features of standard Flex applications, but they also have additional features. For example, as you learned in this chapter, AIR applications can access the local filesystem, utilize local databases, manage system-level copy and paste and drag and drop operations, and load and render HTML content.

In this chapter, you also learned how to build and deploy AIR applications. Using what you've learned in this chapter, you can start building applications for the desktop. This opens new possibilities for you as a Flex developer because you can now build applications that target both the Web *and* the desktop. This chapter is necessarily limited to being an introduction and overview of what is possible with AIR. We set out to provide you with the basics to set a foundation for building AIR applications. If you are interested in learning more, you can continue your study using the online AIR documentation (*http://adobe.com/go/airdocs*).

CHAPTER 22

Building a Flex Application

Throughout this book, you've learned about all the pieces comprising Flex. But you haven't seen how these pieces come together to create a working application. An academic knowledge of Flex is essential to successfully building Flex applications, but that knowledge is of little value unless you also have a concrete understanding of how to use what you've learned in practice. In this chapter, we'll look at how to build a Flex application using everything you learned in the first 21 chapters of the book. We'll walk through building a sample application to illustrate important concepts, and to give you practical experience building a Flex application.

Introducing the Sample Application

In this chapter, we'll take a look at a sample application that illustrates the key points we discuss in the chapter. The sample application is a simple photo viewer that uses the Flickr API from the popular photo-sharing service, Flickr (*http://www.flickr.com*), to allow users to search for photos via keywords and then view photo details. We call this application FlickrFlex.

Figure 22-1 shows the application's home page, which displays a random photo and a search form.

The entire application runs in a web browser, and it supports the browser's back and forward buttons as well as deep linking directly to a search result or to a specific photo's details.

Throughout this chapter, we'll take a look at key parts of the application. What we will not do is go line by line through the code and build the application step by step. Instead, we highlight what we think are important concepts, and then we are leaving it to you, the reader, to download the sample application and review the code in more detail. You may also find that you will gain the most from this chapter if you read it more than once.

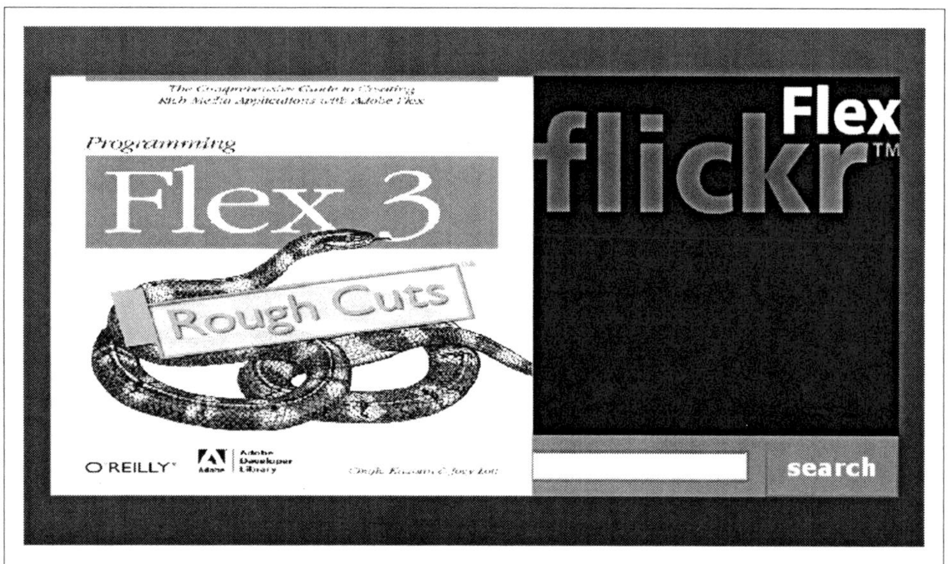

Figure 22-1. The home page of the FlickrFlex application

Once the user searches for photos, the results are shown in a tile grid (see Figure 22-2).

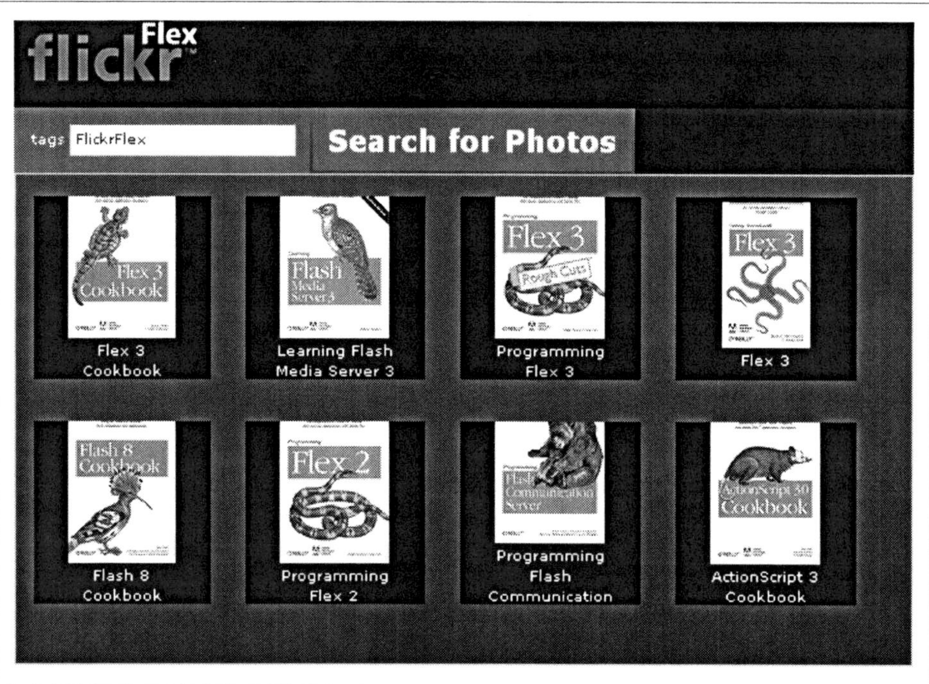

Figure 22-2. The results of a photo search, shown in a tile grid

The user can click a thumbnail to view the photo details screen, as shown in Figure 22-3.

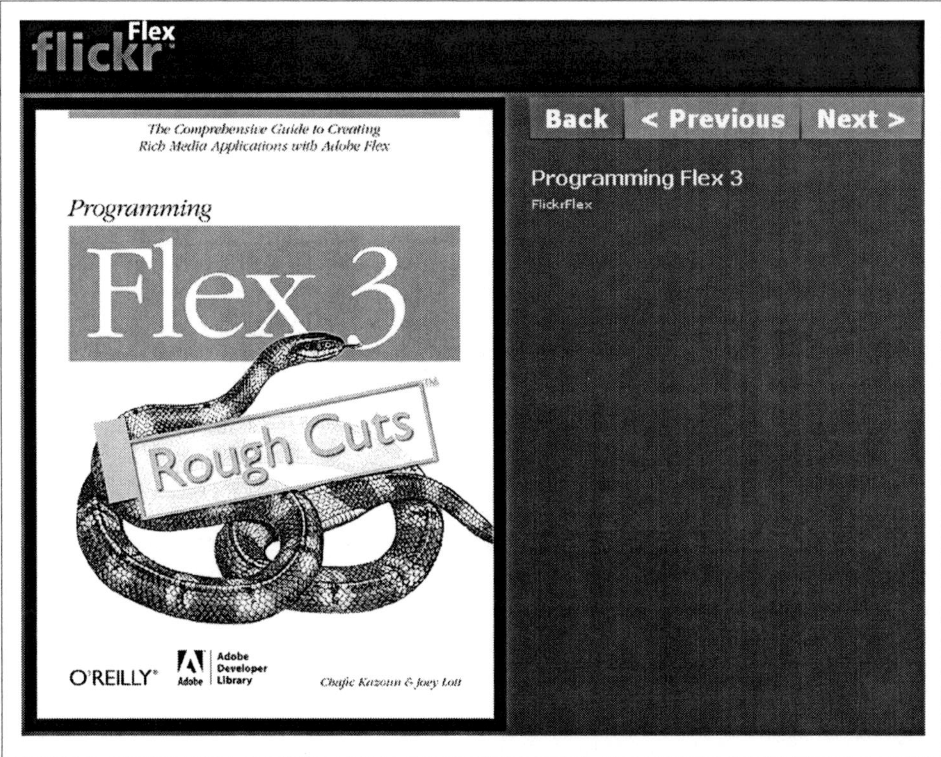

Figure 22-3. The photo details screen

Even though FlickrFlex is a relatively simple application, we think it is complex enough that it encompasses many of the common requirements of Flex web applications. For example, FlickrFlex has to solve problems related to making requests to remote services, which is a very common problem for Flex applications. Also, FlickrFlex has to solve the problems related to browser integration, which is quite a common requirement for Flex applications. By looking at FlickrFlex, we think you'll be able to see ways to solve common problems that you are likely to find in many of your own projects. The purpose of our discussion of FlickrFlex is to look at larger themes and patterns; strategies for solving common application design problems. Therefore, rather than building the entire application one line of code at a time, we'll highlight the important features and patterns.

Every project starts with the basics. You always have to configure the environment, get access to services, and create projects files. In the next few sections, we'll look at the steps required to get started.

Creating a Flickr Account

The sample application runs off the Flickr service. To follow along you will need to have a Flickr account and an API key. Both are free.

- To apply for a Flickr account, go to *http://www.flickr.com/signup*. Flickr is owned by Yahoo!, and a Flickr account is synonymous with a Yahoo! account. If you already have a Yahoo! account, you don't need to apply for a Flickr account because you can use your existing account.
- Once you have logged in with the Flickr account, go to *http://www.flickr.com/services/api/keys/apply* to apply for a new Flickr API key. The Flickr API requires the API key. To follow along with this sample application, you should apply for a noncommercial key.

Once you've created a Flickr API key, you can continue to the next section. You'll next get the source code for the application, and you'll need to edit a configuration file with your Flickr API key.

Retrieving the Source Code

Rather than trying to walk you through the steps for writing all the code for the sample application, we've opted to simply provide you with complete, working source code. You can then spend less time typing code from listings in the book and more time reading about why the code is written the way it is.

To distribute the source code for the sample application, we've created a Google Code project for FlickrFlex. You can view the project site at *http://code.google.com/p/flickrflex/*. From the Google Code project site, you can download the application source code in one of two ways: using Subversion or as a *.zip* file.

We recommend using Subversion to download the source code. You can use any Subversion client to check out the project by using the following repository URL: *http://flickrflex.googlecode.com/svn/trunk/flickrflex-read-only*. This URL will work only with a Subversion client, and not in a web browser.

If you're not comfortable using Subversion (though we highly recommend that you learn how to use it), you can instead download the FlickrFlex application as a *.zip* file from the project's download page, at *http://code.google.com/p/flickrflex/downloads/list*.

Regardless of how you download the project files, we assume that you have downloaded (and extracted, if necessary) all the project files before continuing with the rest of the chapter. Although you can read this chapter and learn much from it without downloading and using the project files, it is likely that you will gain much more if you do follow along with the project files.

Subversion is a version control system. Using a Subversion client and the preceding URL you can download a read-only version of the Flickr-Flex project from the Google Code Subversion server. A detailed description of what Subversion is and how to use it is beyond the scope of this book. However, if you want to learn more about Subversion you can read the entirely free Subversion book, *Version Control with Subversion*, at *http://svnbook.red-bean.com*. You can also find a list of Subversion client programs at *http://subversion.tigris.org/links.html#clients*. Using most of these clients is rather simple, especially when checking out a read-only version of a project, and you can generally find instructions for how to check out a project in the documentation for each client.

Setting Up a New Project

If you are using Flex Builder 3, you can simply import the Flex project, as we've included all the Flex Builder project files along with the source code. If you are not using Flex Builder, you will need to compile the application using `mxmlc`, as you learned how to do in Chapter 2. *Flickr.mxml* is the main application *.mxml* file for FlickrFlex, and *TestRunner.mxml* is the main *.mxml* file for running the unit tests for the project.

Configuring FlickrFlex

The code for the FlickrFlex application is complete and working exactly as downloaded. However, you will need to provide your Flickr API key and secret, both of which you can find at *http://www.flickr.com/services/api/keys/*. You should locate and edit the *assets_embed/xml/flickrconfig.xml* file in the application project files. The file contains the following:

```
<configuration>
    <apiKey>Your API key</apiKey>
    <secret>Your API secret</secret>
</configuration>
```

You should replace your API key and your API secret text with the correct values from the Flickr page.

Compiling the Application

Now that you've downloaded and configured the FlickrFlex project, the next step is to compile it. This is a straightforward step since there is nothing particularly unusual about the project. If you are using Flex Builder and you've imported the Flex project, you'll probably note that two of the *.mxml* files are set to be compilable: *TestRunner.mxml* and *Flick.mxml*. The *Flickr.mxml* file is the file you want to compile, and in Flex Builder the compilation step is automatic unless you've disabled automatic builds for the project. That means all you need to do is run the *Flickr.mxml* file to compile and launch it.

If you're using the Flex SDK without Flex Builder, you will need to compile *Flickr.mxml* using `mxmlc`. FlickrFlex does not require any additional libraries or any unusual compiler options.

Running the Application

When you have successfully followed the preceding steps, you should be able to compile and run the application. You'll know the application is working correctly when you can verify the following user stories:

- The user sees a random "nature" photo on the home page.
- The user can enter a search term on the home page and request search results.
- When search results are returned, the user sees thumbnails and titles for all search results displayed in a scrollable grid.
- When the user clicks on a thumbnail in the search results, she is taken to that photo's details screen in which she sees a large version of the photo along with the title and description (if any exist).
- From the details screen the user can click a button to return to the previous screen.
- From the details screen the user can click Next and Previous buttons to navigate through details of the search results.
- The user can navigate back and forward between viewed pages/screens by using the back and forward web browser buttons.
- The user can copy the address from the browser address bar at any point and paste it into another browser window to see the same page/screen (a process known as *deep linking*).

Utilizing Best Practices

There are lots of ways build Flex applications. This shouldn't surprise you; there are lots of ways to do most things in life, and building Flex applications is no different. Furthermore, it's impossible to say there is exactly one right way to build Flex applications, just as it is impossible to say there is just one right way to do anything else. However, you can employ certain strategies that increase your likelihood of success when building Flex applications. We call these *best practices*, and in the following sections we'll go into a bit more detail regarding a few of the best practices we consider most important. We strongly encourage you to try these out for yourself. Give them a fair chance; you may later discard some of them, but chances are that more than a few will prove to help you and your teams in the long run.

Organizing Files

How you organize project files can have a tremendous impact of the success of a project. File organization might seem unimportant, but don't underrate how influential this factor can be. Organizing files well ensures that not only is it easier to find the files and easier for teams to work together, but also you avoid potential naming conflicts and can facilitate source code versioning (see "Versioning" later in this chapter).

If you use Flex Builder to create Flex projects, you have probably already noticed that Flex Builder provides a degree of organization. Primarily, Flex Builder distinguishes between where it stores source code (*.mxml* and *.as* files) and where it stores deployable application files (*.swf*, *.html*, and runtime assets). The default names for the directories that Flex Builder uses are *src* for source code and *bin-debug* for deployable application files. This high-level structure is important and essential to good project file organization. However, you can do more, and indeed more is required to keep files organized clearly. The following are a few of the key things you can do to organize files:

- Place all *.mxml* and *.as* files (except for the main application *.mxml* file) in packages. As you've learned, Flex treats *.mxml* files as ActionScript classes, and therefore we can think of them and organize them just like we would ActionScript classes. We generally recommend using reverse-domain names for packages. For example, all the classes and *.mxml* files for the sample application in this chapter are organized within a `com.oreilly` package. After the reverse-domain package, we advise using a project subpackage where appropriate. In the sample application, we place all the files in a `pf3` project subpackage. Then it is considered a best practice to further organize files into subpackages. For the sample application, we use the following subpackages:

  `controllers`
  : See "Abstracting Common Patterns" later in this chapter for more information about controllers.

  `events`
  : We use this package for all event types (subclasses of `Event`).

  `models`
  : See "Abstracting Common Patterns" for more information about models.

  `services`
  : This package organizes all the business delegate and related classes.

  `views`
  : See "Abstracting Common Patterns" for more information about views.

- Place all embedded assets in a directory inside the source files directory. In the sample application, we call this directory *assets_embed*. This directory can contain *.css* files, embedded *.swf* files, embedded image files, and generally any sort of file that might be embedded in the application (as opposed to loaded at runtime).

Depending on the number of files, it may make sense to create further subdirectories to better organize everything within the embedded assets directory.

- Any runtime assets that must be deployed with the application should be organized within the deployable application directory (*bin-debug*). These files might include *.xml* files, image files, or any sort of file that the application loads at runtime. Generally, these files should be organized within subdirectories within the deployable application directory.

Using CSS

Flex provides a lot of ways to apply styles to applications. You learned about all of these ways to style applications in Chapter 8. This provides a great deal of flexibility in how to style an application, which is both good and bad. It is good in that it provides lots of options. It is bad in that it allows developers and teams of developers to apply styles without a consistent approach or plan.

We find that in general, it is best to apply most, if not all, styles via external *.css* files. We make exceptions for some layout-related styles such as `verticalAlign` and `horizontalAlign`, which we frequently apply inline. However, we prefer to apply the vast majority of styles via external *.css* files. For the Flickr application, we use only one *.css* file because the application simply isn't complex enough to warrant more than one *.css* file.

If you look at the *FlickrFlex.css* file, you'll notice that we've organized our selectors to make them somewhat easy to locate within the file. We place the `Application` type selector first in the file, followed by the rest of the type selectors in alphabetical order. Then we follow the type selectors with the class selectors, also organized in alphabetical order.

Although it is sometimes tempting to apply styles via inline attributes to MXML tags, we've found it is far better in the long run to take the extra minute or two to apply styles via external *.css*. This has several advantages, some of which are as follows:

- External *.css* cleans up style-related clutter from *.mxml* files.
- External *.css* allows non-Flex developers to work on styling an application.
- External *.css* helps to differentiate between the layout (*view/.mxml*) and style (*.css*).

Application Components

Application components are invaluable and cannot be overrated. Large *.mxml* files or ActionScript classes without clearly defined roles and responsibilities are a good sign that refactoring is necessary. When an application consists of many smaller components, it is often easier to work as a team, to debug an application, and to add new features or make changes to existing features. Too few components, or components that are too large and too complex, make applications difficult to manage. It is generally advisable to err on the side of too many components with responsibilities that are too granular than the other way around. As a rule of thumb, all components should have no more than two or possibly three key responsibilities. If a component has more responsibilities, it should be refactored into several more specialized components.

As we'll see later in this chapter, we use application components extensively for the parts of the application that we call the views and the controllers. Almost universally, developers use application components for views. Our use of application components for controllers is somewhat less usual, but we think it provides a solution to issues that are unique to Flex. You can read more about views and controllers later in this chapter. You can read more about application components in general in Chapter 9.

Versioning

Although versioning may seem like a related practices rather than a core practice, it is nevertheless a core practice that every team should be following for Flex projects. A variety of versioning software tools are available. Some of the most popular are Subversion (which we are using for the sample application), CVS, Mercurial, Git, Team Foundation Server, and Visual SourceSafe (VSS). Every versioning software works slightly differently, and different teams have different philosophies regarding how to manage code repositories. For example, some teams prefer not to add large assets (e.g., videos) to version control repositories, whereas other teams prefer the simplicity of adding everything to one location. What is most important is that you always add all source code to a repository, and you should always keep the repository up-to-date with changes. For the FlickrFlex project and many of our own projects, we like to add everything to the Subversion repository, including source code, Flex Builder project files, runtime assets, and compile time assets (embedded images, fonts, etc.).

Unit Testing

Unit testing involves writing code that runs automated tests on project code. A test will run an assertion that will either pass or fail. A group of tests is known as a *suite* of tests. When running a suite of tests, you can quickly determine whether code is behaving as expected. If all the tests in a suite pass, it indicates that there is a good chance the application is working correctly. If one or more tests fail, it shows you where you should look to correct a problem with the code. Automated tests allow you to run suites of tests frequently, often every time you make a change to the code for an application. The results of the test will help you immediately identify any problems which new code might introduce.

Unit testing does not require that you use a testing framework. However, using an existing testing framework can greatly simplify writing and running test suites. There are two testing frameworks that we know of for use with Flex: FlexUnit (*http://code.google.com/p/as3flexunitlib/*) and AsUnit (*http://www.asunit.org*). We find that FlexUnit is a little easier to use with Flex than AsUnit.

If you're not familiar with unit testing or FlexUnit, you might find the article at *http://www.adobe.com/devnet/flex/articles/unit_testing.html* to be a helpful introduction.

Once you've starting writing unit tests, you're likely to ask yourself exactly what you should be testing. Although it might be possible to write tests for every part of a Flex application, we find that it is generally easiest and most effective to write tests for only certain parts of an application. In particular, we find that tests for the following are most useful:

Data model classes that have custom serialization or deserialization methods
: For example, if a class has a method to deserialize from XML data, it can be very useful to write a test or tests for that.

Business delegates
: These are points of integration that represent relatively high fragility. If the contract with the service changes (e.g., the publisher of the service changes the API), it's possible that the entire Flex application will stop working correctly. Having good unit tests for business delegates helps you to quickly identify where an error is occurring if a service contract changes or if a service simply goes offline or throws an error.

Utility classes/methods
: Any method of a utility class should generally have unit tests.

There is a philosophical approach to software development, known as test-driven development (TDD). This methodology advocates writing tests *before* writing application code. You then write the application code to get it to pass the tests. Some Flex developers find TDD works well for certain types of classes, such as model classes and business delegates. Other Flex developers don't find that TDD is well suited to Flex development. We are mixed on the issue of TDD for Flex development, with one of us liking it and the other not. You'll have to be the judge for yourself.

You can learn much more about test-driven development in the excellent book, *Test Driven Development by Example*, by Kent Beck (Addison-Wesley).

The sample application has a suite of tests that are included in the `com.oreilly.pf3.flickr.test` package, and the application also includes a test runner, *TestRunner.mxml*, to run the tests. You can see that there are two classes in the test package: `PhotoTest` and `FlickrServiceTest`. The `PhotoTest` case runs tests verifying that a `Photo` object correctly deserializes XML data as it is returned by the Flickr service. From a TDD perspective, it is useful to write this test before writing the `Photo` class and its deserialization method. Having the test written first can help to verify that `Photo` does what it is intended to do and that it meets all the requirements placed on it as you write it. However, even after the class has been written, the tests are useful because you can run them to verify that no regressions have occurred as you refactor the application. Likewise, it can be helpful to write the `FlickrServiceTest` class before writing `FlickrService`, and yet it is also useful after writing `FlickrService` to verify that the service works as intended.

Using Blueprints and Microarchitectures

Even with the best practices mentioned in the preceding section, the idea of building a Flex application from scratch can be a bit daunting. Where should you begin? Sometimes too much freedom can be paralyzing. Artists often report that their greatest creativity stems from having boundaries. Likewise, you may find that having structure may provide the right environment for building a successful Flex application. This is the role of a *microarchitecture*.

Microarchitectures are intended to provide a general guideline and structure for building applications. A microarchitecture doesn't deal with the specific requirements of a specific application, but rather concerns itself with a philosophical approach to how applications should be structured and designed in general. Microarchitectures provide these oft-needed boundaries and guidelines that help remove the paralysis you might otherwise experience. To that end they can be useful.

Various individuals and organizations promote many microarchitectures for Flex applications. A few of the more popular of these are as follows:

- Cairngorm (*http://labs.adobe.com/wiki/index.php/Cairngorm*)
- PureMVC (*http://www.puremvc.org*)
- MVCS (*http://www.joeberkovitz.com/mvcs*)

We don't advocate the use of any one microarchitecture over another. In fact, we don't really advocate the use of microarchitectures at all. Instead, we recommend that you find a system that works best for you. For the sample application, we are borrowing some of what we consider to be the best ideas from our own experiences building applications with Flex.

Although any one of these microarchitectures might be helpful and useful, don't be surprised if it is limiting at the same time. The boundaries created by a microarchitecture can provide structure, but they are still boundaries. If you decide to use one of these microarchitectures, it is probably a good idea to follow the rules and build applications exactly as specified by the microarchitecture until you are familiar with the basics and have built several applications successfully. However, at that time you may find it useful to break the rules a little and adapt them to what works best for you. To really take our advice on this matter you'll probably need to be fairly proficient with Flex and with basic design and architectural patterns before you even start working with a microarchitecture. That's not because we think microarchitectures are "advanced" or "difficult." Rather, it's because we think that to be able to have a critical approach to using a microarchitecture (such that you can learn from the patterns without having to adopt the entire system blindly) you need to have a fair amount of Flex and application development experience first. For the sample application in this chapter, you'll find that we're not stressing that you must build your own applications using the same design structure we've used. Instead, we're simply providing one example that uses patterns that we've found to be useful for Flex applications.

Abstracting Common Patterns

Like all software, Flex applications are complex. This requires that developers building Flex applications are able to solve architectural and design problems rather than simply throwing together a bunch of off-the-shelf components. Using a microarchitecture as described in the preceding section can help in this regard. However, when using a microarchitecture you can solve only the problems that the microarchitecture is specifically designed to address. If a problem falls outside that scope, the problem remains unsolved. In this manner, it's perhaps more useful to at least understand some of the common patterns that are used to solve problems. You can then utilize these patterns either as part of or apart from a microarchitecture.

Many papers, articles, and books have been written about design and architectural patterns used in software development. The patterns that you could use when building a Flex application are too numerous to list and detail in this chapter. However, a few patterns are common enough that we would be remiss not to describe them. Notably, nearly every Flex application could profit from the use of the Model-View-Controller pattern and the Business Delegate pattern, both of which we'll discuss in more detail in the following sections. Additionally, we'll start by looking at a pattern for dealing with browser integration, which is a problem that is unique to web-based applications.

Understanding Browser Integration

Shortly we'll look at much of the code in more detail. However, before we do so, you'll need to understand how the FlickrFlex application handles browser integration (deep linking and the back and forward buttons). The principle is rather simple: all significant state change requests are routed through the `BrowserManager` class by updating the address fragment. For example, when the user clicks on a Search button, the FlickrFlex application does not directly change the state to the search results screen or immediately make the request to the search method on the Flickr service. Instead, the application updates the address fragment via `BrowserManager` and waits for `BrowserManager` to dispatch an event notifying the application to update as necessary. We'll see a few specific examples of this later on. However, the basic way in which the application manages this behavior depends on a simple infrastructure provided by a few methods in a few of the *.mxml* files, which we'll look at now.

The main application *.mxml* file is *Flickr.mxml*. This file contains little more than a `Style` tag and an instance of `FlickrController`. The `FlickrController` class is where we start to set up browser integration. Within the `initializeHandler()` method, we tell the application to listen for changes to the URL via the `BrowserManager`:

```
_browserManager.addEventListener(BrowserChangeEvent.APPLICATION_URL_CHANGE,
                                 urlChangeHandler);
_browserManager.addEventListener(BrowserChangeEvent.BROWSER_URL_CHANGE,
                                 urlChangeHandler);
```

When the URL changes, the first thing we do is parse the fragment into an array, using a forward slash as a delimiter:

```
var fragments:Array = _browserManager.fragment.split("/");
```

We then remove the first element from the array and use that to determine what state to set on the view. If, for example, the fragment is `search/nature` (which is what the fragment would be if the user runs a search using the term *nature*), the first element in the array will be `search`, which means we want to tell the view to change to the search screen. In every case, we pass along the remaining fragment to the view:

```
var topFragment:String = fragments.shift();
if(topFragment == "search") {
    view.setMode(FlickrView.MODE_SEARCH_SCREEN, fragments.join("/"));
}
else if(topFragment == "") {
    view.setMode(FlickrView.MODE_HOME, fragments.join("/"));
}
else if(topFragment == "details") {
    view.setMode(FlickrView.MODE_PHOTO_DETAILS, fragments.join("/"));
}
```

Within `FlickrView`'s `setMode()` method, we change the state and then assign the remaining fragment to the `screenFragment` property of the corresponding screen if appropriate:

```
public function setMode(mode:String, fragment:String = null):void {
    currentState = mode;
    if(fragment != null && fragment.length > 0) {
        if(mode == MODE_SEARCH_SCREEN) {
            searchScreen.screenFragment = fragment;
        }
        else if(mode == MODE_PHOTO_DETAILS) {
            photoDetailsScreen.screenFragment = fragment;
        }
    }
}
```

If the entire fragment was `search/nature`, the `setMode()` method would change the state to the search screen state and assign `nature` to the `screenFragment` property of `searchScreen`. Later in the chapter, when we talk about views and controllers, we'll see how the search screen handles the fragment. However, at this point the specifics of how fragments are ultimately utilized in specific views and controllers aren't as important as the overall pattern. To summarize and restate: for FlickrFlex we have a hierarchical structure of objects (`FlickrController` contains `FlickrView`, `FlickrView` contains `HomeController`, etc.). `FlickrController` listens for URL changes, and when the fragment changes, `FlickrController` starts to trickle down the fragment updates by notifying `FlickrView`. `FlickrView` uses the fragment to decide how to change state, and it then passes along the remainder of the fragment to the controller corresponding to the new state. This pattern could theoretically be continued for as many levels of hierarchy that exist.

The Business Delegate Pattern

The majority of Flex applications utilize a service of one sort or another, whether the services are SOAP services, REST services, AMF (Remoting) services, or any other sort. Elements of the Flex application need to interact with these services. For example, a user may request from a service a list of states or provinces for a given country, or a user may fill out a form in Flex and then submit the form to a service method.

In a naïve approach, the actual implementation that a Flex application uses to interact with a service may be exposed directly to all elements within the Flex application. For example, if a part of the application needs to query a SOAP service for a list of states or provinces, it is possible to allow that part of the application to create an instance of the `WebService` component with the appropriate operation, and to bind the results of the operation directly to a UI component. This may work, but it is a shortsighted solution that creates fragility.

Instead of the aforementioned solution, you can use a common pattern known as the Business Delegate pattern. A *business delegate* is a class that serves as a proxy to a remote service, defining an API that the rest of the application can use without having to know anything about the implementation details. That way, the rest of the application only has to know about its contract with the business delegate. If the implementation details change, the rest of the application doesn't have to change as long as the business delegate API remains the same. For example, an application may initially utilize a set of SOAP web services. Later the services may be migrated over to use Remoting (AMF) instead. If the application doesn't use a business delegate, many parts of the application may need updating to work with the new services. However, if the application uses a business delegate, only the business delegate needs to change.

FlickrFlex uses the Business Delegate pattern. In this application, we define a class called `com.oreilly.pf3.flickr.services.FlickrService`. This class allows us to define a simple API for the rest of the FlickrFlex application to use without having to know anything about the implementation details. The `FlickrService` class defines only three methods: `searchPhotosByText()`, `getPhotoDetails()`, and `getPhotoSizes()`. The rest of the application can call these methods without having to know whether FlickrFlex is actually making requests to local XML files or a remote service. However, it turns out that in this example we are going to have the application connect to a remote service.

In the FlickrFlex application, we are connecting to only one service: the Flickr service. We don't want to get too bogged down in the details of the Flickr service since our primary focus in this chapter is to better understand common Flex application design and development problems and solutions. However, to make sense of the code for the sample application we'll need to explain just a few things about working with the Flickr service.

For the purposes of the sample application, we're necessarily using only a small subset of the Flickr API. We're calling only three Flickr service methods: one to search photos, one to get information about a specific photo, and one to get the different sizes of a specific photo.

You can always read more about the Flickr API, including all the available methods and their signatures, at *http://www.flickr.com/services/api*.

The Flickr service uses what is known as *representational state transfer*, more commonly known as REST. REST uses URLs to access resources. The Flickr service allows us to call methods via resources. In the case of the sample application, there are three methods that we relate to business delegate methods: `flickr.photos.search`, `flickr.photos.getInfo`, and `flickr.photos.getSizes`. Next we need to look at how to access these methods.

You must use the same pattern to access any Flickr resources. You must make an HTTP request to the REST resource along with a query string indicating the method and parameters. The REST resource is *http://api.flickr.com/services/rest/*. Therefore, you can see that in `FlickrService` we define a constant called `REST_URL` as follows:

```
static private const REST_URL:String = "http://api.flickr.com/services/rest/?";
```

The trailing ? is there to precede the requisite query string that we will look at next.

The query string for Flickr service requests must always include the method name along with the required parameters for that method. The Flickr API documentation lists the required parameters for each method. All methods require the API key. You can see that in `FlickrService` we define three methods that call REST service methods, each method calling a different service method with different parameters, but each following the same basic pattern. We'll look at `searchPhotosByText()`. This method calls the `flickr.photos.search` method, which requires a `text` parameter, which is a comma-delimited list of words for which to search.

```
public function searchPhotosByText(text:String):PendingOperation {
    text = text.split(" ").join(",");
    var method:String = "flickr.photos.search";
    var parameters:Array = new Array();
    parameters.push(new NameValue("api_key", _apiKey));
    parameters.push(new NameValue("method", method));
    parameters.push(new NameValue("text", text));
    var url:String = REST_URL + createQueryString(parameters);
    var pendingOperation:PendingOperation = new PendingOperation(url);
    return pendingOperation;
}
```

You can see that this method creates an array of NameValue objects, which are simply objects with name and value properties, and then passes that array to createQuery String() to create the query string, which it appends to the REST URL.

If we look next at createQueryString(), we can see that it simply takes all the names and values and strings them together with = and & delimiters:

```
private function createQueryString(parameters:Array):String {
    var queryString:String = "";
    var i:int;
    for(i = 0; i < parameters.length; i++) {
        queryString += parameters[i].name + "=" + parameters[i].value + "&";
    }
    return queryString;
}
```

The searchPhotosByText() method then returns a new PendingOperation object, passing it the newly constructed URL. The PendingOperation class simply makes an HTTP request to the specified URL, and it proxies the response, dispatching an event when the response is returned.

```
package com.oreilly.pf3.flickr.services {

    import flash.events.Event;
    import flash.events.EventDispatcher;
    import flash.events.HTTPStatusEvent;
    import flash.net.URLLoader;
    import flash.net.URLRequest;

    import mx.rpc.events.FaultEvent;
    import mx.rpc.events.ResultEvent;

    public class PendingOperation extends EventDispatcher {

        static public const RESULT:String = "result";
        static public const ERROR:String = "error";

        private var _loader:URLLoader;
        private var _vo:*;

        public function PendingOperation(url:String, vo:* = null) {
            _loader = new URLLoader();
            _loader.addEventListener("complete", resultHandler);
```

```
            _loader.addEventListener(HTTPStatusEvent.HTTP_STATUS, errorHandler);
            _loader.load(new URLRequest(url));
            _vo = vo;
        }

        private function resultHandler(event:Event):void {
            dispatchEvent(new ResultEvent(RESULT, false, true,
ParsingUtility.parse(new XML(_loader.data), _vo)));
        }

        private function errorHandler(event:HTTPStatusEvent):void {
            dispatchEvent(new FaultEvent(ERROR));
        }
    }
}
```

You can see that the `PendingOperation` class relies on a method of the `ParsingUtility` class. We're using this custom `ParsingUtility` class to determine what type of response the service has returned and convert it to the correct type. For example, when the `PendingOperation` object is handling the response from a `flickr.photos.search` method, the `ParsingUtility` class detects the response as such and converts the XML into an `ArrayCollection` of `Photo` objects, which is exactly what the rest of the FlickrFlex application expects.

We've designed the `FlickrService` and `PendingOperation` classes in this way so that the rest of the application needs to know nothing about the implementation details. As far as the controllers and views and the rest of the application are concerned, it makes no difference whether the Flickr service is a REST service. If Flickr decided to change to an AMF service at some point, we could adapt the application with little to no changes to any of the code outside the `services` package.

The Model-View-Controller Pattern

The Model-View-Controller (MVC) architectural pattern is utilized across many languages and platforms. If you have experience building software of any sort, chances are MVC is familiar to you. Volumes have been written about this pattern, and we won't try to repeat much of what has already been said. Instead, we're primarily concerned with the usefulness of the pattern in Flex applications and the nuances of how to implement it practically in Flex. However, if you aren't already familiar with this pattern, we'll outline it briefly.

The principle concern of MVC is to effectively separate the business logic and the user interface code such that they interact with one another only through well-defined programming interfaces. The idea is that this approach reduces fragility because you can make changes to one without having to necessarily make changes to the other.

As the name implies, this pattern typically uses three parts—model, view, and controller:

- The *model* is the way in which data is represented programmatically.
- The *view* is the user interface. Typically, a view does not directly modify the model it represents. Instead, it allows the controller to modify the model, and the view updates itself when the model changes. Additionally, usually a view does not call methods of its controller, nor does it even have a reference to a controller. Instead, a view usually merely dispatches events that a controller can handle.
- The *controller* is the business logic. A controller typically has a reference to a model and a view, and it uses these references to modify the model and call methods of the view directly.

Although it's possible to write models, views, and controllers in a 1:1:1 ratio, it's also possible that a controller could be used with many different views and that a model could likewise be used by many different views and controllers.

You can implement the MVC pattern in many different ways at many different levels. At one level, it is possible to create one model and one controller for an entire application (which uses many different views). It is also possible to implement the pattern at a more granular level, creating controllers, models, and views for all components. How you implement the pattern will depend on the complexity of the application and your preferences as a developer. In the FlickrFlex application, we have opted for a more granular approach.

Next we'll look at creating models, views, and controllers in Flex applications.

Models

Although there are variations on how to implement a model in a Flex application, those variations are relatively narrow in scope, and for the most part Flex developers tend to build models in a very similar fashion. At the core of the model implementation is something called a *business object* (or sometimes more specifically a *value object*). A business object is a type that represents entities (logical groupings of data) within the business domain (application). A value object is a more specific type of business object that has no additional logic applied to it, and merely stores data. In the case of FlickrFlex, we have only one business object, a class called *com.oreilly.pf3.flickr.model.data.Photo*. The `Photo` class is a fairly standard implementation. It models the same basic data as is returned by the various photo-related service methods, defining `private` properties for all of them:

```
private var _id:String;
private var _owner:String;
private var _secret:String;
private var _server:String;
private var _farm:String;
private var _title:String;
private var _thumbnailUrl:String;
```

```
private var _description:String;
private var _tags:ArrayCollection;
private var _imageMediumUrl:String;
private var _imageLargeUrl:String;
```

The class then defines accessor methods for most of the properties, as in the following:

```
public function get id():String {
    return _id;
}
```

Also, a few properties can be updated after the initial creation of the object. Therefore, we create mutator methods as well, and because we want user interface elements (views) to be able to update themselves based on the changes, we set the properties as bindable. The `description` property is an example:

```
[Bindable(event="descriptionChanged")]
public function set description(value:String):void {
    _description = value;
    dispatchEvent(new Event("descriptionChanged"));
}

public function get description():String {
    return _description;
}
```

Various developers have different perspectives on how a business object should be created. Some developers are of the opinion that business objects should not know anything about the manner in which they are created. Other developers prefer to make business objects responsible for creating themselves, given specific input. For `Photo`, we've opted for the latter approach, creating a static `parseFromXml()` method that accepts the return XML from a Flickr photo search, and constructs and returns a corresponding `Photo` object:

```
static public function parseFromXml(xml:XML):Photo {
    var id:String = xml.@id;
    var owner:String = xml.@owner;
    var secret:String = xml.@secret;
    var server:String = xml.@server;
    var farm:String = xml.@farm;
    var title:String = xml.@title;
    return new Photo(id, owner, secret, server, farm, title);
}
```

Frequently, applications require complex models, and it can be useful to maintain an application-wide reference to the models used by various parts of the application. For this purpose, a model locator can be a valuable part of the model. The model locator is typically implemented using the Singleton design pattern, and it stores references to various models in use. For the FlickrFlex application, we've defined a model locator called `com.oreilly.pf3.flickr.model.ApplicationModel`.

The model locator for FlickrFlex is an application-wide repository for stateful model data, including the following:

- The current search term
- The current search results
- The selected photo
- The index of the selected photo in the search results

Controllers and views

The implementation of controllers within Flex applications differs among developers much more widely than does the implementation of models. As we indicated earlier, it is possible to build an application that uses one application-wide controller. This is an approach advocated by some microarchitectures such as MVCS. This is certainly a workable approach, and it has its advantages. However, one drawback of this approach is that the one controller is generalized, and the larger and more complex the application becomes the larger and more complex the controller becomes. Therefore, for many applications it is advantageous to use more granular controllers that are specific to components of the application. This is the approach we use with the FlickrFlex application.

Implementing controllers in Flex can be challenging because of the way Flex is designed. Typically, views are user interface elements and controllers are not. As a result, it may initially seem to make sense to have components create and maintain a reference to their own controller. However, this approach has serious drawbacks; most notably it reverses the typical relationship between views and controllers. A controller should provide the programmatic interface to a component, and it should be able to theoretically control any view that implements the interface the controller expects. By having a view construct a controller, these roles and behaviors are no longer possible.

With the FlickrFlex application we've taken a slightly unconventional approach. We've decided to define controllers using MXML, making controllers extend `UIComponent`. This enables controllers to be added as children of other containers, and it allows controllers to then add views to themselves. If you look in *Flickr.mxml*, you'll notice that it is very simple. In this document, we create an instance of `FlickrController`:

```
<?xml version="1.0" encoding="utf-8"?>
<mx:Application xmlns:mx="http://www.adobe.com/2006/mxml" layout="vertical"
xmlns:views="com.oreilly.pf3.flickr.views.*" xmlns:controllers="com.oreilly.
pf3.flickr.
controllers.*" backgroundColor="#4F5050">
    <mx:Style source="assets_embed/css/FlickrFlex.css"/>
    <controllers:FlickrController/>
</mx:Application>
```

In `FlickrController` we create only one component instance: an instance of `FlickrView`. `FlickrController` is the control for `FlickrView`.

Inside `FlickrView` you can see that in the various states we create instances of different controllers: `HomeController`, `SearchController`, and `PhotoDetailsController`. In each controller document we create just one component instance: `HomeScreen`, `SearchScreen`, and `PhotoDetailsScreen`, respectively. If you look at the code for these views, you'll notice that they don't reference the controllers. Instead, if any communication is necessary with the controllers, it is achieved by dispatching events.

Next we'll look specifically at the `SearchScreen` and `SearchController` to better understand how these two classes are designed and how they work both together and in the context of the application.

In the `com.oreilly.pf3.flickr.views.screens` package you'll see *SearchScreen.mxml*, the view for the search form/search results in the FlickrFlex application. `SearchScreen` is fairly representative of the rest of the views in the application and how we typically build views in general. The key points to notice about `SearchScreen` are as follows:

- The view defines an API to grant access to anything related to its own state, including changes to components within it. You'll notice that `SearchScreen` defines getters and/or setters for the following: `dataProvider`, `searchTerm`, `isSearching`, and `selectedPhoto`. We'll talk more about each in just a moment.
- The view does not have any reference to a controller. You can see that `SearchScreen` doesn't know anything about `SearchController`. However, there are a few instances where `SearchScreen` needs to communicate with its controller. This is achieved through dispatching events. You can see that when the user clicks on an item in the tile list the view dispatches an event, and it dispatches a different event when the user clicks on the Search button.

The `SearchScreen` component, as with all views, is primarily responsible for user interface layout and for relaying user interaction to a controller via events. The `SearchScreen` consists of a search form (a text input and a button) and a tile list, as shown in the following snippet from the code:

```
<mx:HBox width="100%" height="45" backgroundColor="#212122" verticalAlign="middle">
    <mx:HBox styleName="green" height="100%">
        <mx:Label text="tags" />
        <mx:TextInput id="searchTermInput" text="{_searchTerm}" />
        <mx:Spacer width="10" />
        <mx:Button id="searchButton" label="Search for Photos"
            styleName="green" height="100%"
            click="dispatchEvent(new PhotoSearchEvent(searchTermInput.text));" />
    </mx:HBox>
</mx:HBox>
<mx:TileList id="photoList" width="100%" height="100%"
    itemRenderer="com.oreilly.pf3.flickr.views.renderers.PhotoRenderer"
    dataProvider="{_dataProvider}"
    change="dispatchEvent(new PhotoSelectEvent(photoList.selectedItem.id));" />
```

You can see that in the two cases where there is user interactivity (the user clicking on the Search button or selecting an item from the tile list), the view merely dispatches an event.

As mentioned earlier, the view defines an API for reading and writing values and/or state on the view. One of the key getters/setters is `dataProvider`, which is fairly standard for most views. The `dataProvider` getter/setter merely gets/sets the bindable `_dataProvider` property, which is an `ArrayCollection` in the case of `SearchScreen`. The tile list is bound to the `_dataProvider` property such that whenever the property changes, the tile list reflects those changes. We'll look at when and how this property changes when we look at the controller code in just a minute.

The other two getters/setters are `searchTerm` and `isSearching`. The `searchTerm` getter/setter is used to get and set the keyword(s) displayed in the search form, when applicable. The `isSearching` getter/setter is used to change the state to disable the view when a search is running or when the result is returned from the service.

The `selectedPhoto` getter is designed to return a reference to the `Photo` object corresponding to the selected tile list item. This provides a well-defined API such that the controller can access that information without having to know anything about how the view is implemented.

The `SearchController` class is designed to handle all the business logic for searching, displaying results, and navigating to photo details. The `SearchController` has an instance of `SearchScreen` with an ID of `view`:

```
<screens:SearchScreen id="view" photoSearch="photoSearchHandler(event);"
photoSelect="photoSelectHandler(event);" />
```

When the `photoSearch` or `photoSelect` event occurs (dispatched by the view), the controller handles the event. In both cases, the controller handles the event by updating the browser address fragment using `BrowserManager`:

```
private function photoSearchHandler(event:PhotoSearchEvent):void {
    BrowserManager.getInstance().setFragment("search/" + event.searchTerm);
}

private function photoSelectHandler(event:PhotoSelectEvent):void {
    BrowserManager.getInstance().setFragment("details/" + event.photoId);
}
```

You'll recall from earlier in the chapter that state changes are often managed by changes to the browser address (via `BrowserManager`). You may recall from that discussion that when changes are detected in the URL, `FlickrController` tells `FlickrView` to change its state, and `FlickrView` may then pass along part of the address fragment to the corresponding controller via a `screenFragment` property. Therefore, when the fragment is changed to `search/`*`search term`*, the search term gets assigned to the `screenFragment` property of `SearchController`. Therefore, we define a `screenFragment` setter as follows:

```
public function set screenFragment(value:String):void {
    value = unescape(value);
```

```
        ApplicationModel.getInstance().searchTerm = value;
        if(_searchTerm != value) {
            view.searchTerm  = value;
            searchForPhotos(value);
        }
    }
```

You can see that if the search term is the same as the existing search term, no further action is necessary. However, if the search term is different, the controller updates the search term for the view and runs a method (`searchForPhotos()`) that uses the `FlickrService` instance to query the Flickr service for photos with that search term:

```
    private function searchForPhotos(searchTerm:String):void {
        _searchTerm = searchTerm;
        view.isSearching = true;
        var pendingOperation:PendingOperation = _service.searchPhotosByText(_searchTerm);
        pendingOperation.addEventListener(PendingOperation.RESULT,
                                          searchForPhotosResultHandler);
    }
```

You can see that the controller sets `isSearching` to `true`. When the result is returned, not only does the handler method update the `dataProvider` of the view, but it also sets `isSearching` to `false`:

```
    private function searchForPhotosResultHandler(event:ResultEvent):void {
        var photos:ArrayCollection = event.result as ArrayCollection;
        ApplicationModel.getInstance().searchResults = photos;
        view.dataProvider = photos;
        view.isSearching = false;
    }
```

Summary

Throughout this book, you learned a great many things about Flex 3. In this chapter, we tied much of that together with a sample application and looked at a set of simple best practices. In the course of this chapter, you had the opportunity to download a complete Flex 3 sample application that uses the Flickr service to search photos and display results. We then discussed some of the key architectural decisions in the application.

Index

Symbols

A

We'd like to hear your suggestions for improving our indexes. Send email to *index@oreilly.com*.

B

D

E

F

I

J

K

L

N

O

P

R

S

T

U

V

W

X

Z

About the Authors

Chafc Kazoun is co-founder and Chief Software Architect at Atellis. He's worked with Flash technologies since 1998 and with Flex since its inception.

Joey Lott is a founding partner in The Morphic Group (*http://www.themorphicgroup.com*), specializing in Flex application development. Joey has also written many other leading books on Flex and Flash-related technologies, including O'Reilly's *ActionScript 3.0 Cookbook*.

Colophon

The animal on the cover of *Programming Flex 3* is a krait snake. The krait (*Bungarus caeruleus*) is one of the deadliest venomous snakes in the world. Its native habitat is limited to Asia, and it's nocturnal. The snake's bands are white or yellow on a blue/black body. A krait's head is narrow and it can grow to nearly three feet in length.

Fairly common in the fields and jungles of India, Pakistan, and Sri Lanka, the krait is also known to seek shelter in human encampments. It's fond of hiding out in sleeping bags, footwear, and piles of clothing or rags. Its venom contains a neuro-toxin that causes respiratory failure. Victims often feel little pain from the bite itself, but the death rate of victims is 85 percent without administration of anti-venom, and nearly 50 percent even when medication is available.

The 2006 film *Snakes on a Plane* features a snake smuggler named "Kraitler." The krait also makes an appearance in several Sherlock Holmes stories.

The cover image is from the *Dover Pictorial Archive*. The cover font is Adobe ITC Garamond. The text font is Linotype Birka; the heading font is Adobe Myriad Condensed; and the code font is LucasFont's TheSans Mono Condensed.

Breinigsville, PA USA
11 February 2011
255279BV00004B/5/P

9 780596 516215